Blackstone's Statutes

Medical Law

Blackstone's Statutes
Medical Law

Fifth Edition

Edited by

Anne E. Morris
Senior Lecturer in Law at the University of Liverpool

Michael A. Jones
Professor of Common Law at the University of Liverpool

OXFORD
UNIVERSITY PRESS

Great Clarendon Street, Oxford OX2 6DP

Oxford University Press is a department of the University of Oxford.
It furthers the University's objective of excellence in research, scholarship,
and education by publishing worldwide in

Oxford New York

Auckland Cape Town Dar es Salaam Hong Kong Karachi
Kuala Lumpur Madrid Melbourne Mexico City Nairobi
New Delhi Shanghai Taipei Toronto

With offices in

Argentina Austria Brazil Chile Czech Republic France Greece
Guatemala Hungary Italy Japan Poland Portugal Singapore
South Korea Switzerland Thailand Turkey Ukraine Vietnam

Oxford is a registered trade mark of Oxford University Press
in the UK and in certain other countries

Published in the United States
by Oxford University Press Inc., New York

This selection © Anne E. Morris and Michael A. Jones, 2007

The moral rights of the authors have been asserted

Crown copyright material is reproduced under Class Licence
Number C01P0000148 with the permission of OPSI
and the Queen's Printer for Scotland

Database right Oxford University Press (maker)

First published by Blackstone Press
First edition, 1992
Reprinted, 1998
Second edition, 1999
Third edition, 2003
Fourth edition, 2005
Fifth edition, 2007

British Library Cataloguing in Publication Data

Data available

Library of Congress Cataloging in Publication Data

Data available

Typeset by Newgen Imaging Systems (P) Ltd., Chennai, India
Printed in Great Britain
on acid-free paper by
Ashford Colour Press, Gosport, Hampshire

ISBN 978-0-19-921182-1

10 9 8 7 6 5 4 3 2 1

Editors' Preface to the Fifth Edition

When preparing a new edition of these statutes the editors' recurring problem lies not in identifying new material but in deciding what should be omitted in order to keep the book at a manageable length. For this fifth edition we have been guided by the results of surveys undertaken by the publishers. It is clear that Medical Law courses are exceedingly diverse. As a result, material which is essential for one module might be irrelevant for another. A module which encompasses the structure of the health service and regulation of the professions requires rather different information from one which is primarily concerned with the legal regulation of the doctor–patient relationship. We have tried to put together a collection which will meet the needs of most courses but are always open to suggestions for change. We have, for example, departed from previous practice and have included for the first time a small selection of legislation from Scotland. The Acts included (Age of Legal Capacity 1991; Adults with Incapacity 2000 and the Human Tissue Act (Scotland) 2006) were chosen because they offer some interesting comparisons with the law of England and Wales. We hope that these will be of use both north and south of the border.

In terms of the new additions, we have the National Health Service Act 2006 and the National Health Service Redress Act 2006 together with Regulations which begin to implement the Mental Capacity Act 2005 and the Human Tissue Act 2004. As we commented in both 2003 and 2005, however, we still await a new Mental Health Act. As is usual, we have included the new legislation as though it were in force. The General Medical Council has published its new 'Good Medical Practice', while 'Seeking Patients' Consent' is currently under review. As ever we are very grateful to the GMC and also the Human Fertilisation and Embryology Authority for permission to use material which appears on their websites.

The law is printed (as amended) as at April 2007.

Contents

Alphabetical contents list

Chronological contents list

Statutes

Offences Against the Person Act 1861

(1861, c. 100)

18 Shooting or attempting to shoot, or wounding with intent to do grievous bodily harm

Whosoever shall unlawfully and maliciously by any means whatsoever wound or cause any grievous bodily harm to any person, with intent to do some grievous bodily harm to any person, or with intent to resist or prevent the lawful apprehension or detainer of any person, shall be guilty of felony, and being convicted thereof shall be liable to be kept in penal servitude for life.

20 Inflicting bodily injury, with or without weapon

Whosoever shall unlawfully and maliciously wound or inflict any grievous bodily harm upon any other person, either with or without any weapon or instrument, shall be guilty of a misdemeanour, and being convicted thereof shall be liable to be kept in penal servitude.

23 Maliciously administering poison, &c. so as to endanger life or inflict grievous bodily harm

Whosoever shall unlawfully and maliciously administer to or cause to be administered to or taken by any other person any poison or other destructive or noxious thing, so as thereby to endanger the life of such person, or so as thereby to inflict upon such person any grievous bodily harm, shall be guilty of felony, and being convicted thereof shall be liable to be kept in penal servitude for any term not exceeding ten years.

24 Maliciously administering poison, &c. with intent to injure, aggrieve, or annoy any other person

Whosoever shall unlawfully and maliciously administer to or cause to be administered to or taken by any other person any poison or other destructive or noxious thing, with intent to injure, aggrieve, or annoy such person, shall be guilty of a misdemeanor, and being convicted thereof shall be liable to be kept in penal servitude.

47 Assault occasioning bodily harm. Common assault

Whosoever shall be convicted upon an indictment of any assault occasioning actual bodily harm shall be liable to be kept in penal servitude; and whosoever shall be convicted upon an indictment for a common assault shall be liable, at the discretion of the court, to be imprisoned for any term not exceeding one year.

Attempts to procure abortion

58 Administering drugs or using instruments to procure abortion

Every woman, being with child, who, with intent to procure her own miscarriage, shall unlawfully administer to herself any poison or other noxious thing, or shall unlawfully use any instrument or other means whatsoever with the like intent, and whosoever, with intent to procure the miscarriage of any woman, whether she be or be not with child, shall unlawfully administer to her or cause to be taken by her any poison or other noxious thing, or shall unlawfully use any instrument or other means whatsoever with the like intent, shall be guilty of felony, and being convicted thereof shall be liable to be kept in penal servitude for life.

59   Procuring drugs, &c. to cause abortion

Whosoever shall unlawfully supply or procure any poison or other noxious thing, or any instrument or thing whatsoever, knowing that the same is intended to be unlawfully used or employed with intent to procure the miscarriage of any woman, whether she be or be not with child, shall be guilty of a misdemeanor, and being convicted thereof shall be liable to be kept in penal servitude.

Infant Life (Preservation) Act 1929

(1929, c. 34)

1   Punishment for child destruction

(1) Subject as hereinafter in this subsection provided, any person who, with intent to destroy the life of a child capable of being born alive, by any wilful act causes a child to die before it has an existence independent of its mother, shall be guilty of felony, to wit, of child destruction, and shall be liable on conviction thereof on indictment to penal servitude for life:

Provided that no person shall be found guilty of an offence under this section unless it is proved that the act which caused the death of the child was not done in good faith for the purpose only of preserving the life of the mother.

(2) For the purposes of this Act, evidence that a woman had at any material time been pregnant for a period of twenty-eight weeks or more shall be primâ facie proof that she was at that time pregnant of a child capable of being born alive.

2   Prosecution of offences

(2) Where upon the trial of any person for the murder or manslaughter of any child, or for infanticide, or for an offence under section fifty-eight of the Offences against the Person Act 1861 (which relates to administering drugs or using instruments to procure abortion), the jury are of opinion that the person charged is not guilty of murder, manslaughter or infanticide, or of an offence under the said section fifty-eight, as the case may be, but that he is shown by the evidence to be guilty of the felony of child destruction, the jury may find him guilty of that felony, and thereupon the person convicted shall be liable to be punished as if he had been convicted upon an indictment for child destruction.

(3) Where upon the trial of any person for the felony of child destruction the jury are of opinion that the person charged is not guilty of that felony, but that he is shown by the evidence to be guilty of an offence under the said section fifty-eight of the Offences against the Person Act 1861, the jury may find him guilty of that offence, and thereupon the person convicted shall be liable to be punished as if he had been convicted upon an indictment under that section.

Children and Young Persons Act 1933

(1933, c. 12)

1   Cruelty to persons under sixteen

(1) If any person who has attained the age of sixteen years and has responsibility for any child or young person under that age, wilfully assaults, ill-treats, neglects, abandons, or exposes him, or causes or procures him to be assaulted, ill-treated, neglected, abandoned, or exposed, in a manner likely to cause him unnecessary suffering or injury to health (including injury to or loss of sight, or

hearing, or limb, or organ of the body, and any mental derangement), that person shall be guilty of a misdemeanor, and shall be liable –

(a) on conviction on indictment, to a fine or alternatively, or in addition thereto, to imprisonment for any term not exceeding ten years;

(b) on summary conviction, to a fine not exceeding the prescribed sum, or alternatively, or in addition thereto, to imprisonment for any term not exceeding six months.

(2) For the purposes of this section –

(a) a parent or other person legally liable to maintain a child or young person, or the legal guardian of a child or young person, shall be deemed to have neglected him in a manner likely to cause injury to his health if he has failed to provide adequate food, clothing, medical aid or lodging for him, or if, having been unable otherwise to provide such food, clothing, medical aid or lodging, he has failed to take steps to procure it to be provided under the enactments applicable in that behalf;

(3) A person may be convicted of an offence under this section –

(a) notwithstanding that actual suffering or injury to health, or the likelihood of actual suffering or injury to health, was obviated by the action of another person;

(b) notwithstanding the death of the child or young person in question.

National Assistance Act 1948

(1948, c. 29)

47   Removal to suitable premises of persons in need of care and attention

(1) The following provisions of this section shall have effect for the purposes of securing the necessary care and attention for persons who –

(a) are suffering from grave chronic disease or, being aged, infirm or physically incapacitated, are living in insanitary conditions, and

(b) are unable to devote to themselves, and are not receiving from other persons, proper care and attention.

(2) If the medical officer of health certifies in writing to the appropriate authority that he is satisfied after thorough inquiry and consideration that in the interests of any such person as aforesaid residing in the area of the authority, or for preventing injury to the health of, or serious nuisance to, other persons, it is necessary to remove any such person as aforesaid from the premises in which he is residing, the appropriate authority may apply to a court of summary jurisdiction having jurisdiction in the place where the premises are situated for an order under the next following subsection.

(3) On any such application the court may, if satisfied on oral evidence of the allegations in the certificate, and that it is expedient so to do, order the removal of the person to whom the application relates, by such officer of the appropriate authority as may be specified in the order, to a suitable hospital or other place in, or within convenient distance of, the area of the appropriate authority, and his detention and maintenance therein:

Provided that the court shall not order the removal of a person to any premises, unless either the person managing the premises has been heard in the proceedings or seven clear days' notice has been given to him of the intended application and of the time and place at which it is proposed to be made.

(4) An order under the last foregoing subsection may be made so as to authorise a person's detention for any period not exceeding three months, and the court may from time to time by order extend that period for such further period, not exceeding three months, as the court may determine.

(5) An order under subsection (3) of this section may be varied by an order of the court so as to substitute for the place referred to in that subsection such other suitable place in, or within convenient distance of, the area of the appropriate authority as the court may determine, so however

that the proviso to the said subsection (3) shall with the necessary modification apply to any proceedings under this subsection.

(6) At any time after the expiration of six clear weeks from the making of an order under subsection (3) or (4) of this section an application may be made to the court by or on behalf of the person in respect of whom the order was made, and on any such application the court may, if in the circumstances it appears expedient so to do, revoke the order.

(7) No application under this section shall be entertained by the court unless, seven clear days before the making of the application, notice has been given of the intended application and of the time and place at which it is proposed to be made –

(a) where the application is for an order under subsection (3) or (4) of this section, to the person in respect of whom the application is made or to some person in charge of him;

(b) where the application is for the revocation of such an order, to the medical officer of health.

(8) Where in pursuance of an order under this section a person is maintained neither in hospital accommodation provided by the Minister of Health under the National Health Service Act 2006 or the National Health Service (Wales) Act 2006 or by the Secretary of State under the National Health Service (Scotland) Act 1978, nor in premises where accommodation is provided by, or by arrangement with, a local authority under Part III of this Act, the cost of his maintenance shall be borne by the appropriate authority.

(11) Any person who wilfully disobeys, or obstructs the execution of, an order under this section shall be guilty of an offence and liable on summary conviction to a fine not exceeding level 1 on the standard scale.

Suicide Act 1961

(1961, c. 60)

1   Suicide to cease to be a crime

The rule of law whereby it is a crime for a person to commit suicide is hereby abrogated.

2   Criminal liability for complicity in another's suicide

(1) A person who aids, abets, counsels or procures the suicide of another, or an attempt by another to commit suicide, shall be liable on conviction on indictment to imprisonment for a term not exceeding fourteen years.

(2) If on the trial of an indictment for murder or manslaughter it is proved that the accused aided, abetted, counselled or procured the suicide of the person in question, the jury may find him guilty of that offence.

(4) No proceedings shall be instituted for an offence under this section except by or with the consent of the Director of Public Prosecutions.

Abortion Act 1967

(1967, c. 87)

1   Medical termination of pregnancy

(1) Subject to the provisions of this section, a person shall not be guilty of an offence under the law relating to abortion when a pregnancy is terminated by a registered medical practitioner if two registered medical practitioners are of the opinion, formed in good faith –

(a) that the pregnancy has not exceeded its twenty-fourth week and that the continuance of the pregnancy would involve risk, greater than if the pregnancy were terminated, of injury to the physical or mental health of the pregnant woman or any existing children of her family; or

(b) that the termination is necessary to prevent grave permanent injury to the physical or mental health of the pregnant woman; or

(c) that the continuance of the pregnancy would involve risk to the life of the pregnant woman, greater than if the pregnancy were terminated; or

(d) that there is a substantial risk that if the child were born it would suffer from such physical or mental abnormalities as to be seriously handicapped.

(2) In determining whether the continuance of a pregnancy would involve such risk of injury to health as is mentioned in paragraph (a) or (b) of subsection (1) of this section, account may be taken of the pregnant woman's actual or reasonably foreseeable environment.

(3) Except as provided by subsection (4) of this section, any treatment for the termination of pregnancy must be carried out in a hospital vested in a Primary Care Trust or the Secretary of State for the purposes of his functions under the National Health Service Act 2006 or the National Health Service (Scotland) Act 1978 or in a hospital vested in a National Health Service trust or an NHS foundation trust or in a place approved for the purposes of this section by the Secretary of State.

(3A) The power under subsection (3) of this section to approve a place includes power, in relation to treatment consisting primarily in the use of such medicines as may be specified in the approval and carried out in such manner as may be so specified, to approve a class of places.

(4) Subsection (3) of this section, and so much of subsection (1) as relates to the opinion of two registered medical practitioners, shall not apply to the termination of a pregnancy by a registered medical practitioner in a case where he is of the opinion, formed in good faith, that the termination is immediately necessary to save the life or to prevent grave permanent injury to the physical or mental health of the pregnant woman.

2   Notification

(1) The Secretary of State in respect of England and Wales, and the Secretary of State in respect of Scotland, shall by statutory instrument make regulations to provide –

(a) for requiring any such opinion as is referred to in section 1 of this Act to be certified by the practitioners or practitioners concerned in such form and at such time as may be prescribed by the regulations, and for requiring the preservation and disposal of certificates made for the purposes of the regulations;

(b) for requiring any registered medical practitioner who terminates a pregnancy to give notice of the termination and such other information relating to the termination as may be so prescribed;

(c) for prohibiting the disclosure, except to such persons or for such purposes as may be so prescribed, of notices given or information furnished pursuant to the regulations.

(2) The information furnished in pursuance of regulations made by virtue of paragraph (b) of subsection (1) of this section shall be notified solely to the Chief Medical Officer of the Department of Health, or of the Welsh Office, or of the Scottish Administration.

(3) Any person who wilfully contravenes or wilfully fails to comply with the requirements of regulations under subsection (1) of this section shall be liable on summary conviction to a fine not exceeding level 5 on the standard scale.

(4) Any statutory instrument made by virtue of this section shall be subject to annulment in pursuance of a resolution of either House of Parliament.

4   Conscientious objection to participation in treatment

(1) Subject to subsection (2) of this section, no person shall be under any duty, whether by contract or by any statutory or other legal requirement, to participate in any treatment authorised by this Act to which he has a conscientious objection:

Provided that in any legal proceedings the burden of proof of conscientious objection shall rest on the person claiming to rely on it.

(2) Nothing in subsection (1) of this section shall affect any duty to participate in treatment which is necessary to save the life or to prevent grave permanent injury to the physical or mental health of a pregnant woman.

(3) In any proceedings before a court in Scotland, a statement on oath by any person to the effect that he has a conscientious objection to participating in any treatment authorised by this Act shall be sufficient evidence for the purpose of discharging the burden of proof imposed upon him by subsection (1) of this section.

5   Supplementary provisions

(1) No offence under the Infant Life (Preservation) Act 1929 shall be committed by a registered medical practitioner who terminates a pregnancy in accordance with the provisions of this Act.

(2) For the purposes of the law relating to abortion, anything done with intent to procure a woman's miscarriage (or, in the case of a woman carrying more than one foetus, her miscarriage of any foetus) is unlawfully done unless authorised by section I of this Act and, in the case of a woman carrying more than one foetus, anything done with intent to procure her miscarriage of any foetus is authorised by that section if –

>   (a) the ground for termination of the pregnancy specified in subsection (1)(d) of that section applies in relation to any foetus and the thing is done for the purpose of procuring the miscarriage of that foetus, or
>   (b) any of the other grounds for termination of the pregnancy specified in that section applies.

6   Interpretation

In this Act, the following expressions have meanings hereby assigned to them: –

'the law relating to abortion' means sections 58 and 59 of the Offences against the Person Act 1861, and any rule of law relating to the procurement of abortion.

Family Law Reform Act 1969

(1969, c. 46)

1   Reduction of age of majority from 21 to 18

(1) As from the date on which this section comes into force a person shall attain full age on attaining the age of eighteen instead of on attaining the age of twenty-one; and a person shall attain full age on that date if he has then already attained the age of eighteen but not the age of twenty-one.

(2) The foregoing subsection applies for the purposes of any rule of law, and, in the absence of a definition or of any indication of a contrary intention, for the construction of 'full age', 'infant', 'infancy', 'minor', 'minority' and similar expressions in –

>   (a) any statutory provision, whether passed or made before, on or after the date on which this section comes into force; and
>   (b) any deed, will or other instrument of whatever nature (not being a statutory provision) made on or after that date.

8   Consent by persons over 16 to surgical, medical and dental treatment

(1) The consent of a minor who has attained the age of sixteen years to any surgical, medical or dental treatment which, in the absence of consent, would constitute a trespass to his person, shall be as effective as it would be if he were of full age; and where a minor has by virtue of this section given an effective consent to any treatment it shall not be necessary to obtain any consent for it from his parent or guardian.

(2) In this section 'surgical, medical or dental treatment' includes any procedure undertaken for the purposes of diagnosis, and this section applies to any procedure (including, in particular, the administration of an anaesthetic) which is ancillary to any treatment as it applies to that treatment.

(3) Nothing in this section shall be construed as making ineffective any consent which would have been effective if this section had not been enacted.

Congenital Disabilities (Civil Liability) Act 1976

(1976, c. 28)

1   Civil liability to child born disabled

(1) If a child is born disabled as the result of such an occurrence before its birth as is mentioned in subsection (2) below, and a person (other than the child's own mother) is under this section answerable to the child in respect of the occurrence, the child's disabilities are to be regarded as damage resulting from the wrongful act of that person and actionable accordingly at the suit of the child.

(2) An occurrence to which this section applies is one which –

    (a) affected either parent of the child in his or her ability to have a normal, healthy child; or

    (b) affected the mother during her pregnancy, or affected her or the child in the course of its birth, so that the child is born with disabilities which would not otherwise have been present.

(3) Subject to the following subsections, a person (here referred to as 'the defendant') is answerable to the child if he was liable in tort to the parent or would, if sued in due time have been so; and it is no answer that there could not have been such liability because the parent suffered no actionable injury, if there was a breach of legal duty which, accompanied by injury, would have given rise to the liability.

(4) In the case of an occurrence preceding the time of conception, the defendant is not answerable to the child if at that time either or both of the parents knew the risk of their child being born disabled (that it to say, the particular risk created by the occurrence); but should it be the child's father who is the defendant, this subsection does not apply if he knew of the risk and the mother did not.

(5) The defendant is not answerable to the child, for anything he did or omitted to do when responsible in a professional capacity for treating or advising the parent, if he took reasonable care having due regard to then received professional opinion applicable to the particular class of case; but this does not mean that he is answerable only because he departed from received opinion.

(6) Liability to the child under this section may be treated as having been excluded or limited by contract made with the parent affected, to the same extent and subject to the same restrictions as liability in the parent's own case; and a contract term which could have been set up by the defendant in an action by the parent, so as to exclude or limit his liability to him or her, operates in the defendant's favour to the same, but no greater, extent in an action under this section by the child.

(7) If in the child's action under this section it is shown that the parent affected shared the responsibility for the child being born disabled, the damages are to be reduced to such extent as the court thinks just and equitable having regard to the extent of the parent's responsibility.

1A   Extension of section 1 to cover infertility treatments

(1) In any case where –

    (a) a child carried by a woman as the result of the placing in her of an embryo or of sperm and eggs or her artificial insemination is born disabled,

    (b) the disability results from an act or omission in the course of the selection, or the keeping or use outside the body, of the embryo carried by her or of the gametes used to bring about the creation of the embryo, and

    (c) a person is under this section answerable to the child in respect of the act or omission, the child's disabilities are to be regarded as damage resulting from the wrongful act of that person and actionable accordingly at the suit of the child.

(2) Subject to subsection (3) below and the applied provisions of section 1 of this Act, a person (here referred to as 'the defendant') is answerable to the child if he was liable in tort to one or both of the parents (here referred to as 'the parent or parents concerned') or would, if sued in due time, have been so; and it is no answer that there could not have been such liability because the parent or

parents concerned suffered no actionable injury, if there was a breach of legal duty which, accompanied by injury, would have given rise to the liability.

(3) The defendant is not under this section answerable to the child if at the time the embryo, or the sperm and eggs, are placed in the woman or the time of her insemination (as the case may be) either or both of the parents knew the risk of their child being born disabled (that is to say, the particular risk created by the act or omission).

(4) Subsections (5) to (7) of section 1 of this Act apply for the purposes of this section as they apply for the purposes of that but as if references to the parent or the parent affected were references to the parent or parents concerned.

2   Liability of woman driving when pregnant

A woman driving a motor vehicle when she knows (or ought reasonably to know) herself to be pregnant is to be regarded as being under the same duty to take care for the safety of her unborn child as the law imposes on her with respect to the safety of other people; and if in consequence of her breach of that duty her child is born with disabilities which would not otherwise have been present, those disabilities are to be regarded as damage resulting from her wrongful act and actionable accordingly at the suit of the child.

3   Disabled birth due to radiation

(1) Section 1 of this Act does not affect the operation of the Nuclear Installations Act 1965 as to liability for, and compensation in respect of, injury or damage caused by occurrences involving nuclear matter or the emission of ionising radiations.

(2) For the avoidance of doubt anything which –

(a) affects a man in his ability to have a normal, healthy child; or

(b) affects a woman in that ability, or so affects her when she is pregnant that her child is born with disabilities which would not otherwise have been present, is an injury for the purposes of that Act.

(3) If a child is born disabled as the result of an injury to either of its parents caused in breach of a duty imposed by any of sections 7 to 11 of that Act (nuclear site licensees and others to secure that nuclear incidents do not cause injury to persons, etc.), the child's disabilities are to be regarded under the subsequent provisions of that Act (compensation and other matters) as injuries caused on the same occasion, and by the same breach of duty, as was the injury to the parent.

(4) As respects compensation to the child, section 13(6) of that Act (contributory fault of person injured by radiation) is to be applied as if the reference there to fault were to the fault of the parent.

(5) Compensation is not payable in the child's case if the injury to the parent preceded the time of the child's conception and at that time either or both of the parents knew the risk of their child being born disabled (that is to say, the particular risk created by the injury).

4   Interpretation and other supplementary provisions

(1) References in this Act to a child being born disabled or with disabilities are to its being born with any deformity, disease or abnormality, including predisposition (whether or not susceptible of immediate prognosis) to physical or mental defect in the future.

(2) In this Act –

(a) 'born' means born alive (the moment of a child's birth being when it first has a life separate from its mother), and 'birth' has a corresponding meaning; and

(b) 'motor vehicle' means a mechanically propelled vehicle intended or adapted for use on roads.

and reference to embryos shall be construed in accordance with section 1 of the Human Fertilisation and Embryology Act 1990.

(3) Liability to a child under section 1, 1A or 2 of this Act is to be regarded –

(a) as respects all its incidents and any matters arising or to arise out of it; and

(b) subject to any contrary context or intention, for the purpose of construing references in enactments and documents to personal or bodily injuries and cognate matters,

as liability for personal injuries sustained by the child immediately after its birth.

(4) No damages shall be recoverable under any of those sections in respect of any loss of expectation of life, nor shall any such loss be taken into account in the compensation payable in respect of a child under the Nuclear Installations Act 1965 as extended by section 3, unless (in either case) the child lives for at least 48 hours.

(4A) In any case where a child carried by a woman as the result of the placing in her of an embryo or of sperm and eggs or her artificial insemination is born disabled, any reference in section 1 of this Act to a parent includes a reference to a person who would be a parent but for sections 27 to 29 of the Human Fertilisation and Embryology Act 1990.

(5) This Act applies in respect of births after (but not before) its passing, and in respect of any such birth it replaces any law in force before its passing, whereby a person could be liable to a child in respect of disabilities with which it might be born; but in section 1(3) of this Act the expression 'liable in tort' does not include any reference to liability by virtue of this Act, or to liability by virtue of any such law.

5   Crown application
This Act binds the Crown.

Adoption Act 1976

(1976, c. 36)

39   Status conferred by adoption

(1) An adopted child shall be treated in law –

    (a) where the adopters are a married couple, as if he had been born as a child of the marriage (whether or not he was in fact born after the marriage was solemnized);

    (b) in any other case, as if he had been born to the adopter in wedlock (but not as a child of any actual marriage of the adopter).

(2) An adopted child shall, subject to subsections (3) and (3A), be treated in law as if he were not the child of any person other than the adopters or adopter.

(3) In the case of a child adopted by one of its natural parents as sole adoptive parent, subsection (2) has no effect as respects entitlement to property depending on relationship to that parent, or as respects anything else depending on that relationship.

(4) It is hereby declared that this section prevents an adopted child from being illegitimate.

Unfair Contract Terms Act 1977

(1977, c. 50)

1   Scope of Part I

(1) For the purposes of this Part of this Act, 'negligence' means the breach –

    (a) of any obligation, arising from the express or implied terms of a contract, to take reasonable care or exercise reasonable skill in the performance of the contract;

    (b) of any common law duty to take reasonable care or exercise reasonable skill (but not any stricter duty);

(3) In the case of both contract and tort, sections 2 to 7 apply (except where the contrary is stated in section 6(4)) only to business liability, that is liability for breach of obligations or duties arising –

    (a) from things done or to be done by a person in the course of a business (whether his own business or another's) ...

(4) In relation to any breach of duty or obligation, it is immaterial for any purpose of this Part of this Act whether the breach was inadvertent or intentional, or whether liability for it arises directly or vicariously.

2 Negligence liability

(1) A person cannot by reference to any contract term or to a notice given to persons generally or to particular persons exclude or restrict his liability for death or personal injury resulting from negligence.

(2) In the case of other loss or damage, a person cannot so exclude or restrict his liability for negligence except in so far as the term or notice satisfies the requirement of reasonableness.

(3) Where a contract term or notice purports to exclude or restrict liability for negligence a person's agreement to or awareness of it is not of itself to be taken as indicating his voluntary acceptance of any risk.

3 Liability arising in contract

(1) This section applies as between contracting parties where one of them deals as consumer or on the other's written standard terms of business.

(2) As against that party, the other cannot by reference to any contract term –

    (a) when himself in breach of contract, exclude or restrict any liability of his in respect of the breach; or

    (b) claim to be entitled –

        (i) to render a contractual performance substantially different from that which was reasonably expected of him, or

        (ii) in respect of the whole or any part of his contractual obligation, to render no performance at all,

except in so far as (in any of the cases mentioned above in this subsection) the contract term satisfies the requirement of reasonableness.

11 The 'reasonableness' test

(1) In relation to a contract term, the requirement of reasonableness for the purposes of this Part of this Act, section 3 of the Misrepresentation Act 1967 and section 3 of the Misrepresentation Act (Northern Ireland) 1967 is that the term shall have been a fair and reasonable one to be included having regard to the circumstances which were, or ought reasonably to have been, known to or in the contemplation of the parties when the contract was made.

(4) Where by reference to a contract term or notice a person seeks to restrict liability to a specified sum of money, and the question arises (under this or any other Act) whether the term or notice satisfies the requirement of reasonableness, regard shall be had in particular (but without prejudice to subsection (2) above in the case of contract terms) to –

    (a) the resources which he could expect to be available to him for the purpose of meeting the liability should it arise; and

    (b) how far it was open to him to cover himself by insurance.

(5) It is for those claiming that a contract term or notice satisfies the requirement of reasonableness to show that it does.

12 'Dealing as consumer'

(1) A party to a contract 'deals as consumer' in relation to another party if –

    (a) he neither makes the contract in the course of a business nor holds himself out as doing so; and

    (b) the other party does make the contract in the course of a business.

Vaccine Damage Payments Act 1979

(1979, c. 17)

1 Payments to persons severely disabled by vaccination

(1) If, on consideration of a claim, the Secretary of State is satisfied –

    (a) that a person is, or was immediately before his death, severely disabled as a result of vaccination against any of the diseases to which this Act applies; and

(b) that the conditions of entitlement which are applicable in accordance with section 2 below are fulfilled,

he shall in accordance with this Act make a payment of the relevant statutory sum to or for the benefit of that person or to his personal representatives.

(1A) In subsection (1) above 'statutory sum' means £100,000 or such other sum as is specified by the Secretary of State for the purposes of this Act by order made by statutory instrument with the consent of the Treasury; and the relevant statutory sum for the purposes of that subsection is the statutory sum at the time when a claim for payment is first made.

(2) The diseases to which this Act applies are –
- (a) diphtheria,
- (b) tetanus,
- (c) whooping cough,
- (d) poliomyelitis,
- (e) measles,
- (f) mumps,
- (g) rubella,
- (h) tuberculosis,
- (i) smallpox, and
- (j) any other disease which is specified by the Secretary of State for the purpose of this Act by order made by statutory instrument.

(3) Subject to section 2(3) below, this Act has effect with respect to a person who is severely disabled as a result of a vaccination given to his mother before he was born as if the vaccination had been given directly to him and, in such circumstances as may be prescribed by regulations under this Act, this Act has effect with respect to a person who is severely disabled as a result of contracting a disease through contact with a third person who was vaccinated against it as if the vaccination had been given to him and the disablement resulted from it.

(4) For the purposes of this Act, a person is severely disabled if he suffers disablement to the extent of 60 per cent. or more, assessed as for the purposes of section 103 of the Social Security Contributions and Benefits Act 1992 or section 103 of the Social Security Contributions and Benefits (Northern Ireland) Act 1992 (disablement gratuity and pension).

(4A) No order shall be made by virtue of subsection (1A) above unless a draft of the order has been laid before Parliament and been approved by a resolution of each House.

(5) A statutory instrument under subsection (2)(i) above shall be subject to annulment in pursuance of a resolution of either House of Parliament.

2   Conditions of entitlement

(1) Subject to the provisions of this section, the conditions of entitlement referred to in section 1(1)(b) above are –
- (a) that the vaccination in question was carried out –
  - (i) in the United Kingdom or the Isle of Man, and
  - (ii) on or after 5th July 1948, and
  - (iii) in the case of vaccination against smallpox, before 1st August 1971;
- (b) except in the case of vaccination against poliomyelitis or rubella, that the vaccination was carried out either at a time when the person to whom it was given was under the age of eighteen or at the time of an outbreak within the United Kingdom or the Isle of Man of the disease against which the vaccination was given; and
- (c) that the disabled person was over the age of two on the date when the claim was made or, if he died before that date, that he died after 9th May 1978 and was over the age of two when he died.

(2) An order under section 1 (2)(i) above specifying a disease for the purposes of this Act may provide that, in relation to vaccination against that disease, the conditions of entitlement specified in subsection (1) above shall have effect subject to such modifications as may be specified in the order.

(3) In a case where this Act has effect by virtue of section 1(3) above, the reference in sub-section (1)(b) above to the person to whom a vaccination was given is a reference to the person to whom it was actually given and not to the disabled person.

(4) With respect to claims made after such date as may be specified in the order and relating to vaccination against such disease as may be so specified, the Secretary of State may by order made by statutory instrument –

    (a) provide that, in such circumstances as may be specified in the order, one or more of the conditions of entitlement appropriate to vaccination against that disease need not be fulfilled; or

    (b) add to the conditions of entitlement which are appropriate to vaccination against that disease, either generally or in such circumstances as may be specified in the order.

3   Determination of claims

(1) Any reference in this Act, other than section 7, to a claim is a reference to a claim for a payment under section 1(1) above which is made –

    (a) by or on behalf of the disabled person concerned or, as the case may be, by his personal representatives; and

    (b) in the manner prescribed by regulations under this Act; and

    (c) on or before whichever is the later of –

        (i) the date on which the disabled person attains the age of 21, or where he has died, the date on which he would have attained the age of 21; and

        (ii) the end of the period of six years beginning with the date of the vaccination to which the claim relates;

and, in relation to a claim, any reference to the claimant is a reference to the person by whom the claim was made and any reference to the disabled person is a reference to the person in respect of whose disablement a payment under subsection (1) above is claimed to be payable.

(5) If in any case a person is severely disabled, the question whether his severe disablement results from vaccination against any of the diseases to which this Act applies shall be determined for the purposes of this Act on the balance of probability.

4   Appeals to appeal tribunals

(1) The claimant may appeal to an appeal tribunal against any decision of the Secretary of State under section 3 or 3A above.

6   Payments to or for the benefit of disabled persons

(4) The making of a claim for, or the receipt of, a payment under section 1(1) above does not prejudice the right of any person to institute or carry on proceedings in respect of disablement suffered as a result of vaccination against any disease to which this Act applies; but in any civil proceedings brought in respect of disablement resulting from vaccination against such a disease, the court shall treat a payment made to or in respect of the disabled person concerned under section 1(1) above as paid on account of any damages which the court awards in respect of such disablement.

Sale of Goods Act 1979

(1979, c. 54)

14   Implied terms about quality or fitness

(1) Except as provided by this section and section 15 below and subject to any other enact-ment, there is no implied condition or warranty about the quality or fitness for any particular purpose of goods supplied under a contract of sale.

(2) Where the seller sells goods in the course of a business, there is an implied term that the goods supplied under the contract are of satisfactory quality.

(2A) For the purpose of this Act, goods are of satisfactory quality if they meet the standard that a reasonable person would regard as satisfactory, taking account of any description of the goods, the price (if relevant) and all the other relevant circumstances.

(2B) For the purposes of this Act, the quality of goods includes their state and condition and the following (among others) are in appropriate cases aspects of the quality of goods –

> (a) fitness for all the purposes for which goods of the kind in question are commonly supplied,
>
> (b) appearance and finish,
>
> (c) freedom from minor defects,
>
> (d) safety, and
>
> (e) durability.

(2C) The term implied by subsection (2) above does not extend to any matter making the quality of goods unsatisfactory –

> (a) which is specifically drawn to the buyer's attention before the contract is made,
>
> (b) where the buyer examines the goods before the contract is made, which that examination ought to reveal, or
>
> (c) in the case of a contract for sale by sample, which would have been apparent on a reasonable examination of the sample.

(2D) If the buyer deals as consumer or, in Scotland, if a contract of sale is a consumer contract, the relevant circumstances mentioned in subsection (2A) above include any public statements on the specific characteristics of the goods made about them by the seller, the producer or his representative, particularly in advertising or on labelling.

(2E) A public statement is not by virtue of subsection (2D) above a relevant circumstance for the purposes of subsection (2A) above in the case of a contract of sale, if the seller shows that –

> (a) at the time the contract was made, he was not, and could not reasonably have been, aware of the statement,
>
> (b) before the contract was made, the statement had been withdrawn in public or, to the extent that it contained anything which was incorrect or misleading, it had been corrected in public, or
>
> (c) the decision to buy the goods could not have been influenced by the statement.

(2F) Subsections (2D) and (2E) above do not prevent any public statement from being a relevant circumstance for the purposes of subsection (2A) above (whether or not the buyer deals as consumer or, in Scotland, whether or not the contract of sale is a consumer contract) if the statement would have been such a circumstance apart from those subsections.

(3) Where the seller sells goods in the course of a business and the buyer, expressly or by implication, makes known –

> (a) to the seller, or
>
> (b) where the purchase price or part of it is payable by instalments and the goods were previously sold by a credit-broker to the seller, to that credit-broker,

any particular purpose for which the goods are being bought, there is an implied condition that the goods supplied under the contract are reasonably fit for that purpose, whether or not that is a purpose for which such goods are commonly supplied, except where the circumstances show that the buyer does not rely, or that it is unreasonable for him to rely, on the skill or judgement of the seller or credit-broker.

(4) An implied condition or warranty about quality or fitness for a particular purpose may be annexed to a contract of sale by usage.

(5) The preceding provisions of this section apply to a sale by a person who in the course of a business is acting as agent for another as they apply to a sale by a principal in the course of a business and either the buyer knows that fact or reasonable steps are taken to bring it to the notice of the buyer before the contract is made.

(6) Goods of any kind are of merchantable quality within the meaning of subsection (2) above if they are as fit for the purpose or purposes for which goods of that kind are commonly bought as it

is reasonable to expect having regard to any description applied to them, the price (if relevant) and all the other relevant circumstances.

Supreme Court Act 1981

(1981, c. 54)

33   Powers of High Court exercisable before commencement of action

(1) On the application of any person in accordance with rules of court, the High Court shall, in such circumstances as may be specified in the rules, have power to make an order providing for any one or more of the following matters, that is to say –

    (a) the inspection, photographing, preservation, custody and detention of property which appears to the court to be property which may become the subject-matter of subsequent proceedings in the High Court, or as to which any question may arise in any such proceedings; and

    (b) the taking of samples of any such property as is mentioned in paragraph (a), and the carrying out of any experiment on or with any such property.

(2) On the application, in accordance with rules of court, of a person who appears to the High Court to be likely to be a party to subsequent proceedings in that court the High Court shall, in such circumstances as may be specified in the rules, have power to order a person who appears to the court to be likely to be a party to the proceedings and to be likely to have or to have had in his possession, custody or power any documents which are relevant to an issue arising or likely to arise out of that claim –

    (a) to disclose whether those documents are in his possession, custody or power; and

    (b) to produce such of those documents as are in his possession, custody or power to the applicant or, on such conditions as may be specified in the order –

        (i)   to the applicant's legal advisers; or

        (ii) to the applicant's legal advisers and any medical or other professional adviser of the applicant; or

        (iii) if the applicant has no legal adviser, to any medical or other professional adviser of the applicant.

34   Power of High Court to order disclosure of documents, inspection of property etc. in proceedings for personal injuries or death

(2) On the application, in accordance with rules of court, of a party to any proceedings, the High Court shall, in such circumstances as may be specified in the rules, have power to order a person who is not a party to the proceedings and who appears to the court to be likely to have in his possession, custody or power any documents which are relevant to an issue arising out of the said claim –

    (a) to disclose whether those documents are in his possession, custody or power; and

    (b) to produce such of those documents as are in his possession, custody or power to the applicant or, on such conditions as may be specified in the order –

        (i)   to the applicant's legal advisers; or

        (ii) to the applicant's legal advisers and any medical or other professional adviser of the applicant; or

        (iii) if the applicant has no legal adviser, to any medical or other professional adviser of the applicant;

(3) On the application, in accordance with rules of court, of a party to any proceedings, the High Court shall, in such circumstances as may be specified in the rules, have power to make an order providing for any one or more of the following matters, that is to say –

    (a) the inspection, photographing, preservation, custody and detention of property which is not the property of, or in the possession of, any party to the proceedings but which is the subject-matter of the proceedings or as to which any question arises in the proceedings;

(b) the taking of samples of any such property as is mentioned in paragraph (a) and the carrying out of any experiment on or with any such property.

(4) The preceding provisions of this section are without prejudice to the exercise by the High Court of any power to make orders which is exercisable apart from those provisions.

35   Provisions supplementary to ss. 33 and 34

(1) The High Court shall not make an order under section 33 or 34 if it considers that compliance with the order, if made, would be likely to be injurious to the public interest.

(5) In sections 32A, 33 and 34 and this section –

'property' includes any land, chattel or other corporeal property of any description;

'personal injuries' includes any disease and any impairment of a person's physical or mental condition.

41   Wards of court

(1) Subject to the provisions of this section, no minor shall be made a ward of court except by virtue of an order to that effect made by the High Court.

(2) Where an application is made for such an order in respect of a minor, the minor shall become a ward of court on the making of the application, but shall cease to be a ward of court at the end of such period as may be prescribed unless within that period an order has been made in accordance with the application.

(2A) Subsection (2) does not apply with respect to a child who is the subject of a care order (as defined by section 105 of the Children Act 1989).

(3) The High Court may, either upon an application in that behalf or without such an application, order that any minor who is for the time being a ward of court shall cease to be a ward of court.

Supply of Goods and Services Act 1982

(1982, c. 29)

12   The contracts concerned

(1) In this Act a 'contract for the supply of a service' means, subject to subsection (2) below, a contract under which a person ('the supplier') agrees to carry out a service.

(2) For the purposes of this Act, a contract of service or apprenticeship is not a contract for the supply of a service.

(3) Subject to subsection (2) above, a contract is a contract for the supply of a service for the purposes of this Act whether or not goods are also –

(a) transferred or to be transferred, or

(b) bailed or to be bailed by way of hire,

under the contract, and whatever is the nature of the consideration for which the service is to be carried out.

(4) The Secretary of State may by order provide that one or more of sections 13 to 15 below shall not apply to services of a description specified in the order, and such an order may make different provision for different circumstances.

(5) The power to make an order under subsection (4) above shall be exercisable by statutory instrument subject to annulment in pursuance of a resolution of either House of Parliament.

13   Implied term about care and skill

In a contract for the supply of a service where the supplier is acting in the course of a business, there is an implied term that the supplier will carry out the service with reasonable care and skill.

16   Exclusion of implied terms, etc.

(1) Where a right, duty or liability would arise under a contract for the supply of a service by virtue of this Part of this Act, it may (subject to subsection (2) below and the 1977 Act) be negatived or varied by express agreement, or by the course of dealing between the parties, or by such usage as binds both parties to the contract.

(2) An express term does not negative a term implied by this Part of this Act unless inconsistent with it.

(3) Nothing in this Part of this Act prejudices –

(a) any rule of law which imposes on the supplier a duty stricter than that imposed by section 13 or 14 above; or

(b) subject to paragraph (a) above, any rule of law whereby any term not inconsistent with this Part of this Act is to be implied in a contract for the supply of a service.

(4) This Part of this Act has effect subject to any other enactment which defines or restricts the rights, duties or liabilities arising in connection with a service of any description.

Mental Health Act 1983

(1983, c. 20)

Part I Application of Act

1   Application of Act: 'mental disorder'

(1) The provisions of this Act shall have effect with respect to the reception, care and treatment of mentally disordered patients, the management of their property and other related matters.

(2) In this Act –

'mental disorder' means mental illness, arrested or incomplete development of mind, psychopathic disorder and any other disorder or disability of mind and 'mentally disordered' shall be construed accordingly;

'severe mental impairment' means a state of arrested or incomplete development of mind which includes severe impairment of intelligence and social functioning and is associated with abnormally aggressive or seriously irresponsible conduct on the part of the person concerned and 'severely mentally impaired' shall be construed accordingly;

'mental impairment' means a state of arrested or incomplete development of mind (not amounting to severe mental impairment) which includes significant impairment of intelligence and social functioning and is associated with abnormally aggressive or seriously irresponsible conduct on the part of the person concerned and 'mentally impaired' shall be construed accordingly;

'psychopathic disorder' means a persistent disorder or disability of mind (whether or not including significant impairment of intelligence) which results in abnormally aggressive or seriously irresponsible conduct on the part of the person concerned;

and other expressions shall have the meanings assigned to them in section 145 below.

(3) Nothing in subsection (2) above shall be construed as implying that a person may be dealt with under this Act as suffering from mental disorder, or from any form of mental disorder described in this section, by reason only of promiscuity or other immoral conduct, sexual deviancy or dependence on alcohol or drugs.

Part II Compulsory Admission to Hospital and Guardianship

Procedure for hospital admission

2   Admission for assessment

(1) A patient may be admitted to a hospital and detained there for the period allowed by subsection (4) below in pursuance of an application (in this Act referred to as 'an application for admission for assessment') made in accordance with subsections (2) and (3) below.

(2) An application for admission for assessment may be made in respect of a patient on the grounds that –

(a) he is suffering from mental disorder of a nature or degree which warrants the detention of the patient in a hospital for assessment (or for assessment followed by medical treatment) for at least a limited period; and

(b) he ought to be so detained in the interests of his own health or safety or with a view to the protection of other persons.

(3) An application for admission for assessment shall be founded on the written recommendations in the prescribed form of two registered medical practitioners, including in each case a

statement that in the opinion of the practitioner the conditions set out in subsection (2) above are complied with.

(4) Subject to the provisions of section 29(4) below, a patient admitted to hospital in pursuance of an application for admission for assessment may be detained for a period not exceeding 28 days beginning with the day on which he is admitted, but shall not be detained after the expiration of that period unless before it has expired he has become liable to be detained by virtue of a subsequent application, order or direction under the following provisions of this Act.

3   Admission for treatment

(1) A patient may be admitted to a hospital and detained there for the period allowed by the following provisions of this Act in pursuance of an application (in this Act referred to as 'an application for admission for treatment') made in accordance with this section.

(2) An application for admission for treatment may be made in respect of a patient on the grounds that –

(a) he is suffering from mental illness, severe mental impairment, psychopathic disorder or mental impairment and his mental disorder is of a nature or degree which makes it appropriate for him to receive medical treatment in a hospital; and

(b) in the case of psychopathic disorder or mental impairment, such treatment is likely to alleviate or prevent a deterioration of his condition; and

(c) it is necessary for the health or safety of the patient or for the protection of other persons that he should receive such treatment and it cannot be provided unless he is detained under this section.

(3) An application for admission for treatment shall be founded on the written recommendations in the prescribed form of two registered medical practitioners, including in each case a statement that in the opinion of the practitioner the conditions set out in subsection (2) above are complied with; and each such recommendation shall include –

(a) such particulars as may be prescribed of the grounds for that opinion so far as it relates to the conditions set out in paragraphs (a) and (b) of that subsection; and

(b) a statement of the reasons for that opinion so far as it relates to the conditions set out in paragraph (c) of that subsection, specifying whether other methods of dealing with the patient are available and, if so, why they are not appropriate.

4   Admission for assessment in cases of emergency

(1) In any case of urgent necessity, an application for admission for assessment may be made in respect of a patient in accordance with the following provisions of this section, and any application so made is in this Act referred to as 'an emergency application'.

(2) An emergency application may be made either by an approved social worker or by the nearest relative of the patient; and every such application shall include a statement that it is of urgent necessity for the patient to be admitted and detained under section 2 above, and that compliance with the provisions of this Part of this Act relating to applications under that section would involve undesirable delay.

(3) An emergency application shall be sufficient in the first instance if founded on one of the medical recommendations required by section 2 above, given, if practicable, by a practitioner who has previous acquaintance with the patient and otherwise complying with the requirements of section 12 below so far as applicable to a single recommendation, and verifying the statement referred to in subsection (2) above.

(4) An emergency application shall cease to have effect on the expiration of a period of 72 hours from the time when the patient is admitted to the hospital unless –

(a) the second medical recommendation required by section 2 above is given and received by the managers within that period; and

(b) that recommendation and the recommendation referred to in subsection (3) above together comply with all the requirements of section 12 below (other than the requirement as to the time of signature of the second recommendation).

(5) In relation to an emergency application, section 11 below shall have effect as if in sub-section (5) of that section for the words 'the period of 14 days ending with the date of the application' there were substituted the words 'the previous 24 hours'.

5   Application in respect of patient already in hospital

(1) An application for the admission of a patient to a hospital may be made under this Part of this Act notwithstanding that the patient is already an in-patient in that hospital or, in the case of an application for admission for treatment that the patient is for the time being liable to be detained in the hospital in pursuance of an application for admission for assessment; and where an application is so made the patient shall be treated for the purposes of this Part of this Act as if he had been admitted to the hospital at the time when that application was received by the managers.

(2) If, in the case of a patient who is an in-patient in a hospital, it appears to the registered medical practitioner in charge of the treatment of the patient that an application ought to be made under this Part of this Act for the admission of the patient to hospital, he may furnish to the managers a report in writing to that effect; and in any such case the patient may be detained in the hospital for a period of 72 hours from the time when the report is so furnished.

(3) The registered medical practitioner in charge of the treatment of a patient in a hospital may nominate one (but not more than one) other registered medical practitioner on the staff of that hospital to act for him under subsection (2) above in his absence.

(4) If, in the case of a patient who is receiving treatment for mental disorder as an in-patient in a hospital, it appears to a nurse of the prescribed class –

(a) that the patient is suffering from mental disorder to such a degree that it is necessary for his health or safety or for the protection of others for him to be immediately restrained from leaving the hospital; and

(b) that it is not practicable to secure the immediate attendance of a practitioner for the purpose of furnishing a report under subsection (2) above,

the nurse may record that fact in writing; and in that event the patient may be detained in the hospital for a period of six hours from the time when that fact is so recorded or until the earlier arrival at the place where the patient is detained of a practitioner having power to furnish a report under that subsection.

(5) A record made under subsection (4) above shall be delivered by the nurse (or by a person authorised by the nurse in that behalf) to the managers of the hospital as soon as possible after it is made; and where a record is made under that subsection the period mentioned in subsection (2) above shall begin at the time when it is made.

(6) The reference in subsection (1) above to an in-patient does not include an in-patient who is liable to be detained in pursuance of an application under this Part of this Act and the references in subsections (2) and (4) above do not include an in-patient who is liable to be detained in a hospital under this Part of this Act.

(7) In subsection (4) above 'prescribed' means prescribed by an order made by the Secretary of State.

6   Effect of application for admission

(1) An application for the admission of a patient to a hospital under this Part of this Act, duly completed in accordance with the provisions of this Part of this Act, shall be sufficient authority for the applicant, or any person authorised by the applicant, to take the patient and convey him to the hospital at any time within the following period, that is to say –

(a) in the case of an application other than an emergency application, the period of 14 days beginning with the date on which the patient was last examined by a registered medical practitioner before giving a medical recommendation for the purposes of the application;

(b) in the case of an emergency application, the period of 24 hours beginning at the time when the patient was examined by the practitioner giving the medical recommendation which is referred to in section 4(3) above, or at the time when the application is made, whichever is the earlier.

(2) Where a patient is admitted within the said period to the hospital specified in such an application as is mentioned in subsection (1) above, or, being within that hospital, is treated by virtue of section 5 above as if he had been so admitted, the application shall be sufficient authority for the managers to detain the patient in the hospital in accordance with the provisions of this Act.

(3) Any application for the admission of a patient under this Part of this Act which appears to be duly made and to be founded on the necessary medical recommendations may be acted upon without further proof of the signature or qualification of the person by whom the application or any such medical recommendation is made or given or of any matter of fact or opinion stated in it.

(4) Where a patient is admitted to a hospital in pursuance of an application for admission for treatment, any previous application under this Part of this Act by virtue of which he was liable to be detained in a hospital or subject to guardianship shall cease to have effect.

Guardianship

7   Application for guardianship

(1) A patient who has attained the age of 16 years may be received into guardianship, for the period allowed by the following provisions of this Act, in pursuance of an application (in this Act referred to as 'a guardianship application') made in accordance with this section.

(2) A guardianship application may be made in respect of a patient on the grounds that –

(a) he is suffering from mental disorder, being mental illness, severe mental impairment, psychopathic disorder or mental impairment and his mental disorder is of a nature or degree which warrants his reception into guardianship under this section; and

(b) it is necessary in the interests of the welfare of the patient or for the protection of other persons that the patient should be so received.

(3) A guardianship application shall be founded on the written recommendations in the prescribed form of two registered medical practitioners, including in each case a statement that in the opinion of the practitioner the conditions set out in subsection (2) above are complied with; and each such recommendation shall include –

(a) such particulars as may be prescribed of the grounds for that opinion so far as it relates to the conditions set out in paragraph (a) of that subsection; and

(b) a statement of the reasons for that opinion so far as it relates to the conditions set out in paragraph (b) of that subsection.

(4) A guardianship application shall state the age of the patient or, if his exact age is not known to the applicant, shall state (if it be the fact) that the patient is believed to have attained the age of 16 years.

(5) The person named as guardian in a guardianship application may be either a local social services authority or any other person (including the applicant himself); but a guardianship application in which a person other than a local social services authority is named as guardian shall be of no effect unless it is accepted on behalf of that person by the local social services authority for the area in which he resides, and shall be accompanied by a statement in writing by that person that he is willing to act as guardian.

8   Effect of guardianship application, etc.

(1) Where a guardianship application, duly made under the provisions of this Part of this Act and forwarded to the local social services authority within the period allowed by subsection (2) below is accepted by that authority, the application shall, subject to regulations made by the Secretary of State, confer on the authority or person named in the application as guardian, to the exclusion of any other person –

(a) the power to require the patient to reside at a place specified by the authority or person named as guardian;

(b) the power to require the patient to attend at places and times so specified for the purpose of medical treatment, occupation, education or training;

(c) the power to require access to the patient to be given, at any place where the patient is residing, to any registered medical practitioner, approved social worker or other person so specified.

(2) The period within which a guardianship application is required for the purposes of this section to be forwarded to the local social services authority is the period of 14 days beginning with the date on which the patient was last examined by a registered medical practitioner before giving a medical recommendation for the purposes of the application.

(3) A guardianship application which appears to be duly made and to be founded on the necessary medical recommendations may be acted upon without further proof of the signature or qualification of the person by whom the application or any such medical recommendation is made or given, or of any matter of fact or opinion stated in the application.

(4) If within the period of 14 days beginning with the day on which a guardianship application has been accepted by the local social services authority the application, or any medical recommendation given for the purposes of the application, is found to be in any respect incorrect or defective, the application or recommendation may, within that period and with the consent of that authority, be amended by the person by whom it was signed; and upon such amendment being made the application or recommendation shall have effect and shall be deemed to have had effect as if it had been originally made as so amended.

(5) Where a patient is received into gurdianship in pursuance of a guardianship application, any previous application under this Part of this Act by virtue of which he was subject to guardianship or liable to be detained in a hospital shall cease to have effect.

9   Regulations as to guardianship

(1) Subject to the provisions of this Part of this Act, the Secretary of State may make regulations –
(a) for regulating the exercise by the guardians of patients received into guardianship under this Part of this Act of their powers as such; and
(b) for imposing on such guardians, and upon local social services authorities in the case of patients under the guardianship of persons other than local social services authorities, such duties as he considers necessary or expedient in the interests of the patients.

(2) Regulations under this section may in particular make provision for requiring the patients to be visited, on such occasions or at such intervals as may be prescribed by the regulations, on behalf of such local social services authorities as may be so prescribed, and shall provide for the appointment, in the case of every patient subject to the guardianship of a person other than a local social services authority, of a registered medical practitioner to act as the nominated medical attendant of the patient.

10   Transfer of guardianship in case of death, incapacity, etc., of guardian

(1) If any person (other than a local social services authority) who is the guardian of a patient received into guardianship under this Part of this Act –
(a) dies; or
(b) gives notice in writing to the local social services authority that he desires to relinquish the functions of guardian,
the guardianship of the patient shall thereupon vest in the local social services authority, but without prejudice to any power to transfer the patient into the guardianship of another person in pursuance of regulations under section 19 below.

(2) If any such person, not having given notice under subsection (1)(b) above, is incapacitated by illness or any other cause from performing the functions of guardian of the patient, those functions may, during his incapacity, be performed on his behalf by the local social services authority or by any other person approved for the purposes by that authority.

(3) If it appears to the country court, upon application made by an approved social worker, that any person other than a local social services authority having the guardianship of a patient

received into guardianship under this Part of this Act has performed his functions negligently or in a manner contrary to the interests of the welfare of the patient, the court may order that the guardianship of the patient be transferred to the local social services authority or to any other person approved for the purpose by that authority.

(4) Where the guardianship of a patient is transferred to a local social services authority or other person by or under this section, subsection (2)(c) of section 19 below shall apply as if the patient had been transferred into the guardianship of that authority or person in pursuance of regulations under that section.

General provisions as to applications and recommendations

11   General provisions as to applications

(1) Subject to the provisions of this section, an application for admission for assessment, an application for admission for treatment and a guardianship application may be made either by the nearest relative of the patient or by an approved social worker; and every such application shall specify the qualification of the applicant to make the application.

(2) Every application for admission shall be addressed to the managers of the hospital to which admission is sought and every guardianship application shall be forwarded to the local social services authority named in the application as guardian, or, as the case may be, to the local social services authority for the area in which the person so named resides.

(3) Before or within a reasonable time after an application for the admission of a patient for assessment is made by an approved social worker, that social worker shall take such steps as are practicable to inform the person (if any) appearing to be the nearest relative of the patient that the application is to be or has been made and of the power of the nearest relative under section 23(2) (a) below.

(4) Neither an application for admission for treatment nor a guardianship application shall be made by an approved social worker if the nearest relative of the patient has notified that social worker, or the local social services authority by whom that social worker is appointed, that he objects to the application being made and, without prejudice to the foregoing provision, no such application shall be made by such a social worker except after consultation with the person (if any) appearing to be the nearest relative of the patient unless it appears to that social worker that in the circumstances such consultation is not reasonably practicable or would involve unreasonable delay.

(5) None of the applications mentioned in subsection (1) above shall be made by any person in respect of a patient unless that person has personally seen the patient within the period of 14 days ending with the date of the application.

(6) An application for admission for treatment or a guardianship application, and any recommendation given for the purposes of such an application, may describe the patient as suffering from more than one of the following forms of mental disorder, namely mental illness, severe mental impairment, psychopathic disorder or mental impairment; but the application shall be of no effect unless the patient is described in each of the recommendations as suffering from the same form of mental disorder, whether or not he is also described in either of those recommendations as suffering from another form.

(7) Each of the applications mentioned in subsection (1) above shall be sufficient if the recommendations on which it is founded are given either as separate recommendations, each signed by a registered medical practitioner, or as a joint recommendation signed by two such practitioners.

12   General provisions as to medical recommendations

(1) The recommendations required for the purposes of an application for the admission of a patient under this Part of this Act (in this Act referred to as 'medical recommendations') shall be signed on or before the date of the application, and shall be given by practitioners who have personally examined the patient either together or separately, but where they have examined the

patient separately not more than five days must have elapsed between the days on which the separate examination took place.

(2) Of the medical recommendations given for the purposes of any such application, one shall be given by a practitioner approved for the purposes of this section by the Secretary of State as having special experience in the diagnosis or treatment of mental disorder; and unless that practitioner has previous acquaintance with the patient, the other such recommendation shall, if practicable, be given by a registered medical practitioner who has such previous acquaintance.

(3) Subject to subsection (4) below, where the application is for the admission of the patient to a hospital which is not a mental nursing home, one (but not more than one) of the medical recommendations may be given by a practitioner on the staff of that hospital, except where the patient is proposed to be accommodated under section 21(4) or 44(6) of the National Health Service Act 2006, paragraph 15 of Schedule 2 to, or paragraph 11 of Schedule 6 to, that Act, or paragraph 15 of Schedule 2 to, or paragraph 11 of Schedule 5 to, the National Health Service (Wales) Act 2006 (which relate to accommodation for private patients) or otherwise to be accommodated, by virtue of an undertaking to pay in respect of the accommodation, in a hospital vested in an NHS foundation trust.

(4) Subsection (3) above shall not preclude both the medical recommendations being given by practitioners on the staff of the hospital in question if –

(a) compliance with that subsection would result in delay involving serious risk to the health or safety of the patient; and

(b) one of the practitioners giving the recommendations works at the hospital for less than half of the time which he is bound by contract to devote to work in the health service; and

(c) where one of those practitioners is a consultant, the other does not work (whether at the hospital or elsewhere) in a grade in which he is under that consultant's directions.

(5) A medical recommendation for the purposes of an application for the admission of a patient under this Part of this Act shall not be given by –

(a) the applicant;

(b) a partner of the applicant or of a practitioner by whom another medical recommendation is given for the purposes of the same application;

(c) a person employed as an assistant by the applicant or by any such practitioner;

(d) a person who receives or has an interest in the receipt of any payments made on account of the maintenance of the patient; or

(e) except as provided by subsection (3) or (4) above, a practitioner on the staff of the hospital to which the patient is to be admitted,

or by the husband, wife, father, father-in-law, mother, mother-in-law, son, son-in-law, daughter, daughter-in-law, brother, brother-in-law, sister or sister-in-law of the patient, or of any person mentioned in paragraphs (a) to (e) above, or of a practitioner by whom another medical recommendation is given for the purposes of the same application.

(6) A general practitioner who is employed part-time in a hospital shall not for the purposes of this section be regarded as a practitioner on its staff.

(7) Subsections (1), (2) and (5) above shall apply to applications for guardianship as they apply to applications for admission but with the substitution for paragraph (e) of subsection (5) above of the following paragraph –

'(e) the person named as guardian in the application.'.

13   Duty of approved social workers to make applications for admission or guardianship

(1) It shall be the duty of an approved social worker to make an application for admission to hospital or a guardianship application in respect of a patient within the area of the local social services authority by which that officer is appointed in any case where he is satisfied that such an application ought to be made and is of the opinion, having regard to any wishes expressed by

relatives of the patient or any other relevant circumstances, that it is necessary or proper for the application to be made by him.

(2) Before making an application for the admission of a patient to hospital an approved social worker shall interview the patient in a suitable manner and satisfy himself that detention in a hospital is in all the circumstances of the case the most appropriate way of providing the care and medical treatment of which the patient stands in need.

(3) An application under this section by an approved social worker may be made outside the area of the local social services authority by which he is appointed.

(4) It shall be the duty of a local social services authority, if so required by the nearest relative of a patient residing in their area, to direct an approved social worker as soon as practicable to take the patient's case into consideration under subsection (1) above with a view to making an application for his admission to hospital; and if in any such case that approved social worker decides not to make an application he shall inform the nearest relative of his reasons in writing.

(5) Nothing in this section shall be construed as authorising or requiring an application to be made by an approved social worker in contravention of the provisions of section 11(4) above, or as restricting the power of an approved social worker to make any application under this Act.

14   Social reports

Where a patient is admitted to a hospital in pursuance of an application (other than an emergency application) made under this Part of this Act by his nearest relative, the managers of the hospital shall as soon as practicable give notice of that fact to the local social services authority for the area in which the patient resided immediately before his admission; and that authority shall as soon as practicable arrange for a social worker to interview the patient and provide the managers with a report of his social circumstances.

15   Rectification of applications and recommendations

(1) If within the period of 14 days beginning with the day on which a patient has been admitted to a hospital in pursuance of an application for admission for assessment or for treatment the application, or any medical recommendation given for the purpose of the application, is found to be in any respect incorrect or defective, the application or recommendation may, within that period and with the consent of the managers of the hospital, be amended by the person by whom it was signed; and upon such amendment being made the application or recommendation shall have effect and shall be deemed to have had effect as if it had been originally made as so amended.

(2) Without prejudice to subsection (1) above, if within the period mentioned in that subsection it appears to the managers of the hospital that one of the two medical recommendations on which an application for the admission of a patient is founded is insufficient to warrant the detention of the patient in pursuance of the application, they may, within that period, give notice in writing to that effect to the applicant; and where any such notice is given in respect of a medical recommendation, that recommendation shall be disregarded, but the application shall be, and shall be deemed always to have been, sufficient if –

    (a) a fresh medical recommendation complying with the relevant provisions of this Part of this Act (other than the provisions relating to the time of signature and the interval between examinations) is furnished to the managers within that period; and

    (b) that recommendation, and the other recommendation on which the application is founded, together comply with those provisions.

(3) Where the medical recommendations upon which an application for admission is founded are, taken together, insufficient to warrant the detention of the patient in pursuance of the application, a notice under subsection (2) above may be given in respect of either of those recommendations; but this subsection shall not apply in a case where the application is of no effect by virtue of section 11(6) above.

(4) Nothing in this section shall be construed as authorising the giving of notice in respect of an application made as an emergency application, or the detention of a patient admitted in pursuance

of such an application, after the period of 72 hours referred to in section 4(4) above, unless the conditions set out in paragraphs (a) and (b) of that section are complied with or would be complied with apart from any error or defect to which this section applies.

Position of patients subject to detention or guardianship

16   Reclassification of patients

(1) If in the case of a patient who is for the time being detained in a hospital in pursuance of an application for admission for treatment, or subject to guardianship in pursuance of a guardianship application, it appears to the appropriate medical officer that the patient is suffering form a form of mental disorder other than the form or forms specified in the application, he may furnish to the managers of the hospital, or to the guardian, as the case may be, a report to that effect; and where a report is so furnished, the application shall have effect as if that other form of mental disorder were specified in it.

(2) Where a report under subsection (1) above in respect of a patient detained in a hospital is to the effect that he is suffering from psychopathic disorder or mental impairment but not from mental illness or severe mental impairment the appropriate medical officer shall include in the report a statement of his opinion whether further medical treatment in hospital is likely to alleviate or prevent a deterioration of the patient's condition; and if he states that in his opinion such treatment is not likely to have that effect the authority of the managers to detain the patient shall cease.

(3) Before furnishing a report under subsection (1) above the appropriate medical officer shall consult one or more other persons who have been professionally concerned with the patient's medical treatment.

(4) Where a report is furnished under this section in respect of a patient, the managers or guardian shall cause the patient and the nearest relative to be informed.

(5) In this section 'appropriate medical officer' means –

(a) in the case of a patient who is subject to the guardianship of a person other than a local social services authority, the nominated medical attendant of the patient; and

(b) in any other case, the responsible medical officer.

17   Leave of absence from hospital

(1) The responsible medical officer may grant to any patient who is for the time being liable to be detained in a hospital under this Part of this Act leave to be absent from the hospital subject to such conditions (if any) as that officer considers necessary in the interests of the patient or for the protection of other persons.

(2) Leave of absence may be granted to a patient under this section either indefinitely or on specified occasions or for any specified period; and where leave is so granted for a specified period, that period may be extended by further leave granted in the absence of the patient.

(3) Where it appears to the responsible medical officer that it is necessary so to do in the interests of the patient or for the protection of other persons, he may, upon granting leave of absence under this section, direct that the patient remain in custody during his absence; and where leave of absence is so granted the patient may be kept in the custody of any officer on the staff of the hospital, or of any other person authorised in writing by the managers of the hospital or, if the patient is required in accordance with conditions imposed on the grant of leave of absence to reside in another hospital, of any officer on the staff of that other hospital.

(4) In any case where a patient is absent from a hospital in pursuance of leave of absence granted under this section, and it appears to the responsible medical officer that it is necessary so to do in the interests of the patient's health or safety or for the protection of other persons, that officer may, subject to subsection (5) below, by notice in writing given to the patient or to the person for the time being in charge of the patient, revoke the leave of absence and recall the patient to the hospital.

(5) A patient to whom leave of absence is granted under this section shall not be recalled under subsection (4) above after he has ceased to be liable to be detained under this Part of this Act.

18   Return and readmission of patients absent without leave

(1) Where a patient who is for the time being liable to be detained under this Part of this Act in a hospital –

(a) absents himself from the hospital without leave granted under section 17 above; or

(b) fails to return to the hospital on any occasion on which, or at the expiration of any period for which, leave of absence was granted to him under that section, or upon being recalled under that section; or

(c) absents himself without permission from any place where he is required to reside in accordance with conditions imposed on the grant of leave of absence under that section, he may, subject to the provisions of this section, be taken into custody and returned to the hospital or place by any approved social worker, by any officer on the staff of the hospital, by any constable, or by any person authorised in writing by the managers of the hospital.

(2) Where the place referred to in paragraph (c) of subsection (1) above is a hospital other than the one in which the patient is for the time being liable to be detained, the references in that subsection to an officer on the staff of the hospital and the managers of the hospital shall respectively include references to an officer on the staff of the first-mentioned hospital and the managers of that hospital.

(3) Where a patient who is for the time being subject to guardianship under this Part of this Act absents himself without the leave of the guardian from the place at which he is required by the guardian to reside, he may, subject to the provisions of this section, be taken into custody and returned to that place by any officer on the staff of a local social services authority, by any constable, or by any person authorised in writing by the guardian or a local social services authority.

(4) A patient shall not be taken into custody under this section after the later of –

(a) the end of the period of six months beginning with the first day of his absence without leave; and

(b) the end of the period for which (apart from section 21 below) he is liable to be detained or subject to guardianship;

and, in determining for the purposes of paragraph (b) above or any other provision of this Act whether a person who is or has been absent without leave is at any time liable to be detained or subject to guardianship, a report furnished under section 20 or 21B below before the first day of his absence without leave shall not be taken to have renewed the authority for his detention or guardianship unless the period of renewal began before that day.

(5) A patient shall not be taken into custody under this section if the period for which he is liable to be detained is that specified in section 2(4), 4(4) or 5(2) or (4) above and that period has expired.

(6) In this Act 'absent without leave' means absent from any hospital or other place and liable to be taken into custody and returned under this section, and related expressions shall be construed accordingly.

19   Regulations as to transfer of patients

(1) In such circumstances and subject to such conditions as may be prescribed by regulations made by the Secretary of State –

(a) a patient who is for the time being liable to be detained in a hospital by virtue of an application under this Part of this Act may be transferred to another hospital or into the guardianship of a local social services authority or of any person approved by such an authority;

(b) a patient who is for the time being subject to the guardianship of a local social services authority or other person by virtue of an application under this Part of this Act may be transferred into the guardianship of another local social services authority or person, or be transferred to a hospital.

(2) Where a patient is transferred in pursuance of regulations under this section, the provisions of this Part of this Act (including this subsection) shall apply to him as follows, that is to say –

(a) in the case of a patient who is liable to be detained in a hospital by virtue of an application for admission for assessment or for treatment and is transferred to another hospital, as if the application were an application for admission to that other hospital and as if the patient had been admitted to that other hospital at the time when he was originally admitted in pursuance of the application;

(b) in the case of a patient who is liable to be detained in a hospital by virtue of such an application and is transferred into guardianship, as if the application were a guardianship application duly accepted at the said time;

(c) in the case of a patient who is subject to guardianship by virtue of a guardianship application and is transferred into the guardianship of another authority or person, as if the application were for his reception into the guardianship of that authority or person and had been accepted at the time when it was originally accepted;

(d) in the case of a patient who is subject to guardianship by virtue of a guardianship application and is transferred to a hospital, as if the guardianship application were an application for admission to that hospital for treatment and as if the patient had been admitted to the hospital at the time when the application was originally accepted.

(3) Without prejudice to subsections (1) and (2) above, any patient, who is for the time being liable to be detained under this Part of this Act in a hospital vested in the Secretary of State for the purposes of his functions under the National Health Service Act 2006, in a hospital vested in the Welsh Ministers for the purposes of their functions under the National Health Service (Wales) Act 2006, in any accommodation used under either of those Acts by the managers of such a hospital, or in a hospital vested in a National Health Service trust or NHS foundation trust or Primary Care Trust may at any time be removed to any other such hospital or accommodation which is managed by the mangers of, or is vested in the National Health Service trust or NHS foundation trust or Primary Care Trust for, the first mentioned hospital; and paragraph (a) of subsection (2) above shall apply in relation to a patient so removed as it applies in relation to a patient transferred in pursuance of regulations made under this section.

(4) Regulations made under this section may make provision for regulating the conveyance to their destination of patients authorised to be transferred or removed in pursuance of the regulations or under subsection (3) above.

Duration of detention or guardianship and discharge

20   Duration of authority

(1) Subject to the following provisions of this Part of this Act, a patient admitted to hospital in pursuance of an application for admission for treatment, and a patient placed under guardianship in pursuance of a guardianship application, may be detained in a hospital or kept under guardianship for a period not exceeding six months beginning with the day on which he was so admitted, or the day on which the guardianship application was accepted, as the case may be, but shall not be so detained or kept for any longer period unless the authority for his detention or guardianship is renewed under this section.

(2) Authority for the detention or guardianship of a patient may, unless the patient has previously been discharged, be renewed –

(a) from the expiration of the period referred to in subsection (1) above, for a further period of six months;

(b) from the expiration of any period of renewal under paragraph (a) above, for a further period of one year,

and so on for periods of one year at a time.

(3) Within the period of two months ending on the day on which a patient who is liable to be detained in pursuance of an application for admission for treatment would cease under this section to be so liable in default of the renewal of the authority for his detention, it shall be the duty of the responsible medical officer –

(a) to examine the patient; and

(b) if it appears to him that the conditions set out in subsection (4) below are satisfied, to furnish to the managers of the hospital where the patient is detained a report to that effect in the prescribed form;

and where such a report is furnished in respect of a patient the managers shall, unless they discharge the patient, cause him to be informed.

(4) The conditions referred to in subsection (3) above are that –

(a) the patient is suffering from mental illness, severe mental impairment, psychopathic disorder or mental impairment, and his mental disorder is of a nature or degree which makes it appropriate for him to receive medical treatment in a hospital; and

(b) such treatment is likely to alleviate or prevent a deterioration of his condition; and

(c) it is necessary for the health or safety of the patient or for the protection of other persons that he should receive such treatment and that it cannot be provided unless he continues to be detained;

but, in the case of mental illness or severe mental impairment, it shall be an alternative to the condition specified in paragraph (b) above that the patient, if discharged, is unlikely to be able to care for himself, to obtain the care which he needs or to guard himself against serious exploitation.

(5) Before furnishing a report under subsection (3) above the responsible medical officer shall consult one or more other persons who have been professionally concerned with the patient's medical treatment.

(6) Within the period of two months ending with the day on which a patient who is subject to guardianship under this Part of this Act would cease under this section to be so liable in default of the renewal of the authority for his guardianship, it shall be the duty of the appropriate medical officer –

(a) to examine the patient; and

(b) if it appears to him that the conditions set out in subsection (7) below are satisfied, to furnish to the guardian and, where the guardian is a person other than a local social services authority, to the responsible local social services authority a report to that effect in the prescribed form;

and where such a report is furnished in respect of a patient, the local social services authority shall, unless they discharge the patient, cause him to be informed.

(7) The conditions referred to in subsection (6) above are that –

(a) the patient is suffering from mental illness, severe mental impairment, psychopathic disorder or mental impairment and his mental disorder is of a nature or degree which warrants his reception into guardianship; and

(b) it is necessary in the interests of the welfare of the patient or for the protection of other persons that the patient should remain under guardianship.

(8) Where a report is duly furnished under subsection (3) or (6) above, the authority for the detention or guardianship of the patient shall be thereby renewed for the period prescribed in that case by subsection (2) above.

(9) Where the form of mental disorder specified in a report furnished under subsection (3) or (6) above is a form of disorder other than that specified in the application for admission for treatment or, as the case may be, in the guardianship application, that application shall have effect as if that other form of mental disorder were specified in it; and where on any occasion a report specifying such a form of mental disorder is furnished under either of those subsections the appropriate medical officer need not on that occasion furnish a report under section 16 above.

(10) In this section 'appropriate medical officer' has the same meaning as in section 16(5) above.

21   Special provisions as to patients absent without leave

(1) Where a patient is absent without leave –

    (a) on the day on which (apart from this section) he would cease to be liable to be detained or subject to guardianship under this Part of this Act; or

    (b) within the period of one week ending with that day, he shall not cease to be so liable or subject until the relevant time.

(2) For the purposes of subsection (1) above the relevant time –

    (a) where the patient is taken into custody under section 18 above, is the end of the period of one week beginning with the day on which he is returned to the hospital or place where he ought to be;

    (b) where the patient returns himself to the hospital or place where he ought to be within the period during which he can be taken into custody under section 18 above, is the end of the period of one week beginning with the day on which he so returns himself, and

    (c) otherwise, is the end of the period during which he can be taken into custody under section 18 above.

21A   Patients who are taken into custody or return within 28 days

(1) This section applies where a patient who is without leave is taken into custody under section 18 above, or returns himself to the hospital or place where he ought to be, not later than the end of the period of 28 days beginning with the, first day of his absence without leave.

(2) Where the period for which the patient is liable to be detained or subject to guardianship is extended by section 21 above, any examination and report to be made and furnished in respect of the patient under section 20(3) or (6) above may be made and furnished within the period as so extended.

(3) Where the authority for the detention or guardianship of the patient is renewed by virtue of subsection (2) above after the day on which (apart from section 21 above) that authority would have expired, the renewal shall take effect as from that day.

21B   Patients who are taken into custody or return after more than 28 days

(1) This section applies where a patient who is absent without leave is taken into custody under section 18 above, or returns himself to the hospital or place where he ought to be, later than the end of the period of 28 days beginning with the first day of his absence without leave.

(2) It shall be the duty of the appropriate medical officer, within the period of one week beginning with the day on which the patient is returned or returns himself to the hospital or place where he ought to be –

    (a) to examine the patient; and

    (b) if it appears to him that the relevant conditions are satisfied, to furnish to the appropriate body a report to that effect in the prescribed form;

and where such a report is furnished in respect of the patient the appropriate body shall cause him to be informed.

(3) Where the patient is liable to be detained (as opposed to subject to guardianship), the appropriate medical officer shall, before furnishing a report under subsection (2) above, consult –

    (a) one or more other persons who have been professionally concerned with the patient's medical treatment; and

    (b) an approved social worker.

(4) Where the patient would (apart from any renewal of the authority for his detention or guardianship on or after the day on which he is returned or returns himself to the hospital or place where he ought to be) be liable to be detained or subject to guardianship after the end of the period of one week beginning with that day, he shall cease to be so liable or subject at the end of that period unless a report is duly furnished in respect of him under subsection (2) above.

(5) Where the patient would (apart from section 21 above) have ceased to be liable to be detained or subject to guardianship on or before the day on which a report is duly furnished in respect of him under subsection (2) above, the report shall renew the authority for his detention or guardianship for the period prescribed in that case by section 20(2) above.

(6) Where the authority for the detention or guardianship of the patient is renewed by virtue of subsection (5) above –

    (a) the renewal shall take effect as from the day on which (apart from section 21 above and that subsection) the authority would have expired; and

    (b) if (apart from this paragraph) the renewed authority would expire on or before the day on which the report is furnished, the report shall further renew the authority, as from the day on which it would expire, for the period prescribed in that case by section 20(2) above.

(7) Where the authority for the detention or guardianship of the patient would expire within the period of two months beginning with the day on which a report is duly furnished in respect of him under subsection (2) above, the report shall, if it so provides, have effect also as a report duly furnished under section 20(3) or (6) above; and the reference in this subsection to authority includes any authority renewed under subsection (5) above by the report.

(8) Where the form of mental disorder specified in a report furnished under subsection (2) above is a form of disorder other than that specified in the application for admission for treatment or guardianship application concerned (and the report does not have effect as a report furnished under section 20(3) or (6) above), that application shall have effect as if that other form of mental disorder were specified in it.

(9) Where on any occasion a report specifying such a form of mental disorder is furnished under subsection (2) above the appropriate medical officer need not on that occasion furnish a report under section 16 above.

(10) In this section –

'appropriate medical officer' has the same meaning as in section 16(5) above;

'the appropriate body' means –

    (a) in relation to a patient who is liable to be detained in a hospital, the managers of the hospital; and

    (b) in relation to a patient who is subject to guardianship, the responsible local social services authority; and

'the relevant conditions' means –

    (a) in relation to a patient who is liable to be detained in a hospital, the conditions set out in subsection (4) of section 20 above; and

    (b) in relation to a patient who is subject to guardianship, the conditions set out in subsection (7) of that section.

22   Special provisions as to patients sentenced to imprisonment, etc.

(1) Where a patient who is liable to be detained by virtue of an application for admission for treatment or is subject to guardianship by virtue of a guardianship application is detained in custody in pursuance of any sentence or order passed or made by a court in the United Kingdom (including an order committing or remanding him in custody), and is so detained for a period exceeding, or for successive periods exceeding in the aggregate, six months, the application shall cease to have effect at the expiration of that period.

(2) Where any such patient is so detained in custody but the application does not cease to have effect under subsection (1) above, then –

    (a) if apart from this subsection the patient would have ceased to be liable to be so detained or subject to guardianship on or before the day on which he is discharged from custody, he shall not cease and shall be deemed not to have ceased to be so liable or subject until the end of that day; and

    (b) in any case, sections 18, 21 and 21A above shall apply in relation to the patient as if he had absented himself without leave on that day.

(3) In its application by virtue of subsection (2) above section 18(4) above shall have effect with the substitution of the words 'end of the period of 28 days beginning with the first day of his absence without leave'. for the words from 'later of' onwards.

23   Discharge of patients

(1) Subject to the provisions of this section and section 25 below, a patient who is for the time being liable to be detained or subject to guardianship under this Part of this Act shall cease to be so liable or subject if an order in writing discharging him from detention or guardianship (in this Act referred to as 'an order for discharge') is made in accordance with this section.

(2) An order for discharge may be made in respect of a patient –

    (a) where the patient is liable to be detained in a hospital in pursuance of an application for admission for assessment or for treatment by the responsible medical officer, by the managers or by the nearest relative of the patient;

    (b) where the patient is subject to guardianship, by the responsible medical officer, by the responsible local social services authority or by the nearest relative of the patient.

(3) Where the patient is liable to be detained in a mental nursing home in pursuance of an application for admission for assessment or for treatment, an order for his discharge may, without prejudice to subsection (2) above, be made by the Secretary of State and, if the patient is maintained under a contract with a National Health Service trust, NHS foundation trust, Health Authority, Special Health Authority or Primary Care Trust by that National Health Service Trust, NHS foundation trust, Health Authority, Special Health Authority or Primary Care Trust.

(4) The powers conferred by this section on any authority, trust other than an NHS foundation trust or body of persons may be exercised subject to subsection (5) below by any three or more members of that authority, trust or body authorised by them in that behalf or by three or more members of a committee or sub-committee of that authority, trust or body which has been authorised by them in that behalf.

(5) The reference in subsection (4) above to the members of an authority, trust or body or the members of a committee or sub-committee of an authority, trust or body, –

    (a) in the case of a Health Authority, Special Health Authority or Primary Care Trust or a committee or sub-committee of such a Health Authority, Special Health Authority or Primary Care Trust, is a reference only to the chairman of the authority or trust and such members (of the authority, trust, committee or sub-committee, as the case may be) as are not also officers of the authority or trust, within the meaning of the National Health Service Act 2006 or the National Health Service (Wales) Act 2006; and

    (b) in the case of a National Health Service trust or a committee or sub-committee of such a trust, is a reference only to the chairman of the trust and such directors or (in the case of a committee or sub-committee) members as are not also employees of the trust. (6) The powers conferred by this section on any NHS foundation trust may be exercised by any three or more non-executive directors of the board of the trust authorised by the board in that behalf.

(6) The powers conferred by this section on any NHS foundation trust may be exercised by any three or more non-executive directors of the board of the trust authorised by the board in that behalf.

24   Visiting and examination of patients

(1) For the purpose of advising as to the exercise by the nearest relative of a patient who is liable to be detained or subject to guardianship under this Part of this Act of any power to order his discharge, any registered medical practitioner authorised by or on behalf of the nearest relative of the patient may, at any reasonable time, visit the patient and examine him in private.

(2) Any registered medical practitioner authorised for the purposes of subsection (1) above to visit and examine a patient may require the production of and inspect any records relating to the detention or treatment of the patient in any hospital or to any after-care services provided for the patient under section 117 below.

(3) Where application is made by the Secretary of State or a Health Authority, Special Health Authority, Primary Care Trust, National Health Service trust, or NHS foundation trust to exercise, in respect of a patient liable to be detained in a mental nursing home, any power to make an order for his discharge, the following persons, that is to say –

(a) any registered medical practitioner authorised by the Secretary of State or, as the case may be, that Health Authority, Special Health Authority, Primary Care Trust, National Health Service trust or NHS foundation trust; and

(b) any other person (whether a registered medical practitioner or not) authorised under Part II of the Registered Homes Act 1984 to inspect the home,

may at any reasonable time visit the patient and interview him in private.

(4) Any person authorised for the purposes of subsection (3) above to visit a patient may require the production of and inspect any documents constituting or alleged to constitute the authority for the detention of the patient under this Part of this Act; and any person so authorised, who is a registered medical practitioner, may examine the patient in private, and may require the production of and inspect any other records relating to the treatment of the patient in the home or to any after-care services provided for the patient under section 117 below.

25   Restrictions on discharge by nearest relative

(1) An order for the discharge of a patient who is liable to be detained in a hospital shall not be made by his nearest relative except after giving not less than 72 hours' notice in writing to the managers of the hospital; and if, within 72 hours after such notice has been given, the responsible medical officer furnishes to the managers a report certifying that in the opinion of that officer the patient, if discharged, would be likely to act in a manner dangerous to other persons or to himself –

(a) any order for the discharge of the patient made by that relative in pursuance of the notice shall be of no effect; and

(b) no further order for the discharge of the patient shall be made by that relative during the period of six months beginning with the date of the report.

(2) In any case where a report under subsection (1) above is furnished in respect of a patient who is liable to be detained in pursuance of an application for admission for treatment the managers shall cause the nearest relative of the patient to be informed.

After-care under supervision

25A   Application for supervision

(1) Where a patient –

(a) is liable to be detained in a hospital in pursuance of an application for admission for treatment; and

(b) has attained the age of 16 years,

an application may be made for him to be supervised after he leaves hospital, for the period allowed by the following provisions of this Act, with a view to securing that he receives the after-care services provided for him under section 117 below.

(2) In this Act an application for a patient to be so supervised is referred to as a 'supervision application'; and where a supervision application has been duly made and accepted under this Part of this Act in respect of a patient and he has left hospital, he is for the purposes of this Act 'subject to after-care under supervision' (until he ceases to be so subject in accordance with the provisions of this Act).

(3) A supervision application shall be made in accordance with this section and sections 25B and 25C below.

(4) A supervision application may be made in respect of a patient only on the grounds that –

(a) he is suffering from mental disorder, being mental illness, severe mental impairment, psychopathic disorder or mental impairment;

(b) there would be a substantial risk of serious harm to the health or safety of the patient or the safety of other persons, or of the patient being seriously exploited, if he were not to receive the after-care services to be provided for him under section 117 below after he leaves hospital; and

(c) his being subject to after-care under supervision is likely to help to secure that he receives the after-care services to be so provided.

(5) A supervision application may be made only by the responsible medical officer.

(6) A supervision application in respect of a patient shall be addressed to the Primary Care Trust or Health Authority which will have the duty under section 117 below to provide aftercare services for the patient after he leaves hospital.

(7) Before accepting a supervision application in respect of a patient a Primary Care Trust or Health Authority shall consult the local social services authority which will also have that duty.

(8) Where a Primary Care Trust or Health Authority accept a supervision application in respect of a patient the Primary Care Trust or Health Authority shall –

(a) inform the patient both orally and in writing –

(i) that the supervision application has been accepted; and

(ii) of the effect in his case of the provisions of this Act relating to a patient subject to after-care under supervision (including, in particular, what rights of applying to a Mental Health Review Tribunal are available);

(b) inform any person whose name is stated in the supervision application in accordance with subparagraph (i) of paragraph (e) of section 25B(5) below that the supervision application has been accepted; and

(c) inform in writing any person whose name is so stated in accordance with sub-paragraph (ii) of that paragraph that the supervision application has been accepted.

(9) Where a patient in respect of whom a supervision application is made is granted leave of absence from a hospital under section 17 above (whether before or after the supervision application is made), references in –

(a) this section and the following provisions of this Part of this Act; and

(b) Part V of this Act,

to his leaving hospital shall be construed as references to his period of leave expiring (otherwise than on his return to the hospital or transfer to another hospital).

25B   Making of supervision application

(1) The responsible medical officer shall not make a supervision application unless –

(a) subsection (2) below is complied with; and

(b) the responsible medical officer has considered the matters specified in subsection (4) below.

(2) This subsection is complied with if –

(a) the following persons have been consulted about the making of the supervision application –

(i) the patient;

(ii) one or more persons who have been professionally concerned with the patient's medical treatment in hospital;

(iii) one or more persons who will be professionally concerned with the after-care services to be provided for the patient under section 117 below; and

(iv) any person who the responsible medical officer believes will play a substantial part in the care of the patient after he leaves hospital but will not be professionally concerned with any of the after-care services to be so provided;

(b) such steps as are practicable have been taken to consult the person (if any) appearing to be the nearest relative of the patient about the making of the supervision application; and

(c) the responsible medical officer has taken into account any views expressed by the persons consulted.

(3) Where the patient has requested that paragraph (b) of subsection (2) above should not apply, that paragraph shall not apply unless –

(a) the patient has a propensity to violent or dangerous behaviour towards others; and

(b) the responsible medical officer considers that it is appropriate for steps such as are mentioned in that paragraph to be taken.

(4) The matters referred to in subsection (1)(b) above are –

(a) the after-care services to be provided for the patient under section 117 below; and

(b) any requirements to be imposed on him under section 25D below.

(5) A supervision application shall state –

(a) that the patient is liable to be detained in a hospital in pursuance of an application for admission for treatment;

(b) the age of the patient or, if his exact age is not known to the applicant, that the patient is believed to have attained the age of 16 years;

(c) that in the opinion of the applicant (having regard in particular to the patient's history) all of the conditions set out in section 25A(4) above are complied with;

(d) the name of the person who is to be the community responsible medical officer, and of the person who is to be the supervisor, in relation to the patient after he leaves hospital; and

(e) the name of –

(i) any person who has been consulted under paragraph (a)(iv) of subsection (2) above; and

(ii) any person who has been consulted under paragraph (b) of that subsection.

(6) A supervision application shall be accompanied by –

(a) the written recommendation in the prescribed form of a registered medical practitioner who will be professionally concerned with the patient's medical treatment after he leaves hospital or, if no such practitioner other than the responsible medical officer will be so concerned, of any registered medical practitioner; and

(b) the written recommendation in the prescribed form of an approved social worker.

(7) A recommendation under subsection (6)(a) above shall include a statement that in the opinion of the medical practitioner (having regard in particular to the patient's history) all of the conditions set out in section 25A(4) above are complied with.

(8) A recommendation under subsection (6)(b) above shall include a statement that in the opinion of the social worker (having regard in particular to the patient's history) both of the conditions set out in section 25A(4)(b) and (c) above are complied with.

(9) A supervision application shall also be accompanied by –

(a) a statement in writing by the person who is to be the community responsible medical officer in relation to the patient after he leaves hospital that he is to be in charge of the medical treatment provided for the patient as part of the after-care services provided for him under section 117 below;

(b) a statement in writing by the person who is to be the supervisor in relation to the patient after he leaves hospital that he is to supervise the patient with a view to securing that he receives the aftercare services so provided;

(c) details of the after-care services to be provided for the patient under section 117 below; and

(d) details of any requirements to be imposed on him under section 25D below.

(10) On making a supervision application in respect of a patient the responsible medical officer shall –

(a) inform the patient both orally and in writing;

(b) inform any person who has been consulted under paragraph (a)(iv) of subsection (2) above; and

(c) inform in writing any person who has been consulted under paragraph (b) of that subsection,

of the matters specified in subsection (11) below.

(11) The matters referred to in subsection (10) above are –

(a) that the application is being made;

(b) the after-care services to be provided for the patient under section 117 below;

(c) any requirements to be imposed on him under section 25D below; and

(d) the name of the person who is to be the community responsible medical officer, and of the person who is to be the supervisor, in relation to the patient after he leaves hospital.

25C   Supervision applications: supplementary

(1) Subject to subsection (2) below, a supervision application, and the recommendation under section 25B(6)(a) above accompanying it, may describe the patient as suffering from more than one of the following forms of mental disorder, namely, mental illness, severe mental impairment, psychopathic disorder and mental impairment.

(2) A supervision application shall be of no effect unless the patient is described in the application and the recommendation under section 25B(6)(a) above accompanying it as suffering from the same form of mental disorder, whether or not he is also described in the application or the recommendation as suffering from another form.

(3) A registered medical practitioner may at any reasonable time visit a patient and examine him in private for the purpose of deciding whether to make a recommendation under section 25B (6)(a) above.

(4) An approved social worker may at any reasonable time visit and interview a patient for the purpose of deciding whether to make a recommendation under section 25B(6)(b) above.

(5) For the purpose of deciding whether to make a recommendation under section 25B(6) above in respect of a patient, a registered medical practitioner or an approved social worker may require the production of and inspect any records relating to the detention or treatment of the patient in any hospital or to any aftercare services provided for the patient under section 117 below.

(6) If, within the period of 14 days beginning with the day on which a supervision application has been accepted, the application, or any recommendation accompanying it, is found to be in any respect incorrect or defective, the application or recommendation may, within that period and with the consent of the Primary Care Trust or Health Authority which accepted the application, be amended by the person by whom it was made or given.

(7) Where an application or recommendation is amended in accordance with subsection (6) above it shall have effect, and shall be deemed to have had effect, as if it had been originally made or given as so amended.

(8) A supervision application which appears to be duly made and to be accompanied by recommendations under section 25B(6) above may be acted upon without further proof of –

(a) the signature or qualification of the person by whom the application or any such recommendation was made or given; or

(b) any matter of fact or opinion stated in the application or recommendation.

(9) A recommendation under section 25B(6) above accompanying a supervision application in respect of a patient shall not be given by –

(a) the responsible medical officer;

(b) a person who receives or has an interest in the receipt of any payments made on account of the maintenance of the patient; or

(c) a close relative of the patient, of any person mentioned in paragraph (a) or (b) above or of a person by whom the other recommendation is given under section 25B(6) above for the purposes of the application.

(10) In subsection (9)(c) above 'close relative' means husband, wife, father, father-in-law, mother, mother-in-law, son, son-in-law, daughter, daughter-in-law, brother, brother-in-law, sister or sister-in-law.

25D   Requirements to secure receipt of after-care under supervision

(1) Where a patient is subject to after-care under supervision (or, if he has not yet left hospital, is to be so subject after he leaves hospital), the responsible after-care bodies have power to impose

any of the requirements specified in subsection, (3) below for the purpose of securing that the patient receives the after-care services provided for him under section 117 below.

(2) In this Act 'the responsible after-care bodies', in relation to a patient, means the bodies which have (or will have) the duty under section 117 below to provide aftercare services for the patient.

(3) The requirements referred to in subsection (1) above are –

(a) that the patient reside at a specified place;

(b) that the patient attend at specified places and times for the purpose of medical treatment, occupation, education or training; and

(c) that access to the patient be given, at any place where the patient is residing, to the supervisor, any registered medical practitioner or any approved social worker or to any other person authorised by the supervisor.

(4) A patient subject to after-care under supervision may be taken and conveyed by, or by any person authorised by, the supervisor to any place where the patient is required to reside or to attend for the purpose of medical treatment, occupation, education or training.

(5) A person who demands –

(a) to be given access to a patient in whose case a requirement has been imposed under subsection (3)(c) above; or

(b) to take and convey a patient in pursuance of subsection (4) above,

shall, if asked to do so, produce some duly authenticated document to show that he is a person entitled to be given access to, or to take and convey, the patient.

25E   Review of after-care under supervision

(1) The after-care services provided (or to be provided) under section 117 below for a patient who is (or is to be) subject to after-care under supervision, and any requirements imposed on him under section 25D above, shall be kept under review, and (where appropriate) modified, by the responsible after-care bodies.

(2) This subsection applies in relation to a patient who is subject to after-care under supervision where he refuses or neglects –

(a) to receive any or all of the after-care services provided for him under section 117 below; or

(b) to comply with any or all of any requirements imposed on him under section 25D above.

(3) Where subsection (2) above applies in relation to a patient, the responsible after-care bodies shall review, and (where appropriate) modify –

(a) the after-care services provided for him under section 117 below; and

(b) any requirements imposed on him under section 25D above.

(4) Where subsection (2) above applies in relation to a patient, the responsible after-care bodies shall also –

(a) consider whether it might be appropriate for him to cease to be subject to after-care under supervision and, if they conclude that it might be, inform the community responsible medical officer; and

(b) consider whether it might be appropriate for him to be admitted to a hospital for treatment and, if they conclude that it might be, inform an approved social worker.

(5) The responsible after-care bodies shall not modify –

(a) the after-care services provided (or to be provided) under section 117 below for a patient who is (or is to be) subject to after-care under supervision; or

(b) any requirements imposed on him under section 25D above, unless subsection (6) below is complied with.

(6) This subsection is complied with if –

(a) the patient has been consulted about the modifications;

(b) any person who the responsible after-care bodies believe plays (or will play) a substantial part in the care of the patient but is not (or will not be) professionally concerned with the after-care services provided for the patient under section 117 below has been consulted about the modifications;

(c) such steps as are practicable have been taken to consult the person (if any) appearing to be the nearest relative of the patient about the modifications; and

(d) the responsible after-care bodies have taken into account any views expressed by the persons consulted.

(7) Where the patient has requested that paragraph (c) of subsection (6) above should not apply, that paragraph shall not apply unless –

(a) the patient has a propensity to violent or dangerous behaviour towards others; and

(b) the community responsible medical officer (or the person who is to be the community responsible medical officer) considers that it is appropriate for steps such as are mentioned in that paragraph to be taken.

(8) Where the responsible after-care bodies modify the after-care services provided (or to be provided) for the patient under section 117 below or any requirements imposed on him under section 25D above, they shall –

(a) inform the patient both orally and in writing;

(b) inform any person who has been consulted under paragraph (b) of subsection (6) above; and

(c) inform in writing any person who has been consulted under paragraph (c) of that subsection,

that the modifications have been made.

(9) Where –

(a) a person other than the person named in the supervision application becomes the community responsible medical officer when the patient leaves hospital; or

(b) when the patient is subject to after-care under supervision, one person ceases to be, and another becomes, the community responsible medical officer,

the responsible after-care bodies shall comply with subsection (11) below.

(10) Where –

(a) a person other than the person named in the supervision application becomes the supervisor when the patient leaves hospital; or

(b) when the patient is subject to after-care under supervision, one person ceases to be, and another becomes, the supervisor,

the responsible after-care bodies shall comply with subsection (11) below.

(11) The responsible after-care bodies comply with this subsection if they –

(a) inform the patient both orally and in writing;

(b) inform any person who they believe plays a substantial part in the care of the patient but is not professionally concerned with the after-care services provided for the patient under section 117 below; and

(c) unless the patient otherwise requests, take such steps as are practicable to inform in writing the person (if any) appearing to be the nearest relative of the patient, of the name of the person who becomes the community responsible medical officer or the supervisor.

25F   Reclassification of patient subject to after-care under supervision

(1) If it appears to the community responsible medical officer that a patient subject to after-care under supervision is suffering from a form of mental disorder other than the form or forms specified in the supervision application made in respect of the patient, he may furnish a report to that effect to the Primary Care Trust or Health Authority which have the duty under section 117 below to provide after-care services for the patient.

(2) Where a report is so furnished the supervision application shall have effect as if that other form of mental disorder were specified in it.

(3) Unless no-one other than the community responsible medical officer is professionally concerned with the patient's medical treatment, he shall consult one or more persons who are so concerned before furnishing a report under subsection (1) above.

(4) Where a report is furnished under subsection (1) above in respect of a patient, the responsible after-care bodies shall –

    (a) inform the patient both orally and in writing; and

    (b) unless the patient otherwise requests, take such steps as are practicable to inform in writing the person (if any) appearing to be the nearest relative of the patient, that the report has been furnished.

25G   Duration and renewal of after-care under supervision

(1) Subject to sections 25H and 25I below, a patient subject to after-care under supervision shall be so subject for the period –

    (a) beginning when he leaves hospital; and

    (b) ending with the period of six months beginning with the day on which the supervision application was accepted,

but shall not be so subject for any longer period except in accordance with the following provisions of this section.

(2) A patient already subject to after-care under supervision may be made so subject –

    (a) from the end of the period referred to in subsection (1) above, for a further period of six months; and

    (b) from the end of any period of renewal under paragraph (a) above, for a further period of one year,

and so on for periods of one year at a time.

(3) Within the period of two months ending on the day on which a patient who is subject to after-care under supervision would (in default of the operation of subsection (7) below) cease to be so subject, it shall be the duty of the community responsible medical officer –

    (a) to examine the patient; and

    (b) if it appears to him that the conditions set out in subsection (4) below are complied with, to furnish to the responsible after-care bodies a report to that effect in the prescribed form.

(4) The conditions referred to in subsection (3) above are that –

    (a) the patient is suffering from mental disorder, being mental illness, severe mental impairment, psychopathic disorder or mental impairment;

    (b) there would be a substantial risk of serious harm to the health or safety of the patient or the safety of other persons, or of the patient being seriously exploited, if he were not to receive the after-care services provided for him under section 117 below;

    (c) his being subject to after-care under supervision is likely to help to secure that he receives the after-care services so provided.

(5) The community responsible medical officer shall not consider whether the conditions set out in subsection (4) above are complied with unless –

    (a) the following persons have been consulted –

        (i)   the patient;

        (ii) the supervisor;

        (iii) unless no-one other than the community responsible medical officer is professionally concerned with the patient's medical treatment, one or more persons who are so concerned;

        (iv) one or more persons who are professionally concerned with the after-care services (other than medical treatment) provided for the patient under section 117 below; and

        (v) any person who the community responsible medical officer believes plays a substantial part in the care of the patient but is not professionally concerned with the aftercare services so provided;

(b) such steps as are practicable have been taken to consult the person (if any) appearing to be the nearest relative of the patient; and

(c) the community responsible medical officer has taken into account any relevant views expressed by the persons consulted.

(6) Where the patient has requested that paragraph (b) of subsection (5) above should not apply, that paragraph shall not apply unless –

(a) the patient has a propensity to violent or dangerous behaviour towards others; and

(b) the community responsible medical officer considers that it is appropriate for steps such as are mentioned in that paragraph to be taken.

(7) Where a report is duly furnished under subsection (3) above, the patient shall be thereby made subject to after-care under supervision for the further period prescribed in that case by subsection (2) above.

(8) Where a report is furnished under subsection (3) above, the responsible after-care bodies shall –

(a) inform the patient both orally and in writing –

  (i) that the report has been furnished; and

  (ii) of the effect in his case of the provisions of this Act relating to making a patient subject to after-care under supervision for a further period (including, in particular, what rights of applying to a Mental Health Review Tribunal are available);

(b) inform any person who has been consulted under paragraph (a)(v) of subsection (5) above that the report has been furnished; and

(c) inform in writing any person who has been consulted under paragraph (b) of that subsection that the report has been furnished.

(9) Where the form of mental disorder specified in a report furnished under subsection (3) above is a form of disorder other than that specified in the supervision application, that application shall have effect as if that other form of mental disorder were specified in it.

(10) Where on any occasion a report specifying such a form of mental disorder is furnished under subsection (3) above the community responsible medical officer need not on that occasion furnish a report under section 25F above.

25H   Ending of after-care under supervision

(1) The community responsible medical officer may at any time direct that a patient subject to after-care under supervision shall cease to be so subject.

(2) The community responsible medical officer shall not give a direction under subsection (1) above unless subsection (3) below is complied with.

(3) This subsection is complied with if –

(a) the following persons have been consulted about the giving of the direction –

  (i) the patient;

  (ii) the supervisor;

  (iii) unless no-one other than the community responsible medical officer is professionally concerned with the patient's medical treatment, one or more persons who are so concerned;

  (iv) one or more persons who are professionally concerned with the after-care services (other than medical treatment) provided for the patient under section 117 below; and

  (v) any person who the community responsible medical officer believes plays a substantial part in the care of the patient but is not professionally concerned with the aftercare services so provided;

(b) such steps as are practicable have been taken to consult the person (if any) appearing to be the nearest relative of the patient about the giving of the direction; and

(c) the community responsible medical officer has taken into account any views expressed by the persons consulted.

(4) Where the patient has requested that paragraph (b) of subsection (3) above should not apply, that paragraph shall not apply unless –

(a) the patient has a propensity to violent or dangerous behaviour towards others; and

(b) the community responsible medical officer considers that it is appropriate for steps such as are mentioned in that paragraph to be taken.

(5) A patient subject to after-care under supervision shall cease to be so subject if he –

(a) is admitted to a hospital in pursuance of an application for admission for treatment; or

(b) is received into guardianship.

(6) Where a patient (for any reason) ceases to be subject to after-care under supervision the responsible after-care bodies shall –

(a) inform the patient both orally and in writing;

(b) inform any person who they believe plays a substantial part in the care of the patient but is not professionally concerned with the after-care services provided for the patient under section 117 below; and

(c) take such steps as are practicable to inform in writing the person (if any) appearing to be the nearest relative of the patient,

that the patient has ceased to be so subject.

(7) Where the patient has requested that paragraph (c) of subsection (6) above should not apply, that paragraph shall not apply unless subsection (3)(b) above applied in his case by virtue of subsection (4) above.

25I   Special provisions as to patients sentenced to imprisonment etc.

(1) This section applies where a patient who is subject to after-care under supervision –

(a) is detained in custody in pursuance of any sentence or order passed or made by a court in the United Kingdom (including an order committing or remanding him in custody); or

(b) is detained in hospital in pursuance of an application for admission for assessment.

(2) At any time when the patient is detained as mentioned in subsection (1)(a) or (b) above he is not required –

(a) to receive any after-care services provided for him under section 117 below; or

(b) to comply with any requirements imposed on him under section 25D above.

(3) If the patient is detained as mentioned in paragraph (a) of subsection (1) above for a period of, or successive periods amounting in the aggregate to, six months or less, or is detained as mentioned in paragraph (b) of that subsection, and, apart from this subsection, he –

(a) would have ceased to be subject to after-care under supervision during the period for which he is so detained; or

(b) would cease to be so subject during the period of 28 days beginning with the day on which he ceases to be so detained,

he shall be deemed not to have ceased, and shall not cease, to be so subject until the end of that period of 28 days.

(4) Where the period for which the patient is subject to after-care under supervision is extended by subsection (3) above, any examination and report to be made and furnished in respect of the patient under section 25G(3) above may be made and furnished within the period as so extended.

(5) Where, by virtue of subsection (4) above, the patient is made subject to after-care under supervision for a further period after the day on which (apart from subsection (3) above) he would have ceased to be so subject, the further period shall be deemed to have commenced with that day.

25J   Patients moving from Scotland to England and Wales

(1) A supervision application may be made in respect of a patient who is subject to a community care order under the Mental Health (Scotland) Act 1984 and who intends to leave Scotland in order to reside in England and Wales.

(2) Sections 25A to 25I above, section 117 below and any other provision of this Act relating to supervision applications or patients subject to after-care under supervision shall apply in relation to

a patient in respect of whom a supervision application is or is to be made by virtue of this section subject to such modifications as the Secretary of State may by regulations prescribe.

Functions of relatives of patients

26   Definition of 'relative' and 'nearest relative'

(1) In this Part of this Act 'relative' means any of the following persons: –

   (a) husband or wife;

   (b) son or daughter;

   (c) father or mother;

   (d) brother or sister;

   (e) grandparent;

   (f) grandchild;

   (g) uncle or aunt;

   (h) nephew or niece.

(2) In deducing relationships for the purposes of this section, any relationship of the half-blood shall be treated as a relationship of the whole blood, and an illegitimate person shall be treated as the legitimate child of his mother.

(3) In this Part of this Act, subject to the provisions of this section and to the following provisions of this Part of this Act, the 'nearest relative' means the person first described in subsection (1) above who is for the time being surviving, relatives of the whole blood being preferred to relatives of the same description of the half-blood and the elder or eldest of two or more relatives described in any paragraph of that subsection being preferred to the other or others of those relatives, regardless of sex.

(4) Subject to the provisions of this section and to the following provisions of this Part of this Act, where the patient ordinarily resides with or is cared for by one or more of his relatives (or, if he is for the time being an in-patient in a hospital, he last ordinarily resided with or was cared for by one or more of his relatives) his nearest relative shall be determined –

   (a) by giving preference to that relative or those relatives over the other or others; and

   (b) as between two or more such relatives, in accordance with subsection (3) above.

(5) Where the person who, under subsection (3) or (4) above, would be the nearest relative of a patient –

   (a) in the case of a patient ordinarily resident in the United Kingdom, the Channel Islands or the Isle of Man, is not so resident; or

   (b) is the husband or wife of the patient, but is permanently separated from the patient, either by agreement or under an order of a court, or has deserted or has been deserted by the patient for a period which has not come to an end; or

   (c) is a person other than the husband, wife, father or mother of the patient, and is for the time being under 18 years of age;

the nearest relative of the patient shall be ascertained as if that person were dead.

(6) In this section 'husband' and 'wife' include a person who is living with the patient as the patient's husband or wife, as the case may be (or, if the patient is for the time being an in-patient in a hospital, was so living until the patient was admitted), and has been or had been so living for a period of not less than six months; but a person shall not be treated by virtue of this subsection as the nearest relative of a married patient unless the husband or wife of the patient is disregarded by virtue of paragraph (b) of subsection (5) above.

(7) A person, other than a relative, with whom the patient ordinarily resides (or, if the patient is for the time being an in-patient in a hospital, last ordinarily resided before he was admitted), and with whom he has or had been ordinarily residing for a period of not less than five years, shall be treated for the purposes of this Part of this Act as if he were a relative but –

   (a) shall be treated for the purposes of subsection (3) above as if mentioned last in subsection (1) above; and

(b) shall not be treated by virtue of this subsection as the nearest relative of a married patient unless the husband or wife of the patient is disregarded by virtue of paragraph (b) of subsection (5) above.

27   Children and young persons in care

Where –

(a) a patient who is a child or young person is in the care of a local authority by virtue of a care order within the meaning of the Children Act 1989; or

(b) the rights and powers of a parent of a patient who is a child or young person are vested in a local authority by virtue of section 16 of the Social Work (Scotland) Act 1968,

the authority shall be deemed to be the nearest relative of the patient in preference to any person except the patient's husband or wife (if any).

28   Nearest relative of minor under guardianship etc.

(1) Where –

(a) a guardian has been appointed for a person who has not attained the age of eighteen years; or

(b) a residence order (as defined by section 8 of the Children Act 1989) is in force with respect to such a person,

the guardian (or guardians, where there is more than one) or the person named in the residence order shall, to the exclusion of any other person, be deemed to be his nearest relative.

(2) Subsection (5) of section 26 above shall apply in relation to a person who is, or who is one of the persons, deemed to be the nearest relative of a patient by virtue of this section as it applies in relation to a person who would be the nearest relative under subsection (3) of that section.

(3) In this section 'guardian' does not include a guardian under this Part of this Act.

(4) In this section 'court' includes a court in Scotland or Northern Ireland, and 'enactment' includes an enactment of the Parliament of Northern Ireland, a Measure of the Northern Ireland Assembly and an Order in Council under Schedule 1 of the Northern Ireland Act 1974.

29   Appointment by court of acting nearest relative

(1) The country court may, upon application made in accordance with the provisions of this section in respect of a patient, by order direct that the functions of the nearest relative of the patient under this Part of this Act and sections 66 and 69 below shall, during the continuance in force of the order, be exercisable by the applicant, or by any other person specified in the application, being a person who, in the opinion of the court, is a proper person to act as the patient's nearest relative and is willing to do so.

(2) An order under this section may be made on the application of –

(a) any relative of the patient;

(b) any other person with whom the patient is residing (or, if the patient is then an in-patient in a hospital, was last residing before he was admitted); or

(c) an approved social worker; but in relation to an application made by such a social worker, subsection (1) above shall have effect as if for the words 'the applicant' there were substituted the words 'the local social services authority'.

(3) An application for an order under this section may be made upon any of the following grounds, that is to say –

(a) that the patient has no nearest relative within the meaning of this Act, or that it is not reasonably practicable to ascertain whether he has such a relative, or who that relative is;

(b) that the nearest relative of the patient is incapable of acting as such by reason of mental disorder or other illness;

(c) that the nearest relative of the patient unreasonably objects to the making of an application for admission for treatment or a guardianship application in respect of the patient; or

(d) that the nearest relative of the patient has exercised without due regard to the welfare of the patient or the interests of the public his power to discharge the patient from hospital or guardianship under this Part of this Act, or is likely to do so.

(4) If, immediately before the expiration of the period for which a patient is liable to be detained by virtue of an application for admission for assessment, an application under this section, which is an application made on the ground specified in subsection (3)(c) or (d) above, is pending in respect of the patient, that period shall be extended –

(a) in any case, until the application under this section has been finally disposed of; and

(b) if an order is made in pursuance of the application under this section, for a further period of seven days;

and for the purposes of this subsection an application under this section shall be deemed to have been finally disposed of at the expiration of the time allowed for appealing from the decision of the court or, if notice of appeal has been given within that time, when the appeal has been heard or withdrawn, and 'pending' shall be construed accordingly.

(5) An order made on the ground specified in subsection (3)(a) or (b) above may specify a period for which it is to continue in force unless previously discharged under section 30 below.

(6) While an order made under this section is in force, the provisions of this Part of this Act (other than this section and section 30 below) and sections 66, 69, 132(4) and 133 below shall apply in relation to the patient as if for any reference to the nearest relative of the patient there were substituted a reference to the person having the functions of that relative and (without prejudice to section 30 below) shall so apply notwithstanding that the person who was the patient's nearest relative when the order was made is no longer his nearest relative; but this subsection shall not apply to section 66 below in the case mentioned in paragraph (h) of subsection (1) of that section.

30   Discharge and variation of orders under s. 29

(1) An order made under section 29 above in respect of a patient may be discharged by the country court upon application made –

(a) in any case, by the person having the functions of the nearest relative of the patient by virtue of the order;

(b) where the order was made on the ground specified in paragraph (a) or paragraph (b) of section 29(3) above, or where the person who was the nearest relative of the patient when the order was made has ceased to be his nearest relative, on the application of the nearest relative of the patient.

(2) An order made under section 29 above in respect of a patient may be varied by the county court, on the application of the person having the functions of the nearest relative by virtue of the order or on the application of an approved social worker, by substituting for the first-mentioned person a local social services authority or any other person who in the opinion of the court is a proper person to exercise those functions, being an authority or person who is willing to do so.

(3) If the person having the functions of the nearest relative of a patient by virtue of an order under section 29 above dies –

(a) subsections (1) and (2) above shall apply as if for any reference to that person there were substituted a reference to any relative of the patient, and

(b) until the order is discharged or varied under those provisions the functions of the nearest relative under this Part of this Act and sections 66 and 69 below shall not be exercisable by any person.

(4) An order under section 29 above shall, unless previously discharged under subsection (1) above, cease to have effect at the expiration of the period, if any, specified under subsection (5) of that section or, where no such period is specified –

(a) if the patient was on the date of the order liable to be detained in pursuance of an application for admission for treatment or by virtue of an order or direction under Part III of this Act (otherwise than under section 35, 36 or 38) or was subject to guardianship under this Part of this Act or by virtue of such an order or direction, or becomes so liable or subject within the period of three months beginning with that date, when he ceases to be so liable or subject (otherwise than on being transferred in pursuance of regulations under section 19 above);

(b) if the patient was not on the date of the order, and has not within the said period become, so liable or subject, at the expiration of that period.

(5) The discharge or variation under this section of an order made under section 29 above shall not affect the validity of anything previously done in pursuance of the order.

33   Special provisions as to wards of court

(1) An application for the admission to hospital of a minor who is a ward of court may be made under this Part of this Act with the leave of the court; and section 11(4) above shall not apply in relation to an application so made.

(2) Where a minor who is a ward of court is liable to be detained in a hospital by virtue of an application for admission under this Part of this Act, any power exercisable under this Part of this Act or under section 66 below in relation to the patient by his nearest relative shall be exercisable by or with the leave of the court.

(3) Nothing in this Part of this Act shall be construed as authorising the making of a guardianship application in respect of a minor who is a ward of court, or the transfer into guardianship of any such minor.

(4) Where a supervision application has been made in respect of a minor who is a ward of court, the provisions of this Part of this Act relating to after-care under supervision have effect in relation to the minor subject to any order which the court may make in the exercise of its wardship jurisdiction.

34   Interpretation of Part II

(1) In this Part of this Act –

'the community responsible medical officer', in relation to a patient subject to after-care under supervision, means the person who, in accordance with section 117(2A)(a) below, is in charge of medical treatment provided for him;

'the nominated medical attendant', in relation to a patient who is subject to the guardianship of a person other than a local social services authority, means the person appointed in pursuance of regulations made under section 9(2) above to act as the medical attendant of the patient;

'the responsible medical officer' means (except in the phrase the community responsible medical officer) –

(a) in relation to a patient who is liable to be detained by virtue of an application for admission for assessment or an application for admission for treatment, or who is to be subject to after-care supervision after leaving hospital the registered medical practitioner in charge of the treatment of the patient;

(b) in relation to a patient subject to guardianship, the medical officer authorised by the local social services authority to act (either generally or in any particular case or for any particular purpose) as the responsible medical officer.

'the supervisor', in relation to a patient subject to after-care under supervision, means the person who, in accordance with section 117(2A)(b) below, is supervising him.

(1A) Nothing in this Act prevents the same person from acting as more than one of the following in relation to a patient, that is –

(a) the responsible medical officer;

(b) the community responsible medical officer; and

(c) the supervisor.

(2) Except where otherwise expressly provided, this Part of this Act applies in relation to a mental nursing home, being a home in respect of which the particulars of registration are for the time being entered in the separate part of the register kept for the purposes of section 23(5)(b) of the Registered Homes Act 1984, as it applies in relation to a hospital, and references in this Part of this Act to a hospital, and any reference in this Act to a hospital to which this Part of this Act applies, shall be construed accordingly.

(3) In relation to a patient who is subject to guardianship in pursuance of a guardianship application, any reference in this Part of this Act to the responsible local social services authority is a reference –

(a) where the patient is subject to the guardianship of a local social services authority, to that authority;

(b) where the patient is subject to the guardianship of a person other than a local social services authority, to the local social services authority for the area in which that person resides.

Part III Patients Concerned in Criminal Proceedings or Under Sentence

Remands to hospital

35   Remand to hospital for report on accused's mental condition

(1) Subject to the provisions of this section, the Crown Court or a magistrates' court may remand an accused person to a hospital specified by the court for a report on his mental condition.

(2) For the purposes of this section an accused person is –

(a) in relation to the Crown Court, any person who is awaiting trial before the court for an offence punishable with imprisonment or who has been arraigned before the court for such an offence and has not yet been sentenced or otherwise dealt with for the offence on which he has been arraigned;

(b) in relation to a magistrates' court, any person who has been convicted by the court of an offence punishable on summary conviction with imprisonment and any person charged with such an offence if the court is satisfied that he did the act or made the omission charged or he has consented to the exercise by the court of the powers conferred by this section.

(3) Subject to subsection (4) below, the powers conferred by this section may be exercised if –

(a) the court is satisfied, on the written or oral evidence of a registered medical practitioner, that there is reason to suspect that the accused person is suffering from mental illness, psychopathic disorder, severe mental impairment or mental impairment; and

(b) the court is of the opinion that it would be impracticable for a report on his mental condition to be made if he were remanded on bail; but those powers shall not be exercised by the Crown Court in respect of a person who has been convicted before the court if the sentence for the offence of which he has been convicted is fixed by law.

(4) The court shall not remand an accused person to a hospital under this section unless satisfied, on the written or oral evidence of the registered medical practitioner who would be responsible for making the report or of some other person representing the managers of the hospital, that arrangements have been made for his admission to that hospital and for his admission to it within the period of seven days beginning with the date of the remand; and if the court is so satisfied it may, pending his admission, give directions for his conveyance to and detention in a place of safety.

(5) Where a court has remanded an accused person under this section it may further remand him if it appears to the court, on the written or oral evidence of the registered medical practitioner responsible for making the report, that a further remand is necessary for completing the assessment of the accused person's mental condition.

(6) The power of further remanding an accused person under this section may be exercised by the court without his being brought before the court if he is represented by counsel or a solicitor and his counsel or solicitor is given an opportunity of being heard.

(7) An accused person shall not be remanded or further remanded under this section for more than 28 days at a time or for more than 12 weeks in all; and the court may at any time terminate the remand if it appears to the court that it is appropriate to do so.

(8) An accused person remanded to hospital under this section shall be entitled to obtain at his own expense an independent report on his mental condition from a registered medical practitioner chosen by him and to apply to the court on the basis of it for his remand to be terminated under subsection (7) above.

(9) Where an accused person is remanded under this section –

    (a) a constable or any other person directed to do so by the court shall convey the accused person to the hospital specified by the court within the period mentioned in subsection (4) above; and

    (b) the managers of the hospital shall admit him within that period and thereafter detain him in accordance with the provisions of this section.

(10) If an accused person absconds from a hospital to which he has been remanded under this section, or while being conveyed to or from that hospital, he may be arrested without warrant by any constable and shall, after being arrested, be brought as soon as practicable before the court that remanded him; and the court may thereupon terminate the remand and deal with him in any way in which it could have dealt with him if he had not been remanded under this section.

36   Remand of accused person to hospital for treatment

(1) Subject to the provisions of this section, the Crown Court may, instead of remanding an accused person in custody, remand him to a hospital specified by the court if satisfied, on the written or oral evidence of two registered medical practitioners, that he is suffering from mental illness or severe mental impairment of a nature or degree which makes it appropriate for him to be detained in a hospital for medical treatment.

(2) For the purposes of this section an accused person is any person who is in custody awaiting trial before the Crown Court for an offence punishable with imprisonment (other than an offence the sentence for which is fixed by law) or who at any time before sentence is in custody in the course of a trial before that court for such an offence.

(3) The court shall not remand an accused person under this section to a hospital unless it is satisfied, on the written or oral evidence of the registered medical practitioner who would be in charge of his treatment or of some other person representing the managers of the hospital, that arrangements have been made for his admission to that hospital and for his admission to it within the period of seven days beginning with the date of the remand; and if the court is so satisfied it may, pending his admission, give directions for his conveyance to and detention in a place of safety.

(4) Where a court has remanded an accused person under this section it may further remand him if it appears to the court, on the written or oral evidence of the responsible medical officer, that a further remand is warranted.

(5) The power of further remanding an accused person under this section may be exercised by the court without his being brought before the court if he is represented by counsel or a solicitor and his counsel or solicitor is given an opportunity of being heard.

(6) An accused person shall not be remanded or further remanded under this section for more than 28 days at a time or for more than 12 weeks in all; and the court may at any time terminate the remand if it appears to the court that it is appropriate to do so.

(7) An accused person remanded to hospital under this section shall be entitled to obtain at his own expense an independent report on his mental condition from a registered medical practitioner chosen by him and to apply to the court on the basis of it for his remand to be terminated under subsection (6) above.

(8) Subsections (9) and (10) of section 35 above shall have effect in relation to a remand under this section as they have effect in relation to a remand under that section.

Hospital and guardianship orders

37   Powers of courts to order hospital admission or guardianship

(1) Where a person is convicted before the Crown Court of an offence punishable with imprisonment other than an offence the sentence for which is fixed by law, or is convicted by a

magistrates' court of an offence punishable on summary conviction with imprisonment, and the conditions mentioned in subsection (2) below are satisfied, the court may by order authorise his admission to and detention in such hospital as may be specified in the order or, as the case may be, place him under the guardianship of a local social services authority or of such other person approved by a local social services authority as may be so specified.

(2) The conditions referred to in subsection (1) above are that –

    (a) the court is satisfied, on the written or oral evidence of two registered medical practitioners, that the offender is suffering from mental illness, psychopathic disorder, severe mental impairment or mental impairment and that either –

        (i) the mental disorder from which the offender is suffering is of a nature or degree which makes it appropriate for him to be detained in a hospital for medical treatment and, in the case of psychopathic disorder or mental impairment, that such treatment is likely to alleviate or prevent a deterioration of his condition; or

        (ii) in the case of an offender who has attained the age of 16 years, the mental disorder is of a nature or degree which warrants his reception into guardianship under this Act; and

    (b) the court is of the opinion, having regard to all the circumstances including that nature of the offence and the character and antecedents of the offender, and to the other available methods of dealing with him, that the most suitable method of disposing of the case is by means of an order under this section.

(3) Where a person is charged before a magistrates' court with any act or omission as an offence and the court would have power, on convicting him of that offence, to make an order under subsection (1) above in his case as being a person suffering from mental illness or severe mental impairment, then, if the court is satisfied that the accused did the act or made the omission charged, the court may, if it thinks fit, make such an order without convicting him.

(4) An order for the admission of an offender to a hospital (in this Act referred to as 'a hospital order') shall not be made under this section unless the court is satisfied on the written or oral evidence of the registered medical practitioner who would be in charge of his treatment or of some other person representing the managers of the hospital that arrangements have been made for his admission to that hospital in the event of such an order being made by the court, and for his admission to it within the period of 28 days beginning with the date of the making of such an order; and the court may, pending his admission within that period, give such directions as it thinks fit for his conveyance to and detention in a place of safety.

(5) If within the said period of 28 days it appears to the Secretary of State that by reason of an emergency or other special circumstances it is not practicable for the patient to be received into the hospital specified in the order, he may give directions for the admission of the patient to such other hospital as appears to be appropriate instead of the hospital so specified; and where such directions are given –

    (a) the Secretary of State shall cause the person having the custody of the patient to be informed, and

    (b) the hospital order shall have effect as if the hospital specified in the directions were substituted for the hospital specified in the order.

(6) An order placing an offender under the guardianship of a local social services authority or of any other person (in this Act referred to as 'a guardianship order') shall not be made under this section unless the court is satisfied that that authority or person is willing to receive the offender into guardianship.

(7) A hospital order or guardianship order shall specify the form or forms of mental disorder referred to in subsection (2)(a) above from which, upon the evidence taken into account under that subsection, the offender is found by the court to be suffering; and no such order shall be made unless the offender is described by each of the practitioners whose evidence is taken into account under that subsection as suffering from the same one of those forms of mental disorder, whether or not he is also described by either of them as suffering from another of them.

(8) Where an order is made under this section, the court shall not pass sentence of imprisonment or impose a fine or make a probation order in respect of the offence or make any such order as is mentioned in paragraph (b) or (c) of section 7(7) of the Children and Young Persons Act 1969 in respect of the offender, but may make any other order which the court has power to make apart from this section; and for the purposes of this subsection 'sentence of imprisonment' includes any sentence or order for detention.

38   Interim hospital orders

(1) Where a person is convicted before the Crown Court of an offence punishable with imprisonment (other than an offence the sentence for which is fixed by law) or is convicted by a magistrates' court of an offence punishable on summary conviction with imprisonment and the court before or by which he is convicted is satisfied, on the written or oral evidence of two registered medical practitioners –

    (a) that the offender is suffering from mental illness, psychopathic disorder, severe mental impairment or mental impairment; and

    (b) that there is reason to suppose that the mental disorder from which the offender is suffering is such that it may be appropriate for a hospital order to made in his case,

the court may, before making a hospital order or dealing with him in some other way, make an order (in this Act referred to as 'an interim hospital order') authorising his admission to such hospital as may be specified in the order and his detention there in accordance with this section.

(2) In the case of an offender who is subject to an interim hospital order the court may make a hospital order without his being brought before the court if he is represented by counsel or a solicitor and his counsel or solicitor is given an opportunity of being heard.

(3) At least one of the registered medical practitioners whose evidence is taken into account under subsection (1) above shall be employed at the hospital which is to be specified in the order.

(4) An interim hospital order shall not be made for the admission of an offender to a hospital unless the court is satisfied, on the written or oral evidence of the registered medical practitioner who would be in charge of his treatment or of some other person representing the managers of the hospital, that arrangements have been made for his admission to that hospital and for his admission to it within the period of 28 days beginning with the date of the order; and if the court is so satisfied the court may, pending his admission, give directions for his conveyance to and detention in a place of safety.

(5) An interim hospital order –

    (a) shall be in force for such period, not exceeding 12 weeks, as the court may specify when making the order; but

    (b) may be renewed for further periods of not more than 28 days at a time if it appears to the court, on the written or oral evidence of the responsible medical officer, that the continuation of the order is warranted;

but no such order shall continue in force for more than six months in all and the court shall terminate the order if it makes a hospital order in respect of the offender or decides after considering the written or oral evidence of the responsible medical officer to deal with the offender in some other way.

(6) The power of renewing an interim hospital order may be exercised without the offender being brought before the court if he is represented by counsel or a solicitor and his counsel or solicitor is given an opportunity of being heard.

(7) If an offender absconds from a hospital in which he is detained in pursuance of an interim hospital order, or while being conveyed to or from such a hospital, he may be arrested without warrant by a constable and shall, after being arrested, be brought as soon as practicable before the court that made the order; and the court may thereupon terminate the order and deal with him in any way in which it could have dealt with him if no such order had been made.

39   Information as to hospitals

(1) Where a court is minded to make a hospital order or interim hospital order in respect of any person it may request –

(a) the Primary Care Trust or Health Authority for the area in which that person resides or last resided; or

(b) any other Primary Care Trust or Health Authority that appears to the court to be appropriate,

to furnish the court with such information as that Health Authority have or can reasonably obtain with respect to the hospital or hospitals (if any) in their area or elsewhere at which arrangements could be made for the admission of that person in pursuance of the order, and that Health Authority shall comply with any such request.

40   Effect of hospital orders, guardianship orders and interim hospital orders

(1) A hospital order shall be sufficient authority –

(a) for a constable, an approved social worker or any other person directed to do so by the court to convey the patient to the hospital specified in the order within a period of 28 days; and

(b) for the managers of the hospital to admit him at any time within that period and thereafter detain him in accordance with the provisions of this Act.

(2) A guardianship order shall confer on the authority or person named in the order as guardian the same powers as a guardianship application made and accepted under Part II of this Act.

(3) Where an interim hospital order is made in respect of an offender –

(a) a constable or any other person directed to do so by the court shall convey the offender to the hospital specified in the order within the period mentioned in section 38(4) above; and

(b) the managers of the hospital shall admit him within that period and thereafter detain him in accordance with the provisions of section 38 above.

(4) A patient who is admitted to a hospital in pursuance of a hospital order, or placed under guardianship by a guardianship order, shall, subject to the provisions of this subsection, be treated for the purposes of the provisions of this Act mentioned in Part I of Schedule 1 to this Act as if he had been so admitted or placed on the date of the order in pursuance of an application for admission for treatment or a guardianship application, as the case may be, duly made under Part II of this Act, but subject to any modifications of those provisions specified in that Part of that Schedule.

(5) Where a patient is admitted to a hospital in pursuance of a hospital order, or placed under guardianship by a guardianship order, any previous application, hospital order or guardianship order by virtue of which he was liable to be detained in a hospital or subject to guardianship shall cease to have effect; but if the first-mentioned order, or the conviction on which it was made, is quashed on appeal, this subjection shall not apply and section 22 above shall have effect as if during any period for which the patient was liable to be detained or subject to guardianship under the order, he had been detained in custody as mentioned in that section.

(6) Where –

(a) a patient admitted to a hospital in pursuance of a hospital order is absent without leave;

(b) a warrant to arrest him has been issued under section 72 of the Criminal Justice Act 1967; and

(c) he is held pursuant to the warrant in any country or territory other than the United Kingdom, any of the Channel Islands and the Isle of Man,

he shall be treated as having been taken into custody under section 18 above on first being so held.

Restriction orders

41   Power of higher courts to restrict discharge from hospital

(1) Where a hospital order is made in respect of an offender by the Crown Court, and it appears to the court, having regard to the nature of the offence, the antecedents of the offender and the risk of his committing further offences if set at large, that it is necessary for the protection of the public from serious harm so to do, the court may, subject to the provisions of this section, further order

that the offender shall be subject to the special restrictions set out in this section, either without limit of time or during such period as may be specified in the order; and an order under this section shall be known as 'a restriction order'.

(2) A restriction order shall not be made in the case of any person unless at least one of the registered medical practitioners whose evidence is taken into account by the court under section 37 (2)(a) above has given evidence orally before the court.

(3) The special restrictions applicable to a patient in respect of whom a restriction order is in force are as follows –

    (a) none of the provisions of Part II of this Act relating to the duration, renewal and expiration of authority for the detention of patients shall apply, and the patient shall continue to be liable to be detained by virtue of the relevant hospital order until he is duly discharged under the said Part II or absolutely discharged under section 42, 73, 74 or 75 below;

    (aa) none of the provisions of Part II of this Act relating to after-care under supervision shall apply;

    (b) no application shall be made to a Mental Health Review Tribunal in respect of a patient under section 66 or 69(1) below;

    (c) the following powers shall be exercisable only with the consent of the Secretary of State, namely –

        (i) power to grant leave of absence to the patient under section 17 above;

        (ii) power to transfer the patient in pursuance of regulations under section 19 above; and

        (iii) power to order the discharge of the patient under section 23 above;

and if leave of absence is granted under the said section 17 power to recall the patient under that section shall vest in the Secretary of State as well as the responsible medical officer; and

    (d) the power of the Secretary of State to recall the patient under the said section 17 and power to take the patient into custody and return him under section 18 above may be exercised at any time;

and in relation to any such patient section 40(4) above shall have effect as if it referred to Part II of Schedule 1 to this Act instead of Part I of that Schedule.

(4) A hospital order shall not cease to have effect under section 40(5) above if a restriction order in respect of the patient is in force at the material time.

(5) Where a restriction order in respect of a patient ceases to have effect while the relevant hospital order continues in force, the provisions of section 40 above and Part I of Schedule 1 to this Act shall apply to the patient as if he had been admitted to the hospital in pursuance of a hospital order (without a restriction order) made on the date on which the restriction order ceased to have effect.

(6) While a person is subject to a restriction order the responsible medical officer shall at such intervals (not exceeding one year) as the Secretary of State may direct examine and report to the Secretary of State on that person; and every report shall contain such particulars as the Secretary of State may require.

42 Powers of Secretary of State in respect of patients subject to restriction orders

(1) If the Secretary of State is satisfied that in the case of any patient a restriction order is no longer required for the protection of the public from serious harm, he may direct that the patient shall cease to be subject to the special restrictions set out in section 41(3) above; and where the Secretary of State so directs, the restriction order shall cease to have effect, and section 41(5) above shall apply accordingly.

(2) At any time while a restriction order is in force in respect of a patient, the Secretary of State may, if he thinks fit, by warrant discharge the patient from hospital, either absolutely or subject to conditions; and where a person is absolutely discharged under this subsection, he shall thereupon

cease to be liable to be detained by virtue of the relevant hospital order, and the restriction order shall cease to have effect accordingly.

(3) The Secretary of State may at any time during the continuance in force of a restriction order in respect of a patient who has been conditionally discharged under subsection (2) above by warrant recall the patient to such hospital as may be specified in the warrant.

(4) Where a patient is recalled as mentioned in subsection (3) above –

    (a) if the hospital specified in the warrant is not the hospital from which the patient was conditionally discharged, the hospital order and the restriction order shall have effect as if the hospital specified in the warrant were substituted for the hospital specified in the hospital order;

    (b) in any case, the patient shall be treated for the purposes of section 18 above as if he had absented himself without leave from the hospital specified in the warrant, and, if the restriction order was made for a specified period, that period shall not in any event expire until the patient returns to the hospital or is returned to the hospital under that section.

(5) If a restriction order in respect of a patient ceases to have effect after the patient has been conditionally discharged under this section, the patient shall, unless previously recalled under subsection (3) above, be deemed to be absolutely discharged on the date when the order ceases to have effect, and shall cease to be liable to be detained by virtue of the relevant hospital order accordingly.

(6) The Secretary of State may, if satisfied that the attendance at any place in Great Britain of a patient who is subject to a restriction order is desirable in the interests of justice or for the purposes of any public inquiry, direct him to be taken to that place; and where a patient is directed under this subsection to be taken to any place he shall, unless the Secretary of State otherwise directs, be kept in custody while being so taken, while at that place and while being taken back to the hospital in which he is liable to be detained.

43   Power of magistrates' courts to commit for restriction order

(1) If in the case of a person of or over the age of 14 years who is convicted by a magistrates' court of an offence punishable on summary conviction with imprisonment –

    (a) the conditions which under section 37(1) above are required to be satisfied for the making of a hospital order are satisfied in respect of the offender; but

    (b) it appears to the court, having regard to the nature of the offence, the antecedents of the offender and the risk of his committing further offences if set at large, that if a hospital order is made a restriction order should also be made,

the court may, instead of making a hospital order or dealing with him in any other manner, commit him in custody to the Crown Court to be dealt with in respect of the offence.

(2) Where an offender is committed to the Crown Court under this section, the Crown Court shall inquire into the circumstances of the case and may –

    (a) if that court would have power so to do under the foregoing provisions of this Part of this Act upon the conviction of the offender before that court of such an offence as is described in section 37(1) above, make a hospital order in his case, with or without a restriction order;

    (b) if the court does not make such an order, deal with the offender in any other manner in which the magistrates' court might have dealt with him.

(3) The Crown Court shall have the same power to make orders under sections 35, 36 and 38 above in the case of a person committed to the court under this section as the Crown Court has under those sections in the case of an accused person within the meaning of section 35 or 36 above or of a person convicted before that court as mentioned in section 38 above.

(4) The power of a magistrates' court under section 38 of the Magistrates' Courts Act 1980 (which enables such a court to commit an offender to the Crown Court where the court is of the opinion that greater punishment should be inflicted for the offence than the court has power to

inflict) shall also be exercisable by a magistrates' court where it is of the opinion that greater punishment should be inflicted as aforesaid on the offender unless a hospital order is made in his case with a restriction order.

(5) The power of the Crown Court to make a hospital order, with or without a restriction order, in the case of a person convicted before that court of an offence may, in the same circumstances and subject to the same conditions, be exercised by such a court in the case of a person committed to the court under section 5 of the Vagrancy Act 1824 (which provides for the committal to the Crown Court of persons who are incorrigible rogues within the meaning of that section).

44   Committal to hospital under s. 43

(1) Where an offender is committed under section 43(1) above and the magistrates' court by which he is committed is satisfied on written or oral evidence that arrangements have been made for the admission of the offender to a hospital in the event of an order being made under this section, the court may, instead of committing him in custody, by order direct him to be admitted to that hospital, specifying it, and to be detained there until the case is disposed of by the Crown Court, and may give such directions as it thinks fit for his production from the hospital to attend the Crown Court by which his case is to be dealt with.

(2) The evidence required by subsection (1) above shall be given by the registered medical practitioner who would be in charge of the offender's treatment or by some other person representing the managers of the hospital in question.

(3) The power to give directions under section 37(4) above, section 37(5) above and section 40(1) above shall apply in relation to an order under this section as they apply in relation to a hospital order, but as if references to the period of 28 days mentioned in section 40(1) above were omitted; and subject as aforesaid an order under this section shall, until the offender's case is disposed of by the Crown Court, have the same effect as a hospital order together with a restriction order, made without limitation of time.

45   Appeals from magistrates' courts

(1) Where on the trial of an information charging a person with an offence a magistrates' court makes a hospital order or guardianship order in respect of him without convicting him, he shall have the same right of appeal against the order as if it had been made on his conviction; and on any such appeal the Crown Court shall have the same powers as if the appeal had been against both conviction and sentence.

(2) An appeal by a child or young person with respect to whom any such order has been made, whether the appeal is against the order or against the finding upon which the order was made, may be brought by him or by his parent or guardian on his behalf.

Transfer to hospital of prisoners, etc.

47   Removal to hospital of persons serving sentences of imprisonment, etc.

(1) If in the case of a person serving a sentence of imprisonment the Secretary of State is satisfied, by reports from at least two registered medical practitioners –

  (a) that the said person is suffering from mental illness, psychopathic disorder, severe mental impairment or mental impairment; and
  (b) that the mental disorder from which that person is suffering is of a nature or degree which makes it appropriate for him to be detained in a hospital for medical treatment and, in the case of psychopathic disorder or mental impairment, that such treatment is likely to alleviate or prevent a deterioration of his conditions;

the Secretary of State may, if he is of the opinion having regard to the public interest and all the circumstances that it is expedient so to do, by warrant direct that that person be removed to and detained in such hospital (not being a mental nursing home) as may be specified in the direction; and a direction under this section shall be known as 'a transfer direction'.

(2) A transfer direction shall cease to have effect at the expiration of the period of 14 days beginning with the date on which it is given unless within that period the person with respect to whom it was given has been received into the hospital specified in the direction.

(3) A transfer direction with respect to any person shall have the same effect as a hospital order made in his case.

(4) A transfer direction shall specify the form or forms of mental disorder referred to in paragraph (a) of subsection (1) above from which, upon the reports taken into account under that subsection, the patient is found by the Secretary of State to be suffering; and no such direction shall be given unless the patient is described in each of those reports as suffering from the same form of disorder, whether or not he is also described in either of them as suffering from another form.

(5) References in this Part of this Act to a person serving a sentence of imprisonment include references –

> (a) to a person detained in pursuance of any sentence or order for detention made by a court in criminal proceedings (other than an order under any enactment to which section 46 above applies);
>
> (b) to a person committed to custody under section 115(3) of the Magistrates' Courts Act 1980 (which relates to persons who fail to comply with an order to enter into recognisances to keep the peace or be of good behaviour); and
>
> (c) to a person committed by a court to a prison or other institution to which the Prison Act 1952 applies in default of payment of any sum adjudged to be paid on his conviction.

48   Removal to hospital of other prisoners

(1) If in the case of a person to whom this section applies the Secretary of State is satisfied by the same reports as are required for the purposes of section 47 above that that person is suffering from mental impairment of a nature or degree which makes it appropriate for him to be detained in a hospital for medical treatment and that he is in urgent need of such treatment, the Secretary of State shall have the same power of giving a transfer direction in respect of him under that section as if he were serving a sentence of imprisonment.

(2) This section applies to the following persons, that is to say –

> (a) persons detained in a prison or remand centre, not being persons serving a sentence of imprisonment or persons falling within the following paragraphs of this subsection;
>
> (b) persons remanded in custody by a magistrates' court;
>
> (c) civil prisoners, that is to say, persons committed by a court to prison for a limited term (including persons committed to prison in pursuance of a writ of attachment), who are not persons falling to be dealt with under section 47 above;
>
> (d) persons detained under the Immigration Act 1971.

(3) Subsections (2) to (4) of section 47 above shall apply for the purposes of this section and of any transfer direction given by virtue of this section as they apply for the purposes of that section and of any transfer direction under that section.

49   Restriction on discharge of prisoners removed to hospital

(1) Where a transfer direction is given in respect of any person, the Secretary of State, if he thinks fit, may by warrant further direct that that person shall be subject to the special restrictions set out in section 41 above; and where the Secretary of State gives a transfer direction in respect of any such person as is described in paragraph (a) or (b) of section 48(2) above, he shall also give a direction under this section applying those restrictions to him.

(2) A direction under this section shall have the same effect as a restriction order made under section 41 above and shall be known as 'a restriction direction'.

(3) While a person is subject to a restriction direction the responsible medical officer shall at such intervals (not exceeding one year) as the Secretary of State may direct examine and report to the Secretary of State on that person; and every report shall contain such particulars as the Secretary of State may require.

50   Further provisions as to prisoners under sentence

(1) Where a transfer direction and a restriction direction have been given in respect of a person serving a sentence of imprisonment and before the expiration of that person's sentence the Secretary of State is notified by the responsible medical officer, any other registered medical practitioner or a Mental Health Review Tribunal that that person no longer requires treatment in hospital for mental disorder or that no effective treatment for his disorder can be given in the hospital to which he has been removed, the Secretary of State may –

   (a) by warrant direct that he be remitted to any prison or other institution in which he might have been detained if he had not been removed to hospital, there to be dealt with as if he had not been so removed; or

   (b) exercise any power of releasing him on licence or discharging him under supervision which would have been exercisable if he had been remitted to such a prison or institution as aforesaid,

and on his arrival in the prison or other institution or, as the case may be, his release or discharge as aforesaid, the transfer direction and the restriction direction shall cease to have effect.

(2) A restriction direction in the case of a person serving a sentence of imprisonment shall cease to have effect on the expiration of the sentence.

(3) Subject to subsection (4) below, references in this section to the expiration of a person's sentence are references to the expiration of the period during which he would have been liable to be detained in a prison or other institution if the transfer direction had not been given.

(4) For the purposes of section 49(2) of the Prison Act 1952 (which provides for discounting from the sentences of certain prisoners periods while they are unlawfully at large) a patient who, having been transferred in pursuance of a transfer direction from any such institution as is referred to in that section, is at large in circumstances in which he is liable to be taken into custody under any provision of this Act, shall be treated as unlawfully at large and absent from that institution.

51   Further provisions as to detained persons

(1) This section has effect where a transfer direction has been given in respect of any such person as is described in paragraph (a) of section 48(2) above and that person is in this section referred to as 'the detainee'.

(2) The transfer direction shall cease to have effect when the detainee's case is disposed of by the court having jurisdiction to try or otherwise deal with him, but without prejudice to any power of that court to make a hospital order or other order under this Part of this Act in his case.

(3) If the Secretary of State is notified by the responsible medical officer, any other registered medical practitioner or a Mental Health Review Tribunal at any time before the detainee's case is disposed of by that court –

   (a) that the detainee no longer requires treatment in hospital for mental disorder; or

   (b) that no effective treatment for his disorder can be given at the hospital to which he has been removed,

the Secretary of State may by warrant direct that he be remitted to any place where he might have been detained if he had not been removed to hospital, there to be dealt with as if he had not been so removed, and on his arrival at the place to which he is so remitted the transfer direction shall cease to have effect.

(4) If (no direction having been given under subsection (3) above) the court having jurisdiction to try or otherwise deal with the detainee is satisfied on the written or oral evidence of the responsible medical officer –

   (a) that the detainee no longer requires treatment in hospital for mental disorder; or

   (b) that no effective treatment for his disorder can be given at the hospital to which he has been removed,

the court may order him to be remitted to any such place as is mentioned in subsection (3) above or released on bail and on his arrival at that place or, as the case may be, his release on bail the transfer direction shall cease to have effect.

(5) If (no direction or order having been given or made under subsection (3) or (4) above) it appears to the court having jurisdiction to try or otherwise deal with the detainee –

(a) that it is impracticable or inappropriate to bring the detainee before the court; and

(b) that the conditions set out in subsection (6) below are satisfied,

the court may make a hospital order (with or without a restriction order) in his case in his absence and, in the case of a person awaiting trial, without convicting him.

(6) A hospital order may be made in respect of a person under subsection (5) above if the court –

(a) is satisfied, on the written or oral evidence of at least two registered medical practitioners, that the detainee is suffering from mental illness or severe mental impairment of a nature or degree which makes it appropriate for the patient to be detained in a hospital for medical treatment; and

(b) is of the opinion, after considering any depositions or other documents required to be sent to the proper officer of the court, that it is proper to make such an order.

(7) Where a person committed to the Crown Court to be dealt with under section 43 above is admitted to a hospital in pursuance of an order under section 44 above, subsections (5) and (6) above shall apply as if he were a person subject to a transfer direction.

52   Further provisions as to persons remanded by magistrates' courts

(1) This section has effect where a transfer direction has been given in respect of any such person as is described in paragraph (b) of section 48(2) above; and that person is in this section referred to as 'the accused'.

(2) Subject to subsection (5) below, the transfer direction shall cease to have effect on the expiration of the period of remand unless the accused is committed in custody to the Crown Court for trail or to be otherwise dealt with.

(3) Subject to subsection (4) below, the power of further remanding the accused under section 128 of the Magistrates' Courts Act 1980 may be exercised by the court without his being brought before the court; and if the court further remands the accused in custody (whether or not he is brought before the court) the period of remand shall, for the purposes of this section, be deemed not to have expired.

(4) The court shall not under subsection (3) above further remand the accused in his absence unless he has appeared before the court within the previous six months.

(5) If the magistrates' court is satisfied, on the written or oral evidence of the responsible medical officer –

(a) that the accused no longer requires treatment in hospital for mental disorder; or

(b) that no effective treatment for his disorder can be given in the hospital to which he has been removed,

the court may direct that the transfer direction shall cease to have effect notwithstanding that the period of remand has not expired or that the accused is committed to the Crown Court as mentioned in subsection (2) above.

(6) If the accused is committed to the Crown Court as mentioned in subsection (2) above and the transfer direction has not ceased to have effect under subsection (5) above, section 51 above shall apply as if the transfer direction given in his case were a direction given in respect of a person falling within that section.

(7) The magistrates' court may, in the absence of the accused, inquire as examining justices into an offence alleged to have been committed by him and commit him for trial in accordance with section 6 of the Magistrates' Court Act 1980 if –

(a) the court is satisfied, on the written or oral evidence of the responsible medical officer, that the accused is unfit to take part in the proceedings; and

(b) where the court proceeds under subsection (1) of that section, the accused is represented by counsel or a solicitor.

53 Further provisions as to civil prisoners and persons detained under the Immigration Act 1971

(1) Subject to subsection (2) below, a transfer direction given in respect of any such person as is described in paragraph (c) or (d) of section 48(2) above shall cease to have effect on the expiration of the period during which he would, but for his removal to hospital, be liable to be detained in the place from which he was removed.

(2) Where a transfer direction and a restriction direction have been given in respect of any such person as is mentioned in subsection (1) above, then, if the Secretary of State is notified by the responsible medical officer, any other registered medical practitioner or a Mental Health Review Tribunal at any time before the expiration of the period there mentioned –

(a) that that person no longer requires treatment in hospital for mental disorder; or

(b) that no effective treatment for his disorder can be given in the hospital to which he has been removed,

the Secretary of State may be warrant direct that he be remitted to any place where he might have been detained if he had not been removed to hospital, and on his arrival at the place to which he is so remitted the transfer direction and the restriction direction shall cease to have effect.

Supplemental

54 Requirements as to medical evidence

(1) The registered medical practitioner whose evidence is taken into account under section 35(3)(a) above and at least one of the registered medical practitioners whose evidence is taken into account under sections 36(1), 37(2)(a), 38(1) and 51(6)(a) above and whose reports are taken into account under sections 47(1) and 48(1) above shall be a practitioner approved for the purposes of section 12 above by the Secretary of State as having special experience in the diagnosis or treatment of mental disorder.

(2) For the purposes of any provision of this Part of this Act under which a court may act on the written evidence of –

(a) a registered medical practitioner or a registered medical practitioner of any description; or

(b) a person representing the managers of a hospital,

a report in writing purporting to be signed by a registered medical practitioner or a registered medical practitioner of such a description or by a person representing the managers of a hospital may, subject to the provisions of this section, be received in evidence without proof of the signature of the practitioner or that person and without proof that he has the requisite qualifications or authority or is of the requisite description; but the court may require the signatory of any such report to be called to give oral evidence.

(3) Where, in pursuance of a direction of the court, any such report is tendered in evidence otherwise than by or on behalf of the person who is the subject of the report, then –

(a) if that person is represented by counsel or a solicitor, a copy of the report shall be given to his counsel or solicitor;

(b) if that person is not so represented, the substance of the report shall be disclosed to him or, where he is a child or young person, to his parent or guardian if present in court; and

(c) except where the report relates only to arrangements for his admission to a hospital, that person may require the signatory of the report to be called to give oral evidence, and evidence to rebut the evidence contained in the report may be called by or on behalf of that person.

55 Interpretation of Part III

(1) In this Part of this Act –

'child' and 'young person' have the same meaning as in the Children and Young Persons Act 1933;

'civil prisoner' has the meaning given to it by section 48(2)(c) above;

'guardian', in relation to a child or young person, has the same meaning as in the Children and Young Persons Act 1933;

'place of safety', in relation to a person who is not a child or young person, means any police station, prison or remand centre, or any hospital the managers of which are willing temporarily to receive him, and in relation to a child or young person has the same meaning as in the Children and Young Persons Act 1933;

'responsible medical officer', in relation to a person liable to be detained in a hospital within the meaning of Part II of this Act, means the registered medical practitioner in charge of the treatment of the patient.

(2) Any reference in this Part of this Act to an offence punishable on summary conviction with imprisonment shall be construed without regard to any prohibition or restriction imposed by or under any enactment relating to the imprisonment of young offenders.

(3) Where a patient who is liable to be detained in a hospital in pursuance of an order or direction under this Part of this Act is treated by virtue of any provision of this Part of this Act as if he had been admitted to the hospital in pursuance of a subsequent order or direction under this Part of this Act or a subsequent application for admission for treatment under Part II of this Act, he shall be treated as if the subsequent order, direction or application had described him as suffering from the form or forms of mental disorder specified in the earlier order or direction or, where he is treated as if he had been so admitted by virtue of a direction under section 42(1) above, such form of mental disorder as may be specified in the direction under that section.

(4) Any reference to a hospital order, a guardianship order or a restriction order in section 40(2), (4) or (5), section 41(3) to (5), or section 42 above or section 69(1) below shall be construed as including a reference to any order or direction under this Part of this Act having the same effect as the first-mentioned order; and the exceptions and modifications set out in Schedule 1 to this Act in respect of the provisions of this Act described in that Schedule accordingly include those which are consequential on the provisions of this subsection.

(5) Section 34(2) above shall apply for the purposes of this Part of this Act as it applies for the purposes of Part II of this Act.

(6) References in this Part of this Act to persons serving a sentence of imprisonment shall be construed in accordance with section 47(5) above.

(7) Section 99 of the Children and Young Persons Act 1933 (which relates to the presumption and determination of age) shall apply for the purposes of this Part of this Act as it applies for the purposes of that Act.

Part IV Consent to Treatment

56   Patients to whom Part IV applies

(1) This Part of this Act applies to any patient liable to be detained under this Act except –

> (a) a patient who is liable to be detained by virtue of an emergency application and in respect of whom the second medical recommendation referred to in section 4(4)(a) above has not been given and received;
>
> (b) a patient who is liable to be detained by virtue of section 5(2) or (4) or 35 above or section 135 or 136 below or by virtue of a direction under section 37(4) above; and
>
> (c) a patient who has been conditionally discharged under section 42(2) above or section 73 or 74 below and has not been recalled to hospital.

(2) Section 57 and, so far as relevant to that section, sections 59, 60 and 62 below, apply also to any patient who is not liable to be detained under this Act.

57   Treatment requiring consent and a second opinion

(1) This section applies to the following forms of medical treatment for mental disorder –

    (a) any surgical operation for destroying brain tissue or for destroying the functioning of brain tissue; and

    (b) such other forms of treatment as may be specified for the purposes of this section by regulations made by the Secretary of State.

(2) Subject to section 62 below, a patient shall not be given any form of treatment to which this section applies unless he has consented to it and –

    (a) a registered medical practitioner appointed for the purposes of this Part of this Act by the Secretary of State (not being the responsible medical officer) and two other persons appointed for the purposes of this paragraph by the Secretary of State (not being registered medical practitioners) have certified in writing that the patient is capable of understanding the nature, purpose and likely effects of the treatment in question and has consented to it; and

    (b) the registered medical practitioner referred to in paragraph (a) above has certified in writing that, having regard to the likelihood of the treatment alleviating or preventing a deterioration of the patient's condition, the treatment should be given.

(3) Before giving a certificate under subsection (2)(b) above the registered medical practitioner concerned shall consult two other persons who have been professionally concerned with the patient's medical treatment, and of those persons one shall be a nurse and the other shall be neither a nurse nor a registered medical practitioner.

(4) Before making any regulations for the purpose of this section the Secretary of State shall consult such bodies as appear to him to be concerned.

58   Treatment requiring consent or a second opinion

(1) This section applies to the following forms of medical treatment for mental disorder –

    (a) such forms of treatment as may be specified for the purposes of this section by regulations made by the Secretary of State;

    (b) the administration of medicine to a patient by any means (not being a form of treatment specified under paragraph (a) above or section 57 above) at any time during a period for which he is liable to be detained as a patient to whom this Part of this Act applies if three months or more have elapsed since the first occasion in that period when medicine was administered to him by any means for his mental disorder.

(2) The Secretary of State may by order vary the length of the period mentioned in subsection (1)(b) above.

(3) Subject to section 62 below, a patient shall not be given any form of treatment to which this section applies unless –

    (a) he has consented to that treatment and either the responsible medical officer or a registered medical practitioner appointed for the purposes of this Part of this Act by the Secretary of State has certified in writing that the patient is capable of understanding its nature, purpose and likely effects and has consented to it; or

    (b) a registered medical practitioner appointed as aforesaid (not being the responsible medical officer) has certified in writing that the patient is not capable of understanding the nature, purpose and likely effects of that treatment or has not consented to it but that, having regard to the likelihood of its alleviating or preventing a deterioration of his condition, the treatment should be given.

(4) Before giving a certificate under subsection (3)(b) above the registered medical practitioner concerned shall consult two other persons who have been professionally concerned with the patient's medical treatment, and of those persons one shall be a nurse and the other shall be neither a nurse nor a registered medical practitioner.

(5) Before making any regulations for the purposes of this section the Secretary of State shall consult such bodies as appear to him to be concerned.

59   Plans of treatment

Any consent or certificate under section 57 or 58 above may relate to a plan of treatment under which the patient is to be given (whether within a specified period or otherwise) one or more of the forms of treatment to which that section applies.

60   Withdrawal of consent

(1) Where the consent of a patient to any treatment has been given for the purposes of section 57 or 58 above, the patient may, subject to section 62 below, at any time before the completion of the treatment withdraw his consent, and those sections shall then apply as if the remainder of the treatment were a separate form of treatment.

(2) Without prejudice to the application of subsection (1) above to any treatment given under the plan of treatment to which a patient has consented, a patient who has consented to such a plan may, subject to section 62 below, at any time withdraw his consent to further treatment, or to further treatment of any description, under the plan.

61   Review of treatment

(1) Where a patient is given treatment in accordance with section 57(2) or 58(3)(b) above a report on the treatment and the patient's condition shall be given by the responsible medical officer to the Secretary of State –

    (a) on the next occasion on which the responsible medical officer furnishes a report in respect of the patient under section 20(3) or 21B(2) above renewing the authority for the detention of the patient; and

    (b) at any other time if so required by the Secretary of State.

(2) In relation to a patient who is subject to a restriction order or restriction direction subsection (1) above shall have effect as if paragraph (a) required the report to be made –

    (a) in the case of treatment in the period of six months beginning with the date of the order or direction, at the end of that period;

    (b) in the case of treatment at any subsequent time, on the next occasion on which the responsible medical officer makes a report in respect of the patient under section 41(6) or 49(3) above.

(3) The Secretary of State may at any time give notice to the responsible medical officer directing that, subject to section 62 below, a certificate given in respect of a patient under section 57(2) or 58(3)(b) above shall not apply to treatment given to him after a date specified in the notice and sections 57 and 58 above shall then apply to any such treatment as if that certificate had not been given.

62   Urgent treatment

(1) Sections 57 and 58 above shall not apply to any treatment –

    (a) which is immediately necessary to save the patient's life; or

    (b) which (not being irreversible) is immediately necessary to prevent a serious deterioration of his condition; or

    (c) which (not being irreversible or hazardous) is immediately necessary to alleviate serious suffering by the patient; or

    (d) which (not being irreversible or hazardous) is immediately necessary and represents the minimum interference necessary to prevent the patient from behaving violently or being a danger to himself or to others.

(2) Sections 60 and 61(3) above shall not preclude the continuation of any treatment or of treatment under any plan pending compliance with section 57 or 58 above if the responsible medical officer considers that the discontinuance of the treatment or of treatment under the plan would cause serious suffering to the patient.

(3) For the purposes of this section treatment is irreversible if it has unfavourable irreversible physical or psychological consequences and hazardous if it entails significant physical hazard.

63   Treatment not requiring consent

The consent of a patient shall not be required for any medical treatment given to him for the mental disorder from which he is suffering, not being treatment falling within section 57 or 58 above, if the treatment is given by or under the direction of the responsible medical officer.

64   Supplementary provisions for Part IV

(1) In this Part of this Act 'the responsible medical officer' means the registered medical practitioner in charge of the treatment of the patient in question and 'hospital' includes a mental nursing home.

(2) Any certificate for the purposes of this Part of this Act shall be in such form as may be prescribed by regulations made by the Secretary of State.

Part V Mental Health Review Tribunals

Constitution etc.

65   Mental Health Review Tribunals

(1) There shall be tribunals known as Mental Health Review Tribunals for the purpose of dealing with applications and references by and in respect of patients under the provisions of this Act.

(1A) There shall be –

(a) one tribunal for each region of England, and

(b) one tribunal for Wales.

(1B) The Secretary of State –

(a) shall by order determine regions for the purpose of subsection (1A)(a) above; and

(b) may by order vary a region determined for that purpose;

and the Secretary of State shall act under this subsection so as to secure that the regions together comprise the whole of England.

(1C) Any order made under subsection (1B) above may make such transitional, consequential, incidental or supplemental provision as the Secretary of State considers appropriate.

(2) The provisions of Schedule 2 to this Act shall have effect with respect to the constitution of Mental Health Review Tribunals.

(3) Subject to the provisions of Schedule 2 to this Act, and to rules made by the Lord Chancellor under this Act, the jurisdiction of a Mental Health Review Tribunal may be exercised by any three or more of its members, and references in this Act to a Mental Health Review Tribunal shall be construed accordingly.

(4) The Secretary of State may pay to the members of Mental Health Review Tribunals such remuneration and allowances as he may with the consent of the Treasury determine, and defray the expenses of such tribunals to such amount as he may with the consent of the Treasury determine, and may provide for each such tribunal such officers and servants, and such accommodation, as the tribunal may require.

Applications and references concerning Part II patients

66   Applications to tribunals

(1) Where –

(a) a patient is admitted to a hospital in pursuance of an application for admission for assessment; or

(b) a patient is admitted to a hospital in pursuance of an application for admission for treatment; or

(c) a patient is received into guardianship in pursuance of a guardianship application; or

(d) a report is furnished under section 16 above in respect of a patient; or

(e) a patient is transferred from guardianship to a hospital in pursuance of regulations made under section 19 above; or

(f) a report is furnished under section 20 above in respect of a patient and the patient is not discharged; or

(fa) a report is furnished under subsection (2) of section 21B above in respect of a patient and subsection (5) of the section applies (or subsections (5) and (6)(b) of that section apply) in the case of the report; or

(fb) a report is furnished under subsection (2) of section 21B above in respect of a patient and subsection (8) of that section applies in the case of the report; or

(g) a report is furnished under section 25 above in respect of a patient who is detained in pursuance of an application for admission for treatment; or

(ga) a supervision application is accepted in respect of a patient; or

(gb) a report is furnished under section 25F above in respect of a patient; or

(gc) a report is furnished under section 25G above in respect of a patient; or

(h) an order is made under section 29 above in respect of a patient who is or subsequently becomes liable to be detained or subject to guardianship under Part II of this Act, an application may be made to a Mental Health Review Tribunal within the relevant period –

  (i) by the patient (except in the cases mentioned in paragraphs (g) and (h) above) or, in the cases mentioned in paragraphs (d), (ga), (gb) and (gc) by his nearest relative if he has been (or was entitled to be) informed under this Act of the report or acceptance.

  (ii) in the cases mentioned in paragraphs (g) and (h) above, by his nearest relative.

(2) In subsection (1) above 'the relevant period' means –

(a) in the cases mentioned in paragraph (a) of that subsection, 14 days beginning with the day on which the patient is admitted as so mentioned;

(b) in the case mentioned in paragraph (b) of that subsection, six months beginning with the day on which the patient is admitted as so mentioned;

(c) in the cases mentioned in paragraphs (c) and (ga) of that subsection, six months beginning with the day on which the application is accepted;

(d) in the cases mentioned in paragraphs (d), (fb), (g) and (gb) of that subsection, 28 days beginning with the day on which the applicant is informed that the report has been furnished;

(e) in the case mentioned in paragraph (e) of that subsection, six months beginning with the day on which the patient is transferred;

(f) in the case mentioned in paragraph (f) or (fa) of that subsection, the period or periods for which authority for the patient's detention or guardianship is renewed by virtue of the report;

(fa) in the case mentioned in paragraph (gc) of that subsection, the further period for which the patient is made subject to after-care under supervision by virtue of the report;

(g) in the case mentioned in paragraph (h) of that subsection, 12 months beginning with the date of the order, and in any subsequent period of 12 months during which the order continues in force.

(3) Section 32 above shall apply for the purposes of this section as it applies for the purposes of Part II of this Act.

67 References to tribunals by Secretary of State concerning Part II patients

(1) The Secretary of State may, if he thinks fit, at any time refer to a Mental Health Review Tribunal the case of any patient who is liable to be detained or subject to guardianship or to after-care under supervision under Part II of this Act.

(2) For the purpose of furnishing information for the purposes of a reference under subsection (1) above any registered medical practitioner authorised by or on behalf of the patient may, at any reasonable time, visit the patient and examine him in private and require the production of and inspect any records relating to the detention or treatment of the patient in any hospital or to any after-care services provided for the patient under section 117 below.

(3) Section 32 above shall apply for the purposes of this section as it applies for the purposes of Part II of this Act.

68   Duty of managers of hospitals to refer cases to tribunal

(1) Where a patient who is admitted to a hospital in pursuance of an application for admission for treatment or a patient who is transferred from guardianship to hospital does not exercise his right to apply to a Mental Health Review Tribunal under section 66(1) above by virtue of his case falling within paragraph (b) or, as the case may be, paragraph (e) of that section, the managers of the hospital shall at the expiration of the period for making such an application refer the patient's case to such a tribunal unless an application or reference in respect of the patient has then been made under section 66(1) above by virtue of his case falling within paragraph (d), (g) or (h) of that section or under section 67(1) above.

(2) If the authority for the detention of a patient in a hospital is renewed under section 20 or 21B above and a period of three years (or, if the patient has not attained the age of sixteen years, one year) has elapsed since his case was last considered by a Mental Health Review Tribunal, whether on his own application or otherwise, the managers of the hospital shall refer his case to such a tribunal.

(3) For the purpose of furnishing information for the purposes of any reference under this section, any registered medical practitioner authorised by or on behalf of the patient may at any reasonable time visit and examine the patient in private and require the production of and inspect any records relating to the detention or treatment of the patient in any hospital.

(4) The Secretary of State may by order vary the length of the periods mentioned in subsection (2) above.

(5) For the purposes of subsection (1) above a person who applies to a tribunal but subsequently withdraws his application shall be treated as not having exercised his right to apply, and where a person withdraws his application on a date after the expiration of the period mentioned in that subsection, the managers shall refer the patient's case as soon as possible after that date.

Applications and references concerning Part III patients

69   Applications to tribunals concerning patients subject to hospital and guardianship orders

(1) Without prejudice to any provision of section 66(1) above as applied by section 40(4) above, an application to a Mental Health Review Tribunal may also be made –

- (a) in respect of a patient admitted to a hospital in pursuance of a hospital order, by the nearest relative of the patient in the period between the expiration of six months and the expiration of 12 months beginning with the date of the order and in any subsequent period of 12 months; and
- (b) in respect of a patient placed under guardianship by a guardianship order –
  - (i)   by the patient, within the period of six months beginning with the date of the order;
  - (ii) by the nearest relative of the patient, within the period of 12 months beginning with the date of the order and in any subsequent period of 12 months.

(2) Where a person detained in a hospital –

- (a) is treated as subject to a hospital order or transfer direction by virtue of section 41 (5) above, 82(2) or 85(2) below, section 77(2) of the Mental Health (Scotland) Act 1984 or section 5(1) of the Criminal Procedure (Insanity) Act 1964; or
- (b) is subject to a direction having the same effect as a hospital order by virtue of section 46(3), 47(3) or 48(3) above,

then, without prejudice to any provision of Part II of this Act as applied by section 40 above, that person may make an application to a Mental Health Review Tribunal in the period of six months beginning with the date of the order or direction mentioned in paragraph (a) above or, as the case may be, the date of the direction mentioned in paragraph (b) above.

70   Applications to tribunals concerning restricted patients

A patient who is a restricted patient within the meaning of section 79 below and is detained in a hospital may apply to a Mental Health Review Tribunal –

    (a) in the period between the expiration of six months and the expiration of 12 months beginning with the date of the relevant hospital order or transfer direction; and

    (b) in any subsequent period of 12 months.

71   References by Secretary of State concerning restricted patients

(1) The Secretary of State may at any time refer the case of a restricted patient to a Mental Health Review Tribunal.

(2) The Secretary of State shall refer to a Mental Health Review Tribunal the case of any restricted patient detained in a hospital whose case has not been considered by such a tribunal, whether on his own application or otherwise, within the last three years.

(3) The Secretary of State may by order vary the length of the period mentioned in subsection (2) above.

(4) Any reference under subsection (1) above in respect of a patient who has been conditionally discharged and not recalled to hospital shall be made to the tribunal for the area in which the patient resides.

(5) Where a person who is treated as subject to a hospital order and a restriction order by virtue of an order under section 5(1) of the Criminal Procedure (Insanity) Act 1964 does not exercise his right to apply to a Mental Health Review Tribunal in the period of six months beginning with the date of that order, the Secretary of State shall at the expiration of that period refer his case to a tribunal.

(6) For the purposes of subsection (5) above a person who applies to a tribunal but subsequently withdraws his application shall be treated as not having exercised his right to apply, and where a patient withdraws his application on a date after the expiration of the period there mentioned the Secretary of State shall refer his case as soon as possible after that date.

Discharge of patients

72   Powers of tribunals

(1) Where application is made to a Mental Health Review Tribunal by or in respect of a patient who is liable to be detained under this Act, the tribunal may in any case direct that the patient be discharged, and –

    (a) the tribunal shall direct the discharge of a patient liable to be detained under section 2 above if they are not satisfied –

        (i) that he is then suffering from mental disorder or from mental disorder of a nature or degree which warrants his detention in a hospital for assessment (or for assessment followed by medical treatment) for at least a limited period; or

        (ii) that his detention as aforesaid is justified in the interests of his own health or safety or with a view to the protection of other persons;

    (b) the tribunal shall direct the discharge of a patient liable to be detained otherwise than under section 2 above if they are not satisfied –

        (i) that he is then suffering from mental illness, psychopathic disorder, severe mental impairment or mental impairment or from any of those forms of disorder of a nature or degree which makes it appropriate for him to be liable to be detained in a hospital for medical treatment; or

        (ii) that it is necessary for the health of safety of the patient or for the protection of other persons that he should receive such treatment; or

        (iii) in the case of an application by virtue of paragraph (g) of section 66(1) above, that the patient, if released, would be likely to act in a manner dangerous to other persons or to himself.

(2) In determining whether to direct the discharge of a patient detained otherwise than under section 2 above in a case not falling within paragraph (b) of subsection (1) above, the tribunal shall have regard –

(a) to the likelihood of medical treatment alleviating or preventing a deterioration of the patient's condition; and

(b) in the case of a patient suffering from mental illness or severe mental impairment, to the likelihood of the patient, if discharged, being able to care for himself, to obtain the care he needs or to guard himself against serious exploitation.

(3) A tribunal may under subsection (1) above direct the discharge of a patient on a future date specified in the direction; and where a tribunal do not direct the discharge of a patient under that subsection the tribunal may –

(a) with a view to facilitating his discharge on a future date, recommend that he be granted leave of absence or transferred to another hospital or into guardianship; and

(b) further consider his case in the event of any such recommendation not being complied with.

(3A) Where, in the case of an application to a tribunal by or in respect of a patient who is liable to be detained in pursuance of an application for admission for treatment or by virtue of an order or direction for his admission or removal to hospital under Part III of this Act, the tribunal do not direct the discharge of the patient under subsection (1) above, the tribunal may –

(a) recommend that the responsible medical officer consider whether to make a supervision application in respect of the patient; and

(b) further consider his case in the event of no such application being made.

(4) Where application is made to a Mental Health Review Tribunal by or in respect of a patient who is subject to guardianship under this Act, the tribunal may in any case direct that the patient be discharged, and shall so direct if they are satisfied –

(a) that he is not then suffering from mental illness, psychopathic disorder, severe mental impairment or mental impairment; or

(b) that it is not necessary in the interests of the welfare of the patient, or for the protection of other persons, that the patient should remain under such guardianship.

(4A) Where application is made to a Mental Health Review Tribunal by or in respect of a patient who is subject to after-care under supervision (or, if he has not yet left hospital, is to be so subject after he leaves hospital), the tribunal may in any case direct that the patient shall cease to be so subject (or not become so subject), and shall so direct if they are satisfied –

(a) in a case where the patient has not yet left hospital, that the conditions set out in section 25A(4) above are not complied with; or

(b) in any other case, that the conditions set out in section 25G(4) above are not complied with.

(5) Where application is made to a Mental Health Review Tribunal under any provision of this Act by or in respect of a patient and the tribunal do not direct that the patient be discharged, or, if he is (or is to be) subject to after-care under supervision, that he cease to be so subject (or not become so subject) the tribunal may, if satisfied that the patient is suffering from a form of mental disorder other than the form specified in the application, order or direction relating to him, direct that that application, order or direction be amended by substituting for the form of mental disorder specified in it such other form of mental disorder as appears to the tribunal to be appropriate.

(6) Subsections (1) to (5) above apply in relation to references to a Mental Health Review Tribunal as they apply in relation to applications made to such a tribunal by or in respect of a patient.

(7) Subsection (1) above shall not apply in the case of a restricted patient except as provided in section 73 and 74 below.

73   Power to discharge restricted patients

(1) Where an application to a Mental Health Review Tribunal is made by a restricted patient who is subject to a restriction order, or where the case of such a patient is referred to such a tribunal, the tribunal shall direct the absolute discharge of the patient if –

      (a) the tribunal are not satisfied as to the matters mentioned in paragraph (b)(i) or (ii) of section 72(1) above; and

      (b) the tribunal are satisfied that it is not appropriate for the patient to remain liable to be recalled to hospital for further treatment.

(2) Where in the case of any such patient as is mentioned in subsection (1) above –

      (a) paragraph (a) of that subsection applies; but

      (b) paragraph (b) of that subsection does not apply,

the tribunal shall direct the conditional discharge of the patient.

(3) Where a patient is absolutely discharged under this section he shall thereupon cease to be liable to be detained by virtue of the relevant hospital order, and the restriction order shall cease to have effect accordingly.

(4) Where a patient is conditionally discharged under this section –

      (a) he may be recalled by the Secretary of State under subsection (3) of section 42 above as if he had been conditionally discharged under subsection (2) of that section; and

      (b) the patient shall comply with such conditions (if any) as may be imposed at the time of discharge by the tribunal or at any subsequent time by the Secretary of State.

(5) The Secretary of State may from time to time vary any condition imposed (whether by the tribunal or by him) under subsection (4) above.

(6) Where a restriction order in respect of a patient ceases to have effect after he has been conditionally discharged under his section the patient shall, unless previously recalled, be deemed to be absolutely discharged on the date when the order ceases to have effect and shall cease to be liable to be detained by virtue of the relevant hospital order.

(7) A tribunal may defer a direction for the conditional discharge of a patient until such arrangements as appear to the tribunal to be necessary for that purpose have been made to their satisfaction; and where by virtue of any such deferment no direction has been given on an application or reference before the time when the patient's case comes before the tribunal on a subsequent application or reference, the previous application or reference shall be treated as one on which no direction under this section can be given.

(8) This section is without prejudice to section 42 above.

74   Restricted patients subject to restriction directions

(1) Where an application to a Mental Health Review Tribunal is made by a restricted patient who is subject to a restriction direction, or where the case of such a patient is referred to such a tribunal, the tribunal –

      (a) shall notify the Secretary of State whether, in their opinion, the patient would, if subject to a restriction order, be entitled to be absolutely or conditionally discharged under section 73 above; and

      (b) if they notify him that the patient would be entitled to be conditionally discharged, may recommend that in the event of his not being discharged under his section he should continue to be detained in hospital.

(2) If in the case of a patient not falling within subsection (4) below –

      (a) the tribunal notify the Secretary of State that the patient would be entitled to be absolutely or conditionally discharged; and

      (b) within the period of 90 days beginning with the date of that notification the Secretary of State gives notice to the tribunal that the patient may be so discharged,

the tribunal shall direct the absolute or, as the case may be, the conditional discharge of the patient.

(3) Where a patient continues to be liable to be detained in a hospital at the end of the period referred to in subsection (2)(b) above because the Secretary of State has not given the notice there mentioned, the managers of the hospital shall, unless the tribunal have made a recommendation under subsection (1)(b) above, transfer the patient to a prison or other institution in which he might have been detained if he had not been removed to hospital, there to be dealt with as if he had not been so removed.

(4) If, in the case of a patient who is subject to a transfer direction under section 48 above, the tribunal notify the Secretary of State that the patient would be entitled to be absolutely or conditionally discharged, the Secretary of State shall, unless the tribunal have made a recommendation under subsection (1)(b) above, by warrant direct that the patient be remitted to a prison or other institution in which he might have been detained if he had not been removed to hospital, there to be dealt with as if he had not been so removed.

(5) Where a patient is transferred or remitted under subsection (3) or (4) above the relevant transfer direction and the restriction direction shall cease to have effect on his arrival in the prison or other institution.

(6) Subsections (3) to (8) of section 73 above shall have effect in relation to this section as they have effect in relation to that section, taking references to the relevant hospital order and the restriction order as references to the transfer direction and the restriction direction.

(7) This section is without prejudice to sections 50 to 53 above in their application to patients who are not discharged under this section.

75   Applications and references concerning conditionally discharged restricted patients

(1) Where a restricted patient has been conditionally discharged under section 42(2), 73 or 74 above and is subsequently recalled to hospital –
> (a) the Secretary of State shall, within one month of the day on which the patient returns or is returned to hospital, refer his case to a Mental Health Review Tribunal; and
> (b) section 70 above shall apply to the patient as if the relevant hospital order or transfer direction had been made on that day.

(2) Where a restricted patient has been conditionally discharged as aforesaid but has not been recalled to hospital he may apply to a Mental Health Review Tribunal –
> (a) in the period between the expiration of 12 months and the expiration of two years beginning with the date on which he was conditionally discharged; and
> (b) in any subsequent period of two years.

(3) Sections 73 and 74 above shall not apply to an application under subsection (2) above but on any such application the tribunal may –
> (a) vary any condition to which the patient is subject in connection with his discharge or impose any condition which might have been imposed in connection therewith; or
> (b) direct that the restriction order or restriction direction to which he is subject shall cease to have effect;

and if the tribunal give a direction under paragraph (b) above the patient shall cease to be liable to be detained by virtue of the relevant hospital order or transfer direction.

General

76   Visiting and examination of patients

(1) For the purpose of advising whether an application to a Mental Health Review Tribunal should be made by or in respect of a patient who is liable to be detained or subject to guardianship or to after-care under supervision (or, if he has not yet left hospital, is to be subject to after-care under supervision after he leaves hospital) under Part II of this Act or of furnishing information as to the condition of a patient for the purposes of such an application, any registered medical practitioner authorised by or on behalf of the patient or other person who is entitled to make or has made the application –
> (a) may at any reasonable time visit the patient and examine him in private, and
> (b) may require the production of and inspect any records relating to the detention or treatment of the patient in any hospital or to any after-care services provided for the patient under section 117 below.

(2) Section 32 above shall apply for the purposes of this section as it applies for the purposes of Part II of this Act.

77 General provisions concerning tribunal applications

(1) No application shall be made to a Mental Health Review Tribunal by or in respect of a patient except in such cases and at such times as are expressly provided by this Act.

(2) Where under this Act any person is authorised to make an application to a Mental Health Review Tribunal within a specified period, not more than one such application shall be made by that person within that period but for that purpose there shall be disregarded any application which is withdrawn in accordance with rules made under section 78 below.

(3) Subject to subsection (4) below an application to a Mental Health Review Tribunal authorised to be made by or in respect of a patient under this Act shall be made by notice in writing addressed to the tribunal for the area in which the hospital in which the patient is detained is situated or in which the patient is residing under guardianship or when subject to after-care under supervision (or in which he is to reside on becoming so subject after leaving hospital) as the case may be.

(4) Any application under section 75(2) above shall be made to the tribunal for the area in which the patient resides.

78 Procedure of tribunals

(1) The Lord Chancellor may make rules with respect to the making of applications to Mental Health Review Tribunals and with respect to the proceedings of such tribunals and matters incidental to or consequential on such proceedings.

(2) Rules made under this section may in particular make provision –

    (a) for enabling a tribunal, or the chairman of a tribunal, to postpone the consideration of any application by or in respect of a patient, or of any such application of any specified class, until the expiration of such period (not exceeding 12 months) as may be specified in the rules from the date on which an application by or in respect of the same patient was last considered and determined by that or any other tribunal under this Act;

    (b) for the transfer of proceedings from one tribunal to another in any case where, after the making of the application, the patient is removed out of the area of the tribunal to which it was made;

    (c) for restricting the persons qualified to serve as members of a tribunal for the consideration of any application, or of an application of any specified class;

    (d) for enabling a tribunal to dispose of an application without a formal hearing where such a hearing is not requested by the applicant or it appears to the tribunal that such a hearing would be detrimental to the health of the patient;

    (e) for enabling a tribunal to exclude members of the public, or any specified class of members of the public, from any proceedings of the tribunal, or to prohibit the publication of reports of any such proceedings or the names of any persons concerned in such proceedings;

    (f) for regulating the circumstances in which, and the persons by whom, applicants and patients in respect of whom applications are made to a tribunal may, if not desiring to conduct their own case, be represented for the purposes of those applications;

    (g) for regulating the methods by which information relevant to an application may be obtained by or furnished to the tribunal, and in particular for authorising the members of a tribunal, or any one or more of them, to visit and interview in private any patient by or in respect of whom an application has been made;

    (h) for making available to any applicant, and to any patient in respect of whom an application is made to a tribunal, copies of any documents obtained by or furnished to the tribunal in connection with the application, and a statement of the substance of any oral information so obtained or furnished except where the tribunal considers it undesirable in the interests of the patient or for other special reasons;

    (i) for requiring a tribunal, if so requested in accordance with the rules, to furnish such statements of the reasons for any decision given by the tribunal as may be prescribed by the rules, subject to any provision made by the rules for withholding such a statement from a patient or any other person in cases where the tribunal considers that furnishing it would be undesirable in the interests of the patient or for other special reasons;

(j) for conferring on the tribunals such ancillary powers as the Lord Chancellor thinks necessary for the purposes of the exercise of their functions under this Act;

(k) for enabling any functions of a tribunal which relate to matters preliminary or incidental to an application to be performed by the chairman of the tribunal.

(3) Subsections (1) and (2) above apply in relation to references to Mental Health Review Tribunals as they apply in relation to applications to such tribunals by or in respect of patients.

(4) Rules under this section may make provision as to the procedure to be adopted in cases concerning restricted patients and, in particular –

(a) for restricting the persons qualified to serve as president of a tribunal for the consideration of an application or reference relating to a restricted patient;

(b) for the transfer of proceedings from one tribunal to another in any case where, after the making of a reference or application in accordance with section 71(4) or 77(4) above, the patient ceases to reside in the area of the tribunal to which the reference or application was made.

(5) Rules under this section may be so framed as to apply to all applications or references or to applications or references of any specified class and may make different provision in relation to different cases.

(6) Any functions conferred on the chairman of a Mental Health Review Tribunal by rules under this section may, if for any reason he is unable to act, be exercised by another member of that tribunal appointed by him for the purpose.

(7) A Mental Health Review Tribunal may pay allowances in respect of travelling expenses, subsistence and loss of earnings to any person attending the tribunal as an applicant or witness, to the patient who is the subject of the proceedings if he attends otherwise than as the applicant or a witness and to any person (other than counsel or a solicitor) who attends as the representative of an applicant.

(8) A Mental Health Review Tribunal may, and if so required by the High Court shall, state in the form of a special case for determination by the High Court any question of law which may arise before them.

(9) The Arbitration Act 1950 shall not apply to any proceedings before a Mental Health Review Tribunal except so far as any provisions of that Act may be applied, with or without modifications, by rules made under this section.

79   Interpretation of Part V

(1) In this Part of this Act 'restricted patient' means a patient who is subject to a restriction order or restriction direction and this Part of this Act shall, subject to the provisions of this section, have effect in relation to any person who –

(a) is subject to a direction which by virtue of section 46(3) above has the same effect as a hospital order and a restriction order; or

(b) is treated as subject to a hospital order and a restriction order by virtue of an order under section 5(1) of the Criminal Procedure (Insanity) Act 1964 or section 6 or 14(1) of the Criminal Appeal Act 1968; or

(c) is treated as subject to a hospital order and a restriction order or to a transfer direction and a restriction direction by virtue of section 82(2) or 85(2) below or section 77(2) of the Mental Health (Scotland) Act 1984,

as it has effect in relation to a restricted patient.

(2) Subject to the following provisions of this section, in this Part of this Act 'the relevant hospital order' and 'the relevant transfer direction', in relation to a restricted patient, mean the hospital order or transfer direction by virtue of which he is liable to be detained in a hospital.

(3) In the case of a person within paragraph (a) of subsection (1) above, references in this Part of this Act to the relevant hospital order or restriction order shall be construed as references to the direction referred to in that paragraph.

(4) In the case of a person within paragraph (b) of subsection (1) above, reference in this Part of this Act to the relevant hospital order or restriction order shall be construed as references to the order under the provisions mentioned in that paragraph.

(5) In the case of a person within paragraph (c) of subsection (1) above, references in this Part of this Act to the relevant hospital order, the relevant transfer direction, the restriction order or the restriction direction or to a transfer direction under section 48 above shall be construed as references to the hospital order, transfer direction, restriction order, restriction direction or transfer direction under that section to which that person is treated as subject by virtue of the provisions mentioned in that paragraph.

(6) In this Part of this Act, unless the context otherwise requires, 'hospital' means a hospital and 'the responsible medical officer' means the responsible medical officer within the meaning of Part II of this Act.

(7) In this Part of this Act any reference to the area of a tribunal is –
 (a) in relation to a tribunal for a region of England, a reference to that region; and
 (b) in relation to the tribunal for Wales, a reference to Wales.

Part VIII Miscellaneous Functions of Local Authorities and the Secretary of State

Approved social workers

114 Appointment of approved social workers

(1) A local social services authority shall appoint a sufficient number of approved social workers for the purpose of discharging the functions conferred on them by this Act.

(2) No person shall be appointed by a local social services authority as an approved social worker unless he is approved by the authority as having appropriate competence in dealing with persons who are suffering from mental disorder.

(3) In approving a person for appointment as an approved social worker a local social services authority shall have regard to such matters as the Secretary of State may direct.

115 Powers of entry and inspection

An approved social worker of a local social services authority may at all reasonable times after producing, if asked to do so, some duly authenticated document showing that he is such a social worker, enter and inspect any premises (not being a hospital) in the area of that authority in which a mentally disordered patient is living, if he has reasonable cause to believe that the patient is not under proper care.

Visiting patients

116 Welfare of certain hospital patients

(1) Where a patient to whom this section applies is admitted to a hospital or nursing home in England and Wales (whether for treatment for mental disorder or for any other reason) then, without prejudice to their duties in relation to the patient apart from the provisions of this section, the authority shall arrange for visits to be made to him on behalf of the authority, and shall take such other steps in relation to the patient while in the hospital or nursing home as would be expected to be taken by his parents.

(2) This section applies to –
 (a) a child or young person –
  (i) who is in the care of a local authority by virtue of a care order within the meaning of the Children Act 1989, or

> (ii) in respect of whom the rights and powers of a parent are vested in a local authority by virtue of section 16 of the Social Work (Scotland) Act 1968;

(b) a person who is subject to the guardianship of a local social services authority under the provisions of this Act or the Mental Health (Scotland) Act 1984; or

(c) a person the functions of whose nearest relative under this Act or under the Mental Health (Scotland) Act 1984 are for the time being transferred to a local social services authority.

After-care

117   After-care

(1) This section applies to persons who are detained under section 3 above, or admitted to a hospital in pursuance of a hospital order made under section 37 above, or transferred to a hospital in pursuance of a transfer direction made under section 47 or 48 above, and then cease to be detained and (whether or not immediately after so ceasing) leave hospital.

(2) It shall be the duty of the Primary Care Trust or Health Authority and of the local social services authority to provide, in co-operation with relevant voluntary agencies, after-care services for any person to whom this section applies until such time as the Health Authority and the local social services authority are satisfied that the person concerned is no longer in need of such services; but they shall not be so satisfied in the case of a patient who is subject to after-care under supervision at any time while he remains so subject.

(2A) It shall be the duty of the Primary Care Trust or Health Authority to secure that at all times while a patient is subject to after-care under supervision –

(a) a person who is a registered medical practitioner approved for the purposes of section 12 above by the Secretary of State as having special experience in the diagnosis or treatment of mental disorder is in charge of the medical treatment provided for the patient as part of the after-care services provided for him under this section; and

(b) a person professionally concerned with any of the after-care services so provided is supervising him with a view to securing that he receives the after-care services so provided.

(2B) Section 32 above shall apply for the purposes of this section as it applies for the purposes of Part II of this Act.

(3) In this section 'Primary Care Trust' or 'the Health Authority' means the Primary Care Trust or Health Authority, and 'the local social services authority' means the local social services authority, for the area in which the person concerned is resident or to which he is sent on discharge by the hospital in which he was detained.

Functions of the Secretary of State

118   Code of practice

(1) The Secretary of State shall prepare, and from time to time revise, a code of practice –

(a) for the guidance of registered medical practitioners, managers and staff of hospitals and mental nursing homes and approved social workers in relation to the admission of patients to hospitals and mental nursing homes under this Act and to guardianship and after-care under supervision under this Act; and

(b) for the guidance of registered medical practitioners and members of other professions in relation to the medical treatment of patients suffering from mental disorder.

(2) The code shall, in particular, specify forms of medical treatment in addition to any specified by regulations made for the purposes of section 57 above which in the opinion of the Secretary of State give rise to special concern and which should accordingly not be given by a registered medical practitioner unless the patient has consented to the treatment (or to a plan of treatment including that treatment) and a certificate in writing as to the matters mentioned in subsection (2)(a) and(b) of that section has been given by another registered medical practitioner, being a practitioner appointed for the purposes of this section by the Secretary of State.

(3) Before preparing the code or making any alteration in it the Secretary of State shall consult such bodies as appear to him to be concerned.

(4) The Secretary of State shall lay copies of the code and of any alteration in the code before Parliament; and if either House of Parliament passes a resolution requiring the code or any alteration in it to be withdrawn the Secretary of State shall withdraw the code or alteration and, where he withdraws the code, shall prepare a code in substitution for the one which is withdrawn.

(5) No resolution shall be passed by either House of Parliament under subsection (4) above in respect of a code or alteration after the expiration of the period of 40 days beginning with the day on which a copy of the code or alteration was laid before that House; but for the purposes of this subsection no account shall be taken of any time during which Parliament is dissolved or prorogued or during which both Houses are adjourned for more than four days.

(6) The Secretary of State shall publish the code as for the time being in force.

119   Practitioners approved for Part IV and s. 118

(1) The Secretary of State may make such provision as he may with the approval of the Treasury determine for the payment of remuneration, allowances, pensions or gratuities to or in respect of registered medical practitioners appointed by him for the purposes of Part IV of this Act and section 118 above and to or in respect of other persons appointed for the purposes of section 57(2)(a) above.

(2) A registered medical practitioner or other person appointed by the Secretary of State for the purposes of the provisions mentioned in subsection (1) above may, for the purpose of exercising his functions under those provisions, at any reasonable time –

> (a) visit and interview and, in the case of a registered medical practitioner, examine in private any patient detained in a mental nursing home; and
> (b) require the production of and inspect any records relating to the treatment of the patient in that home.

120   General protection of detained patients

(1) The Secretary of State shall keep under review the exercise of the powers and the discharge of the duties conferred or imposed by this Act so far as relating to the detention of patients or to patients liable to be detained under this Act and shall make arrangements for persons authorised by him in that behalf –

> (a) to visit and interview in private patients detained under this Act in hospitals and mental nursing homes; and
> (b) to investigate –
> > (i)   any complaint made by a person in respect of a matter that occurred while he was detained under this Act in a hospital or mental nursing home and which he considers has not been satisfactorily dealt with by the managers of that hospital or mental nursing home; and
> > (ii)   any other complaint as to the exercise of the powers or the discharge of the duties conferred or imposed by this Act in respect of a person who is or has been so detained.

(2) The arrangements made under this section in respect of the investigation of complaints may exclude matters from investigation in specified circumstances and shall not require any person exercising functions under the arrangements to undertake or continue with any investigation where he does not consider it appropriate to do so.

(3) Where any such complaint as is mentioned in subsection (1)(b)(ii) above is made by a Member of Parliament and investigated under the arrangements made under this section the results of the investigation shall be reported to him.

(4) For the purpose of any such review as is mentioned in subsection (1) above or of carrying out his functions under arrangements made under this section any person authorised in that behalf by the Secretary of State may at any reasonable time –

(a) visit and interview and, if he is a registered medical practitioner, examine in private any patient in a mental nursing home; and

(7) The powers and duties referred to in subsection (1) above do not include any power or duty conferred or imposed by Part VII of this Act.

121   Mental Health Act Commission

(1) Without prejudice to section 273(1) of the National Health Service Act 2006, or section 204(1) of the National Health Service (Wales) Act 2006 (power to vary or revoke orders or directions) there shall continue to be a special health authority known as the Mental Health Act Commission established under section 11 of that Act.

(2) Without prejudice to the generality of his powers under section 13 of that Act, the Secretary of State shall direct the Commission to perform on his behalf –

(a) the function of appointing registered medical practitioners for the purposes of Part IV of this Act and section 118 above and of appointing other persons for the purposes of section 57(2)(a) above; and

(b) the functions of the Secretary of State under sections 61 and 120(1) and (4) above.

(3) The registered medical practitioners and other persons appointed for the purposes mentioned in subsection (2)(a) above may include members of the Commission.

(4) The Secretary of State may, at the request of or after consultation with the Commission and after consulting such other bodies as appear to him to be concerned, direct the Commission to keep under review the care and treatment, or any aspect of the care and treatment, in hospitals and mental nursing homes of patients who are not liable to be detained under this Act.

(5) For the purpose of any such review as is mentioned in subsection (4) above any person authorised in that behalf by the Commission may at any reasonable time –

(a) visit and interview and, if he is a registered medical practitioner, examine in private any patient in a mental nursing home; and

(b) require the production of and inspect any records relating to the treatment of any person who is or has been a patient in a mental nursing home.

(6) The Secretary of State may make such provision as he may with the approval of the Treasury determine for the payment of remuneration, allowances, pensions or gratuities to or in respect of persons exercising functions in relation to any such review as is mentioned in subsection (4) above.

(7) The Commission shall review any decision to withhold a postal packet (or anything contained in it) under subsection (1)(b) or (2) of section 134 below if an application in that behalf is made –

(a) in a case under subsection (1)(b), by the patient; or

(b) in a case under subsection (2), either by the patient or by the person by whom the postal packet was sent;

and any such application shall be made within six months of the receipt by the applicant of the notice referred to in subsection (6) of that section.

(8) On an application under subsection (7) above the Commission may direct that the postal packet which is the subject of the application (or anything contained in it) shall not be withheld and the managers in question shall comply with any such direction.

(9) The Secretary of State may be regulations make provision with respect to the making and determination of applications under subsection (7) above, including provision for the production to the Commission of any postal packet which is the subject of such an application.

(10) The Commission shall in the second year after its establishment and subsequently in every second year publish a report on its activities; and copies of every such report shall be sent by the Commission to the Secretary of State who shall lay a copy before each House of Parliament.

122   Provision of pocket-money for in-patients in hospital

(1) The Secretary of State may pay to persons who are receiving treatment as in-patients (whether liable to be detained or not) in hospitals wholly or mainly used for the treatment of persons suffering from mental disorder, such amounts as he thinks fit in respect of their occasional

personal expenses where it appears to him that they would otherwise be without resources to meet those expenses.

(2) For the purposes of National Health Service Act 2006 and the National Health Service (Wales) Act 2006, the making of payments under this section to persons for whom hospital services are provided under either of those Acts shall be treated as included among those services.

123   Transfers to and from special hospitals

(1) Without prejudice to any other provisions of this Act with respect to the transfer of patients, any patient who is for the time being liable to be detained under this Act (other than under section 35, 36 or 38 above) in a hospital at which high security psychiatric services are provided may, upon the directions of the Secretary of State, at any time be removed into any other hospital at which those services are provided.

(2) Without prejudice to any such provision, the Secretary of State may give directions for the transfer of any patient who is for the time being liable to be so detained into a hospital at which those services are not provided.

(3) Subsections (2) and (4) of section 19 above shall apply in relation to the transfer or removal of a patient under this section as they apply in relation to the transfer or removal of a patient from one hospital to another under that section.

125   Inquiries

(1) The Secretary of State may cause an inquiry to be held in any case where he thinks it advisable to do so in connection with any matter arising under this Act.

(2) Subsections (2) to (5) of section 250 of the Local Government Act 1972 shall apply to any inquiry held under this Act, except that no local authority shall be ordered to pay costs under subsection (4) of that section in the case of any inquiry unless the authority is a party to the inquiry.

Part IX Offences

126   Forgery, false statements, etc.

(1) Any person who without lawful authority or excuse has in his custody or under his control any document to which this subsection applies, which is, and which he knows or believes to be, false within the meaning of Part I of the Forgery and Counterfeiting Act 1981, shall be guilty of an offence.

(2) Any person who without lawful authority or excuse makes or has in his custody or under his control, any document so closely resembling a document to which subsection (1) above applies as to be calculated to deceive shall be guilty of an offence.

(3) The documents to which subsection (1) above applies are any documents purporting to be –

    (a) an application under Part II of this Act;

    (b) a medical or other recommendation or report under this Act; and

    (c) any other document required or authorised to be made for any of the purposes of this Act.

(4) Any person who –

    (a) wilfully makes a false entry or statement in any application, recommendation, report, record or other document required or authorised to be made for any of the purposes of this Act; or

    (b) with intent to deceive, makes use of any such entry or statement which he knows to be false,

shall be guilty of an offence.

(5) Any person guilty of an offence under this section shall be liable –

    (a) on summary conviction, to imprisonment for a term not exceeding six months or to a fine not exceeding the statutory maximum, or to both;

(b) on conviction on indictment, to imprisonment for a term not exceeding two years or to a fine of any amount, or to both.

127   Ill-treatment of patients

(1) It shall be an offence for any person who is an officer on the staff of or otherwise employed in, or who is one of the managers of, a hospital or mental nursing home –

(a) to ill-treat or wilfully to neglect a patient for the time being receiving treatment for mental disorder as an in-patient in that hospital or home; or

(b) to ill-treat or wilfully to neglect, on the premises of which the hospital or home forms part, a patient for the time being receiving such treatment there as an out-patient.

(2) It shall be an offence for any individual to ill-treat or wilfully to neglect a mentally disordered patient who is for the time being subject to his guardianship under this Act or otherwise in his custody or care (whether by virtue of any legal or moral obligation or otherwise).

(2A) It shall be an offence for any individual to ill-treat or wilfully to neglect a mentally disordered patient who is for the time being subject to after-care under supervision.

(3) Any person guilty of an offence under this section shall be liable –

(a) on summary conviction, to imprisonment for a term not exceeding six months or to a fine not exceeding the statutory maximum, or to both;

(b) on conviction on indictment, to imprisonment for a term not exceeding two years or to a fine of any amount, or to both.

(4) No proceedings shall be instituted for an offence under this section except by or with the consent of the Director of Public Prosecutions.

128   Assisting patients to absent themselves without leave, etc.

(1) Where any person induces or knowingly assists another person who is liable to be detained in a hospital within the meaning of Part II of this Act or is subject to guardianship under this Act to absent himself without leave he shall be guilty of an offence.

(2) Where any person induces or knowingly assists another person who is in legal custody by virtue of section 137 below to escape from such custody he shall be guilty of an offence.

(3) Where any person knowingly harbours a patient who is absent without leave or is otherwise at large and liable to be retaken under this Act or gives him any assistance with intent to prevent, hinder or interfere with his being taken into custody or returned to the hospital or other place where he ought to be he shall be guilty of an offence.

(4) Any person guilty of an offence under this section shall be liable –

(a) on summary conviction, to imprisonment for a term not exceeding six months or to a fine not exceeding the statutory maximum, or to both;

(b) on conviction on indictment, to imprisonment for a term not exceeding two years or to a fine of any amount, or to both.

129   Obstruction

(1) Any person who without reasonable cause –

(a) refuses to allow the inspection of any premises; or

(b) refuses to allow the visiting, interviewing or examination of any person by a person authorised in that behalf by or under this Act or to give access to any person to a person so authorised; or

(c) refuses to produce for the inspection of any person so authorised any document or record the production of which is duly required by him; or

(d) otherwise obstructs any such person in the exercise of his functions, shall be guilty of an offence.

(2) Without prejudice to the generality of subsection (1) above, any person who insists on being present when required to withdraw by a person authorised by or under this Act to interview or examine a person in private shall be guilty of an offence.

(3) Any person guilty of an offence under this section shall be liable on summary conviction to imprisonment for a term not exceeding three months or to a fine not exceeding level 4 on the standard scale or to both.

130   Prosecutions by local authorities

A local social services authority may institute proceedings for any offence under this Part of this Act, but without prejudice to any provision of this Part of this Act requiring the consent of the Director of Public Prosecutions for the institution of such proceedings.

Part X Miscellaneous and Supplementary

Miscellaneous provisions

131   Informal admission of patients

(1) Nothing in this Act shall be construed as preventing a patient who requires treatment for mental disorder from being admitted to any hospital or mental nursing home in pursuance of arrangements made in that behalf and without any application, order or direction rendering him liable to be detained under this Act, or from remaining in any hospital or mental nursing home in pursuance of such arrangements after he has ceased to be so liable to be detained.

(2) In the case of a minor who has attained the age of 16 years and is capable of expressing his own wishes, any such arrangements as are mentioned in subsection (1) above may be made, carried out and determined even though there are one or more persons who have parental responsibility for him (within the meaning of the Children Act 1989).

132   Duty of managers of hospitals to give information to detained patients

(1) The managers of a hospital or mental nursing home in which a patient is detained under this Act shall take such steps as are practicable to ensure that the patient understands –

  (a) under which of the provisions of this Act he is for the time being detained and the effect of that provision; and

  (b) what rights of applying to a Mental Health Review Tribunal are available to him in respect of his detention under that provision;

and those steps shall be taken as soon as practicable after the commencement of the patient's detention under the provision in question.

(2) The managers of a hospital or mental nursing home in which a patient is detained as aforesaid shall also take such steps as are practicable to ensure that the patient understands the effect, so far as relevant in his case, of sections 23, 25, 56 to 64, 66(1)(g), 118 and 120 above and section 134 below; and those steps shall be taken as soon as practicable after the commencement of the patient's detention in the hospital or nursing home.

(3) The steps to be taken under subsections (1) and (2) above shall include giving the requisite information both orally and in writing.

(4) The managers of a hospital or mental nursing home in which a patient is detained as aforesaid shall, except where the patient otherwise requests, take such steps as are practicable to furnish the person (if any) appearing to them to be his nearest relative with a copy of any information given to him in writing under subsections (1) and (2) above; and those steps shall be taken when the information is given to the patient or within a reasonable time thereafter.

133   Duty of managers of hospitals to inform nearest relatives of discharge

(1) Where a patient liable to be detained under this Act in a hospital or mental nursing home is to be discharged otherwise than by virtue of an order for discharge made by his nearest relative, the managers of the hospital or mental nursing home shall, subject to subsection (2) below, take such steps as are practicable to inform the person (if any) appearing to them to be the nearest relative of the patient; and that information shall, if practicable, be given at least seven days before the date of discharge.

(2) Subsection (1) above shall not apply if the patient or his nearest relative has requested that information about the patient's discharge should not be given under this section.

134   Correspondence of patients

(1) A postal packet addressed to any person by a patient detained in a hospital under this Act and delivered by the patient for dispatch may be withheld from the Post Office –

    (a) if that person has requested that communications addressed to him by the patient should be withheld; or

    (b) subject to subsection (3) below, if the hospital is one at which high security psychiatric services are provided and the managers of the hospital consider that the postal packet is likely –

        (i) to cause distress to the person to whom it is addressed or to any other person (not being a person on the staff of the hospital); or

        (ii) to cause danger to any person;

and any request for the purposes of paragraph (a) above shall be made by a notice in writing given to the managers of the hospital, the registered medical practitioner in charge of the treatment of the patient or the Secretary of State.

(2) Subject to subsection (3) below, a postal packet addressed to a patient detained under this Act in a hospital at which high security psychiatric services are provided may be withheld from the patient if, in the opinion of the managers of the hospital, it is necessary to do so in the interests of the safety of the patient or for the protection of other persons.

(3) Subsections (1)(b) and (2) above do not apply to any postal packet addressed by a patient to, or sent to a patient by or on behalf of –

    (a) any Minister of the Crown or Member of either House of Parliament or of the Northern Ireland Assembly;

    (b) any judge or officer of the Court of Protection, any of the Court of Protection Visitors or any person asked by that Court for a report under section 49 of the Mental Capacity Act 2005 concerning the patient;

    (c) the Parliamentary Commissioner for Administration, the Welsh Administration Ombudsman, the Health Service Commissioner for England, the Health Service Commissioner for Wales or a Local Commissioner within the meaning of Part III of the Local Government Act 1974;

    (d) a Mental Health Review Tribunal;

    (e) a Strategic Health Authority, Health Authority, Special Health Authority or Primary Care Trust, a local social services authority, a Community Health Council, a Patients Forum or a probation committee (within the meaning of the Probation Service Act 1993);

    (ea) a provider of a patient advocacy and liaison service for the assistance of patients at the hospital and their families and carers;

    (eb) a provider of independent advocacy services for the patient;

    (f) the managers of the hospital in which the patient is detained;

    (g) any legally qualified person instructed by the patient to act as his legal adviser; or

    (h) the European Commission of Human Rights or the European Court of Human Rights.

(3A) In subsection (3) above –

    (a) 'patient advocacy and liaison service' means a service of a description prescribed by regulations made by the Secretary of State, and

    (b) 'independent advocacy services' means services provided under arrangements under section 248 of the National Health Service Act 2006 or section 187 of the National Health Service (Wales) Act 2006.

(4) The managers of a hospital may inspect and open any postal packet for the purposes of determining –

    (a) whether it is one to which subsection (1) or (2) applies, and

    (b) in the case of a postal packet to which subsection (1) or (2) above applies, whether or not if should be withheld under that subsection;

and the power to withhold a postal packet under either of those subsections includes power to withhold anything contained in it.

(5) Where a postal packet or anything contained in it is withheld under subsection (1) or (2) above the managers of the hospital shall record that fact in writing.

(6) Where a postal packet or anything contained in it is withheld under subsection (1)(b) or (2) above the managers of the hospital shall within seven days give notice of that fact to the patient and, in the case of a packet withheld under subsection (2) above, to the person (if known) by whom the postal packet was sent; and any such notice shall be given in writing and shall contain a statement of the effect of section 121(7) and (8) above.

(7) The functions of the managers of a hospital under this section shall be discharged on their behalf by a person on the staff of the hospital appointed by them for that purpose and different persons may be appointed to discharge different functions.

(8) The Secretary of State may make regulations with respect to the exercise of the powers conferred by this section.

(9) In this section 'hospital' has the same meaning as in Part II of this Act, 'postal packet' has the same meaning as in the Post Office Act 1953 and the provisions of this section shall have effect notwithstanding anything in section 56 of that Act.

135   Warrant to search for and remove patients

(1) If it appears to a justice of the peace, on information on oath laid by an approved social worker, that there is reasonable cause to suspect that a person believed to be suffering from mental disorder –

    (a) has been, or is being, ill-treated, neglected or kept otherwise than under proper control, in any place within the jurisdiction of the justice, or

    (b) being unable to care for himself, is living alone in any such place,

the justice may issue a warrant authorising any constable to enter, if need be by force, any premises specified in the warrant in which that person is believed to be, and, if thought fit, to remove him to a place of safety with a view to the making of an application in respect of him under Part II of this Act, or of other arrangements for his treatment or care.

(2) If it appears to a justice of the peace, on information on oath laid by any constable or other person who is authorised by or under this Act or under section 83 of the Mental Health (Scotland) Act 1984 to take a patient to any place, or to take into custody or retake a patient who is liable under this Act or under the said section 83 to be so taken or retaken –

    (a) that there is reasonable cause to believe that the patient is to be found on premises within the jurisdiction of the justice; and

    (b) that admission to the premises has been refused or that a refusal of such admission is apprehended,

the justice may issue a warrant authorising any constable to enter the premises, if need be by force, and remove the patient.

(3) A patient who is removed to a place of safety in the execution of a warrant issued under this section may be detained there for a period not exceeding 72 hours.

(4) In the execution of a warrant issued under subsection (1) above, a constable shall be accompanied by an approved social worker and by a registered medical practitioner, and in the execution of a warrant issued under subsection (2) above a constable may be accompanied –

    (a) by a registered medical practitioner;

    (b) by any person authorised by or under this Act or under section 83 of the Mental Health (Scotland) Act 1984 to take or retake the patient.

(5) It shall not be necessary in any information or warrant under subsection (1) above to name the patient concerned.

(6) In this section 'place of safety' means residential accommodation provided by a local social services authority under Part III of the National Assistance Act 1948, a hospital as defined by this

Act, a police station, a mental nursing home or residential home for mentally disordered persons or any other suitable place the occupier of which is willing temporarily to receive the patient.

136 Mentally disordered persons found in public places

(1) If a constable finds in a place to which the public have access a person who appears to him to be suffering from mental disorder and to be in immediate need of care or control, the constable may, if he thinks it necessary to do so in the interests of that person or for the protection of other persons, remove that person to a place of safety within the meaning of section 135 above.

(2) A person removed to a place of safety under this section may be detained there for a period not exceeding 72 hours for the purpose of enabling him to be examined by a registered medical practitioner and to be interviewed by an approved social worker and of making any necessary arrangements for his treatment or care.

137 Provisions as to custody, conveyance and detention

(1) Any person required or authorised by or by virtue of this Act to be conveyed to any place or to be kept in custody or detained in a place of safety or at any place to which he is taken under section 42(6) above shall, while being so conveyed, detained or kept, as the case may be, be deemed to be in legal custody.

(2) A constable or any other person required or authorised by or by virtue of this Act to take any person into custody, or to convey or detain any person shall, for the purposes of taking him into custody or conveying or detaining him, have all the powers, authorities, protection and privileges which a constable has within the area for which he acts as constable.

(3) In this section 'convey' includes any other expression denoting removal from one place to another.

138 Retaking of patients escaping from custody

(1) If any person who is in legal custody by virtue of section 137 above escapes, he may, subject to the provisions of this section, be retaken –
  (a) in any case, by the person who had his custody immediately before the escape, or by any constable or approved social worker;
  (b) if at the time of the escape he was liable to be detained in a hospital within the meaning of Part II of this Act, or subject to guardianship under this Act, by any other person who could take him into custody under section 18 above if he had absented himself without leave.

(2) A person to whom paragraph (b) of subsection (1) above applies shall not be retaken under this section after the expiration of the period within which he could be retaken under section 18 above if he had absented himself without leave on the day of the escape unless he is subject to a restriction order under Part III of this Act or an order or direction having the same effect as such an order; and subsection (4) of the said section 18 shall apply with the necessary modifications accordingly.

(3) A person who escapes while being taken to or detained in a place of safety under section 135 or 136 above shall not be retaken under this section after the expiration of the period of 72 hours beginning with the time when he escapes or the period during which he is liable to be so detained, whichever expires first.

(4) This section, so far as it relates to the escape of a person liable to be detained in a hospital within the meaning of Part II of this Act, shall apply in relation to a person who escapes –
  (a) while being taken to or from such a hospital in pursuance of regulations under section 19 above, or of any order, direction or authorisation under Part III or VI of this Act (other than under section 35, 36, 38, 53, 83 or 85) or under section 123 above; or
  (b) while being taken to or detained in a place of safety in pursuance of an order under Part III of this Act (other than under section 35, 36 or 38 above) pending his admission to such a hospital,
as if he were liable to be detained in that hospital and, if he had not previously been received in that hospital, as if he had been so received.

(5) In computing for the purposes of the power to give directions under section 37(4) above and for the purposes of sections 37(5) and 40(1) above the period of 28 days mentioned in those

sections, no account shall be taken of any time during which the patient is at large and liable to be retaken by virtue of this section.

(6) Section 21 above shall, with any necessary modifications, apply in relation to a patient who is at large and liable to be retaken by virtue of this section as it applies in relation to a patient who is absent without leave and references in that section to section 18 above shall be construed accordingly.

139   Protection for acts done in pursuance of this Act

(1) No person shall be liable, whether on the ground of want of jurisdiction or on any other ground, to any civil or criminal proceedings to which he would have been liable apart from this section in respect of any act purporting to be done in pursuance of this Act or any regulations or rules made under this Act, unless the act was done in bad faith or without reasonable care.

(2) No civil proceedings shall be brought against any person in any court in respect of any such act without the leave of the High Court; and no criminal proceedings shall be brought against any person in any court in respect of any such act except by or with the consent of the Director of Public Prosecutions.

(3) This section does not apply to proceedings for an offence under this Act, being proceedings which, under any other provision of this Act, can be instituted only by or with the consent of the Director of Public Prosecutions.

(4) This section does not apply to proceedings against the Secretary of State or against a Strategic Health Authority, Health Authority, Special Health Authority, Primary Care Trust or against a National Health Service trust established under the National Health Service Act 2006 or the National Health Service (Wales) Act 2006 or an NHS foundation trust.

(5) In relation to Northern Ireland the reference in this section to the Director of Public Prosecutions shall be construed as a reference to the Director of Public Prosecutions for Northern Ireland.

140   Notification of hospitals having arrangements for reception of urgent cases

It shall be the duty of every Primary Care Trust or Health Authority to give notice to every local social services authority for an area wholly or partly comprised within the Health Authority's area of the Authority specifying the hospital or hospitals administered by or otherwise available to the Health Authority in which arrangements are from time to time in force for the reception, in case of special urgency, of patients requiring treatment for mental disorder.

145   Interpretation

(1) In this Act, unless the context otherwise requires –

'absent without leave' has the meaning given to it by section 18 above and related expressions shall be construed accordingly;

'application for admission for assessment' has the meaning given in section 2 above;

'application for admission for treatment' has the meaning given in section 3 above;

'approved social worker' means an officer of a local social services authority appointed to act as an approved social worker for the purposes of this Act;

'high security psychiatric services' has the same meaning as in section 4 of the National Health Service Act 2006 or section 4 of the National Health Service (Wales) Act 2006;

'hospital' means –

(a) any health service hospital within the meaning of the National Health Service Act 2006 or the National Health Service (Wales) Act 2006; and

(b) any accommodation provided by a local authority and used as a hospital by or on behalf of the Secretary of State under that Act;

and 'hospital within the meaning of Part II of this Act' has the meaning given in section 34 above;

'hospital order' and 'guardianship order' have the meanings respectively given in section 37 above;

'interim hospital order' has the meaning given in section 38 above;

'local social services authority' means a council which is a local authority for the purpose of the Local Authority Social Services Act 1970;

'the managers' means –

    (a) in relation to a hospital vested in the Secretary of State for the purposes of his functions under the National Health Service Act 2006, or in the Welsh Ministers for the purposes of their functions under the National Health Service (Wales) Act 2006, and in relation to any accommodation provided by a local authority and used as a hospital by or on behalf of the Secretary of State under the National Health Service Act 2006, or of the Welsh Ministers under the National Health Service (Wales) Act 2006, the Primary Care Trust, Strategic Health Authority, Health Authority, or special health authority responsible for the administration of the hospital;

    (bb) in relation to a hospital vested in a Primary Care Trust or a National Health Service Trust, the trust;

    (bc) in relation to a hospital vested in an NHS foundation trust, the trust;

    (c) in relation to a mental nursing home registered in pursuance of the Registered Homes Act 1984, the person or persons registered in respect of the home; and in this definition 'hospital' means a hospital within the meaning of Part II of this Act;

'medical treatment' includes nursing, and also includes care, habilitation and rehabilitation under medical supervision;

'mental disorder', 'severe mental impairment', 'mental impairment' and 'psychopathic disorder' have the meanings given in section 1 above;

'mental nursing home' has the same meaning as in the Registered Homes Act 1984;

'nearest relative', in relation to a patient, has the meaning given in Part II of this Act;

'patient' means a person suffering or appearing to be suffering from mental disorder;

'Primary Care Trust' means a Primary Care Trust established under section 18 of the National Health Service Act 2006;

'the responsible after-care bodies' has the meaning given in section 25D above;

'restriction direction' has the meaning given to it by section 49 above;

'restriction order' has the meaning given to it by section 41 above;

'standard scale' has the meaning given in section 75 of the Criminal Justice Act 1982;

'Strategic Health Authority' means a Strategic Health Authority established under section 13 of the National Health Service Act 2006;

'supervision application' has the meaning given in section 25A above;

'transfer direction' has the meaning given to it by section 47 above.

(1A) References in this Act to a patient being subject to after-care under supervision (or to after-care under supervision) shall be construed in accordance with section 25A above.

(1AA) Where high security psychiatric services and other services are provided at a hospital, the part of the hospital at which high security psychiatric services are provided and the other part shall be treated as separate hospitals for the purposes of this Act.

(2) 'Statutory maximum' has the meaning given in section 74 of the Criminal Justice Act 1982.

(3) In relation to a person who is liable to be detained or subject to guardianship by virtue of an order or direction under Part III of this Act (other than under section 35, 36 or 38), any reference in this Act to any enactment contained in Part II of this Act or in section 66 or 67 above shall be construed as a reference to that enactment as it applies to that person by virtue of Part III of this Act.

Schedule

Schedule 1 Application of Certain Provisions to Patients Subject to Hospital and Guardianship Orders

Part I Patients not Subject to Special Restrictions

1. Sections 9, 10, 17, 21 to 21B, 24(3) and (4), 25C to 28, 31, 32, 34, 67 and 76 shall apply in relation to the patient without modification.

2. Sections 16, 18, 19, 20, 22, 23, 25A, 25B and 66 shall apply in relation to the patient with the modifications specified in paragraphs 3 to 9 below.

3. In section 16(1) for references to an application for admission or a guardianship application there shall be substituted references to the order or direction under Part III of this Act by virtue of which the patient is liable to be detained or subject to guardianship.

4. In section 18 subsection (5) shall be omitted.

5. In section 19(2) for the words from 'as follows' to the end of the subsection there shall be substituted the words 'as if the order or direction under Part III of this Act by virtue of which he was liable to be detained or subject to guardianship before being transferred were an order or direction for his admission or removal to the hospital to which he is transferred, or placing him under the guardianship of the authority or person into whose guardianship he is transferred, as the case may be'.

6. In section 20 –

    (a) in subsection (1) for the words from 'day on which he was' to 'as the case may be' there shall be substituted the words 'date of the relevant order or direction under Part III of this Act'; and

    (b) in subsection (9) for the words 'the application for admission for treatment or, as the case may be, in the guardianship application, that application' there shall be substituted the words 'the relevant order or direction under Part III of this Act, that order or direction'.

7. In section 22 for references to an application for admission or a guardianship application there shall be substituted references to the order or direction under Part III of this Act by virtue of which the patient is liable to be detained or subject to guardianship.

8. In Section 23(2) –

    (a) in paragraph (a) the words 'for assessment or' shall be omitted; and

    (b) in paragraphs (a) and (b) the references to the nearest relative shall be omitted.

8A. In section 25A(1)(a) and 25B(5)(a) for the words 'in pursuance of an application for admission for treatment' there shall be substituted the words 'by virtue of an order or direction for his admission or removal to hospital under Part III of this Act'.

9. In section 66 –

    (a) in subsection (1), paragraphs (a), (b), (c), (g) and (h), the words in parenthesis in paragraph (i) and paragraph (ii) shall be omitted; and

    (b) in subsection (2), paragraphs (a), (b), (c) and (g), and in paragraph (d) ', (g)' shall be omitted.

Part II Patients Subject to Special Restrictions

1. Sections 24(3) and (4), 32 and 76 shall apply in relation to the patient without modification.

2. Sections 17 to 19, 22, 23 and 34 shall apply in relation to the patient with the modifications specified in paragraphs 3 to 8 below.

3. In section 17 –

    (a) in subsection (1) after the word 'may' there shall be inserted the words 'with the consent of the Secretary of State';

(b) in subsection (4) after the words 'the responsible medical officer' and after the words 'that officer' there shall be inserted the words 'or the Secretary of State'; and

(c) in subsection (5) after the word 'recalled' there shall be inserted the words 'by the responsible medical officer', and for the words from 'he has ceased' to the end of the subsection there shall be substituted the words 'the expiration of the period of twelve months beginning with the first day of his absence on leave'.

4. In section 18 there shall be omitted –

(a) in subsection (1) the words 'subject to the provisions of this section'; and

(b) subsections (3), (4) and (5).

5. In section 19 –

(a) in subsection (1) after the word 'may' in paragraph (a) there shall be inserted the words 'with the consent of the Secretary of State', and the words from 'or into' to the end of the subsection shall be omitted; and

(b) in subsection (2) for the words from 'as follows' to the end of the subsection there shall be substituted the words 'as if the order or direction under Part III of this Act by virtue of which he was liable to be detained before being transferred were an order or direction for his admission or removal to the hospital to which he is transferred'.

6. In section 22 subsection (1) and paragraph (a) of subsection (2) shall not apply.

7. In section 23 –

(a) in subsection (1) references to guardianship shall be omitted and after the word 'made' there shall be inserted the words 'with the consent of the Secretary of State and' and

(b) in subsection (2) –

(i) in paragraph (a) the words 'for assessment or' and 'or by the nearest relative of the patient' shall be omitted; and

(ii) paragraph (b) shall be omitted.

8. In section 34, in subsection (1) the definition of 'the nominated medical attendant' and subsection (3) shall be omitted.

Medical Act 1983

(1983, c. 54)

Part I Preliminary

The General Medical Council

1   The General Medical Council

(1) There shall continue to be a body corporate known as the General Medical Council (in this Act referred to as 'the General Council') having the functions assigned to them by this Act.

(1A) The main objective of the General Council in exercising their functions is to protect, promote and maintain the health and safety of the public.

(2) The General Council shall be constituted as provided by Her Majesty by Order in Council under this section subject to the provisions of Part I of Schedule 1 to this Act.

(3) The General Council shall have the following committees –

(a) the Education Committee,

(b) one or more Interim Orders Panels,

(c) one or more Registration Panels,

(d) one or more Registration Appeals Panels,

(e) the Investigation Committee,

(f) one or more Fitness to Practise Panels,

constituted in accordance with Part III of Schedule 1 to this Act and having the functions assigned to them by or under this Act. (3A) The committees of the General Council specified in paragraphs (a) to (f) of subsection (3) above are referred to in this Act as 'the statutory committees'.

2   Registration of medical practitioners

(1) There shall continue to be kept by the registrar of the General Council (in this Act referred to as 'the Registrar') a register of medical practitioners registered under this Act containing the names of those registered and the qualifications they are entitled to have registered under this Act.

(2) The register referred to is 'the register of medical practitioners' consisting of three lists, namely –

   (a) the principal list,
   (c) the visiting overseas doctors list, and
   (d) the visiting EEA practitioners list.

(3) Medical practitioners shall be registered as fully registered medical practitioners or provisionally as provided in Parts II and III of this Act and in the appropriate list of the register of medical practitioners as provided in Part IV of this Act.

Part V Fitness To Practise and Medical Ethics

35   General Council's power to advise on conduct, performance or ethics

The powers of the General Council shall include the power to provide, in such manner as the Council think fit, advice for members of the medical profession on –

   (a) standards of professional conduct;
   (b) standards of professional performance; or
   (c) medical ethics.

35A   General Council's power to require disclosure of information

(1) For the purpose of assisting the General Council or any of their committees in carrying out functions in respect of professional conduct, professional performance or fitness to practise, a person authorised by the Council may require –

   (a) a practitioner (except the practitioner in respect of whose professional conduct, professional performance or fitness to practise the information or document is sought); or
   (b) any other person,

who in his opinion is able to supply information or produce any document which appears relevant to the discharge of any such function, to supply such information or produce such a document.

(2) As soon as is reasonably practicable after the relevant date, the General Council shall require, from a practitioner in respect of whom a decision mentioned in subsection (3) has been made, details of any person –

   (a) by whom the practitioner is employed to provide services in, or in relation to, any area of medicine; or
   (b) with whom he has an arrangement to do so.

(3) For the purposes of this section and section 35B the relevant date is the date specified by the General Council by rules under paragraph 1 of Schedule 4 of this Act.

(4) Nothing in this section shall require or permit any disclosure of information which is prohibited by or under any other enactment.

(5) But where information is held in a form in which the prohibition operates because the information is capable of identifying an individual, the person referred to in subsection (1) may, in exercising his functions under that subsection, require that the information be put into a form which is not capable of identifying that individual.

(5A) In determining for the purposes of sub-section (4) above whether a disclosure is not prohibited, by reason of being a disclosure of personal data which is exempt from non-disclosure provisions of the Data Protection Act 1998 by virtue of section 35(1) of that Act, it shall be assumed that the disclosure is required by this section.

(6) Subsection (1) above does not apply in relation to the supplying of information or the production of any document which a person could not be compelled to supply or produce in civil proceedings before the court (within the meaning of section 40(5)).

(6A) If a person fails to supply any information or produce any document within 14 days of his being required to do so under subsection (1) above, the General Council may seek an order of the relevant court requiring the information to be supplied or the document to be produced.

(6B) For the purposes of subsection (6A), 'the relevant court' means the county court or, in Scotland, the sheriff in whose sheriffdom is situated the address—

(a) which is shown in the register as the address of the person concerned; or

(b) which would have been so shown if the person concerned were registered.

(8) For the purposes of this section and section 35B, a 'practitioner' means a fully registered person or a provisionally registered person.

35B   Notification and disclosure by the General Council

(1) As soon as is reasonably practicable after the relevant date, the General Council shall notify the following of an investigation by the General Council of a practitioner's fitness to practise –

(a) the Secretary of State, the Scottish Ministers and the National Assembly for Wales; and

(b) any person in the United Kingdom of whom the General Council are aware –

(i) by whom the practitioner concerned is employed to provide services in, or in relation to, any area of medicine, or

(ii) with whom he has an arrangement to do so.

(2) The General Council may disclose to any person any information relating to a practitioner's fitness to practise which they consider it to be in the public interest to disclose.

35C   Functions of the Investigation Committee

(1) This section applies where an allegation is made to the General Council against –

(a) a fully registered person; or

(b) a person who is provisionally registered, that his fitness to practise is impaired.

(2) The General Council may, if they consider it to be in the public interest to do so, publish, or disclose to any person, information—

(a) which relates to a particular practitioner's fitness to practise, whether the matter to which the information relates arose before or after his registration, or arose in the United Kingdom or elsewhere; or

(b) of a particular description related to fitness to practise in relation to every practitioner, or to every practitioner of a particular description.

(3) For the purposes of subsection (2)(b) above, the General Council need not consider whether it is in the public interest to publish or disclose the information in question in relation to each individual practitioner to whom it relates.

(4) Subject to subsection (5), the General Council shall publish in such manner as they see fit—

(a) decisions of a Fitness to Practise Panel that relate to a finding that a person's fitness to practise is impaired (including decisions in respect of a direction relating to such a finding that follow a review of an earlier direction relating to such a finding);

(b) decisions of a Fitness to Practise Panel to make an order under section 38(1) or (2) below;

(c) decisions of a Fitness to Practise Panel to refuse an application for restoration to the register or to give a direction under section 41(9) below;

(d) decisions of an Interim Orders Panel or a Fitness to Practise Panel to make an order under section 41A below (including decisions in respect of orders varying earlier orders under that section);

(e) warnings of a Fitness to Practise Panel regarding a person's future conduct or performance;

(f) warnings of the Investigation Committee regarding a person's future conduct or performance; and

(g) undertakings that have been agreed in accordance with rules made under paragraph 1(2A) of Schedule 4.

(5) The General Council may withhold from publication under subsection (4) above information concerning the physical or mental health of a person which the General Council consider to be confidential.

(3) This section is not prevented from applying because the allegation is based on a matter alleged to have occurred –

(a) outside the United Kingdom; or

(b) at a time when the person was not registered.

(4) The Investigation Committee shall investigate the allegation and decide whether it should be considered by a Fitness to Practise Panel.

(5) If the Investigation Committee decide that the allegation ought to be considered by a Fitness to Practise Panel –

(a) they shall give a direction to that effect to the Registrar;

(b) the Registrar shall refer the allegation to a Fitness to Practise Panel; and

(c) the Registrar shall serve a notification of the Committee's decision on the person who is the subject of the allegation and the person making the allegation (if any).

(6) If the Investigation Committee decide that the allegation ought not to be considered by a Fitness to Practise Panel, they may give a warning to the person who is the subject of the allegation regarding his future conduct or performance.

(7) If the Investigation Committee decide that the allegation ought not to be considered by a Fitness to Practise Panel, but that no warning should be given under subsection (6) above –

(a) they shall give a direction to that effect to the Registrar; and

(b) the Registrar shall serve a notification of the Committee's decision on the person who is the subject of the allegation and the person making the allegation (if any).

(8) If the Investigation Committee are of the opinion that an Interim Orders Panel or a Fitness to Practise Panel should consider making an order for interim suspension or interim conditional registration under section 41A below in relation to the person who is the subject of the allegation –

(a) they shall give a direction to that effect to the Registrar;

(b) the Registrar shall refer the matter to an Interim Orders Panel or a Fitness to Practise Panel for the Panel to decide whether to make such an order; and

(c) the Registrar shall serve notification of the decision on the person who is the subject of the allegation and the person making the allegation (if any).

(9) In this section –

'enactment' includes –

(a) an enactment comprised in, or in an instrument made under, an Act of the Scottish Parliament; and

(b) any provision of, or any instrument made under, Northern Ireland legislation; and 'regulatory body' means a regulatory body which has the function of authorising persons to practise as a member of a health or social care profession.

35D   Functions of a Fitness to Practise Panel

(1) Where an allegation against a person is referred under section 35C above to a Fitness to Practise Panel, subsections (2) and (3) below shall apply.

(2) Where the Panel find that the person's fitness to practise is impaired they may, if they think fit –

(a) except in a health case, direct that the person's name shall be erased from the register;

(b) direct that his registration in the register shall be suspended (that is to say, shall not have effect) during such period not exceeding twelve months as may be specified in the direction; or

(c) direct that his registration shall be conditional on his compliance, during such period not exceeding three years as may be specified in the direction, with such requirements so specified as the Panel think fit to impose for the protection of members of the public or in his interests.

(3) Where the Panel find that the person's fitness to practise is not impaired they may nevertheless give him a warning regarding his future conduct or performance.

(4) Where a Fitness to Practise Panel have given a direction that a person's registration be suspended –

  (a) under subsection (2) above;
  (b) under subsection (10) or (12) below; or
  (c) under rules made by virtue of paragraph 5A(3) of Schedule 4 to this Act, subsection (5) below applies.

(5) In such a case, a Fitness to Practise Panel may, if they think fit –

  (a) direct that the current period of suspension shall be extended for such further period from the time when it would otherwise expire as may be specified in the direction;
  (b) except in a health case, direct that the person's name shall be erased from the register; or
  (c) direct that the person's registration shall, as from the expiry of the current period of suspension, be conditional on his compliance, during such period not exceeding three years as may be specified in the direction, with such requirements so specified as the Panel think fit to impose for the protection of members of the public or in his interests,

but, subject to subsection (6) below, the Panel shall not extend any period of suspension under this section for more than twelve months at a time.

(6) In a health case, a Fitness to Practise Panel may give a direction in relation to a person whose registration has been suspended under this section extending his period of suspension indefinitely where –

  (a) the period of suspension will, on the date on which the direction takes effect, have lasted for at least two years; and
  (b) the direction is made not more than two months before the date on which the period of suspension would otherwise expire.

(7) Where a Fitness to Practise Panel have given a direction under subsection (6) above for a person's period of suspension to be extended indefinitely, a Fitness to Practise Panel shall review the direction if –

  (a) the person requests them to do so;
  (b) at least two years have elapsed since the date on which the direction took effect; and
  (c) if the direction has previously been reviewed under this subsection, at least two years have elapsed since the date of the previous review.

(8) On such a review the Panel may –

  (a) confirm the direction;
  (b) direct that the suspension be terminated; or
  (c) direct that the person's registration be conditional on his compliance, during such period not exceeding three years as may be specified in the direction, with such requirements so specified as the Panel think fit to impose for the protection of members of the public or in his interests.

(9) Where –

  (a) a direction that a person's registration be subject to conditions has been given under –
      (i)   subsection (2), (5) or (8) above,
      (ii) subsection (12) below,
      (iii) rules made by virtue of paragraph 5A(3) of Schedule 4 to this Act, or
      (iv) section 41A below; and
  (b) that person is judged by a Fitness to Practise Panel to have failed to comply with any requirement imposed on him as such a condition,

subsection (10) below applies.

(10) In such a case, the Panel may, if they think fit –

    (a) except in a health case, direct that the person's name shall be erased from the register; or

    (b) direct that the person's registration in the register shall be suspended during such period not exceeding twelve months as may be specified in the direction.

(11) Where a direction that a person's registration be subject to conditions has been given under –

    (a) subsection (2), (5) or (8) above; or

    (b) rules made by virtue of paragraph 5A(3) of Schedule 4 to this Act,

subsection (12) below applies.

(12) In such a case, a Fitness to Practise Panel may, if they think fit –

    (a) except in a health case, direct that the person's name shall be erased from the register;

    (b) direct that the person's registration in the Register shall be suspended during such period not exceeding twelve months as may be specified in the direction;

    (c) direct that the current period of conditional registration shall be extended for such further period from the time when it would otherwise expire as may be specified in the direction; or

    (d) revoke the direction, or revoke or vary any of the conditions imposed by the direction, for the remainder of the current period of conditional registration,

but the Panel shall not extend any period of conditional registration under this section for more than three years at a time.

38 Power to order immediate suspension etc. after a finding of impairment of fitness to practise

(1) On giving a direction for erasure or a direction for suspension under section 35D(2), (10) or (12) above, or under rules made by virtue of paragraph 5A(3) of Schedule 4 to this Act, in respect of any person the Fitness to Practise Panel, if satisfied that to do so is necessary for the protection of members of the public or is otherwise in the public interest, or is in the best interests of that person, may order that his registration in the register shall be suspended forthwith in accordance with this section.

(2) On giving a direction for conditional registration under section 35D(2) above, or under rules made by virtue of paragraph 5A(3) of Schedule 4 to this Act, in respect of any person the Fitness to Practise Panel, if satisfied that to do so is necessary for the protection of members of the public or is otherwise in the public interest, or is in the best interests of that person, may order that his registration be made conditional forthwith in accordance with this section.

(3) Where, on the giving of a direction, an order under subsection (1) or (2) above is made in respect of a person, his registration in the register shall, subject to subsection (4) below, be suspended (that is to say, shall not have effect) or made conditional, as the case may be, from the time when the order is made until the time when –

    (a) the direction takes effect in accordance with –

        (i) paragraph 10 of Schedule 4 to this Act; or

        (ii) rules made by virtue of paragraph 5A(3) of that Schedule; or

    (b) an appeal against it under section 40 below or paragraph 5A(4) of that Schedule is (otherwise than by the dismissal of the appeal) determined.

(4) Where a Fitness to Practise Panel make an order under subsection (1) or (2) above, the Registrar shall forthwith serve a notification of the order on the person to whom it applies.

(5) If, when an order under subsection (1) or (2) above is made, the person to whom it applies is neither present nor represented at the proceedings, subsection (3) above shall have effect as if, for the reference to the time when the order is made, there were substituted a reference to the time of service of a notification of the order as determined for the purposes of paragraph to this Act.

(6) Except as provided in subsection (7) below, while a person's registration in the register is suspended by virtue of subsection (1) above, he shall be treated as not being registered in the register notwithstanding that his name still appears in it.

(7) Notwithstanding subsection (6) above, sections 35C to 35E above shall continue to apply to a person whose registration in the register is suspended.

(8) The relevant court may terminate any suspension of a person's registration in the register imposed under subsection (1) above or any conditional registration imposed under subsection (2) above, and the decision of the court on any application under this subsection shall be final.

(9) In this section 'the relevant court' has the same meaning as in section 40(5) below.

39.— Fraud or error in relation to registration

(1) If the Registrar is satisfied that any entry in the register has been fraudulently procured or incorrectly made, he may erase the entry from the register.

(2) Where the Registrar decides to erase a person's name under this section, the Registrar shall forthwith serve on that person notification of the decision and of his right to appeal against the decision under Schedule 3A to this Act.

40   Appeals

(1) The following decisions are appealable decisions for the purposes of this section, that is to say –
   (a) a decision of a Fitness to Practise Panel under section 35D above giving a direction for erasure, for suspension or for conditional registration or varying the conditions imposed by a direction for conditional registration;
   (b) a decision of a Fitness to Practise Panel under section 41(9) below giving a direction that the right to make further application under that section shall be suspended indefinitely; or
   (c) a decision of the General Council under section 45(6) below giving a direction that the right to make further applications under that section shall be suspended indefinitely.

(1A) A decision under regulations made—
   (a) under section 31 above by virtue of subsection (8) of that section; or
   (b) under section 31A(1)(c) above,
not to restore a person's name to the register for a reason that relates to his fitness to practise is also an appealable decision for the purposes of this section.

(3) In subsection (1) above –
   (a) references to a direction for suspension include a reference to a direction extending a period of suspension; and
   (b) references to a direction for conditional registration include a reference to a direction extending a period of conditional registration.

(4) A person in respect of whom an appealable decision falling within subsection (1) has been taken may, before the end of the period of 28 days beginning with the date on which notification of the decision was served under section 35E(1) above, or section 41(10) or 45(7) below, appeal against the decision to the relevant court.

(4A) A person in respect of whom an appealable decision falling within subsection (1A) has been taken may, before the end of the period of 28 days beginning with the date on which notification of the decision was served, appeal against the decision to the relevant court.

(5) In subsections (4) and (4A) above, 'the relevant court' –
   (a) in the case of a person whose address in the register is (or if he were registered would be) in Scotland, means the Court of Session;
   (b) in the case of a person whose address in the register is (or if he were registered would be) in Northern Ireland, means the High Court of Justice in Northern Ireland; and
   (c) in the case of any other person (including one appealing against a decision falling within subsection (1)(c) above), means the High Court of Justice in England and Wales.

(7) On an appeal under this section from a Fitness to Practise Panel, the court may –
(a) dismiss the appeal;
(b) allow the appeal and quash the direction or variation appealed against;
(c) substitute for the direction or variation appealed against any other direction or variation which could have been given or made by a Fitness to Practise Panel; or
(d) remit the case to the Registrar for him to refer it to a Fitness to Practise Panel to dispose of the case in accordance with the directions of the court,

and may make such order as to costs (or, in Scotland, expenses) as it thinks fit.

(8) On an appeal under this section from the General Council, the court (or the sheriff) may –
(a) dismiss the appeal;
(b) allow the appeal and quash the direction appealed against; or
(c) remit the case to the General Council to dispose of the case in accordance with the directions of the court (or the sheriff),

and may make such order as to costs (or, in Scotland, expenses) as it (or he) thinks fit.

(9) On an appeal under this section from a Fitness to Practise Panel, the General Council may appear as respondent; and for the purpose of enabling directions to be given as to the costs of any such appeal the Council shall be deemed to be a party thereto, whether they appear on the hearing of the appeal or not.

41   Restoration of names to the register

(1) Subject to subsections (2) and (6) below, where the name of a person has been erased from the register under section 35D above, or section 44B(4)(b) below, a Fitness to Practise Panel may, if they think fit, direct that his name be restored to the register.

(2) No application for the restoration of a name to the register under this section shall be made to a Fitness to Practise Panel –
(a) before the expiration of five years from the date of erasure; or
(b) in any period of twelve months in which an application for the restoration of his name has already been made by or on behalf of the person whose name has been erased.

(3) An application under this section shall be made to the Registrar who shall refer the application to a Fitness to Practise Panel.

(4) In the case of a person who was provisionally registered under section 15, 15A, 21 or 21C above before his name was erased, a direction under subsection (1) above shall be a direction that his name be restored by way of provisional registration under section 15, 15A, 21 or 21C above, as the case requires.

(5) The requirements of Part II or Part III of this Act as to the experience required for registration as a fully registered medical practitioner shall not apply to registration in pursuance of a direction under subsection (1) above.

(6) Before determining whether to give a direction under subsection (1) above, a Fitness to Practise Panel shall require an applicant for restoration to provide such evidence as they direct as to his fitness to practise; and they shall not give such a direction if that evidence does not satisfy them.

(7) A Fitness to Practise Panel shall not give a direction under subsection (1) above unless at the same time in accordance with regulations made by the General Council under this subsection, they direct the Registrar to restore the practitioner's licence to practise.

(8) Subsections (3) to (5) of section 29J above apply to regulations made under subsection (7) above as they apply in relation to regulations made under section 29A above.

(9) Where, during the same period of erasure, a second or subsequent application for the restoration of a name to the register, made by or on behalf of the person whose name has been erased, is unsuccessful, a Fitness to Practise Panel may direct that his right to make any further such applications shall be suspended indefinitely.

(10) Where a Fitness to Practise Panel give a direction under subsection (9) above, the Registrar shall without delay serve on the person in respect of whom it has been made a notification of the direction and of his right to appeal against it in accordance with section 40 above.

(11) Any person in respect of whom a direction has been given under subsection (9) above may, after the expiration of three years from the date on which the direction was given, apply to the Registrar for that direction to be reviewed by a Fitness to Practise Panel and, thereafter, may make further applications for review; but no such application may be made before the expiration of three years from the date of the most recent review decision.

41A   Interim orders

(1) Where an Interim Orders Panel or a Fitness to Practise Panel are satisfied that it is necessary for the protection of members of the public or is otherwise in the public interest, or is in the interests of a fully registered person, for the registration of that person to be suspended or to be made subject to conditions, the Panel may make an order –

    (a) that his registration in the register shall be suspended (that is to say, shall not have effect) during such period not exceeding eighteen months as may be specified in the order (an 'interim suspension order'); or

    (b) that his registration shall be conditional on his compliance, during such period not exceeding eighteen months as may be specified in the order, with such requirements so specified as the Panel think fit to impose (an 'order for interim conditional registration').

(2) Subject to subsection (9) below, where an Interim Orders Panel or a Fitness to Practise Panel have made an order under subsection (1) above, an Interim Orders Panel or a Fitness to Practise Panel –

    (a) shall review it within the period of six months beginning on the date on which the order was made, and shall thereafter, for so long as the order continues in force, further review it –

        (i) before the end of the period of six months beginning on the date of the decision of the immediately preceding review; or

        (ii) if after the end of the period of three months beginning on the date of the decision of the immediately preceding review the person concerned requests an earlier review, as soon as practicable after that request; and

    (b) may review it where new evidence relevant to the order has become available after the making of the order.

(3) Where an interim suspension order or an order for interim conditional registration has been made in relation to any person under any provision of this section (including this subsection), an Interim Orders Panel or a Fitness to Practise Panel may, subject to subsection (4) below –

    (a) revoke the order or revoke any condition imposed by the order;

    (b) vary any condition imposed by the order;

    (c) if satisfied that to do so is necessary for the protection of members of the public or is otherwise in the public interest, or is in the interests of the person concerned, replace an order for interim conditional registration with an interim suspension order having effect for the remainder of the term of the former; or

    (d) if satisfied that to do so is necessary for the protection of members of the public, or is otherwise in the public interest, or is in the interests of the person concerned, replace an interim suspension order with an order for interim conditional registration having effect for the remainder of the term of the former.

(4) No order under subsection (1) or (3)(b) to (d) above shall be made by any Panel in respect of any person unless he has been afforded an opportunity of appearing before the Panel and being heard on the question of whether such an order should be made in his case; and for the purposes of this subsection a person may be represented before the Panel by counsel or a solicitor, or (if rules made under paragraph 1 of Schedule 4 to this Act so provide and he so elects) by a person of such other description as may be specified in the rules.

(5) If an order is made under any provision of this section, the Registrar shall without delay serve a notification of the order on the person to whose registration it relates.

(6) The General Council may apply to the relevant court for an order made by an Interim Orders Panel or a Fitness to Practise Panel under subsection (1) or (3) above to be extended, and may apply again for further extensions.

(7) On such an application the relevant court may extend (or further extend) for up to 12 months the period for which the order has effect.

(8) Any reference in this section to an interim suspension order, or to an order for interim conditional registration, includes a reference to such an order as so extended.

(9) For the purposes of subsection (2) above the first review after the relevant court's extension of an order made by an Interim Orders Panel or a Fitness to Practise Panel or after a replacement order made by an Interim Orders Panel or a Fitness to Practise Panel under subsection (3)(c) or (d) above shall take place –

> (a) if the order (or the order which has been replaced) had not been reviewed at all under subsection (2), within the period of six months beginning on the date on which the relevant court ordered the extension or on which a replacement order under subsection (3)(c) or (d) was made; and
>
> (b) if it had been reviewed under the provision, within the period of three months beginning on that date.

(10) Where an order has effect under any provision of this section, the relevant court may –

> (a) in the case of an interim suspension order, terminate the suspension;
>
> (b) in the case of an order for interim conditional registration, revoke or vary any condition imposed by the order;
>
> (c) in either case, substitute for the period specified in the order (or in the order extending it) some other period which could have been specified in the order when it was made (or in the order extending it),

and the decision of the relevant court under any application under this subsection shall be final.

(11) Except as provided in subsection (12) below, while a person's registration in the register is suspended by virtue of an interim suspension order under this section he shall be treated as not being registered in the register notwithstanding that his name still appears in the register.

(12) Notwithstanding subsection (11) above, sections 31A, 35C to 35E and 39 above shall continue to apply to a person whose registration in the register is suspended.

(13) This section applies to a provisionally registered person whether or not the circumstances are such that he falls within the meaning in this Act of the expression 'fully registered person'.

(14) In this section 'the relevant court' has the same meaning as in section 40(5) above.

43 Proceedings before the Investigation Committee, Interim Orders Panels and Fitness to Practise Panels

Schedule 4 to this Act (which contains supplementary provisions about proceedings before the Investigation Committee, Interim Orders Panels and Fitness to Practise Panels) shall have effect.

44 Effect of disqualification in another member State on registration in the United Kingdom

(1) A person who is subject to a disqualifying decision in an EEA State in which he is or has been established in medical practice shall not be entitled to be registered by virtue of section 3(1)(b) above for so long as the decision remains in force in relation to him.

(2) A disqualifying decision in respect of a person is a decision, made by responsible authorities of the EEA State in which he was established in medical practice or in which he acquired a primary United Kingdom or primary European qualification, and –

> (a) expressed to be made on the grounds that he has committed a criminal offence or on grounds related to his professional conduct, professional performance or physical or mental health; and
>
> (b) having in that State the effect either that he is no longer registered or otherwise officially recognised as a medical practitioner, or that he is prohibited from practising medicine there.

(3) If a person has been registered by virtue of section 3(1)(b) above and it is subsequently shown to the satisfaction of the Registrar that he was subject to a disqualifying decision in force at the time of registration, and that the decision remains in force, the Registrar shall remove the person's name from the register.

(4) A decision under –

(a) subsection (1) above not to register a person; or

(b) subsection (3) above to remove a person's name from the register, is an appealable registration decision for the purposes of Schedule 3A to this Act.

(5) If a person has been registered as a fully registered medical practitioner by virtue of section 3(1)(b) above at a time when a disqualifying decision was in force in respect of him, and he has been so registered for a period of not less than one month throughout which the decision had effect –

(a) a Fitness to Practise Panel may direct that his registration be suspended for such period, not exceeding the length of the first-mentioned period, as the Panel think fit, and the period of suspension shall begin on a date to be specified in the Panel's direction; and

(b) sections 35E(1) and (3) and 40 and paragraphs 1, 2, 8, 9, 10, 12 and 13 of Schedule 4 to this Act shall have effect, with any necessary modifications, in relation to suspension under this subsection.

(6) Where on or after the date on which a person was registered by virtue of section 3(1)(b) above a disqualifying decision relating to him comes into force, this Part of this Act shall apply, with any necessary modifications, as if it had been found that he had been convicted of the criminal offence referred to in the disqualifying decision, or that his professional performance or physical or mental health had been such as is imputed to him by that decision, as the case may be.

(7) Subsection (1) of section 18 above shall not apply to a person and that person shall not be registered as a visiting EEA practitioner at any time when he is subject to a disqualifying decision imposed by a member State or its competent authority (within the meaning of that section).

44B.– Provision of information in respect of fitness to practise matters

(1) If a person has been registered by virtue of any provision of this Act and it is subsequently shown to the satisfaction of the Registrar that—

(a) his fitness to practise was impaired at the time of his registration because of his involvement in a serious matter or a problem with his physical or mental health; and

(b) he had not informed the Registrar of that matter or problem before his registration, the Registrar may erase that person's name from the register.

(2) The General Council may by regulations make provision for the information to be provided to the Registrar—

(a) by or in respect of a person seeking registration by virtue of any provision of this Act, other than section 18 above, for the purpose of determining whether his fitness to practise is impaired;

(b) by or in respect of a person who is fully registered or provisionally registered, for the purpose of determining whether his fitness to practise was impaired at the time of his registration because of his involvement in a serious matter or a problem with his physical or mental health.

(3) In subsections (1) and (2) above, 'serious matter' has the same meaning as in article 12(2) of Directive 93/16/EEC.

(4) The Registrar may—

(a) refuse to register (even if he is directed by the General Council to do so) any person who fails to comply with, or in respect of whom there is a failure to comply with, regulations made under subsection (2)(a) above;

(b) erase from the register the name of any person who fails to comply with, or in respect of whom there is a failure to comply with, regulations made under subsection (2)(b) above.

(5) For the purpose of determining whether an exempt person ('E') should be registered under this Act, the General Council or the Registrar, as the case may be, shall accept as sufficient evidence that his fitness to practise is not impaired a document—

(a) to which subsection (6) below applies, as regards his physical or mental health; or

(b) to which subsection (8) below applies, as regards any other relevant matter, if it is presented to the Registrar within the period of three months beginning with its date of issue.

(6) This subsection applies to a document that attests to E's good physical and mental health, and—

(a) which would be required in E's EEA State of origin or the EEA State from which he comes ('E's attesting State'), if he wished to start practising medicine there; or

(b) if no such document is required there, which is issued by a competent authority in E's attesting State (and which, if relevant, is in the form mentioned in subsection (7) below).

(7) If regulations made under subsection (2) above require a certificate which attests to an applicant's good physical and mental health to be in a particular form, a document referred to in subsection (6)(b) above must be in that form or in a form which corresponds to it.

(8) Except as mentioned in subsection (9) below, this subsection applies to a document—

(a) containing an extract from the judicial record issued by a competent authority in E's attesting State; or

(b) which is a certificate issued by a competent authority in E's attesting State, in either case attesting to E's good character and good repute.

(9) Subsection (8) above does not apply to a document which may be, or has been, revised or rescinded as a consequence of an approach made by the General Council to the competent authority which issued it, in accordance with article 11(3) of Directive 93/16/EEC.

(10) Regulations under subsection (2) above shall not have effect until approved by order of the Privy Council.

44C.– Indemnity arrangements

(1) A person who holds a licence to practise shall have in force in relation to him an adequate and appropriate indemnity arrangement which provides cover in respect of liabilities which may be incurred in carrying out work as a medical practitioner.

(2) For the purposes of this section, an 'indemnity arrangement' may comprise—

(a) a policy of insurance;

(b) an arrangement made for the purposes of indemnifying a person; or

(c) a combination of a policy of insurance and an arrangement made for the purposes of indemnifying a person.

(3) The General Council may make regulations about what is an 'adequate and appropriate indemnity arrangement' for the purposes of this section, and the regulations may make different provision for different cases.

(4) The General Council may make regulations about the information to be provided to the Registrar—

(a) by or in respect of a person seeking a licence to practise for the purpose of determining whether, if he is granted a licence to practise, there will be in force in relation to him an adequate and appropriate indemnity arrangement which commences, at the latest, on the date on which he is granted a licence to practise; and

(b) by or in respect of a person who holds a licence to practise for the purpose of deter-mining whether there is in force in relation to him an adequate and appropriate indemnity arrangement.

(5) Regulations made under subsection (4)(b) above may require the information mentioned there to be provided—

    (a) at the request of the Registrar; or

    (b) on such dates or at such intervals as the Registrar may determine, either generally or in relation to individual practitioners or practitioners of a particular description.

(6) The General Council may also make regulations requiring a person who holds a licence to practise to inform the Registrar if there ceases to be in force in relation to him an adequate and appropriate indemnity arrangement.

(7) A licensing authority may refuse to grant a licence to practise to any person who fails to comply, or in respect of whom there is a failure to comply, with regulations made under subsection (4)(a) above.

(8) If a person who holds a licence to practise is in breach of subsection (1) above or fails to comply with regulations made under subsection (4)(b) or (6) above, or there is a failure to comply with regulations made under subsection (4)(b) in respect of him—

    (a) a licensing authority may withdraw that person's licence to practise; or

    (b) the breach or failure may be treated as misconduct for the purposes of section 35C(2)(a) above, and the Registrar may refer the matter to the Investigation Committee for investigation by them under section 35C(4) above.

(9) Regulations under subsection (3), (4) or (6) above shall not have effect until approved by order of the Privy Council.

44D.– Approved practice settings

(1) Unless the Registrar otherwise directs in relation to a particular person, a person who is registered under section 3(1)(a) or 21B above after the coming into force of this section shall, before his first revalidation in accordance with Part 3A above after he is registered, practise medicine in the United Kingdom only in a practice setting—

    (a) where he is subject to a governance system that includes, but is not limited to, provision for appropriate supervision and appraisal arrangements or assessments; and

    (b) which is, or which is of a type which is, for the time being recognised by the General Council, either generally or in relation to him or to practitioners of his class, as being acceptable for a practitioner who is newly fully registered.

(2) Unless the Registrar otherwise directs in relation to a particular person, a person whose name is restored to the register after the coming into force of this section shall, before his first revalidation in accordance with Part 3A above after his name is restored to the register, practise medicine in the United Kingdom only in a practice setting—

    (a) where he is subject to a governance system that includes, but is not limited to, provision for appropriate supervision and appraisal arrangements or assessments; and

    (b) which is, or which is of a type which is, for the time being recognised by the General Council, either generally or in relation to him or to practitioners of his class, as being acceptable for a practitioner who is newly restored to the register.

(3) The General Council may limit their recognition of—

    (a) a particular practice setting so that it is recognised in relation only to one or more particular practitioners or particular classes of practitioner;

    (b) a particular type of practice setting so that it is recognised in relation only to one or more particular classes of practitioner.

(4) The General Council may exclude a particular practice setting from their recognition of a particular type of practice setting—

    (a) in relation to all practitioners; or

    (b) in relation to one or more particular classes of practitioner.

(5) The General Council may at any time vary or withdraw their recognition from a particular practice setting or a particular type of practice setting.

(6) An example of a valid reason for withdrawing recognition from a particular practice setting, or excluding a particular practice setting from recognition of a particular type of practice

setting, is that the relevant governance system operated there is not quality assured by a body that is acceptable to the General Council as a provider of quality assurance.

(7) If—

(a) a person starts practising medicine in a practice setting that is, or is of a type that is, recognised under whichever is appropriate of subsection (1)(b) or (2)(b) above, either generally or in relation to practitioners of his class; and

(b) while he is practising medicine there, it ceases to be so recognised, it is to be treated as continuing to be recognised in relation to the particular practitioner while he continues to practise medicine there.

(8) The General Council may by regulations make provision for the information to be provided to the Registrar by or in respect of a fully registered person for the purposes of determining whether or not he is in breach of subsection (1) or (2) above.

(9) If a fully registered person—

(a) is in breach of subsection (1) or (2) above; or

(b) fails to comply with regulations made under subsection (8) above, or there is a failure to comply with those regulations in respect of him, the breach or failure may be treated as misconduct for the purposes of section 35C(2)(a) above, and the Registrar may refer the matter to the Investigation Committee for investigation by them under section 35C(4) above.

(10) Regulations under subsection (8) above shall not have effect until approved by order of the Privy Council.

(11) The General Council may publish guidance for practitioners who—

(a) are newly fully registered or whose names are newly restored to the register; but

(b) are not subject to the requirements imposed by subsection (1) and (2),

on what are suitable practice settings for them before their first revalidation in accordance with Part 3A above after being registered or before their names are restored to the register.

45   Disciplinary provisions affecting practitioners who render services while visiting the United Kingdom

(1) If a national of an EEA State who has medical qualifications entitling him to registration under section 3 above but is not so registered and who renders medical services while visiting the United Kingdom (whether or not registered as a visiting EEA practitioner) –

(a) is found by a Fitness to Practise Panel to have been convicted of a criminal offence in any EEA State where he was practising medicine; or

(b) is subject to a finding that his fitness to practise is impaired,

the Committee may, if they think fit, impose on him a prohibition in respect of the rendering of medical services in the United Kingdom in the future.

(2) A prohibition imposed under this section shall either relate to a period specified by a Fitness to Practise Panel or be expressed to continue for an indefinite period.

(3) A person may apply to the General Council for termination of a prohibition imposed on him under this section and the Council may, on any such application, terminate the prohibition or reduce the period of it; but no application may be made under this subsection –

(a) earlier than five years from the date on which the prohibition was imposed; or

(b) in the period of twelve months following a decision made on an earlier application.

(4) Section 18(1) above does not apply to a person and that person shall not be registered as a visiting EEA practitioner at a time when he is subject to a prohibition imposed by a Fitness to Practise Panel under this section.

(5) Before determining whether to terminate a prohibition under subsection (3), the General Council shall require the person applying for its termination to provide such evidence as they direct as to his fitness to practise; and they shall not terminate the prohibition if that evidence does not satisfy them.

(6) Where, during the same period of prohibition, a second or subsequent application for termination of the prohibition, made by or on behalf of a person on whom the prohibition has been imposed, is unsuccessful, the General Council may direct that his right to make any further such applications shall be suspended indefinitely.

(7) Where the General Council give a direction under subsection (6), the Registrar shall without delay serve on the person in respect of whom it has been made a notification of the direction and of his right to appeal against it in accordance with section 40.

(8) Any person in respect of whom a direction has been given under subsection (6) may, after the expiration of three years from the date on which the direction was made, apply to the General Council for that direction to be reviewed by the General Council and, thereafter, may make further applications for review; but no such application may be made before the expiration of three years from the date of the most recent review decision.

Part VI Privileges of Registered Practitioners

46   Recovery of fees

(1) Except as provided in subsection (2) or (2A) below, no person shall be entitled to recover any charge in any court of law for any medical advice or attendance, or for the performance of any operation, unless he proves that he is fully registered and holds a licence to practise.

(2) Subsection (1) above shall not apply to fees in respect of medical services lawfully rendered in the United Kingdom by a person who is a national of any EEA State without first being registered under this Act if he has previously complied with the requirements of subsection (2) of section 18 above or subsequently complies with those requirements as modified in respect of urgent cases by subsection (3) of that section.

(2A) Subsection (1) above shall not apply to fees in respect of medical services lawfully provided—

(a) under arrangements to provide services as part of the health service, the Northern Ireland health service or the Scottish health service (those terms having the same meaning here as in section 29G(3) above);

(b) by any person who is not a medical practitioner but who is entitled to provide those medical services by virtue of an enforceable Community right;

(c) by a person who is a member of a profession regulated by a body, apart from the General Council, mentioned in section 25(3) of the National Health Service Reform and Health Care Professions Act 2002.

(3) Where a practitioner is a fellow of a college of physicians, fellows of which are prohibited by byelaw from recovering by law their expenses, charges or fees, then, notwithstanding that he is fully registered, the prohibitory byelaw, so long as it is in force, may be pleaded in bar of any legal proceedings instituted by him for the recovery of expenses, charges or fees.

47   Appointments not to be held except by fully registered practitioners who hold licences to practise

(1) Subject to subsection (2) below, only a person who is fully registered and who holds a licence to practise may hold any appointment as physician, surgeon or other medical officer –

(a) in the naval, military or air service,

(b) in any hospital or other place for the reception of persons suffering from mental disorder, or in any other hospital, infirmary or dispensary not supported wholly by voluntary contributions,

(c) in any prison, or

(d) in any other public establishment, body or institution, or to any friendly or other society for providing mutual relief in sickness, infirmity or old age.

(2) Nothing in this section shall prevent any person who is not a Commonwealth citizen from being and acting as the resident physician or medical officer of any hospital established exclusively for the relief of foreigners in sickness, so long as he –

(a) has obtained from a foreign university a degree or diploma of doctor in medicine and has passed the regular examinations entitling him to practise medicine in his own country, and

(b) is engaged in no medical practise except as such a resident physician or medical officer.

(3) None of the suspension events mentioned in subsection (4) below shall terminate any appointment such as is mentioned in subsection (1) above but the person suspended shall not perform the duties of such an appointment during the suspension.

(4) The suspension events are –

(a) the suspension of registration of a person by a Fitness to Practise Panel –

(i) following a finding of impairment of fitness to practise by reason of deficient professional performance or adverse physical or mental health under section 35D above, or

(ii) under rules made by virtue of paragraph 5A(3) of Schedule 4 to this Act;

(b) an order for immediate suspension by a Fitness to Practise Panel under section 38(1) above; or

(c) an interim suspension order by an Interim Orders Panel or a Fitness to Practise Panel under section 41A above (or such an order as extended under that section).

48   Certificates invalid if not signed by fully registered practitioners who hold licences to practise

A certificate required by any enactment, whether passed before or after the commencement of this Act, from any physician, surgeon, licentiate in medicine and surgery or other medical practitioner shall not be valid unless the person signing it is fully registered and holds a licence to practise.

49   Penalty for pretending to be registered

(1) Subject to subsection (2) below, any person who wilfully and falsely pretends to be or takes or uses the name or title of physician, doctor of medicine, licentiate in medicine and surgery, bachelor of medicine, surgeon, general practitioner or apothecary, or any name, title, addition or description implying that he is registered under any provision of this Act, or that he is recognised by law as a physician or surgeon or licentiate in medicine and surgery or a practitioner in medicine or an apothecary, shall be liable on summary conviction to a fine not exceeding level 5 on the standard scale (as defined in section 75 of the Criminal Justice Act 1982); and for the purposes of this subsection –

(a) section 37 of that Act; and

(b) an order under section 143 of the Magistrates' Courts Act 1980 which alters the sums specified in subsection (2) of the said section 37,

shall extend to Northern Ireland and the said section 75 shall have effect as if after the words 'England and Wales' there were inserted the words 'or Northern Ireland'.

(2) Subsection (1) above shall not apply to anything done by a person who is a national of any EEA State for the purposes of or in connection with the lawful rendering of medical services by him without first being registered under this Act if he has previously complied with the requirements of subsection (2) of section 18 above or subsequently complies with its requirements as modified in respect of urgent cases by subsection (3) of that section.

Public Health (Control of Disease) Act 1984

(1984, c. 22)

10   Notifiable diseases

In this Act, 'notifiable disease' means any of the following diseases –

(a) cholera;

(b) plague;

(c) relapsing fever;

(d) smallpox; and

(e) typhus.

11   Cases of notifiable disease and food poisoning to be reported

(1) If a registered medical practitioner becomes aware, or suspects, that a patient whom he is attending within the district of a local authority is suffering from a notifiable disease or from food poisoning, he shall, unless he believes, and has reasonable grounds for believing, that some other registered medical practitioner has complied with this subsection with respect to the patient, forthwith send to the proper officer of the local authority for that district a certificate stating –

(a) the name, age and sex of the patient and the address of the premises where the patient is,

(b) the disease or, as the case may be, particulars of the poisoning from which the patient is, or is suspected to be, suffering and the date, or approximate date, of its onset, and

(c) if the premises are a hospital, the day on which the patient was admitted, the address of the premises from which he came there and whether or not, in the opinion of the person giving the certificate, the disease or poisoning from which the patient is, or is suspected to be, suffering was contracted in the hospital.

(2) A local authority shall, upon application, supply forms of certificate for use under this section free of charge to any registered medical practitioner practising in their district.

(3) The officer who receives the certificate shall, on the day of its receipt (if possible) and in any case within 48 hours after is receipt, send a copy –

(a) to the Primary Care Trust or Health Authority within whose area are situated the premises whose address is specified in the certificate in accordance with subsection (1)(a) above, and

(b) if the certificate is given with respect to a patient in a hospital who came there from premises outside the district of the local authority within whose district the hospital is situated and the certificate states that the patient did not contract the disease or the poisoning in the hospital –

(i)   to the proper officer of the local authority for the district within which the premises from which the patient came are situated, and

(ii) to the Primary Care Trust or Health Authority for the area in which those premises are situated, if that Primary Care Trust or Health Authority are not responsible for the administration of the hospital, and

(iii) to the proper officer of the relevant port health authority, if those premises were a ship or hovercraft situated within the port health district for which that authority is constituted.

(4) A person who fails to comply with an obligation imposed on him by subsection (1) above shall be liable on summary conviction to a fine not exceeding level 1 on the standard scale.

(5) In this section, 'hospital' means any institution for the reception and treatment of persons suffering from illness, any maternity home and any institution for the reception and treatment of persons during convalescence or persons requiring medical rehabilitation, and 'illness' includes mental disorder within the meaning of the Mental Health Act 1983 and any injury or disability requiring medical, surgical or dental treatment or nursing.

13   Regulations for control of certain diseases

(1) Subject to the provisions of this section, the Secretary of State may, as respects the whole or any part of England and Wales, including coastal waters, make regulations –

(a) with a view to the treatment of persons affected with any epidemic, endemic or infectious disease and for preventing the spread of such diseases,

(b) for preventing danger to public health from vessels or aircraft arriving at any place, and

(c) for preventing the spread of infection by means of any vessel or aircraft leaving any place, so far as may be necessary or expedient for the purpose of carrying out any treaty, convention, arrangement or engagement with any other country.

(2) Without prejudice to the generality of subsection (1) above, the Secretary of State may by any such regulations apply, with or without modifications, to any disease to which the regulations relate any enactment (including any enactment in this Act) relating to the notification of disease or to notifiable diseases.

15   Contravention of regulations under s. 13

Any person who wilfully neglects or refuses to obey or carry out, or obstructs the execution of, any regulations made under section 13 above shall, in a case where no provision is made in the regulations for his punishment, be liable on summary conviction –

(a) to a fine not exceeding level 5 on the standard scale, and

(b) in the case of a continuing offence, to a further fine not exceeding £50 for every day on which the offence continues after conviction.

17   Exposure of persons and articles liable to convey notifiable disease

(1) A person who –

(a) knowing that he is suffering from a notifiable disease, exposes other persons to the risk of infection by his presence or conduct in any street, public place, place of entertainment or assembly, club, hotel, inn or shop,

(b) having the care of a person whom he knows to be suffering from a notifiable disease, causes or permits that person to expose other persons to the risk of infection by his presence or conduct in any such place as aforesaid, or

(c) gives, lends, sells, transmits or exposes, without previous disinfection, any clothing, bedding or rags which he knows to have been exposed to infection from any such disease, or any other article which he knows to have been so exposed and which is liable to carry such infection,

shall be liable on summary conviction to a fine not exceeding level 1 on the standard scale.

(2) A person shall not incur any liability under this section by transmitting with proper precautions any article for the purpose of having it disinfected.

Infectious persons

35   Medical examination

(1) If a justice of the peace (acting, if he deems it necessary, ex parte) is satisfied, on a written certificate issued by a registered medical practitioner nominated by the local authority for a district –

(a) that there is reason to believe that some person in the district –

    (i)   is or has been suffering from a notifiable disease, or

    (ii) though not suffering from such a disease, is carrying an organism that is capable of causing it, and

(b) that in his own interest, or in the interest of his family, or in the public interest, it is expedient that he should be medically examined, and

(c) that he is not under the treatment of a registered medical practitioner or that the registered medical practitioner who is treating him consents to the making of an order under this section,

the justice may order him to be medically examined by a registered medical practitioner so nominated.

(2) An order under this section may be combined with a warrant under subsection (3) or section 61 below authorising a registered medical practitioner nominated by the local authority to enter any premises, and for the purposes of that subsection that practitioner shall, if not an officer of the local authority, be treated as one.

(3) In this section, references to a person's being medically examined shall be construed as including references to his being submitted to bacteriological and radiological tests and similar investigations.

36 Medical examination of group of persons believed to comprise carrier of notifiable disease

(1) If a justice of the peace (acting, if he deems it necessary, ex parte) is satisfied, on a written certificate issued by the proper officer of the local authority for a district –

(a) that there is reason to believe that one of a group of persons, though not suffering from a notifiable disease, is carrying an organism that is capable of causing it, and

(b) that in the interest of those persons or their families, or in the public interest, it is expedient that those persons should be medically examined, the justice may order them to be medically examined by a registered medical practitioner nominated by the local authority for that district.

(2) Subsections (2) and (3) of section 35 above apply in relation to subsection (1) above as they apply in relation to subsection (1) of that section.

37 Removal to hospital of person with notifiable disease

(1) Where a justice of the peace (acting, if he deems it necessary, ex parte) is satisfied, on the application of the local authority, that a person is suffering from a notifiable disease and –

(a) that his circumstances are such that proper precautions to prevent the spread of infection cannot be taken, or that such precautions are not being taken, and

(b) that serious risk of infection is thereby caused to other persons, and

(c) that accommodation for him is available in a suitable hospital vested in the Secretary of State, or, pursuant to arrangements made by a Health Authority or Primary Care Trust (whether under an NHS contract or otherwise) in a suitable hospital vested in a NHS trust, NHS foundation trust, Primary Care Trust or other person the justice may, with the consent mentioned in subsection 1A below, order him to be removed to it.

(1A) The consent referred to in subsection (1) above is that of a Primary Care Trust or Health Authority –

(a) any part of whose area falls within that of the local authority, and

(b) which appears to the local authority to be an appropriate Primary Care Trust or Health Authority from whom to obtain consent.

(2) An order under this section may be addressed to such officer of the local authority as the justice may think expedient, and that officer and any officer of the hospital may do all acts necessary for giving effect to the order.

38 Detention in hospital of person with notifiable disease

(1) Where a justice of the peace (acting, if he deems it necessary, ex parte) in and for the place in which a hospital for infectious diseases is situated is satisfied, on the application of any local authority, that an inmate of the hospital who is suffering from a notifiable disease would not on leaving the hospital be provided with lodging or accommodation in which proper precautions could be taken to prevent the spread of the disease by him, the justice may order him to be detained in the hospital.

(2) An order made under subsection (1) above may direct detention for a period specified in the order, but any justice of the peace acting in and for the same place may extend a period so specified as often as it appears to him to be necessary to do so.

(3) Any person who leaves a hospital contrary to an order made under this section for his detention there shall be liable on summary conviction to a fine not exceeding level 1 on the standard scale, and the court may order him to be taken back to the hospital.

(4) An order under this section may be addressed –

(a) in the case of an order for a person's detention, to such officer of the hospital, and

(b) in the case of an order made under subsection (3) above, to such officer of the local authority on whose application the order for detention was made,

as the justice may think expedient, and that officer and any officer of the hospital may do all acts necessary for giving effect to the order.

Surrogacy Arrangements Act 1985

(1985, c. 49)

1   Meaning of 'surrogate mother', 'surrogacy arrangement' and other terms

(1) The following provisions shall have effect for the interpretation of this Act.

(2) 'Surrogate mother' means a woman who carries a child in pursuance of an arrangement –

(a) made before she began to carry the child, and

(b) made with a view to any child carried in pursuance of it being handed over to, and parental responsibility being met (so far as practicable) by, another person or other persons.

(3) An arrangement is a surrogacy arrangement if, were a woman to whom the arrangement relates to carry a child in pursuance of it, she would be a surrogate mother.

(4) In determining whether an arrangement is made with such a view as is mentioned in subsection (2) above regard may be had to the circumstances as a whole (and, in particular, where there is a promise or understanding that any payment will or may be made to the woman or for her benefit in respect of the carrying of any child in pursuance of the arrangement, to that promise or understanding).

(5) An arrangement may be regarded as made with such a view though subject to conditions relating to the handing over of any child.

(6) A woman who carries a child is to be treated for the purposes of subsection (2)(a) above as beginning to carry it at the time of the insemination or of the placing in her of an embryo, of an egg in the process of fertilisation or of sperm and eggs, as the case may be, that results in her carrying the child.

(7) 'Body of persons' means a body of persons corporate or unincorporate.

(8) 'Payment' means payment in money or money's worth.

(9) This Act applies to arrangements whether or not they are lawful.

1A   Surrogacy arrangements unenforceable

No surrogacy arrangement is enforceable by or against any of the persons making it.

2   Negotiating surrogacy arrangements on a commercial basis, etc.

(1) No person shall on a commercial basis do any of the following acts in the United Kingdom, that is –

(a) initiate or take part in any negotiations with a view to the making of a surrogacy arrangement,

(b) offer or agree to negotiate the making of a surrogacy arrangement, or

(c) compile any information with a view to its use in making, or negotiating the making of, surrogacy arrangements;

and no person shall in the United Kingdom knowingly cause another to do any of those acts on a commercial basis.

(2) A person who contravenes subsection (1) above is guilty of an offence; but it is not a contravention of that subsection –

(a) for a woman, with a view to becoming a surrogate mother herself, to do any act mentioned in that subsection or to cause such an act to be done, or

(b) for any person, with a view to a surrogate mother carrying a child for him, to do such an act or to cause such an act to be done.

(3) For the purposes of this section, a person does an act on a commercial basis (subject to subsection (4) below) if –

(a) any payment is at any time received by himself or another in respect of it, or

      (b) he does it with a view to any payment being received by himself or another in respect of making, or negotiating or facilitating the making of, any surrogacy arrangement.

In this subsection 'payment' does not include payment to or for the benefit of a surrogate mother or prospective surrogate mother.

    (4) In proceedings against a person for an offence under subsection (1) above, he is not to be treated as doing an act on a commercial basis by reason of any payment received by another in respect of the act if it is proved that –

      (a) in a case where the payment was received before he did the act, he did not do the act knowing or having reasonable cause to suspect that any payment had been received in respect of the act; and

      (b) in any other case, he did not do the act with a view to any payment being received in respect of it.

    (5) Where –

      (a) a person acting on behalf of a body of persons takes any part in negotiating or facilitating the making of a surrogacy arrangement in the United Kingdom, and

      (b) negotiating or facilitating the making of surrogacy arrangements is an activity of the body,

then, if the body at any time receives any payment made by or on behalf of –

      (i)   a woman who carries a child in pursuance of the arrangement,

      (ii) the person or persons for whom she carries it, or

      (iii) any person connected with the woman or with that person or those persons,

the body is guilty of an offence.

  For the purposes of this subsection, a payment received by a person connected with a body is to be treated as received by the body.

    (6) In proceedings against a body for an offence under subsection (5) above, it is a defence to prove that the payment concerned was not made in respect of the arrangement mentioned in paragraph (a) of that subsection.

    (7) A person who in the United Kingdom takes part in the management or control –

      (a) of any body of persons, or

      (b) of any of the activities of any body of persons,

is guilty of an offence if the activity described in subsection (8) below is an activity of the body concerned.

    (8) The activity referred to in subsection (7) above is negotiating or facilitating the making of surrogacy arrangements in the United Kingdom, being –

      (a) arrangements the making of which is negotiated or facilitated on a commercial basis, or

      (b) arrangements in the case of which payments are received (or treated for the purposes of subsection (5) above as received) by the body concerned in contravention of subsection (5) above.

    (9) In proceedings against a person for an offence under subsection (7) above, it is a defence to prove that he neither knew nor had reasonable cause to suspect that the activity described in subsection (8) above was an activity of the body concerned; and for the purposes of such proceedings any arrangement falling within subsection (8)(b) above shall be disregarded if it is proved that the payment concerned was not made in respect of the arrangement.

3   Advertisements about surrogacy

    (1) This section applies to any advertisement containing an indication (however expressed) –

      (a) that any person is or may be willing to enter into a surrogacy arrangement or to negotiate or facilitate the making of a surrogacy arrangement, or

      (b) that any person is looking for a woman willing to become a surrogate mother or for persons wanting a woman to carry a child as a surrogate mother.

    (2) Where a newspaper or periodical containing an advertisement to which this section applies is published in the United Kingdom, any proprietor, editor or publisher of the newspaper or periodical is guilty of an offence.

(3) Where an advertisement to which this section applies is conveyed by means of a tele-communication system so as to be seen or heard (or both) in the United Kingdom, any person who in the United Kingdom causes it to be so conveyed knowing it to contain such an indication as is mentioned in subsection (1) above is guilty of an offence.

(4) A person who publishes or causes to be published in the United Kingdom an advertisement to which this section applies (not being an advertisement contained in a newspaper or periodical or conveyed by means of a telecommunication system) is guilty of an offence.

(5) A person who distributes or causes to be distributed in the United Kingdom an adver-tisement to which this section applies (not being an advertisement contained in a newspaper or periodical published outside the United Kingdom or an advertisement conveyed by means of a telecommunication system) knowing it to contain such an indication as is mentioned in subsection (1) above is guilty of an offence.

4   Offences

(1) A person guilty of an offence under this Act shall be liable on summary conviction –
> (a) in the case of an offence under section 2 to a fine not exceeding level 5 on the standard scale or to imprisonment for a term not exceeding 3 months or both,
> (b) in the case of an offence under section 3 to a fine not exceeding level 5 on the standard scale.

In this subsection 'the standard scale' has the meaning given by section 75 of the Criminal Justice Act 1982.

(2) No proceedings for an offence under this Act shall be instituted –
> (a) in England and Wales, except by or with the consent of the Director of Public Pros-ecutions; and
> (b) in Northern Ireland, except by or with the consent of the Director of Public Prosecutions for Northern Ireland.

(3) Where an offence under this Act committed by a body corporate is proved to have been committed with the consent or connivance of, or to be attributable to any neglect on the part of, any director, manager, secretary or other similar officer of the body corporate or any person who was purporting to act in any such capacity, he as well as the body corporate is guilty of the offence and is liable to be proceeded against and punished accordingly.

(4) Where the affairs of a body corporate are managed by its members, subsection (3) above shall apply in relation to the acts and defaults of a member in connection with his functions of management as if he were a director of the body corporate.

(5) In any proceedings for an offence under section 2 of this Act, proof of things done or of words written, spoken or published (whether or not in the presence of any party to the proceedings) by any person taking part in the management or control of a body of persons or of any of the activities of the body, or by any person doing any of the acts mentioned in subsection (1)(a) to (c) of that section on behalf of the body, shall be admissible as evidence of the activities of the body.

(6) In relation to an offence under this Act, section 127(1) of the Magistrates' Courts Act 1980 (information must be laid within six months of commission offence), section 331(1) of the Criminal Procedure (Scotland) Act 1975 (proceedings must be commenced within that time) and Article 19(1) of the Magistrates' Courts (Northern Ireland) Order 1981 (complaint must be made within that time) shall have effect as if for the reference to six months there were substituted a reference to two years.

Family Law Reform Act 1987

(1987, c. 42)

27   Artificial insemination

(1) Where after the coming into force of this section a child is born in England and Wales as the result of the artificial insemination of a woman who –

    (a) was at the time of the insemination a party to a marriage (being a marriage which had
        not at that time been dissolved or annulled); and

    (b) was artificially inseminated with the semen of some person other than the other party
        to that marriage,

then, unless it is proved to the satisfaction of any court by which the matter has to be determined
that the other party to that marriage did not consent to the insemination, the child shall be treated
in law as the child of the parties to that marriage and shall not be treated as the child of any person
other than the parties to that marriage.

    (2) Any reference in this section to a marriage includes a reference to a void marriage if at the
time of the insemination resulting in the birth of the child both or either of the parties reasonably
believed that the marriage was valid; and for the purposes of this section it shall be presumed, unless
the contrary is shown, that one of the parties so believed at that time that the marriage was valid.

    (3) Nothing in this section shall affect the succession to any dignity or title of honour or render
any person capable of succeeding to or transmitting a right to succeed to any such dignity or title.

    [Note: see the Human Fertilisation and Embryology Act 1990 ss. 28 and 49(3)(4)]

Consumer Protection Act 1987

(1987, c. 43)

Part I Product Liability

1   Purpose and construction of Part I

    (1) This Part shall have effect for the purpose of making such provision as is necessary in order
to comply with the product liability Directive and shall be construed accordingly.

    (2) In this Part, except in so far as the context otherwise requires –

'dependant' and 'relative' have the same meaning as they have in, respectively, the Fatal Accidents
Act 1976 and the Damages (Scotland) Act 1976;

'producer', in relation to a product, means –

    (a) the person who manufactured it;

    (b) in the case of a substance which has not been manufactured but has been won or
        abstracted, the person who won or abstracted it;

    (c) in the case of a product which has not been manufactured, won or abstracted but
        essential characteristics of which are attributable to an industrial or other process
        having been carried out (for example, in relation to agricultural produce), the person
        who carried out that process;

'product' means any goods or electricity and (subject to subsection (3) below) includes a product
which is comprised in another product, whether by virtue of being a component part or raw
material or otherwise; and

'the product liability Directive' means the Directive of the Council of the European Communities,
dated 25th July 1985 (No. 85/374/EEC) on the approximation of the laws, regulations and
administrative provisions of the member States concerning liability for defective products.

    (3) For the purposes of this Part a person who supplies any product in which products are
comprised, whether by virtue of being component parts or raw materials or otherwise, shall not be
treated by reason only of his supply of that product as supplying any of the products so comprised.

2   Liability for defective products

    (1) Subject to the following provisions of this Part, where any damage is caused wholly or
partly by a defect in a product, every person to whom subsection (2) below applies shall be liable for
the damage.

    (2) This subsection applies to –

(a) the producer of the product;

(b) any person who, by putting his name on the product or using a trade mark or other distinguishing mark in relation to the product, has held himself out to be the producer of the product;

(c) any person who has imported the product into a member State from a place outside the member States in order, in the course of any business of his, to supply it to another.

(3) Subject as aforesaid, where any damage is caused wholly or partly by a defect in a product, any person who supplied the product (whether to the person who suffered the damage, to the producer of any product in which the product in question is comprised or to any other person) shall be liable for the damage if –

(a) the person who suffered the damage requests the supplier to identify one or more of the persons (whether still in existence or not) to whom subsection (2) above applies in relation to the product;

(b) that request is made within a reasonable period after the damage occurs and at a time when it is not reasonably practicable for the person making the request to identify all those persons; and

(c) the supplier fails, within a reasonable period after receiving the request, either to comply with the request or to identify the person who supplied the product to him.

(5) Where two or more persons are liable by virtue of this Part for the same damage, their liability shall be joint and several.

(6) This section shall be without prejudice to any liability arising otherwise than by virtue of this Part.

3   Meaning of 'defect'

(1) Subject to the following provisions of this section, there is a defect in a product for the purposes of this Part if the safety of the product is not such as persons generally are entitled to expect; and for those purposes 'safety', in relation to a product, shall include safety with respect to products comprised in that product and safety in the context of risks of damage to property, as well as in the context of risks of death or personal injury.

(2) In determining for the purposes of subsection (1) above what persons generally are entitled to expect in relation to a product all the circumstances shall be taken into account, including –

(a) the manner in which, and purposes for which, the product has been marketed, its get-up, the use of any mark in relation to the product and any instructions for, or warnings with respect to, doing or refraining from doing anything with or in relation to the product;

(b) what might reasonably be expected to be done with or in relation to the product; and

(c) the time when the product was supplied by its producer to another;

and nothing in this section shall require a defect to be inferred from the fact alone that the safety of a product which is supplied after that time is greater than the safety of the product in question.

4   Defences

(1) In any civil proceedings by virtue of this Part against any person ('the person proceeded against') in respect of a defect in a product it shall be a defence for him to show –

(a) that the defect is attributable to compliance with any requirement imposed by or under any enactment or with any Community obligation; or

(b) that the person proceeded against did not at any time supply the product to another; or

(c) that the following conditions are satisfied, that is to say –

(i)   that the only supply of the product to another by the person proceeded against was otherwise than in the course of a business of that person's; and

(ii) that section 2(2) above does not apply to that person or applies to him by virtue only of things done otherwise than with a view to profit; or

(d) that the defect did not exist in the product at the relevant time; or

(e) that the state of scientific and technical knowledge at the relevant time was not such that a producer of products of the same description as the product in question might be expected to have discovered the defect if it had existed in his products while they were under his control; or

(f) that the defect –

    (i) constituted a defect in a product ('the subsequent product') in which the product in question had been comprised; and

    (ii) was wholly attributable to the design of the subsequent product or to compliance by the producer of the product in question with instructions given by the producer of the subsequent product.

(2) In this section 'the relevant time', in relation to electricity, means the time at which it was generated, being a time before it was transmitted or distributed, and in relation to any other product, means –

(a) if the person proceeded against is a person to whom subsection (2) of section 2 above applies in relation to the product, the time when he supplied the product to another;

(b) if that subsection does not apply to that person in relation to the product, the time when the product was last supplied by a person to whom that subsection does apply in relation to the product.

5   Damage giving rise to liability

(1) Subject to the following provisions of this section, in this Part 'damage' means death or personal injury or any loss of or damage to any property (including land).

(2) A person shall not be liable under section 2 above in respect of any defect in a product for the loss of or any damage to the product itself or for the loss of or any damage to the whole or any part of any product which has been supplied with the product in question comprised in it.

(3) A person shall not be liable under section 2 above for any loss of or damage to any property which, at the time it is lost or damaged, is not –

(a) of a description of property ordinarily intended for private use, occupation or consumption; and

(b) intended by the person suffering the loss or damage mainly for his own private use, occupation or consumption.

(4) No damages shall be awarded to any person by virtue of this Part in respect of any loss of or damage to any property if the amount which would fall to be so awarded to that person, apart from this subsection and any liability for interest, does not exceed £275.

(5) In determining for the purposes of this Part who has suffered any loss of or damage to property and when any such loss or damage occurred, the loss or damage shall be regarded as having occurred at the earliest time at which a person with an interest in the property had knowledge of the material facts about the loss or damage.

(6) For the purposes of subsection (5) above the material facts about any loss of or damage to any property are such facts about the loss or damage as would lead a reasonable person with an interest in the property to consider the loss or damage sufficiently serious to justify his instituting proceedings for damages against a defendant who did not dispute liability and was able to satisfy a judgment.

(7) For the purposes of subsection (5) above a person's knowledge includes knowledge which he might reasonably have been expected to acquire –

(a) from facts observable or ascertainable by him; or

(b) from facts ascertainable by him with the help of appropriate expert advice which it is reasonable for him to seek;

but a person shall not be taken by virtue of this subsection to have knowledge of a fact ascertainable by him only with the help of expert advice unless he has failed to take all reasonable steps to obtain (and, where appropriate, to act on) that advice.

(8) Subsections (5) to (7) above shall not extend to Scotland.

6   Application of certain enactments etc.

(1) Any damage for which a person is liable under section 2 above shall be deemed to have been caused –

    (a) for the purposes of the Fatal Accidents Act 1976, by that person's wrongful act, neglect or default;

(2) Where –

    (a) a person's death is caused wholly or partly by a defect in a product, or a person dies after suffering damage which has been so caused;

    (b) a request such as mentioned in paragraph (a) of subsection (3) of section 2 above is made to a supplier of the product by that person's personal representatives or, in the case of a person whose death is caused wholly or partly by the defect, by any dependant or relative of that person; and

    (c) the conditions specified in paragraphs (b) and (c) of that subsection are satisfied in relation to that request,

this Part shall have effect for the purposes of the Law Reform (Miscellaneous Provisions) Act 1934, the Fatal Accidents Act 1976 and the Damages (Scotland) Act 1976 as if liability of the supplier to that person under that subsection did not depend on that person having requested the supplier to identify certain persons or on the said conditions having been satisfied in relation to a request made by that person.

(3) Section 1 of the Congenital Disabilities (Civil Liability) Act 1976 shall have effect for the purposes of this Part as if –

    (a) a person were answerable to a child in respect of an occurrence caused wholly or partly by a defect in a product if he is or has been liable under section 2 above in respect of any effect of the occurrence on a parent of the child, or would be so liable if the occurrence caused a parent of the child to suffer damage;

    (b) the provisions of this Part relating to liability under section 2 above applied in relation to liability by virtue of paragraph (a) above under the said section 1; and

    (c) subsection (6) of the said section 1 (exclusion of liability) were omitted.

(4) Where any damage is caused partly by a defect in a product and partly by the fault of the person suffering the damage, the Law Reform (Contributory Negligence) Act 1945 and section 5 of the Fatal Accidents Act 1976 (contributory negligence) shall have effect as if the defect were the fault of every person liable by virtue of this Part for the damage caused by the defect.

(5) In subsection (4) above 'fault' has the same meaning as in the said Act of 1945.

(7) It is hereby declared that liability by virtue of this Part is to be treated as liability in tort for the purposes of any enactment conferring jurisdiction on any court with respect to any matter.

(8) Nothing in this Part shall prejudice the operation of section 12 of the Nuclear Installations Act 1965 (rights to compensation for certain breaches of duties confined to rights under that Act).

7   Prohibition on exclusions from liability

The liability of a person by virtue of this Part to a person who has suffered damage caused wholly or partly by a defect in a product, or to a dependant or relative of such a person, shall not be limited or excluded by any contract term, by any notice or by any other provision.

46   Meaning of 'supply'

(1) Subject to the following provisions of this section, references in this Act to supplying goods shall be construed as references to doing any of the following, whether as principal or agent, that is to say –

    (a) selling, hiring out or lending the goods;

    (b) entering into a hire-purchase agreement to furnish the goods;

    (c) the performance of any contract for work and materials to furnish the goods;

    (d) providing the goods in exchange for any consideration (including trading stamps) other than money;

(e) providing the goods in or in connection with the performance of any statutory function; or

(f) giving the goods as a prize or otherwise making a gift of the goods; and, in relation to gas or water, those references shall be construed as including references to providing the service by which the gas or water is made available for use.

(2) For the purposes of any reference in this Act to supplying goods, where a person ('the ostensible supplier') supplies goods to another person ('the customer') under a hire-purchase agreement, conditional sale agreement or credit-sale agreement or under an agreement for the hiring of goods (other than a hire-purchase agreement) and the ostensible supplier –

(a) carries on the business of financing the provision of goods for others by means of such agreement; and

(b) in the course of that business acquired his interest in the goods supplied to the customer as a means of financing the provision of them for the customer by a further person ('the effective supplier'),

the effective supplier and not the ostensible supplier shall be treated as supplying the goods to the customer.

Access to Medical Reports Act 1988

(1988, c. 28)

1   Right of access

It shall be the right of an individual to have access, in accordance with the provisions of this Act, to any medical report relating to the individual which is to be, or has been, supplied by a medical practitioner for employment purposes or insurance purposes.

2   Interpretation

(1) In this Act –

'the applicant' means the person referred to in section 3(1) below;

'care' includes examination, investigation or diagnosis for the purposes of, or in connection with, any form of medical treatment;

'employment purposes', in the case of any individual, means the purposes in relation to the individual of any person by whom he is or has been, or is seeking to be, employed (whether under a contract of service or otherwise);

'health professional' has the same meaning as in the Data Protection Act 1998.

'insurance purposes', in a case of any individual who has entered into, or is seeking to enter into, a contract of insurance with an insurer, means the purposes of that insurer in relation to that individual;

'insurer' means –

(a) a person who has permission under Part 4 of the Financial Services and Markets Act 2000 to effect or carry out contracts of insurance;

(b) an EEA firm of the kind mentioned in paragraph 5(d) of Schedule 3 to that Act, which has permission under paragraph 15 of that Schedule (as a result of qualifying for authorisation under paragraph 12 of that Schedule) to effect or carry out relevant contracts of insurance;

'medical practitioner' means a person registered under the Medical Act 1983;

'medical report', in the case of an individual, means a report relating to the physical or mental health of the individual prepared by a medical practitioner who is or has been responsible for the clinical care of the individual.

(1A) The definitions of 'insurance purposes' and 'insurer' in subsection (1) must be read with –

(a) section 22 of the Financial Services and Markets Act 2002;

(b) any relevant order under that section; and

(c) Schedule 2 to that Act.

(2) Any reference in this Act to the supply of a medical report for employment or insurance purposes shall be construed –

>   (a) as a reference to the supply of such a report for employment or insurance purposes which are purposes of the person who is seeking to be supplied with it; or
>
>   (b) (in the case of a report that has already been supplied) as a reference to the supply of such a report for employment or insurance purposes which, at the time of its being supplied, were purposes of the person to whom it was supplied.

3   Consent to applications for medical reports for employment or insurance purposes

(1) A person shall not apply to a medical practitioner for a medical report relating to any individual to be supplied to him for employment or insurance purposes unless –

>   (a) that person ('the applicant') has notified the individual that he proposes to make the application; and
>
>   (b) the individual has notified the applicant that he consents to the making of the application.

(2) Any notification given under subsection (1)(a) above must inform the individual of his right to withhold his consent to the making of the application, and of the following rights under this Act, namely –

>   (a) the rights arising under sections 4(1) to (3) and 6(2) below with respect to access to the report before or after it is supplied,
>
>   (b) the right to withhold consent under subsection (1) of section 5 below, and
>
>   (c) the right to request the amendment of the report under subsection (2) of that section,

as well as of the effect of section 7 below.

4   Access to reports before they are supplied

(1) An individual who gives his consent under section 3 above to the making of an application shall be entitled, when giving his consent, to state that he wishes to have access to the report to be supplied in response to the application before it is so supplied; and, if he does so, the applicant shall –

>   (a) notify the medical practitioner of that fact at the time when the application is made, and
>
>   (b) at the same time notify the individual of the making of the application;

and each such notification shall contain a statement of the effect of subsection (2) below.

(2) Where a medical practitioner is notified by the applicant under subsection (1) above that the individual in question wishes to have access to the report before it is supplied, the practitioner shall not supply the report unless –

>   (a) he has given the individual access to it and any requirements of section 5 below have been complied with, or
>
>   (b) the period of 21 days beginning with the date of the making of the application has elapsed without his having received any communication from the individual concerning arrangements for the individual to have access to it.

(3) Where a medical practitioner –

>   (a) receives an application for a medical report to be supplied for employment or insurance purposes without being notified by the applicant as mentioned in subsection (1) above, but
>
>   (b) before supplying the report receives a notification from the individual that he wishes to have access to the report before it is supplied,

the practitioner shall not supply the report unless –

>   (i) he has given the individual access to it and any requirements of section 5 below have been complied with, or
>
>   (ii) the period of 21 days beginning with the date of that notification has elapsed without his having received (either with that notification or otherwise) any communication from the individual concerning arrangements for the individual to have access to it.

(4) References in this section and section 5 below to giving an individual access to a medical report are references to –

      (a) making the report or a copy of it available for his inspection; or

      (b) supplying him with a copy of it;

and where a copy is supplied at the request, or otherwise with the consent, of the individual the practitioner may charge a reasonable fee to cover the costs of supplying it.

5   Consent to supplying of report and correction of errors

(1) Where an individual has been given access to a report under section 4 above the report shall not be supplied in response to the application in question unless the individual has notified the medical practitioner that he consents to its being so supplied.

(2) The individual shall be entitled, before giving his consent under subsection (1) above, to request the medical practitioner to amend any part of the report which the individual considers to be incorrect or misleading; and, if the individual does so, the practitioner –

      (a) if he is to any extent prepared to accede to the individual's request, shall amend the report accordingly;

      (b) if he is to any extent not prepared to accede to it but the individual requests him to attach to the report a statement of the individual's views in respect of any part of the report which he is declining to amend, shall attach such a statement to the report.

(3) Any request made by an individual under subsection (2) above shall be made in writing.

6   Retention of reports

(1) A copy of any medical report which a medical practitioner has supplied for employment or insurance purposes shall be retained by him for at least six months from the date on which it was supplied.

(2) A medical practitioner shall, if so requested by an individual, give the individual access to any medical report relating to him which the practitioner has supplied for employment or insurance purposes in the previous six months.

(3) The reference in subsection (2) above to giving an individual access to a medical report is a reference to –

      (a) making a copy of the report available for his inspection; or

      (b) supplying him with a copy of it;

and where a copy is supplied at the request, or otherwise with the consent, of the individual the practitioner may charge a reasonable fee to cover the costs of supplying it.

7   Exemptions

(1) A medical practitioner shall not be obliged to give an individual access, in accordance with the provisions of section 4(4) or 6(3) above, to any part of a medical report whose disclosure would in the opinion of the practitioner be likely to cause serious harm to the physical or mental health of the individual or others or would indicate the intentions of the practitioner in respect of the individual.

(2) A medical practitioner shall not be obliged to give an individual access, in accordance with those provisions, to any part of a medical report whose disclosure would be likely to reveal information about another person, or to reveal the identity of another person who has supplied information to the practitioner about the individual, unless –

      (a) that person has consented; or

      (b) that person is a health professional who has been involved in the care of the individual and the information relates to or has been provided by the professional in that capacity.

(3) Where it appears to a medical practitioner that subsection (1) or (2) above is applicable to any part (but not the whole) of a medical report –

      (a) he shall notify the individual of that fact; and

(b) references in the preceding sections of this Act to the individual being given access to the report shall be construed as references to his being given access to the remainder of it; and other references to the report in sections 4(4), 5(2) and 6(3) above shall similarly be construed as references to the remainder of the report.

(4) Where it appears to a medical practitioner that subsection (1) or (2) above is applicable to the whole of a medical report –

(a) he shall notify the individual of that fact; but

(b) he shall not supply the report unless he is notified by the individual that the individual consents to its being supplied;

and accordingly, if he is so notified by the individual, the restrictions imposed by section 4(2) and (3) above on the supply of the report shall not have effect in relation to it.

8   Application to the court

(1) If a court is satisfied on the application of an individual that any person, in connection with a medical report relating to that individual, has failed or is likely to fail to comply with any requirement of this Act, the court may order that person to comply with that requirement.

(2) The jurisdiction conferred by this section shall be exercisable by a county court or, in Scotland, by the sheriff.

9   Notifications under this Act

Any notification required or authorised to be given under this Act –

(a) shall be given in writing; and

(b) may be given by post.

Health and Medicines Act 1988

(1988, c. 49)

HIV testing kits and services

23   HIV testing kits and services

(1) The Secretary of State may provide by regulations that a person –

(a) who sells or supplies to another an HIV testing kit or any component part of such a kit;

(b) who provides another with HIV testing services; or

(c) who advertises such kits or component parts or such services,

shall be guilty of an offence.

(4) If any person contravenes regulations under this section, he shall be liable –

(a) on summary conviction to a fine not exceeding the statutory maximum; and

(b) on conviction on indictment to a fine or to imprisonment for a term of not more than two years, or to both.

(5) Where an offence under this section which is committed by a body corporate is proved to have been committed with the consent or connivance of, or to be attributable to any neglect on the part of, any director, manager, secretary or other similar officer of the body corporate, or any person who was purporting to act in any such capacity, he as well as the body corporate shall be guilty of that offence and shall be liable to be proceeded against and punished accordingly.

(6) In this section –

'HIV' means Human Immunodeficiency Virus of any type;

'HIV testing kit' means a diagnostic kit the purpose of which is to detect the presence of HIV or HIV antibodies; and

'HIV testing services' means diagnostic services the purpose of which is to detect the presence of HIV or HIV antibodies in identifiable individuals.

Children Act 1989

(1989, c. 41)

Part I Introductory

1 Welfare of the child

(1) When a court determines any question with respect to –

(a) the upbringing of a child; or

(b) the administration of a child's property or the application of any income arising from it,

the child's welfare shall be the court's paramount consideration.

(2) In any proceedings in which any question with respect to the upbringing of a child arises, the court shall have regard to the general principle that any delay in determining the question is likely to prejudice the welfare of the child.

(3) In the circumstances mentioned in subsection (4), a court shall have regard in particular to –

(a) the ascertainable wishes and feelings of the child concerned (considered in the light of his age and understanding);

(b) his physical, emotional and educational needs;

(c) the likely effect on him of any change in his circumstances;

(d) his age, sex, background and any characteristics of his which the court considers relevant;

(e) any harm which he has suffered or is at risk of suffering;

(f) how capable each of his parents, and any other person in relation to whom the court considers the question to be relevant, is of meeting his needs;

(g) the range of powers available to the court under this Act in the proceedings in question.

(4) The circumstances are that –

(a) the court is considering whether to make, vary or discharge a section 8 order, and the making, variation or discharge of the order is opposed by any party to the proceedings; or

(b) the court is considering whether to make, vary or discharge a special guardianship order or an order under Part IV.

(5) Where a court is considering whether or not to make one or more orders under this Act with respect to a child, it shall not make the order or any of the orders unless it considers that doing so would be better for the child than making no order at all.

2 Parental responsibility for children

(1) Where a child's father and mother were married to each other at the time of his birth, they shall each have parental responsibility for the child.

(2) Where a child's father and mother were not married to each other at the time of his birth –

(a) the mother shall have parental responsibility for the child;

(b) the father shall have parental responsibility for the child if he has acquired it (and has not ceased to have it) in accordance with the provisions of this Act.

(3) References in this Act to a child whose father and mother were, or (as the case may be) were not, married to each other at the time of his birth must be read with section 1 of the Family Law Reform Act 1987 (which extends their meaning).

(4) The rule of law that a father is the natural guardian of his legitimate child is abolished.

(5) More than one person may have parental responsibility for the same child at the same time.

(6) A person who has parental responsibility for a child at any time shall not cease to have that responsibility solely because some other person subsequently acquires parental responsibility for the child.

(7) Where more than one person has parental responsibility for a child, each of them may act alone and without the other (or others) in meeting that responsibility; but nothing in this Part shall be taken to affect the operation of any enactment which requires the consent of more than one person in a matter affecting the child.

(8) The fact that a person has parental responsibility for a child shall not entitle him to act in any way which would be incompatible with any order made with respect to the child under this Act.

(9) A person who has parental responsibility for a child may not surrender or transfer any part of that responsibility to another but may arrange for some or all of it to be met by one or more persons acting on his behalf.

(10) The person with whom any such arrangement is made may himself be a person who already has parental responsibility for the child concerned.

(11) The making of any such arrangement shall not affect any liability of the person making it which may arise from any failure to meet any part of his parental responsibility for the child concerned.

3   Meaning of 'parental responsibility'

(1) In this Act 'parental responsibility' means all the rights, duties, powers, responsibilities and authority which by law a parent of a child has in relation to the child and his property.

(2) It also includes the rights, powers and duties which a guardian of the child's estate (appointed, before the commencement of section 5, to act generally) would have had in relation to the child and his property.

(3) The rights referred to in subsection (2) include, in particular, the right of the guardian to receive or recover in his own name, for the benefit of the child, property of whatever description and wherever situated which the child is entitled to receive or recover.

(4) The fact that a person has, or does not have, parental responsibility for a child shall not affect –

    (a) any obligation which he may have in relation to the child (such as a statutory duty to maintain the child); or

    (b) any rights which, in the event of the child's death, he (or any other person) may have in relation to the child's property.

(5) A person who –

    (a) does not have parental responsibility for a particular child; but

    (b) has care of the child,

may (subject to the provisions of this Act) do what is reasonable in all the circumstances of the case for the purpose of safeguarding or promoting the child's welfare.

4   Acquisition of parental responsibility by father

(1) Where a child's father and mother were not married to each other at the time of his birth the father shall acquire parental responsibility if –

    (a) he becomes registered as the child's father under any of the enactments specified in subsection (1A);

    (b) he and the child's mother make an agreement (a 'parental responsibility agreement') providing for him to have parental responsibility for the child; or

    (c) the court, on his application, orders that he shall have parental responsibility for the child.

(1A) The enactments referred to in subsection (1)(a) are –

    (a) paragraphs (a), (b) and (c) of section 10(1) and of section 10A(1) of the Births and Deaths Registration Act 1953;

(2) No parental responsibility agreement shall have effect for the purposes of this Act unless –

    (a) it is made in the form prescribed by regulations made by the Secretary of State; and

    (b) where regulations are made by the Secretary of State prescribing the manner in which such agreements must be recorded, it is recorded in the prescribed manner.

(2A) A person who has acquired parental responsibility under subsection (1) shall cease to have that responsibility only if the court so orders.

(3) The court may make an order under subsection (2A) on the application –

(a) of any person who has parental responsibility for the child; or

(b) with the leave of the court, of the child himself,

subject, in the case of parental responsibility acquired under subsection (1)(c), to section 12(4).

(4) The court may only grant leave under subsection (3)(b) if it is satisfied that the child has sufficient understanding to make the proposed application.

5 Appointment of guardians

(1) Where an application with respect to a child is made to the court by any individual, the court may by order appoint that individual to be the child's guardian if –

(a) the child has no parent with parental responsibility for him; or

(b) a residence order has been made with respect to the child in favour of a parent or guardian or special guardian of his who has died while the order was in force; or

(c) paragraph (b) does not apply, and the child's only or last surviving special guardian dies.

(2) The power conferred by subsection (1) may also be exercised in any family proceedings if the court considers that the order should be made even though no application has been made for it.

(3) A parent who has parental responsibility for his child may appoint another individual to be the child's guardian in the event of his death.

(4) A guardian of a child may appoint another individual to take his place as the child's guardian in the event of his death; and a special guardian of a child may appoint another individual to be the child's guardian in the event of his death.

(5) An appointment under subsection (3) or (4) shall not have effect unless it is made in writing, is dated and is signed by the person making the appointment or –

(a) in the case of an appointment made by a will which is not signed by the testator, is signed at the direction of the testator in accordance with the requirements of section 9 of the Wills Act 1837; or

(b) in any other case, is signed at the direction of the person making the appointment, in his presence and in the presence of two witnesses who each attest the signature.

(6) A person appointed as a child's guardian under this section shall have parental responsibility for the child concerned.

(7) Where –

(a) on the death of any person making an appointment under subsection (3) or (4), the child concerned has no parent with parental responsibility for him; or

(b) immediately before the death of any person making such an appointment, a residence order in his favour was in force with respect to the child, or he was the child's only (or last surviving) special guardian,

the appointment shall take effect on the death of that person.

(8) Where, on the death of any person making an appointment under subsection (3) or (4) –

(a) the child concerned has a parent with parental responsibility for him; and

(b) subsection (7)(b) does not apply,

the appointment shall take effect when the child no longer has a parent who has parental responsibility for him.

(9) Subsections (1) and (7) do not apply if the residence order referred to in paragraph (b) of those subsections was also made in favour of a surviving parent of the child.

(10) Nothing in this section shall be taken to prevent an appointment under subsection (3) or (4) being made by two or more persons acting jointly.

(11) Subject to any provision made by rules of court, no court shall exercise the High Court's inherent jurisdiction to appoint a guardian of the estate of any child.

(12) Where rules of court are made under subsection (11) they may prescribe the circumstances in which, and conditions subject to which, an appointment of such a guardian may be made.

(13) A guardian of a child may only be appointed in accordance with the provisions of this section.

Part II Orders with Respect to Children in Family Proceedings

General

8   Residence, contact and other orders with respect to children

(1) In this Act –

'a contact order' means an order requiring the person with whom a child lives, or is to live, to allow the child to visit or stay with the person named in the order, or for that person and the child otherwise to have contact with each other;

'a prohibited steps order' means an order that no step which could be taken by a parent in meeting his parental responsibility for a child, and which is of a kind specified in the order, shall be taken by any person without the consent of the court;

'a residence order' means an order settling the arrangements to be made as to the person with whom a child is to live; and

'a specific issue order' means an order giving directions for the purpose of determining a specific question which has arisen, or which may arise, in connection with any aspect of parental responsibility for a child.

(2) In this Act 'a section 8 order' means any of the orders mentioned in subsection (1) and any order varying or discharging such an order.

(3) For the purposes of this Act 'family proceedings' means (subject to subsection (5)) any proceedings –

(a) under the inherent jurisdiction of the High Court in relation to children; and

(b) under the enactments mentioned in subsection (4),

but does not include proceedings on an application for leave under section 100(3).

(4) The enactments are –

(a) Parts I, II and IV of this Act;

(b) the Matrimonial Causes Act 1973;

(ba) Schedule 5 to the Civil Partnership Act 2004;

(d) the Adoption and Children Act 2002;

(e) the Domestic Proceedings and Magistrates' Courts Act 1978;

(ea) Schedule 6 to the Civil Partnership Act 2004;

(g) Part III of the Matrimonial and Family Proceedings Act 1984;

(h) the Family Law Act 1996;

(i) sections 11 and 12 of the Crime and Disorder Act 1998.

9   Restrictions on making section 8 orders

(1) No court shall make any section 8 order, other than a residence order, with respect to a child who is in the care of a local authority.

(2) No application may be made by a local authority for a residence order or contact order and no court shall make such an order in favour of a local authority.

(3) A person who is, or was at any time within the last six months, a local authority foster parent of a child may not apply for leave to apply for a section 8 order with respect to the child unless –

(a) he has the consent of the authority;

(b) he is a relative of the child; or

(c) the child has lived with him for at least three years preceding the application.

(5) No court shall exercise its powers to make a specific issue order or prohibited steps order –

    (a) with a view to achieving a result which could be achieved by making a residence or contact order; or

    (b) in any way which is denied to the High Court (by section 100(2)) in the exercise of its inherent jurisdiction with respect to children.

(6) Subject to section 12(5) no court shall make any section 8 order which is to have effect for a period which will end after the child has reached the age of sixteen unless it is satisfied that the circumstances of the case are exceptional.

(7) No court shall make any section 8 order, other than one varying or discharging such an order, with respect to a child who has reached the age of sixteen unless it is satisfied that the circumstances of the case are exceptional.

10   Power of court to make section 8 orders

(1) In any family proceedings in which a question arises with respect to the welfare of any child, the court may make a section 8 order with respect to the child if –

    (a) an application for the order has been made by a person who –

        (i)   is entitled to apply for a section 8 order with respect to the child; or

        (ii) has obtained the leave of the court to make the application; or

    (b) the court considers that the order should be made even though no such application has been made.

(2) The court may also make a section 8 order with respect to any child on the application of a person who –

    (a) is entitled to apply for a section 8 order with respect to the child; or

    (b) has obtained the leave of the court to make the application.

(3) This section is subject to the restrictions imposed by section 9.

(4) The following persons are entitled to apply to the court for any section 8 order with respect to a child –

    (a) any parent or guardian, or special guardian of the child;

    (aa)any person who by virtue of section 4A has parental responsibility for the child;

    (b) any person in whose favour a residence order is in force with respect to the child.

(5) The following persons are entitled to apply for a residence or contact order with respect to a child –

    (a) any party to a marriage (whether or not subsisting) in relation to whom the child is a child of the family;

    (aa)any person with whom the child has lived for a period of at least three years;

    (b) any person who –

        (i)   in any case where a residence order is in force with respect to the child, has the consent of each of the persons in whose favour the order was made;

        (ii) in any case where the child is in the care of a local authority, has the consent of that authority; or

        (iii) in any other case, has the consent of each of those (if any) who have parental responsibility for the child.

(5A) A local authority foster parent is entitled to apply for a residence order with respect to a child if the child has lived with him for a period of at least one year immediately preceding the application.

(6) A person who would not otherwise be entitled (under the previous provisions of this section) to apply for the variation or discharge of a section 8 order shall be entitled to do so if –

    (a) the order was made on his application; or

    (b) in the case of a contact order, he is named in the order.

(7) Any person who falls within a category of person prescribed by rules of court is entitled to apply for any such section 8 order as may be prescribed in relation to that category of person.

(7A) If a special guardianship order is in force with respect to a child, an application for a residence order may only be made with respect to him, if, apart from this subsection the leave of the court is not required, with such leave.

(8) Where the person applying for leave to make an application for a section 8 order is the child concerned, the court may only grant leave if it is satisfied that he has sufficient understanding to make the proposed application for the section 8 order.

(9) Where the person applying for leave to make an application for a section 8 order is not the child concerned, the court shall, in deciding whether or not to grant leave, have particular regard to –

    (a) the nature of the proposed application for the section 8 order;

    (b) the applicant's connection with the child;

    (c) any risk there might be of that proposed application disrupting the child's life to such an extent that he would be harmed by it; and

    (d) where the child is being looked after by a local authority –

        (i) the authority's plans for the child's future; and

        (ii) the wishes and feelings of the child's parents.

(10) The period of three years mentioned in subsection (5)(b) need not be continuous but must not have begun more than five years before, or ended more than three months before, the making of the application.

Part IV Care and Supervision

General

31   Care and supervision orders

    (1) On the application of any local authority or authorised person, the court may make an order –

        (a) placing the child with respect to whom the application is made in the care of a designated local authority.

    (2) A court may only make a care order or supervision order if it is satisfied –

        (a) that the child concerned is suffering, or is likely to suffer, significant harm; and

        (b) that the harm, or likelihood of harm, is attributable to –

            (i) the care given to the child, or likely to be given to him if the order were not made, not being what it would be reasonable to expect a parent to give to him; or

            (ii) the child's being beyond parental control.

    (3) No care order or supervision order may be made with respect to a child who has reached the age of seventeen (or sixteen, in the case of a child who is married).

    (5) The court may –

        (a) on an application for a care order, make a supervision order;

        (b) on an application for a supervision order, make a care order.

    (6) Where an authorised person proposes to make an application under this section he shall –

        (a) if it is reasonably practicable to do so; and

        (b) before making the application,

consult the local authority appearing to him to be the authority in whose area the child concerned is ordinarily resident.

    (8) The local authority designated in a care order must be –

        (a) the authority within whose area the child is ordinarily resident; or

        (b) where the child does not reside in the area of a local authority, the authority within whose area any circumstances arose in consequence of which the order is being made.

    (9) In this section –

'authorised person' means –

        (a) the National Society for the Prevention of Cruelty to Children and any of its officers; and

(b) any person authorised by order of the Secretary of State to bring proceedings under this section and any officer of a body which is so authorised;

'harm' means ill-treatment or the impairment of health or development including, for example, impairment suffered from seeing or hearing the ill-treatment of another;

'development' means physical, intellectual, emotional, social or behavioural development;

'health' means physical or mental health; and

'ill-treatment' includes sexual abuse and forms of ill-treatment which are not physical.

(10) Where the question of whether harm suffered by a child is significant turns on the child's health or development, his health or development shall be compared with that which could reasonably be expected of a similar child.

(11) In this Act –

'a care order' means (subject to section 105(1)) an order under subsection (1)(a) and (except where express provision to the contrary is made) includes an interim care order made under section 38; and

'a supervision order' means an order under subsection (1)(b) and (except where express provision to the contrary is made) includes an interim supervision order made under section 38.

Care orders

33   Effect of care order

(1) Where a care order is made with respect to a child it shall be the duty of the local authority designated by the order to receive the child into their care and to keep him in their care while the order remains in force.

(2) Where –

(a) a care order has been made with respect to a child on the application of an authorised person; but

(b) the local authority designated by the order was not informed that that person proposed to make the application,

the child may be kept in the care of that person until received into the care of the authority.

(3) While a care order is in force with respect to a child, the local authority designated by the order shall –

(a) have parental responsibility for the child; and

(b) have the power (subject to the following provisions of this section) to determine the extent to which

(i)   a parent, guardian or special guardian of the child; or

(ii)   a person who by virtue of section 4A has parental responsibility for the child,

may meet his parental responsibility for him.

(4) The authority may not exercise the power in subsection (3)(b) unless they are satisfied that it is necessary to do so in order to safeguard or promote the child's welfare.

(5) Nothing in subsection (3)(b) shall prevent a person mentioned in that provision who has care of the child from doing what is reasonable in all the circumstances of the case for the purpose of safeguarding or promoting his welfare.

(6) While a care order is in force with respect to a child, the local authority designated by the order shall not –

(a) cause the child to be brought up in any religious persuasion other than that in which he would have been brought up if the order had not been made; or

(b) have the right –

(ii)   to agree or refuse to agree to the making of an adoption order, or an order under section 84 of the Adoption and Children Act 2002, with respect to the child; or

(iii) to appoint a guardian for the child.

(7) While a care order is in force with respect to a child, no person may –

(a) cause the child to be known by a new surname; or

(b) remove him from the United Kingdom,

without either the written consent of every person who has parental responsibility for the child or the leave of the court.

(8) Subsection (7)(b) does not –

(a) prevent the removal of such a child, for a period of less than one month, by the authority in whose care he is; or

(b) apply to arrangements for such a child to live outside England and Wales (which are governed by paragraph 19 of Schedule 2).

(9) The power in subsection (3)(b) is subject (in addition to being subject to the provisions of this section) to any right, duty, power, responsibility or authority which a person mentioned in that provision has in relation to the child and his property by virtue of any other enactment.

Part V Protection of Children

43   Child assessment orders

(1) On the application of a local authority or authorised person for an order to be made under this section with respect to a child, the court may make the order if, but only if, it is satisfied that –

(a) the applicant has reasonable cause to suspect that the child is suffering, or is likely to suffer, significant harm;

(b) an assessment of the state of the child's health or development, or of the way in which he has been treated, is required to enable the applicant to determine whether or not the child is suffering, or is likely to suffer, significant harm; and

(c) it is unlikely that such an assessment will be made, or be satisfactory, in the absence of an order under this section.

(2) In this Act 'a child assessment order' means an order under this section.

(3) A court may treat an application under this section as an application for an emergency protection order.

(4) No court shall make a child assessment order if it is satisfied –

(a) that there are grounds for making an emergency protection order with respect to the child; and

(b) that it ought to make such an order rather than a child assessment order.

(5) A child assessment order shall –

(a) specify the date by which the assessment is to begin; and

(b) have effect for such period, not exceeding 7 days beginning with that date, as may be specified in the order.

(6) Where a child assessment order is in force with respect to a child it shall be the duty of any person who is in a position to produce the child –

(a) to produce him to such person as may be named in the order; and

(b) to comply with such directions relating to the assessment of the child as the court thinks fit to specify in the order.

(7) A child assessment order authorises any person carrying out the assessment, or any part of the assessment, to do so in accordance with the terms of the order.

(8) Regardless of subsection (7), if the child is of sufficient understanding to make an informed decision he may refuse to submit to a medical or psychiatric examination or other assessment.

(9) The child may only be kept away from home –

(a) in accordance with directions specified in the order;

(b) if it is necessary for the purposes of the assessment; and

(c) for such period or periods as may be specified in the order.

(10) Where the child is to be kept away from home, the order shall contain such directions as the court thinks fit with regard to the contact that he must be allowed to have with other persons while away from home.

(11) Any person making an application for a child assessment order shall take such steps as are reasonably practicable to ensure that notice of the application is given to –

    (a) the child's parents;

    (b) any person who is not a parent of his but who has parental responsibility for him;

    (c) any other person caring for the child;

    (d) any person in whose favour a contact order is in force with respect to the child;

    (e) any person who is allowed to have contact with the child by virtue of an order under section 34; and

    (f) the child,

before the hearing of the application.

(12) Rules of court may make provision as to the circumstances in which –

    (a) any of the persons mentioned in subsection (11); or

    (b) such other person as may be specified in the rules,

may apply to the court for a child assessment order to be varied or discharged.

(13) In this section 'authorised person' means a person who is an authorised person for the purposes of section 31.

100 Restrictions on use of wardship jurisdiction

(1) Section 7 of the Family Law Reform Act 1969 (which gives the High Court power to place a ward of court in the care, or under the supervision, of a local authority) shall cease to have effect.

(2) No court shall exercise the High Court's inherent jurisdiction with respect to children –

    (a) so as to require a child to be placed in the care, or put under the supervision, of a local authority;

    (b) so as to require a child to be accommodated by or on behalf of a local authority;

    (c) so as to make a child who is the subject of a care order a ward of court; or

    (d) for the purpose of conferring on any local authority power to determine any question which has arisen, or which may arise, in connection with any aspect of parental responsibility for a child.

(3) No application for any exercise of the court's inherent jurisdiction with respect to children may be made by a local authority unless the authority have obtained the leave of the court.

(4) The court may only grant leave if it is satisfied that –

    (a) the result which the authority wish to achieve could not be achieved through the making of any order of a kind to which subsection (5) applies; and

    (b) there is reasonable cause to believe that if the court's inherent jurisdiction is not exercised with respect to the child he is likely to suffer significant harm.

(5) This subsection applies to any order –

    (a) made otherwise than in the exercise of the court's inherent jurisdiction; and

    (b) which the local authority is entitled to apply for (assuming, in the case of any application which may only be made with leave, that leave is granted).

Schedule 3 Supervision Orders

Meaning of 'responsible person'

1. In this Schedule, 'the responsible person', in relation to a supervised child, means –

    (a) any person who has parental responsibility for the child; and

    (b) any other person with whom the child is living.

Power of supervisor to give directions to supervised child

2.—(1) A supervision order may require the supervised child to comply with any directions given from time to time by the supervisor which require him to do all or any of the following things –

    (a) to live at a place or places specified in the directions for a period or periods so specified;

    (b) to present himself to a person or persons specified in the directions at a place or places and on a day or days so specified;

    (c) to participate in activities specified in the directions on a day or days so specified.

(2) It shall be for the supervisor to decide whether, and to what extent, he exercises his power to give directions and to decide the form of any directions which he gives.

(3) Sub-paragraph (1) does not confer on a supervisor power to give directions in respect of any medical or psychiatric examination or treatment (which are matters dealt with in paragraphs 4 and 5).

Psychiatric and medical examinations

4.—(1) A supervision order may require the supervised child –

    (a) to submit to a medical or psychiatric examination; or

    (b) to submit to any such examination from time to time as directed by the supervisor.

(2) Any such examination shall be required to be conducted –

    (a) by, or under the direction of, such registered medical practitioner as may be specified in the order;

    (b) at a place specified in the order and at which the supervised child is to attend as a non-resident patient; or

    (c) at –

        (i) a health service hospital; or

        (ii) in the case of a psychiatric examination, a hospital, independent hospital or care home, at which the child is, or is to attend as, a resident patient.

(3) A requirement of a kind mentioned in sub-paragraph (2)(c) shall not be included unless the court is satisfied, on the evidence of a registered medical practitioner, that –

    (a) the child may be suffering from a physical or mental condition that requires, and may be susceptible to, treatment; and

    (b) a period as a resident patient is necessary if the examination is to be carried out properly.

(4) No court shall include a requirement under this paragraph in a supervision order unless it is satisfied that –

    (a) where the child has sufficient understanding to make an informed decision, he consents to its inclusion; and

    (b) satisfactory arrangements have been, or can be, made for the examination.

Psychiatric and medical treatment

5.—(1) Where a court which proposes to make or vary a supervision order is satisfied, on the evidence of a registered medical practitioner approved for the purposes of section 12 of the Mental Health Act 1983, that the mental condition of the supervised child –

    (a) is such as requires, and may be susceptible to, treatment; but

    (b) is not such as to warrant his detention in pursuance of a hospital order under Part III of that Act,

the court may include in the order a requirement that the supervised child shall, for a period specified in the order, submit to such treatment as is so specified.

(2) The treatment specified in accordance with sub-paragraph (1) must be –

    (a) by, or under the direction of, such registered medical practitioner as may be specified in the order;

    (b) as a non-resident patient at such a place as may be so specified; or

    (c) as a resident patient in a hospital, independent hospital or care home.

(3) Where a court which proposes to make or vary a supervision order is satisfied, on the evidence of a registered medical practitioner, that the physical condition of the supervised child is such as requires, and may be susceptible to, treatment, the court may include in the order a requirement that the supervised child shall, for a period specified in the order, submit to such treatment as is so specified.

(4) The treatment specified in accordance with sub-paragraph (3) must be –

    (a) by, or under the direction of, such registered medical practitioner as may be specified in the order;

    (b) as a non-resident patient at such place as may be so specified; or

    (c) as a resident patient in a health service hospital.

(5) No court shall include a requirement under this paragraph in a supervision order unless it is satisfied –

    (a) where the child has sufficient understanding to make an informed decision, that he consents to its inclusion; and

    (b) that satisfactory arrangements have been, or can be, made for the treatment.

(6) If a medical practitioner by whom or under whose direction a supervised person is being treated in pursuance of a requirement included in a supervision order by virtue of this paragraph is unwilling to continue to treat or direct the treatment of the supervised child or is of the opinion that –

    (a) the treatment should be continued beyond the period specified in the order;

    (b) the supervised child needs different treatment;

    (c) he is not susceptible to treatment; or

    (d) he does not require further treatment,

the practitioner shall make a report in writing to that effect to the supervisor.

Access to Health Records Act 1990

(1990, c. 23)

Preliminary

1   'Health record' and related expressions

(1) In this Act 'health record' means a record which –

    (a) consists of information relating to the physical or mental health of an individual who can be identified from that information, or from that and other information in the possession of the holder of the record; and

    (b) has been made by or on behalf of a health professional in connection with the care of that individual.

(2) In this Act 'holder', in relation to a health record, means –

    (a) in the case of a record made by a health professional performing primary medical services under a general medical services contract made with a Primary Care Trust or Local Health Board, the person or body who entered into the contract with the Trust or Board (or, in a case where more than one person so entered into the contract, any such person);

    (aa) in the case of a record made by a health professional performing such services in accordance with arrangements under section 92 or 107 of the National Health Service Act 2006, or section 50 or 64 of the National Health Service (Wales) Act 2006 with a Primary Care Trust, Strategic Health Authority or Local Health Board, the person or body which made the arrangements with the Trust, Authority or Board (or, in a case where more than one person so made the arrangements, any such person);

    (b) in the case of a record made by a health professional for purposes connected with the provision of health services by a health service body (and not falling within paragraph (aa) above), the health service body by which or on whose behalf the record is held;

    (c) in any other case, the health professional by whom or on whose behalf the record is held;

(3) In this Act 'patient', in relation to a health record, means the individual in connection with whose care the record has been made.

2   Health professionals

In this Act 'health professional' has the same meaning as in the Data Protection Act 1998.

Main provisions

3   Right of access to health records

(1) An application for access to a health record, or to any part of a health record, may be made to the holder of the record by any of the following, namely –

  (f) where the patient has died, the patient's personal representative and any person who may have a claim arising out of the patient's death.

(2) Subject to section 4 below, where an application is made under subsection (1) above the holder shall, within the requisite period, give access to the record, or the part of a record, to which the application relates –

  (a) in the case of a record, by allowing the applicant to inspect the record or, where section 5 below applies, an extract setting out so much of the record as is not excluded by that section;

  (b) in the case of a part of a record, by allowing the applicant to inspect an extract setting out that part or, where that section applies, so much of that part as is not so excluded; or

  (c) in either case, if the applicant so requires, by supplying him with a copy of the record or extract.

(3) Where any information contained in a record or extract which is so allowed to be inspected, or a copy of which is so supplied, is expressed in terms which are not intelligible without explanation, an explanation of those terms shall be provided with the record or extract, or supplied with the copy.

(4) No fee shall be required for giving access under subsection (2) above other than the following, namely –

  (a) where access is given to a record, or part of a record, none of which was made after the beginning of the period of 40 days immediately preceding the date of the application, a fee not exceeding such maximum as may be prescribed for the purposes of this section by regulations under section 7 of the Data Protection Act 1998; and

  (b) where a copy of a record or extract is supplied to the applicant, a fee not exceeding the cost of making the copy and (where applicable) the cost of posting it to him.

(5) For the purposes of subsection (2) above the requisite period is –

  (a) where the application relates to a record, or part of a record, none of which was made before the beginning of the period of 40 days immediately preceding the date of the application, the period of 21 days beginning with that date;

  (b) in any other case, the period of 40 days beginning with that date.

(6) Where –

  (a) an application under subsection (1) above does not contain sufficient information to enable the holder of the record to identify the patient or, to satisfy himself that the applicant is entitled to make the application; and

  (b) within the period of 14 days beginning with the date of the application, the holder of the record requests the applicant to furnish him with such further information as he may reasonably require for that purpose,

subsection (5) above shall have effect as if for any reference to that date there were substituted a reference to the date on which that further information is so furnished.

4   Cases where right of access may be wholly excluded

(3) Where an application is made under subsection (1)(f) of section 3 above, access shall not be given under subsection (2) of that section if the record includes a note, made at the patient's request, that he did not wish access to be given on such an application.

5   Cases where right of access may be partially excluded

(1) Access shall not be given under section 3(2) above to any part of a health record –

    (a) which, in the opinion of the holder of the record, would disclose –

        (i) information likely to cause serious harm to the physical or mental health of any individual; or

        (ii) information relating to or provided by an individual, other than the patient, who could be identified from that information; or

    (b) which was made before the commencement of this Act.

(2) Subsection (1)(a)(ii) above shall not apply –

    (a) where the individual concerned has consented to the application; or

    (b) where that individual is a health professional who has been involved in the care of the patient;

and subsection (1)(b) above shall not apply where and to the extent that, in the opinion of the holder of the record, the giving of access is necessary in order to make intelligible any part of the record to which access is required to be given under section 3(2) above.

(3) Access shall not be given under section 3(2) to any part of a health record which, in the opinion of the holder of the record, would disclose –

    (a) information provided by the patient in the expectation that it would not be disclosed to the applicant; or

    (b) information obtained as a result of any examination or investigation to which the patient consented in the expectation that the information would not be so disclosed.

(4) Where an application is made under subsection (1)(f) of section 3 above, access shall not be given under subsection (2) of that section to any part of the record which, in the opinion of the holder of the record, would disclose information which is not relevant to any claim which may arise out of the patient's death.

(5) The Secretary of State may be regulations provide that, in such circumstances as may be prescribed by the regulations, access shall not be given under section 3(2) above to any part of a health record which satisfies such conditions as may be so prescribed.

6   Correction of inaccurate health records

(1) Where a person considers that any information contained in a health record, or any part of a health record, to which he has been given access under section 3(2) above is inaccurate, he may apply to the holder of the record for the necessary correction to be made.

(2) On an application under subsection (1) above, the holder of the record shall –

    (a) if he is satisfied that the information is inaccurate, make the necessary correction;

    (b) if he is not so satisfied, make in the part of the record in which the information is contained a note of the matters in respect of which the information is considered by the applicant to be inaccurate; and

    (c) in either case, without requiring any fee, supply the applicant with a copy of the correction or note.

(3) In this section 'inaccurate' means incorrect, misleading or incomplete.

7   Duty of health service bodies etc. to take advice

(1) A health service body shall take advice from the appropriate health professional before they decide whether they are satisfied as to any matter for the purposes of this Act, or form an opinion as to any matter for those purposes.

(2) In this section 'the appropriate health professional', in relation to a health service body means –

    (a) where, for purposes connected with the provision of health services by the body, one or more medical or dental practitioners are currently responsible for the clinical care of the patient, that practitioner or, as the case may be, such one of those practitioners as is the most suitable to advise the body on the matter in question;

(b) where paragraph (a) above does not apply but one or more medical or dental practitioners are available who, for purposes connected with the provision of such services by the body, have been responsible for the clinical care of the patient, that practitioner or, as the case may be, such one of those practitioners as was most recently so responsible; and

(c) where neither paragraph (a) nor paragraph (b) above applies, a health professional who has the necessary experience and qualifications to advise the body on the matter in question.

Supplemental

8   Applications to the court

(1) Subject to subsection (2) below, where the court is satisfied, on an application made by the person concerned within such period as may be prescribed by rules of court, that the holder of a health record has failed to comply with any requirement of this Act, the court may order the holder to comply with that requirement.

(2) The court shall not entertain an application under subsection (1) above unless it is satisfied that the applicant has taken all such steps to secure compliance with the requirement as may be prescribed by regulations made by the Secretary of State.

(3) For the purposes of subsection (2) above, the Secretary of State may by regulations require the holders of health records to make such arrangements for dealing with complaints that they have failed to comply with any requirements of this Act as may be prescribed by the regulations.

(4) For the purpose of determining any question whether an applicant is entitled to be given access under section 3(2) above to any health record, or any part of a health record, the court –

(a) may require the record or part to be made available for its own inspection; but

(b) shall not, pending determination of that question in the applicant's favour, require the record or part to be disclosed to him or his representatives whether by discovery (or, in Scotland, recovery) or otherwise.

(5) The jurisdiction conferred by this section shall be exercisable by the High Court or a county court or, in Scotland, by the Court of Session or the sheriff.

9   Avoidance of certain contractual terms

Any term or condition of a contract shall be void in so far as it purports to require an individual to supply any other person with a copy of a health record, or of an extract from a health record, to which he has been given access under section 3(2) above.

10   Regulations and orders

(1) Regulations under this Act may make different provision for different cases or classes of cases including, in particular, different provision for different health records or classes of health records.

11   Interpretation

In this Act –

'application' means an application in writing and 'apply' shall be construed accordingly;

'care' includes examination, investigation, diagnosis and treatment;

'general medical services contract' means a contract under section 84 of the National Health Service Act 2006 or section 42 of the National Health Service (Wales) Act 2006;

'health service body' means –

(a) a Strategic Health Authority, Health Authority, Special Health Authority or Primary Care Trust;

(b) a Health Board;

(c) a State Hospital Management Committee constituted under section 91 of the Mental Health (Scotland) Act 1984;

(d) a National Health Service trust first established under section 5 of the National Health Service and Community Care Act 1990, section 25 of the National Health Service Act 2006 or section 18 of the National Health Service (Wales) Act 2006 or section 12A of the National Health Service (Scotland) Act 1978;

(e) an NHS foundation trust;

'information', in relation to a health record, includes any expression of opinion about the patient;

'make', in relation to such a record, includes compile;

'Primary Care Trust' means a Primary Care Trust established under section 18 of the National Health Service Act 2006.

'Special Health Authority' means a Special Health Authority established under section 28 of the National Health Service Act 2006 or section 22 of the National Health Service (Wales) Act 2006.

'Strategic Health Authority' means a Strategic Health Authority established under section 13 of the National Health Service Act 2006.

Human Fertilisation and Embryology Act 1990

(1990, c. 37)

Principal terms used

1   Meaning of 'embryo', 'gamete' and associated expressions

(1) In this Act, except where otherwise stated –

(a) embryo means a live human embryo where fertilisation is complete, and

(b) references to an embryo include an egg in the process of fertilisation,

and, for this purpose, fertilisation is not complete until the appearance of a two cell zygote.

(2) This Act, so far as it governs bringing about the creation of an embryo, applies only to bringing about the creation of an embryo outside the human body; and in this Act –

(a) references to embryos the creation of which was brought about *in vitro* (in their application to those where fertilisation is complete) are to those where fertilisation began outside the human body whether or not it was completed there, and

(b) references to embryos taken from a woman do not include embryos whose creation was brought about *in vitro*.

(3) This Act, so far as it governs the keeping or use of an embryo, applies only to keeping or using an embryo outside the human body.

(4) References in this Act to gametes, eggs or sperm, except where otherwise stated, are to live human gametes, eggs or sperm but references below in this Act to gametes or eggs do not include eggs in the process of fertilisation.

2   Other terms

(1) In this Act –

'the Authority' means the Human Fertilisation and Embryology Authority established under section 5 of this Act,

'directions' means directions under section 23 of this Act,

'licence' means a licence under Schedule 2 to this Act and, in relation to a licence,

'the person responsible' has the meaning given by section 17 of this Act, and

'treatment services' means medical, surgical or obstetric services provided to the public or a section of the public for the purpose of assisting women to carry children.

(2) References in this Act to keeping, in relation to embryos or gametes, include keeping while preserved, whether preserved by cryopreservation or in any other way; and embryos or gametes so kept are referred to in this Act as 'stored' (and 'store' and 'storage' are to be interpreted accordingly).

(3) For the purpose of this Act, a woman is not to be treated as carrying a child until the embryo has become implanted.

Activities governed by the Act

3   Prohibitions in connection with embryos

(1) No person shall –

    (a) bring about the creation of an embryo, or

    (b) keep or use an embryo,

except in pursuance of a licence.

(2) No person shall place in a woman –

    (a) a live embryo other than a human embryo, or

    (b) any live gametes other than human gametes.

(3) A licence cannot authorise –

    (a) keeping or using an embryo after the appearance of the primitive streak,

    (b) placing an embryo in any animal,

    (c) keeping or using an embryo in any circumstances in which regulations prohibit its keeping or use, or

    (d) replacing a nucleus of a cell of an embryo with a nucleus taken from a cell of any person, embryo or subsequent development of an embryo.

(4) For the purposes of subsection (3)(a) above, the primitive streak is to be taken to have appeared in an embryo not later than the end of the period of 14 days beginning with the day when the gametes are mixed, not counting any time during which the embryo is stored.

3A—(1) No person shall, for the purpose of providing fertility services for any woman, use female germ cells taken or derived from an embryo or a foetus or use embryos created by using such cells.

(2) In this section –

'female germ cells' means cells of the female germ line and includes such cells at any stage of maturity and accordingly includes eggs; and

'fertility services' means medical, surgical or obstetric services provided for the purpose of assisting women to carry children.

4   Prohibitions in connection with gametes

(1) No person shall –

    (a) store any gametes, or

    (b) in the course of providing treatment services for any woman, use the sperm of any man unless the services are being provided for the woman and the man together or use the eggs of any other woman, or

    (c) mix gametes with the live gametes of any animal,

except in pursuance of a licence.

(2) A licence cannot authorise storing or using gametes in any circumstances in which regulations prohibit their storage or use.

(3) No person shall place sperm and eggs in a woman in any circumstances specified in regulations except in pursuance of a licence.

(4) Regulations made by virtue of subsection (3) above may provide that, in relation to licences only to place sperm and eggs in a woman in such circumstances, sections 12 to 22 of this Act shall have effect with such modifications as may be specified in the regulations.

(5) Activities regulated by this section or section 3 of this Act are referred to in this Act as 'activities governed by this Act'.

The Human Fertilisation and Embryology Authority, its functions and procedure

5   The Human Fertilisation and Embryology Authority

(1) There shall be a body corporate called the Human Fertilisation and Embryology Authority.

(2) The Authority shall consist of –

(a) a chairman and deputy chairman, and

(b) such number of other members as the Secretary of State appoints.

(3) Schedule 1 to this Act (which deals with the membership of the Authority, etc.) shall have effect.

6   Accounts and audit

(1) The Authority shall keep proper accounts and proper records in relation to the accounts and shall prepare for each accounting year a statement of accounts.

(2) The annual statement of accounts shall comply with any direction given by the Secretary of State, with the approval of the Treasury, as to the information to be contained in the statement, the way in which the information is to be presented or the methods and principles according to which the statement is to be prepared.

(3) Not later than five months after the end of an accounting year, the Authority shall send a copy of the statement of accounts for that year to the Secretary of State and to the Comptroller and Auditor General.

(4) The Comptroller and Auditor General shall examine, certify and report on every statement of accounts received by him under subsection (3) above and shall lay a copy of the statement and of his report before each House of Parliament.

(5) The Secretary of State and the Comptroller and Auditor General may inspect any records relating to the accounts.

(6) In this section 'accounting year' means the period beginning with the day when the Authority is established and ending with the following 31st March, or any later period of twelve months ending with the 31st March.

7   Reports to Secretary of State

(1) The Authority shall prepare a report for the first twelve months of its existence, and a report for each succeeding period of twelve months, and shall send each report to the Secretary of State as soon as practicable after the end of the period for which it is prepared.

(2) A report prepared under this section for any period shall deal with the activities of the Authority in the period and the activities the Authority proposes to undertake in the succeeding period of twelve months.

(3) The Secretary of State shall lay before each House of Parliament a copy of every report received by him under this section.

8   General functions of the authority

The Authority shall –

(a) keep under review information about embryos and any subsequent development of embryos and about the provision of treatment services and activities governed by this Act, and advise the Secretary of State, if he asks it to do so, about those matters,

(b) publicise the services provided to the public by the Authority or provided in pursuance of licences,

(c) provide, to such extent as it considers appropriate, advice and information for persons to whom licences apply or who are receiving treatment services or providing gametes or embryos for use for the purposes of activities governed by this Act, or may wish to do so, and

(d) perform such other functions as may be specified in regulations.

9   Licence committees and other committees

(1) The Authority shall maintain one or more committees to discharge the Authority's functions relating to the grant, variation, suspension and revocation of licences, and a committee discharging those functions is referred to in this Act as a 'licence committee'.

(2) The Authority may provide for the discharge of any of its other functions by committees or by members or employees of the Authority.

(3) A committee (other than a licence committee) may appoint sub-committees.

(4) Persons, committees or sub-committees discharging functions of the Authority shall do so in accordance with any general directions of the Authority.

(5) A licence committee shall consist of such number of persons as may be specified in or determined in accordance with regulations, all being members of the Authority, and shall include at least one person who is not authorised to carry on or participate in any activity under the authority of a licence and would not be so authorised if outstanding applications were granted.

(6) A committee (other than a licence committee) or a sub-committee may include a minority of persons who are not members of the Authority.

(7) Subject to subsection (10) below, a licence committee, before considering an application for authority –

   (a) for a person to carry on an activity governed by this Act which he is not then authorised to carry on, or

   (b) for a person to carry on any such activity on premises where he is not then authorised to carry it on,

shall arrange for the premises where the activity is to be carried on to be inspected on its behalf, and for a report on the inspection to be made to it.

(8) Subject to subsection (9) below, a licence committee shall arrange for any premises to which a licence relates to be inspected on its behalf once in each calendar year, and for a report on the inspection to be made to it.

(9) Any particular premises need not be inspected in any particular year if the licence committee considers an inspection in that year unnecessary.

(10) A licence committee need not comply with subsection (7) above where the premises in question have been inspected in pursuance of that subsection or subsection (8) above at some time during the period of one year ending with the date of the application, and the licence committee considers that a further inspection is not necessary.

(11) An inspection in pursuance of subsection (7) or (8) above may be carried out by a person who is not a member of a licence committee.

10   Licensing procedure

(1) Regulations may make such provision as appears to the Secretary of State to be necessary or desirable about the proceedings of licence committees and of the Authority on any appeal from such a committee.

(2) The regulations may in particular include provision –

   (a) for requiring persons to give evidence or to produce documents, and

   (b) about the admissibility of evidence.

Scope of licences

11   Licences for treatment, storage and research

(1) The Authority may grant the following and no other licences –

   (a) licences under paragraph 1 of Schedule 2 to this Act authorising activities in the course of providing treatment services,

   (b) licences under that Schedule authorising the storage of gametes and embryos, and

   (c) licences under paragraph 3 of that Schedule authorising activities for the purpose of a project of research.

(2) Paragraph 4 of that Schedule has effect in the case of all licences.

Licence conditions

12   General conditions

The following shall be conditions of every licence granted under this Act –

   (a) that the activities authorised by the licence shall be carried on only on the premises to which the licence relates and under the supervision of the person responsible,

(b) that any member or employee of the Authority, on production, if so required, of a document identifying the person as such, shall at all reasonable times be permitted to enter those premises and inspect them (which includes inspecting any equipment or records and observing any activity),

(c) that the provisions of Schedule 3 to this Act shall be complied with,

(d) that proper records shall be maintained in such form as the Authority may specify in directions,

(e) that no money or other benefit shall be given or received in respect of any supply of gametes or embryos unless authorised by directions,

(f) that, where gametes or embryos are supplied to a person to whom another licence applies, that person shall also be provided with such information as the Authority may specify in directions, and

(g) that the Authority shall be provided, in such form and at such intervals as it may specify in directions, with such copies of or extracts from the records, or such other information, as the directions may specify.

13   Conditions of licences for treatment

(1) The following shall be conditions of every licence under paragraph 1 of Schedule 2 to this Act.

(2) Such information shall be recorded as the Authority may specify in directions about the following –

(a) the persons for whom services are provided in pursuance of the licence,

(b) the services provided for them,

(c) the persons whose gametes are kept or used for the purposes of services provided in pursuance of the licence or whose gametes have been used in bringing about the creation of embryos so kept or used,

(d) any child appearing to the person responsible to have been born as a result of treatment in pursuance of the licence,

(e) any mixing of egg and sperm and any taking of an embryo from a woman or other acquisition of an embryo, and

(f) such other matters as the Authority may specify in directions.

(3) The records maintained in pursuance of the licence shall include any information recorded in pursuance of subsection (2) above and any consent of a person whose consent is required under Schedule 3 to this Act.

(4) No information shall be removed from any records maintained in pursuance of the licence before the expiry of such period as may be specified in directions for records of the class in question.

(5) A woman shall not be provided with treatment services unless account has been taken of the welfare of any child who may be born as a result of the treatment (including the need of that child for a father), and of any other child who may be affected by the birth.

(6) A woman shall not be provided with any treatment services involving –

(a) the use of any gametes of any person, if that person's consent is required under paragraph 5 of Schedule 3 to this Act for the use in question,

(b) the use of any embryo the creation of which was brought about *in vitro*, or

(c) the use of any embryo taken from a woman, if the consent of the woman from whom it was taken is required under paragraph 7 of that Schedule for the use in question,

unless the woman being treated and, where she is being treated together with a man, the man have been given a suitable opportunity to receive proper counselling about the implications of taking the proposed steps, and have been provided with such relevant information as is proper.

(7) Suitable procedures shall be maintained –

(a) for determining the persons providing gametes or from whom embryos are taken for use in pursuance of the licence, and

(b) for the purpose of securing that consideration is given to the use of practices not requiring the authority of a licence as well as those requiring such authority.

14 Conditions of storage licences

(1) The following shall be conditions of every licence authorising the storage of gametes or embryos –

(a) that gametes of a person or an embryo taken from a woman shall be placed in storage only if received from that person or woman or acquired from a person to whom a licence applies and that an embryo the creation of which has been brought about *in vitro* otherwise than in pursuance of that licence shall be placed in storage only if acquired from a person to whom a licence applies,

(b) that gametes or embryos which are or have been stored shall not be supplied to a person otherwise than in the course of providing treatment services unless that person is a person to whom a licence applies,

(c) that no gametes or embryos shall be kept in storage for longer than the statutory storage period and, if stored at the end of the period, shall be allowed to perish, and

(d) that such information as the Authority may specify in directions as to the persons whose consent is required under Schedule 3 to this Act, the terms of their consent and the circumstances of the storage and as to such other matters as the Authority may specify in directions shall be included in the records maintained in pursuance of the licence.

(2) No information shall be removed from any record maintained in pursuance of such a licence before the expiry of such period as may be specified in directions for records of the class in question.

(3) The statutory storage period in respect of gametes is such period not exceeding ten years as the licence may specify.

(4) The statutory storage period in respect of embryos is such period not exceeding five years as the licence may specify.

(5) Regulations may provide that subsection (3) or (4) above shall have effect as if for ten years or, as the case may be, five years there were substituted –

(a) such shorter period, or

(b) in such circumstances as may be specified in the regulations, such longer period,

as may be specified in the regulations.

15 Conditions of research licences

(1) The following shall be conditions of every licence under paragraph 3 of Schedule 2 to this Act.

(2) The records maintained in pursuance of the licence shall include such information as the Authority may specify in directions about such matters as the Authority may so specify.

(3) No information shall be removed from any records maintained in pursuance of the licence before the expiry of such period as may be specified in directions for records of the class in question.

(4) No embryo appropriated for the purposes of any project of research shall be kept or used otherwise than for the purpose of such a project.

Grant, revocation and suspension of licences

16 Grant of licence

(1) Where application is made to the Authority in a form approved for the purpose by it accompanied by the initial fee, a licence may be granted to any person by a licence committee if the requirements of subsection (2) below are met and any additional fee is paid.

(2) The requirements mentioned in subsection (1) above are –

(a) that the application is for a licence designating an individual as the person under whose supervision the activities to be authorised by the licence are to be carried on,

(b) that either that individual is the applicant or –
    (i) the application is made with the consent of that individual, and
    (ii) the licence committee is satisfied that the applicant is a suitable person to hold a licence,
(c) that the licence committee is satisfied that the character, qualifications and experience of that individual are such as are required for the supervision of the activities and that the individual will discharge the duty under section 17 of this Act,
(d) that the licence committee is satisfied that the premises in respect of which the licence is to be granted are suitable for the activities, and
(e) that all the other requirements of this Act in relation to the granting of the licence are satisfied.

(3) The grant of a licence to any person may be by way of renewal of a licence granted to that person, whether on the same or different terms.

(4) Where the licence committee is of the opinion that the information provided in the application is insufficient to enable it to determine the application, it need not consider the application until the applicant has provided it with such further information as it may require him to provide.

(5) The licence committee shall not grant a licence unless a copy of the conditions to be imposed by the licence has been shown to, and acknowledged in writing by, the applicant and (where different) the person under whose supervision the activities are to be carried on.

(6) In subsection (1) above 'initial fee' and 'additional fee' mean a fee of such amount as may be fixed from time to time by the Authority with the approval of the Secretary of State and the Treasury, and in determining any such amount, the Authority may have regard to the costs of performing all its functions.

(7) Different fees may be fixed for different circumstances and fees paid under this section are not repayable.

17   The person responsible

(1) It shall be the duty of the individual under whose supervision the activities authorised by a licence are carried on (referred to in this Act as the 'person responsible') to secure –
(a) that the other persons to whom the licence applies are of such character, and are so qualified by training and experience, as to be suitable persons to participate in the activities authorised by the licence,
(b) that proper equipment is used,
(c) that proper arrangements are made for the keeping of gametes and embryos and for the disposal of gametes or embryos that have been allowed to perish,
(d) that suitable practices are used in the course of the activities, and
(e) that the conditions of the licence are complied with.

(2) References in this Act to the persons to whom a licence applies are to –
(a) the person responsible,
(b) any person designated in the licence, or in a notice given to the Authority by the person who holds the licence or the person responsible, as a person to whom the licence applies, and
(c) any person acting under the direction of the person responsible or of any person so designated.

(3) References below in this Act to the nominal licensee are to a person who holds a licence under which a different person is the person responsible.

18   Revocation and variation of licence

(1) A licence committee may revoke a licence if it is satisfied –
(a) that any information given for the purposes of the application for the grant of the licence was in any material respect false or misleading,

    (b) that the premises to which the licence relates are no longer suitable for the activities authorised by the licence,

    (c) that the person responsible has failed to discharge, or is unable because of incapacity to discharge, the duty under section 17 of this Act or has failed to comply with directions given in connection with any licence, or

    (d) that there has been any other material change of circumstances since the licence was granted.

(2) A licence committee may also revoke a licence if –

    (a) it ceases to be satisfied that the character of the person responsible is such as is required for the supervision of those activities or that the nominal licensee is a suitable person to hold a licence, or

    (b) the person responsible dies or is convicted of an offence under this Act.

(3) Where a licence committee has power to revoke a licence under subsection (1) above it may instead vary any terms of the licence.

(4) A licence committee may, on an application by the person responsible or the nominal licensee, vary or revoke a licence.

(5) A licence committee may, on an application by the nominal licensee, vary the licence so as to designate another individual in place of the person responsible if –

    (a) the committee is satisfied that the character, qualifications and experience of the other individual are such as are required for the supervision of the activities authorised by the licence and that the individual will discharge the duty under section 17 of this Act, and

    (b) the application is made with the consent of the other individual.

(6) Except on an application under subsection (5) above, a licence can only be varied under this section –

    (a) so far as it relates to the activities authorised by the licence, the manner in which they are conducted or the conditions of the licence, or

    (b) so as to extend or restrict the premises to which the licence relates.

19   Procedure for refusal, variation or revocation of licence

(1) Where a licence committee proposes to refuse a licence or to refuse to vary a licence so as to designate another individual in place of the person responsible, the committee shall give notice of the proposal, the reasons for it and the effect of subsection (3) below to the applicant.

(2) Where a licence committee proposes to vary or revoke a licence, the committee shall give notice of the proposal, the reasons for it and the effect of subsection (3) below to the person responsible and the nominal licensee (but not to any person who has applied for the variation or revocation).

(3) If, within the period of twenty-eight days beginning with the day on which notice of the proposal is given, any person to whom notice was given under subsection (1) or (2) above gives notice to the committee of a wish to make to the committee representations about the proposal in any way mentioned in subsection (4) below, the committee shall, before making its determination, give the person an opportunity to make representations in that way.

(4) The representations may be –

    (a) oral representations made by the person, or another acting on behalf of the person, at a meeting of the committee, and

    (b) written representations made by the person.

(5) A licence committee shall –

    (a) in the case of a determination to grant a licence, give notice of the determination to the person responsible and the nominal licensee,

    (b) in the case of a determination to refuse a licence, or to refuse to vary a licence so as to designate another individual in place of the person responsible, give such notice to the applicant, and

(c) in the case of a determination to vary or revoke a licence, give such notice to the person responsible and the nominal licensee.

(6) A licence committee giving notice of a determination to refuse a licence or to refuse to vary a licence so as to designate another individual in place of the person responsible, or of a determination to vary or revoke a licence otherwise than on an application by the person responsible or the nominal licensee, shall give in the notice the reasons for its decision.

20   Appeal to Authority against determinations of licence committee

(1) Where a licence committee determines to refuse a licence or to refuse to vary a licence so as to designate another individual in place of the person responsible, the applicant may appeal to the Authority if notice has been given to the committee and to the Authority before the end of the period of twenty-eight days beginning with the date on which notice of the committee's determination was served on the applicant.

(2) Where a licence committee determines to vary or revoke a licence, any person on whom notice of the determination was served (other than a person who applied for the variation or revocation) may appeal to the Authority if notice has been given to the committee and to the Authority before the end of the period of twenty-eight days beginning with the date on which notice of the committee's determination was served.

(3) An appeal under this section shall be by way of rehearing by the Authority and no member of the Authority who took any part in the proceedings resulting in the determination appealed against shall take any part in the proceedings on appeal.

(4) On the appeal –
  (a) the appellant shall be entitled to appear or be represented,
  (b) the members of the licence committee shall be entitled to appear, or the committee shall be entitled to be represented, and
  (c) the Authority shall consider any written representations received from the appellant or any member of the committee and may take into account any matter that could be taken into account by a licence committee,
and the Authority may make such determination on the appeal as it thinks fit.

(5) The Authority shall give notice of its determination to the appellant and, if it is a determination to refuse a licence or to refuse to vary a licence so as to designate another individual in place of the person responsible or a determination to vary or revoke a licence, shall include in the notice the reasons for the decision.

(6) The functions of the Authority on an appeal under this section cannot be discharged by any committee, member or employee of the Authority and, for the purposes of the appeal, the quorum shall not be less than five.

21   Appeals to High Court or Court of Session

Where the Authority determines under section 20 of this Act –
  (a) to refuse a licence or to refuse to vary a licence so as to designate another individual in place of the person responsible, or
  (b) to vary or revoke a licence,
any person on whom notice of the determination was served may appeal to the High Court or, in Scotland, the Court of Session on a point of law.

22   Temporary suspension of licence

(1) Where a licence committee –
  (a) has reasonable grounds to suspect that there are grounds for revoking the licence under section 18 of this Act, and
  (b) is of the opinion that the licence should immediately be suspended,
it may by notice suspend the licence for such period not exceeding three months as may be specified in the notice.

(2) Notice under subsection (1) above shall be given to the person responsible or, where the person responsible has died or appears to the licence committee to be unable because of incapacity to discharge the duty under section 17 of this Act, to some other person to whom the licence applies or the nominal licensee and a licence committee may, by a further notice to that person, renew or further renew the notice under subsection (1) above for such further period not exceeding three months as may be specified in the renewal notice.

(3) While suspended under this section a licence shall be of no effect, but application may be made under section 18(5) of this Act by the nominal licensee to designate another individual as the person responsible.

Directions and guidance

23   Directions: general

(1) The Authority may from time to time give directions for any purpose for which directions may be given under this Act or directions varying or revoking such directions.

(2) A person to whom any requirement contained in directions is applicable shall comply with the requirement.

(3) Anything done by a person in pursuance of directions is to be treated for the purposes of this Act as done in pursuance of a licence.

(4) Where directions are to be given to a particular person, they shall be given by serving notice of the directions on the person.

(5) In any other case, directions may be given –

   (a) in respect of any licence (including a licence which has ceased to have effect), by serving notice of the directions on the person who is or was the person responsible or the nominal licensee, or

   (b) if the directions appear to the Authority to be general directions or it appears to the Authority that it is not practicable to give notice in pursuance of paragraph (a) above, by publishing the directions in such way as, in the opinion of the Authority, is likely to bring the directions to the attention of the persons to whom they are applicable.

(6) This section does not apply to directions under section 9(4) of this Act.

24   Directions as to particular matters

(1) If, in the case of any information about persons for whom treatment services were provided, the person responsible does not know that any child was born following the treatment, the period specified in directions by virtue of section 13(4) of this Act shall not expire less than 50 years after the information was first recorded.

(2) In the case of every licence under paragraph 1 of Schedule 2 to this Act, directions shall require information to be recorded and given to the Authority about each of the matters referred to in section 13(2)(a) to (e) of this Act.

(3) Directions may authorise, in such circumstances and subject to such conditions as may be specified in the directions, the keeping, by or on behalf of a person to whom a licence applies, of gametes or embryos in the course of their carriage to or from any premises.

(4) Directions may authorise any person to whom a licence applies to receive gametes or embryos from outside the United Kingdom or to send gametes or embryos outside the United Kingdom in such circumstances and subject to such conditions as may be specified in the directions, and directions made by virtue of this subsection may provide for sections 12 to 14 of this Act to have effect with such modifications as may be specified in the directions.

(5) A licence committee may from time to time give such directions as are mentioned in subsection (7) below where a licence has been varied or has ceased to have effect (whether by expiry, suspension, revocation or otherwise).

(6) A licence committee proposing to suspend, revoke or vary a licence may give such directions as are mentioned in subsection (7) below.

(7) The directions referred to in subsections (5) and (6) above are directions given for the purpose of securing the continued discharge of the duties of the person responsible under the licence concerned ('the old licence'), and such directions may, in particular –

(a) require anything kept or information held in pursuance of the old licence to be transferred to the Authority or any other person, or

(b) provide for the discharge of the duties in question by any individual, being an individual whose character, qualifications and experience are, in the opinion of the committee, such as are required for the supervision of the activities authorised by the old licence, and authorise those activities to be carried on under the supervision of that individual,

but cannot require any individual to discharge any of those duties unless the individual has consented in writing to do so.

(8) Directions for the purpose referred to in subsection (7)(a) above shall be given to the person responsible under the old licence or, where that person has died or appears to the licence committee to have become unable because of incapacity to discharge the duties in question, to some other person to whom the old licence applies or applied or to the nominal licensee.

(9) Directions for the purpose referred to in subsection (7)(b) above shall be given to the individual who under the directions is to discharge the duty.

(10) Where a person who holds a licence dies, anything done subsequently by an individual which that individual would have been authorised to do if the licence had continued in force shall, until directions are given by virtue of this section, be treated as authorised by a licence.

(11) Where the Authority proposes to give directions specifying any animal for the purposes of paragraph 1(1)(f) or 3(5) of Schedule 2 to this Act, it shall report the proposal to the Secretary of State; and the directions shall not be given until the Secretary of State has laid a copy of the report before each House of Parliament.

25   Code of practice

(1) The Authority shall maintain a code of practice giving guidance about the proper conduct of activities carried on in pursuance of a licence under this Act and the proper discharge of the functions of the person responsible and other persons to whom the licence applies.

(2) The guidance given by the code shall include guidance for those providing treatment services about the account to be taken of the welfare of children who may be born as a result of treatment services (including a child's need for a father), and of other children who may be affected by such births.

(3) The code may also give guidance about the use of any technique involving the placing of sperm and eggs in a woman.

(4) The Authority may from time to time revise the whole or any part of the code.

(5) The Authority shall publish the code as for the time being in force.

(6) A failure on the part of any person to observe any provision of the code shall not of itself render the person liable to any proceedings, but –

(a) a licence committee shall, in considering whether there has been any failure to comply with any conditions of a licence and, in particular, conditions requiring anything to be 'proper' or 'suitable', take account of any relevant provision of the code, and

(b) a licence committee may, in considering, where it has power to do so, whether or not to vary or revoke a licence, take into account any observance of or failure to observe the provisions of the code.

26   Procedure for approval of code

(1) The Authority shall send a draft of the proposed first code of practice under section 25 of this Act to the Secretary of State within twelve months of the commencement of section 5 of this Act.

(2) If the Authority proposes to revise the code or, if the Secretary of State does not approve a draft of the proposed first code, to submit a further draft, the Authority shall send a draft of the revised code or, as the case may be, a further draft of the proposed first code to the Secretary of State.

(3) Before preparing any draft, the Authority shall consult such persons as the Secretary of State may require it to consult and such other persons (if any) as it considers appropriate.

(4) If the Secretary of State approves a draft, he shall lay it before Parliament and, if he does not approve it, he shall give reasons to the Authority.

(5) A draft approved by the Secretary of State shall come into force in accordance with directions.

Status

27   Meaning of 'mother'

(1) The woman who is carrying or has carried a child as a result of the placing in her of an embryo or of sperm and eggs, and no other woman, is to be treated as the mother of the child.

(2) Subsection (1) above does not apply to any child to the extent that the child is treated by virtue of adoption as not being the woman's child.

(3) Subsection (1) above applies whether the woman was in the United Kingdom or elsewhere at the time of the placing in her of the embryo or the sperm and eggs.

28   Meaning of 'father'

(1) Subject to subsections (5A) to (5I) below, this section applies in the case of a child who is being or has been carried by a woman as the result of the placing in her of an embryo or of sperm and eggs or her artificial insemination.

(2) If –

  (a) at the time of the placing in her of the embryo or the sperm and eggs or of her insemination, the woman was a party to a marriage, and

  (b) the creation of the embryo carried by her was not brought about with the sperm of the other party to the marriage,

then, subject to subsection (5) below, the other party to the marriage shall be treated as the father of the child unless it is shown that he did not consent to the placing in her of the embryo or the sperm and eggs or to her insemination (as the case may be).

(3) If no man is treated, by virtue of subsection (2) above, as the father of the child but –

  (a) the embryo or the sperm and eggs were placed in the woman, or she was artificially inseminated, in the course of treatment services provided for her and a man together by a person to whom a licence applies, and

  (b) the creation of the embryo carried by her was not brought about with the sperm of that man,

then, subject to subsection (5) below, that man shall be treated as the father of the child.

(4) Where a person is treated as the father of the child by virtue of subsection (2) or (3) above, no other person is to be treated as the father of the child.

(5) Subsections (2) and (3) above do not apply –

  (a) in relation to England and Wales and Northern Ireland, to any child who, by virtue of the rules of common law, is treated as the legitimate child of the parties to a marriage,

  (b) in relation to Scotland, to any child who, by virtue of any enactment or other rule of law, is treated as the child of the parties to a marriage, or

  (c) to any child to the extent that the child is treated by virtue of adoption as not being the man's child.

(5A) If –

  (a) a child has been carried by a woman as the result of the placing in her of an embryo or of sperm and eggs or her artificial insemination,

(b) the creation of the embryo carried by her was brought about by using the sperm of a man after his death, or the creation of the embryo was brought about using the sperm of a man before his death but the embryo was placed in the woman after his death,

(c) the woman was a party to a marriage with the man immediately before his death,

(d) the man consented in writing (and did not withdraw the consent) –

  (i) to the use of his sperm after his death which brought about the creation of the embryo carried by the woman or (as the case may be) to the placing in the woman after his death of the embryo which was brought about using his sperm before his death, and

  (ii) to being treated for the purpose mentioned in subsection (5I) below as the father of any resulting child,

(e) the woman has elected in writing not later than the end of the period of 42 days from the day on which the child was born for the man to be treated for the purpose mentioned in subsection (5I) below as the father of the child, and

(f) no-one else is to be treated as the father of the child by virtue of subsection (2) or (3) above or by virtue of adoption or the child being treated as mentioned in paragraph (a) or (b) of subsection (5) above, then the man shall be treated for the purpose mentioned in subsection (5I) below as the father of the child.

(5B) If –

(a) a child has been carried by a woman as the result of the placing in her of an embryo or of sperm and eggs or her artificial insemination,

(b) the creation of the embryo carried by her was brought about by using the sperm of a man after his death, or the creation of the embryo was brought about using the sperm of a man before his death but the embryo was placed in the woman after his death,

(c) the woman was not a party to a marriage with the man immediately before his death but treatment services were being provided for the woman and the man together before his death either by a person to whom a licence applies or outside the United Kingdom,

(d) the man consented in writing (and did not withdraw the consent) –

  (i) to the use of his sperm after his death which brought about the creation of the embryo carried by the woman or (as the case may be) to the placing in the woman after his death of the embryo which was brought about using his sperm before his death, and

  (ii) to being treated for the purpose mentioned in subsection (5I) below as the father of any resulting child,

(e) the woman has elected in writing not later than the end of the period of 42 days from the day on which the child was born for the man to be treated for the purpose mentioned in subsection (5I) below as the father of the child, and

(f) no-one else is to be treated as the father of the child by virtue of subsection (2) or (3) above or by virtue of adoption or the child being treated as mentioned in paragraph (a) or (b) of subsection (5) above, then the man shall be treated for the purpose mentioned in subsection (5I) below as the father of the child.

(5C) If –

(a) a child has been carried by a woman as the result of the placing in her of an embryo,

(b) the embryo was created at a time when the woman was a party to a marriage,

(c) the creation of the embryo was not brought about with the sperm of the other party to the marriage,

(d) the other party to the marriage died before the placing of the embryo in the woman,

(e) the other party to the marriage consented in writing (and did not withdraw the consent) –

  (i) to the placing of the embryo in the woman after his death, and

  (ii) to being treated for the purpose mentioned in subsection (5I) below as the father of any resulting child,

(f) the woman has elected in writing not later than the end of the period of 42 days from the day on which the child was born for the other party to the marriage to be treated for the purpose mentioned in subsection (5I) below as the father of the child, and

(g) no-one else is to be treated as the father of the child by virtue of subsection (2) or (3) above or by virtue of adoption or the child being treated as mentioned in paragraph (a) or (b) of subsection (5) above,

then the other party to the marriage shall be treated for the purpose mentioned in subsection (5I) below as the father of the child.

(5D) If –

(a) a child has been carried by a woman as the result of the placing in her of an embryo,

(b) the embryo was not created at a time when the woman was a party to a marriage but was created in the course of treatment services provided for the woman and a man together either by a person to whom a licence applies or outside the United Kingdom,

(c) the creation of the embryo was not brought about with the sperm of that man,

(d) the man died before the placing of the embryo in the woman,

(e) the man consented in writing (and did not withdraw the consent) –

    (i) to the placing of the embryo in the woman after his death, and

    (ii) to being treated for the purpose mentioned in subsection (5I) below as the father of any resulting child,

(f) the woman has elected in writing not later than the end of the period of 42 days from the day on which the child was born for the man to be treated for the purpose mentioned in subsection (5I) below as the father of the child, and

(g) no-one else is to be treated as the father of the child by virtue of subsection (2) or (3) above or by virtue of adoption or the child being treated as mentioned in paragraph (a) or (b) of subsection (5) above, then the man shall be treated for the purpose mentioned in subsection (5I) below as the father of the child.

(5E) In the application of subsections (5A) to (5D) above to Scotland, for any reference to a period of 42 days there shall be substituted a reference to a period of 21 days.

(5F) The requirement under subsection (5A), (5B), (5C) or (5D) above as to the making of an election (which requires an election to be made either on or before the day on which the child was born or within the period of 42 or, as the case may be, 21 days from that day) shall nevertheless be treated as satisfied if the required election is made after the end of that period but with the consent of the Registrar General under subsection (5G) below.

(5G) The Registrar General may at any time consent to the making of an election after the end of the period mentioned in subsection (5F) above if, on an application made to him in accordance with such requirements as he may specify, he is satisfied that there is a compelling reason for giving his consent to the making of such an election.

(5H) In subsections (5F) and (5G) above 'the Registrar General' means the Registrar General for England and Wales, the Registrar General of Births, Deaths and Marriages for Scotland or (as the case may be) the Registrar General for Northern Ireland.

(5I) The purpose referred to in subsections (5A) to (5D) above is the purpose of enabling the man's particulars to be entered as the particulars of the child's father in (as the case may be) a register of live-births or still-births kept under the Births and Deaths Registration Act 1953 or the Births and Deaths Registration (Northern Ireland) Order 1976 or a register of births or still-births kept under the Registration of Births, Deaths and Marriages (Scotland) Act 1965.

(6) Where –

(a) the sperm of a man who had given such consent as is required by paragraph 5 of Schedule 3 to this Act was used for a purpose for which such consent was required, or

(b) the sperm of a man, or any embryo the creation of which was brought about with his sperm, was used after his death,

he is not, subject to subsections (5A) and (5B) above, to be treated as the father of the child.

(7) The references in subsection (2) above and subsections (5A) to (5D) above to the parties to a marriage at the time there referred to –

    (a) are to the parties to a marriage subsisting at that time, unless a judicial separation was then in force, but

    (b) include the parties to a void marriage if either or both of them reasonably believed at that time that the marriage was valid; and for the purposes of this subsection it shall be presumed, unless the contrary is shown, that one of them reasonably believed at the time that the marriage was valid.

(8) This section applies whether the woman was in the United Kingdom or elsewhere at the time of the placing in her of the embryo or the sperm and eggs or her artificial insemination.

(9) In subsection (7)(a) above, 'judicial separation' includes a legal separation obtained in a country outside the British Islands and recognised in the United Kingdom.

29   Effect of sections 27 and 28

(1) Where by virtue of section 27 or 28 of this Act a person is to be treated as the mother or father of a child, that person is to be treated in law as the mother or, as the case may be, father of the child for all purposes.

(2) Where by virtue of section 27 or 28 of this Act a person is not be be treated as the mother or father of a child, that person is to be treated in law as not being the mother or, as the case may be, father of the child for any purpose.

(3) Where subsection (1) or (2) above has effect, references to any relationship between two people in any enactment, deed or other instrument or document (whenever passed or made) are to be read accordingly.

(3A) Subsections (1) to (3) above do not apply in relation to the treatment in law of a deceased man in a case to which section 28 (5A), (5B), (5C) or (5D) of this Act applies.

(3B) Where subsection (5A), (5B), (5C) or (5D) of section 28 of this Act applies, the deceased man –

    (a) is to be treated in law as the father of the child for the purpose referred to in that subsection, but

    (b) is to be treated in law as not being the father of the child for any other purpose.

(3C) Where subsection (3B) above has effect, references to any relationship between two people in any enactment, deed or other instrument or document (whenever passed or made) are to be read accordingly.

(3D) In subsection (3C) above 'enactment' includes an enactment comprised in, or in an instrument made under, an Act of the Scottish Parliament or Northern Ireland legislation.

(4) In relation to England and Wales and Northern Ireland, nothing in the provisions of section 27(1) or 28(2) to (4) or (5A) to (5I), read with this section, affects –

    (a) the succession to any dignity or title of honour or renders any person capable of succeeding to or transmitting a right to succeed to any such dignity or title, or

    (b) the devolution of any property limited (expressly or not) to devolve (as nearly as the law permits) along with any dignity or title of honour.

(5) In relation to Scotland –

    (a) those provisions do not apply to any title, coat of arms, honour or dignity transmissible on the death of the holder thereof or affect the succession thereto or the devolution thereof, and

    (b) where the terms of any deed provide that any property or interest in property shall devolve along with a title, coat of arms, honour or dignity, nothing in those provisions shall prevent that property or interest from so devolving.

30   Parental orders in favour of gamete donors

(1) The court may make an order providing for a child to be treated in law as the child of the parties to a marriage (referred to in this section as 'the husband' and 'the wife') if –

(a) the child has been carried by a woman other than the wife as the result of the placing in her of an embryo or sperm and eggs or her artificial insemination,

(b) the gametes of the husband or the wife, or both, were used to bring about the creation of the embryo, and

(c) the conditions in subsections (2) to (7) below are satisfied.

(2) The husband and the wife must apply for the order within six months of the birth of the child or, in the case of a child born before the coming into force of this Act, within six months of such coming into force.

(3) At the time of the application and of the making of the order –

(a) the child's home must be with the husband and the wife, and

(b) the husband or the wife, or both of them, must be domiciled in a part of the United Kingdom or in the Channel Islands or the Isle of Man.

(4) At the time of the making of the order both the husband and the wife must have attained the age of eighteen.

(5) The court must be satisfied that both the father of the child (including a person who is the father by virtue of section 28 of this Act), where he is not the husband, and the woman who carried the child have freely, and with full understanding of what is involved, agreed unconditionally to the making of the order.

(6) Subsection (5) above does not require the agreement of a person who cannot be found or is incapable of giving agreement and the agreement of the woman who carried the child is ineffective for the purposes of that subsection if given by her less than six weeks after the child's birth.

(7) The court must be satisfied that no money or other benefit (other than for expenses reasonably incurred) has been given or received by the husband or the wife for or in consideration of –

(a) the making of the order,

(b) any agreement required by subsection (5) above,

(c) the handing over of the child to the husband and the wife, or

(d) the making of any arrangements with a view to the making of the order, unless authorised by the court.

(8) For the purposes of an application under this section –

(a) in relation to England and Wales, section 92(7) to (10) of, and Part I of Schedule 11 to, the Children Act 1989 (jurisdiction of courts) shall apply for the purposes of this section to determine the meaning of 'the court' as they apply for the purposes of that Act and proceedings on the application shall be 'family proceedings' for the purposes of that Act,

(b) in relation to Scotland, 'the court' means the Court of Session or the sheriff court of the sheriffdom within which the child is, and

(c) in relation to Northern Ireland, 'the court' means the High Court or any county court within whose division the child is.

(9) Regulations may provide –

(a) for any provision of the enactments about adoption to have effect, with such modifications (if any) as may be specified in the regulations, in relation to orders under this section, and applications for such orders, as it has effect in relation to adoption, and applications for adoption orders, and

(b) for references in any enactment to adoption, an adopted child or an adoptive relationship to be read (respectively) as references to the effect of an order under this section, a child to whom such an order applies and a relationship arising by virtue of the enactments about adoption, as applied by the regulations, and for similar expressions in connection with adoption to be read accordingly,

and the regulations may include such incidental or supplemental provision as appears to the Secretary of State necessary or desirable in consequence of any provision made by virtue of paragraph (a) or (b) above.

(10) In this section 'the enactments about adoption' means the Adoption and Children Act 2002, the Adoption (Scotland) Act 1978 and the Adoption (Northern Ireland) Order 1987.

(11) Subsection (1)(a) above applies whether the woman was in the United Kingdom or elsewhere at the time of the placing in her of the embryo or the sperm and eggs or her artificial insemination.

Information

31   The Authority's register of information

(1) The Authority shall keep a register which shall contain any information obtained by the Authority which falls within subsection (2) below.

(2) Information falls within this subsection if it relates to –

    (a) the provision of treatment services for any identifiable individual, or

    (b) the keeping or use of the gametes of any identifiable individual or of an embryo taken from any identifiable woman,

or if it shows that any identifiable individual was, or may have been, born in consequence of treatment services.

(3) A person who has attained the age of eighteen ('the applicant') may be notice to the Authority require the Authority to comply with a request under subsection (4) below, and the Authority shall do so if –

    (a) the information contained in the register shows that the applicant was, or may have been, born in consequence of treatment services, and

    (b) the applicant has been given a suitable opportunity to receive proper counselling about the implications of compliance with the request.

(4) The applicant may request the Authority to give the applicant notice stating whether or not the information contained in the register shows that a person other than a parent of the applicant would or might, but for sections 27 to 29 of this Act, be a parent of the applicant and, if it does show that –

    (a) giving the applicant so much of that information as relates to the person concerned as the Authority is required by regulations to give (but no other information), or

    (b) stating whether or not that information shows that, but for sections 27 to 29 of this Act, the applicant, and a person specified in the request as a person whom the applicant proposes to marry, would or might be related.

(5) Regulations cannot require the Authority to give any information as to the identity of a person whose gametes have been used or from whom an embryo has been taken if a person to whom a licence applied was provided with the information at a time when the Authority could not have been required to give information of the kind in question.

(6) A person who has not attained the age of eighteen ('the minor') may by notice to the Authority specifying another person ('the intended spouse') as a person whom the minor proposes to marry require the Authority to comply with a request under subsection (7) below, and the Authority shall do so if –

    (a) the information contained in the register shows that the minor was, or may have been, born in consequence of treatment services, and

    (b) the minor has been given a suitable opportunity to receive proper counselling about the implications of compliance with the request.

(7) The minor may request the Authority to give the minor notice stating whether or not the information contained in the register shows that, but for sections 27 to 29 of this Act, the minor and the intended spouse would or might be related.

32   Information to be provided to Registrar General

(1) This section applies where a claim is made before the Registrar General that a man is or is not the father of a child and it is necessary or desirable for the purpose of any function of the Registrar General to determine whether the claim is or may be well-founded.

(2) The Authority shall comply with any request made by the Registrar General by notice to the Authority to disclose whether any information on the register kept in pursuance of section 31 of this

Act tends to show that the man may be the father of the child by virtue of section 28 of this Act and, if it does, disclose that information.

(3) In this section and section 33 of this Act, 'the Registrar General' means the Registrar General for England and Wales, the Registrar General of Births, Deaths and Marriages for Scotland or the Registrar General for Northern Ireland, as the case may be.

33   Restrictions on disclosure of information

(1) No person who is or has been a member or employee of the Authority shall disclose any information mentioned in subsection (2) below which he holds or has held as such a member or employee.

(2) The information referred to in subsection (1) above is –

(a) any information contained or required to be contained in the register kept in pursuance of section 31 of this Act, and

(b) any other information obtained by any member or employee of the Authority on terms or in circumstances requiring it to be held in confidence.

(3) Subsection (1) above does not apply to any disclosure of information mentioned in subsection (2)(a) above made –

(a) to a person as a member or employee of the Authority,

(b) to a person to whom a licence applies for the purposes of his functions as such,

(c) so that no individual to whom the information relates can be identified,

(d) in pursuance of an order of a court under section 34 or 35 of this Act,

(e) to the Registrar General in pursuance of a request under section 32 of this Act, or

(f) in accordance with section 31 of this Act.

(4) Subsection (1) above does not apply to any disclosure of information mentioned in subsection (2)(b) above –

(a) made to a person as a member or employee of the Authority,

(b) made with the consent of the person or persons whose confidence would otherwise be protected, or

(c) which has been lawfully made available to the public before the disclosure is made.

(5) No person who is or has been a person to whom a licence applies and no person to whom directions have been given shall disclose any information falling within section 31(2) of this Act which he holds or has held as such a person.

(6) Subsection (5) above does not apply to any disclosure of information made –

(a) to a person as a member or employee of the Authority,

(b) to a person to whom a licence applies for the purposes of his functions as such,

(c) so far as it identifies a person who, but for sections 27 to 29 of this Act, would or might be a parent of a person who instituted proceedings under section 1A of the Congenital Disabilities (Civil Liability) Act 1976, but only for the purpose of defending such proceedings, or instituting connected proceedings for compensation against that parent,

(d) so that no individual to whom the information relates can be identified,

(e) in pursuance of directions given by virtue of section 24(5) or (6) of this Act.

(f) necessarily –

(i)   for any purpose preliminary to proceedings, or

(ii) for the purposes of, or in connection with, any proceedings,

(g) for the purpose of establishing, in any proceedings relating to an application for an order under subsection (1) of section 30 of this Act, whether the condition specified in paragraph (a) or (b) of that subsection is met, or

(h) under section 3 of the Access to Health Records Act 1990 (right of access to health records).

(6A) Paragraph (f) of subsection (6) above, so far as relating to disclosure for the purposes of, or in connection with, any proceedings, does not apply –

(a) to disclosure of information enabling a person to be identified as a person whose gametes were used, in accordance with consent given under paragraph 5 of Schedule 3 to this Act, for the purposes of treatment services in consequence of which an identifiable individual was, or may have been, born, or

(b) to disclosure, in circumstances in which subsection (1) of section 34 of this Act applies, of information relevant to the determination of the question mentioned in that subsection.

(6B) In the case of information relating to the provision of treatment services for any identifiable individual –

(a) where one individual is identifiable, subsection (5) above does not apply to disclosure with the consent of that individual;

(b) where both a woman and a man treated together with her are identifiable, subsection (5) above does not apply –

(i) to disclosure with the consent of them both, or

(ii) if disclosure is made for the purpose of disclosing information about the provision of treatment services for one of them, to disclosure with the consent of that individual.

(6C) For the purposes of subsection (6B) above, consent must be to disclosure to a specific person, except where disclosure is to a person who needs to know –

(a) in connection with the provision of treatment services, or any other description of medical, surgical or obstetric services, for the individual giving the consent,

(b) in connection with the carrying out of an audit of clinical practice, or

(c) in connection with the auditing of accounts.

(6D) For the purposes of subsection (6B) above, consent to disclosure given at the request of another shall be disregarded unless, before it is given, the person requesting it takes reasonable steps to explain to the individual from whom it is requested the implications of compliance with the request.

(6E) In the case of information which relates to the provision of treatment services for any identifiable individual, subsection (5) above does not apply to disclosure in an emergency, that is to say, to disclosure made –

(a) by a person who is satisfied that it is necessary to make the disclosure to avert an imminent danger to the health of an individual with whose consent the information could be disclosed under subsection (6B) above, and

(b) in circumstances where it is not reasonably practicable to obtain that individual's consent.

(6F) In the case of information which shows that any identifiable individual was, or may have been, born in consequence of treatment services, subsection (5) above does not apply to any disclosure which is necessarily incidental to disclosure under subsection (6B) or (6E) above.

(6G) Regulations may provide for additional exceptions from subsection (5) above, but no exception may be made under this subsection –

(a) for disclosure of a kind mentioned in paragraph (a) or (b) of subsection (6A) above, or

(b) for disclosure, in circumstances in which section 32 of this Act applies, of information having the tendency mentioned in subsection (2) of that section.

(7) This section does not apply to the disclosure to any individual of information which –

(a) falls within section 31(2) of this Act by virtue of paragraph (a) or (b) of that subsection, and

(b) relates only to that individual or, in the case of an individual treated together with another, only to that individual and that other.

(9) In subsection (6)(f) above, references to proceedings include any formal procedure for dealing with a complaint.

34   Disclosure in interests of justice

(1) Where in any proceedings before a court the question whether a person is or is not the parent of a child by virtue of sections 27 to 29 of this Act falls to be determined, the court may on the application of any party to the proceedings make an order requiring the Authority –

(a) to disclose whether or not any information relevant to that question is contained in the register kept in pursuance of section 31 of this Act, and

(b) if it is, to disclose so much of it as is specified in the order,

but such an order may not require the Authority to disclose any information falling within section 31(2)(b) of this Act.

(2) The court must not make an order under subsection (1) above unless it is satisfied that the interests of justice require it to do so, taking into account –

    (a) any representations made by any individual who may be affected by the disclosure, and

    (b) the welfare of the child, if under 18 years old, and of any other person under that age who may be affected by the disclosure.

(3) If the proceedings before the court are civil proceedings, it –

    (a) may direct that the whole or any part of the proceedings on the application for an order under subsection (2) above shall be heard in camera, and

    (b) if it makes such an order, may then or later direct that the whole or any part of any later stage of the proceedings shall be heard in camera.

(4) An application for a direction under subsection (3) above shall be heard in camera unless the court otherwise directs.

35   Disclosure in interests of justice: congenital disabilities, etc.

(1) Where for the purpose of instituting proceedings under section 1 of the Congenital Disabilities (Civil Liability) Act 1976 (civil liability to child born disabled) it is necessary to identify a person who would or might be the parent of a child but for sections 27 to 29 of this Act, the court may, on the application of the child, make an order requiring the Authority to disclose any information contained in the register kept in pursuance of section 31 of this Act identifying that person.

(2) Where, for the purposes of any action for damages in Scotland (including any such action which is likely to be brought) in which the damages claimed consist of or include damages or solatium in respect of personal injury (including any disease and any impairment of physical or mental condition), it is necessary to identify a person who would or might be the parent of a child but for sections 27 to 29 of this Act, the court may, on the application of any party to the action or, if the proceedings have not been commenced, the prospective pursuer, make an order requiring the Authority to disclose any information contained in the register kept in pursuance of section 31 of this Act identifying that person.

(3) Subsections (2) to (4) of section 34 of this Act apply for the purposes of this section as they apply for the purposes of that.

Conscientious objection

38   Conscientious objection

(1) No person who has a conscientious objection to participating in any activity governed by this Act shall be under any duty, however arising, to do so.

(2) In any legal proceedings the burden of proof of conscientious objection shall rest on the person claiming to rely on it.

(3) In any proceedings before a court in Scotland, a statement on oath by any person to the effect that he has a conscientious objection to participating in a particular activity governed by this Act shall be sufficient evidence of that fact for the purpose of discharging the burden of proof imposed by subsection (2) above.

Enforcement

39   Powers of members and employees of Authority

(1) Any member or employee of the Authority entering and inspecting premises to which a licence relates may –

    (a) take possession of anything which he has reasonable grounds to believe may be required –

        (i) for the purpose of the functions of the Authority relating to the grant, variation, suspension and revocation of licences, or

(ii) for the purpose of being used in evidence in any proceedings for an offence under this Act, and retain it for so long as it may be required for the purpose in question, and

(b) for the purpose in question, take such steps as appear to be necessary for preserving any such thing or preventing interference with it, including requiring any person having the power to do so to give such assistance as may reasonably be required.

(2) In subsection (1) above –

(a) the references to things include information recorded in any form, and

(b) the reference to taking possession of anything includes, in the case of information recorded otherwise than in legible form, requiring any person having the power to do so to produce a copy of the information in legible form and taking possession of the copy.

(3) Nothing in this Act makes it unlawful for a member or employee of the Authority to keep any embryo or gametes in pursuance of that person's functions as such.

40   Power to enter premises

(1) A justice of the peace (including, in Scotland, a sheriff) may issue a warrant under this section if satisfied by the evidence on oath of a member or employee of the Authority that there are reasonable grounds for suspecting that an offence under this Act is being, or has been, committed on any premises.

(2) A warrant under this section shall authorise any named member or employee of the Authority (who must, if so required, produce a document identifying himself), together with any constables –

(a) to enter the premises specified in the warrant, using such force as is reasonably necessary for the purpose, and

(b) to search the premises and –

(i)   take possession of anything which he has reasonable grounds to believe may be required to be used in evidence in any proceedings for an offence under this Act, or

(ii) take such steps as appear to be necessary for preserving any such thing or preventing interference with it, including requiring any person having the power to do so to give such assistance as may reasonably be required.

(3) A warrant under this section shall continue in force until the end of the period of one month beginning with the day on which it is issued.

(4) Anything of which possession is taken under this section may be retained –

(a) for a period of six months, or

(b) if within that period proceedings to which the thing is relevant are commenced against any person for an offence under this Act, until the conclusion of those proceedings.

(5) In this section –

(a) the references to things include information recorded in any form, and

(b) the reference in subsection (2)(b)(i) above to taking possession of anything includes, in the case of information recorded otherwise than in legible form, requiring any person having the power to do so to produce a copy of the information in legible form and taking possession of the copy.

Offences

41   Offences

(1) A person who –

(a) contravenes section 3(2), 3A or 4(1)(c) of this Act, or

(b) does anything which, by virtue of section 3(3) of this Act, cannot be authorised by a licence,

is guilty of an offence and liable on conviction on indictment to imprisonment for a term not exceeding ten years or a fine or both.

(2) A person who –

(a) contravenes section 3(1) of this Act, otherwise than by doing something which, by virtue of section 3(3) of this Act, cannot be authorised by a licence,

(b) keeps or uses any gametes in contravention of section 4(1)(a) or (b) of this Act,

(c) contravenes section 4(3) of this Act, or

(d) fails to comply with any directions given by virtue of section 24(7)(a) of this Act, is guilty of an offence.

(3) If a person –

(a) provides any information for the purposes of the grant of a licence, being information which is false or misleading in a material particular, and

(b) either he knows the information to be false or misleading in a material particular or he provides the information recklessly, he is guilty of an offence.

(4) A person guilty of an offence under subsection (2) or (3) above is liable –

(a) on conviction on indictment, to imprisonment for a term not exceeding two years or a fine or both, and

(b) on summary conviction, to imprisonment for a term not exceeding six months or a fine not exceeding the statutory maximum or both.

(5) A person who discloses any information in contravention of section 33 of this Act is guilty of an offence and liable –

(a) on conviction on indictment, to imprisonment for a term not exceeding two years or a fine or both, and

(b) on summary conviction, to imprisonment for a term not exceeding six months or a fine not exceeding the statutory maximum or both.

(6) A person who –

(a) fails to comply with a requirement made by virtue of section 39(1)(b) or (2)(b) or 40(2)(b)(ii) or (5)(b) of this Act, or

(b) intentionally obstructs the exercise of any rights conferred by a warrant issued under section 40 of this Act,

is guilty of an offence.

(7) A person who without reasonable excuse fails to comply with a requirement imposed by regulations made by virtue of section 10(2)(a) of this Act is guilty of an offence.

(8) Where a person to whom a licence applies or the nominal licensee gives or receives any money or other benefit, not authorised by directions, in respect of any supply of gametes or embryos, he is guilty of an offence.

(9) A person guilty of an offence under subsection (6), (7) or (8) above is liable on summary conviction to imprisonment for a term not exceeding six months or a fine not exceeding level five on the standard scale or both.

(10) It is a defence for a person ('the defendant') charged with an offence of doing anything which, under section 3(1) or 4(1) of this Act, cannot be done except in pursuance of a licence to prove –

(a) that the defendant was acting under the direction of another, and

(b) that the defendant believed on reasonable grounds –

(i) that the other person was at the material time the person responsible under a licence, a person designated by virtue of section 17(2)(b) of this Act as a person to whom a licence applied, or a person to whom directions had been given by virtue of section 24(9) of this Act, and

(ii) that the defendant was authorised by virtue of the licence or directions to do the thing in question.

(11) It is a defence for a person charged with an offence under this Act to prove –

(a) that at the material time he was a person to whom a licence applied or to whom directions had been given, and

(b) that he took all such steps as were reasonable and exercised all due diligence to avoid committing the offence.

42   Consent to prosecution

No proceedings for an offence under this Act shall be instituted –

    (a) in England and Wales, except by or with the consent of the Director of Public Prosecutions, and

    (b) in Northern Ireland, except by or with the consent of the Director of Public Prosecutions for Northern Ireland.

Miscellaneous and General

43   Keeping and examining gametes and embryos in connection with crime, etc.

    (1) Regulations may provide –

        (a) for the keeping and examination of gametes or embryos, in such manner and on such conditions (if any) as may be specified in regulations, in connection with the investigation of, or proceedings for, an offence (wherever committed), or

        (b) for the storage of gametes, in such manner and on such conditions (if any) as may be specified in regulations, where they are to be used only for such purposes, other than treatment services, as may be specified in regulations.

    (2) Nothing in this Act makes unlawful the keeping or examination of any gametes or embryos in pursuance of regulations made by virtue of this section.

    (3) In this section 'examination' includes use for the purposes of any test.

47   Index

The expressions listed in the left-hand column below are respectively defined or (as the case may be) are to be interpreted in accordance with the provisions of this Act listed in the right-hand column in relation to those expressions.

Expression	*Relevant provision*
Activities governed by this Act	Section 4(5)
Authority	Section 2(1)
Carry, in relation to a child	Section 2(3)
Directions	Section 2(1)
Embryo	Section 1
Gametes, eggs or sperm	Section 1
Keeping, in relation to embryos or gametes	Section 2(2)
Licence	Section 2(1)
Licence committee	Section 9(1)
Nominal licensee	Section 17(3)
Person responsible	Section 17(1)
Person to whom a licence applies	Section 17(2)
Statutory storage period	Section 14(3) to (5)
Store, and similar expressions, in relation to embryos or gametes	Section 2(2)
Treatment services	Section 2(1)

49   Short title, commencement, etc.

    (3) Section 27 to 29 of this Act shall have effect only in relation to children carried by women as a result of the placing in them of embryos or of sperm and eggs, or of their artificial insemination (as the case may be), after the commencement of those sections.

(4) Section 27 of the Family Law Reform Act 1987 (artificial insemination) does not have effect in relation to children carried by women as the result of their artificial insemination after the commencement of sections 27 to 29 of this Act.

Schedules

Schedule 2 Activities for Which Licences may be Granted

Licences for treatment

1.—(1) A licence under this paragraph may authorise any of the following in the course of providing treatment services –

    (a) bringing about the creation of embryos *in vitro*,

    (b) keeping embryos,

    (c) using gametes,

    (d) practices designed to secure that embryos are in a suitable condition to be placed in a woman or to determine whether embryos are suitable for that purpose,

    (e) placing any embryo in a woman,

    (f) mixing sperm with the egg of a hamster, or other animal specified in directions, for the purpose of testing the fertility or normality of the sperm, but only where anything which forms is destroyed when the test is complete and, in any event, not later than the two cell stage, and

    (g) such other practices as may be specified in, or determined in accordance with, regulations.

(2) Subject to the provisions of this Act, a licence under this paragraph may be granted subject to such conditions as may be specified in the licence and may authorise the performance of any of the activities referred to in sub-paragraph (1) above in such manner as may be so specified.

(3) A licence under this paragraph cannot authorise any activity unless it appears to the Authority to be necessary or desirable for the purpose of providing treatment services.

(4) A licence under this paragraph cannot authorise altering the genetic structure of any cell while it forms part of an embryo.

(5) A licence under this paragraph shall be granted for such period not exceeding five years as may be specified in the licence.

Licences for storage

2.—(1) A licence under this paragraph or paragraph 1 or 3 of this Schedule may authorise the storage of gametes or embryos or both.

(2) Subject to the provisions of this Act, a licence authorising such storage may be granted subject to such conditions as may be specified in the licence and may authorise storage in such manner as may be so specified.

(3) A licence under this paragraph shall be granted for such period not exceeding five years as may be specified in the licence.

Licences for research

3.—(1) A licence under this paragraph may authorise any of the following –

    (a) bringing about the creation of embryos *in vitro*, and

    (b) keeping or using embryos,

for the purposes of a project of research specified in the licence.

(2) A licence under this paragraph cannot authorise any activity unless it appears to the Authority to be necessary or desirable for the purpose of –

    (a) promoting advances in the treatment of infertility,

    (b) increasing knowledge about the causes of congenital disease,

(c) increasing knowledge about the causes of miscarriages,

(d) developing more effective techniques of contraception, or

(e) developing methods for detecting the presence of gene or chromosome abnormalities in embryos before implantation,

or for such other purposes as may be specified in regulations.

(3) Purposes may only be so specified with a view to the authorisation of projects of research which increase knowledge about the creation and development of embryos, or about disease, or enable such knowledge to be applied.

(4) A licence under this paragraph cannot authorise altering the genetic structure of any cell while it forms part of an embryo, except in such circumstances (if any) as may be specified in or determined in pursuance of regulations.

(5) A licence under this paragraph may authorise mixing sperm with the egg of a hamster, or other animal specified in directions, for the purpose of developing more effective techniques for determining the fertility or normality of sperm, but only where anything which forms is destroyed when the research is complete and, in any event, not later than the two cell stage.

(6) No licence under this paragraph shall be granted unless the Authority is satisfied that any proposed use of embryos is necessary for the purposes of the research.

(7) Subject to the provisions of this Act, a licence under this paragraph may be granted subject to such conditions as may be specified in the licence.

(8) A licence under this paragraph may authorise the performance of any of the activities referred to in sub-paragraph (1) or (5) above in such manner as may be so specified.

(9) A licence under this paragraph shall be granted for such period not exceeding three years as may be specified in the licence.

General

4.—(1) A licence under this Schedule can only authorise activities to be carried on on premises specified in the licence and under the supervision of an individual designated in the licence.

(2) A licence cannot –

(a) authorise activities falling within both paragraph 1 and paragraph 3 above,

(b) apply to more than one project of research,

(c) authorise activities to be carried on under the supervision of more than one individual, or

(d) apply to premises in different places.

Schedule 3 Consents to Use of Gametes or Embryos

Consent

1. A consent under this Schedule must be given in writing and, in this Schedule, 'effective consent' means a consent under this Schedule which has not been withdrawn.

2.—(1) A consent to the use of any embryo must specify one or more of the following purposes –

(a) use in providing treatment services to the person giving consent, or that person and another specified person together,

(b) use in providing treatment services to persons not including the person giving consent, or

(c) use for the purposes of any project of research,

and may specify conditions subject to which the embryo may be so used.

(2) A consent to the storage of any gametes or any embryo must –

(a) specify the maximum period of storage (if less than the statutory storage period), and

(b) state what is to be done with the gametes or embryo if the person who gave the consent dies or is unable because of incapacity to vary the terms of the consent or to revoke it,

and may specify conditions subject to which the gametes or embryo may remain in storage.

(3) A consent under this Schedule must provide for such other matters as the Authority may specify in directions.

(4) A consent under this Schedule may apply –

(a) to the use or storage of a particular embryo, or

(b) in the case of a person providing gametes, to the use or storage of any embryo whose creation may be brought about using those gametes,

and in the paragraph (b) case the terms of the consent may be varied, or the consent may be withdrawn, in accordance with this Schedule either generally or in relation to a particular embryo or particular embryos.

Procedure for giving consent

3.—(1) Before a person gives consent under this Schedule –

(a) he must be given a suitable opportunity to receive proper counselling about the implications of taking the proposed steps, and

(b) he must be provided with such relevant information as is proper.

(2) Before a person gives consent under this Schedule he must be informed of the effect of paragraph 4 below.

Variation and withdrawal of consent

4.—(1) The terms of any consent under this Schedule may from time to time be varied, and the consent may be withdrawn, by notice given by the person who gave the consent to the person keeping the gametes or embryo to which the consent is relevant.

(2) The terms of any consent to the use of any embryo cannot be varied, and such consent cannot be withdrawn, once the embryo has been used –

(a) in providing treatment services, or

(b) for the purposes of any project of research.

Use of gametes for treatment of others

5.—(1) A person's gametes must not be used for the purposes of treatment services unless there is an effective consent by that person to their being so used and they are used in accordance with the terms of the consent.

(2) A person's gametes must not be received for use for those purposes unless there is an effective consent by that person to their being so used.

(3) This paragraph does not apply to the use of a person's gametes for the purpose of that person, or that person and another together, receiving treatment services.

In vitro fertilisation and subsequent use of embryo

6.—(1) A person's gametes must not be used to bring about the creation of any embryo *in vitro* unless there is an effective consent by that person to any embryo the creation of which may be brought about with the use of those gametes being used for one or more of the purposes mentioned in paragraph 2(1) above.

(2) An embryo the creation of which was brought about *in vitro* must not be received by any person unless there is an effective consent by each person whose gametes were used to bring about the creation of the embryo to the use for one or more of the purposes mentioned in paragraph 2(1) above of the embryo.

(3) An embryo the creation of which was brought about *in vitro* must not be used for any purpose unless there is an effective consent by each person whose gametes were used to bring about the creation of the embryo to the use for that purpose of the embryo and the embryo is used in accordance with those consents.

(4) Any consent required by this paragraph is in addition to any consent that may be required by paragraph 5 above.

Embryos obtained by lavage, etc.

7.—(1) An embryo taken from a woman must not be used for any purpose unless there is an effective consent by her to the use of the embryo for that purpose and it is used in accordance with the consent.

(2) An embryo taken from a woman must not be received by any person for use for any purpose unless there is an effective consent by her to the use of the embryo for that purpose.

(3) This paragraph does not apply to the use, for the purpose of providing a woman with treatment services, of an embryo taken from her.

Storage of gametes and embryos

8.—(1) A person's gametes must not be kept in storage unless there is an effective consent by that person to their storage and they are stored in accordance with the consent.

(2) An embryo the creation of which was brought about *in vitro* must not be kept in storage unless there is an effective consent, by each person whose gametes were used to bring about the creation of the embryo, to the storage of the embryo and the embryo is stored in accordance with those consents.

(3) An embryo taken from a woman must not be kept in storage unless there is an effective consent by her to its storage and it is stored in accordance with the consent.

Health Service Commissioners Act 1993

(1993, c. 46)

Health Service Commissioners

1   The Commissioners

(1) For the purpose of conducting investigations in accordance with this Act, there shall continue to be –

(a) a Health Service Commissioner for England,

(b) a Health Service Commissioner for Wales.

Health service bodies subject to investigation

2   The bodies subject to investigation

(1) The bodies subject to investigation by the Health Service Commissioner for England are –

(a) Strategic Health Authorities,

(c) Special Health Authorities to which this section applies not exercising functions only or mainly in Wales,

(d) National Health Service trusts managing a hospital, or other establishment or facility, in England,

(da)Primary Care Trusts,

(db)NHS foundation trusts.

(2) The bodies subject to investigation by the Health Service Commissioner for Wales are –

(a) Health Authorities,

(aa)Local Health Boards,

(b) Special Health Authorities to which this section applies not exercising functions only or mainly in England,

(c) National Health Service trusts managing a hospital, or other establishment or facility, in Wales, and

(ca)the National Assembly for Wales ('the Assembly').

Persons subject to investigation

2A   Health service providers subject to investigation

(1) Persons are subject to investigation by the Health Service Commissioner for England if they are or were at the time of the action complained of –

(a) persons (whether individuals or bodies) providing services under a contract entered into by them with a Primary Care Trust under section 84 or 100 of the National Health Service Act 2006;

(b) persons (whether individuals or bodies) undertaking to provide in England pharmaceutical services under that Act; or

(c) individuals performing in England primary medical services or primary dental services in accordance with arrangements made under section section 92 or 107 of that Act (except as employees of, or otherwise on behalf of, a health service body or an independent provider).

(4) In this Act –

(a) references to a family health service provider are to any person mentioned in subsection (1) or (2);

(b) references to family health services are to any of the services so mentioned.

2B   Independent providers subject to investigation

(1) Persons are subject to investigation by the Health Service Commissioner for England if –

(a) they are or were at the time of the action complained of persons (whether individuals or bodies) providing services in England under arrangements with health service bodies or family health service providers, and

(b) they are not or were not at the time of the action complained of themselves health service bodies or family health service providers.

(4) The services provided under arrangements mentioned in subsection (1)(a) or (2)(a) may be services of any kind.

(5) In this Act references to an independent provider are to any person providing services as mentioned in subsection (1) or (2).

Matters subject to investigation

3   General remit of Commissioners

(1) On a complaint duly made to a Commissioner by or on behalf of a person that he has sustained injustice or hardship in consequence of –

(a) a failure in a service provided by a health service body,

(b) a failure of such a body to provide a service which it was a function of the body to provide, or

(c) maladministration connected with any other action taken by or on behalf of such a body,

the Commissioner may, subject to the provisions of this Act, investigate the alleged failure or other action.

(1A) Where a family health service provider has undertaken to provide any family health services and a complaint is duly made to a Commissioner by or on behalf of a person that he has sustained injustice or hardship in consequence of –

(a) action taken by the family health service provider in connection with the services,

(b) action taken in connection with the services by a person employed by the family health service provider in respect of the services,

(c) action taken in connection with the services by a person acting on behalf of the family health service provider in respect of the services, or

(d) action taken in connection with the services by a person to whom the family health service provider has delegated any functions in respect of the services,

the Commissioner may, subject to the provisions of this Act, investigate the alleged action.

(1C) Where an independent provider has made an arrangement with a health service body or a family health service provider to provide a service (of whatever kind) and a complaint is duly made to a Commissioner by or on behalf of a person that he has sustained injustice or hardship in consequence of –

(a) a failure in the service provided by the independent provider,

(b) a failure of the independent provider to provide the service, or

(c) maladministration connected with any other action taken in relation to the service,

the Commissioner may, subject to the provisions of this Act, investigate the alleged failure or other action.

(1D) Any failure or maladministration mentioned in subsection (1C) may arise from action of –

(a) the independent provider,

(b) a person employed by the provider,

(c) a person acting on behalf of the provider, or

(d) a person to whom the provider has delegated any functions.

(1E) Where a complaint is duly made to a Commissioner by or on behalf of a person that the person has sustained injustice or hardship in consequence of maladministration by any person or body in the exercise of any function under section 113 of the Health and Social Care (Community Health and Standards) Act 2003 (complaints about health care), the Commissioner may, subject to the provisions of this Act, investigate the alleged maladministration.

(1F) Where a complaint is duly made to the Commissioner by or on behalf of a person that the person has sustained injustice or hardship in consequence of maladministration by any person or body –

(a) in the exercise of any functions under a scheme established under section 1 of the NHS Redress Act 2006,

(b) in connection with a settlement agreement entered into under such a scheme, or

(c) in the exercise of any functions under regulations made under section 14 of that Act (complaints about maladministration in connection with redress scheme), the Commissioner may, subject to the provisions of this Act, investigate the alleged mal-administration.

(2) In determining whether to initiate, continue or discontinue an investigation under this Act, a Commissioner shall act in accordance with his own discretion.

(3) Any question whether a complaint is duly made to a Commissioner shall be determined by him.

(4) Nothing in this Act authorises or requires a Commissioner to question the merits of a decision taken without maladministration by a health service body in the exercise of a discretion vested in that body.

(5) Nothing in this Act authorises or requires a Commissioner to question the merits of a decision taken without maladministration by –

(a) a family health service provider,

(b) a person employed by a family health service provider,

(c) a person acting on behalf of a family health service provider, or

(d) a person to whom a family health service provider has delegated any functions.

(6) Nothing in this Act authorises or requires a Commissioner to question the merits of a decision taken without maladministration by –

(a) an independent provider,

(b) a person employed by an independent provider,

(c) a person acting on behalf of an independent provider, or

(d) a person to whom an independent provider has delegated any functions.

Matters excluded from investigation

4   Availability of other remedy

(1) A Commissioner shall not conduct an investigation in respect of action in relation to which the person aggrieved has or had –

(a) a right of appeal, reference or review to or before a tribunal constituted by or under any enactment or by virtue of Her Majesty's prerogative, or

(b) a remedy by way of proceedings in any court of law,

unless the Commissioner is satisfied that in the particular circumstances it is not reasonable to expect that person to resort or have resorted to it.

(2) A Commissioner shall not conduct an investigation in respect of action which has been, or is, the subject of an inquiry under section 84 of the National Health Service Act 1977.

(4) Subsection (5) applies where –

> (a) action by reference to which a complaint is made under section 3(1), (1A) , (1C) or (1F)(a) or (b) is action by reference to which a complaint can be made under section 113(1) or (2) of the Health and Social Care (Community Health and Standards) Act 2003 under section 14 of the NHS Redress Act 2006 or under a procedure operated by a health service body, a family health service provider or an independent provider, and
> (b) subsection (1), (2) or (3) does not apply as regards the action.

(5) In such a case a Commissioner shall not conduct an investigation in respect of the action unless he is satisfied that –

> (a) the other procedure has been invoked and exhausted, or
> (b) in the particular circumstances it is not reasonable to expect that procedure to be invoked or (as the case may be) exhausted.

6   General health services and service committees

(3) A Commissioner shall not conduct an investigation in respect of action taken by a Primary Care Trust or Health Authority in the exercise of its functions under the National Health Service (Service Committees and Tribunal) Regulations 1992, or any instrument amending or replacing those regulations.

(5) A Commissioner shall not conduct an investigation in respect of action taken by a Primary Care Trust or Health Authority in the exercise of its functions under regulations made under section 126 or 129 of the National Health Service Act 2006 by virtue of section 17 of the Health and Medicines Act 1988 (investigations of matters relating to services).

7   Personnel, contracts etc.

(1) A Commissioner shall not conduct an investigation in respect of action taken in respect of appointments or removals, pay, discipline, superannuation or other personnel matters in relation to service under the National Health Service Act 2006 or the National Health Service (Wales) Act 2006.

(2) A Commissioner shall not conduct an investigation in respect of action taken in matters relating to contractual or other commercial transactions, except for –

> (a) matters relating to NHS contracts (as defined by section 9 of the National Health Service Act 2006),
> (b) matters arising from arrangements between a health service body and an independent provider for the provision of services by the provider,
> (c) matters arising from arrangements between a family health service provider and an independent provider for the provision of services by the independent provider and,
> (d) matters arising from settlement agreements entered into under a scheme established under section 1 of the NHS Redress Act 2006.

(3) In determining what matters arise from arrangements mentioned in subsection (2)(b) the Health Service Commissioners for England and for Wales shall disregard any arrangements for the provision of services at an establishment maintained by a Minister of the Crown mainly for patients who are members of the armed forces of the Crown.

(3A) A Commissioner shall not conduct an investigation in pursuance of a complaint if –

> (a) the complaint is in respect of action taken in any matter relating to arrangements made by a health service body and a family health service provider for the provision of family health services,
> (b) the action is taken by or on behalf of the body or by the provider, and
> (c) the complaint is made by the provider or the body.

(3B) Nothing in the preceding provisions of this section prevents a Commissioner conducting an investigation in respect of action taken by a health service body in operating a procedure established to examine complaint.

Complaints

8   Individuals or bodies entitled to complain

(1) A complaint under this Act may be made by an individual or a body of persons, whether incorporated or not, other than a public authority.

9   Requirements to be complied with

(1) The following requirements apply in relation to a complaint, made to a Commissioner.

(2) A complaint must be made in writing.

(3) The complaint shall not be entertained unless it is made –

(a) by the person aggrieved, or

(b) where the person by whom a complaint might have been made has died or is for any reason unable to act for himself, by –

(i)   his personal representative,

(ii) a member of his family, or

(iii) some body or individual suitable to represent him.

(4) The Commissioner shall not entertain the complaint if it is made more than a year after the day on which the person aggrieved first had notice of the matters alleged in the complaint, unless he considers it reasonable to do so.

(4A) In the case of a complaint against a person who is no longer of a description set out in section 2A(1) or (2), but was of such a description at the time of the action complained of, the Commissioner shall not entertain the complaint if it is made more than three years after the last day on which the person was a family health service provider.

(4B) In the case of a complaint against a person falling within section 2B(1) or (2) in relation to whom there are no longer any such arrangements as are mentioned there, the Commissioner shall not entertain the complaint if it is made more than three years after the last day on which the person was an independent provider.

10   Referral of complaint by health service body

(1) A health service body may itself refer to a Commissioner a complaint made to that body that a person has, in consequence of a failure or maladministration for which the body is responsible, sustained such injustice or hardship as is mentioned in section 3(1).

(2) A complaint may not be so referred unless it was made –

(a) in writing,

(b) by the person aggrieved or by a person authorised by section 9(3)(b) to complain to the Commissioner on his behalf, and

(c) not more than a year after the person aggrieved first had notice of the matters alleged in the complaint, or such later date as the Commissioner considers appropriate in any particular case.

(3) A health service body may not refer a complaint under this section after the period of one year beginning with the day on which the body received the complaint.

(4) Any question whether a complaint has been duly referred to a Commissioner under this section shall be determined by him.

(5) A complaint referred to a Commissioner under this section shall be deemed to be duly made to him.

Investigations

11   Procedure in respect of investigations

(1) Where a Commissioner proposes to conduct an investigation pursuant to a complaint under section 3(1), he shall afford –

   (a) to the health service body concerned, and
   (b) to any other person who is alleged in the complaint to have taken or authorised the
       action complained of,
an opportunity to comment on any allegations contained in the complaint.
   (1A) Where a Commissioner proposes to conduct an investigation pursuant to a complaint
under section 3(1A), he shall afford –
   (a) to the family health service provider, and
   (b) to any person by reference to whose action the complaint is made (if different from the
       family health service provider),
an opportunity to comment on any allegations contained in the complaint.
   (1B) Where a Commissioner proposes to conduct an investigation pursuant to a complaint
under section 3(1C) he shall afford –
   (a) to the independent provider concerned, and
   (b) to any other person who is alleged in the complaint to have taken or authorised the
       action complained of,
an opportunity to comment on any allegations contained in the complaint.
   (1C) Where a Commissioner proposes to conduct an investigation pursuant to a
complaint under section 3(1E) or (1F), he shall afford to the person or body whose maladministration is complained of an opportunity to comment on any allegations contained in
the complaint.
   (2) An investigation shall be conducted in private.
   (3) In other respects, the procedure for conducting an investigation shall be such as the
Commissioner considers appropriate in the circumstances of the case, and in particular –
   (a) he may obtain information from such persons and in such manner, and make such
       inquiries, as he thinks fit, and
   (b) he may determine whether any person may be represented, by counsel or solicitor or
       otherwise, in the investigation.
   (4) A Commissioner may, if he thinks fit, pay to the person by whom the complaint was made
and to any other person who attends or supplies information for the purposes of an investigation –
   (a) sums in respect of expenses properly incurred by them, and
   (b) allowances by way of compensation for the loss of their time.
Payments under this subsection shall be in accordance with such scales and subject to such conditions as may be determined by the Treasury.
   (5) The conduct of an investigation pursuant to a complaint under section 3(1) shall not affect
any action taken by the health service body concerned, or any power or duty of that body to take
further action with respect to any matters subject to the investigation.
   (5A) The conduct of an investigation pursuant to a complaint under section 3(1A) or (1C) shall
not affect any action taken by the family health service provider or independent provider concerned, or any power or duty of that provider to take further action with respect to any matters
subject to the investigation.
   (6) Where the person aggrieved has been removed from the United Kingdom under any order
in force under the Immigration Act 1971 he shall, if the Commissioner so directs, be permitted to re-
enter and remain in the United Kingdom, subject to such conditions as the Secretary of State may
direct, for the purposes of the investigation.

12   Evidence
   (1) For the purposes of an investigation pursuant to a complaint under section 3(1) a Commissioner may require any officer or member of the health service body concerned or any other
person who in his opinion is able to supply information or produce documents relevant to the
investigation to supply any such information or Produce any such document.
   (1A) For the purposes of an investigation pursuant to a complaint under section 3(1A) or (1C),
(1E) or (1F) a Commissioner may require any person who in his opinion is able to supply information

or produce documents relevant to the investigation to supply any such information or produce any such document.

(2) For the purposes of an investigation a Commissioner shall have the same powers as the Court in respect of –

(a) the attendance and examination of witnesses (including the administration of oaths and affirmations and the examination of witnesses abroad), and

(b) the production of documents.

(3) No obligation to maintain secrecy or other restriction on the disclosure of information obtained by or supplied to persons in Her Majesty's service, whether imposed by any enactment or by any rule of law, shall apply to the disclosure of information for the purposes of an investigation.

(4) The Crown shall not be entitled in relation to an investigation to any such privilege in respect of the production of documents or the giving of evidence as is allowed by law in legal proceedings.

(5) No person shall be required or authorised by this Act –

(a) to supply any information or answer any question relating to proceedings of the Cabinet or of any Committee of the Cabinet, or

(b) to produce so much of any document as relates to such proceedings;

and for the purposes of this subsection a certificate issued by the Secretary of the Cabinet with the approval of the Prime Minister and certifying that any information, question, document or part of a document relates to such proceedings shall be conclusive.

(6) Subject to subsections (3) and (4), no person shall be compelled for the purposes of an investigation to give any evidence or produce any document which he could not be compelled to give or produce in civil proceedings before the Court.

13   Obstruction and contempt

(1) A Commissioner may certify an offence to the Court where –

(a) a person without lawful excuse obstructs him or any of his officers in the performance of his functions, or

(b) a person is guilty of any act or omission in relation to an investigation which, if that investigation were a proceeding in the Court, would constitute contempt of court.

(2) Where an offence is so certified the Court may inquire into the matter and after hearing –

(a) any witnesses who may be produced against or on behalf of the person charged with the offence, and

(b) any statement that may be offered in defence,

the Court may deal with the person charged with the offence in any manner in which it could deal with him if he had committed the like offence in relation to the Court.

(3) Nothing in this section shall be construed as applying to the taking of any such action as is mentioned in section 11(5).

Reports

14   Reports by Commissioners

(1) In any case where the Health Service Commissioner for England conducts an investigation pursuant to a complaint under section 3(1) he shall send a report of the results of the investigation –

(a) to the person who made the complaint,

(b) to any member of the House of Commons who to the Commissioner's knowledge assisted in the making of the complaint (or if he is no longer a member to such other member as the Commissioner thinks appropriate),

(c) to the health service body who at the time the report is made provides the service, or has the function, in relation to which the complaint was made,

(d) to any person who is alleged in the complaint to have taken or authorised the action complained of, and

(e) to the Secretary of State,

(2) In any case pursuant to a complaint under section 3(1) where the Health Service Commissioner for England decides not to conduct an investigation pursuant to a complaint under section 3(1) he shall send a statement of his reasons –

(a) to the person who made the complaint,

(b) to any such member of the House of Commons as is mentioned in subsection (1)(b), and

(2A) In any case where the Health Service Commissioner for England conducts an investigation pursuant to a complaint under section 3(1A) he shall send a report of the results of the investigation –

(a) to the person who made the complaint,

(b) to any member of the House of Commons who to the Commissioner's knowledge assisted in the making of the complaint (or if he is no longer a member to such other member as the Commissioner thinks appropriate),

(c) to any person by reference to whose action the complaint is made,

(d) to the family health service provider (if he does not fall within paragraph (c)),

(e) to any health service body with whom the family health service provider is subject to an undertaking to provide family health services, and

(f) to the Secretary of State.

(2B) In any case where the Health Service Commissioner for England decides not to conduct an investigation pursuant to a complaint under section 3(1A) he shall send a statement of his reasons –

(a) to the person who made the complaint, and

(b) to any such member of the House of Commons as is mentioned in subsection (2A)(b).

(2C) In any case where the Health Service Commissioner for England conducts an investigation pursuant to a complaint under section 3(1C) he shall send a report of the results of the investigation –

(a) to the person who made the complaint,

(b) to any member of the House of Commons who to the Commissioner's knowledge assisted in the making of the complaint (or if he is no longer a member to such other member as the Commissioner thinks appropriate),

(c) to any person who is alleged in the complaint to have taken or authorised the action complained of,

(d) to the independent provider,

(e) to the health service body or family health service provider with whom the independent provider made the arrangement to provide the service concerned, and

(f) to the Secretary of State.

(2D) In any case where the Health Service Commissioner for England decides not to conduct an investigation pursuant to a complaint under section 3(1C) he shall send a statement of his reasons –

(a) to the person who made the complaint, and

(b) to any such member of the House of Commons as is mentioned in subsection (2C)(b).

(2E) In any case where the Health Service Commissioner for England conducts an investigation pursuant to a complaint under section 3(1E) he shall send a report of the results of the investigation –

(a) to the person who made the complaint;

(b) to any member of the House of Commons who to the Commissioner's knowledge assisted in the making of the complaint (or if he is no longer a member to such other member as the Commissioner thinks appropriate);

(c) to the person or body whose maladministration is complained of;

(d) to any person or body whose action was complained of in the complaint made to the person or body whose maladministration is complained of;

(e) to the Secretary of State.

(2F) In any case where the Health Service Commissioner for England decides not to conduct an investigation pursuant to a complaint under section 3(1E) he shall send a statement of his reasons –

(a) to the person who made the complaint; or

(b) to any such member of the House of Commons as is mentioned in subsection (2E)(b).

(3) If after conducting an investigation it appears to the Health Service Commissioner for England that –

    (a) the person aggrieved has sustained such injustice or hardship as is mentioned in section 3(1), (1A) or (1C) and

    (b) the injustice or hardship has not been and will not be remedied,

he may if he thinks fit lay before each House of Parliament a special report on the case.

(4) The Health Service Commissioner –

    (a) shall annually lay before each House of Parliament a general report on the performance of his functions under this Act, and

    (b) may from time to time lay before each House of Parliament such other reports with respect to those functions as he thinks fit.

(5) For the purposes of the law of defamation, the publication of any matter by a Commissioner in sending or making a report or statement in pursuance of this section shall be absolutely privileged.

(2G) In any case where the Commissioner conducts an investigation pursuant to a complaint under section 3(1F) he shall send a report of the results of the investigation –

    (a) to the person who made the complaint,

    (b) to any member of the House of Commons who to the Commissioner's knowledge assisted in the making of the complaint (or if he is no longer a member to such other member as the Commissioner thinks appropriate),

    (c) to the person or body whose maladministration is complained of,

    (d) in the case of a complaint under section 3(1F)(c), to any person or body whose action was complained of in the complaint made to the person or body whose maladministration is complained of, and

    (e) to the Secretary of State.

(2H) In any case where the Commissioner decides not to conduct an investigation pursuant to a complaint under section 3(1F) he shall send a statement of his reasons –

    (a) to the person who made the complaint, and

    (b) to any such member of the House of Commons as is mentioned in subsection (2G)(b).

Information and consultation

15   Confidentiality of information

(1) Information obtained by a Commissioner or his officers in the course of or for the purposes of an investigation shall not be disclosed except –

    (a) for the purposes of the investigation and any report to be made in respect of it,

    (b) for the purposes of any proceedings for –

        (i) an offence under the Official Secrets Acts 1911 to 1989 alleged to have been committed in respect of information obtained by virtue of this Act by a Commissioner or any of his officers, or

        (ii) an offence of perjury alleged to have been committed in the course of the investigation,

    (c) for the purposes of an inquiry with a view to the taking of such proceedings as are mentioned in paragraph (b),

    (d) for the purposes of any proceedings under section 13 (offences of obstruction and contempt) or

    (e) where the information is to the effect that any person is likely to constitute a threat to the health or safety of patients as permitted by subsection (1B).

(1B) In a case within subsection (1)(e) the Commissioner may disclose the information to any persons to whom he thinks it should be disclosed in the interests of the health and safety of patients.

(1C) If a Commissioner discloses information as permitted by subsection (1B) he shall –

(a) where he knows the identity of the person mentioned in subsection (1)(e), inform that person that he has disclosed the information and of the identity of any person to whom he has disclosed it, and

(b) inform the person from whom the information was obtained that he has disclosed it.

(2) Neither a Commissioner nor his officers nor his advisers shall be called on to give evidence in any proceedings, other than proceedings mentioned in subsection (1), of matters coming to his or their knowledge in the course of an investigation under this Act.

(3) The reference in subsection (2) to a Commissioner's advisers is a reference to persons from whom the Commissioner obtains advice under paragraph 13 of Schedule 1.

(4) Information obtained from the Information Commissioner by virtue of section 76 of the Freedom of Information Act 2000 shall be treated for the purposes of subsection (1) as obtained for the purposes of an investigation and, in relation to such information, the reference in paragraph (a) of that subsection to the investigation shall have effect as a reference to any investigation.

16   Information prejudicial to the safety of the State

(1) A Minister of the Crown may give notice in writing to a Commissioner with respect to any document or information specified in the notice that in the Minister's opinion the disclosure of the document or information would be prejudicial to the safety of the State or otherwise contrary to the public interest.

(2) Where such a notice is given to a Commissioner, nothing in this Act shall be construed as authorising or requiring him or any of his officers to communicate to any person or for any purpose any document or information specified in the notice.

(3) References above to a document or information include references to a class of document or a class of information.

17   Use of information by Commissioner in other capacity

(1) This section applies where a Commissioner also holds any of the other offices of Health Service Commissioner or the office of Parliamentary Commissioner (an 'additional office').

(2) Where –

(a) a person initiates a complaint to the Commissioner as the holder of the additional office, and

(b) the complaint relates partly to a matter with respect to which that person has previously initiated, or subsequently initiates, a complaint to the Commissioner in his capacity as such,

information obtained by the Commissioner or his officers in the course of or for the purposes of the investigation of that other complaint may be disclosed for the purposes of carrying out his functions in relation to the complaint initiated to him as the holder of the additional office.

18   Consultation during investigation

(1) Where a Commissioner, at any stage in the course of conducting an investigation, forms the opinion that the complaint relates partly to a matter which could be the subject of an investigation –

(a) by either of the other Health Service Commissioners under this Act,

(b) by the Parliamentary Commissioner under the Parliamentary Commissioner Act 1967,

(c) by a Local Commissioner under Part III of the Local Government Act 1974,

he shall consult about the complaint with the appropriate Commissioner and, if he considers it necessary, he shall inform the person initiating the complaint of the steps necessary to initiate a complaint to that Commissioner.

(2) Where a Commissioner consults with another Commissioner in accordance with this section, the consultations may extend to any matter relating to the complaint, including –

(a) the conduct of any investigation into the complaint, and

(b) the form, content and publication of any report of the results of such an investigation.

(3) Nothing in section 15 (confidentiality of information) applies in relation to the disclosure of information by a Commissioner or his officers in the course of consultations held in accordance with this section.

18A   Disclosure of information to Information Commissioner

(1) The Health Service Commissioner for England or the Health Service Commissioner for Wales may disclose to the Information Commissioner any information obtained by, or furnished to, the Health Service Commissioner under or for the purposes of this Act if the information appears to the Health Service Commissioner to relate to –

(a) a matter in respect of which the Information Commissioner could exercise any power conferred by –

(i)   Part V of the Data Protection Act 1998 (enforcement),

(ii) section 48 of the Freedom of Information Act 2000 (practice recommendations), or

(iii) Part IV of that Act (enforcement), or

(b) the commission of an offence under –

(i)   any provision of the Data Protection Act 1998 other than paragraph 12 of Schedule 9 (obstruction of execution of warrant), or

(ii) section 77 of the Freedom of Information Act 2000 (offence of altering etc. records with intent to prevent disclosure).

(3) Nothing in section 15 (confidentiality of information) applies in relation to the disclosure of information in accordance with this section.

Schedule

Schedule 1 The English Commissioners

Ineligibility of certain persons for appointment

3.—(1) A person who is a member of a relevant health service body shall not be appointed a Commissioner or acting Commissioner; and a person so appointed shall not, during his appointment, become a member of such a body.

3A.—(1) A person who is a relevant family health service provider shall not be appointed a Commissioner or acting Commissioner; and a person so appointed shall not, during his appointment, become a relevant family health service provider.

Family Law Act 1996

(1996, c. 27)

48   Remand for medical examination and report

(1) If the relevant judicial authority has reason to consider that a medical report will be required, any power to remand a person under section 47(7)(b) or (10) may be exercised for the purpose of enabling a medical examination and report to be made.

(2) If such a power is so exercised, the adjournment must not be for more than 4 weeks at a time unless the relevant judicial authority remands the accused in custody.

(3) If the relevant judicial authority so remands the accused, the adjournment must not be for more than 3 weeks at a time.

(4) If there is reason to suspect that a person who has been arrested –

(a) under section 47(6), or

(b) under a warrant issued on an application made under section 47(8),

is suffering from mental illness or severe mental impairment, the relevant judicial authority has the same power to make an order under section 35 of the Mental Health Act 1983 (remand for report on accused's mental condition) as the Crown Court has under section 35 of the Act of 1983 in the case of an accused person within the meaning of that section.

51　Power of magistrates' court to order hospital admission or guardianship

(1) A magistrates' court has the same power to make a hospital order or guardianship order under section 37 of the Mental Health Act 1983 or an interim hospital order under section 38 of that Act in the case of a person suffering from mental illness or severe mental impairment who could otherwise be committed to custody for breach of a relevant requirement as a magistrates' court has under those sections in the case of a person convicted of an offence punishable on summary conviction with imprisonment.

Data Protection Act 1998

(1998, c. 29)

Part I Preliminary

1　Basic interpretative provisions

(1) In this Act, unless the context otherwise requires –

'data' means information which –

(a) is being processed by means of equipment operating automatically in response to instructions given for that purpose,

(b) is recorded with the intention that it should be processed by means of such equipment,

(c) is recorded as part of a relevant filing system or with the intention that it should form part of a relevant filing system,

(d) does not fall within paragraph (a), (b) or (c) but forms part of an accessible record as defined by section 68; or

(e) is recorded information held by a public authority and does not fall within any of the paragraphs (a) to (d);

'public authority' has the same meaning as in the Freedom of Information Act 2000;

'data controller' means, subject to subsection (4), a person who (either alone or jointly or in common with other persons) determines the purposes for which and the manner in which any personal data are, or are to be, processed;

'data processor', in relation to personal data, means any person (other than an employee of the data controller) who processes the data on behalf of the data controller;

'data subject' means an individual who is the subject of personal data;

'personal data' means data which relate to a living individual who can be identified –

(a) from those data, or

(b) from those data and other information which is in the possession of, or is likely to come into the possession of, the data controller,

and includes any expression of opinion about the individual and any indication of the intentions of the data controller or any other person in respect of the individual;

'processing', in relation to information or data, means obtaining, recording or holding the information or data or carrying out any operation or set of operations on the information or data, including –

(a) organisation, adaptation or alteration of the information or data,

(b) retrieval, consultation or use of the information or data,

(c) disclosure of the information or data by transmission, dissemination or otherwise making available, or

(d) alignment, combination, blocking, erasure or destruction of the information or data;

'relevant filing system' means any set of information relating to individuals to the extent that, although the information is not processed by means of equipment operating automatically in response to instructions given for that purpose, the set is structured, either by reference to individuals or by reference to criteria relating to individuals, in such a way that specific information relating to a particular individual is readily accessible.

(2) In this Act, unless the context otherwise requires –

    (a) 'obtaining' or 'recording', in relation to personal data, includes obtaining or recording the information to be contained in the data, and

    (b) 'using' or 'disclosing', in relation to personal data, includes using or disclosing the information contained in the data.

(3) In determining for the purposes of this Act whether any information is recorded with the intention –

    (a) that it should be processed by means of equipment operating automatically in response to instructions given for that purpose, or

    (b) that it should form part of a relevant filing system, it is immaterial that it is intended to be so processed or to form part of such a system only after being transferred to a country or territory outside the European Economic Area.

(4) Where personal data are processed only for purposes for which they are required by or under any enactment to be processed, the person on whom the obligation to process the data is imposed by or under that enactment is for the purposes of this Act the data controller.

2   Sensitive personal data

In this Act 'sensitive personal data' means personal data consisting of information as to –

    (a) the racial or ethnic origin of data subject,

    (b) his political opinions,

    (c) his religious beliefs or other beliefs of a similar nature,

    (d) whether he is a member of a trade union (within the meaning of the Trade Union and Labour Relations (Consolidation) Act 1992),

    (e) his physical or mental health or condition,

    (f) his sexual life,

    (g) the commission or alleged commission by him of any offence, or

    (h) any proceedings for any offence committed or alleged to have been committed by him, the disposal of such proceedings or the sentence of any court in such proceedings.

3   The special purposes

In this Act 'the special purposes' means any one or more of the following –

    (a) the purposes of journalism,

    (b) artistic purposes, and

    (c) literary purposes.

4   The data protection principles

(1) References in this Act to the data protection principles are to the principles set out in Part I of Schedule 1.

(2) Those principles are to be interpreted in accordance with Part II of Schedule 1.

(3) Schedule 2 (which applies to all personal data) and Schedule 3 (which applies only to sensitive personal data) set out conditions applying for the purposes of the first principle; and Schedule 4 sets out cases in which the eighth principle does not apply.

(4) Subject to section 27(1), it shall be the duty of a data controller to comply with the data protection principles in relation to all personal data with respect to which he is the data controller.

5   Application of Act

(1) Except as otherwise provided by or under section 54, this Act applies to a data controller in respect of any data only if –

    (a) the data controller is established in the United Kingdom and the data are processed in the context of that establishment, or

    (b) the data controller is established neither in the United Kingdom nor in any other EEA State but uses equipment in the United Kingdom for processing the data otherwise than for the purposes of transit through the United Kingdom.

(2) A data controller falling within subsection (1)(b) must nominate for the purposes of this Act a representative established in the United Kingdom.

(3) For the purposes of subsections (1) and (2), each of the following is to be treated as established in the United Kingdom –

(a) an individual who is ordinarily resident in the United Kingdom,

(b) a body incorporated under the law of, or of any part of, the United Kingdom,

(c) a partnership or other unincorporated association formed under the law of any part of the United Kingdom, and

(d) any person who does not fall within paragraph (a), (b) or (c) but maintains in the United Kingdom –

(i) an office, branch or agency through which he carries on any activity, or

(ii) a regular practice;

and the reference to establishment in any other EEA State has a corresponding meaning.

6   The Commissioner and the Tribunal

(1) For the purposes of this Act and of the Freedom of Information Act 2000 there shall be an officer known as the Information Commissioner (in this Act referred to as the Commissioner).

(3) For the purposes of this Act and of the Freedom of Information Act 2000 there shall be a tribunal known as the Information Tribunal (in this Act referred to as the Tribunal).

(4) The Tribunal shall consist of –

(a) a chairman appointed by the Lord Chancellor after consultation with the Secretary of State,

(b) such number of deputy chairmen so appointed as the Lord Chancellor may determine, and

(c) such number of other members appointed by the Lord Chancellor as he may determine.

(6) The members of the Tribunal appointed under subsection 4(c) shall be –

(a) persons to represent the interests of data subjects,

(aa) persons to represent the interests of those who make requests for information under the Freedom of Information Act 2000,

(b) persons to represent the interests of data controllers, and

(bb) persons to represent the interests of public authorities.

Part II Rights of Data Subjects and Others

7   Right of access to personal data

(1) Subject to the following provisions of this section and to sections 8 and 9 and 9A, an individual is entitled –

(a) to be informed by any data controller whether personal data of which that individual is the data subject are being processed by or on behalf of that data controller,

(b) if that is the case, to be given by the data controller a description of –

(i) the personal data of which that individual is the data subject,

(ii) the purposes for which they are being or are to be processed, and

(iii) the recipients or classes of recipients to whom they are or may be disclosed,

(c) to have communicated to him in an intelligible form –

(i) the information constituting any personal data of which that individual is the data subject, and

(ii) any information available to the data controller as to the source of those data, and

(d) where the processing by automatic means of personal data of which that individual is the data subject for the purpose of evaluating matters relating to him such as, for example, his performance at work, his creditworthiness, his reliability or his conduct, has constituted or is likely to constitute the sole basis for any decision significantly affecting him, to be informed by the data controller of the logic involved in that decision-taking.

(2) A data controller is not obliged to supply any information under subsection (1) unless he has received –

(a) a request in writing, and

(b) except in prescribed cases, such fee (not exceeding the prescribed maximum) as he may require.

(3) Where a data controller –

(a) reasonably requires further information in order to satisfy himself as to the identity of the person making a request under this section and to locate the information which that person seeks, and

(b) has informed him of that requirement, the data controller is not obliged to comply with the request unless he is supplied with that further information.

(4) Where a data controller cannot comply with the request without disclosing information relating to another individual who can be identified from that information, he is not obliged to comply with the request unless –

(a) the other individual has consented to the disclosure of the information to the person making the request, or

(b) it is reasonable in all the circumstances to comply with the request without the consent of the other individual.

(5) In subsection (4) the reference to information relating to another individual includes a reference to information identifying that individual as the source of the information sought by the request; and that subsection is not to be construed as excusing a data controller from communicating so much of the information sought by the request as can be communicated without disclosing the identity of the other individual concerned, whether by the omission of names or other identifying particulars or otherwise.

(6) In determining for the purposes of subsection (4)(b) whether it is reasonable in all the circumstances to comply with the request without the consent of the other individual concerned, regard shall be had, in particular, to –

(a) any duty of confidentiality owed to the other individual,

(b) any steps taken by the data controller with a view to seeking the consent of the other individual,

(c) whether the other individual is capable of giving consent, and

(d) any express refusal of consent by the other individual.

(7) An individual making a request under this section may, in such cases as may be prescribed, specify that his request is limited to personal data of any prescribed description.

(8) Subject to subsection (4), a data controller shall comply with a request under this section promptly and in any event before the end of the prescribed period beginning with the relevant day.

(9) If a court is satisfied on the application of any person who has made a request under the foregoing provisions of this section that the data controller in question has failed to comply with the request in contravention of those provisions, the court may order him to comply with the request.

(10) In this section –

'prescribed' means prescribed by the Secretary of State by regulations;

'the prescribed maximum' means such amount as may be prescribed;

'prescribed period' means forty days or such other period as may be prescribed;

'the relevant day', in relation to a request under this section, means the day on which the data controller receives the request or, if later, the first day on which the data controller has both the required fee and the information referred to in subsection (3).

(11) Different amounts or periods may be prescribed under this section in relation to different cases.

8   Provisions supplementary to section 7

(1) The Secretary of State may by regulations provide that, in such cases as may be prescribed, a request for information under any provision of subsection (1) of section 7 is to be treated as extending also to information under other provisions of that subsection.

(2) The obligation imposed by section 7(1)(c)(i) must be complied with by supplying the data subject with a copy of the information in permanent form unless –

   (a) the supply of such a copy is not possible or would involve disproportionate effort, or

   (b) the data subject agrees otherwise;

and where any of the information referred to in section 7(1)(c)(i) is expressed in terms which are not intelligible without explanation the copy must be accompanied by an explanation of those terms.

(3) Where a data controller has previously complied with a request made under section 7 by an individual, the data controller is not obliged to comply with a subsequent identical or similar request under that section by that individual unless a reasonable interval has elapsed between compliance with the previous request and the making of the current request.

(4) In determining for the purposes of subsection (3) whether requests under section 7 are made at reasonable intervals, regard shall be had to the nature of the data, the purpose for which the data are processed and the frequency with which data are altered.

(5) Section 7(1)(d) is not to be regarded as requiring the provision of information as to the logic involved in any decision-taking if, and to the extent that, the information constitutes a trade secret.

(6) The information to be supplied pursuant to a request under section 7 must be supplied by reference to the data in question at the time when the request is received, except that it may take account of any amendment or deletion made between that time and the time when the information is supplied, being an amendment or deletion that would have been made regardless of the receipt of the request.

(7) For the purposes of section 7(4) and (5) another individual can be identified from the information being disclosed if he can be identified from that information, or from that and any other information which, in the reasonable belief of the data controller, is likely to be in, or to come into, the possession of the data subject making the request.

10   Right to prevent processing likely to cause damage or distress

(1) Subject to subsection (2), an individual is entitled at any time by notice in writing to a data controller to require the data controller at the end of such period as is reasonable in the circumstances to cease, or not to begin, processing, or processing for a specified purpose or in a specified manner, any personal data in respect of which he is the data subject, on the ground that, for specified reasons –

   (a) the processing of those data or their processing for that purpose or in that manner is causing or is likely to cause substantial damage or substantial distress to him or to another, and

   (b) that damage or distress is or would be unwarranted.

(2) Subsection (1) does not apply –

   (a) in a case where any of the conditions in paragraphs 1 to 4 of Schedule 2 is met, or

   (b) in such other cases as may be prescribed by the Secretary of State by order.

(3) The data controller must within twenty-one days of receiving a notice under subsection (1) ('the data subject notice') give the individual who gave it a written notice –

   (a) stating that he has complied or intends to comply with the data subject notice, or

   (b) stating his reasons for regarding the data subject notice as to any extent unjustified and the extent (if any) to which he has complied or intends to comply with it.

(4) If a court is satisfied, on the application of any person who has given a notice under subsection (1) which appears to the court to be justified (or to be justified to any extent), that the data controller in question has failed to comply with the notice, the court may order him to take

such steps for complying with the notice (or for complying with it to that extent) as the court thinks fit.

(5) The failure by a data subject to exercise the right conferred by subsection (1) or section 11 (1) does not affect any other right conferred on him by this Part.

13   Compensation for failure to comply with certain requirements

(1) An individual who suffers damage by reason of any contravention by a data controller of any of the requirements of this Act is entitled to compensation from the data controller for that damage.

(2) An individual who suffers distress by reason of any contravention by a data controller of any of the requirements of this Act is entitled to compensation from the data controller for that distress if –

    (a) the individual also suffers damage by reason of the contravention, or

    (b) the contravention relates to the processing of personal data for the special purposes.

(3) In proceedings brought against a person by virtue of this section it is a defence to prove that he had taken such care as in all the circumstances was reasonably required to comply with the requirement concerned.

14   Rectification, blocking, erasure and destruction

(1) If a court is satisfied on the application of a data subject that personal data of which the applicant is the subject are inaccurate, the court may order the data controller to rectify, block, erase or destroy those data and any other personal data in respect of which he is the data controller and which contain an expression of opinion which appears to the court to be based on the inaccurate data.

Part III Notification by Data Controllers

16   Preliminary

(1) In this Part 'the registrable particulars', in relation to a data controller, means –

    (a) his name and address,

    (b) if he has nominated a representative for the purposes of this Act, the name and address of the representative,

    (c) a description of the personal data being or to be processed by or on behalf of the data controller and of the category or categories of data subject to which they relate,

    (d) a description of the purpose or purposes for which the data are being or are to be processed,

    (e) a description of any recipient or recipients to whom the data controller intends or may wish to disclose the data,

    (f) the names, or a description of, any countries or territories outside the European Economic Area to which the data controller directly or indirectly transfers, or intends or may wish directly or indirectly to transfer, the data, and

    (ff) where the data controller is a public authority, a statement of that fact, and

    (g) in any case where –

        (i)   personal data are being, or are intended to be, processed in circumstances in which the prohibition in subsection (1) of section 17 is excluded by subsection (2) or (3) of that section, and

        (ii) the notification does not extend to those data, a statement of that fact.

(2) In this Part –

'fees regulations' means regulations made by the Secretary of State under section 18(5) or 19(4) or (7);

'notification regulations' means regulations made by the Secretary of State under the other provisions of this Part;

'prescribed', except where used in relation to fees regulations, means prescribed by notification regulations.

(3) For the purposes of this Part, so far as it relates to the addresses of data controllers –

 (a) the address of a registered company is that of its registered office, and

 (b) the address of a person (other than a registered company) carrying on a business is that of his principal place of business in the United Kingdom.

17 Prohibition on processing without registration

(1) Subject to the following provisions of this section, personal data must not be processed unless an entry in respect of the data controller is included in the register maintained by the Commissioner under section 19 (or is treated by notification regulations made by virtue of section 19(3) as being so included).

(2) Except where the processing is assessable processing for the purposes of section 22, subsection (1) does not apply in relation to personal data consisting of information which falls neither within paragraph (a) of the definition of 'data' in section 1(1) nor within paragraph (b) of that definition.

(3) If it appears to the Secretary of State that processing of a particular description is unlikely to prejudice the rights and freedoms of data subjects, notification regulations may provide that, in such cases as may be prescribed, subsection (1) is not to apply in relation to processing of that description.

(4) Subsection (1) does not apply in relation to any processing whose sole purpose is the maintenance of a public register.

18 Notification by data controllers

(1) Any data controller who wishes to be included in the register maintained under section 19 shall give a notification to the Commissioner under this section.

19 Register of notifications

(1) The Commissioner shall –

 (a) maintain a register of persons who have given notification under section 18, and

 (b) make an entry in the register in pursuance of each notification received by him under that section from a person in respect of whom no entry as data controller was for the time being included in the register.

20 Duty to notify changes

(1) For the purpose specified in subsection (2), notification regulations shall include provision imposing on every person in respect of whom an entry as a data controller is for the time being included in the register maintained under section 19 a duty to notify to the Commissioner, in such circumstances and at such time or times and in such form as may be prescribed, such matters relating to the registrable particulars and measures taken as mentioned in section 18(2)(b) as may be prescribed.

(2) The purpose referred to in subsection (1) is that of ensuring, so far as practicable, that at any time –

 (a) the entries in the register maintained under section 19 contain current names and addresses and describe the current practice or intentions of the data controller with respect to the processing of personal data, and

 (b) the Commissioner is provided with a general description of measures currently being taken as mentioned in section 18(2)(b).

(3) Subsection (3) of section 18 has effect in relation to notification regulations made by virtue of subsection (1) as it has effect in relation to notification regulations made by virtue of subsection (2) of that section.

(4) On receiving any notification under notification regulations made by virtue of subsection (1), the Commissioner shall make such amendments of the relevant entry in the register maintained under section 19 as are necessary to take account of the notification.

21 Offences

(1) If section 17(1) is contravened, the data controller is guilty of an offence.

(2) Any person who fails to comply with the duty imposed by notification regulations made by virtue of section 20(1) is guilty of an offence.

(3) It shall be a defence for a person charged with an offence under subsection (2) to show that he exercised all due diligence to comply with the duty.

22   Preliminary assessment by the Commissioner

(1) In this section 'assessable processing' means processing which is of a description specified in an order made by the Secretary of State as appearing to him to be particularly likely –

(a) to cause substantial damage or substantial distress to data subjects, or

(b) otherwise significantly to prejudice the rights and freedoms of data subjects.

(2) On receiving notification from any data controller under section 18 or under notification regulations made by virtue of section 20 the Commissioner shall consider –

(a) whether any of the processing to which the notification relates is assessable processing, and

(b) if so, whether the assessable processing is likely to comply with the provisions of this Act.

(3) Subject to subsection (4), the Commissioner shall, within the period of twenty-eight days beginning with the day on which he receives a notification which relates to assessable processing, give a notice to the data controller stating the extent to which the Commissioner is of the opinion that the processing is likely or unlikely to comply with the provisions of this Act.

(4) Before the end of the period referred to in subsection (3) the Commissioner may, by reason of special circumstances, extend that period on one occasion only by notice to the data controller by such further period not exceeding fourteen days as the Commissioner may specify in the notice.

(5) No assessable processing in respect of which a notification has been given to the Commissioner as mentioned in subsection (2) shall be carried on unless either –

(a) the period of twenty-eight days beginning with the day on which the notification is received by the Commissioner (or, in a case falling within subsection (4), that period as extended under that subsection) has elapsed, or

(b) before the end of that period (or that period as so extended) the data controller has received a notice from the Commissioner under subsection (3) in respect of the processing.

(6) Where subsection (5) is contravened, the data controller is guilty of an offence.

(7) The Secretary of State may by order amend subsections (3), (4) and (5) by substituting for the number of days for the time being specified there a different number specified in the order.

23   Power to make provision for appointment of data protection supervisors

(1) The Secretary of State may by order –

(a) make provision under which a data controller may appoint a person to act as a data protection supervisor responsible in particular for monitoring in an independent manner the data controller's compliance with the provisions of this Act, and

(b) provide that, in relation to any data controller who has appointed a data protection supervisor in accordance with the provisions of the order and who complies with such conditions as may be specified in the order, the provisions of this Part are to have effect subject to such exemptions or other modifications as may be specified in the order.

(2) An order under this section may –

(a) impose duties on data protection supervisors in relation to the Commissioner, and

(b) confer functions on the Commissioner in relation to data protection supervisors.

24   Duty of certain data controllers to make certain information available

(1) Subject to subsection (3), where personal data are processed in a case where –

(a) by virtue of subsection (2) or (3) of section 17, subsection (1) of that section does not apply to the processing, and

(b) the data controller has not notified the relevant particulars in respect of that processing under section 18, the data controller must, within twenty-one days of receiving a written request from any person, make the relevant particulars available to that person in writing free of charge.

(2) In this section 'the relevant particulars' means the particulars referred to in paragraphs (a) to (f) of section 16(1).

(3) This section has effect subject to any exemption conferred for the purposes of this section by notification regulations.

(4) Any data controller who fails to comply with the duty imposed by subsection (1) is guilty of an offence.

(5) It shall be a defence for a person charged with an offence under subsection (4) to show that he exercised all due diligence to comply with the duty.

30   Health education and social work

(1) The Secretary of State may by order exempt from the subject information provisions, or modify those provisions in relation to, personal data consisting of information as to the physical or mental health or condition of the data subject.

31   Regulatory activity

(1) Personal data processed for the purposes of discharging functions to which this subsection applies are exempt from the subject information provisions in any case to the extent to which the application of those provisions to the data would be likely to prejudice the proper discharge of those functions.

(2) Subsection (1) applies to any relevant function which is designed –
    (a) for protecting members of the public against –
        (ii) dishonesty, malpractice or other seriously improper conduct by, or the unfitness or incompetence of, persons authorised to carry on any profession or other activity,
    (b) for protecting charities against misconduct or mismanagement (whether by trustees or other persons) in their administration,
    (c) for protecting the property of charities from loss or misapplication,
    (d) for the recovery of the property of charities,
    (e) for securing the health, safety and welfare of persons at work, or
    (f) for protecting persons other than persons at work against risk to health or safety arising out of or in connection with the actions of persons at work.

(3) In subsection (2) 'relevant function' means –
    (a) any function conferred on any person by or under any enactment,
    (b) any function of the Crown, a Minister of the Crown or a government department, or
    (c) any other function which is of a public nature and is exercised in the public interest.

(4) Personal data processed for the purpose of discharging any function which –
    (a) is conferred by or under any enactment on –
        (ii) the Health Service Commissioner for England, the Health Service Commissioner for Wales or the Health Service Commissioner for Scotland, and
    (b) is designed for protecting members of the public against –
        (i) maladministration by public bodies,
        (ii) failures in services provided by public bodies, or
        (iii) a failure of a public body to provide a service which it was a function of the body to provide,
are exempt from the subject information provisions in any case to the extent to which the application of those provisions to the data would be likely to prejudice the proper discharge of that function.

(6) Personal data processed for the purpose of the function of considering a complaint under section 14 of the NHS Redress Act 2006, section 113(1) or (2) or 114(1) or (3) of the Health and Social Care (Community Health and Standards) Act 2003, or section 24D, 26, 26ZA or 26ZB of the

Children Act 1989, are exempt from the subject information provisions in any case to the extent to which the application of those provisions to the data would be likely to prejudice the proper discharge of that function.

32   Journalism, literature and art

(1) Personal data which are processed only for the special purposes are exempt from any provision to which this subsection relates if –

    (a) the processing is undertaken with a view to the publication by any person of any journalistic, literary or artistic material,

    (b) the data controller reasonably believes that, having regard in particular to the special importance of the public interest in freedom of expression, publication would be in the public interest, and

    (c) the data controller reasonably believes that, in all the circumstances, compliance with that provision is incompatible with the special purposes.

(2) Subsection (1) relates to the provisions of –

    (a) the data protection principles except the seventh data protection principle,

    (b) section 7,

    (c) section 10,

    (d) sections 12, 9,

    (dd) section 12A, and

    (e) section 14(1) to (3).

(3) In considering for the purposes of subsection (1)(b) whether the belief of a data controller that publication would be in the public interest was or is a reasonable one, regard may be had to his compliance with any code of practice which –

    (a) is relevant to the publication in question, and

    (b) is designated by the Secretary of State by order for the purposes of this subsection.

(4) Where at any time ('the relevant time') in any proceedings against a data controller under section 7(9), 10(4), 12(8), 12A(3) or 14 or by virtue of section 13 the data controller claims, or it appears to the court, that any personal data to which the proceedings relate are being processed –

    (a) only for the special purposes, and

    (b) with a view to the publication by any person of any journalistic, literary or artistic material which, at the time twenty-four hours immediately before the relevant time, had not previously been published by the data controller,

the court shall stay the proceedings until either of the conditions in subsection (5) is met.

(5) Those conditions are –

    (a) that a determination of the Commissioner under section 45 with respect to the data in question takes effect, or

    (b) in a case where the proceedings were stayed on the making of a claim, that the claim is withdrawn.

(6) For the purposes of this Act 'publish', in relation to journalistic, literary or artistic material, means make available to the public or any section of the public.

33   Research, history and statistics

(1) In this section –

'research purposes' includes statistical or historical purposes;

'the relevant conditions', in relation to any processing of personal data, means the conditions –

    (a) that the data are not processed to support measures or decisions with respect to particular individuals, and

    (b) that the data are not processed in such a way that substantial damage or substantial distress is, or is likely to be, caused to any data subject.

(2) For the purposes of the second data protection principle, the further processing of personal data only for research purposes in compliance with the relevant conditions is not to be regarded as incompatible with the purposes for which they were obtained.

(3) Personal data which are processed only for research purposes in compliance with the relevant conditions may, notwithstanding the fifth data protection principle, be kept indefinitely.

(4) Personal data which are processed only for research purposes are exempt from section 7 if –

(a) they are processed in compliance with the relevant conditions, and

(b) the results of the research or any resulting statistics are not made available in a form which identifies data subjects or any of them.

(5) For the purposes of subsections (2) to (4) personal data are not to be treated as processed otherwise than for research purposes merely because the data are disclosed –

(a) to any person, for research purposes only,

(b) to the data subject or a person acting on his behalf,

(c) at the request, or with the consent, of the data subject or a person acting on his behalf, or

(d) in circumstances in which the person making the disclosure has reasonable grounds for believing that the disclosure falls within paragraph (a), (b) or (c).

33A   Manual data held by public authorities

(1) Personal data falling within paragraph (e) of the definition of 'data' in section 1(1) are exempt from –

(a) the first, second, third, fifth, seventh and eighth data protection principles,

(b) the sixth data protection principle except so far as it relates to the rights conferred on data subjects by sections 7 and 14,

(c) sections 10 to 12,

(d) section 13, except so far as it relates to damage caused by a contravention of section 7 or of the fourth data protection principle and to any distress which is also suffered by reason of that contravention,

(e) Part III, and

(f) section 55.

(2) Personal data which fall within paragraph (e) of the definition of 'data' in section 1(1) and relate to appointments or removals, pay, discipline, superannuation or other personnel matters, in relation to –

(a) service in any of the armed forces of the Crown,

(b) service in any office or employment under the Crown or under any public authority, or

(c) service in any office or employment, or under any contract for services, in respect of which power to take action, or to determine or approve the action taken, in such matters is vested in Her Majesty, any Minister of the Crown, the National Assembly for Wales, any Northern Ireland Minister (within the meaning of the Freedom of Information Act 2000) or any public authority, are also exempt from the remaining data protection principles and the remaining provisions of Part II.

35   Disclosures required by law or made in connection with legal proceedings etc.

(1) Personal data are exempt from the non-disclosure provisions where the disclosure is required by or under any enactment, by any rule of law or by the order of a court.

(2) Personal data are exempt from the non-disclosure provisions where the disclosure is necessary

(a) for the purpose of, or in connection with, any legal proceedings (including prospective legal proceedings), or

(b) for the purpose of obtaining legal advice,

or is otherwise necessary for the purposes of establishing, exercising or defending legal rights.

Part V Enforcement

40   Enforcement notices

(1) If the Commissioner is satisfied that a data controller has contravened or is contravening any of the data protection principles, the Commissioner may serve him with a notice (in this Act

referred to as 'an enforcement notice') requiring him, for complying with the principle or principles in question, to do either or both of the following –

    (a) to take within such time as may be specified in the notice, or to refrain from taking after such time as may be so specified, such steps as are so specified, or

    (b) to refrain from processing any personal data, or any personal data of a description specified in the notice, or to refrain from processing them for a purpose so specified or in a manner so specified, after such time as may be so specified.

(2) In deciding whether to serve an enforcement notice, the Commissioner shall consider whether the contravention has caused or is likely to cause any person damage or distress.

Unlawful obtaining etc. of personal data

55   Unlawful obtaining etc. of personal data

(1) A person must not knowingly or recklessly, without the consent of the data controller –

    (a) obtain or disclose personal data or the information contained in personal data, or

    (b) procure the disclosure to another person of the information contained in personal data.

(2) Subsection (1) does not apply to a person who shows –

    (a) that the obtaining, disclosing or procuring –

        (i)   was necessary for the purpose of preventing or detecting crime, or

        (ii) was required or authorised by or under any enactment, by any rule of law or by the order of a court,

    (b) that he acted in the reasonable belief that he had in law the right to obtain or disclose the data or information or, as the case may be, to procure the disclosure of the information to the other person,

    (c) that he acted in the reasonable belief that he would have had the consent of the data controller if the data controller had known of the obtaining, disclosing or procuring and the circumstances of it, or

    (d) that in the particular circumstances the obtaining, disclosing or procuring was justified as being in the public interest.

(3) A person who contravenes subsection (1) is guilty of an offence.

(4) A person who sells personal data is guilty of an offence if he has obtained the data in contravention of subsection (1).

(5) A person who offers to sell personal data is guilty of an offence if –

    (a) he has obtained the data in contravention of subsection (1), or

    (b) he subsequently obtains the data in contravention of that subsection.

(6) For the purposes of subsection (5), an advertisement indicating that personal data are or may be for sale is an offer to sell the data.

(7) Section 1(2) does not apply for the purposes of this section; and for the purposes of subsections (4) to (6), 'personal data' includes information extracted from personal data.

(8) References in this section to personal data do not include references to personal data which by virtue of section 28 or 33A are exempt from this section.

57   Avoidance of certain contractual terms relating to health record

(1) Any term or condition of a contract is void in so far as it purports to require an individual –

    (a) to supply any other person with a record to which this section applies, or with a copy of such a record or a part of such a record, or

    (b) to produce to any other person such a record, copy or part.

(2) This section applies to any record which –

    (a) has been or is to be obtained by a data subject in the exercise of the right conferred by section 7, and

    (b) consists of the information contained in any health record as defined by section 68(2).

68   Meaning of 'accessible record'

(1) In this Act 'accessible record' means –

    (a) a health record as defined by subsection (2),

    (b) an educational record as defined by Schedule 11, or

    (c) an accessible public record as defined by Schedule 12.

(2) In subsection (1)(a) 'health record' means any record which –

    (a) consists of information relating to the physical or mental health or condition of an individual, and

    (b) has been made by or on behalf of a health professional in connection with the care of that individual.

69   Meaning of 'health professional'

(1) In this Act 'health professional' means any of the following –

    (a) a registered medical practitioner,

    (b) a registered dentist as defined by section 53(1) of the Dentists Act 1984,

    (c) a registered optician as defined by section 36(1) of the Opticians Act 1989,

    (d) a registered pharmaceutical chemist as defined by section 24(1) of the Pharmacy Act 1954 or a registered person as defined by Article 2(2) of the Pharmacy (Northern Ireland) Order 1976,

    (e) a registered nurse or midwife,

    (f) a registered osteopath as defined by section 41 of the Osteopaths Act 1993,

    (g) a registered chiropractor as defined by section 43 of the Chiropractors Act 1994,

    (h) any person who is registered as a member of a profession to which the Professions Supplementary to Medicine Act 1960 for the time being extends,

    (i) a clinical psychologist, child psychotherapist or speech therapist,

    (j) a music therapist employed by a health service body, and

    (k) a scientist employed by such a body as head of a department.

(2) In subsection (1)(a) 'registered medical practitioner' includes any person who is provisionally registered under section 15 or 21 of the Medical Act 1983 and is engaged in such employment as is mentioned in subsection (3) of that section.

(3) In subsection (1) 'health service body' means –

    (a) a Strategic Health Authority established under section 13 of the National Health Service Act 2006,

    (b) a Special Health Authority established under section 28 of that Act, or section 22 of the National Health Service (Wales) Act 2006,

    (bb) a Primary Care Trust established under section 18 of the National Health Service Act 2006,

    (bbb) a Local Health Board established under section 11 of the National Health Service (Wales) Act 2006,

    (c) a Health Board within the meaning of the National Health Service (Scotland) Act 1978,

    (d) a Special Health Board within the meaning of that Act,

    (e) the managers of a State Hospital provided under section 102 of that Act,

    (f) a National Health Service trust first established under section 5 of the National Health Service and Community Care Act 1990, section 25 of the National Health Service Act 2006, section 18 of the National Health Service (Wales) Act 2006or section 12A of the National Health Service (Scotland) Act 1978,

    (fa) an NHS foundation trust,

    (g) a Health and Social Services Board established under Article 16 of the Health and Personal Social Services (Northern Ireland) Order 1972,

    (h) a special health and social services agency established under the Health and Personal Social Services (Special Agencies) (Northern Ireland) Order 1990, or

    (i) a Health and Social Services trust established under Article 10 of the Health and Personal Social Services (Northern Ireland) Order 1991.

70   Supplementary definitions

(1) In this Act, unless the context otherwise requires –

'business' includes any trade or profession;

'the Commissioner' means the Information Commissioner;

'the Data Protection Directive' means Directive 95/46/EC on the protection of individuals with regard to the processing of personal data and on the free movement of such data;

'EEA State' means a State which is a contracting party to the Agreement on the European Economic Area signed at Oporto on 2nd May 1992 as adjusted by the Protocol signed at Brussels on 17th March 1993:

'public register' means any register which pursuant to a requirement imposed –

(a) by or under any enactment, or

(b) in pursuance of any international agreement,

is open to public inspection or open to inspection by any person having a legitimate interest;

'recipient', in relation to any personal data, means any person to whom the data are disclosed, including any person (such as an employee or agent of the data controller, a data processor or an employee or agent of a data processor) to whom they are disclosed in the course of processing the data for the data controller, but does not include any person to whom disclosure is or may be made as a result of, or with a view to, a particular inquiry by or on behalf of that person made in the exercise of any power conferred by law;

'third party', in relation to personal data, means any person other than –

(a) the data subject,

(b) the data controller, or

(c) any data processor or other person authorised to process data for the data controller or processor;

'the Tribunal' means the Information Tribunal.

(2) For the purposes of this Act data are inaccurate if they are incorrect or misleading as to any matter of fact.

Schedules

Schedule 1 The Data Protection Principles

Part I The Principles

1. Personal data shall be processed fairly and lawfully and, in particular, shall not be processed unless –

(a) at least one of the conditions in Schedule 2 is met, and

(b) in the case of sensitive personal data, at least one of the conditions in Schedule 3 is also met.

2. Personal data shall be obtained only for one or more specified and lawful purposes, and shall not be further processed in any manner incompatible with that purpose or those purposes.

3. Personal data shall be adequate, relevant and not excessive in relation to the purpose or purposes for which they are processed.

4. Personal data shall be accurate and, where necessary, kept up to date.

5. Personal data processed for any purpose or purposes shall not be kept for longer than is necessary for that purpose or those purposes.

6. Personal data shall be processed in accordance with the rights of data subjects under this Act.

7. Appropriate technical and organisational measures shall be taken against unauthorised or unlawful processing of personal data and against accidental loss or destruction of, or damage to, personal data.

8. Personal data shall not be transferred to a country or territory outside the European Economic Area unless that country or territory ensures an adequate level of protection for the rights and freedoms of data subjects in relation to the processing of personal data.

Part II Interpretation of the Principles in Part I

The first principle

1.—(1) In determining for the purposes of the first principle whether personal data are processed fairly, regard is to be had to the method by which they are obtained, including in particular whether any person from whom they are obtained is deceived or misled as to the purpose or purposes for which they are to be processed.

(2) Subject to paragraph 2, for the purposes of the first principle data are to be treated as obtained fairly if they consist of information obtained from a person who –

    (a) is authorised by or under any enactment to supply it, or

    (b) is required to supply it by or under any enactment or by any convention or other instrument imposing an international obligation on the United Kingdom.

2.—(1) Subject to paragraph 3, for the purposes of the first principle personal data are not to be treated as processed fairly unless –

    (a) in the case of data obtained from the data subject, the data controller ensures so far as practicable that the data subject has, is provided with, or has made readily available to him, the information specified in subparagraph (3), and

    (b) in any other case, the data controller ensures so far as practicable that, before the relevant time or as soon as practicable after that time, the data subject has, is provided with, or has made readily available to him, the information specified in sub-paragraph (3).

(2) In sub-paragraph (1)(b) 'the relevant time' means –

    (a) the time when the data controller first processes the data, or

    (b) in a case where at that time disclosure to a third party within a reasonable period is envisaged –

        (i) if the data are in fact disclosed to such a person within that period, the time when the data are first disclosed,

        (ii) if within that period the data controller becomes, or ought to become, aware that the data are unlikely to be disclosed to such a person within that period, the time when the data controller does become, or ought to become, so aware, or

        (iii) in any other case, the end of that period.

(3) The information referred to in sub-paragraph (1) is as follows, namely –

    (a) the identity of the data controller,

    (b) if he has nominated a representative for the purposes of this Act, the identity of that representative,

    (c) the purpose or purposes for which the data are intended to be processed, and

    (d) any further information which is necessary, having regard to the specific circumstances in which the data are or are to be processed, to enable processing in respect of the data subject to be fair.

3.—(1) Paragraph 2(1)(b) does not apply where either of the primary conditions in sub-paragraph (2), together with such further conditions as may be prescribed by the Secretary of State by order, are met.

(2) The primary conditions referred to in sub-paragraph (1) are –

    (a) that the provision of that information would involve a disproportionate effort, or

    (b) that the recording of the information to be contained in the data by, or the disclosure of the data by, the data controller is necessary for compliance with any legal obligation to which the data controller is subject, other than an obligation imposed by contract.

4.—(1) Personal data which contain a general identifier falling within a description prescribed by the Secretary of State by order are not to be treated as processed fairly and lawfully unless they are processed in compliance with any conditions so prescribed in relation to general identifiers of that description.

(2) In sub-paragraph (1) 'a general identifier' means any identifier (such as, for example, a number or code used for identification purposes) which –

(a) relates to an individual, and

(b) forms part of a set of similar identifiers which is of general application.

The second principle

5. The purpose or purposes for which personal data are obtained may in particular be specified –

(a) in a notice given for the purposes of paragraph 2 by the data controller to the data subject, or

(b) in a notification given to the Commissioner under Part III of this Act.

6. In determining whether any disclosure of personal data is compatible with the purpose or purposes for which the data were obtained, regard is to be had to the purpose or purposes for which the personal data are intended to be processed by any person to whom they are disclosed.

The fourth principle

7. The fourth principle is not to be regarded as being contravened by reason of any inaccuracy in personal data which accurately record information obtained by the data controller from the data subject or a third party in a case where –

(a) having regard to the purpose or purposes for which the data were obtained and further processed, the data controller has taken reasonable steps to ensure the accuracy of the data, and

(b) if the data subject has notified the data controller of the data subject's view that the data are inaccurate, the data indicate that fact.

The sixth principle

8. A person is to be regarded as contravening the sixth principle if, but only if –

(a) he contravenes section 7 by failing to supply information in accordance with that section,

(b) he contravenes section 10 by failing to comply with a notice given under subsection (1) of that section to the extent that the notice is justified or by failing to give a notice under subsection (3) of that section,

(c) he contravenes section 11 by failing to comply with a notice given under subsection (1) of that section, or

(d) he contravenes section 12 by failing to comply with a notice given under subsection (1) or (2)(b) of that section or by failing to give a notification under subsection (2)(a) of that section or a notice under subsection (3) of that section.

The seventh principle

9. Having regard to the state of technological development and the cost of implementing any measures, the measures must ensure a level of security appropriate to –

(a) the harm that might result from such unauthorised or unlawful processing or accidental loss, destruction or damage as are mentioned in the seventh principle, and

(b) the nature of the data to be protected.

10. The data controller must take reasonable steps to ensure the reliability of any employees of his who have access to the personal data.

11. Where processing of personal data is carried out by a data processor on behalf of a data controller, the data controller must in order to comply with the seventh principle –

(a) choose a data processor providing sufficient guarantees in respect of the technical and organisational security measures governing the processing to be carried out, and

(b) take reasonable steps to ensure compliance with those measures.

12. Where processing of personal data is carried out by a data processor on behalf of a data controller, the data controller is not to be regarded as complying with the seventh principle unless –

> (a) the processing is carried out under a contract –
>> (i) which is made or evidenced in writing, and
>> (ii) under which the data processor is to act only on instructions from the data controller, and
> (b) the contract requires the data processor to comply with obligations equivalent to those imposed on a data controller by the seventh principle.

The eighth principle

13. An adequate level of protection is one which is adequate in all the circumstances of the case, having regard in particular to –

> (a) the nature of the personal data,
> (b) the country or territory of origin of the information contained in the data,
> (c) the country or territory of final destination of that information,
> (d) the purposes for which and period during which the data are intended to be processed,
> (e) the law in force in the country or territory in question,
> (f) the international obligations of that country or territory,
> (g) any relevant codes of conduct or other rules which are enforceable in that country or territory (whether generally or by arrangement in particular cases), and
> (h) any security measures taken in respect of the data in that country or territory.

14. The eighth principle does not apply to a transfer falling within any paragraph of Schedule 4, except in such circumstances and to such extent as the Secretary of State may by order provide.

15.—(1) Where –

> (a) in any proceedings under this Act any question arises as to whether the requirement of the eighth principle as to an adequate level of protection is met in relation to the transfer of any personal data to a country or territory outside the European Economic Area, and
> (b) a Community finding has been made in relation to transfers of the kind in question,

that question is to be determined in accordance with that finding.

(2) In sub-paragraph (1) 'Community finding' means a finding of the European Commission, under the procedure provided for in Article 31(2) of the Data Protection Directive, that a country or territory outside the European Economic Area does, or does not, ensure an adequate level of protection within the meaning of Article 25(2) of the Directive.

Schedule 2 Conditions Relevant for Purposes of the First Principle: Processing of Any Personal Data

1. The data subject has given his consent to the processing.
2. The processing is necessary –

> (a) for the performance of a contract to which the data subject is a party, or
> (b) for the taking of steps at the request of the data subject with a view to entering into a contract.

3. The processing is necessary for compliance with any legal obligation to which the data controller is subject, other than an obligation imposed by contract.
4. The processing is necessary in order to protect the vital interests of the data subject.
5. The processing is necessary –

> (a) for the administration of justice,
> (aa) for the exercise of any functions of either House of Parliament,
> (b) for the exercise of any functions conferred on any person by or under any enactment,

(c) for the exercise of any functions of the Crown, a Minister of the Crown or a government department, or

(d) for the exercise of any other functions of a public nature exercised in the public interest by any person.

6.—(1) The processing is necessary for the purposes of legitimate interests pursued by the data controller or by the third party or parties to whom the data are disclosed, except where the processing is unwarranted in any particular case by reason of prejudice to the rights and freedoms or legitimate interests of the data subject.

(2) The Secretary of State may by order specify particular circumstances in which this condition is, or is not, to be taken to be satisfied.

Schedule 3 Conditions Relevant for Purposes of the First Principle: Processing of Sensitive Personal Data

1. The data subject has given his explicit consent to the processing of the personal data.

2.—(1) The processing is necessary for the purposes of exercising or performing any right or obligation which is conferred or imposed by law on the data controller in connection with employment.

(2) The Secretary of State may by order –

(a) exclude the application of sub-paragraph (1) in such cases as may be specified, or

(b) provide that, in such cases as may be specified, the condition in sub-paragraph (1) is not to be regarded as satisfied unless such further conditions as may be specified in the order are also satisfied.

3. The processing is necessary –

(a) in order to protect the vital interests of the data subject or another person, in a case where –

(i)   consent cannot be given by or on behalf of the data subject, or

(ii) the data controller cannot reasonably be expected to obtain the consent of the data subject, or

(b) in order to protect the vital interests of another person, in a case where consent by or on behalf of the data subject has been unreasonably withheld.

4. The processing –

(a) is carried out in the course of its legitimate activities by any body or association which –

(i)   is not established or conducted for profit, and

(ii) exists for political, philosophical, religious or trade-union purposes,

(b) is carried out with appropriate safeguards for the rights and freedoms of data subjects,

(c) relates only to individuals who either are members of the body or association or have regular contact with it in connection with its purposes, and

(d) does not involve disclosure of the personal data to a third party without the consent of the data subject.

5. The information contained in the personal data has been made public as a result of steps deliberately taken by the data subject.

6. The processing –

(a) is necessary for the purpose of, or in connection with, any legal proceedings (including prospective legal proceedings),

(b) is necessary for the purpose of obtaining legal advice, or

(c) is otherwise necessary for the purposes of establishing, exercising or defending legal rights.

7.—(1) The processing is necessary –

(a) for the administration of justice,

(b) for the exercise of any functions of either House of Parliament,

(c) for the exercise of any functions conferred on any person by or under an enactment, or

(d) for the exercise of any functions of the Crown, a Minister of the Crown or a government department.

(2) The Secretary of State may by order –

(a) exclude the application of sub-paragraph (1) in such cases as may be specified, or

(b) provide that, in such cases as may be specified, the condition in sub-paragraph (1) is not to be regarded as satisfied unless such further conditions as may be specified in the order are also satisfied.

8.—(1) The processing is necessary for medical purposes and is undertaken by –

(a) a health professional, or

(b) a person who in the circumstances owes a duty of confidentiality which is equivalent to that which would arise if that person were a health professional.

(2) In this paragraph 'medical purposes' includes the purposes of preventative medicine, medical diagnosis, medical research, the provision of care and treatment and the management of healthcare services.

9.—(1) The processing –

(a) is of sensitive personal data consisting of information as to racial or ethnic origin,

(b) is necessary for the purpose of identifying or keeping under review the existence or absence of equality of opportunity or treatment between persons of different racial or ethnic origins, with a view to enabling such equality to be promoted or maintained, and

(c) is carried out with appropriate safeguards for the rights and freedoms of data subjects.

(2) The Secretary of State may by order specify circumstances in which processing falling within sub-paragraph (1)(a) and (b) is, or is not, to be taken for the purposes of sub-paragraph (1) (c) to be carried out with appropriate safeguards for the rights and freedoms of data subjects.

10. The personal data are processed in circumstances specified in an order made by the Secretary of State for the purposes of this paragraph.

Schedule 4 Cases Where the Eighth Principle Does Not Apply

1. The data subject has given his consent to the transfer.

2. The transfer is necessary –

(a) for the performance of a contract between the data subject and the data controller, or

(b) for the taking of steps at the request of the data subject with a view to his entering into a contract with the data controller.

3. The transfer is necessary –

(a) for the conclusion of a contract between the data controller and a person other than the data subject which –

(i)   is entered into at the request of the data subject, or

(ii) is in the interests of the data subject, or

(b) for the performance of such a contract.

4.—(1) The transfer is necessary for reasons of substantial public interest.

(2) The Secretary of State may by order specify –

(a) circumstances in which a transfer is to be taken for the purposes of sub-paragraph (1) to be necessary for reasons of substantial public interest, and

(b) circumstances in which a transfer which is not required by or under an enactment is not to be taken for the purpose of sub-paragraph (1) to be necessary for reasons of substantial public interest.

5. The transfer –

(a) is necessary for the purpose of, or in connection with, any legal proceedings (including prospective legal proceedings),

(b) is necessary for the purpose of obtaining legal advice, or

(c) is otherwise necessary for the purposes of establishing, exercising or defending legal rights.

6. The transfer is necessary in order to protect the vital interests of the data subject.

7. The transfer is of part of the personal data on a public register and any conditions subject to which the register is open to inspection are complied with by any person to whom the data are or may be disclosed after the transfer.

8. The transfer is made on terms which are of a kind approved by the Commissioner as ensuring adequate safeguards for the rights and freedoms of data subjects.

9. The transfer has been authorised by the Commissioner as being made in such a manner as to ensure adequate safeguards for the rights and freedoms of data subjects.

Schedule 7 Miscellaneous Exemptions

Confidential references given by the data controller

1. Personal data are exempt from section 7 if they consist of a reference given or to be given in confidence by the data controller for the purposes of –

  (a) the education, training or employment, or prospective education, training or employment, of the data subject,

  (b) the appointment, or prospective appointment, of the data subject to any office, or

  (c) the provision, or prospective provision, by the data subject of any service.

Human Rights Act 1998

(1998, c. 42)

Introduction

1—(1) In this Act 'the Convention rights' means the rights and fundamental freedoms set out in –

  (a) Articles 2 to 12 and 14 of the Convention,

  (b) Articles 1 to 3 of the First Protocol, and

  (c) Articles 1 and 2 of the Sixth Protocol, as read with Articles 16 to 18 of the Convention.

  (2) Those Articles are to have effect for the purposes of this Act subject to any designated derogation or reservation (as to which see sections 14 and 15).

  (3) The Articles are set out in Schedule 1.

2—(1) A court or tribunal determining a question which has arisen in connection with a Convention right must take into account any –

  (a) judgment, decision, declaration or advisory opinion of the European Court of Human Rights,

  (b) opinion of the Commission given in a report adopted under Article 31 of the Convention, or

  (c) decision of the Commission in connection with Article 26 or 27(2) of the Convention, or

  (d) decision of the Committee of Ministers taken under Article 46 of the Convention,

whenever made or given, so far as, in the opinion of the court or tribunal, it is relevant to the proceedings in which that question has arisen.

Legislation

3—(1) So far as it is possible to do so, primary legislation and subordinate legislation must be read and given effect in a way which is compatible with the Convention rights.

Public authorities

6—(1) It is unlawful for a public authority to act in a way which is incompatible with a Convention right.

  (2) Subsection (1) does not apply to an act if –

  (a) as the result of one or more provisions of primary legislation, the authority could not have acted differently; or

  (b) in the case of one or more provisions of, or made under, primary legislation which cannot be read or given effect in a way which is compatible with the Convention rights, the authority was acting so as to give effect to or enforce those provisions.

(3) In this section 'public authority' includes –

    (a) a court or tribunal, and

    (b) any person certain of whose functions are functions of a public nature,

but does not include either House of Parliament or a person exercising functions in connection with proceedings in Parliament.

(4) In subsection (3) 'Parliament' does not include the House of Lords in its judicial capacity.

7—(1) A person who claims that a public authority has acted (or proposes to act) in a way which is made unlawful by section 6(1) may –

    (a) bring proceedings against the authority under this Act in the appropriate court or tribunal, or

    (b) rely on the Convention right or rights concerned in any legal proceedings, but only if he is (or would be) a victim of the unlawful act.

(2) In subsection (1)(a) 'appropriate court or tribunal' means such court or tribunal as may be determined in accordance with rules; and proceedings against an authority include a counterclaim or similar proceeding.

(3) If the proceedings are brought on an application for judicial review, the applicant is to be taken to have a sufficient interest in relation to the unlawful act only if he is, or would be, a victim of that act.

(7) For the purposes of this section, a person is a victim of an unlawful act only if he would be a victim for the purposes of Article 34 of the Convention if proceedings were brought in the European Court of Human Rights in respect of that act.

(8) Nothing in this Act creates a criminal offence.

8—(1) In relation to any act (or proposed act) of a public authority which the court finds is (or would be) unlawful, it may grant such relief or remedy, or make such order, within its powers as it considers just and appropriate.

(2) But damages may be awarded only by a court which has power to award damages, or to order the payment of compensation, in civil proceedings.

(3) No award of damages is to be made unless, taking account of all the circumstances of the case, including –

    (a) any other relief or remedy granted, or order made, in relation to the act in question (by that or any other court), and

    (b) the consequences of any decision (of that or any other court) in respect of that act,

the court is satisfied that the award is necessary to afford just satisfaction to the person in whose favour it is made.

(4) In determining –

    (a) whether to award damages, or

    (b) the amount of an award,

the court must take into account the principles applied by the European Court of Human Rights in relation to the award of compensation under Article 41 of the Convention.

Schedule

Schedule 1 The Articles

Part I The Convention

Rights and Freedoms

Article 2 Right to life

1. Everyone's right to life shall be protected by law. No one shall be deprived of his life intentionally save in the execution of a sentence of a court following his conviction of a crime for which this penalty is provided by law.

2. Deprivation of life shall not be regarded as inflicted in contravention of this Article when it results from the use of force which is no more than absolutely necessary:

    (a) in defence of any person from unlawful violence;

    (b) in order to effect a lawful arrest or to prevent the escape of a person lawfully detained;

    (c) in action lawfully taken for the purpose of quelling a riot or insurrection.

Article 3   Prohibition of torture

No one shall be subjected to torture or to inhuman or degrading treatment or punishment.

Article 5   Right to liberty and security

1. Everyone has the right to liberty and security of person. No one shall be deprived of his liberty save in the following cases and in accordance with a procedure prescribed by law:

    (e) the lawful detention of persons for the prevention of the spreading of infectious diseases, of persons of unsound mind, alcoholics or drug addicts or vagrants;

2. Everyone who is arrested shall be informed promptly, in a language which he understands, of the reasons for his arrest and of any charge against him.

4. Everyone who is deprived of his liberty by arrest or detention shall be entitled to take proceedings by which the lawfulness of his detention shall be decided speedily by a court and his release ordered if the detention is not lawful.

5. Everyone who has been the victim of arrest or detention in contravention of the provisions of this Article shall have an enforceable right to compensation.

Article 8   Right to respect for private and family life

1. Everyone has the right to respect for his private and family life, his home and his correspondence.

2. There shall be no interference by a public authority with the exercise of this right except such as is in accordance with the law and is necessary in a democratic society in the interests of national security, public safety or the economic well-being of the country, for the prevention of disorder or crime, for the protection of health or morals, or for the protection of the rights and freedoms of others.

Article 9   Freedom of thought, conscience and religion

1. Everyone has the right to freedom of thought, conscience and religion; this right includes freedom to change his religion or belief and freedom, either alone or in community with others and in public or private, to manifest his religion or belief, in worship, teaching, practice and observance.

2. Freedom to manifest one's religion or beliefs shall be subject only to such limitations as are prescribed by law and are necessary in a democratic society in the interests of public safety, for the protection of public order, health or morals, or for the protection of the rights and freedoms of others.

Article 10   Freedom of expression

1. Everyone has the right to freedom of expression. This right shall include freedom to hold opinions and to receive and impart information and ideas without interference by public authority and regardless of frontiers. This Article shall not prevent States from requiring the licensing of broadcasting, television or cinema enterprises.

2. The exercise of these freedoms, since it carries with it duties and responsibilities, may be subject to such formalities, conditions, restrictions or penalties as are prescribed by law and are necessary in a democratic society, in the interests of national security, territorial integrity or public safety, for the prevention of disorder or crime, for the protection of health or morals, for the protection of the reputation or rights of others, for preventing the disclosure of information received in confidence, or for maintaining the authority and impartiality of the judiciary.

Article 12   Right to marry

Men and women of marriageable age have the right to marry and to found a family, according to the national laws governing the exercise of this right.

Article 14   Prohibition of discrimination

The enjoyment of the rights and freedom set forth In this Convention shall be secured without discrimination on any ground such as sex, race, colour, language, religion, political or other opinion, national or social origin, association with a national minority, property, birth or other status.

Health Act 1999

(1999, c. 8)

Part III Miscellaneous and Supplementary

Miscellaneous

60   Regulation of health care and associated professions

(1) Her Majesty may by Order in Council make provision –

    (a) modifying the regulation of any profession to which subsection (2) applies, so far as appears to Her to be necessary or expedient for the purpose of securing or improving the regulation of the profession or the services which the profession provides or to which it contributes,

    (b) regulating any other profession which appears to Her to be concerned (wholly or partly) with the physical or mental health of individuals and to require regulation in pursuance of this section,

    (c) modifying the functions, powers or duties of the Council for the Regulation of Health Care Professionals,

    (d) modifying the list of regulatory bodies (in section 25(3) of the National Health Service Reform and Health Care Professions Act 2002) in relation to which that Council performs its functions,

    (e) modifying, as respects any such regulatory body, the range of functions of that body in relation to which the Council performs its functions.

(2) The professions referred to in subsection (1)(a) are –

    (a) the professions regulated by the Pharmacy Act 1954, the Medical Act 1983, the Dentists Act 1984, the Opticians Act 1989, the Osteopaths Act 1993 and the Chiropractors Act 1994,

    (b) the professions regulated by the Nursing and Midwifery Order 2001,

    (c) the professions regulated by the Health Professions Order 2001,

    (d) any other profession regulated by Order in Council under this section.

Schedules

Schedule 3 Regulation of Health Care and Associated Professions

Matters generally within the scope of the Orders

1. An Order may make provision, in relation to any profession, for any of the following matters (among others) –

    (a) the establishment and continuance of a regulatory body,

    (b) keeping a register of members admitted to practice,

    (c) education and training before and after admission to practice,

    (d) privileges of members admitted to practice,

    (e) standards of conduct and performance,

    (f) discipline and fitness to practise,

    (g) investigation and enforcement by or on behalf of the regulatory body,

(h) appeals,

(i) default powers exercisable by a person other than the regulatory body.

Matters outside the scope of the Orders

7.—(1) An Order may not abolish the regulatory body of any profession to which section 60(2)(a) applies, any regulatory body established by an Order as the successor to the Council for Professions Supplementary to Medicine or the United Kingdom Central Council for Nursing, Midwifery and Health Visiting or any other regulatory body established by an Order.

(2) An Order may not impose any requirement which would have the effect that a majority of the members of the regulatory body of any profession would be persons not included in the register of members admitted to practice.

(3) An Order may not provide for any function conferred on the Privy Council, in relation to any profession to which section 60(2)(a) applies, to be exercised by a different person.

8.—(1) Where an enactment provides, in relation to any profession, for any function mentioned in sub-paragraph (2) to be exercised by the regulatory body or any of its committees or officers, an Order may not provide for any person other than that regulatory body or any of its committees or officers to exercise that function.

(2) The functions are –

(a) keeping the register of members admitted to practice,

(b) determining standards of education and training for admission to practice,

(c) giving advice about standards of conduct and performance,

(d) administering procedures (including making rules) relating to misconduct, unfitness to practise and similar matters.

Human Reproductive Cloning Act 2001

(2001, c. 23)

1   The offence

(1) A person who places in a woman a human embryo which has been created otherwise than by fertilisation is guilty of an offence.

(2) A person who is guilty of the offence is liable on conviction on indictment to imprisonment for a term not exceeding 10 years or a fine or both.

(3) No proceedings for the offence may be instituted –

(a) in England and Wales, except with the consent of the Director of Public Prosecutions

. . .

National Health Service Reform and Health Care Professions Act 2002

(2002, c. 17)

Part 2 Health Care Professions

The Council for the Regulation of Health Care Professionals

25   The Council for the Regulation of Health Care Professionals

(1) There shall be a body corporate known as the Council for the Regulation of Health Care Professionals (in this group of sections referred to as 'the Council').

(2) The general functions of the Council are –

(a) to promote the interests of patients and other members of the public in relation to the performance of their functions by the bodies mentioned in subsection (3) (in this group of sections referred to as 'regulatory bodies'), and by their committees and officers,

(b) to promote best practice in the performance of those functions,

(c) to formulate principles relating to good professional self-regulation, and to encourage regulatory bodies to conform to them, and

(d) to promote co-operation between regulatory bodies; and between them, or any of them, and other bodies performing corresponding functions.

(3) The bodies referred to in subsection (2)(a) are –

(a) the General Medical Council,

(b) the General Dental Council,

(c) the General Optical Council,

(d) the General Osteopathic Council,

(e) the General Chiropractic Council,

(f) subject to section 26(5), the Royal Pharmaceutical Society of Great Britain,

(g) subject to section 26(6), the Pharmaceutical Society of Northern Ireland,

(i) any regulatory body (within the meaning of Schedule 3 to the 1999 Act) established by an Order in Council under section 60 of that Act as the successor to a body mentioned in paragraph (h), and

(j) any other regulatory body (within that meaning) established by an Order in Council under that section.

29   Reference of disciplinary cases by Council to court

(1) This section applies to –

(c) a direction by a Fitness to Practise Panel of the General Medical Council under section 35D of the Medical Act 1983 (c. 54) that the fitness to practise of a medical practitioner was impaired otherwise than by reason of his physical or mental health.

(2) This section also applies to –

(a) a final decision of the relevant committee not to take any disciplinary measure under the provision referred to in whichever of paragraphs (a) to (h) of subsection (1) applies,

(b) a decision of the relevant regulatory body, or one of its committees or officers, to restore a person to the register following his removal from it in accordance with any of the measures referred to in paragraphs (a) to (j) of subsection (1).

(3) The things to which this section applies are referred to below as 'relevant decisions'.

(4) If the Council considers that –

(a) a relevant decision falling within subsection (1) has been unduly lenient, whether as to any finding of professional misconduct or fitness to practise on the part of the practitioner concerned (or lack of such a finding), or as to any penalty imposed, or both, or

(b) a relevant decision falling within subsection (2) should not have been made, and that it would be desirable for the protection of members of the public for the Council to take action under this section, the Council may refer the case to the relevant court.

Adoption and Children Act 2002

(2002, c. 38)

Part 1 Adoption

Chapter 1 Introductory

1   Considerations applying to the exercise of powers

(1) This section applies whenever a court or adoption agency is coming to a decision relating to the adoption of a child.

(2) The paramount consideration of the court or adoption agency must be the child's welfare, throughout his life.

(3) The court or adoption agency must at all times bear in mind that, in general, any delay in coming to the decision is likely to prejudice the child's welfare.

(4) The court or adoption agency must have regard to the following matters (among others) –

    (a) the child's ascertainable wishes and feelings regarding the decision (considered in the light of the child's age and understanding),

    (b) the child's particular needs,

    (c) the likely effect on the child (throughout his life) of having ceased to be a member of the original family and become an adopted person,

    (d) the child's age, sex, background and any of the child's characteristics which the court or agency considers relevant,

    (e) any harm (within the meaning of the Children Act 1989 (c. 41)) which the child has suffered or is at risk of suffering,

    (f) the relationship which the child has with relatives, and with any other person in relation to whom the court or agency considers the relationship to be relevant, including –

        (i) the likelihood of any such relationship continuing and the value to the child of its doing so,

        (ii) the ability and willingness of any of the child's relatives, or of any such person, to provide the child with a secure environment in which the child can develop, and otherwise to meet the child's needs,

        (iii) the wishes and feelings of any of the child's relatives, or of any such person, regarding the child.

(5) In placing the child for adoption, the adoption agency must give due consideration to the child's religious persuasion, racial origin and cultural and linguistic background.

(6) The court or adoption agency must always consider the whole range of powers available to it in the child's case (whether under this Act or the Children Act 1989); and the court must not make any order under this Act unless it considers that making the order would be better for the child than not doing so.

(8) For the purposes of this section –

    (a) references to relationships are not confined to legal relationships,

    (b) references to a relative, in relation to a child, include the child's mother and father.

Chapter 3 Placement for Adoption and Adoption Orders

45   Suitability of adopters

(1) Regulations under section 9 may make provision as to the matters to be taken into account by an adoption agency in determining, or making any report in respect of, the suitability of any persons to adopt a child.

(2) In particular, the regulations may make provision for the purpose of securing that, in determining the suitability of a couple to adopt a child, proper regard is had to the need for stability and permanence in their relationship.

The making of adoption orders

46   Adoption orders

(1) An adoption order is an order made by the court on an application under section 50 or 51 giving parental responsibility for a child to the adopters or adopter.

(2) The making of an adoption order operates to extinguish –

    (a) the parental responsibility which any person other than the adopters or adopter has for the adopted child immediately before the making of the order,

    (b) any order under the 1989 Act . . .,

(6) Before making an adoption order, the court must consider whether there should be arrangements for allowing any person contact with the child; and for that purpose the court must consider any existing or proposed arrangements and obtain any views of the parties to the proceedings.

49   Applications for adoption

(1) An application for an adoption order may be made by –
  (a) a couple, or
  (b) one person,
but only if it is made under section 50 or 51 and one of the following conditions is met.

(2) The first condition is that at least one of the couple (in the case of an application under section 50) or the applicant (in the case of an application under section 51) is domiciled in a part of the British Islands.

(3) The second condition is that both of the couple (in the case of an application under section 50) or the applicant (in the case of an application under section 51) have been habitually resident in a part of the British Islands for a period of not less than one year ending with the date of the application.

(4) An application for an adoption order may only be made if the person to be adopted has not attained the age of 18 years on the date of the application.

(5) References in this Act to a child, in connection with any proceedings (whether or not concluded) for adoption, (such as 'child to be adopted' or 'adopted child') include a person who has attained the age of 18 years before the proceedings are concluded.

50   Adoption by couple

(1) An adoption order may be made on the application of a couple where both of them have attained the age of 21 years.

(2) An adoption order may be made on the application of a couple where –
  (a) one of the couple is the mother or the father of the person to be adopted and has attained the age of 18 years, and
  (b) the other has attained the age of 21 years.

51   Adoption by one person

(1) An adoption order may be made on the application of one person who has attained the age of 21 years and is not married.

(2) An adoption order may be made on the application of one person who has attained the age of 21 years if the court is satisfied that the person is the partner of a parent of the person to be adopted.

(3) An adoption order may be made on the application of one person who has attained the age of 21 years and is married if the court is satisfied that –
  (a) the person's spouse cannot be found,
  (b) the spouses have separated and are living apart, and the separation is likely to be permanent, or
  (c) the person's spouse is by reason of ill-health, whether physical or mental, incapable of making an application for an adoption order.

(4) An adoption order may not be made on an application under this section by the mother or the father of the person to be adopted unless the court is satisfied that –
  (a) the other natural parent is dead or cannot be found,
  (b) by virtue of section 28 of the Human Fertilisation and Embryology Act 1990 (c. 37) (disregarding subsections (5A) to (5I) of that section), there is no other parent, or
  (c) there is some other reason justifying the child's being adopted by the applicant alone,
and where the court makes an adoption order on such an application, the court must record that it is satisfied as to the fact mentioned in paragraph (a) or (b) or, in the case of paragraph (c), record the reason.

Chapter 4 Status of Adopted Children

67   Status conferred by adoption

(1) An adopted person is to be treated in law as if born as the child of the adopters or adopter.

(2) An adopted person is the legitimate child of the adopters or adopter and, if adopted by –

    (a) a couple, or

    (b) one of a couple under section 51(2),

is to be treated as the child of the relationship of the couple in question.

(3) An adopted person –

    (a) if adopted by one of a couple under section 51(2), is to be treated in law as not being the child of any person other than the adopter and the other one of the couple, and

    (b) in any other case, is to be treated in law, subject to subsection (4), as not being the child of any person other than the adopters or adopter;

but this subsection does not affect any reference in this Act to a person's natural parent or to any other natural relationship.

(4) In the case of a person adopted by one of the person's natural parents as sole adoptive parent, subsection (3)(b) has no effect as respects entitlement to property depending on relationship to that parent, or as respects anything else depending on that relationship.

(5) This section has effect from the date of the adoption.

68   Adoptive relatives

(1) A relationship existing by virtue of section 67 may be referred to as an adoptive relationship, and –

    (a) an adopter may be referred to as an adoptive parent or (as the case may be) as an adoptive father or adoptive mother,

    (b) any other relative of any degree under an adoptive relationship may be referred to as an adoptive relative of that degree.

(2) Subsection (1) does not affect the interpretation of any reference, not qualified by the word 'adoptive', to a relationship.

(3) A reference (however expressed) to the adoptive mother and father of a child adopted by –

    (a) a couple of the same sex, or

    (b) a partner of the child's parent, where the couple are of the same sex,

is to be read as a reference to the child's adoptive parents.

Chapter 5 The Registers

Adopted Children Register etc.

77   Adopted Children Register

(1) The Registrar General must continue to maintain in the General Register Office a register, to be called the Adopted Children Register.

(2) The Adopted Children Register is not to be open to public inspection or search.

(3) No entries may be made in the Adopted Children Register other than entries –

    (a) directed to be made in it by adoption orders, or

    (b) required to be made under Schedule 1.

78   Searches and copies

(1) The Registrar General must continue to maintain at the General Register Office an index of the Adopted Children Register.

(2) Any person may –

    (a) search the index,

(b) have a certified copy of any entry in the Adopted Children Register.

(3) But a person is not entitled to have a certified copy of an entry in the Adopted Children Register relating to an adopted person who has not attained the age of 18 years unless the applicant has provided the Registrar General with the prescribed particulars.

'Prescribed' means prescribed by regulations made by the Registrar General with the approval of the Chancellor of the Exchequer.

79   Connections between the register and birth records

(1) The Registrar General must make traceable the connection between any entry in the registers of live-births or other records which has been marked 'Adopted' and any corresponding entry in the Adopted Children Register.

(2) Information kept by the Registrar General for the purposes of subsection (1) is not to be open to public inspection or search.

(3) Any such information, and any other information which would enable an adopted person to obtain a certified copy of the record of his birth, may only be disclosed by the Registrar General in accordance with this section.

(4) In relation to a person adopted before the appointed day the court may, in exceptional circumstances, order the Registrar General to give any information mentioned in subsection (3) to a person.

(5) On an application made in the prescribed manner by the appropriate adoption agency in respect of an adopted person a record of whose birth is kept by the Registrar General, the Registrar General must give the agency any information relating to the adopted person which is mentioned in subsection (3).

(7) On an application made in the prescribed manner by an adopted person a record of whose birth is kept by the Registrar General and who –

(a) is under the age of 18 years, and

(b) intends to be married,

the Registrar General must inform the applicant whether or not it appears from information contained in the registers of live-births or other records that the applicant and the person whom the applicant intends to marry may be within the prohibited degrees of relationship for the purposes of the Marriage Act 1949 (c. 76).

Part 3 Miscellaneous and Final Provisions

Chapter 1 Miscellaneous

Advertisements in the United Kingdom

123   Restriction on advertisements etc.

(1) A person must not –

(a) publish or distribute an advertisement or information to which this section applies, or

(b) cause such an advertisement or information to be published or distributed.

(2) This section applies to an advertisement indicating that –

(a) the parent or guardian of a child wants the child to be adopted,

(b) a person wants to adopt a child,

(c) a person other than an adoption agency is willing to take any step mentioned in paragraphs (a) to (e), (g) and (h) and (so far as relating to those paragraphs) (i) of section 92(2),

(d) a person other than an adoption agency is willing to receive a child handed over to him with a view to the child's adoption by him or another, or

(e) a person is willing to remove a child from the United Kingdom for the purposes of adoption.

(4) For the purposes of this section and section 124 –

    (a) publishing or distributing an advertisement or information means publishing it or distributing it to the public and includes doing so by electronic means (for example, by means of the internet),

    (b) the public includes selected members of the public as well as the public generally or any section of the public.

(5) Subsection (1) does not apply to publication or distribution by or on behalf of an adoption agency.

124 Offence of breaching restriction under section 123

(1) A person who contravenes section 123(1) is guilty of an offence.

(3) A person guilty of an offence under this section is liable on summary conviction to imprisonment for a term not exceeding three months, or a fine not exceeding level 5 on the standard scale, or both.

144 General interpretation etc.

(1) In this Act –

'child', except where used to express a relationship, means a person who has not attained the age of 18 years,

'guardian' has the same meaning as in the 1989 Act and includes a special guardian within the meaning of that Act,

'information' means information recorded in any form,

'relative', in relation to a child, means a grandparent, brother, sister, uncle or aunt, whether of the full blood or half-blood or by marriage.

(4) In this Act, a couple means –

    (a) a married couple, or

    (b) two people (whether of different sexes or the same sex) living as partners in an enduring family relationship.

(5) Subsection (4)(b) does not include two people one of whom is the other's parent, grandparent, sister, brother, aunt or uncle.

(6) References to relationships in subsection (5) –

    (a) are to relationships of the full blood or half blood or, in the case of an adopted person, such of those relationships as would exist but for adoption, and

    (b) include the relationship of a child with his adoptive, or former adoptive, parents, but do not include any other adoptive relationships.

(7) For the purposes of this Act, a person is the partner of a child's parent if the person and the parent are a couple but the person is not the child's parent.

Female Genital Mutilation Act 2003

(2003, c. 31)

1 Offence of female genital mutilation

(1) A person is guilty of an offence if he excises, infibulates or otherwise mutilates the whole or any part of a girl's labia majora, labia minora or clitoris.

(2) But no offence is committed by an approved person who performs –

    (a) a surgical operation on a girl which is necessary for her physical or mental health, or

    (b) a surgical operation on a girl who is in any stage of labour, or has just given birth, for purposes connected with the labour or birth.

(3) The following are approved persons –

    (a) in relation to an operation falling within subsection (2)(a), a registered medical practitioner,

(b) in relation to an operation falling within subsection (2)(b), a registered medical practitioner, a registered midwife or a person undergoing a course of training with a view to becoming such a practitioner or midwife.

(4) There is also no offence committed by a person who –

(a) performs a surgical operation falling within subsection (2)(a) or (b) outside the United Kingdom, and

(b) in relation to such an operation exercises functions corresponding to those of an approved person.

(5) For the purpose of determining whether an operation is necessary for the mental health of a girl it is immaterial whether she or any other person believes that the operation is required as a matter of custom or ritual.

2   Offence of assisting a girl to mutilate her own genitalia

A person is guilty of an offence if he aids, abets, counsels or procures a girl to excise, infibulate or otherwise mutilate the whole or any part of her own labia majora, labia minora or clitoris.

3   Offence of assisting a non-UK person to mutilate overseas a girl's genitalia

(1) A person is guilty of an offence if he aids, abets, counsels or procures a person who is not a United Kingdom national or permanent United Kingdom resident to do a relevant act of female genital mutilation outside the United Kingdom.

(2) An act is a relevant act of female genital mutilation if –

(a) it is done in relation to a United Kingdom national or permanent United Kingdom resident, and

(b) it would, if done by such a person, constitute an offence under section 1.

(3) But no offence is committed if the relevant act of female genital mutilation –

(a) is a surgical operation falling within section 1(2)(a) or (b), and

(b) is performed by a person who, in relation to such an operation, is an approved person or exercises functions corresponding to those of an approved person.

Health and Social Care (Community Health and Standards) Act 2003

(2003, c. 43)

Part 2 Standards

Regulatory Bodies

41   The Commission for Healthcare Audit and Inspection

(1) There is to be a body corporate known as the Commission for Healthcare Audit and Inspection (in this Part referred to as the CHAI).

42   The Commission for Social Care Inspection

(1) There is to be a body corporate known as the Commission for Social Care Inspection (in this Part referred to as the CSCI).

44   Abolition of former regulatory bodies

(1) The Commission for Health Improvement is abolished.

(2) The National Care Standards Commission is abolished.

NHS Health Care: Introductory

45   Quality in health care

(1) It is the duty of each NHS body to put and keep in place arrangements for the purpose of monitoring and improving the quality of health care provided by and for that body.

(2) In this Part 'health care' means –

    (a) services provided to individuals for or in connection with the prevention, diagnosis or treatment of illness; and

    (b) the promotion and protection of public health.

(3) In subsection (2)(a), 'illness' has the meaning given by section 275 of the 2006 Act.

46 Standards set by Secretary of State

(1) The Secretary of State may prepare and publish statements of standards in relation to the provision of health care by and for English NHS bodies and cross-border SHAs.

47A Code of practice relating to health care associated infections

(1) The Secretary of State may issue a code of practice–

    (a) applying to bodies within subsection (2), and

    (b) relating to the prevention and control of health care associated infections in connection with health care provided by or for those bodies.

(2) The bodies within this subsection are –

    (a) English NHS bodies other than Strategic Health Authorities; and

    (b) cross-border SHAs.

(3) The code may provide for provisions of the code to apply to –

    (a) such description or descriptions of bodies within subsection (2) as may be specified in the code;

    (b) such body or bodies within that subsection as may be so specified.

(4) The code may in particular –

    (a) make such provision as the Secretary of State considers appropriate for the purpose of safeguarding individuals (whether receiving health care or otherwise) from the risk, or any increased risk, of being exposed to health care associated infections or of being made susceptible, or more susceptible, to them;

    (b) contain provisions imposing on bodies to which the provisions apply requirements in relation to health care provided for such bodies by other persons as well as in relation to health care provided by such bodies.

(8) In this section 'health care associated infection' means any infection to which an individual may be exposed or made susceptible (or more susceptible) in circumstances where –

    (a) health care is being, or has been, provided to that or any other individual, and

    (b) the risk of exposure to the infection, or of susceptibility (or increased susceptibility) to it, is directly or indirectly attributable to the provision of the health care.

(9) But subsection (8) does not include an infection to which the individual is deliberately exposed as part of any health care.

47C Effect of code under section 47A

(1) Where any provisions of a code of practice issued under section 47A apply to an NHS body, the body must observe those provisions in discharging its duty under section 45.

(2) A failure to observe any provision of a code of practice issued under section 47A does not of itself make a person liable to any criminal or civil proceedings.

(3) A code of practice issued under section 47A is admissible in evidence in any criminal or civil proceedings.

NHS Health Care: Functions of CHAI

Healthcare provided by and for NHS bodies

48 Introductory

(1) The CHAI has the general function of encouraging improvement in the provision of health care by and for NHS bodies.

(2) In exercising its functions under subsection (1) and sections 49 to 56 in relation to such provision, the CHAI shall be concerned in particular with –

  (a) the availability of, and access to, the health care;
  (b) the quality and effectiveness of the health care;
  (c) the economy and efficiency of the provision of the health care;
  (d) the availability and quality of information provided to the public about the health care;
  (e) the need to safeguard and promote the rights and welfare of children; and
  (f) the effectiveness of measures taken for the purpose of paragraph (e) by the body in question and any person who provides, or is to provide, health care for that body.

49   National performance data

The CHAI has the function of publishing data relating to the provision of health care by and for NHS bodies.

50   Annual reviews

(1) In each financial year the CHAI must conduct a review of the provision of health care by and for –

  (a) each English NHS body, and
  (b) each cross-border SHA,

and must award a performance rating to each such body.

(2) The CHAI is to exercise its function under subsection (1) by reference to criteria from time to time devised by it and approved by the Secretary of State.

(3) The CHAI must publish the criteria devised and approved from time to time under subsection (2).

51   Reviews: England and Wales

(1) The CHAI has the function of conducting reviews of –

  (a) the overall provision of health care by and for NHS bodies;
  (b) the overall provision of particular kinds of health care by and for NHS bodies;
  (c) the provision of health care, or a particular kind of health care, by and for NHS bodies of a particular description.

(2) If the Secretary of State so requests, the CHAI must conduct –

  (a) a review under subsection (1)(a);
  (b) a review under subsection (1)(b) of the overall provision of a kind of health care specified in the request; or
  (c) a review under subsection (1)(c) of the provision of health care, or health care of a kind specified in the request, by or for NHS bodies of a description so specified.

(5) For the purposes of this section the CHAI may carry out an inspection of –

  (a) any NHS body; and
  (b) any person who provides, or is to provide, health care for an NHS body (wherever the health care is or is to be provided).

(6) Where the CHAI conducts a review under this section it must publish a report.

52   Reviews and investigations: England

(1) The CHAI has the function of conducting other reviews of, and investigations into, the provision of health care by and for English NHS bodies and cross-border SHAs.

(2) The CHAI may in particular under this section conduct –

  (a) a review of the overall provision of health care by and for English NHS bodies and cross-border SHAs;
  (b) a review of the overall provision of a particular kind of health care by and for English NHS bodies and cross-border SHAs;
  (c) a review of, or investigation into, the provision of any health care by or for a particular English NHS body or cross-border SHA.

(4) If the Secretary of State so requests, the CHAI must conduct –

(a) a review under subsection (2)(a);

(b) a review under subsection (2)(b) of the overall provision of a kind of health care specified in the request;

(c) a review or investigation under subsection (2)(c), or a review under subsection (3), in relation to the provision of such health care by or for such body as may be specified in the request.

(7) Where the CHAI conducts a review or investigation under this section it must publish a report.

53 Failings

(1) This section applies where the CHAI conducts –

(a) a review under section 50 or 51; or

(b) a review or investigation under section 52.

(2) The CHAI must make a report to the Secretary of State if it is of the view that –

(a) there are significant failings in relation to the provision of health care by or for an English NHS body or cross-border SHA;

(b) there are significant failings in the running of an English NHS body or cross-border SHA; or

(c) there are significant failings in the running of any body, or the practice of any individual, providing health care for an English NHS body or cross-border SHA.

(6) The CHAI must also make a report to the regulator where it is of the view that –

(a) there are significant failings in relation to the provision of health care by or for an NHS foundation trust;

(b) there are significant failings in the running of an NHS foundation trust; or

(c) there are significant failings in the running of any body, or the practice of any individual, providing health care for an NHS foundation trust.

54 Functions relating to Secretary of State and Assembly

(1) The CHAI is to keep the appropriate authority informed about the provision of health care by and for any NHS body.

(2) The CHAI may at any time give advice to the appropriate authority on any matter connected with the provision of such health care (including, in particular, advice on any changes which it thinks should be made to the standards under section 46 or 47 for the purpose of securing improvement in the quality of the health care).

57 Studies as to economy, efficiency etc

(1) The CHAI has the function of promoting or undertaking comparative or other studies designed to enable it to make recommendations for improving economy, efficiency and effectiveness in the exercise of any of the functions of an English NHS body, other than a Special Health Authority (whether the functions are exercised by the English NHS body or by another person).

(2) The CHAI may exercise its function under subsection (1) in relation to a body on the CHAI's own initiative or at the request of the body concerned.

Complaints

113 Complaints about health care

(1) The Secretary of State may by regulations make provision about the handling and consideration of complaints made under the regulations about –

(a) the exercise of any of the functions of an English NHS body or a cross-border SHA;

(b) the provision of health care by or for such a body;

(c) the provision of services by such a body or any other person in pursuance of arrangements made by the body under section 75 of the National Health Service Act 2006 or section 33 of the National Health Service (Wales) Act 2006 in relation to the exercise of the health-related functions of a local authority.

(3) Regulations under this section may provide for a complaint to be considered by one or more of the following –

(a) an NHS body;

(b) the CHAI;

(c) an independent lay person;

(d) an independent panel established under the regulations;

(e) any other person or body.

(4) Regulations under this section may make provision for a complaint or any matter raised by a complaint –

(a) to be referred to a Health Service Commissioner for him to consider whether to investigate the complaint or matter under the Health Service Commissioners Act 1993 (c. 46) (and to be treated by him as a complaint duly referred to him under section 10 of that Act);

(b) to be referred to any other person or body for him or it to consider whether to take any action otherwise than under the regulations.

148   Interpretation of Part 2

In this Part –

'Audit Commission' means the Audit Commission for Local Authorities and the National Health Service in England and Wales;

'the CHAI' means the Commission for Healthcare Audit and Inspection;

'cross-border SHA' means a Special Health Authority not performing functions only or mainly in respect of England or only or mainly in respect of Wales;

'the CSCI' means the Commission for Social Care Inspection;

'English NHS body' means –

(a) a Primary Care Trust;

(b) a Strategic Health Authority;

(c) an NHS trust all or most of whose hospitals, establishments and facilities are situated in England;

(d) an NHS foundation trust;

(e) a Special Health Authority performing functions only or mainly in respect of England;

'health care' has the meaning given by section 45(2);

'local authority' has the same meaning as in the Local Authority Social Services Act 1970 (c. 42) (see section 1 of that Act);

'NHS body' means –

(a) an English NHS body;

(b) a Welsh NHS body;

(c) a cross-border SHA;

'NHS trust' has the same meaning as in the 2006 Act;

'personal records' includes medical records;

'regulator' means the Independent Regulator of NHS Foundation Trusts.

Human Fertilisation and Embryology (Deceased Fathers) Act 2003

(2003, c. 24)

1   Certain deceased men to be registered as fathers

[See section 28 and section 29 of the Human Fertilisation and Embryology Act 1990]

3   Retrospective, transitional and transitory provision

(1) This Act shall (in addition to any case where the sperm or embryo is used on or after the coming into force of section 1) apply to any case where the sperm of a man, or any embryo the

creation of which was brought about with the sperm of a man, was used on or after 1st August 1991 and before the coming into force of that section.

(2) Where the child concerned was born before the coming into force of section 1 of this Act, section 28(5A) or (as the case may be) (5B) of the Human Fertilisation and Embryology Act 1990 (c. 37) shall have effect as if for paragraph (e) there were substituted –

'(e) the woman has elected in writing not later than the end of the period of six months beginning with the coming into force of this subsection for the man to be treated for the purpose mentioned in subsection (5I) below as the father of the child,'.

(3) Where the child concerned was born before the coming into force of section 1 of this Act, section 28(5C) of the Act of 1990 shall have effect as if for paragraph (f) there were substituted –

'(f) the woman has elected in writing not later than the end of the period of six months beginning with the coming into force of this subsection for the other party to the marriage to be treated for the purpose mentioned in subsection (5I) below as the father of the child,'.

(4) Where the child concerned was born before the coming into force of section 1 of this Act, section 28(5D) of the Act of 1990 shall have effect as if for paragraph (f) there were substituted –

'(f) the woman has elected in writing not later than the end of the period of six months beginning with the coming into force of this subsection for the man to be treated for the purpose mentioned in subsection (5I) below as the father of the child,'.

(5) Where the child concerned was born before the coming into force of section 1 of this Act, section 28 of the Act of 1990 shall have effect as if –

    (a) subsection (5E) were omitted; and

    (b) in subsection (5F) for the words from '(which requires' to 'that day)' there were substituted '(which requires an election to be made not later than the end of a period of six months)'.

(6) Where the man who might be treated as the father of the child died before the passing of this Act –

    (a) subsections (5A) and (5B) of section 28 of the Act of 1990 shall have effect as if paragraph (d) of each subsection were omitted;

    (b) subsections (5C) and (5D) of that section of that Act shall have effect as if paragraph (e) of each subsection were omitted.

Health Protection Agency Act 2004

(2004, c. 17)

1 Health Protection Agency

    (1) There shall be a body corporate to be known as the Health Protection Agency.

2 Health functions

    (1) The Agency has the following functions in relation to health –

        (a) the protection of the community (or any part of the community) against infectious disease and other dangers to health;

        (b) the prevention of the spread of infectious disease;

        (c) the provision of assistance to any other person who exercises functions in relation to the matters mentioned in paragraphs (a) and (b).

4 Functions: supplementary

    (1) For the purpose of the exercise of its functions the Agency may do any of the following –

        (a) engage in or commission research;

        (b) obtain and analyse data and other information;

(c) provide laboratory services;

(d) provide other technical and clinical services;

(e) provide training in relation to matters in respect of which the Agency has functions;

(f) make available to any other body such persons, materials and facilities as it thinks appropriate;

(g) provide information and advice.

(6) The Agency must exercise its functions efficiently and cost-effectively.

Human Tissue Act 2004

(2004, c. 30)

Part 1 Removal, Storage and Use of Human Organs and Other Tissue for Scheduled Purposes

1   Authorisation of activities for scheduled purposes

(1) The following activities shall be lawful if done with appropriate consent –

    (a) the storage of the body of a deceased person for use for a purpose specified in Schedule 1, other than anatomical examination;

    (b) the use of the body of a deceased person for a purpose so specified, other than anatomical examination;

    (c) the removal from the body of a deceased person, for use for a purpose specified in Schedule 1, of any relevant material of which the body consists or which it contains;

    (d) the storage for use for a purpose specified in Part 1 of Schedule 1 of any relevant material which has come from a human body;

    (e) the storage for use for a purpose specified in Part 2 of Schedule 1 of any relevant material which has come from the body of a deceased person;

    (f) the use for a purpose specified in Part 1 of Schedule 1 of any relevant material which has come from a human body;

    (g) the use for a purpose specified in Part 2 of Schedule 1 of any relevant material which has come from the body of a deceased person.

(2) The storage of the body of a deceased person for use for the purpose of anatomical examination shall be lawful if done –

    (a) with appropriate consent, and

    (b) after the signing of a certificate –

        (i)   under section 22(1) of the Births and Deaths Registration Act 1953 (c. 20), or

        (ii)   under Article 25(2) of the Births and Deaths Registration (Northern Ireland) Order 1976 (S.I. 1976/1041 (N.I. 14)), of the cause of death of the person.

(3) The use of the body of a deceased person for the purpose of anatomical examination shall be lawful if done –

    (a) with appropriate consent, and

    (b) after the death of the person has been registered –

        (i)   under section 15 of the Births and Deaths Registration Act 1953.

(4) Subsections (1) to (3) do not apply to an activity of a kind mentioned there if it is done in relation to –

    (a) a body to which subsection (5) applies, or

    (b) relevant material to which subsection (6) applies.

(5) This subsection applies to a body if –

    (a) it has been imported, or

    (b) it is the body of a person who died before the day on which this section comes into force and at least one hundred years have elapsed since the date of the person's death.

(6) This subsection applies to relevant material if –

    (a) it has been imported,

    (b) it has come from a body which has been imported, or

    (c) it is material which has come from the body of a person who died before the day on which this section comes into force and at least one hundred years have elapsed since the date of the person's death.

(7) Subsection (1)(d) does not apply to the storage of relevant material for use for the purpose of research in connection with disorders, or the functioning, of the human body if –

    (a) the material has come from the body of a living person, and

    (b) the research falls within subsection (9).

(8) Subsection (1)(f) does not apply to the use of relevant material for the purpose of research in connection with disorders, or the functioning, of the human body if –

(a) the material has come from the body of a living person, and

(b) the research falls within subsection (9).

(9) Research falls within this subsection if –

(a) it is ethically approved in accordance with regulations made by the Secretary of State, and

(b) it is to be, or is, carried out in circumstances such that the person carrying it out is not in possession, and not likely to come into possession, of information from which the person from whose body the material has come can be identified.

(10) The following activities shall be lawful –

(a) the storage for use for a purpose specified in Part 2 of Schedule 1 of any relevant material which has come from the body of a living person;

(b) the use for such a purpose of any relevant material which has come from the body of a living person;

(c) an activity in relation to which subsection (4), (7) or (8) has effect.

(11) The Secretary of State may by order –

(a) vary or omit any of the purposes specified in Part 1 or 2 of Schedule 1, or

(b) add to the purposes specified in Part 1 or 2 of that Schedule.

(12) Nothing in this section applies to –

(a) the use of relevant material in connection with a device to which Directive 98/79/EC of the European Parliament and of the Council on *in vitro* diagnostic medical devices applies, where the use falls within the Directive, or

(b) the storage of relevant material for use falling within paragraph (a).

(13) In this section, the references to a body or material which has been imported do not include a body or material which has been imported after having been exported with a view to its subsequently being re-imported.

2   'Appropriate consent': children

(1) This section makes provision for the interpretation of 'appropriate consent' in section 1 in relation to an activity involving the body, or material from the body, of a person who is a child or has died a child ('the child concerned').

(2) Subject to subsection (3), where the child concerned is alive, 'appropriate consent' means his consent.

(3) Where –

(a) the child concerned is alive,

(b) neither a decision of his to consent to the activity, nor a decision of his not to consent to it, is in force, and

(c) either he is not competent to deal with the issue of consent in relation to the activity or, though he is competent to deal with that issue, he fails to do so,

'appropriate consent' means the consent of a person who has parental responsibility for him.

(4) Where the child concerned has died and the activity is one to which subsection (5) applies, 'appropriate consent' means his consent in writing.

(5) This subsection applies to an activity involving storage for use, or use, for the purpose of –

(a) public display, or

(b) where the subject-matter of the activity is not excepted material, anatomical examination.

(6) Consent in writing for the purposes of subsection (4) is only valid if –

(a) it is signed by the child concerned in the presence of at least one witness who attests the signature, or

(b) it is signed at the direction of the child concerned, in his presence and in the presence of at least one witness who attests the signature.

(7) Where the child concerned has died and the activity is not one to which subsection (5) applies, 'appropriate consent' means –

(a) if a decision of his to consent to the activity, or a decision of his not to consent to it, was in force immediately before he died, his consent;

(b) if paragraph (a) does not apply –

   (i) the consent of a person who had parental responsibility for him immediately before he died, or

   (ii) where no person had parental responsibility for him immediately before he died, the consent of a person who stood in a qualifying relationship to him at that time.

3   'Appropriate consent': adults

(1) This section makes provision for the interpretation of 'appropriate consent' in section 1 in relation to an activity involving the body, or material from the body, of a person who is an adult or has died an adult ('the person concerned').

(2) Where the person concerned is alive, 'appropriate consent' means his consent.

(3) Where the person concerned has died and the activity is one to which subsection (4) applies, 'appropriate consent' means his consent in writing.

(4) This subsection applies to an activity involving storage for use, or use, for the purpose of –

(a) public display, or

(b) where the subject-matter of the activity is not excepted material, anatomical examination.

(5) Consent in writing for the purposes of subsection (3) is only valid if –

(a) it is signed by the person concerned in the presence of at least one witness who attests the signature,

(b) it is signed at the direction of the person concerned, in his presence and in the presence of at least one witness who attests the signature, or

(c) it is contained in a will of the person concerned made in accordance with the requirements of –

   (i) section 9 of the Wills Act 1837 (c. 26).

(6) Where the person concerned has died and the activity is not one to which subsection (4) applies, 'appropriate consent' means –

(a) if a decision of his to consent to the activity, or a decision of his not to consent to it, was in force immediately before he died, his consent;

(b) if –

   (i) paragraph (a) does not apply, and

   (ii) he has appointed a person or persons under section 4 to deal after his death with the issue of consent in relation to the activity, consent given under the appointment;

(c) if neither paragraph (a) nor paragraph (b) applies, the consent of a person who stood in a qualifying relationship to him immediately before he died.

(7) Where the person concerned has appointed a person or persons under section 4 to deal after his death with the issue of consent in relation to the activity, the appointment shall be disregarded for the purposes of subsection (6) if no one is able to give consent under it.

(8) If it is not reasonably practicable to communicate with a person appointed under section 4 within the time available if consent in relation to the activity is to be acted on, he shall be treated for the purposes of subsection (7) as not able to give consent under the appointment in relation to it.

4   Nominated representatives

(1) An adult may appoint one or more persons to represent him after his death in relation to consent for the purposes of section 1.

(2) An appointment under this section may be general or limited to consent in relation to such one or more activities as may be specified in the appointment.

(3) An appointment under this section may be made orally or in writing.

(4) An oral appointment under this section is only valid if made in the presence of at least two witnesses present at the same time.

(5) A written appointment under this section is only valid if –

(a) it is signed by the person making it in the presence of at least one witness who attests the signature,

(b) it is signed at the direction of the person making it, in his presence and in the presence of at least one witness who attests the signature, or

(c) it is contained in a will of the person making it, being a will which is made in accordance with the requirements of –

    (i) section 9 of the Wills Act 1837 (c. 26).

(6) Where a person appoints two or more persons under this section in relation to the same activity, they shall be regarded as appointed to act jointly and severally unless the appointment provides that they are appointed to act jointly.

(7) An appointment under this section may be revoked at any time.

(8) Subsections (3) to (5) apply to the revocation of an appointment under this section as they apply to the making of such an appointment.

(9) A person appointed under this section may at any time renounce his appointment.

(10) A person may not act under an appointment under this section if –

(a) he is not an adult, or

(b) he is of a description prescribed for the purposes of this provision by regulations made by the Secretary of State.

5   Prohibition of activities without consent etc.

(1) A person commits an offence if, without appropriate consent, he does an activity to which subsection (1), (2) or (3) of section 1 applies, unless he reasonably believes –

(a) that he does the activity with appropriate consent, or

(b) that what he does is not an activity to which the subsection applies.

(2) A person commits an offence if –

(a) he falsely represents to a person whom he knows or believes is going to, or may, do an activity to which subsection (1), (2) or (3) of section 1 applies –

    (i) that there is appropriate consent to the doing of the activity, or

    (ii) that the activity is not one to which the subsection applies, and

(b) he knows that the representation is false or does not believe it to be true.

(3) Subject to subsection (4), a person commits an offence if, when he does an activity to which section 1(2) applies, neither of the following has been signed in relation to the cause of death of the person concerned –

(a) a certificate under section 22(1) of the Births and Deaths Registration Act 1953 (c. 20).

(4) Subsection (3) does not apply –

(a) where the person reasonably believes –

    (i) that a certificate under either of those provisions has been signed in relation to the cause of death of the person concerned, or

    (ii) that what he does is not an activity to which section 1(2) applies, or

(b) where the person comes into lawful possession of the body immediately after death and stores it prior to its removal to a place where anatomical examination is to take place.

(5) Subject to subsection (6), a person commits an offence if, when he does an activity to which section 1(3) applies, the death of the person concerned has not been registered under either of the following provisions –

(a) section 15 of the Births and Deaths Registration Act 1953.

(6) Subsection (5) does not apply where the person reasonably believes –

(a) that the death of the person concerned has been registered under either of those provisions, or

(b) that what he does is not an activity to which section 1(3) applies.

(7) A person guilty of an offence under this section shall be liable –

(a) on summary conviction to a fine not exceeding the statutory maximum;

(b) on conviction on indictment –

(i) to imprisonment for a term not exceeding 3 years, or

(ii) to a fine, or

(iii) to both.

(8) In this section, 'appropriate consent' has the same meaning as in section 1.

6 Activities involving material from adults who lack capacity to consent

Where –

(a) an activity of a kind mentioned in section 1(1)(d) or (f) involves material from the body of a person who –

(i) is an adult, and

(ii) lacks capacity to consent to the activity, and

(b) neither a decision of his to consent to the activity, nor a decision of his not to consent to it, is in force,

there shall for the purposes of this Part be deemed to be consent of his to the activity if it is done in circumstances of a kind specified by regulations made by the Secretary of State.

7 Powers to dispense with need for consent

(1) If the Authority is satisfied –

(a) that relevant material has come from the body of a living person,

(b) that it is not reasonably possible to trace the person from whose body the material has come ('the donor'),

(c) that it is desirable in the interests of another person (including a future person) that the material be used for the purpose of obtaining scientific or medical information about the donor, and

(d) that there is no reason to believe –

(i) that the donor has died,

(ii) that a decision of the donor to refuse to consent to the use of the material for that purpose is in force, or

(iii) that the donor lacks capacity to consent to the use of the material for that purpose, it may direct that subsection (3) apply to the material for the benefit of the other person.

(2) If the Authority is satisfied –

(a) that relevant material has come from the body of a living person,

(b) that it is desirable in the interests of another person (including a future person) that the material be used for the purpose of obtaining scientific or medical information about the person from whose body the material has come ('the donor'),

(c) that reasonable efforts have been made to get the donor to decide whether to consent to the use of the material for that purpose,

(d) that there is no reason to believe –

(i) that the donor has died,

(ii) that a decision of the donor to refuse to consent to the use of the material for that purpose is in force, or

(iii) that the donor lacks capacity to consent to the use of the material for that purpose, and

(e) that the donor has been given notice of the application for the exercise of the power conferred by this subsection,

it may direct that subsection (3) apply to the material for the benefit of the other person.

(3) Where material is the subject of a direction under subsection (1) or (2), there shall for the purposes of this Part be deemed to be consent of the donor to the use of the material for the purpose of obtaining scientific or medical information about him which may be relevant to the person for whose benefit the direction is given.

(4) The Secretary of State may by regulations enable the High Court, in such circumstances as the regulations may provide, to make an order deeming there for the purposes of this Part to be appropriate consent to an activity consisting of –

(a) the storage of the body of a deceased person for use for the purpose of research in connection with disorders, or the functioning, of the human body,

(b) the use of the body of a deceased person for that purpose,

(c) the removal from the body of a deceased person, for use for that purpose, of any relevant material of which the body consists or which it contains,

(d) the storage for use for that purpose of any relevant material which has come from a human body, or

(e) the use for that purpose of any relevant material which has come from a human body.

8   Restriction of activities in relation to donated material

(1) Subject to subsection (2), a person commits an offence if he –

(a) uses donated material for a purpose which is not a qualifying purpose, or

(b) stores donated material for use for a purpose which is not a qualifying purpose.

(2) Subsection (1) does not apply where the person reasonably believes that what he uses, or stores, is not donated material.

(3) A person guilty of an offence under this section shall be liable –

(a) on summary conviction to a fine not exceeding the statutory maximum;

(b) on conviction on indictment –

(i)   to imprisonment for a term not exceeding 3 years, or

(ii) to a fine, or

(iii) to both.

(4) In subsection (1), references to a qualifying purpose are to –

(a) a purpose specified in Schedule 1,

(b) the purpose of medical diagnosis or treatment,

(c) the purpose of decent disposal, or

(d) a purpose specified in regulations made by the Secretary of State.

(5) In this section, references to donated material are to –

(a) the body of a deceased person, or

(b) relevant material which has come from a human body, which is, or has been, the subject of donation.

(6) For the purposes of subsection (5), a body, or material, is the subject of donation if authority under section 1(1) to (3) exists in relation to it.

9   Existing holdings

(1) In its application to the following activities, section 1(1) shall have effect with the omission of the words 'if done with appropriate consent' –

(a) the storage of an existing holding for use for a purpose specified in Schedule 1;

(b) the use of an existing holding for a purpose so specified.

(2) Subsection (1) does not apply where the existing holding is a body, or separated part of a body, in relation to which section 10(3) or (5) has effect.

(3) Section 5(1) and (2) shall have effect as if the activities mentioned in subsection (1) were not activities to which section 1(1) applies.

(4) In this section, 'existing holding' means –

(a) the body of a deceased person, or

(b) relevant material which has come from a human body,

held, immediately before the day on which section 1(1) comes into force, for use for a purpose specified in Schedule 1.

10   Existing anatomical specimens

(1) This section applies where a person dies during the three years immediately preceding the coming into force of section 1.

(2) Subsection (3) applies where –

    (a) before section 1 comes into force, authority is given under section 4(2) or (3) of the Anatomy Act 1984 (c. 14) for the person's body to be used for anatomical examination, and

    (b) section 1 comes into force before anatomical examination of the person's body is concluded.

(3) During so much of the relevant period as falls after section 1 comes into force, that authority shall be treated for the purposes of section 1 as appropriate consent in relation to –

    (a) the storage of the person's body, or separated parts of his body, for use for the purpose of anatomical examination, and

    (b) the use of his body, or separated parts of his body, for that purpose.

(4) Subsection (5) applies where –

    (a) before section 1 comes into force, authority is given under section 6(2) or (3) of the Anatomy Act 1984 for possession of parts (or any specified parts) of the person's body to be held after anatomical examination of his body is concluded, and

    (b) anatomical examination of the person's body is concluded –

        (i) after section 1 comes into force, but

        (ii) before the end of the period of three years beginning with the date of the person's death.

(5) With effect from the conclusion of the anatomical examination of the person's body, that authority shall be treated for the purposes of section 1 as appropriate consent in relation to –

    (a) the storage for use for a qualifying purpose of a part of the person's body which –

        (i) is a part to which that authority relates, and

        (ii) is such that the person cannot be recognised simply by examination of the part, and

    (b) the use for a qualifying purpose of such a part of the person's body.

(6) Where for the purposes of section 1 there would not be appropriate consent in relation to an activity but for authority given under the Anatomy Act 1984 (c. 14) being treated for those purposes as appropriate consent in relation to the activity, section 1(1) to (3) do not authorise the doing of the activity otherwise than in accordance with that authority.

(7) In subsection (3), 'the relevant period', in relation to a person, means whichever is the shorter of –

    (a) the period of three years beginning with the date of the person's death, and

    (b) the period beginning with that date and ending when anatomical examination of the person's body is concluded.

(8) In subsection (5), 'qualifying purpose' means a purpose specified in paragraph 6 or 9 of Schedule 1.

(9) The Secretary of State may by order amend subsection (8).

11   Coroners

(1) Nothing in this Part applies to anything done for purposes of functions of a coroner or under the authority of a coroner.

(2) Where a person knows, or has reason to believe, that –

    (a) the body of a deceased person, or

    (b) relevant material which has come from the body of a deceased person,

is, or may be, required for purposes of functions of a coroner, he shall not act on authority under section 1 in relation to the body, or material, except with the consent of the coroner.

12   Interpretation of Part 1

In this Part, 'excepted material' means material which has –

    (a) come from the body of a living person, or

    (b) come from the body of a deceased person otherwise than in the course of use of the body for the purpose of anatomical examination.

Part 2 Regulation of Activities Involving Human Tissue

The Human Tissue Authority

13   The Human Tissue Authority

(1) There shall be a body corporate to be known as the Human Tissue Authority (referred to in this Act as 'the Authority').

14   Remit

(1) The following are the activities within the remit of the Authority –

(a) the removal from a human body, for use for a scheduled purpose, of any relevant material of which the body consists or which it contains;

(b) the use, for a scheduled purpose, of –

(i)   the body of a deceased person, or

(ii) relevant material which has come from a human body;

(c) the storage of an anatomical specimen or former anatomical specimen;

(d) the storage (in any case not falling within paragraph (c)) of –

(i)   the body of a deceased person, or

(ii) relevant material which has come from a human body, for use for a scheduled purpose;

(e) the import or export of –

(i)   the body of a deceased person, or

(ii) relevant material which has come from a human body, for use for a scheduled purpose;

(f) the disposal of the body of a deceased person which has been –

(i)   imported for use,

(ii) stored for use, or

(iii) used, for a scheduled purpose;

(g) the disposal of relevant material which –

(i)   has been removed from a person's body for the purposes of his medical treatment,

(ii) has been removed from the body of a deceased person for the purposes of an anatomical, or post-mortem, examination,

(iii) has been removed from a human body (otherwise than as mentioned in sub-paragraph (ii)) for use for a scheduled purpose,

(iv) has come from a human body and been imported for use for a scheduled purpose, or

(v)   has come from the body of a deceased person which has been imported for use for a scheduled purpose.

(2) Without prejudice to the generality of subsection (1)(a) and (b), the activities within the remit of the Authority include, in particular –

(a) the carrying-out of an anatomical examination, and

(b) the making of a post-mortem examination.

(3) An activity is excluded from the remit of the Authority if –

(a) it relates to the body of a person who died before the day on which this section comes into force or to material which has come from the body of such a person, and

(b) at least one hundred years have elapsed since the date of the person's death.

(4) The Secretary of State may by order amend this section for the purpose of adding to the activities within the remit of the Authority.

(5) In this section, 'relevant material', in relation to use for the scheduled purpose of transplantation, does not include blood or anything derived from blood.

15   General functions

The Authority shall have the following general functions –

    (a) maintaining a statement of the general principles which it considers should be followed –
        (i)   in the carrying-on of activities within its remit, and
        (ii) in the carrying-out of its functions in relation to such activities;

    (b) providing in relation to activities within its remit such general oversight and guidance as it considers appropriate;

    (c) superintending, in relation to activities within its remit, compliance with –
        (i)   requirements imposed by or under Part 1 or this Part, and
        (ii) codes of practice under this Act;

    (d) providing to the public, and to persons carrying on activities within its remit, such information and advice as it considers appropriate about the nature and purpose of such activities;

    (e) monitoring developments relating to activities within its remit and advising the Secretary of State, the National Assembly for Wales and the relevant Northern Ireland department on issues relating to such developments;

    (f) advising the Secretary of State, the National Assembly for Wales or the relevant Northern Ireland department on such other issues relating to activities within its remit as he, the Assembly or the department may require.

Licensing

16   Licence requirement

    (1) No person shall do an activity to which this section applies otherwise than under the authority of a licence granted for the purposes of this section.

    (2) This section applies to the following activities –
        (a) the carrying-out of an anatomical examination;
        (b) the making of a post-mortem examination;
        (c) the removal from the body of a deceased person (otherwise than in the course of an activity mentioned in paragraph (a) or (b)) of relevant material of which the body consists or which it contains, for use for a scheduled purpose other than transplantation;
        (d) the storage of an anatomical specimen;
        (e) the storage (in any case not falling within paragraph (d)) of –
            (i)   the body of a deceased person, or
            (ii) relevant material which has come from a human body, for use for a scheduled purpose;
        (f) the use, for the purpose of public display, of –
            (i)   the body of a deceased person, or
            (ii) relevant material which has come from the body of a deceased person.

    (3) The Secretary of State may by regulations specify circumstances in which storage of relevant material by a person who intends to use it for a scheduled purpose is excepted from subsection (2)(e)(ii).

    (4) An activity is excluded from subsection (2) if –
        (a) it relates to the body of a person who died before the day on which this section comes into force or to material which has come from the body of such a person, and
        (b) at least one hundred years have elapsed since the date of the person's death.

    (5) The Secretary of State may by regulations amend this section for the purpose of –
        (a) adding to the activities to which this section applies,
        (b) removing an activity from the activities to which this section applies, or
        (c) altering the description of an activity to which this section applies.

    (6) Schedule 3 (which makes provision about licences for the purposes of this section) has effect.

(7) In subsection (2) –

    (a) references to storage do not include storage which is incidental to transportation, and

    (b) 'relevant material', in relation to use for the scheduled purpose of transplantation, does not include blood or anything derived from blood.

25   Breach of licence requirement

(1) A person who contravenes section 16(1) commits an offence, unless he reasonably believes –

    (a) that what he does is not an activity to which section 16 applies, or

    (b) that he acts under the authority of a licence.

(2) A person guilty of an offence under subsection (1) shall be liable –

    (a) on summary conviction to a fine not exceeding the statutory maximum;

    (b) on conviction on indictment –

        (i)   to imprisonment for a term not exceeding 3 years, or

        (ii) to a fine, or

        (iii) to both.

Codes of practice

26   Preparation of codes

(1) The Authority may prepare and issue codes of practice for the purpose of –

    (a) giving practical guidance to persons carrying on activities within its remit, and

    (b) laying down the standards expected in relation to the carrying-on of such activities.

(2) The Authority shall deal under subsection (1) with the following matters –

    (a) the carrying-out of anatomical examinations;

    (b) the storage of anatomical specimens;

    (c) the storage and disposal of former anatomical specimens;

    (d) the definition of death for the purposes of this Act;

    (e) communication with the family of the deceased in relation to the making of a post-mortem examination;

    (f) the making of post-mortem examinations;

    (g) communication with the family of the deceased in relation to the removal from the body of the deceased, for use for a scheduled purpose, of any relevant material of which the body consists or which it contains;

    (h) the removal from a human body, for use for a scheduled purpose, of any relevant material of which the body consists or which it contains;

    (i) the storage for use for a scheduled purpose, and the use for such a purpose, of –

        (i)   the body of a deceased person, or

        (ii) relevant material which has come from a human body;

    (j) the storage for use for a scheduled purpose, and the use for such a purpose, of an existing holding within the meaning of section 9;

    (k) the import, and the export, of –

        (i)   the body of a deceased person, or

        (ii) relevant material which has come from a human body, for use for a scheduled purpose;

    (l) the disposal of relevant material which –

        (i)   has been removed from a human body for use for a scheduled purpose, or

        (ii) has come from a human body and is an existing holding for the purposes of section 9.

(3) In dealing under subsection (1) with the matters mentioned in subsection (2)(h) and (i), the Authority shall, in particular, deal with consent.

(4) The Authority shall –

    (a) keep any code of practice under this section under review, and

    (b) prepare a revised code of practice when appropriate.

27   Provision with respect to consent

(1) The duty under section 26(3) shall have effect, in particular, to require the Authority to lay down the standards expected in relation to the obtaining of consent where consent falls by virtue of section 2(7)(b)(ii) or 3(6)(c) to be obtained from a person in a qualifying relationship.

(2) Subject to subsection (3), the standards required to be laid down by subsection (1) shall include provision to the effect set out in subsections (4) to (8).

(3) The standards required to be laid down by subsection (1) may include provision to different effect in relation to cases which appear to the Authority to be exceptional.

(4) The qualifying relationships for the purpose of sections 2(7)(b)(ii) and 3(6)(c) should be ranked in the following order –

    (a) spouse or partner;

    (b) parent or child;

    (c) brother or sister;

    (d) grandparent or grandchild;

    (e) child of a person falling within paragraph (c);

    (f) stepfather or stepmother;

    (g) half-brother or half-sister;

    (h) friend of longstanding.

(5) Relationships in the same paragraph of subsection (4) should be accorded equal ranking.

(6) Consent should be obtained from the person whose relationship to the person concerned is accorded the highest ranking in accordance with subsections (4) and (5).

(7) If the relationship of each of two or more persons to the person concerned is accorded equal highest ranking in accordance with subsections (4) and (5), it is sufficient to obtain the consent of any of them.

(8) In applying the principles set out above, a person's relationship shall be left out of account if –

    (a) he does not wish to deal with the issue of consent,

    (b) he is not able to deal with that issue, or

    (c) having regard to the activity in relation to which consent is sought, it is not reasonably practicable to communicate with him within the time available if consent in relation to the activity is to be acted on.

(9) The Secretary of State may by order amend subsection (4).

28   Effect of codes

(1) A failure on the part of any person to observe any provision of a code of practice under section 26 shall not of itself render the person liable to any proceedings.

(2) The Authority may, in carrying out its functions with respect to licences, take into account any relevant observance of, or failure to observe, a code of practice under section 26, so far as dealing with a matter mentioned in any of paragraphs (a) to (c) and (e) to (j) of subsection (2) of that section.

Anatomy

30   Possession of anatomical specimens away from licensed premises

(1) Subject to subsections (2) to (6), a person commits an offence if –

    (a) he has possession of an anatomical specimen, and

    (b) the specimen is not on premises in respect of which an anatomy licence is in force.

(2) Subsection (1) does not apply where –

    (a) the specimen has come from premises in respect of which a storage licence is in force, and

    (b) the person –

        (i) is authorised in writing by the designated individual to have possession of the specimen, and

        (ii) has possession of the specimen only for a purpose for which he is so authorised to have possession of it.

(3) Subsection (1) does not apply where –

    (a) the specimen is the body of a deceased person which is to be used for the purpose of anatomical examination,

    (b) the person who has possession of the body has come into lawful possession of it immediately after the deceased's death, and

    (c) he retains possession of the body prior to its removal to premises in respect of which an anatomy licence is in force.

(4) Subsection (1) does not apply where the person has possession of the specimen only for the purpose of transporting it to premises –

    (a) in respect of which an anatomy licence is in force, or

    (b) where the specimen is to be used for the purpose of education, training or research.

(5) Subsection (1) does not apply where the person has possession of the specimen for purposes of functions of, or under the authority of, a coroner.

(6) Subsection (1) does not apply where the person reasonably believes –

    (a) that what he has possession of is not an anatomical specimen,

    (b) that the specimen is on premises in respect of which an anatomy licence is in force, or

    (c) that any of subsections (2) to (5) applies.

(7) A person guilty of an offence under subsection (1) shall be liable –

    (a) on summary conviction to a fine not exceeding the statutory maximum;

    (b) on conviction on indictment –

        (i) to imprisonment for a term not exceeding 3 years, or

        (ii) to a fine, or

        (iii) to both.

(8) In this section –

'anatomy licence' means a licence authorising –

    (a) the carrying-out of an anatomical examination, or

    (b) the storage of anatomical specimens;

'storage licence' means a licence authorising the storage of anatomical specimens.

31   Possession of former anatomical specimens away from licensed premises

(1) Subject to subsections (2) to (5), a person commits an offence if –

    (a) he has possession of a former anatomical specimen, and

    (b) the specimen is not on premises in respect of which a storage licence is in force.

(2) Subsection (1) does not apply where –

    (a) the specimen has come from premises in respect of which a storage licence is in force, and

    (b) the person –

        (i) is authorised in writing by the designated individual to have possession of the specimen, and

        (ii) has possession of the specimen only for a purpose for which he is so authorised to have possession of it.

(3) Subsection (1) does not apply where the person has possession of the specimen only for the purpose of transporting it to premises –

    (a) in respect of which a storage licence is in force, or

    (b) where the specimen is to be used for the purpose of education, training or research.

(4) Subsection (1) does not apply where the person has possession of the specimen –

    (a) only for the purpose of its decent disposal, or

    (b) for purposes of functions of, or under the authority of, a coroner.

(5) Subsection (1) does not apply where the person reasonably believes –

    (a) that what he has possession of is not a former anatomical specimen,

    (b) that the specimen is on premises in respect of which a storage licence is in force, or

    (c) that any of subsections (2) to (4) applies.

(6) A person guilty of an offence under subsection (1) shall be liable –

    (a) on summary conviction to a fine not exceeding the statutory maximum;

    (b) on conviction on indictment –

        (i)   to imprisonment for a term not exceeding 3 years, or

        (ii) to a fine, or

        (iii) to both.

(7) In this section, 'storage licence' means a licence authorising the storage, for use for a scheduled purpose, of relevant material which has come from a human body.

Trafficking

32   Prohibition of commercial dealings in human material for transplantation

(1) A person commits an offence if he –

    (a) gives or receives a reward for the supply of, or for an offer to supply, any controlled material;

    (b) seeks to find a person willing to supply any controlled material for reward;

    (c) offers to supply any controlled material for reward;

    (d) initiates or negotiates any arrangement involving the giving of a reward for the supply of, or for an offer to supply, any controlled material;

    (e) takes part in the management or control of a body of persons corporate or unincorporate whose activities consist of or include the initiation or negotiation of such arrangements.

(2) Without prejudice to subsection (1)(b) and (c), a person commits an offence if he causes to be published or distributed, or knowingly publishes or distributes, an advertisement –

    (a) inviting persons to supply, or offering to supply, any controlled material for reward, or

    (b) indicating that the advertiser is willing to initiate or negotiate any such arrangement as is mentioned in subsection (1)(d).

(3) A person who engages in an activity to which subsection (1) or (2) applies does not commit an offence under that subsection if he is designated by the Authority as a person who may lawfully engage in the activity.

(4) A person guilty of an offence under subsection (1) shall be liable –

    (a) on summary conviction –

        (i)   to imprisonment for a term not exceeding 12 months, or

        (ii) to a fine not exceeding the statutory maximum, or

        (iii) to both;

    (b) on conviction on indictment –

        (i)   to imprisonment for a term not exceeding 3 years, or

        (ii) to a fine, or

        (iii) to both.

(5) A person guilty of an offence under subsection (2) shall be liable on summary conviction –

    (a) to imprisonment for a term not exceeding 51 weeks, or

    (b) to a fine not exceeding level 5 on the standard scale, or

    (c) to both.

(6) For the purposes of subsections (1) and (2), payment in money or money's worth to the holder of a licence shall be treated as not being a reward where –

    (a) it is in consideration for transporting, removing, preparing, preserving or storing controlled material, and

    (b) its receipt by the holder of the licence is not expressly prohibited by the terms of the licence.

(7) References in subsections (1) and (2) to reward, in relation to the supply of any controlled material, do not include payment in money or money's worth for defraying or reimbursing –

    (a) any expenses incurred in, or in connection with, transporting, removing, preparing, preserving or storing the material,

(b) any liability incurred in respect of –
    (i) expenses incurred by a third party in, or in connection with, any of the activities mentioned in paragraph (a), or
    (ii) a payment in relation to which subsection (6) has effect, or
(c) any expenses or loss of earnings incurred by the person from whose body the material comes so far as reasonably and directly attributable to his supplying the material from his body.

(8) For the purposes of this section, controlled material is any material which –
    (a) consists of or includes human cells,
    (b) is, or is intended to be removed, from a human body,
    (c) is intended to be used for the purpose of transplantation, and
    (d) is not of a kind excepted under subsection (9).

(9) The following kinds of material are excepted –
    (a) gametes,
    (b) embryos, and
    (c) material which is the subject of property because of an application of human skill.

(10) Where the body of a deceased person is intended to be used to provide material which –
    (a) consists of or includes human cells, and
    (b) is not of a kind excepted under subsection (9), for use for the purpose of transplantation, the body shall be treated as controlled material for the purposes of this section.

(11) In this section –

'advertisement' includes any form of advertising whether to the public generally, to any section of the public or individually to selected persons;

'reward' means any description of financial or other material advantage.

Transplants

33　Restriction on transplants involving a live donor

(1) Subject to subsections (3) and (5), a person commits an offence if –
    (a) he removes any transplantable material from the body of a living person intending that the material be used for the purpose of transplantation, and
    (b) when he removes the material, he knows, or might reasonably be expected to know, that the person from whose body he removes the material is alive.

(2) Subject to subsections (3) and (5), a person commits an offence if –
    (a) he uses for the purpose of transplantation any transplantable material which has come from the body of a living person, and
    (b) when he does so, he knows, or might reasonably be expected to know, that the transplantable material has come from the body of a living person.

(3) The Secretary of State may by regulations provide that subsection (1) or (2) shall not apply in a case where –
    (a) the Authority is satisfied –
        (i) that no reward has been or is to be given in contravention of section 32, and
        (ii) that such other conditions as are specified in the regulations are satisfied, and
    (b) such other requirements as are specified in the regulations are complied with.

(4) Regulations under subsection (3) shall include provision for decisions of the Authority in relation to matters which fall to be decided by it under the regulations to be subject, in such circumstances as the regulations may provide, to reconsideration in accordance with such procedure as the regulations may provide.

(5) Where under subsection (3) an exception from subsection (1) or (2) is in force, a person does not commit an offence under that subsection if he reasonably believes that the exception applies.

(6) A person guilty of an offence under this section is liable on summary conviction –

(a) to imprisonment for a term not exceeding 51 weeks, or

(b) to a fine not exceeding level 5 on the standard scale, or

(c) to both.

(7) In this section –

'reward' has the same meaning as in section 32;

'transplantable material' means material of a description specified by regulations made by the Secretary of State.

34   Information about transplant operations

(1) The Secretary of State may make regulations requiring such persons as may be specified in the regulations to supply to such authority as may be so specified such information as may be so specified with respect to transplants that have been or are proposed to be carried out using transplantable material removed from a human body.

(2) Any such authority shall keep a record of information supplied to it in pursuance of regulations under this section.

(3) A person commits an offence if –

(a) he fails without reasonable excuse to comply with regulations under this section, or

(b) in purported compliance with such regulations, he knowingly or recklessly supplies information which is false or misleading in a material respect.

(4) A person guilty of an offence under subsection (3)(a) is liable on summary conviction to a fine not exceeding level 3 on the standard scale.

(5) A person guilty of an offence under subsection (3)(b) is liable on summary conviction to a fine not exceeding level 5 on the standard scale.

(6) In this section, 'transplantable material' has the same meaning as in section 33.

General

35   Agency arrangements and provision of services

(1) Arrangements may be made between the Authority and a government department, a public authority or the holder of a public office ('the other authority') for –

(a) any functions of the Authority to be carried out by, or by members of staff of, the other authority, or

(b) the provision by the other authority of administrative, professional or technical services to the Authority.

(2) Arrangements under subsection (1)(a) shall not affect responsibility for the carrying-out of the Authority's functions.

(3) Subsection (1)(a) shall not apply to functions of making subordinate legislation (within the meaning of the Interpretation Act 1978 (c. 30)).

38   Duties in relation to carrying out functions

(1) The Authority must carry out its functions effectively, efficiently and economically.

(2) In carrying out its functions, the Authority must, so far as relevant, have regard to the principles of best regulatory practice (including the principles under which regulatory activities should be transparent, accountable, proportionate, consistent and targeted only at cases in which action is needed).

Exceptions

39   Criminal justice purposes

(1) Subject to subsection (2), nothing in section 14(1) or 16(2) applies to anything done for purposes related to –

(a) the prevention or detection of crime, or

(b) the conduct of a prosecution.

(2) Subsection (1) does not except from section 14(1) or 16(2) the carrying-out of a post-mortem examination for purposes of functions of a coroner.

(3) The reference in subsection (2) to the carrying-out of a post-mortem examination does not include the removal of relevant material from the body of a deceased person, or from a part of the body of a deceased person, at the first place where the body or part is situated to be attended by a constable.

(4) For the purposes of subsection (1)(a), detecting crime shall be taken to include –

    (a) establishing by whom, for what purpose, by what means and generally in what circumstances any crime was committed, and

    (b) the apprehension of the person by whom any crime was committed; and the reference in subsection (1)(a) to the detection of crime includes any detection outside the United Kingdom of any crime or suspected crime.

(5) In subsection (1)(b), the reference to a prosecution includes a prosecution brought in respect of any crime in a country or territory outside the United Kingdom.

(6) In this section, references to crime include a reference to any conduct which –

    (a) constitutes one or more criminal offences (whether under the law of a part of the United Kingdom or of a country or territory outside the United Kingdom),

    (b) is, or corresponds to, any conduct which, if it all took place in any one part of the United Kingdom, would constitute one or more criminal offences, or

    (c) constitutes one or more offences of a kind triable by court-martial under the Army Act 1955 (3 & 4 Eliz. 2 c. 18), the Air Force Act 1955 (3 & 4 Eliz. 2 c. 19) or the Naval Discipline Act 1957 (c. 53).

40   Religious relics

(1) This section applies –

    (a) to the use of –

       (i) the body of a deceased person, or

       (ii) relevant material which has come from a human body, for the purpose of public display at a place of public religious worship or at a place associated with such a place, and

    (b) to the storage of –

       (i) the body of a deceased person, or

       (ii) relevant material which has come from a human body, for use for the purpose mentioned in paragraph (a).

(2) An activity to which this section applies is excluded from sections 14(1) and 16(2) if there is a connection between –

    (a) the body or material to which the activity relates, and

    (b) the religious worship which takes place at the place of public religious worship concerned.

(3) For the purposes of this section, a place is associated with a place of public religious worship if it is used for purposes associated with the religious worship which takes place there.

Supplementary

41   Interpretation of Part 2

(1) In this Part –

'anatomical specimen' means –

    (a) the body of a deceased person to be used for the purpose of anatomical examination, or

    (b) the body of a deceased person in the course of being used for the purpose of anatomical examination (including separated parts of such a body);

'designated individual', in relation to a licence, means the individual designated in the licence as the person under whose supervision the licensed activity is authorised to be carried on;

'export' means export from England, Wales or Northern Ireland to a place outside England, Wales and Northern Ireland;

'import' means import into England, Wales or Northern Ireland from a place outside England, Wales and Northern Ireland;

'scheduled purpose' means a purpose specified in Schedule 1.

(2) In this Part, references to the carrying-out of an anatomical examination are to the carrying-out of a macroscopic examination by dissection for anatomical purposes of the body of a deceased person, and, where parts of the body of a deceased person are separated in the course of such an examination, include the carrying-out of a macroscopic examination by dissection of the parts for those purposes.

(3) In this Part, references to a person to whom a licence applies are to a person to whom the authority conferred by the licence extends (as provided by section 17).

Part 3 Miscellaneous and General

Miscellaneous

43   Preservation for transplantation

(1) Where part of a body lying in a hospital, nursing home or other institution is or may be suitable for use for transplantation, it shall be lawful for the person having the control and management of the institution –

  (a) to take steps for the purpose of preserving the part for use for transplantation, and

  (b) to retain the body for that purpose.

(2) Authority under subsection (1)(a) shall only extend –

  (a) to the taking of the minimum steps necessary for the purpose mentioned in that provision, and

  (b) to the use of the least invasive procedure.

(3) Authority under subsection (1) ceases to apply once it has been established that consent making removal of the part for transplantation lawful has not been, and will not be, given.

(4) Authority under subsection (1) shall extend to any person authorised to act under the authority by –

  (a) the person on whom the authority is conferred by that subsection, or

  (b) a person authorised under this subsection to act under the authority.

(5) An activity done with authority under subsection (1) shall be treated –

  (a) for the purposes of Part 1, as not being an activity to which section 1(1) applies;

  (b) for the purposes of Part 2, as not being an activity to which section 16 applies.

(6) In this section, 'body' means the body of a deceased person.

44   Surplus tissue

(1) It shall be lawful for material to which subsection (2) or (3) applies to be dealt with as waste.

(2) This subsection applies to any material which consists of or includes human cells and which has come from a person's body in the course of his –

  (a) receiving medical treatment,

  (b) undergoing diagnostic testing, or

  (c) participating in research.

(3) This subsection applies to any relevant material which –

  (a) has come from a human body, and

  (b) ceases to be used, or stored for use, for a purpose specified in Schedule 1.

(4) This section shall not be read as making unlawful anything which is lawful apart from this section.

45   Non-consensual analysis of DNA

(1) A person commits an offence if –

  (a) he has any bodily material intending –

      (i)   that any human DNA in the material be analysed without qualifying consent, and

      (ii)   that the results of the analysis be used otherwise than for an excepted purpose,

  (b) the material is not of a kind excepted under subsection (2), and

  (c) he does not reasonably believe the material to be of a kind so excepted.

(2) Bodily material is excepted if –

  (a) it is material which has come from the body of a person who died before the day on which this section comes into force and at least one hundred years have elapsed since the date of the person's death,

  (b) it is an existing holding and the person who has it is not in possession, and not likely to come into possession, of information from which the individual from whose body the material has come can be identified, or

  (c) it is an embryo outside the human body.

(3) A person guilty of an offence under this section –

  (a) is liable on summary conviction to a fine not exceeding the statutory maximum;

  (b) is liable on conviction on indictment –

      (i)   to imprisonment for a term not exceeding 3 years, or

      (ii)   to a fine, or

      (iii)   both.

(4) Schedule 4 (which makes provision for the interpretation of 'qualifying consent' and 'use for an excepted purpose' in subsection (1)(a)) has effect.

(5) In this section (and Schedule 4) –

'bodily material' means material which –

  (a) has come from a human body, and

  (b) consists of or includes human cells;

'existing holding' means bodily material held immediately before the day on which this section comes into force.

General

50   Prosecutions

No proceedings for an offence under section 5, 32 or 33 shall be instituted –

     (a) in England and Wales, except by or with the consent of the Director of Public Prosecutions.

53   'Relevant material'

(1) In this Act, 'relevant material' means material, other than gametes, which consists of or includes human cells.

(2) In this Act, references to relevant material from a human body do not include –

  (a) embryos outside the human body, or

  (b) hair and nail from the body of a living person.

54   General interpretation

(1) In this Act –

'adult' means a person who has attained the age of 18 years;

'anatomical examination' means macroscopic examination by dissection for anatomical purposes;

'anatomical purposes' means purposes of teaching or studying, or researching into, the gross structure of the human body;

'the Authority' has the meaning given by section 13(1);

'child', except in the context of qualifying relationships, means a person who has not attained the age of 18 years;

'licence' means a licence under paragraph 1 of Schedule 3;

'licensed activity', in relation to a licence, means the activity which the licence authorises to be carried on;

'parental responsibility' –

    (a) in relation to England and Wales, has the same meaning as in the Children Act 1989 (c. 41).

(2) In this Act –

    (a) references to material from the body of a living person are to material from the body of a person alive at the point of separation, and

    (b) references to material from the body of a deceased person are to material from the body of a person not alive at the point of separation.

(3) In this Act, references to transplantation are to transplantation to a human body and include transfusion.

(4) In this Act, references to decent disposal include, in relation to disposal of material which has come from a human body, disposal as waste.

(5) In this Act, references to public display, in relation to the body of a deceased person, do not include –

    (a) display for the purpose of enabling people to pay their final respects to the deceased, or

    (b) display which is incidental to the deceased's funeral.

(6) Subsections (1) and (4) of section 1 of the Human Fertilisation and Embryology Act 1990 (c. 37) (definitions of 'embryo' and 'gametes') have effect for the purposes of this Act as they have effect for the purposes of that Act (other than that section).

(7) For the purposes of this Act, material shall not be regarded as from a human body if it is created outside the human body.

(8) For the purposes of this Act, except section 49, a person is another's partner if the two of them (whether of different sexes or the same sex) live as partners in an enduring family relationship.

(9) The following are qualifying relationships for the purposes of this Act, spouse, partner, parent, child, brother, sister, grandparent, grandchild, child of a brother or sister, stepfather, stepmother, half-brother, half-sister and friend of long standing.

(10) The Secretary of State may by order amend subsection (9).

Schedule 1

Section 1 Scheduled Purposes

Part 1 Purposes Requiring Consent: General

1   Anatomical examination.

2   Determining the cause of death.

3   Establishing after a person's death the efficacy of any drug or other treatment administered to him.

4   Obtaining scientific or medical information about a living or deceased person which may be relevant to any other person (including a future person).

5   Public display.

6   Research in connection with disorders, or the functioning, of the human body.

7   Transplantation.

Part 2 Purposes Requiring Consent: Deceased Persons

8   Clinical audit.

9   Education or training relating to human health.

10 Performance assessment.

11 Public health monitoring.

12 Quality assurance.

Schedule 4

Section 45: Supplementary

Part 1 Qualifying Consent

Introductory

1 This Part of this Schedule makes provision for the interpretation of 'qualifying consent' in section 45(1)(a)(i).

Qualifying consent

2 (1) In relation to analysis of DNA manufactured by the body of a person who is alive, 'qualifying consent' means his consent, except where sub-paragraph (2) applies.

(2) Where –

(a) the person is a child,

(b) neither a decision of his to consent, nor a decision of his not to consent, is in force, and

(c) either he is not competent to deal with the issue of consent or, though he is competent to deal with that issue, he fails to do so,

'qualifying consent' means the consent of a person who has parental responsibility for him.

(3) In relation to analysis of DNA manufactured by the body of a person who has died an adult, 'qualifying consent' means –

(a) if a decision of his to consent, or a decision of his not to consent, was in force immediately before he died, his consent;

(b) if paragraph (a) does not apply, the consent of a person who stood in a qualifying relationship to him immediately before he died.

(4) In relation to analysis of DNA manufactured by the body of a person who has died a child, 'qualifying consent' means –

(a) if a decision of his to consent, or a decision of his not to consent, was in force immediately before he died, his consent;

(b) if paragraph (a) does not apply –

(i)   the consent of a person who had parental responsibility for him immediately before he died, or

(ii) where no person had parental responsibility for him immediately before he died, the consent of a person who stood in a qualifying relationship to him at that time.

Part 2 Use for an Excepted Purpose

Introductory

This Part of this Schedule makes provision for the interpretation of 'use for an excepted purpose' in section 45(1)(a)(ii).

Purposes of general application

5 (1) Use of the results of an analysis of DNA for any of the following purposes is use for an excepted purpose –

(a) the medical diagnosis or treatment of the person whose body manufactured the DNA;

(b) purposes of functions of a coroner;

(c) purposes of functions of a procurator fiscal in connection with the investigation of deaths;

(d) the prevention or detection of crime;

(e) the conduct of a prosecution;

(f) purposes of national security;

(g) implementing an order or direction of a court or tribunal, including one outside the United Kingdom.

(2) For the purposes of sub-paragraph (1)(d), detecting crime shall be taken to include –

(a) establishing by whom, for what purpose, by what means and generally in what circumstances any crime was committed, and

(b) the apprehension of the person by whom any crime was committed; and the reference in sub-paragraph (1)(d) to the detection of crime includes any detection outside the United Kingdom of any crime or suspected crime.

(3) In sub-paragraph (1)(e), the reference to a prosecution includes a prosecution brought in respect of a crime in a country or territory outside the United Kingdom.

(4) In this paragraph, a reference to a crime includes a reference to any conduct which –

(a) constitutes one or more criminal offences (whether under the law of a part of the United Kingdom or a country or territory outside the United Kingdom),

(b) is, or corresponds to, conduct which, if it all took place in any one part of the United Kingdom, would constitute one or more criminal offences, or

(c) constitutes one or more offences of a kind triable by court-martial under the Army Act 1955 (3 & 4 Eliz. 2 c. 18), the Air Force Act 1955 (3 & 4 Eliz. 2 c. 19) or the Naval Discipline Act 1957 (c. 53).

(5) Sub-paragraph (1)(g) shall not be taken to confer any power to make orders or give directions.

Purpose of research in connection with disorders, or functioning, of the human body

6 (1) Use of the results of an analysis of DNA for the purpose of research in connection with disorders, or the functioning, of the human body is use for an excepted purpose if the bodily material concerned is the subject of an order under sub-paragraph (2).

Purposes relating to existing holdings

7 Use of the results of an analysis of DNA for any of the following purposes is use for an excepted purpose if the bodily material concerned is an existing holding –

(a) clinical audit;

(b) determining the cause of death;

(c) education or training relating to human health;

(d) establishing after a person's death the efficacy of any drug or other treatment administered to him;

(e) obtaining scientific or medical information about a living or deceased person which may be relevant to any other person (including a future person);

(f) performance assessment;

(g) public health monitoring;

(h) quality assurance;

(i) research in connection with disorders, or the functioning, of the human body;

(j) transplantation.

Purposes relating to material from body of a living person

8 Use of the results of an analysis of DNA for any of the following purposes is use for an excepted purpose if the bodily material concerned is from the body of a living person –

(a) clinical audit;

(b) education or training relating to human health;

(c) performance assessment;

(d) public health monitoring;

(e) quality assurance.

9 (1) Use of the results of an analysis of DNA for the purpose of obtaining scientific or medical information about the person whose body manufactured the DNA is use for an excepted purpose if –

      (a) the bodily material concerned is the subject of a direction under sub-paragraph (2) or (3) or an order under sub-paragraph (4) or (5), and

      (b) the information may be relevant to the person for whose benefit the direction is given or order is made.

(2) If the Authority is satisfied –

      (a) that bodily material has come from the body of a living person,

      (b) that it is not reasonably possible to trace the person from whose body the material has come ('the donor'),

      (c) that it is desirable in the interests of another person (including a future person) that DNA in the material be analysed for the purpose of obtaining scientific or medical information about the donor, and

      (d) that there is no reason to believe –

         (i)   that the donor has died,

         (ii) that a decision of the donor to refuse consent to the use of the material for that purpose is in force, or

         (iii) that the donor lacks capacity to consent to the use of the material for that purpose,

it may direct that this paragraph apply to the material for the benefit of the other person.

(3) If the Authority is satisfied –

      (a) that bodily material has come from the body of a living person,

      (b) that it is desirable in the interests of another person (including a future person) that DNA in the material be analysed for the purpose of obtaining scientific or medical information about the person from whose body the material has come ('the donor'),

      (c) that reasonable efforts have been made to get the donor to decide whether to consent to the use of the material for that purpose,

      (d) that there is no reason to believe –

         (i)   that the donor has died,

         (ii) that a decision of the donor to refuse to consent to the use of the material for that purpose is in force, or

         (iii) that the donor lacks capacity to consent to the use of the material for that purpose, and

      (e) that the donor has been given notice of the application for the exercise of the power conferred by this sub-paragraph,

it may direct that this paragraph apply to the material for the benefit of the other person.

(4) If the Court of Session is satisfied –

      (a) that bodily material has come from the body of a living person,

      (b) that it is not reasonably possible to trace the person from whose body the material has come ('the donor'),

      (c) that it is desirable in the interests of another person (including a future person) that DNA in the material be analysed for the purpose of obtaining scientific or medical information about the donor, and

      (d) that there is no reason to believe –

         (i)   that the donor has died,

         (ii) that a decision of the donor to refuse consent to the use of the material for that purpose is in force, or

         (iii) that the donor is an incapable adult within the meaning of the Adults with Incapacity (Scotland) Act 2000 (asp 4), it may order that this paragraph apply to the material for the benefit of the other person.

10 Use of the results of an analysis of DNA for the purpose of research in connection with disorders, or the functioning, of the human body is use for an excepted purpose if –

      (a) the bodily material concerned is from the body of a living person,

      (b) the research is ethically approved in accordance with regulations made by the Secretary of State, and

(c) the analysis is to be carried out in circumstances such that the person carrying it out is not in possession, and not likely to come into possession, of information from which the individual from whose body the material has come can be identified.

Purpose authorised under section 1

11 Use of the results of an analysis of DNA for a purpose specified in paragraph 7 is use for an excepted purpose if the use in England and Wales, or Northern Ireland, for that purpose of the bodily material concerned is authorised by section 1(1) or (10)(c).

Purposes relating to DNA of adults who lack capacity to consent

12 (1) Use of the results of an analysis of DNA for a purpose specified under sub-paragraph (2) is use for an excepted purpose if –

(a) the DNA has been manufactured by the body of a person who –

(i) has attained the age of 18 years and, under the law of England and Wales or Northern Ireland, lacks capacity to consent to analysis of the DNA, or

(ii) under the law of Scotland, is an adult with incapacity within the meaning of the Adults with Incapacity (Scotland) Act 2000 and

(b) neither a decision of his to consent to analysis of the DNA for that purpose, nor a decision of his not to consent to analysis of it for that purpose, is in force.

(2) The Secretary of State may by regulations specify for the purposes of this paragraph purposes for which DNA may be analysed.

Children Act 2004

(2004, c. 31)

Part 1 Children's Commissioner

1   Establishment

(1) There is to be an office of Children's Commissioner.

2   General function

(1) The Children's Commissioner has the function of promoting awareness of the views and interests of children in England.

(3) The Children's Commissioner is to be concerned in particular under this section with the views and interests of children so far as relating to the following aspects of their well-being –

(c) physical and mental health and emotional well-being;

(d) protection from harm and neglect;

(e) education, training and recreation;

(f) the contribution made by them to society;

(g) social and economic well-being.

11   Arrangements to safeguard and promote welfare

(1) This section applies to each of the following –

(c) a Strategic Health Authority;

(d) a Special Health Authority, so far as exercising functions in relation to England, designated by order made by the Secretary of State for the purposes of this section;

(e) a Primary Care Trust;

(f) an NHS trust all or most of whose hospitals, establishments and facilities are situated in England;

(g) an NHS foundation trust.

(2) Each person and body to whom this section applies must make arrangements for ensuring that –

(a) their functions are discharged having regard to the need to safeguard and promote the welfare of children; and

(b) any services provided by another person pursuant to arrangements made by the person or body in the discharge of their functions are provided having regard to that need.

Mental Capacity Act 2005

(2005, c. 9)

Part 1 Persons Who Lack Capacity

The principles

1   The principles

(1) The following principles apply for the purposes of this Act.

(2) A person must be assumed to have capacity unless it is established that he lacks capacity.

(3) A person is not to be treated as unable to make a decision unless all practicable steps to help him to do so have been taken without success.

(4) A person is not to be treated as unable to make a decision merely because he makes an unwise decision.

(5) An act done, or decision made, under this Act for or on behalf of a person who lacks capacity must be done, or made, in his best interests.

(6) Before the act is done, or the decision is made, regard must be had to whether the purpose for which it is needed can be as effectively achieved in a way that is less restrictive of the person's rights and freedom of action.

Preliminary

2   People who lack capacity

(1) For the purposes of this Act, a person lacks capacity in relation to a matter if at the material time he is unable to make a decision for himself in relation to the matter because of an impairment of, or a disturbance in the functioning of, the mind or brain.

(2) It does not matter whether the impairment or disturbance is permanent or temporary.

(3) A lack of capacity cannot be established merely by reference to –

(a) a person's age or appearance, or

(b) a condition of his, or an aspect of his behaviour, which might lead others to make unjustified assumptions about his capacity.

(4) In proceedings under this Act or any other enactment, any question whether a person lacks capacity within the meaning of this Act must be decided on the balance of probabilities.

(5) No power which a person ('D') may exercise under this Act –

(a) in relation to a person who lacks capacity, or

(b) where D reasonably thinks that a person lacks capacity,

is exercisable in relation to a person under 16.

3   Inability to make decisions

(1) For the purposes of section 2, a person is unable to make a decision for himself if he is unable –

(a) to understand the information relevant to the decision,

(b) to retain that information,

(c) to use or weigh that information as part of the process of making the decision, or

(d) to communicate his decision (whether by talking, using sign language or any other means).

(2) A person is not to be regarded as unable to understand the information relevant to a decision if he is able to understand an explanation of it given to him in a way that is appropriate to his circumstances (using simple language, visual aids or any other means).

(3) The fact that a person is able to retain the information relevant to a decision for a short period only does not prevent him from being regarded as able to make the decision.

(4) The information relevant to a decision includes information about the reasonably fore-seeable consequences of –

    (a) deciding one way or another, or

    (b) failing to make the decision.

4　Best interests

(1) In determining for the purposes of this Act what is in a person's best interests, the person making the determination must not make it merely on the basis of –

    (a) the person's age or appearance, or

    (b) a condition of his, or an aspect of his behaviour, which might lead others to make unjustified assumptions about what might be in his best interests.

(2) The person making the determination must consider all the relevant circumstances and, in particular, take the following steps.

(3) He must consider –

    (a) whether it is likely that the person will at some time have capacity in relation to the matter in question, and

    (b) if it appears likely that he will, when that is likely to be.

(4) He must, so far as reasonably practicable, permit and encourage the person to participate, or to improve his ability to participate, as fully as possible in any act done for him and any decision affecting him.

(5) Where the determination relates to life-sustaining treatment he must not, in considering whether the treatment is in the best interests of the person concerned, be motivated by a desire to bring about his death.

(6) He must consider, so far as is reasonably ascertainable –

    (a) the person's past and present wishes and feelings (and, in particular, any relevant written statement made by him when he had capacity),

    (b) the beliefs and values that would be likely to influence his decision if he had capacity, and

    (c) the other factors that he would be likely to consider if he were able to do so.

(7) He must take into account, if it is practicable and appropriate to consult them, the views of –

    (a) anyone named by the person as someone to be consulted on the matter in question or on matters of that kind,

    (b) anyone engaged in caring for the person or interested in his welfare,

    (c) any donee of a lasting power of attorney granted by the person, and

    (d) any deputy appointed for the person by the court, as to what would be in the person's best interests and, in particular, as to the matters mentioned in subsection (6).

(8) The duties imposed by subsections (1) to (7) also apply in relation to the exercise of any powers which –

    (a) are exercisable under a lasting power of attorney, or

    (b) are exercisable by a person under this Act where he reasonably believes that another person lacks capacity.

(9) In the case of an act done, or a decision made, by a person other than the court, there is sufficient compliance with this section if (having complied with the requirements of subsections (1) to (7)) he reasonably believes that what he does or decides is in the best interests of the person concerned.

(10) 'Life-sustaining treatment' means treatment which in the view of a person providing health care for the person concerned is necessary to sustain life.

(11) 'Relevant circumstances' are those –

    (a) of which the person making the determination is aware, and

    (b) which it would be reasonable to regard as relevant.

5   Acts in connection with care or treatment

(1) If a person ('D') does an act in connection with the care or treatment of another person ('P'), the act is one to which this section applies if –

    (a) before doing the act, D takes reasonable steps to establish whether P lacks capacity in relation to the matter in question, and

    (b) when doing the act, D reasonably believes –

        (i) that P lacks capacity in relation to the matter, and

        (ii) that it will be in P's best interests for the act to be done.

(2) D does not incur any liability in relation to the act that he would not have incurred if P –

    (a) had had capacity to consent in relation to the matter, and

    (b) had consented to D's doing the act.

(3) Nothing in this section excludes a person's civil liability for loss or damage, or his criminal liability, resulting from his negligence in doing the act.

(4) Nothing in this section affects the operation of sections 24 to 26 (advance decisions to refuse treatment).

6   Section 5 acts: limitations

(1) If D does an act that is intended to restrain P, it is not an act to which section 5 applies unless two further conditions are satisfied.

(2) The first condition is that D reasonably believes that it is necessary to do the act in order to prevent harm to P.

(3) The second is that the act is a proportionate response to –

    (a) the likelihood of P's suffering harm, and

    (b) the seriousness of that harm.

(4) For the purposes of this section D restrains P if he –

    (a) uses, or threatens to use, force to secure the doing of an act which P resists, or

    (b) restricts P's liberty of movement, whether or not P resists.

(5) But D does more than merely restrain P if he deprives P of his liberty within the meaning of Article 5(1) of the Human Rights Convention (whether or not D is a public authority).

(6) Section 5 does not authorise a person to do an act which conflicts with a decision made, within the scope of his authority and in accordance with this Part, by –

    (a) a donee of a lasting power of attorney granted by P, or

    (b) a deputy appointed for P by the court.

(7) But nothing in subsection (6) stops a person –

    (a) providing life-sustaining treatment, or

    (b) doing any act which he reasonably believes to be necessary to prevent a serious deterioration in P's condition, while a decision as respects any relevant issue is sought from the court.

Lasting powers of attorney

9   Lasting powers of attorney

(1) A lasting power of attorney is a power of attorney under which the donor ('P') confers on the donee (or donees) authority to make decisions about all or any of the following –

    (a) P's personal welfare or specified matters concerning P's personal welfare, and

    (b) P's property and affairs or specified matters concerning P's property and affairs, and which includes authority to make such decisions in circumstances where P no longer has capacity.

(2) A lasting power of attorney is not created unless –

    (a) section 10 is complied with,

(b) an instrument conferring authority of the kind mentioned in subsection (1) is made and registered in accordance with Schedule 1, and

(c) at the time when P executes the instrument, P has reached 18 and has capacity to execute it.

(4) The authority conferred by a lasting power of attorney is subject to –

(a) the provisions of this Act and, in particular, sections 1 (the principles) and 4 (best interests), and

(b) any conditions or restrictions specified in the instrument.

10   Appointment of donees

(1) A donee of a lasting power of attorney must be –

(a) an individual who has reached 18, or

(b) if the power relates only to P's property and affairs, either such an individual or a trust corporation.

11   Lasting powers of attorney: restrictions

(1) A lasting power of attorney does not authorise the donee (or, if more than one, any of them) to do an act that is intended to restrain P, unless three conditions are satisfied.

(2) The first condition is that P lacks, or the donee reasonably believes that P lacks, capacity in relation to the matter in question.

(3) The second is that the donee reasonably believes that it is necessary to do the act in order to prevent harm to P.

(4) The third is that the act is a proportionate response to –

(a) the likelihood of P's suffering harm, and

(b) the seriousness of that harm.

(5) For the purposes of this section, the donee restrains P if he –

(a) uses, or threatens to use, force to secure the doing of an act which P resists, or

(b) restricts P's liberty of movement, whether or not P resists, or if he authorises another person to do any of those things.

(6) But the donee does more than merely restrain P if he deprives P of his liberty within the meaning of Article 5(1) of the Human Rights Convention.

(7) Where a lasting power of attorney authorises the donee (or, if more than one, any of them) to make decisions about P's personal welfare, the authority –

(a) does not extend to making such decisions in circumstances other than those where P lacks, or the donee reasonably believes that P lacks, capacity,

(b) is subject to sections 24 to 26 (advance decisions to refuse treatment), and

(c) extends to giving or refusing consent to the carrying out or continuation of a treatment by a person providing health care for P.

(8) But subsection (7)(c) –

(a) does not authorise the giving or refusing of consent to the carrying out or continuation of life-sustaining treatment, unless the instrument contains express provision to that effect, and

(b) is subject to any conditions or restrictions in the instrument.

13   Revocation of lasting powers of attorney etc.

(1) This section applies if –

(a) P has executed an instrument with a view to creating a lasting power of attorney, or

(b) a lasting power of attorney is registered as having been conferred by P, and in this section references to revoking the power include revoking the instrument.

(2) P may, at any time when he has capacity to do so, revoke the power.

General powers of the court and appointment of deputies

15   Power to make declarations

(1) The court may make declarations as to –

(a) whether a person has or lacks capacity to make a decision specified in the declaration;

(b) whether a person has or lacks capacity to make decisions on such matters as are described in the declaration;

(c) the lawfulness or otherwise of any act done, or yet to be done, in relation to that person.

(2) 'Act' includes an omission and a course of conduct.

16 Powers to make decisions and appoint deputies: general

(1) This section applies if a person ('P') lacks capacity in relation to a matter or matters concerning –

(a) P's personal welfare, or

(b) P's property and affairs.

(2) The court may –

(a) by making an order, make the decision or decisions on P's behalf in relation to the matter or matters, or

(b) appoint a person (a 'deputy') to make decisions on P's behalf in relation to the matter or matters.

(3) The powers of the court under this section are subject to the provisions of this Act and, in particular, to sections 1 (the principles) and 4 (best interests).

(4) When deciding whether it is in P's best interests to appoint a deputy, the court must have regard (in addition to the matters mentioned in section 4) to the principles that –

(a) a decision by the court is to be preferred to the appointment of a deputy to make a decision, and

(b) the powers conferred on a deputy should be as limited in scope and duration as is reasonably practicable in the circumstances.

(5) The court may make such further orders or give such directions, and confer on a deputy such powers or impose on him such duties, as it thinks necessary or expedient for giving effect to, or otherwise in connection with, an order or appointment made by it under subsection (2).

(6) Without prejudice to section 4, the court may make the order, give the directions or make the appointment on such terms as it considers are in P's best interests, even though no application is before the court for an order, directions or an appointment on those terms.

(7) An order of the court may be varied or discharged by a subsequent order.

(8) The court may, in particular, revoke the appointment of a deputy or vary the powers conferred on him if it is satisfied that the deputy –

(a) has behaved, or is behaving, in a way that contravenes the authority conferred on him by the court or is not in P's best interests, or

(b) proposes to behave in a way that would contravene that authority or would not be in P's best interests.

17 Section 16 powers: personal welfare

(1) The powers under section 16 as respects P's personal welfare extend in particular to –

(a) deciding where P is to live;

(b) deciding what contact, if any, P is to have with any specified persons;

(c) making an order prohibiting a named person from having contact with P;

(d) giving or refusing consent to the carrying out or continuation of a treatment by a person providing health care for P;

(e) giving a direction that a person responsible for P's health care allow a different person to take over that responsibility.

(2) Subsection (1) is subject to section 20 (restrictions on deputies).

20 Restrictions on deputies

(1) A deputy does not have power to make a decision on behalf of P in relation to a matter if he knows or has reasonable grounds for believing that P has capacity in relation to the matter.

(2) Nothing in section 16(5) or 17 permits a deputy to be given power –

(a) to prohibit a named person from having contact with P;

(b) to direct a person responsible for P's health care to allow a different person to take over that responsibility.

(4) A deputy may not be given power to make a decision on behalf of P which is inconsistent with a decision made, within the scope of his authority and in accordance with this Act, by the donee of a lasting power of attorney granted by P (or, if there is more than one donee, by any of them).

(5) A deputy may not refuse consent to the carrying out or continuation of life-sustaining treatment in relation to P.

(6) The authority conferred on a deputy is subject to the provisions of this Act and, in particular, sections 1 (the principles) and 4 (best interests).

(7) A deputy may not do an act that is intended to restrain P unless four conditions are satisfied.

(8) The first condition is that, in doing the act, the deputy is acting within the scope of an authority expressly conferred on him by the court.

(9) The second is that P lacks, or the deputy reasonably believes that P lacks, capacity in relation to the matter in question.

(10) The third is that the deputy reasonably believes that it is necessary to do the act in order to prevent harm to P.

(11) The fourth is that the act is a proportionate response to –

(a) the likelihood of P's suffering harm, or

(b) the seriousness of that harm.

(12) For the purposes of this section, a deputy restrains P if he –

(a) uses, or threatens to use, force to secure the doing of an act which P resists, or

(b) restricts P's liberty of movement, whether or not P resists,

or if he authorises another person to do any of those things.

(13) But a deputy does more than merely restrain P if he deprives P of his liberty within the meaning of Article 5(1) of the Human Rights Convention (whether or not the deputy is a public authority).

Advance decisions to refuse treatment

24   Advance decisions to refuse treatment: general

(1) 'Advance decision' means a decision made by a person ('P'), after he has reached 18 and when he has capacity to do so, that if –

(a) at a later time and in such circumstances as he may specify, a specified treatment is proposed to be carried out or continued by a person providing health care for him, and

(b) at that time he lacks capacity to consent to the carrying out or continuation of the treatment, the specified treatment is not to be carried out or continued.

(2) For the purposes of subsection (1)(a), a decision may be regarded as specifying a treatment or circumstances even though expressed in layman's terms.

(3) P may withdraw or alter an advance decision at any time when he has capacity to do so.

(4) A withdrawal (including a partial withdrawal) need not be in writing.

(5) An alteration of an advance decision need not be in writing (unless section 25(5) applies in relation to the decision resulting from the alteration).

25   Validity and applicability of advance decisions

(1) An advance decision does not affect the liability which a person may incur for carrying out or continuing a treatment in relation to P unless the decision is at the material time –

(a) valid, and

(b) applicable to the treatment.

(2) An advance decision is not valid if P –

(a) has withdrawn the decision at a time when he had capacity to do so,

(b) has, under a lasting power of attorney created after the advance decision was made, conferred authority on the donee (or, if more than one, any of them) to give or refuse consent to the treatment to which the advance decision relates, or

(c) has done anything else clearly inconsistent with the advance decision remaining his fixed decision.

(3) An advance decision is not applicable to the treatment in question if at the material time P has capacity to give or refuse consent to it.

(4) An advance decision is not applicable to the treatment in question if –

(a) that treatment is not the treatment specified in the advance decision,

(b) any circumstances specified in the advance decision are absent, or

(c) there are reasonable grounds for believing that circumstances exist which P did not anticipate at the time of the advance decision and which would have affected his decision had he anticipated them.

(5) An advance decision is not applicable to life-sustaining treatment unless –

(a) the decision is verified by a statement by P to the effect that it is to apply to that treatment even if life is at risk, and

(b) the decision and statement comply with subsection (6).

(6) A decision or statement complies with this subsection only if –

(a) it is in writing,

(b) it is signed by P or by another person in P's presence and by P's direction,

(c) the signature is made or acknowledged by P in the presence of a witness, and

(d) the witness signs it, or acknowledges his signature, in P's presence.

(7) The existence of any lasting power of attorney other than one of a description mentioned in subsection (2)(b) does not prevent the advance decision from being regarded as valid and applicable.

26   Effect of advance decisions

(1) If P has made an advance decision which is –

(a) valid, and

(b) applicable to a treatment, the decision has effect as if he had made it, and had had capacity to make it, at the time when the question arises whether the treatment should be carried out or continued.

(2) A person does not incur liability for carrying out or continuing the treatment unless, at the time, he is satisfied that an advance decision exists which is valid and applicable to the treatment.

(3) A person does not incur liability for the consequences of withholding or withdrawing a treatment from P if, at the time, he reasonably believes that an advance decision exists which is valid and applicable to the treatment.

(4) The court may make a declaration as to whether an advance decision –

(a) exists;

(b) is valid;

(c) is applicable to a treatment.

(5) Nothing in an apparent advance decision stops a person –

(a) providing life-sustaining treatment, or

(b) doing any act he reasonably believes to be necessary to prevent a serious deterioration in P's condition, while a decision as respects any relevant issue is sought from the court.

28   Mental Health Act matters

(1) Nothing in this Act authorises anyone –

(a) to give a patient medical treatment for mental disorder, or

(b) to consent to a patient's being given medical treatment for mental disorder, if, at the time when it is proposed to treat the patient, his treatment is regulated by Part 4 of the Mental Health Act.

(2) 'Medical treatment', 'mental disorder' and 'patient' have the same meaning as in that Act.

Research

30   Research

(1) Intrusive research carried out on, or in relation to, a person who lacks capacity to consent to it is unlawful unless it is carried out –

> (a) as part of a research project which is for the time being approved by the appropriate body for the purposes of this Act in accordance with section 31, and
>
> (b) in accordance with sections 32 and 33.

(2) Research is intrusive if it is of a kind that would be unlawful if it was carried out –

> (a) on or in relation to a person who had capacity to consent to it, but
>
> (b) without his consent.

(3) A clinical trial which is subject to the provisions of clinical trials regulations is not to be treated as research for the purposes of this section.

(4) 'Appropriate body', in relation to a research project, means the person, committee or other body specified in regulations made by the appropriate authority as the appropriate body in relation to a project of the kind in question.

(5) 'Clinical trials regulations' means –

> (a) the Medicines for Human Use (Clinical Trials) Regulations 2004 (S.I. 2004/1031) and any other regulations replacing those regulations or amending them, and
>
> (b) any other regulations relating to clinical trials and designated by the Secretary of State as clinical trials regulations for the purposes of this section.

(6) In this section, section 32 and section 34, 'appropriate authority' means –

> (a) in relation to the carrying out of research in England, the Secretary of State, and
>
> (b) in relation to the carrying out of research in Wales, the National Assembly for Wales.

31   Requirements for approval

(1) The appropriate body may not approve a research project for the purposes of this Act unless satisfied that the following requirements will be met in relation to research carried out as part of the project on, or in relation to, a person who lacks capacity to consent to taking part in the project ('P').

(2) The research must be connected with –

> (a) an impairing condition affecting P, or
>
> (b) its treatment.

(3) 'Impairing condition' means a condition which is (or may be) attributable to, or which causes or contributes to (or may cause or contribute to), the impairment of, or disturbance in the functioning of, the mind or brain.

(4) There must be reasonable grounds for believing that research of comparable effectiveness cannot be carried out if the project has to be confined to, or relate only to, persons who have capacity to consent to taking part in it.

(5) The research must –

> (a) have the potential to benefit P without imposing on P a burden that is disproportionate to the potential benefit to P, or
>
> (b) be intended to provide knowledge of the causes or treatment of, or of the care of persons affected by, the same or a similar condition.

(6) If the research falls within paragraph (b) of subsection (5) but not within paragraph (a), there must be reasonable grounds for believing –

> (a) that the risk to P from taking part in the project is likely to be negligible, and
>
> (b) that anything done to, or in relation to, P will not –
>
>> (i)   interfere with P's freedom of action or privacy in a significant way, or
>>
>> (ii) be unduly invasive or restrictive.

(7) There must be reasonable arrangements in place for ensuring that the requirements of sections 32 and 33 will be met.

32   Consulting carers etc.

(1) This section applies if a person ('R') –

    (a) is conducting an approved research project, and

    (b) wishes to carry out research, as part of the project, on or in relation to a person ('P') who lacks capacity to consent to taking part in the project.

(2) R must take reasonable steps to identify a person who –

    (a) otherwise than in a professional capacity or for remuneration, is engaged in caring for P or is interested in P's welfare, and

    (b) is prepared to be consulted by R under this section.

(3) If R is unable to identify such a person he must, in accordance with guidance issued by the appropriate authority, nominate a person who –

    (a) is prepared to be consulted by R under this section, but

    (b) has no connection with the project.

(4) R must provide the person identified under subsection (2), or nominated under subsection (3), with information about the project and ask him –

    (a) for advice as to whether P should take part in the project, and

    (b) what, in his opinion, P's wishes and feelings about taking part in the project would be likely to be if P had capacity in relation to the matter.

(5) If, at any time, the person consulted advises R that in his opinion P's wishes and feelings would be likely to lead him to decline to take part in the project (or to wish to withdraw from it) if he had capacity in relation to the matter, R must ensure –

    (a) if P is not already taking part in the project, that he does not take part in it;

    (b) if P is taking part in the project, that he is withdrawn from it.

(6) But subsection (5)(b) does not require treatment that P has been receiving as part of the project to be discontinued if R has reasonable grounds for believing that there would be a significant risk to P's health if it were discontinued.

(7) The fact that a person is the donee of a lasting power of attorney given by P, or is P's deputy, does not prevent him from being the person consulted under this section.

(8) Subsection (9) applies if treatment is being, or is about to be, provided for P as a matter of urgency and R considers that, having regard to the nature of the research and of the particular circumstances of the case –

    (a) it is also necessary to take action for the purposes of the research as a matter of urgency, but

    (b) it is not reasonably practicable to consult under the previous provisions of this section.

(9) R may take the action if –

    (a) he has the agreement of a registered medical practitioner who is not involved in the organisation or conduct of the research project, or

    (b) where it is not reasonably practicable in the time available to obtain that agreement, he acts in accordance with a procedure approved by the appropriate body at the time when the research project was approved under section 31.

(10) But R may not continue to act in reliance on subsection (9) if he has reasonable grounds for believing that it is no longer necessary to take the action as a matter of urgency.

33   Additional safeguards

(1) This section applies in relation to a person who is taking part in an approved research project even though he lacks capacity to consent to taking part.

(2) Nothing may be done to, or in relation to, him in the course of the research –

    (a) to which he appears to object (whether by showing signs of resistance or otherwise) except where what is being done is intended to protect him from harm or to reduce or prevent pain or discomfort, or

    (b) which would be contrary to –

        (i) an advance decision of his which has effect, or

(ii) any other form of statement made by him and not subsequently withdrawn, of which R is aware.

(3) The interests of the person must be assumed to outweigh those of science and society.

(4) If he indicates (in any way) that he wishes to be withdrawn from the project he must be withdrawn without delay.

(5) P must be withdrawn from the project, without delay, if at any time the person conducting the research has reasonable grounds for believing that one or more of the requirements set out in section 31(2) to (7) is no longer met in relation to research being carried out on, or in relation to, P.

(6) But neither subsection (4) nor subsection (5) requires treatment that P has been receiving as part of the project to be discontinued if R has reasonable grounds for believing that there would be a significant risk to P's health if it were discontinued.

34 Loss of capacity during research project

(1) This section applies where a person ('P') –

    (a) has consented to take part in a research project begun before the commencement of section 30, but

    (b) before the conclusion of the project, loses capacity to consent to continue to take part in it.

(2) The appropriate authority may by regulations provide that, despite P's loss of capacity, research of a prescribed kind may be carried out on, or in relation to, P if –

    (a) the project satisfies prescribed requirements,

    (b) any information or material relating to P which is used in the research is of a prescribed description and was obtained before P's loss of capacity, and

    (c) the person conducting the project takes in relation to P such steps as may be prescribed for the purpose of protecting him.

(3) The regulations may, in particular, –

    (a) make provision about when, for the purposes of the regulations, a project is to be treated as having begun;

    (b) include provision similar to any made by section 31, 32 or 33.

Independent mental capacity advocate service

35 Appointment of independent mental capacity advocates

(1) The appropriate authority must make such arrangements as it considers reasonable to enable persons ('independent mental capacity advocates') to be available to represent and support persons to whom acts or decisions proposed under sections 37, 38 and 39 relate.

(4) In making arrangements under subsection (1), the appropriate authority must have regard to the principle that a person to whom a proposed act or decision relates should, so far as practicable, be represented and supported by a person who is independent of any person who will be responsible for the act or decision.

(6) For the purpose of enabling him to carry out his functions, an independent mental capacity advocate –

    (a) may interview in private the person whom he has been instructed to represent, and

    (b) may, at all reasonable times, examine and take copies of –

        (i) any health record,

        (ii) any record of, or held by, a local authority and compiled in connection with a social services function, and

        (iii) any record held by a person registered under Part 2 of the Care Standards Act 2000 (c. 14), which the person holding the record considers may be relevant to the independent mental capacity advocate's investigation.

(7) In this section, section 36 and section 37, 'the appropriate authority' means –

    (a) in relation to the provision of the services of independent mental capacity advocates in England, the Secretary of State, and

(b) in relation to the provision of the services of independent mental capacity advocates in Wales, the National Assembly for Wales.

36   Functions of independent mental capacity advocates

(1) The appropriate authority may make regulations as to the functions of independent mental capacity advocates.

(2) The regulations may, in particular, make provision requiring an advocate to take such steps as may be prescribed for the purpose of –

(a) providing support to the person whom he has been instructed to represent ('P') so that P may participate as fully as possible in any relevant decision;

(b) obtaining and evaluating relevant information;

(c) ascertaining what P's wishes and feelings would be likely to be, and the beliefs and values that would be likely to influence P, if he had capacity;

(d) ascertaining what alternative courses of action are available in relation to P;

(e) obtaining a further medical opinion where treatment is proposed and the advocate thinks that one should be obtained.

(3) The regulations may also make provision as to circumstances in which the advocate may challenge, or provide assistance for the purpose of challenging, any relevant decision.

37   Provision of serious medical treatment by NHS body

(1) This section applies if an NHS body –

(a) is proposing to provide, or secure the provision of, serious medical treatment for a person ('P') who lacks capacity to consent to the treatment, and

(b) is satisfied that there is no person, other than one engaged in providing care or treatment for P in a professional capacity or for remuneration, whom it would be appropriate to consult in determining what would be in P's best interests.

(2) But this section does not apply if P's treatment is regulated by Part 4 of the Mental Health Act.

(3) Before the treatment is provided, the NHS body must instruct an independent mental capacity advocate to represent P.

(4) If the treatment needs to be provided as a matter of urgency, it may be provided even though the NHS body has not been able to comply with subsection (3).

(5) The NHS body must, in providing or securing the provision of treatment for P, take into account any information given, or submissions made, by the independent mental capacity advocate.

(6) 'Serious medical treatment' means treatment which involves providing, withholding or withdrawing treatment of a kind prescribed by regulations made by the appropriate authority.

(7) 'NHS body' has such meaning as may be prescribed by regulations made for the purposes of this section by –

(a) the Secretary of State, in relation to bodies in England, or

(b) the National Assembly for Wales, in relation to bodies in Wales.

38   Provision of accommodation by NHS body

(1) This section applies if an NHS body proposes to make arrangements –

(a) for the provision of accommodation in a hospital or care home for a person ('P') who lacks capacity to agree to the arrangements, or

(b) for a change in P's accommodation to another hospital or care home,

and is satisfied that there is no person, other than one engaged in providing care or treatment for P in a professional capacity or for remuneration, whom it would be appropriate for it to consult in determining what would be in P's best interests.

(2) But this section does not apply if P is accommodated as a result of an obligation imposed on him under the Mental Health Act.

(3) Before making the arrangements, the NHS body must instruct an independent mental capacity advocate to represent P unless it is satisfied that –

    (a) the accommodation is likely to be provided for a continuous period which is less than the applicable period, or

    (b) the arrangements need to be made as a matter of urgency.

(4) If the NHS body –

    (a) did not instruct an independent mental capacity advocate to represent P before making the arrangements because it was satisfied that subsection (3)(a) or (b) applied, but

    (b) subsequently has reason to believe that the accommodation is likely to be provided for a continuous period –

        (i) beginning with the day on which accommodation was first provided in accordance with the arrangements, and

        (ii) ending on or after the expiry of the applicable period,

it must instruct an independent mental capacity advocate to represent P.

(5) The NHS body must, in deciding what arrangements to make for P, take into account any information given, or submissions made, by the independent mental capacity advocate.

(6) 'Care home' has the meaning given in section 3 of the Care Standards Act 2000 (c. 14).

(7) 'Hospital' means –

    (a) a health service hospital as defined by section 275 of the National Health Service Act 2006 or section 206 of the National Health Service (Wales) Act 2006, or

    (b) an independent hospital as defined by section 2 of the Care Standards Act 2000.

(8) 'NHS body' has such meaning as may be prescribed by regulations made for the purposes of this section by –

    (a) the Secretary of State, in relation to bodies in England, or

    (b) the National Assembly for Wales, in relation to bodies in Wales.

(9) 'Applicable period' means –

    (a) in relation to accommodation in a hospital, 28 days, and

    (b) in relation to accommodation in a care home, 8 weeks.

40   Exceptions

Sections 37(3), 38(3) and (4) and 39(4) and (5) do not apply if there is –

    (a) a person nominated by P (in whatever manner) as a person to be consulted in matters affecting his interests,

    (b) a donee of a lasting power of attorney created by P,

    (c) a deputy appointed by the court for P, or

    (d) a donee of an enduring power of attorney (within the meaning of Schedule 4) created by P.

Miscellaneous and supplementary

42   Codes of practice

(1) The Lord Chancellor must prepare and issue one or more codes of practice –

    (a) for the guidance of persons assessing whether a person has capacity in relation to any matter,

    (b) for the guidance of persons acting in connection with the care or treatment of another person (see section 5),

    (c) for the guidance of donees of lasting powers of attorney,

    (d) for the guidance of deputies appointed by the court,

    (e) for the guidance of persons carrying out research in reliance on any provision made by or under this Act (and otherwise with respect to sections 30 to 34),

    (f) for the guidance of independent mental capacity advocates,

    (g) with respect to the provisions of sections 24 to 26 (advance decisions and apparent advance decisions), and

    (h) with respect to such other matters concerned with this Act as he thinks fit.

(4) It is the duty of a person to have regard to any relevant code if he is acting in relation to a person who lacks capacity and is doing so in one or more of the following ways –

    (a) as the donee of a lasting power of attorney,

    (b) as a deputy appointed by the court,

    (c) as a person carrying out research in reliance on any provision made by or under this Act (see sections 30 to 34),

    (d) as an independent mental capacity advocate,

    (e) in a professional capacity,

    (f) for remuneration.

(5) If it appears to a court or tribunal conducting any criminal or civil proceedings that –

    (a) a provision of a code, or

    (b) a failure to comply with a code, is relevant to a question arising in the proceedings, the provision or failure must be taken into account in deciding the question.

44   Ill-treatment or neglect

(1) Subsection (2) applies if a person ('D') –

    (a) has the care of a person ('P') who lacks, or whom D reasonably believes to lack, capacity,

    (b) is the donee of a lasting power of attorney, or an enduring power of attorney (within the meaning of Schedule 4), created by P, or

    (c) is a deputy appointed by the court for P.

(2) D is guilty of an offence if he ill-treats or wilfully neglects P.

(3) A person guilty of an offence under this section is liable –

    (a) on summary conviction, to imprisonment for a term not exceeding 12 months or a fine not exceeding the statutory maximum or both;

    (b) on conviction on indictment, to imprisonment for a term not exceeding 5 years or a fine or both.

Part 2 The Court of Protection and the Public Guardian

The Court of Protection

45   The Court of Protection

(1) There is to be a superior court of record known as the Court of Protection.

(6) The office of the Supreme Court called the Court of Protection ceases to exist.

The Public Guardian

57   The Public Guardian

(1) For the purposes of this Act, there is to be an officer, to be known as the Public Guardian.

58   Functions of the Public Guardian

(1) The Public Guardian has the following functions –

    (a) establishing and maintaining a register of lasting powers of attorney,

    (b) establishing and maintaining a register of orders appointing deputies,

    (c) supervising deputies appointed by the court,

    (d) directing a Court of Protection Visitor to visit –

        (i) a donee of a lasting power of attorney,

        (ii) a deputy appointed by the court, or

        (iii) the person granting the power of attorney or for whom the deputy is appointed ('P'), and to make a report to the Public Guardian on such matters as he may direct,

    (e) receiving security which the court requires a person to give for the discharge of his functions,

    (f) receiving reports from donees of lasting powers of attorney and deputies appointed by the court,

(g) reporting to the court on such matters relating to proceedings under this Act as the court requires,

(h) dealing with representations (including complaints) about the way in which a donee of a lasting power of attorney or a deputy appointed by the court is exercising his powers,

(i) publishing, in any manner the Public Guardian thinks appropriate, any information he thinks appropriate about the discharge of his functions.

59   Public Guardian Board

(1) There is to be a body, to be known as the Public Guardian Board.

(2) The Board's duty is to scrutinise and review the way in which the Public Guardian discharges his functions and to make such recommendations to the Lord Chancellor about that matter as it thinks appropriate.

Part 3 Miscellaneous and General

Declaratory provision

62   Scope of the Act

For the avoidance of doubt, it is hereby declared that nothing in this Act is to be taken to affect the law relating to murder or manslaughter or the operation of section 2 of the Suicide Act 1961 (c. 60) (assisting suicide).

General

64   Interpretation

(1) In this Act –

'treatment' includes a diagnostic or other procedure.

National Health Service Act 2006

2006 Chapter 41

Part 1

Promotion and Provision of the Health Service in England

The Secretary of State and the health service in England

1   Secretary of State's duty to promote health service

(1) The Secretary of State must continue the promotion in England of a comprehensive health service designed to secure improvement –

(a) in the physical and mental health of the people of England, and

(b) in the prevention, diagnosis and treatment of illness.

(3) The services so provided must be free of charge except in so far as the making and recovery of charges is expressly provided for by or under any enactment, whenever passed.

General power to provide services

2 Secretary of State's general power

(1) The Secretary of State may –

(a) provide such services as he considers appropriate for the purpose of discharging any duty imposed on him by this Act, and

(b) do anything else which is calculated to facilitate, or is conducive or incidental to, the discharge of such a duty.

Provision of particular services

3   Secretary of State's duty as to provision of certain services

(1) The Secretary of State must provide throughout England, to such extent as he considers necessary to meet all reasonable requirements –

(a) hospital accommodation,

(b) other accommodation for the purpose of any service provided under this Act,

(c) medical, dental, ophthalmic, nursing and ambulance services,

(d) such other services or facilities for the care of pregnant women, women who are breastfeeding and young children as he considers are appropriate as part of the health service,

(e) such other services or facilities for the prevention of illness, the care of persons suffering from illness and the after-care of persons who have suffered from illness as he considers are appropriate as part of the health service,

(f) such other services or facilities as are required for the diagnosis and treatment of illness.

(2) For the purposes of the duty in subsection (1), services provided under –

(a) section 83(2) (primary medical services), section 99(2) (primary dental services) or section 115(4) (primary ophthalmic services), or

(b) a general medical services contract, a general dental services contract or a general ophthalmic services contract, must be regarded as provided by the Secretary of State.

4   High security psychiatric services

(1) The Secretary of State's duty under section 1 includes a duty to provide hospital accommodation and services for persons who –

(a) are liable to be detained under the Mental Health Act 1983, and

(b) in the opinion of the Secretary of State require treatment under conditions of high security on account of their dangerous, violent or criminal propensities.

(2) The hospital accommodation and services mentioned in subsection (1) are referred to in this section and paragraph 15 of Schedule 4 (NHS trusts) as 'high security psychiatric services'.

(3) High security psychiatric services may be provided only at hospital premises at which services are provided only for the persons mentioned in subsection (1).

(4) 'Hospital premises' means –

    (a) a hospital, or

    (b) any part of a hospital which is treated as a separate unit.

5   Other services

Schedule 1 makes further provision about the Secretary of State and services under this Act.

NHS contracts

9   NHS contracts

(1) In this Act, an NHS contract is an arrangement under which one health service body ('the commissioner') arranges for the provision to it by another health service body ('the provider') of goods or services which it reasonably requires for the purposes of its functions.

(5) Whether or not an arrangement which constitutes an NHS contract would apart from this subsection be a contract in law, it must not be regarded for any purpose as giving rise to contractual rights or liabilities.

Provision of services otherwise than by the Secretary of State

12   Secretary of State's arrangements with other bodies

(1) The Secretary of State may arrange with any person or body to provide, or assist in providing, any service under this Act.

(2) Arrangements may be made under subsection (1) with voluntary organisations.

(3) The Secretary of State may make available any facilities provided by him for any service under this Act –

    (a) to any person or body carrying out any arrangements under subsection (1), or

    (b) to any voluntary organisation eligible for assistance under section 64 or section 65 of the Health Services and Public Health Act 1968.

(4) Where facilities are made available under subsection (3), the Secretary of State may make available the services of any person employed in connection with the facilities by –

    (a) the Secretary of State,

    (b) a Strategic Health Authority,

    (c) a Primary Care Trust,

    (d) a Special Health Authority, or

    (e) a Local Health Board.

(5) Powers under this section may be exercised on such terms as may be agreed, including terms as to the making of payments by or to the Secretary of State.

Part 2
Health Service Bodies

Chapter 1
Strategic Health Authorities

13   Strategic Health Authorities

(1) The Strategic Health Authorities established by the Secretary of State continue in existence.

(2) But the Secretary of State may by order –

    (a) vary the area in England for which a Strategic Health Authority is established,

    (b) abolish a Strategic Health Authority,

    (c) establish a new Strategic Health Authority for an area in England,

(d) change the name by which a Strategic Health Authority is known.

(4) No order may be made under this section until after the completion of such consultation as may be prescribed.

(5) Consultation requirements in regulations under subsection (4) are in addition to, and not in substitution for, any other consultation requirements which may apply.

(6) The Secretary of State must act under this section so as to ensure that the areas for which Strategic Health Authorities are at any time established together comprise the whole of England.

17   Advice for Strategic Health Authorities

Each Strategic Health Authority must make arrangements with a view to securing that it receives advice appropriate for enabling it effectively to exercise the functions exercisable by it from persons with professional expertise relating to the physical or mental health of individuals.

Chapter 2
Primary Care Trusts

18   Primary Care Trusts

(1) The Primary Care Trusts established by the Secretary of State continue in existence.

(2) But the Secretary of State may by order (a 'PCT order') –

    (a) vary the area in England for which a Primary Care Trust is established,

    (b) abolish a Primary Care Trust,

    (c) establish a new Primary Care Trust for the area in England specified in the order with a view to it exercising functions in relation to the health service.

(3) The Secretary of State must act under this section so as to ensure that the areas for which Primary Care Trusts are at any time established together comprise the whole of England.

20   Strategic Health Authority directions to Primary Care Trusts

(1) A Strategic Health Authority may give directions to a Primary Care Trust about its exercise of any function.

(2) Directions under this section are subject to any directions given under section 8.

22   Administration and management of services

Each Primary Care Trust must, in accordance with regulations –

    (a) administer the arrangements made in pursuance of this Act for the provision for its area of primary medical services, primary dental services, primary ophthalmic services, pharmaceutical services and local pharmaceutical services, and

    (b) perform such management and other functions relating to those services as may be prescribed.

23   Advice for Primary Care Trusts

Each Primary Care Trust must make arrangements with a view to securing that it receives advice appropriate for enabling it effectively to exercise the functions exercisable by it from persons with professional expertise relating to the physical or mental health of individuals.

24   Plans for improving health etc

(1) Each Primary Care Trust must, at such times as the Secretary of State may direct, prepare a plan which sets out a strategy for improving –

    (a) the health of the people for whom it is responsible, and

    (b) the provision of health care to such people.

(2) Each Primary Care Trust must keep under review any plan prepared by it under this section.

(3) Each local authority whose area falls wholly or partly within the area of a Primary Care Trust must participate in the preparation or review by the Primary Care Trust of any plan under this section.

Chapter 3

NHS Trusts

25   NHS trusts

(1) The Secretary of State may by order establish bodies, called National Health Service trusts ('NHS trusts'), to provide goods and services for the purposes of the health service.

(2) An order under subsection (1) is referred to in this Act as 'an NHS trust order'.

26   General duty of NHS trusts

An NHS trust must exercise its functions effectively, efficiently and economically.

Chapter 4

Special Health Authorities

28   Special Health Authorities

(1) The Secretary of State may by order establish special bodies for the purpose of exercising any functions which may be conferred on them by or under this Act.

(3) A body established under this section is called a Special Health Authority.

Chapter 5

NHS Foundation Trusts

Introductory

30   NHS foundation trusts

(1) An NHS foundation trust is a public benefit corporation which is authorised under this Chapter to provide goods and services for the purposes of the health service in England.

(2) A public benefit corporation is a body corporate which, in pursuance of an application under this Chapter, is constituted in accordance with Schedule 7.

31   Independent Regulator of NHS Foundation Trusts

(1) There continues to be a body corporate known as the Independent Regulator of NHS Foundation Trusts (referred to in this Act as 'the regulator').

Authorisation

33   Applications by NHS trusts

(1) An NHS trust may make an application to the regulator for authorisation to become an NHS foundation trust, if the application is supported by the Secretary of State.

(2) The application must –

    (a) describe the goods and services which the applicant proposes should be provided by the NHS foundation trust, and

    (b) be accompanied by a copy of the proposed constitution of the NHS foundation trust, and must give any further information which the regulator requires the applicant to give.

34   Other applications

(1) An application may be made to the regulator by persons (other than an NHS trust) to be incorporated as a public benefit corporation and authorised to become an NHS foundation trust, if the application is supported by the Secretary of State.

(2) The application must –

(a) describe the goods and services which the applicants propose should be provided by the NHS foundation trust, and

(b) be accompanied by a copy of the proposed constitution of the NHS foundation trust, and must give any further information which the regulator requires the applicants to give.

39   Register of NHS foundation trusts

(1) The regulator must continue to maintain a register of NHS foundation trusts.

Functions

43   Authorised services

(1) An authorisation must authorise the NHS foundation trust to provide goods and services for purposes related to the provision of health care.

(2) But the authorisation must secure that the principal purpose of the NHS foundation trust is the provision of goods and services for the purposes of the health service in England.

(3) The NHS foundation trust may also carry on activities other than those mentioned in subsection (1), subject to any restrictions in the authorisation, for the purpose of making additional income available in order better to carry on its principal purpose.

(4) The authorisation may require the provision, wholly or partly for the purposes of the health service in England, of goods and services by the NHS foundation trust.

(5) The authorisation must authorise and may require the NHS foundation trust –

(a) to carry out research in connection with the provision of health care,

(b) to make facilities and staff available for the purposes of education, training or research carried on by others, and, in deciding how to exercise its functions under this subsection in a case where any of the corporation's hospitals includes a medical or dental school provided by a university, the regulator must have regard to the need to establish and maintain appropriate arrangements within the university.

44   Private health care

(1) An authorisation may restrict the provision, for purposes other than those of the health service in England, of goods and services by an NHS foundation trust.

(2) The power must be exercised, in particular, with a view to securing that the proportion of the total income of an NHS foundation trust which was an NHS trust in any financial year derived from private charges is not greater than the proportion of the total income of the NHS trust derived from such charges in the base financial year.

(4) 'Private charges' means charges imposed in respect of goods and services provided to patients other than patients being provided with goods and services for the purposes of the health service.

(6) According to the nature of its functions, an NHS foundation trust may, in the case of patients being provided with goods and services for the purposes of the health service, make accommodation or further services available for patients who give undertakings (or for whom undertakings are given) to pay any charges imposed by the NHS foundation trust in respect of the accommodation or services.

(7) An NHS foundation trust may exercise the power conferred by subsection (6) only to the extent that its exercise does not to any significant extent interfere with the performance by the NHS foundation trust of its functions.

Failure

52   Failing NHS foundation trusts

(1) If the regulator is satisfied –

(a) that an NHS foundation trust is contravening, or failing to comply with, any term of its authorisation or any requirement imposed on it under any enactment and that the contravention or failure is significant, or

(b) that an NHS foundation trust has contravened, or failed to comply with, any such term or requirement and is likely to do so again and that the contravention or failure was significant, the regulator may by a notice to the trust exercise one or more of the powers in subsections (3) and (4).

(3) The regulator may require the trust, the directors or the board of governors to do, or not to do, specified things or things of a specified description within a specified period.

(4) The regulator may remove any or all of the directors or members of the board of governors and appoint interim directors or members of the board.

63   General duty of NHS foundation trusts

An NHS foundation trust must exercise its functions effectively, efficiently and economically.

Chapter 6
Miscellaneous

Intervention orders and default powers

66   Intervention orders

(1) This section applies to NHS bodies other than NHS foundation trusts.

(2) If the Secretary of State –

(a) considers that a body to which this section applies is not performing one or more of its functions adequately or at all, or that there are significant failings in the way the body is being run, and

(b) is satisfied that it is appropriate for him to intervene under this section, he may make an order under this section in respect of the body (an 'intervention order').

(3) An intervention order may make any provision authorised by section 67 (including any combination of such provisions).

Co-operation between NHS bodies

72   Co-operation between NHS bodies

It is the duty of NHS bodies to co-operate with each other in exercising their functions.

Part 4
Medical Services

Duty of Primary Care Trusts in relation to primary medical services

83   Primary medical services

(1) Each Primary Care Trust must, to the extent that it considers necessary to meet all reasonable requirements, exercise its powers so as to provide primary medical services within its area, or secure their provision within its area.

(2) A Primary Care Trust may (in addition to any other power conferred on it) –

(a) provide primary medical services itself (whether within or outside its area),

(b) make such arrangements for their provision (whether within or outside its area) as it considers appropriate, and may in particular make contractual arrangements with any person.

(3) Each Primary Care Trust must publish information about such matters as may be prescribed in relation to the primary medical services provided under this Act.

(4) Each Primary Care Trust must co-operate with each other Primary Care Trust and each Local Health Board in the discharge of their respective functions relating to the provision of primary medical services under this Act and the National Health Service (Wales) Act 2006 (c. 42).

(5) Regulations may provide that services of a prescribed description must, or must not, be regarded as primary medical services for the purposes of this Act.

(6) Regulations under this section may in particular describe services by reference to the manner or circumstances in which they are provided.

General medical services contracts

84   General medical services contracts: introductory

(1) A Primary Care Trust may enter into a contract under which primary medical services are provided in accordance with the following provisions of this Part.

(2) A contract under this section is called in this Act a 'general medical services contract'.

(3) A general medical services contract may make such provision as may be agreed between the Primary Care Trust and the contractor or contractors in relation to –

    (a) the services to be provided under the contract,

    (b) remuneration under the contract, and

    (c) any other matters.

(4) The services to be provided under a general medical services contract may include –

    (a) services which are not primary medical services,

    (b) services to be provided outside the area of the Primary Care Trust.

(5) In this Part, 'contractor', in relation to a general medical services contract, means any person entering into the contract with the Primary Care Trust.

85   Requirement to provide certain primary medical services

(1) A general medical services contract must require the contractor or contractors to provide, for his or their patients, primary medical services of such descriptions as may be prescribed.

(2) Regulations under subsection (1) may in particular describe services by reference to the manner or circumstances in which they are provided.

86   Persons eligible to enter into GMS contracts

(1) A Primary Care Trust may, subject to such conditions as may be prescribed, enter into a general medical services contract with –

    (a) a medical practitioner,

    (b) two or more individuals practising in partnership where the conditions in subsection (2) are satisfied, or

    (c) a company limited by shares where the conditions in subsection (3) are satisfied.

(2) The conditions referred to in subsection (1)(b) are that –

    (a) at least one partner is a medical practitioner, and

    (b) any partner who is not a medical practitioner is either –

        (i)   an NHS employee,

        (ii) a section 92 employee, section 107 employee, section 50 employee, section 64 employee, section 17C employee or Article 15B employee,

        (iii) a health care professional who is engaged in the provision of services under this Act or the National Health Service (Wales) Act 2006 (c. 42), or

        (iv) an individual falling within section 93(1)(d).

(3) The conditions referred to in subsection (1)(c) are that –

    (a) at least one share in the company is legally and beneficially owned by a medical practitioner, and

    (b) any share which is not so owned is legally and beneficially owned by a person referred to in subsection (2)(b).

(4) Regulations may make provision as to the effect, in relation to a general medical services contract entered into by individuals practising in partnership, of a change in the membership of the partnership.

(5) In this section –

'health care professional', 'NHS employee', 'section 92 employee', 'section 107 employee', 'section 50 employee', 'section 64 employee', 'section 17C employee' and 'Article 15B employee' have the meaning given by section 93.

87   GMS contracts: payments

(1) The Secretary of State may give directions as to payments to be made under general medical services contracts.

(2) A general medical services contract must require payments to be made under the contract in accordance with directions under this section.

(3) Directions under subsection (1) may in particular –

    (a) provide for payments to be made by reference to compliance with standards or the achievement of levels of performance,

    (b) provide for payments to be made by reference to –

        (i)   any scheme or scale specified in the direction, or

        (ii) a determination made by any person in accordance with factors specified in the direction,

    (c) provide for the making of payments in respect of individual practitioners,

    (d) provide that the whole or any part of a payment is subject to conditions (and may provide that payments are payable by a Primary Care Trust only if it is satisfied as to certain conditions),

    (e) make provision having effect from a date before the date of the direction, provided that, having regard to the direction as a whole, the provision is not detrimental to the persons to whose remuneration it relates.

(4) Before giving a direction under subsection (1), the Secretary of State –

    (a) must consult any body appearing to him to be representative of persons to whose remuneration the direction would relate, and

    (b) may consult such other persons as he considers appropriate.

(5) 'Payments' includes fees, allowances, reimbursements, loans and repayments.

88   GMS contracts: prescription of drugs, etc

(1) A general medical services contract must contain provision requiring the contractor or contractors to comply with any directions given by the Secretary of State for the purposes of this section as to the drugs, medicines or other substances which may or may not be ordered for patients in the provision of medical services under the contract.

89   GMS contracts: other required terms

(1) A general medical services contract must contain such provision as may be prescribed (in addition to the provision required by the preceding provisions of this Part).

(2) Regulations under subsection (1) may in particular make provision as to –

    (a) the manner in which, and standards to which, services must be provided,

    (b) the persons who perform services,

    (c) the persons to whom services will be provided,

    (d) the variation of contract terms (other than terms required by or under this Part),

    (e) rights of entry and inspection (including inspection of clinical records and other documents),

    (f) the circumstances in which, and the manner in which, the contract may be terminated,

    (g) enforcement,

    (h) the adjudication of disputes.

(3) Regulations making provision under subsection (2)(c) may make provision as to the circumstances in which a contractor or contractors –

    (a) must or may accept a person as a patient to whom services are provided under the contract,

    (b) may decline to accept a person as such a patient, or

    (c) may terminate his or their responsibility for a patient.

(6) Regulations under subsection (1) must make provision as to the right of patients to choose the persons from whom they receive services.

90   GMS contracts: disputes and enforcement

(1) Regulations may make provision for the resolution of disputes as to the terms of a proposed general medical services contract.

Performance of primary medical services

91   Persons performing primary medical services

(1) Regulations may provide that a health care professional of a prescribed description may not perform any primary medical service for which a Primary Care Trust is responsible unless he is included in a list maintained under the regulations by a Primary Care Trust.

(2) For the purposes of this section –

- (a) 'health care professional' means a person who is a member of a profession regulated by a body mentioned in section 25(3) of the National Health Service Reform and Health Care Professions Act 2002,
- (b) a Primary Care Trust is responsible for a medical service if it provides the service, or secures its provision, by or under any enactment.

Other arrangements for the provision of primary medical services

92   Arrangements by Strategic Health Authorities for the provision of primary medical services

(1) A Strategic Health Authority may make one or more agreements with respect to its area under which primary medical services are provided (otherwise than by the Strategic Health Authority).

(2) An agreement must be in accordance with regulations under section 94.

94   Regulations about section 92 arrangements

(1) The Secretary of State may make regulations about the provision of services in accordance with section 92 arrangements.

(2) The regulations must include provision for participants other than Strategic Health Authorities to withdraw from section 92 arrangements if they wish to do so.

Assistance and support

96   Assistance and support: primary medical services

(1) A Primary Care Trust may provide assistance or support to any person providing or proposing to provide –

- (a) primary medical services under a general medical services contract, or
- (b) primary medical services in accordance with section 92 arrangements.

(2) Assistance or support provided by a Primary Care Trust under subsection (1) is provided on such terms, including terms as to payment, as the Primary Care Trust considers appropriate.

(3) 'Assistance' includes financial assistance.

Local Medical Committees

97   Local Medical Committees

(1) A Primary Care Trust may recognise a committee formed for its area, or for its area and that of one or more other Primary Care Trusts, which it is satisfied is representative of –

- (a) the persons to whom subsection (2) applies, and
- (b) the persons to whom subsection (3) applies.

(2) This subsection applies to –

- (a) each medical practitioner who, under a general medical services contract entered into by him, is providing primary medical services in the area for which the committee is formed, and

(b) each medical practitioner who, under a general ophthalmic services contract entered into by him, is providing primary ophthalmic services in that area.

(3) This subsection applies to each other medical practitioner –

    (a) who is performing primary medical services or primary ophthalmic services in the area for which the committee is formed –

        (i) pursuant to section 83(2)(a) or section 115(4)(a),

        (ii) in accordance with section 92 arrangements, or

        (iii) under a general medical services contract or a general ophthalmic services contract, and

    (b) who has notified the Primary Care Trust that he wishes to be represented by the committee (and has not notified it that he wishes to cease to be so represented).

(4) A committee recognised under this section is called the Local Medical Committee for the area for which it is formed.

Provision of accommodation by the Secretary of State

98   Use of accommodation: provision of primary medical services

If the Secretary of State considers that any accommodation provided by him by virtue of this Act is suitable for use in connection with the provision of primary medical services, he may make the accommodation available on such terms as he considers appropriate to persons providing those services.

Part 8

Family Health Services Appeal Authority

169   FHSAA

(1) There continues to be a body known as the Family Health Services Appeal Authority ('FHSAA').

(2) The FHSAA has such functions as are conferred on it by this Act or by any other enactment.

(3) The Secretary of State may direct the FHSAA to exercise any of his functions relating to the determination of appeals to him which are specified in the directions.

(4) The Secretary of State may make available to the FHSAA any facilities provided by him or by an NHS trust or Special Health Authority for any service under this Act, and the services of persons employed by the Secretary of State or by an NHS trust or Special Health Authority.

(5) Schedule 13 makes further provision about the FHSAA.

Part 9

Charging

Power to charge generally

172   Charges for drugs, medicines or appliances, or pharmaceutical services

(1) Regulations may provide for the making and recovery in such manner as may be prescribed of such charges as may be prescribed in respect of –

    (a) the supply under this Act (otherwise than under Chapter 1 of Part 7) of drugs, medicines or appliances (including the replacement and repair of those appliances), and

    (b) such of the pharmaceutical services referred to in that Chapter as may be prescribed.

(2) Regulations under this section may in particular make provision in relation to the supply of contraceptive substances and appliances under paragraph 8 of Schedule 1.

173   Exemptions from general charging

(1) No charge may be made under regulations under section 172(1) in respect of –

    (a) the supply of any drug, medicine or appliance for a patient who is resident in hospital,

    (b) the supply of any drug or medicine for the treatment of sexually transmitted disease (otherwise than in the provision of primary medical services or in accordance with a pilot scheme or an LPS scheme),

(c) the supply of any appliance (otherwise than in pursuance of paragraph 8(d) of Schedule 1) for a person who is under 16 years of age or is under 19 years of age and receiving qualifying full-time education, or

(d) the replacement or repair of any appliance in consequence of a defect in the appliance as supplied.

(2) In subsection (1)(c) 'qualifying full-time education' means full-time instruction at a recognised educational establishment or by other means accepted as comparable by the Secretary of State.

(3) For the purposes of subsection (2) –

(a) 'recognised educational establishment' means an establishment recognised by the Secretary of State as being, or as comparable to, a school, college or university, and

(b) regulations may prescribe the circumstances in which a person must, or must not, be treated as receiving full-time instruction.

Part 12
Public Involvement and Scrutiny

Chapter 1
Patients' Forums

237   Establishment of Patients' Forums

(1) The Patients' Forums established by the Secretary of State continue in existence, and he must establish a Patients' Forum –

(a) for each NHS trust all or most of whose hospitals, establishments and facilities are situated in England,

(b) for each Primary Care Trust, and

(c) for each NHS foundation trust.

(2) The members of each Patients' Forum must be appointed by the Commission for Patient and Public Involvement in Health.

(3) A Patients' Forum must –

(a) monitor and review the range and operation of services provided by, or under arrangements made by, the trust for which it is established,

(b) obtain the views of patients and their carers about those matters and report on those views to the trust,

(c) provide advice, and make reports and recommendations, about matters relating to the range and operation of those services to the trust,

(d) make available to patients and their carers advice and information about those services,

(e) in prescribed circumstances, perform any prescribed function of the trust with respect to the provision of a service affording assistance to patients and their families and carers,

(f) carry out such other functions as may be prescribed.

(4) In providing advice or making recommendations under subsection (3)(c), a Patients' Forum must have regard to the views of patients and their carers.

(5) If, in the course of exercising its functions, a Patients' Forum becomes aware of any matter which in its view –

(a) should be considered by a relevant overview and scrutiny committee, or

(b) should be brought to the attention of the Commission for Patient and Public Involvement in Health, the Forum may refer that matter to the committee, or to the Commission.

(6) Subsection (5) does not affect the power of a Patients' Forum to make such other representations or referrals as it considers appropriate, to such persons or bodies as it considers appropriate, about matters arising in the course of it exercising its functions.

'carer', in relation to a patient, means a person who provides care for the patient, but who is not employed to do so by any body in the exercise of its functions under any enactment,

'relevant overview and scrutiny committee', in relation to a Patients' Forum, means any overview and scrutiny committee in relation to which the Primary Care Trust, NHS trust or NHS foundation trust for which the Forum is established is a local NHS body by virtue of regulations made under section 244 (3) (including that provision as read with section 245(5) and as applied by section 247(2)),

238   Additional functions of PCT Patients' Forums

(1) A Patients' Forum established for a Primary Care Trust (a 'PCT Patients' Forum') has the following additional functions –

>   (a) providing independent advocacy services to persons in the Primary Care Trust's area or persons to whom services have been provided by, or under arrangements with, the Primary Care Trust,
>
>   (b) making available to patients and their carers advice and information about the making of complaints in relation to services provided by or under arrangements with the Primary Care Trust, and
>
>   (c) representing to persons and bodies which exercise functions in relation to the area of the Primary Care Trust (including, in particular, any relevant overview and scrutiny committee) the views of members of the public in the Primary Care Trust's area about matters affecting their health.

(2) In subsection (1), references to services have the meaning given by section 237(8).

(3) It is also the function of a PCT Patients' Forum –

>   (a) to promote the involvement of members of the public in the area of the Primary Care Trust in consultations or processes leading (or potentially leading) to decisions by those mentioned in subsection (4), or the formulation of policies by them, which would or might affect (whether directly or not) the health of those members of the public,
>
>   (b) to make available advice and information to such members of the public about such involvement,
>
>   (c) to advise those mentioned in subsection (4) about how to encourage such involvement (including, in the case of bodies mentioned in subsection (4) to which section 242 applies, advising them how to comply with the requirements of that section in relation to the area of the Primary Care Trust), and
>
>   (d) to monitor how successful those mentioned in subsection (4) are at achieving such involvement.

(4) Those referred to in subsection (3) are –

>   (a) Strategic Health Authorities whose areas include any part of the area of the Primary Care Trust,
>
>   (b) the Primary Care Trust itself,
>
>   (c) NHS trusts which provide services to patients in the area of the Primary Care Trust,
>
>   (d) other public bodies, and
>
>   (e) others providing services to the public or a section of the public.

(5) In this section –

'carer' and 'patient' have the meaning given by section 237,

'independent advocacy services' means services provided under section 248,

'relevant overview and scrutiny committee' has the meaning given by section 237.

Chapter 2
Public Involvement and Consultation

242   Public involvement and consultation

(1) This section applies to –

>   (a) Strategic Health Authorities,

    (b) Primary Care Trusts,

    (c) NHS trusts, and

    (d) NHS foundation trusts.

(2) Each body to which this section applies must make arrangements with a view to securing, as respects health services for which it is responsible, that persons to whom those services are being or may be provided are, directly or through representatives, involved in and consulted on–

    (a) the planning of the provision of those services,

    (b) the development and consideration of proposals for changes in the way those services are provided, and

    (c) decisions to be made by that body affecting the operation of those services.

(3) For the purposes of this section a body is responsible for health services –

    (a) if the body provides or will provide those services to individuals, or

    (b) if another person provides, or will provide, those services to individuals –

        (i) at that body's direction,

        (ii) on its behalf, or

        (iii) in accordance with an agreement or arrangements made by that body with that other person, and references in this section to the provision of services include references to the provision of services jointly with another person.

243   The Commission for Patient and Public Involvement in Health

(1) There continues to be a body corporate known as the Commission for Patient and Public Involvement in Health ('the Commission') to exercise the functions set out in subsections (2) to (5) (in addition to its function of appointing members of Patients' Forums).

(2) The Commission has the following functions –

    (a) advising the Secretary of State, and such bodies as may be prescribed, about arrangements for public involvement in, and consultation on, matters relating to the health service in England,

    (b) advising the Secretary of State, and such bodies as may be prescribed, about arrangements for the provision in England of independent advocacy services,

    (c) representing to the Secretary of State and such bodies as may be prescribed, and advising him and them on, the views, as respects the arrangements referred to in paragraphs (a) and (b), of Patients' Forums and those voluntary organisations and other bodies appearing to the Commission to represent the interests of patients of the health service in England and their carers,

    (d) providing staff to Patients' Forums established for Primary Care Trusts, and advice and assistance to Patients' Forums and facilitating the co-ordination of their activities,

    (e) advising and assisting providers of independent advocacy services in England,

    (f) setting quality standards relating to any aspect of –

        (i) the way Patients Forums exercise their functions, and

        (ii) the services provided by independent advocacy services in England, monitoring how successfully they meet those standards, and making recommendations to them about how to improve their performance against those standards,

    (g) such other functions in relation to England as may be prescribed.

(3) It is also the function of the Commission to promote the involvement of members of the public in England in consultations or processes leading (or potentially leading) to decisions by those mentioned in subsection (4), or the formulation of policies by them, which would or might affect (whether directly or not) the health of those members of the public.

(4) The decisions in question are those made by –

    (a) health service bodies,

    (b) other public bodies, and

    (c) others providing services to the public or a section of the public.

(5) It is also the function of the Commission –

(a) to review the annual reports of Patients' Forums made under section 240, and

(b) to make, to the Secretary of State or to such other persons or bodies as the Commission considers appropriate, such reports or recommendations as the Commission considers appropriate concerning any matters arising from those annual reports.

(6) If the Commission –

(a) becomes aware in the course of exercising its functions of any matter connected with the health service in England which in its opinion gives rise to concerns about the safety or welfare of patients, and

(b) is not satisfied that the matter is being dealt with, or about the way it is being dealt with, the Commission must report the matter to whichever person or body it considers most appropriate (or, if it considers it appropriate to do so, to more than one person or body).

(7) Bodies to whom the Commission might report a matter include –

(a) the regulatory body for the profession of a person working in the health service,

(b) the Commission for Healthcare Audit and Inspection.

(8) The Commission may make such charges as it considers appropriate for the provision of advice and other services (but this is subject to any prescribed limitation).

(12) In this section –

'carer' and 'patient' have the same meaning as in section 237,

'health service bodies' means Strategic Health Authorities, Primary Care Trusts, NHS trusts and NHS foundation trusts,

'independent advocacy services' means services provided under section 248,

Part 13
Miscellaneous

Independent advocacy services

248   Independent advocacy services

(1) The Secretary of State must arrange, to such extent as he considers necessary to meet all reasonable requirements, for the provision of independent advocacy services.

(2) 'Independent advocacy services' are services providing assistance (by way of representation or otherwise) to individuals making or intending to make –

(a) a complaint under a procedure operated by a health service body or independent provider,

(b) a complaint under section 113(1) or (2) of the Health and Social Care (Community Health and Standards) Act 2003,

(c) a complaint to the Health Service Commissioner for England or the Public Services Ombudsman for Wales,

(d) a complaint of a prescribed description which relates to the provision of services as part of the health service and –

(i)   is made under a procedure of a prescribed description, or

(ii) gives rise, or may give rise, to proceedings of a prescribed description.

(5) In making arrangements under this section the Secretary of State must have regard to the principle that the provision of services under the arrangements should, so far as practicable, be independent of any person who is –

(a) the subject of a relevant complaint, or

(b) involved in investigating or adjudicating on such a complaint.

(6) The Secretary of State may make payments to any person in pursuance of arrangements under this section.

Patient information

251   Control of patient information

(1) The Secretary of State may by regulations make such provision for and in connection with requiring or regulating the processing of prescribed patient information for medical purposes as he considers necessary or expedient –

    (a) in the interests of improving patient care, or

    (b) in the public interest.

(2) Regulations under subsection (1) may, in particular, make provision –

    (a) for requiring prescribed communications of any nature which contain patient information to be disclosed by health service bodies in prescribed circumstances –

        (i) to the person to whom the information relates,

        (ii) (where it relates to more than one person) to the person to whom it principally relates, or

        (iii) to a prescribed person on behalf of any such person as is mentioned in subparagraph (i) or (ii), in such manner as may be prescribed,

    (b) for requiring or authorising the disclosure or other processing of prescribed patient information to or by persons of any prescribed description subject to compliance with any prescribed conditions (including conditions requiring prescribed undertakings to be obtained from such persons as to the processing of such information),

    (c) for securing that, where prescribed patient information is processed by a person in accordance with the regulations, anything done by him in so processing the information must be taken to be lawfully done despite any obligation of confidence owed by him in respect of it,

    (d) for creating offences punishable on summary conviction by a fine not exceeding level 5 on the standard scale or such other level as is prescribed or for creating other procedures for enforcing any provisions of the regulations.

(3) Subsections (1) and (2) are subject to subsections (4) to (7).

(6) Regulations under subsection (1) may not make provision for requiring the processing of confidential patient information solely or principally for the purpose of determining the care and treatment to be given to particular individuals.

(7) Regulations under this section may not make provision for or in connection with the processing of prescribed patient information in a manner inconsistent with any provision made by or under the Data Protection Act 1998 (c 29).

(8) Subsection (7) does not affect the operation of provisions made under subsection (2)(c).

(10) In this section 'patient information' means –

    (a) information (however recorded) which relates to the physical or mental health or condition of an individual, to the diagnosis of his condition or to his care or treatment, and

    (b) information (however recorded) which is to any extent derived, directly or indirectly, from such information, whether or not the identity of the individual in question is ascertainable from the information.

(11) For the purposes of this section, patient information is 'confidential patient information' where –

    (a) the identity of the individual in question is ascertainable –

        (i) from that information, or

        (ii) from that information and other information which is in the possession of, or is likely to come into the possession of, the person processing that information, and

    (b) that information was obtained or generated by a person who, in the circumstances, owed an obligation of confidence to that individual.

(12) In this section 'medical purposes' means the purposes of any of –

(a) preventative medicine, medical diagnosis, medical research, the provision of care and treatment and the management of health and social care services, and

(b) informing individuals about their physical or mental health or condition, the diagnosis of their condition or their care and treatment.

(13) In this section –

'health service body' means any body (including a government department) or person engaged in the provision of the health service that is prescribed, or of a description prescribed, for the purposes of this definition,

'processing', in relation to information, means the use, disclosure or obtaining of the information or the doing of such other things in relation to it as may be prescribed for the purposes of this definition.

252   Patient Information Advisory Group

(1) For the purposes of subsections (2) and (3), there continues to be a committee known as the Patient Information Advisory Group ('the Advisory Group').

(2) Before laying before Parliament a draft of any statutory instrument containing regulations under section 251(1), or making any regulations pursuant to section 251(5)(b), the Secretary of State must seek and have regard to the views of the Advisory Group on the proposed regulations.

(3) The Secretary of State may seek the views of the Advisory Group on such other matters connected with the processing of patient information or of any information (other than patient information) obtained or generated in the course of the provision of the health service as he considers appropriate.

Emergency powers

253   Emergency powers

(1) The Secretary of State may give directions under this section if he considers that by reason of an emergency it is necessary to do so in order to ensure that a service falling to be provided under or by virtue of this Act is provided.

(2) Directions under this section may direct that, during the period specified by the directions, a function conferred on any body or person under or by virtue of this Act is to the exclusion of or concurrently with that body or person to be performed by another body or person.

(3) The powers conferred on the Secretary of State by this section are in addition to any other powers exercisable by him.

(4) The references in this section to this Act do not include a reference to Chapter 5 of Part 2 (NHS foundation trusts).

Supplies by the Secretary of State

255   Supplies not readily obtainable

(1) Where the Secretary of State has acquired –

(a) supplies of human blood for the purposes of any service under this Act,

(b) any part of a human body for the purpose of, or in the course of providing, any such service, or

(c) supplies of any other substances or preparations not readily obtainable, he may arrange to make such supplies or that part available (on such terms, including terms as to charges, as he considers appropriate) to any person.

(2) The Secretary of State may exercise the powers conferred by subsection (1) only if, and to the extent that, he is satisfied that anything which he proposes to do or allow under those powers –

(a) will not to a significant extent interfere with the performance by him of any duty imposed on him by this Act to provide accommodation or services of any kind, and

(b) will not to a significant extent operate to the disadvantage of persons seeking or afforded admission or access to accommodation or services at health service hospitals (whether as resident or non-resident patients) otherwise than as private patients.

(3) 'Health service hospital' includes such a hospital within the meaning of section 206 of the National Health Service (Wales) Act 2006 (c. 42).

Universities

258   University clinical teaching and research

(1) The Secretary of State must exercise his functions under this Act so as to secure that there are made available such facilities as he considers are reasonably required by any university which has a medical or dental school, in connection with –

(a) clinical teaching, and

(b) research connected with clinical medicine or clinical dentistry.

(2) Regulations may provide for any functions –

(a) exercisable by a Strategic Health Authority, Primary Care Trust, Special Health Authority or Local Health Board,

(b) in relation to the provision of facilities such as are mentioned in subsection (1), to be exercisable by the body jointly with one or more NHS body other than an NHS foundation trust.

Sale of medical practices

259   Sale of medical practices

(1) It is unlawful to sell the goodwill of the medical practice of a person to whom any of subsections (2) to (4) applies, unless the person –

(a) no longer provides or performs the services mentioned, and

(b) has never carried on the practice in a relevant area.

(2) This subsection applies to a person who has at any time provided general medical services under arrangements made –

(a) with any Council, Committee or Authority under the National Health Service Act 1946 or the National Health Service Reorganisation Act 1973, or

(b) with any Primary Care Trust, Health Authority or Local Health Board under section 29 of the National Health Service Act 1977.

(3) This subsection applies to a person who has at any time provided or performed personal medical services in accordance with section 28C of the National Health Service Act 1977 (prior to the coming into force of section 16CC of that Act).

(4) This subsection applies to a person who has at any time, in prescribed circumstances or, if regulations so provide, in all circumstances, provided or performed primary medical services –

(a) in accordance with section 28C arrangements (within the meaning given by section 28D of the National Health Service Act 1977),

(b) in accordance with arrangements under section 16CC(2)(b) of that Act,

(c) under a general medical services contract (within the meaning of section 28Q(2) of that Act),

(d) in accordance with section 92 arrangements or section 50 arrangements,

(e) in accordance with arrangements under section 83(2)(b) of this Act, or section 41(2)(b) of the National Health Service (Wales) Act 2006 (c. 42),

(f) under a general medical services contract or a Welsh general medical services contract.

(5) In this section –

'goodwill' includes any part of goodwill and, in relation to a person practising in partnership, means his share of the goodwill of the partnership practice,

'medical practice' includes any part of a medical practice,

'relevant area', in relation to any Council, Committee, Primary Care Trust, Local Health Board or Authority by arrangement or contract with whom a person has at any time provided or performed services, means the area, district or locality of that Council, Committee, Primary Care Trust, Local Health Board or Authority (at that time) . . .

262   Power to control prices

(1) The Secretary of State may, after consultation with the industry body –

(a) limit any price which may be charged by any manufacturer or supplier for the supply of any health service medicine, and

(b) provide for any amount representing sums charged by that person for that medicine in excess of the limit to be paid to the Secretary of State within a specified period.

(2) The powers conferred by this section are not exercisable at any time in relation to a manufacturer or supplier to whom at that time a voluntary scheme applies.

263   Statutory schemes

(1) The Secretary of State may, after consultation with the industry body, make a scheme (referred to in this section and section 264 as a statutory scheme) for the purpose of –

(a) limiting the prices which may be charged by any manufacturer or supplier for the supply of any health service medicines, or

(b) limiting the profits which may accrue to any manufacturer or supplier in connection with the manufacture or supply of any health service medicines.

(2) A statutory scheme may, in particular, make any provision mentioned in subsections (3) to (6).

(3) The scheme may require any manufacturer or supplier to whom it applies to –

(a) record and keep information, and

(b) provide information to the Secretary of State.

(4) The scheme may provide for any amount representing sums charged by any manufacturer or supplier to whom the scheme applies, in excess of the limits determined under the scheme, for health service medicines covered by the scheme to be paid by that person to the Secretary of State within a specified period.

(5) The scheme may provide for any amount representing the profits, in excess of the limits determined under the scheme, accruing to any manufacturer or supplier to whom the scheme applies in connection with the manufacture or supply of health service medicines covered by the scheme to be paid by that person to the Secretary of State within a specified period.

(6) The scheme may –

(a) prohibit any manufacturer or supplier to whom the scheme applies from increasing, without the approval of the Secretary of State, any price charged by him for the supply of any health service medicine covered by the scheme, and

(b) provide for any amount representing any increase in contravention of that prohibition in the sums charged by that person for that medicine, so far as the increase is attributable to supplies to the health service, to be paid to the Secretary of State within a specified period.

(7) A statutory scheme may not apply to a manufacturer or supplier to whom a voluntary scheme applies.

265   Enforcement

(1) Regulations may provide for a person who contravenes any provision of regulations or directions under sections 261 to 264 to be liable to pay a penalty to the Secretary of State.

(2) The penalty may be –

(a) a single penalty not exceeding £100,000, or

(b) a daily penalty not exceeding £10,000 for every day on which the contravention occurs or continues.

Use of facilities in private practice

267   Permission for use of facilities in private practice

(1) A person to whom this section applies who wishes to use any relevant health service accommodation or facilities for the purpose of providing medical, dental, pharmaceutical, ophthalmic or chiropody services to non-resident private patients may apply in writing to the Secretary of State for permission under this section.

(2) Any application for permission under this section must specify –

    (a) which of the relevant health service accommodation or facilities the applicant wishes to use for the purpose of providing services to such patients, and

    (b) which of the kinds of services mentioned in subsection (1) he wishes the permission to cover.

(3) On receiving an application under this section the Secretary of State –

    (a) must consider whether anything for which permission is sought would interfere with the giving of full and proper attention to persons seeking or afforded access otherwise than as private patients to any services provided under this Act, and

    (b) must grant the permission applied for unless in his opinion anything for which permission is sought would so interfere.

(4) Any grant of permission under this section is on such terms (including terms as to the payment of charges for the use of the relevant health service accommodation or facilities pursuant to the permission) as the Secretary of State may from time to time determine.

(5) The persons to whom this section applies are –

    (a) medical practitioners, registered pharmacists or other persons who provide pharmaceutical services under Chapter 1 of Part 7,

    (b) chiropodists who provide services under this Act at premises where services are provided under that Chapter,

    (c) persons providing primary medical services, primary dental services or primary ophthalmic services under a general medical services contract, a general dental services contract or a general ophthalmic services contract, or in accordance with section 92 arrangements or section 107 arrangements.

(6) 'Relevant health service accommodation or facilities', in relation to a person to whom this section applies, means –

    (a) any accommodation or facilities available at premises provided by the Secretary of State by virtue of this Act, being accommodation or facilities which that person is authorised to use for purposes of this Act, or

    (b) in the case of a person to whom this section applies by virtue of subsection (5)(b), accommodation or facilities which that person is authorised to use for purposes of this Act at premises where services are provided under Chapter 1 of Part 7.

Registration of information, etc

269   Special notices of births and deaths

(1) The requirements of this section with respect to the notification of births and deaths are in addition to, and not in substitution for, the requirements of any Act relating to the registration of births and deaths.

(2) Each registrar of births and deaths must furnish, to the Primary Care Trust the area of which includes the whole or part of the registrar's sub-district, such particulars of each birth and death which occurred in the area of the Primary Care Trust as are entered in a register of births or deaths kept for that sub-district.

(3) Regulations may provide as to the manner in which and the times at which particulars must be furnished under subsection (2).

(4) In the case of each child born –

    (a) the child's father, if at the time of the birth he is residing on the premises where the birth takes place, and

    (b) any person in attendance upon the mother at the time of, or within six hours after, the birth, must give notice of the birth to the Primary Care Trust for the area in which the birth takes place.

(5) Subsection (4) applies to any child which is born after the expiry of the twenty-fourth week of pregnancy whether alive or dead.

(6) Notice under subsection (4) must be given either –

(a) by posting within 36 hours after the birth a prepaid letter or postcard addressed to the Primary Care Trust at its offices and containing the required information, or

(b) by delivering within that period at the offices of the Primary Care Trust a written notice containing the required information.

(7) A Primary Care Trust must, upon application to it, supply without charge to any medical practitioner or midwife residing or practising within its area prepaid addressed envelopes together with the forms of notice.

(8) Any person who fails to give notice of a birth in accordance with subsection (4) is liable on summary conviction to a fine not exceeding level 1 on the standard scale, unless he satisfies the court that he believed, and had reasonable grounds for believing, that notice had been duly given by some other person.

(9) Proceedings in respect of an offence under subsection (8) must not, without the Attorney-General's written consent, be taken by any person other than a party aggrieved or the Primary Care Trust concerned.

(10) A registrar of births and deaths must, for the purpose of obtaining information concerning births which have occurred in his sub-district, have access at all reasonable times to –

(a) notices of births received by a Primary Care Trust under this section, or

(b) any book in which those notices may be recorded.

Part 14

Supplementary

275   Interpretation

(1) In this Act (except where the context otherwise requires) –

'facilities' includes the provision of (or the use of) premises, goods, materials, vehicles, plant or apparatus,

'the FHSAA' means the Family Health Services Appeal Authority,

'functions' includes powers and duties,

'goods' include accommodation,

'the health service' means the health service continued under section 1(1) and under section 1(1) of the National Health Service (Wales) Act 2006,

'health service hospital' means a hospital vested in the Secretary of State for the purposes of his functions under this Act or vested in a Primary Care Trust, an NHS trust or an NHS foundation trust,

'hospital' means –

(a) any institution for the reception and treatment of persons suffering from illness,

(b) any maternity home, and

(c) any institution for the reception and treatment of persons during convalescence or persons requiring medical rehabilitation, and includes clinics, dispensaries and out-patient departments maintained in connection with any such home or institution, and 'hospital accommodation' must be construed accordingly,

'illness' includes mental disorder within the meaning of the Mental Health Act 1983 and any injury or disability requiring medical or dental treatment or nursing,

'Local Health Board' means a body established under section 11 of the National Health Service (Wales) Act 2006 (c. 42),

'medical' includes surgical,

'medical practitioner' means a registered medical practitioner within the meaning of Schedule 1 to the Interpretation Act 1978 (c. 30),

'medicine' includes such chemical re-agents as are included in a list approved by the Secretary of State for the purposes of section 126,

'modifications' includes additions, omissions and amendments,

'NHS trust' includes an NHS trust established under the National Health Service (Wales) Act 2006,

'officer' includes servant,

'patient' includes a woman who is pregnant or breast-feeding or who has recently given birth,

'prescribed' means prescribed by regulations made by the Secretary of State,

'property' includes rights,

'regulations' means regulations made by the Secretary of State,

'university' includes a university college,

'voluntary organisation' means a body the activities of which are carried on otherwise than for profit, but does not include any public or local authority.

(2) In this Act (except where the context otherwise requires) any reference to a body established under this Act or the National Health Service (Wales) Act 2006 includes a reference to a body continued in existence by virtue of this Act or that Act.

278 Short title, extent and application

(2) Subject to this section, this Act extends to England and Wales only.

(3) Sections 261 to 266 in Part 13 (price of medical supplies) extend also to Scotland and Northern Ireland.

NHS Redress Act 2006

2006 Chapter 44

England

1 Power to establish redress scheme

(1) The Secretary of State may by regulations establish a scheme for the purpose of enabling redress to be provided without recourse to civil proceedings in circumstances in which this section applies.

(2) This section applies where under the law of England and Wales qualifying liability in tort on the part of a body or other person mentioned in subsection (3) arises in connection with the provision, as part of the health service in England, of qualifying services.

(3) The bodies and other persons referred to are –

(a) the Secretary of State,

(b) a Primary Care Trust,

(c) a designated Strategic Health Authority, and

(d) a body or other person providing, or arranging for the provision of, services whose provision is the subject of arrangements with a body or other person mentioned in paragraph (a), (b) or (c).

(4) The reference in subsection (2) to qualifying liability in tort is to liability in tort owed –

(a) in respect of or consequent upon personal injury or loss arising out of or in connection with breach of a duty of care owed to any person in connection with the diagnosis of illness, or the care or treatment of any patient, and

(b) in consequence of any act or omission by a health care professional.

(5) For the purposes of subsection (2), services are qualifying services if –

(a) they are provided in a hospital (in England or elsewhere), or

(b) they are of such other description (including a description involving provision outside England) as the Secretary of State may specify by regulations.

(11) In this section, 'hospital' has the same meaning as in the National Health Service Act 2006.

2   Application of scheme

(1) Subject to subsection (2), a scheme may make such provision defining its application as the Secretary of State thinks fit.

(2) A scheme must provide that it does not apply in relation to a liability that is or has been the subject of civil proceedings.

3   Redress under scheme

(1) Subject to subsections (2) and (5), a scheme may make such provision as the Secretary of State thinks fit about redress under the scheme.

(2) A scheme must provide for redress ordinarily to comprise –

(a) the making of an offer of compensation in satisfaction of any right to bring civil proceedings in respect of the liability concerned,

(b) the giving of an explanation,

(c) the giving of an apology, and

(d) the giving of a report on the action which has been, or will be, taken to prevent similar cases arising, but may specify circumstances in which one or more of those forms of redress is not required.

(3) A scheme may, in particular –

(a) make provision for the compensation that may be offered to take the form of entry into a contract to provide care or treatment or of financial compensation, or both;

(b) make provision about the circumstances in which different forms of compensation may be offered.

(4) A scheme that provides for financial compensation to be offered may, in particular –

(a) make provision about the matters in respect of which financial compensation may be offered;

(b) make provision with respect to the assessment of the amount of any financial compensation.

(5) A scheme that provides for financial compensation to be offered –

(a) may specify an upper limit on the amount of financial compensation that may be included in an offer under the scheme;

(b) if it does not specify a limit under paragraph (a), must specify an upper limit on the amount of financial compensation that may be included in such an offer in respect of pain and suffering;

(c) may not specify any other limit on what may be included in such an offer by way of financial compensation.

4   Commencement of proceedings under scheme

(1) A scheme may make such provision as the Secretary of State thinks fit about the commencement of proceedings under the scheme.

(2) A scheme may, in particular, make provision –

(a) about who may commence proceedings under the scheme;

(b) about how proceedings under the scheme may be commenced;

(c) for time limits in relation to the commencement of proceedings under the scheme;

(d) about circumstances in which proceedings under the scheme may not be commenced;

(e) requiring proceedings under the scheme to be commenced in specified circumstances;

(f) for notification of the commencement of proceedings under the scheme in specified circumstances.

5   Duty to consider potential application of scheme

(1) The Secretary of State may by regulations make provision requiring any body or other person mentioned in subsection (2) –

    (a) to consider, in such circumstances as the regulations may provide, whether a case that the body or other person is investigating or reviewing involves liability to which a scheme applies, and

    (b) if it appears that it does, to take such steps as the regulations may provide.

(2) The bodies and other persons referred to are –

    (a) any body or other person to whose liability a scheme applies, and

    (b) the Commission for Healthcare Audit and Inspection.

6   Proceedings under scheme

(1) Subject to subsections (3) to (6), a scheme may make such provision as the Secretary of State thinks fit about proceedings under the scheme.

(2) A scheme may, in particular, make provision –

    (a) about the investigation of cases under the scheme (including provision for the over-seeing of the investigation by an individual of a specified description);

    (b) about the making of decisions about the application of the scheme;

    (c) for time limits in relation to acceptance of an offer of compensation under the scheme;

    (d) about the form and content of settlement agreements under the scheme;

    (e) for settlement agreements under the scheme to be subject in cases of a specified description to approval by a court;

    (f) about the termination of proceedings under the scheme.

(3) A scheme must –

    (a) make provision for the findings of an investigation of a case under the scheme to be recorded in a report, and

    (b) subject to subsection (4), make provision for a copy of the report to be provided on request to the individual seeking redress.

(4) A scheme may provide that no copy of an investigation report need be provided –

    (a) before an offer is made under the scheme or proceedings under the scheme are ter-minated, or

    (b) in such other circumstances as may be specified.

(5) A scheme must provide for a settlement agreement under the scheme to include a waiver of the right to bring civil proceedings in respect of the liability to which the settlement relates.

(6) A scheme must provide for the termination of proceedings under the scheme if the liability to which the proceedings relate becomes the subject of civil proceedings.

7   Suspension of limitation period

(1) A scheme must make provision for the period during which a liability is the subject of proceedings under the scheme to be disregarded for the purposes of calculating whether any relevant limitation period has expired.

(2) In subsection (1), the reference to any relevant limitation period is to any period of time for the bringing of civil proceedings in respect of the liability which is prescribed by or under the Limitation Act 1980 or any other enactment.

(3) A scheme may define for the purposes of provision in pursuance of subsection (1) when liability is the subject of proceedings under the scheme.

8   Legal advice etc.

(1) Subject to subsections (2) and (4), a scheme may make such provision as the Secretary of State thinks fit –

    (a) for the provision of legal advice without charge to individuals seeking redress under the scheme;

(b) for the provision in connection with proceedings under the scheme of other services, including the services of medical experts.

(2) A scheme must make such provision as the Secretary of State considers appropriate in order to secure that individuals to whom an offer under the scheme is made have access to legal advice without charge in relation to –

(a) the offer, and

(b) any settlement agreement.

(3) Provision under subsection (1)(a) or (2) about who may provide the legal advice may operate by reference to whether a potential provider is included in a list prepared by a specified person.

(4) A scheme that makes provision for the provision of the services of medical experts must provide for such experts to be instructed jointly by the scheme authority and the individual seeking redress under the scheme.

9   Assistance for individuals seeking redress under scheme

(1) It is the duty of the Secretary of State to arrange, to such extent as he considers necessary to meet all reasonable requirements, for the provision of assistance (by way of representation or otherwise) to individuals seeking, or intending to seek, redress under a scheme.

(2) The Secretary of State may make such other arrangements as he thinks fit for the provision of assistance to individuals in connection with cases which are the subject of proceedings under a scheme.

(3) The Secretary of State may make payments to any person in pursuance of arrangements under this section.

(4) In making arrangements under this section, the Secretary of State must have regard to the principle that the provision of services under the arrangements in connection with a particular case should, so far as practicable, be independent of any person to whose conduct the case relates or who is involved in dealing with the case.

10   Scheme members

(1) Subject to subsection (3), a scheme may make such provision as the Secretary of State thinks fit –

(a) about membership of the scheme on the part of any body or other person to whose liability the scheme applies, and

(b) about the functions of members in connection with the scheme.

(2) A scheme may, in particular –

(a) require or permit a specified body or other person to be a member of the scheme;

(b) require a member of the scheme to carry out specified functions in relation to specified proceedings under the scheme;

(c) authorise members of the scheme to make arrangements under which functions under the scheme are carried out by one member on behalf of another;

(d) require members of the scheme to have regard, in relation to the carrying out of functions under the scheme, to any relevant advice or other guidance issued by the scheme authority;

(e) require, or enable the scheme authority to require, members of the scheme to keep specified records in relation to the carrying out of functions under the scheme;

(f) require, or enable the scheme authority to require, members of the scheme to provide the authority with information or documents relevant to its functions;

(g) require members of the scheme to make payments in accordance with the scheme by way of contribution to specified costs of its operation;

(h) require a member of the scheme to charge an individual of a specified description with responsibility for overseeing the carrying out of specified functions conferred on the member under this Act;

(i) require a member of the scheme to charge an individual of a specified description with responsibility for advising the member about lessons to be learnt from cases involving the member that are dealt with under the scheme.

(3) A scheme must require a member of the scheme to prepare and publish an annual report about cases involving the member that are dealt with under the scheme and the lessons to be learnt from them.

(4) The provision that may be made under this section includes provision which has the effect that a member of a scheme who has arranged for the provision of services has functions under the scheme which relate to someone else's liability in connection with the provision of the services.

11 Scheme authority

(1) A scheme must make provision for a specified Special Health Authority (in this Act referred to as 'the scheme authority') to have such functions in connection with the scheme as the Secretary of State thinks fit.

(2) A scheme may, in particular, provide for the scheme authority to have functions in relation to –

(a) proceedings under the scheme;

(b) payments under settlement agreements under the scheme;

(c) the provision in connection with the scheme of advice or other guidance about specified matters;

(d) the provision in connection with the scheme of legal advice without charge;

(e) the assessment and payment of contributions by members of the scheme;

(f) the monitoring of the carrying out by members of the scheme of their functions under it;

(g) the provision to the Independent Regulator of Foundation Trusts of reports with respect to failure by NHS foundation trusts to carry out functions under the scheme;

(h) the publication of annual data about the scheme.

(3) Section 28(1) of the National Health Service Act 2006 (power to establish special bodies for the purpose of exercising any functions which may be conferred on them by or under that Act) shall have effect as if the provisions of this Act were contained in that Act.

12 General duty to promote resolution under scheme

A scheme must include provision requiring the scheme authority and the members of the scheme, in carrying out their functions under the scheme, to have regard in particular to the desirability of redress being provided without recourse to civil proceedings.

13 Duties of co-operation

(1) The scheme authority under a scheme and the Commission for Healthcare Audit and Inspection must co-operate with each other where it appears to them that it is appropriate to do so for the efficient and effective discharge of their respective functions.

(2) The scheme authority under a scheme and the National Patient Safety Agency must co-operate with each other where it appears to them that it is appropriate to do so for the efficient and effective discharge of their respective functions.

14 Complaints

(1) The Secretary of State may by regulations make provision about the handling and consideration of complaints made under the regulations about maladministration by any body or other person –

(a) in the exercise of functions under a scheme,

(b) in the exercise of other functions relating to proceedings under a scheme, or

(c) in connection with a settlement agreement entered into under a scheme.

(2) Regulations under subsection (1) must provide for complaints to be considered by –

(a) the scheme authority, or

(b) a member of the scheme.

(3) Without prejudice to the generality of subsection (1), regulations under that subsection may make the following provision.

(4) The regulations may make provision about –

    (a) the persons who may make a complaint;

    (b) the complaints which may, or may not, be made under the regulations;

    (c) the persons to whom complaints may be made;

    (d) complaints which need not be considered;

    (e) the period within which complaints must be made;

    (f) the procedures to be followed in making, handling and considering a complaint;

    (g) matters which are excluded from consideration;

    (h) the making of a report or recommendations about a complaint;

    (i) the action to be taken as a result of a complaint.

(5) The regulations may impose on the scheme authority, or a member of the scheme, obligations with respect to producing, or making available to the public, information about the procedures to be followed under the regulations.

(6) The regulations may also –

    (a) provide for different parts or aspects of a complaint to be treated differently;

    (b) require the production of information or documents in order to enable a complaint to be properly considered;

    (c) authorise the disclosure of information or documents relevant to a complaint to a person who is considering a complaint under the regulations, notwithstanding any rule of common law that would otherwise prohibit or restrict the disclosure.

(7) The regulations may make provision about complaints which raise both matters falling to be considered under the regulations and matters falling to be considered under other statutory complaints procedures, including in particular provision for enabling such a complaint to be made under the regulations.

(8) The regulations may, in relation to complaints in connection with a scheme which are made or purport to be made under the regulations, make provision for securing –

    (a) that any matters raised in such complaints which fall to be considered under other statutory complaints procedures are referred to the body or other person operating the appropriate procedures;

    (b) that any such matters are treated as if they had been raised in a complaint made under the appropriate procedures.

(9) In subsections (7) and (8), 'statutory complaints procedures' means complaints procedures established by or under any enactment.

Supplementary

18   Interpretation

(1) In this Act –

'designated Strategic Health Authority' means a Strategic Health Authority designated for the purposes of this Act by regulations made by the Secretary of State;

'health service' has the same meaning as in the National Health Service Act 2006;

'illness' has the same meaning as in the National Health Service Act 2006;

'patient' has the same meaning as in the National Health Service Act 2006;

'personal injury' includes any disease and any impairment of a person's physical or mental health;

'scheme', except in section 1, means a scheme established under that section;

'scheme authority' has the meaning given by section 11(1);

'specified', in relation to a scheme, means specified in the scheme.

(2) In this Act, references to functions in connection with a scheme include functions in relation to settlement agreements under the scheme.

19   Short title, commencement and extent

(5) This Act extends to England and Wales only.

Part II

Statutory Instruments

National Health Service (Venereal Diseases) Regulations 1974

(SI 1974, No. 29)

Confidentiality of information

2 Every Strategic Health Authority, NHS Trust, NHS foundation trust and Primary Care Trust shall take all necessary steps to secure that any information capable of identifying an individual obtained by officers of the Authority or Trust with respect to persons examined or treated for any sexually transmitted disease shall not be disclosed except –

  (a) for the purpose of communicating that information to a medical practitioner, or to a person employed under the direction of a medical practitioner in connection with the treatment of persons suffering from such disease or the prevention of the spread thereof, and

  (b) for the purpose of such treatment or prevention.

Mental Health (Hospital, Guardianship and Consent to Treatment) Regulations 1983

(SI 1983, No. 893)

Part I

Interpretation

2 (1) In these regulations, unless the context otherwise requires

  'the Act' means the Mental Health Act 1983;

  'appropriate medical officer' has the same meaning as in section 16(5) of the Act;

  'the Commission' means the Mental Health Act Commission;

  'document' means any application, recommendation, record, report, order, notice or other document;

  'private guardian', in relation to a patient, means a person, other than a local social services authority, who acts as guardian under the Act;

  'served', in relation to a document, includes addressed, delivered, given, forwarded, furnished or sent.

  (2) Except insofar as the context otherwise requires, any reference in these regulations to –

  (a) a numbered section is to the section of the Act bearing that number;

  (b) a numbered regulation or Schedule is to the regulation in or Schedule to these regulations bearing that number and any reference in a regulation to a numbered paragraph is a reference to the paragraph of that regulation bearing that number;

  (c) a numbered form is a reference to the form in Schedule 1 bearing that number.

Part III Functions of Guardians and Nearest Relatives

Duties of private guardians

12 It shall be the duty of a private guardian –

(a) to appoint a registered medical practitioner to act as the nominated medical attendant of the patient;

(b) to notify the responsible local social services authority of the name and address of the nominated medical attendant;

(c) in exercising the powers and duties conferred or imposed upon him by the Act and these regulations, to comply with such directions as that authority may give;

(d) to furnish that authority with all such reports or other information with regard to the patient as the authority may from time to time require;

(e) to notify the authority

(i) on the reception of the patient into guardianship of his address and the address of the patient,

(ii) except in a case to which paragraph (f) applies, of any permanent change of either address, before or not later than 7 days after the change takes place;

(f) where on any permanent change of his address, the new address is in the area of a different local social services authority, to notify that authority

(i) of his address and that of the patient,

(ii) of the particulars mentioned in paragraph (b), and to send a copy of the notification to the authority which was formerly responsible; and

(g) in the event of the death of the patient, or the termination of the guardianship by discharge, transfer or otherwise, to notify the responsible local social services authority as soon as reasonably practicable.

Visits to patients subject to guardianship

13 The responsible local social services authority shall arrange for every patient received into guardianship under Part II of the Act to be visited at such intervals as the authority may decide, but in any case at intervals of not more than 3 months, and at least one such visit in any year shall be made by a practitioner approved by the Secretary of State for the purposes of section 12 (general provisions as to medical recommendations).

Performance of functions of nearest relative

14—(1) Subject to the conditions of paragraph (2), the nearest relative of a patient may authorise in writing any person other than the patient or a person mentioned in section 26(5) (persons deemed not to be nearest relative) to perform in respect of the patient the functions conferred upon the nearest relative by or under Part II of the Act or these regulations and may revoke such authority.

(2) The conditions mentioned in paragraph (1) are that, on making or revoking such authority, the nearest relative shall forthwith give the authority, or give notice in writing of the revocation of such authority, to

(a) the person authorised;

(b) in the case of a patient liable to be detained in a hospital, the managers of that hospital;

(c) in the case of a patient subject to guardianship, the responsible local social services authority and to the private guardian, if any.

(3) Any such authority shall take effect upon receipt of the authority by the person authorised, and any revocation of such authority shall take effect upon the receipt of the notice by the person authorised.

(4) A person for the time being authorised in accordance with the preceding paragraphs shall exercise the functions mentioned in paragraph (1) on behalf of the nearest relative.

Discharge by nearest relative

15—(1) Any order made by the nearest relative of the patient under section 23 for the discharge of a patient who is liable to be detained under Part II of the Act shall be served upon the managers of the hospital where the patient is liable to be detained and may be in the form set out in Form 34.

(2) Any order made by the nearest relative of the patient under section 23 for discharge of a patient subject to guardianship under the Act shall be served upon the responsible local social services authority and may be in the form set out in Form 35.

(3) Any report given by the responsible medical officer for the purposes of section 25 (restrictions on discharge by nearest relative) shall be in the form set out in Part I of Form 36 and the receipt of that report by the managers of the hospital in which the patient is liable to be detained shall be in the form set out in Part II of Form 36.

Part IV Consent to Treatment

Consent to treatment

16—(1) For the purposes of section 57 (treatment requiring consent and a second opinion) –
- (a) the form of treatment to which that section shall apply, in addition to the treatment mentioned in subsection (1)(a) of that section (any surgical operation for destroying brain tissue or for destroying the functioning of brain tissue), shall be the surgical implantation of hormones for the purpose of reducing male sexual drive;
- (b) the certificates required for the purposes of subsection (2)(a) and (b) of that section shall be in the form set out in Form 37.

(2) For the purposes of section 58 (treatment requiring consent or a second opinion) –
- (a) the form of treatment to which that section shall apply, in addition to the administration of medicine mentioned in subsection (1)(b) of that section, shall be electroconvulsive therapy; and
- (b) the certificates required for the purposes of subsection (3)(a) and (b) of that section shall be in the form set out in Forms 38 and 39 respectively.

Part V Correspondence of Patients

Inspection and opening of postal packets

17—(1) Where under section 134(4) (inspection and opening of postal packets addressed to or by patients in hospital) any postal packet is inspected and opened, but neither the packet nor anything contained in it is withheld under section 134(1) or (2), the person who so inspected and opened it, being a person appointed under section 134(7) to perform the functions of the managers of the hospital under that section ('the person appointed'), shall record in writing –
- (a) that the packet had been so inspected and opened;
- (b) that nothing in the packet has been withheld; and
- (c) his name and the name of the hospital, and shall, before resealing the packet, place the record in that packet.

(2) Where under section 134(1) or (2) any postal packet or anything contained in it is withheld by the person appointed
- (a) he shall record in a register kept for the purpose
    - (i) that the packet or anything contained in it has been withheld,
    - (ii) the date on which it was so withheld,
    - (iii) the grounds on which it was so withheld,
    - (iv) a description of the contents of the packet withheld or of any item withheld,
    - (v) his name; and

(b) if anything contained in the packet is withheld, he shall record in writing
    (i) that the packet has been inspected and opened,
    (ii) that an item or items contained in the packet have been withheld,
    (iii) a description of any such item,
    (iv) his name and the name of the hospital, and
    (v) in any case to which section 134(1)(b) or (2) applies, the further particulars required for the purposes of section 134(6), and shall, before resealing the packet, place the record in that packet.

(3) In a case to which section 134(1)(b) or (2) applies
    (a) the notice required for the purposes of section 134(6) shall include
      (i) a statement of the grounds on which the packet in question or anything contained in it was withheld, and
      (ii) the name of the person appointed who so decided to withhold that packet or anything contained in it and the name of the hospital; and
    (b) where anything contained in a packet is withheld the record required by paragraph (2)(b) above shall, if the provisions of section 134(6) are otherwise satisfied, be sufficient notice to the person to whom the packet is addressed for the purposes of section 134(6).

Review of decisions to withhold postal packets

18—(1) Every application for review by the Commission under section 121(7) (review of any decision to withhold a postal packet, or anything contained in it, under section 134) –
    (a) shall be made in such manner as the Commission may accept as sufficient in the circumstances of any particular case or class of case and may be made otherwise than in writing; and
    (b) shall be made, delivered or sent to an office of the Commission.

(2) Any person making such an application shall furnish to the Commission the notice of the withholding of the postal packet or anything contained in it, given under section 134(6), or a copy of that notice.

(3) For the purpose of determining any such application the Commission may direct the production of such documents, information and evidence as it may reasonably require.

Mental Health Review Tribunal Rules 1983

(SI 1983, No. 942)

Part I Introduction

Interpretation

2—(1) In these Rules, unless the context otherwise requires –

'the Act' means the Mental Health Act 1983;

'admission papers' means the application for admission under section 2 of the Act and the written recommendations of the two registered medical practitioners on which it is founded;

'assessment application' means an application by a patient who is detained for assessment and entitled to apply under section 66(1)(a) of the Act or who, being so entitled, has applied;

'the authority's statement' means the statement provided by the responsible authority pursuant to rule 6(1);

'chairman' means the legal member appointed by the Lord Chancellor as chairman of the Mental Health Review Tribunal under paragraph 3 of Schedule 2 to the Act or another member of the tribunal appointed to act on his behalf in accordance with paragraph 4 of that Schedule or section 78(6) of the Act as the case may be;

'decision with recommendations' means a decision with recommendations in accordance with section 72(3)(a) or (3A)(a) of the Act;

'health authority' has the same meaning as in the National Health Service Act 1977;

'National Health Service trust' means a body established under section 5(1) of the National Health Service and Community Care Act 1990;

'nearest relative' means a person who has for the time being the functions under the Act of the nearest relative of a patient who is not a restricted patient;

'NHS foundation trust' has the same meaning as in section 1(1) of the Health and Social Care (Community Health and Standards) Act 2003;

'party' means the applicant, the patient, the responsible authority, any other person to whom a notice under rule 7 or rule 31(c) is sent or who is added as a party by direction of the tribunal;

'president' means the president of the tribunal as defined in paragraph 6 of Schedule 2 to the Act;

'private guardian' in relation to a patient means a person, other than a local social services authority, who acts as guardian under the Act;

'proceedings' includes any proceedings of a tribunal following an application or reference in relation to a patient;

'provisional decision' includes a deferred direction for conditional charge in accordance with section 73(7) of the Act and a notification to the Secretary of State in accordance with section 74(1) of the Act;

'reference' means a reference under section 67(1), 68(1) or (2), 71(1), (2) or (5) or 75(1) of the Act;

'registration authority' means the authority exercising the functions of the Secretary of State under the Nursing Homes Act 1975;

'responsible authority' means –

    (a) in relation to a patient liable to be detained under the Act in a hospital or mental nursing home, the managers of the hospital or home as defined in section 145(1) of the Act; and

    (b) in relation to a patient subject to guardianship, the responsible local social services authority as defined in section 34(3) of the Act;

    (c) in relation to a patient subject to after-care under supervision, the Health Authority or Primary Care Trust which has the duty under section 117 of the Act to provide after-care services for the patient.

'the Secretary of State's statement' means a statement provided by the Secretary of State pursuant to rule 6(2) or (3);

'tribunal' in relation to an application or a reference means the Mental Health Review Tribunal constituted under section 65 of the Act which has jurisdiction in the area in which the patient, at the time the application or reference is made, is detained or is liable to be detained or is subject to guardianship or is (or is to be) subject to after-care under supervision, or the tribunal to which the proceedings are transferred in accordance with rule 17(2), or, in the case of a conditionally discharged patient, the tribunal for the area in which the patient resides.

Part II Preliminary Matters

Making an application

3—(1) An application shall be made to the tribunal in writing, signed by the applicant or any person authorised by him to do so on his behalf.

    (2) The application shall wherever possible include the following information –

        (a) the name of the patient;

        (b) the patient's address, which shall include –

            (i) the address of the hospital or mental nursing home where the patient is detained; or

            (ii) the name and address of the patient's private guardian; or

(iii) in the case of a conditionally discharged patient or a patient to whom leave of absence from hospital has been granted, the address of the hospital or mental nursing home where the patient was last detained or is liable to be detained; together with the patient's current address;

(c) where the application is made by the patient's nearest relative, the name and address of the applicant and his relationship to the patient;

(d) the section of the Act under which the patient is detained or is liable to be detained;

(e) the name and address of any representative authorised in accordance with rule 10 or, if none has yet been authorised, whether the applicant intends to authorise a representative or wishes to conduct his own case.

(f) in the case of a patient subject (or to be subject) to after-care under supervision –

(i) the names of the persons who are (or who are to be) the patient's supervisor and community responsible medical officer:

(ii) the name and address of any place at which the patient is (or will be receiving medical treatment;

(iii) where the patient is subject to after-care under supervision his current address, or in the case of a patient who is to be subject to after-care under supervision upon leaving hospital, the address of the hospital where he is, or was last, detained or is liable to be detained.

(3) If any of the information specified in paragraph (2) is not included in the application, it shall in so far as is practicable be provided by the responsible authority or, in the case of a restricted patient, the Secretary of State, at the request of the tribunal.

Notice of application

4—(1) On receipt of an application, the tribunal shall send notice of the application to –

(a) the responsible authority;

(b) the patient (where he is not the applicant); and

(c) if the patient is a restricted patient, the Secretary of State.

(2) Paragraph (1) shall apply whether or not the power to postpone consideration of the application under rule 9 is exercised.

Statements by the responsible authority and the Secretary of State

6—(1) The responsible authority shall send a statement to the tribunal and, in the case of a restricted patient, the Secretary of State, as soon as practicable and in any case within 3 weeks of its receipt of the notice of application; and such statement shall contain –

(a) the information specified in Part A of Schedule 1 to these Rules, in so far as it is within the knowledge of the Secretary of State; and

(b) the report specified in paragraph 1 of Part B of that Schedule; and

(c) the other reports specified in Part B of that Schedule, in so far as it is reasonably practicable to provide them.

(2) Where the patient is a restricted patient, the Secretary of State shall send to the tribunal, as soon as practicable and in any case within 3 weeks of receipt by him of the authority's statement, a statement of such further information relevant to the application as may be available to him.

(3) Where the patient is a conditionally discharged patient, paragraphs (1) and (2) shall not apply and the Secretary of State shall send to the tribunal as soon as practicable, and in any case within 6 weeks of receipt by him of the notice of application, a statement which shall contain –

(a) the information specified in Part C of Schedule 1 to these Rules, in so far as it is within the knowledge of the responsible authority;

(b) the reports specified in Part D of that Schedule, in so far as it is reasonably practicable to provide them.

(3A) Where the patient is (or is to be) subject to after-care under supervision paragraph (1) shall not apply and the responsible authority shall send a statement to the tribunal as soon as practicable, and in any case within 3 weeks of the responsible authority's receipt of the notice of application, and this statement shall contain –

    (a) the information specified in Part E of Schedule 1 to these Rules, in so far as it is within the knowledge of the responsible authority;

    (b) the reports specified in Part F of that Schedule;

    (c) the details of the after-care services being (or to be) provided under section 117 of the Act; and

    (d) details of any requirements imposed (or to be imposed) on the patient under section 25D of the Act; and shall be accompanied by copies of the documents specified in paragraph 3 of Part E of that Schedule.

(4) Any part of the authority's statement or the Secretary of State's statement which, in the opinion of –

    (a) (in the case of the authority's statement) the responsible authority; or

    (b) (in the case of the Secretary of State's statement) the Secretary of State,

should be withheld from the applicant or (where he is not the applicant) the patient on the ground that its disclosure would adversely affect the health or welfare of the patient or others, shall be made in a separate document in which shall be set out the reasons for believing that its disclosure would have that effect.

(5) On receipt of any statement provided in accordance with paragraph (1), (2) or (3), the tribunal shall send a copy to the applicant and (where he is not the applicant) the patient, excluding any part of any statement which is contained in a separate document in accordance with paragraph (4).

Notice to other persons interested

7 On receipt of the authority's statement or, in the case of a conditionally discharged patient, the Secretary of State's statement, the tribunal shall give notice of the proceedings –

    (a) where the patient is liable to be detained in a mental nursing home, to the registration authority of that home;

    (b) where the patient is subject to the guardianship of a private guardian, to the guardian;

    (bb) where the patient is, or will upon leaving hospital be, subject to aftercare under supervision, to the person who appears to be the patient's nearest relative, and the persons who are, or will be, the patient's supervisor and community responsible medical officer and in the case of a patient who has not yet left hospital, the person who has prepared the medical report referred to in paragraph 1 of Part F of Schedule 1 to these Rules;

    (c) where the patient's financial affairs are under the control of the Court of Protection, to the Court of Protection;

    (d) where any person other than the applicant is named in the authority's statement as exercising the functions of the nearest relative, to that person;

    (e) where a health authority, Primary Care Trust, National Health Service trust, or NHS foundation trust has a right to discharge the patient under the provisions of section 23 (3) of the Act, to that authority or trust;

    (f) to any other person who, in the opinion of the tribunal, should have an opportunity of being heard.

Appointment of the tribunal

8—(1) Unless the application belongs to a class or group of proceedings for which members have already been appointed, the members of the tribunal who are to hear the application shall be appointed by the chairman.

(2) A person shall not be qualified to serve as a member of a tribunal for the purpose of any proceedings where –

    (a) he is a member or officer of the responsible authority or of the registration authority concerned in the proceedings; or

(b) he is a member or officer of a health authority, or Primary Care Trust or National Health Service trust, or NHS foundation trust which has the right to discharge the patient under section 23(3) of the Act; or

(c) he has a personal connection with the patient or has recently treated the patient in a professional medical capacity.

(3) The persons qualified to serve as president of the tribunal for the consideration of an application or reference relating to a restricted patient shall be restricted to those legal members who have been approved for that purpose by the Lord Chancellor.

Powers to postpone consideration of an application

9—(1) Where an application or reference by or in respect of a patient has been considered and determined by a tribunal for the same or any other area, the tribunal may, subject to the provisions of this rule, postpone the consideration of a further application by or in respect of that patient until such date as it may direct, not being later than –

(a) the expiration of the period of six months from the date on which the previous application was determined; or

(b) the expiration of the current period of detention, whichever shall be the earlier.

(2) The power of postponement shall not be exercised unless the tribunal is satisfied, after making appropriate inquiries of the applicant and (where he is not the applicant) the patient, that postponement would be in the interests of the patient.

(3) The power of postponement shall not apply to –

(a) an application under section 66(1)(d) or (gb) of the Act;

(b) an application under section 66(1)(f) of the Act in respect of a renewal of authority for detention of the patient for a period of six months or an application under section 66(1) (gc) of the Act in respect of a report furnished under section 25G(3) concerning renewal of after-care under supervision, unless the previous application or reference was made to the tribunal more than three months after the patient's admission to hospital, reception into guardianship or becoming subject to after-care under supervision;

(c) an application under section 66(1)(g) of the Act;

(d) any application where the previous application or reference was determined before a break or change in the authority for the patient's detention or guardianship or his being (or being about to be) subject to after-care under supervision as defined in paragraph (7).

(4) Where the consideration of an application is postponed, the tribunal shall state in writing the reasons for postponement and the period for which the application is postponed and shall send a copy of the statement to all the parties and, in the case of a restricted patient, the Secretary of State.

(5) Where the consideration of an application is postponed, the tribunal shall send a further notice of the application in accordance with rule 4 not less than 7 days before the end of the period of postponement and consideration of the application shall proceed thereafter, unless before the end of the period of postponement the application has been withdrawn or is deemed to be withdrawn in accordance with the provisions of rule 19 or has been determined in accordance with the next following paragraph.

(6) Where a new application which is not postponed under this rule or a reference is made in respect of a patient, the tribunal may direct that any postponed application in respect of the same patient shall be considered and determined at the same time as the new application or reference.

(7) For the purpose of paragraph (3)(d) a break or change in the authority for the detention or guardianship or his being (or being about to be) subject to after-care under supervision of a patient shall be deemed to have occurred only –

(a) on his admission to hospital in pursuance of an application for treatment or in pursuance of a hospital order without an order restricting his discharge; or

(b) on his reception into guardianship in pursuance of a guardianship application or a guardianship order; or

(c) on the application to him of the provisions of Part II or Part III of the Act as if he had been so admitted or received following –

    (i) the making of a transfer direction, or

    (ii) the ceasing of effect of a transfer direction or an order or direction restricting his discharge; or

(d) on his transfer from guardianship to hospital in pursuance of regulations made under section 19 of the Act;

(e) on his ceasing to be subject to after-care under supervision on his reception into guardianship in accordance with section 25H(5)(b).

Part III General Provisions

Representation, etc.

10—(1) Any party may be represented by any person whom he has authorised for that purpose not being a person liable to be detained or subject to guardianship or after-care under supervision under the Act or a person receiving treatment for mental disorder at the same hospital or mental nursing home as the patient.

(2) Any representative authorised in accordance with paragraph (1) shall notify the tribunal of his authorisation and postal address.

(3) As regards the representation of any patient who does not desire to conduct his own case and does not authorise a representative in accordance with paragraph (1) the tribunal may appoint some person to act for him as his authorised representative.

(4) Without prejudice to rule 12(3), the tribunal shall send to an authorised representative copies of all notices and documents which are by these Rules required or authorised to be sent to the person whom he represents and such representative may take all such steps and do all such things relating to the proceedings as the person whom he represents is by these Rules required or authorised to take or do.

(5) Any document required or authorised by these Rules to be sent or given to any person shall, if sent or given to the authorised representative of that person, be deemed to have been sent or given to that person.

(6) Unless the tribunal otherwise directs, a patient or any other party appearing before the tribunal may be accompanied by such other person or persons as he wishes, in addition to any representative he may have authorised.

Medical examination

11 At any time before the hearing of the application, the medical member or, where the tribunal includes more than one, at least one of them shall examine the patient and take such other steps as he considers necessary to form an opinion of the patient's mental condition; and for this purpose the patient may be seen in private and all his medical records may be examined by the medical member, who may take such notes and copies of them as he may require, for use in connection with the application and in the case of a patient subject to after-care under supervision this rule shall also apply to such other records relating to any after-care services provided under section 117 of the Act.

Disclosure of documents

12—(1) Subject to paragraph (2), the tribunal shall, as soon as practicable, send a copy of every document it receives which is relevant to the application to the applicant, and (where he is not the applicant) the patient, the responsible authority and, in the case of a restricted patient, the Secretary of State and any of those persons may submit comments thereon in writing to the tribunal.

(2) As regards any documents which have been received by the tribunal but which have not been copied to the applicant or the patient, including documents withheld in accordance with

rule 6, the tribunal shall consider whether disclosure of such documents would adversely affect the health or welfare of the patient or others and, if satisfied that it would, shall record in writing its decision not to disclose such documents.

(3) Where the tribunal is minded not to disclose any document to which paragraph (1) applies to an applicant or a patient who has an authorised representative it shall nevertheless disclose it as soon as practicable to that representative if he is –

(a) a barrister or solicitor,

(b) a registered medical practitioner;

(c) in the opinion of the tribunal, a suitable person by virtue of his experience or professional qualification;

provided that no information disclosed in accordance with this paragraph shall be disclosed either directly or indirectly to the applicant or (whether he is not the applicant) to the patient or to any other person without the authority of the tribunal or used otherwise than in connection with the application.

Evidence

14—(1) For the purpose of obtaining information, the tribunal may take evidence on oath and subpoena any witness to appear before it or to produce documents, and the president of the tribunal shall have the powers of an arbitrator under section 12(3) of the Arbitration Act 1950 and the powers of a party to a reference under an arbitration agreement under subsection (4) of that section, but no person shall be compelled to give any evidence or produce any document which he could not be compelled to give or produce on the trial of an action.

(2) The tribunal may receive in evidence any document or information notwithstanding that such document or information would be inadmissible in a court of law.

Further information

15—(1) Before or during any hearing the tribunal may call for such further information or reports as it may think desirable, and may give directions as to the manner in which and the persons by whom such material is to be furnished.

(2) Rule 12 shall apply to any further information or reports obtained by the tribunal.

Adjournment

16—(1) The tribunal may at any time adjourn a hearing for the purpose of obtaining further information or for such other purposes as it may think appropriate.

(2) Before adjourning any hearing, the tribunal may give such directions as it thinks fit for ensuring the prompt consideration of the application at an adjourned hearing.

(3) Where the applicant or the patient (where he is not the applicant) or the responsible authority requests that a hearing adjourned in accordance with this rule be resumed, the hearing shall be resumed provided that the tribunal is satisfied that resumption would be in the interests of the patient.

(4) Before the tribunal resumes any hearing which has been adjourned without a further hearing date being fixed it shall give to all parties and, in the case of a restricted patient, the Secretary of State, not less than 14 days' notice (or such shorter notice as all parties may consent to) of the date, time and place of the resumed hearing.

Withdrawal of application

19—(1) An application may be withdrawn at any time at the request of the applicant provided that the request is made in writing and the tribunal agrees.

(2) If a patient ceases to be liable to be detained or subject to guardianship or after-care under supervision in England and Wales, any application relating to that patient shall be deemed to be withdrawn.

(2A) Where a patient subject to after-care under supervision fails without reasonable explanation to undergo a medical examination under rule 11, any application relating to that patient may be deemed by the tribunal to be withdrawn.

(3) Where an application is withdrawn or deemed to be withdrawn, the tribunal shall so inform the parties and, in the case of a restricted patient, the Secretary of State.

Part IV The Hearing

Notice of hearing

20 The tribunal shall give at least 14 days' notice of the date, time and place fixed for the hearing (or such shorter notice as all parties may consent to) to all the parties and, in the case of a restricted patient, the Secretary of State.

Privacy of proceedings

21—(1) The tribunal shall sit in private unless the patient requests a hearing in public and the tribunal is satisfied that a hearing in public would not be contrary to the interests of the patient.

(2) Where the tribunal refuses a request for a public hearing or directs that a hearing which has begun in public shall continue in private the tribunal shall record its reasons in writing and shall inform the patient of those reasons.

(3) When the tribunal sits in private it may admit to the hearing such persons on such terms and conditions as it considers appropriate.

(4) The tribunal may exclude from any hearing or part of a hearing any person or class of persons, other than a representative of the applicant or of the patient to whom documents would be disclosed in accordance with rule 12(3), and in any case where the tribunal decides to exclude the applicant or the patient or their representative or a representative of the responsible authority, it shall inform the person excluded of its reasons and record those reasons in writing.

(5) Except in so far as the tribunal may direct, information about proceedings before the tribunal and the names of any persons concerned in the proceedings shall not be made public.

(6) Nothing in this rule shall prevent a member of the Council on Tribunals from attending the proceedings of a tribunal in his capacity as such provided that he takes no part in those proceedings or in the deliberations of the tribunal.

Hearing procedure

22—(1) The tribunal may conduct the hearing in such manner as it considers most suitable bearing in mind the health and interests of the patient and it shall, so far as appears to it appropriate, seek to avoid formality in its proceedings.

(2) At any time before the application is determined, the tribunal or any one or more of its members may interview the patient, and shall interview him if he so requests, and the interview may, and shall if the patient so requests, take place in the absence of any other person.

(3) At the beginning of the hearing the president shall explain the manner of proceeding which the tribunal proposes to adopt.

(4) Subject to rule 21(4), any part and, with the permission of the tribunal, any other person, may appear at the hearing and take such part in the proceedings as the tribunal thinks proper; and the tribunal shall in particular hear and take evidence from the applicant, the patient (where he is not the applicant) and the responsible authority who may hear each other's evidence, put questions to each other, call witnesses and put questions to any witness or other person appearing before the tribunal.

(5) After all the evidence has been given, the applicant and (where he is not the applicant) the patient shall be given a further opportunity to address the tribunal.

Part V Decisions, Further Consideration and Miscellaneous Provisions

Decisions

23—(1) Any decision of the majority of the members of a tribunal shall be the decision of the tribunal and, in the event of an equality of votes, the president of the tribunal shall have a second or casting vote.

(2) The decision by which the tribunal determines an application shall be recorded in writing; the record shall be signed by the president and shall give the reasons for the decision and, in

particular, where the tribunal relies upon any of the matters set out in section 72(1), (4) or (4A) or section 73(1) or (2) of the Act, shall state its reasons for being satisfied as to those matters.

(3) Paragraphs (1) and (2) shall apply to provisional decisions and decisions with recommendations as they apply to decisions by which applications are determined.

Communication of decisions

24—(1) The decision by which the tribunal determines an application may, at the discretion of the tribunal, be announced by the president immediately after the hearing of the case and, subject to paragraph (2), the written decision of the tribunal, including the reasons, shall be communicated in writing within 7 days of the hearing to all the parties and, in the case of a restricted patient, the Secretary of State.

(2) Where the tribunal considers that the full disclosure of the recorded reasons for its decision to the patient in accordance with paragraph (1) would adversely affect the health or welfare of the patient or others, the tribunal may instead communicate its decision to him in such manner as it thinks appropriate and may communicate its decision to the other parties subject to any conditions it may think appropriate as to the disclosure thereof to the patient; provided that, where the applicant or the patient was represented at the hearing by a person to whom documents would be disclosed in accordance with rule 12(3), the tribunal shall disclose the full recorded grounds of its decision to such a person, subject to any conditions it may think appropriate as to disclosure thereof to the patient.

(3) Paragraphs (1) and (2) shall apply to provisional decisions and decisions with recommendations as they apply to decisions by which applications are determined.

(4) Where the tribunal makes a decision with recommendations, the decision shall specify the period at the expiration of which the tribunal will consider the case further in the event of those recommendations not being complied with.

Part VI References and Applications By Patients Detained for Assessment

References

29   The tribunal shall consider a reference as if there had been an application by the patient and the provisions of these Rules shall apply with the following modifications –

    (a) rules 3, 4, 9 and 19 shall not apply and where a reference is made under section 75(1) of the Act rule 20 shall also not apply;

    (b) the tribunal shall, on receipt of the reference, send notice thereof to the patient and the responsible authority; provided that where the reference has been made by the responsible authority, instead of the notice of reference there shall be sent to the responsible authority a request for the authority's statement;

    (c) rules 5, 6 and 7 shall apply as if rule 6(1) referred to the notice of reference, or the request for the authority's statement, as the case may be, instead of the notice of application and

where a reference is made under section 75(1) of the Act –

        (i) rule 6(2) shall apply as if the period of time specified therein was 2 weeks instead of 3 weeks; and

        (ii) on receipt of the authority's statement, the tribunal shall give notice of the date, time and place fixed for the hearing to any person whom the tribunal notifies of the proceedings under rule 7;

    (cc) where a reference is made under section 75(1) of the Act, on receipt of the reference the tribunal shall –

        (i) fix a date for the hearing being not later than eight weeks, nor earlier than five weeks, from the date on which the reference was received;

(ii) fix the time and place for the hearing; and

(iii) give notice of the date, time and place of the hearing to the patient, the responsible authority and the Secretary of State;

(d) a reference made by the Secretary of State in circumstances in which he is not by the terms of the Act obliged to make a reference may be withdrawn by him at any time before it is considered by the tribunal and, where a reference is so withdrawn, the tribunal shall inform the patient and the other parties that the reference has been withdrawn.

Making an assessment application

30—(1) An assessment application shall be made to the tribunal in writing signed by the patient or any person authorised by him to do so on his behalf.

(2) An assessment application shall indicate that it is made by or on behalf of a patient detained for assessment and shall wherever possible include the following information –

(a) the name of the patient;

(b) the address of the hospital or mental nursing home where the patient is detained;

(c) the name and address of the patient's nearest relative and his relationship to the patient;

(d) the name and address of any representative authorised by the patient in accordance with rule 10 or, if none has yet been authorised, whether the patient intends to authorise a representative or wishes to conduct his own case.

(3) If any of the information specified in paragraph (2) is not included in the assessment application, it shall in so far as is practicable be provided by the responsible authority at the request of the tribunal.

Appointment of a tribunal and hearing date

31 On receipt of an assessment application the tribunal shall –

(a) fix a date for the hearing, being not later than 7 days from the date on which the application was received, and the time and place for the hearing;

(b) give notice of the date, time and place fixed for the hearing to the patient;

(c) give notice of the application and of the date, time and place fixed for the hearing to the responsible authority, the nearest relative (where practicable) and any other person who, in the opinion of the tribunal, should have an opportunity of being heard;

and the chairman shall appoint the members of the tribunal to deal with the case in accordance with rule 8.

Provision of admission papers, etc.

32—(1) On receipt of the notice of an assessment application, or a request from the tribunal, whichever may be the earlier, the responsible authority shall provide for the tribunal copies of the admission papers, together with such of the information specified in Part A of Schedule 1 to these Rules as is within the knowledge of the responsible authority and can reasonably be provided in the time available and such of the reports specified in Part B of that Schedule as can reasonably be provided in the time available.

(2) The responsible authority shall indicate if any part of the admission papers or other documents supplied in accordance with paragraph (1) should, in their opinion, be withheld from the patient on the ground that its disclosure would adversely affect the health or welfare of the patient or others and shall state their reasons for believing that its disclosure would have that effect.

(3) The tribunal shall make available to the patient copies of the admission papers and any other documents supplied in accordance with paragraph (1), excluding any part indicated by the responsible authority in accordance with paragraph (2).

General procedure, hearing procedure and decisions

33   Rule 5, rule 8 and Parts III, IV and V of these Rules shall apply to assessment applications as they apply to applications in so far as the circumstances of the case permit and subject to the following modifications –

(a) rule 12 shall apply as if any reference to a document being withheld in accordance with rule 6 was a reference to part of the admission papers or other documents supplied in accordance with rule 32 being withheld;

(b) rule 16 shall apply with the substitution, for the reference to 14 days' notice, of a reference to such notice as is reasonably practicable;

(c) rule 20 shall not apply;

(d) rule 24 shall apply as if the period of time specified therein was 3 days instead of 7 days.

Public Health (Infectious Diseases) Regulations 1988

(SI 1988, No. 1546)

Interpretation

2—(1) In these Regulations, unless the context otherwise requires –

'the Act' means the Public Health (Control of Disease) Act 1984;

'appropriate health authority' means –

(a) in Wales, the Health Authority within which a district of a local authority or a port health district is wholly or partly situated; and

(b) in England, the Primary Care Trust –

(i) any part of whose area falls within that of the local authority or port health district of the proper officer; and

(ii) which appears to the proper officer to be the relevant Primary Care Trust;

'appropriate medical officer' means –

(a) in a case where the Health Authority or Primary Care Trust has appointed a Director of Public Health, the Director of Public Health, and

(b) in any other case, the registered medical practitioner designated by the Health Authority or Primary Care Trust for the purposes of these Regulations;

'certificate' means a certificate required by section 11 of the Act to be sent by a registered medical practitioner to a proper officer;

'International Health Regulations' means the International Health Regulations (1969) as adopted by the World Health Assembly on 25th July 1969 and as amended by the 26th World Health Assembly in 1973 and by the 34th World Health Assembly in 1981;

'port health authority' means a port health authority constituted by an order made, or having effect as if made, by the Secretary of State under section 2 of the Act, and includes the port health authority for the Port of London as constituted under section 7 of the Act;

'port health district' means the district of a port health authority.

Public health enactments applied to certain diseases

3 There shall apply to the diseases listed in column (1) of Schedule 1 the enactments in the Act listed in column (2) of that Schedule with the modifications specified in column (2).

Modification of section 35 of the Act as it is applied to certain diseases

4   Where in Schedule 1 reference is made to section 35 of the Act as modified by this regulation, that section shall apply to the disease specified with the modification that in subsection (1)(a) the words 'or

(ii) though not suffering from such a disease, is carrying an organism that is capable of causing it,'

shall be omitted.

Modification of section 38 of the Act as it is applied to acquired immune deficiency syndrome

5   In its application to acquired immune deficiency syndrome section 38(1) of the Act shall apply so that a justice of the peace (acting if he deems it necessary ex parte) may on the application of any

local authority make an order for the detention in hospital of an inmate of that hospital suffering from acquired immune deficiency syndrome, in addition to the circumstances specified in that section, if the justice is satisfied that on his leaving the hospital proper precautions to prevent the spread of that disease would not be taken by him –

    (a) in his lodging or accommodation, or

    (b) in other places to which he may be expected to go if not detained in the hospital.

Cases of infectious disease to be specially reported

6—(1) In this regulation 'a disease subject to the International Health Regulations' means cholera, including cholera due to the *eltor* vibrio, plague, smallpox, including variola minor (alastrim), and yellow fever.

    (2) Without prejudice to paragraph (3), a proper officer shall, if his district or port health district is in England immediately inform the Chief Medical Officer for England, or, if his district or port health district is in Wales immediately inform the Chief Medical Officer for Wales of –

        (a) any case or suspected case of a disease subject to the International Health Regulations and

        (b) any serious outbreak of any disease (including food poisoning)

which to his knowledge has occurred in his district or port health district, and he shall similarly inform the appropriate medical officer of the appropriate District Health Authority.

    (3) A proper officer who receives a certificate in respect of any case of –

        (a) a disease subject to the International Health Regulations,

        (b) leprosy,

        (c) malaria or rabies contracted in Great Britain, or

        (d) a viral haemorrhagic fever

shall immediately send a copy to the Chief Medical Officer for England if the address of the patient in the certificate is in England or to the Chief Medical Officer for Wales if such address is in Wales.

Immunisation and vaccination

10 Where a case of any notifiable disease or of any disease mentioned in Schedule 1 (other than tuberculosis) occurs in a district or port health district, the proper officer of that district or port health district and of any adjacent district or port health district may, if he considers it in the public interest, arrange for the vaccination or immunisation, without charge, of any person in his district or port health district who has come or may have come or may come in contact with the infection and is willing to be vaccinated or immunised.

Confidentiality of documents

12 Any certificate, or copy, and any accompanying or related document, shall be sent in such a manner that its contents cannot be read during transmission; and the information contained therein shall not be divulged to any person except –

    (a) so far as is necessary for compliance with the requirements of any enactment (including these Regulations), or

    (b) for the purposes of such action as any proper officer considers reasonably necessary for preventing the spread of disease.

Enforcement and publication

13—(1) These Regulations shall be enforced and executed –

    (a) in the district of a local authority, by the local authority thereof; and

    (b) in a port health district, by the port health authority thereof, so far as these Regulations are in terms applicable thereto.

    (2) Every local authority shall send to any registered medical practitioner who after due enquiry is ascertained to be practising in their district –

    (a) a copy of these Regulations and

    (b) a copy of sections 10 and 11 of the Act.

Schedule 1 The Enactments in the Act Applied to Particular Diseases

(1) *Diseases*	(2) *Enactments applied*
Acquired immune deficiency syndrome	Sections 35, 37, 38 (as modified by regulation 5), 43 and 44.
Acute encephalitis	Sections 11, 12, 17 to 24, 26, 28 to 30, 33 to 35 (as modified by regulation 4), 37, 38, 44 and 45.
Acute poliomyelitis Meningitis	
Meningococcal septicaemia (without meningitis)	
Anthrax	Sections 11, 12, 17 to 22, 24, 26, 28 to 30, 33 to 35 (as modified by regulation 4), 37, 38 and 43 to 45.
Diphtheria	Sections 11, 12, 17 to 24, 26, 28 to 30, 33 to 38, 44 and 45.
Dysentery (amoebic or bacillary)	
Paratyphoid fever	
Typhoid fever	
Viral hepatitis	
Leprosy	Sections 11, 12, 17, 19 to 21, 28 to 30, 35 (as modified by regulation 4) 37, 38 and 44.
Leptospirosis	Sections 11, 12, 17 to 22, 24, 26, 28 to 30, 33 to 35 (as modified by regulation 4), 37, 38, 44 and 45.
Measles	
Mumps	
Rubella	
Whooping cough	
Malaria	Sections 11, 12, 18 and 35 (as modified by regulation 4).
Tetanus	
Yellow fever	
Ophthalmia neonatorum	Sections 11, 12, 17, 24 and 26.
Rabies	Sections 11, 12, 17 to 26, 28 to 30 and 32 to 38.
Scarlet fever	Sections 11, 12, 17 to 22, 24, 26, 28 to 30, 33 to 38, 44 and 45.
Tuberculosis	Sections 12, 17 to 24, 26, 28 to 30, 35 (as modified by regulation 4), 44 and 45; in addition— (a) section 11 shall apply where the opinion of the registered medical practitioner that a person is suffering from tuberculosis is formed from evidence not derived solely from tuberculin tests, and (b) sections 25, 37 and 38 shall apply to tuberculosis of the respiratory tract in an infectious state.
Viral haemorrhagic fever	Sections 11, 12, 17 to 38, 43 to 45 and 48.

Abortion Regulations 1991

(SI 1991, No. 499)

Interpretation

2 In these Regulations 'the Act' means the Abortion Act 1967 and 'practitioner' means a registered medical practitioner.

Certificate of opinion

3—(1) Any opinion to which section 1 of the Act refers shall be certified –
> (a) in the case of a pregnancy terminated in accordance with section 1(1) of the Act, either –
>> (i) in the form set out in Part I of Schedule 1 to these Regulations; or
>> (ii) in a certificate signed and dated by both practitioners jointly or in separate certificates signed and dated by each practitioner stating: –
>>> (a) the full name and address of each practitioner;
>>> (b) the full name and address of the pregnant woman;
>>> (c) whether or not each practitioner has seen or examined, or seen and examined, the pregnant woman; and
>>> (d) that each practitioner is of the opinion formed in good faith that at least one and the same ground mentioned in paragraph (a) to (d) of section 1(1) of the Act is fulfilled.
> (b) in the case of a pregnancy terminated in accordance with section 1(4) of the Act, either –
>> (i) in the form set out in Part II of Schedule 1 to these Regulations; or
>> (ii) in a certificate giving the full name and address of the practitioner and containing the full name and address of the pregnant woman and stating that the practitioner is of the opinion formed in good faith that one of the grounds mentioned in section 1(4) of the Act is fulfilled.

(2) Any certificate of an opinion referred to in section 1(1) of the Act shall be given before the commencement of the treatment for the termination of the pregnancy to which it relates.

(3) Any certificate of an opinion referred to in section 1(4) of the Act shall be given before the commencement of the treatment for the termination of the pregnancy to which it relates or, if that is not reasonably practicable, not later than 24 hours after such termination.

(4) Any such certificate as is referred to in paragraphs (2) and (3) of this regulation shall be preserved by the practitioner who terminated the pregnancy to which it relates for a period of not less than three years beginning with the date of the termination.

(5) A certificate which is no longer to be preserved shall be destroyed by the person in whose custody it then is.

Notice of termination of pregnancy and information relating to the termination

4—(1) Any practitioner who terminates a pregnancy in England or Wales shall give to the appropriate Chief Medical Officer –
> (a) notice of the termination, and
> (b) such other information relating to the termination as is specified in Schedule 2 to these Regulations,

and shall do so by sending them to him within 14 days of the termination either in a sealed envelope or by an electronic communication transmitted by an electronic communications system used solely for the transfer of confidential information to him.

(2) The appropriate Chief Medical Officer is –
> (a) where the pregnancy was terminated in England, the Chief Medical Officer of the Department of Health, Richmond House, 79 Whitehall, London, SW1A 2NS; or
> (b) where the pregnancy was terminated in Wales, the Chief Medical Officer of the Welsh Office, Cathays Park, Cardiff CF1 3NQ.

Restriction on disclosure of information

5 A notice given or any information furnished to a Chief Medical Officer in pursuance of these Regulations shall not be disclosed except that disclosure may be made –

    (a) for the purposes of carrying out their duties –

        (i) to an officer of the Department of Health authorised by the Chief Medical Officer of that Department, or to an officer of the Welsh Office authorised by the Chief Medical Officer of that Office, as the case may be, or

        (ii) to the Registrar General or a member of his staff authorised by him; or

        (iii) to an individual authorised by the Chief Medical Officer who is engaged in setting up, maintaining and supporting a computer system used for the purpose of recording, processing and holding such notice or information;

    (d) pursuant to a court order, for the purposes of proceedings which have begun; or

    (e) for the purposes of bona fide scientific research; or

    (f) to the practitioner who terminated the pregnancy; or

    (g) to a practitioner, with the consent in writing of the woman whose pregnancy was terminated; or

    (h) when requested by the President of the General Medical Council for the purpose of investigating whether the fitness to practise of the practitioner is impaired, to the President of the General Medical Council or a member of its staff authorised by him –

(i) to the woman whose pregnancy was terminated, on her supplying to the Chief Medical Officer written details of her date of birth, the date and place of the termination and a copy of the certificate of registration of her birth certified as a true copy of the original by a solicitor or a practitioner.

IN CONFIDENCE

ABORTION ACT 1967

Not to be destroyed within three years of the date of operation

**Certificate to be completed before an abortion is
performed under Section 1(1) of the Act**

I, ...
(Name and qualifications of practitioner in block capitals)

of ....

....
(Full address of practitioner)

Have/have not* seen/and examined* the pregnant woman to whom this certificate relates at

....

....
(full address of place at which patient was seen or examined)

on ....

and I ....
(Name and qualifications of practitioner in block capitals)

of ....

....
(Full address of practitioner)

Have/have not* seen/and examined* the pregnant woman to whom this certificate relates at

....

....
(Full address of place at which patient was seen or examined)

on ....

We hereby certify that we are of the opinion, formed in good faith, that in the case

of ....
(Full name of pregnant woman in block capitals)

of ....

....
(Usual place of residence of pregnant woman in block capitals)

(Ring appro- priate letter(s))		
	A	the continuance of the pregnancy would involve risk to the life of the pregnant woman greater than if the pregnancy were terminated;
	B	the termination is necessary to prevent grave permanent injury to the physical or mental health of the pregnant woman;
	C	the pregnancy has NOT exceeded its 24th week and that the continuance of the pregnancy would involve risk, greater than if the pregnancy were terminated, of injury to the physical or mental health of the pregnant woman;
	D	the pregnancy has NOT exceeded its 24th week and that the continuance of the pregnancy would involve risk, greater than if the pregnancy were terminated, of injury to the physical or mental health of any existing child(ren) of the family of the pregnant woman;
	E	there is a substantial risk that if the child were born it would suffer from such physical or mental abnormalities as to be seriously handicapped.

This certificate of opinion is given before the commencement of the treatment for the termination of pregnancy to which it refers and relates to the circumstances of the pregnant woman's individual case.

Signed ....   **Date** ....

Signed ....   **Date** ....

* Delete as appropriate   DH/DH005329 4/94 C8000 CC38806   Form HSA1 (revised 1991)

IN CONFIDENCE   **Certificate B**

Not to be destroyed within three years of the date of operation

ABORTION ACT 1967

**Certificate to be completed in relation to abortion performed
in emergency under Section I (4) of the Act**

I, ...

(Name and qualifications of practitioner in block capitals)

of   ....

....

(Full address of practitioner)

hereby certify that I *am/was of the opinion formed in good faith that it *is/was necessary

immediately to terminate the pregnancy of

....

(Full name of pregnant woman in block capitals)

of   ....

....

(Usual place of residence of pregnant woman in block capitals)

(Ring appropriate number)

In order I.   to save the life of the pregnant woman : or

　　　　　2.   to prevent grave permanent injury to the physical or mental health of the
　　　　　　　pregnant woman.

This certificate of opinion is given :—

(Ring appropriate letter)

A.   before the commencement of the treatment for the termination of the pregnancy to

　　　which it relates ; or, if that is not reasonably practicable, then

B.   not later than 24 hours after such termination.

Signed   ....

　　　　　　　　　　　　　　　　　　　　　　　Date...

*Delete as appropriate

FORM H.S.A. 2   15985 8003903 30m (2) 11/79 WPLtd Gp709

16468 PC1 10k 2P AUG 99 (0)

Schedule 2

Regulation 4

Information to be supplied in an Abortion Notification

1. Full name and address (including postcode) of the practitioner who terminated the pregnancy and the General Medical Council registration number of the practitioner.

2. In non-emergency cases particulars of the practitioners who gave a certificate of opinion pursuant to section 1(1) of the Act and whether they saw or examined, or saw and examined the patient before giving the certificate.

3. Patient's details –
   (a) patient's hospital or clinic number or National Health Service number or (if unavailable) patient's full name;
   (b) date of birth;
   (c) in the case of a patient resident in the United Kingdom, her full postcode or, if the postcode is unavailable, her address;
   (d) in the case of a patient resident outside the United Kingdom, her country of residence;
   (e) ethnicity (if disclosed by the patient);
   (f) marital status; and
   (g) parity.

4. Name and address of place of termination.

5. Whether the termination was paid for privately or not.

6. Date and method of foeticide if appropriate.

7. In a case where the termination is by surgery –
   (a) date of termination;
   (b) the method of termination used; and
   (c) in cases where the dates are different, the date of admission to the place of termination and the date of discharge from the place of termination.

8. In a case where the termination is by non-surgical means –
   (a) the date of treatment with antiprogestrone;
   (b) the date of treatment with prostaglandin;
   (c) the date on which the termination is confirmed;
   (d) in cases where the place of treatment with prostaglandin is different from the place of treatment with antiprogestrone, the name and address at which the prostaglandin was administered;
   (e) details of other agents used and the date of administration; and
   (f) the date of discharge if an overnight stay is required.

9. Number of complete weeks of gestation.

10. The ground(s) certified for terminating the pregnancy contained in the certificate of opinion given pursuant to section 1(1) of the Act together with the following additional information in the case of –
   (a) the ground specified in paragraph (a), whether or not there was a risk to the patient's mental health and if not, her main medical conditions;
   (b) the grounds specified in paragraphs (b) and (c), the main medical condition(s) of the patient;
   (c) the ground specified in paragraph (d), any foetal abnormalities diagnosed, together with method of diagnosis used, and any other reasons for termination.

11. The ground(s) certified for terminating the pregnancy contained in the certificate of opinion given pursuant to section 1(4) of the Act and the patient's main medical conditions.

12. In cases of selective termination the original number of foetuses and the number of foetuses remaining.

13. Whether or not the patient was offered chlamydia screening.

14. Particulars of any complications experienced by the patient up to the date of discharge.

15. In the case of the death of the patient the date and cause of death.

Access to Health Records (Control of Access) Regulations 1993

(SI 1993, No. 746)

1   Citation, commencement and interpretation

(2) In these Regulations, 'the Act' means the Access to Health Records Act 1990.

2   Restriction of right of access to health records

Access shall not be given under section 3(2) of the Act to any part of a health record which would disclose information showing that an identifiable individual was, or may have been, born in consequence of treatment services within the meaning of the Human Fertilisation and Embryology Act 1990.

National Health Service (Clinical Negligence Scheme) Regulations 1996

(SI 1996, No. 251)

1   Citation, commencement and interpretation

(2) In these Regulations, unless the context otherwise requires –

'the Act' means the National Health Service and Community Care Act 1990;

'an eligible body' means a body of a kind described in regulation 3 or a body which before 1 October 2002 was a Health Authority which area was situated in England;

'member' means an eligible body which is a member of the Scheme;

'membership year' means, in relation to an eligible body, any period of 12 months beginning on 1st April during any part of which that body is a member of the Scheme;

'preceding year' means, in relation to a membership year, the period of 12 months immediately preceding that membership year;

'qualifying liability' means a liability of a kind described in regulation 4;

'relevant function' means the function of providing services in England or securing the provision of services for the purposes of the National Health Service Act 1977 or by virtue of section 7 of the Health and Medicines Act 1988 or under paragraphs 13, 14, 15 or 15A of Schedule 2 to the Act;

'the Scheme' means the Clinical Negligence Scheme for Trusts established by regulation 2.

2   Establishment of scheme

There is hereby established a scheme, to be known as the Clinical Negligence Scheme for Trusts, whereby an eligible body may, in accordance with the following provisions of these Regulations, make provision to meet qualifying liabilities.

3   Eligible bodies

(1) A body is eligible to participate in the Scheme if it is –

    (a) a National Health Service trust,

    (aa) an NHS foundation trust,

    (b) a Strategic Health Authority,

    (c) a Special Health Authority,

    (d) a Primary Care Trust, or

    (e) the Health Protection Agency.

4   Liabilities to which the Scheme applies

(1) The Scheme applies to any liability in tort owed by a member to a third party in respect of or consequent upon personal injury or loss arising out of or in connection with any breach of a duty of care owed by that body to any person in connection with the diagnosis of any illness, or the care or treatment of any patient, in consequence of any act or omission to act on the part of a person employed or engaged by a member in connection with any relevant function of that member.

5   Administration of the Scheme

The Scheme shall be administered by the Secretary of State.

8   Members' contributions to the Scheme

(1) A member shall pay to the Secretary of State in respect of each membership year such amount as shall be determined in relation to that member, and notified to it, in accordance with this regulation.

(2) When determining in relation to any member the amount of the payment to be made under paragraph (1), the Secretary of State shall have regard to –

(a) his estimate of the total amount which will, by virtue of regulation 9 (payments under the Scheme), fall to be paid during that membership year in respect of all qualifying liabilities under the Scheme;

(b) the nature of the member's relevant functions;

(c) the number of employees of the member who are engaged in its performance of a relevant function, or any part of such a function, and the qualifications and experience of those employees;

(d) any agreement between the Secretary of State and the member that regulation 9(2)(b) or (c) is not to apply in relation to certain liabilities incurred by the member; and

9   Payments under the Scheme

(1) Where, in any membership year, a payment falls to be made by any member in connection with a claim in respect of a qualifying liability, the Secretary of State may, subject to paragraph (2), pay to or on behalf of that member an amount to be determined by him in accordance with paragraph (3).

(3) The amount of any payment under paragraph (1) shall be determined by reference to –

(a) where an award of damages has been made against the member by a Court, the amount of that award, together with the amounts of the legal and associated, costs awarded to the plaintiff and of any such costs incurred by or on behalf of the member;

(b) where legal proceedings have been compromised by the member, the amount of –

(i) any sum paid or payable by the member in relation to the plaintiff's claim for damages,

(ii) the member's contribution towards any legal and associated costs incurred by or on behalf of the plaintiff, and

(iii) any such costs incurred by or on behalf of the member;

(c) where, in any legal proceedings, a Court has declined to award damages against the member, the amount of any legal and associated costs incurred by or on behalf of the member, to the extent that such costs are not recoverable from the plaintiff or from the Legal Services Commission under the Access to Justice Act 1999;

(d) where, otherwise than in the course of legal proceedings –

(i) a member has agreed to make a payment in settlement of a claim, the amount of that payment,

(ii) a member has agreed to make any contribution towards legal or associated costs incurred by a person in connection with that person's claim against the member in respect of a qualifying liability, the amount of that contribution, and the amount of any legal or associated costs incurred by or on behalf of the member in connection with the claim; or

(e) where a member has agreed to be bound by the determination of any person or body as to the making of a payment by that member in respect of a qualifying liability, the amount of the payment and the amount of any legal or associated costs incurred by the person making the claim and any such costs incurred by or on behalf of the member in connection with the claim.

(f) where the member has decided to make a payment into court, the amount of that payment;

10   Provision of information

A member shall, at such times and in such manner as the Secretary of State may require, furnish to the Secretary of State such information as he may request, about –

(a) the nature of any relevant function being carried on, or to be carried on, by the member in any membership year which the Secretary of State may specify;

(b) the number of employees of the member who are engaged in its performance of any relevant function, or such part of any relevant function as the Secretary of State may specify, and the qualifications and experience of those employees; and

(c) any event of which the member is aware which it considers might give rise to a qualifying liability.

National Health Service (Existing Liabilities Scheme) Regulations 1996

(SI 1996, No. 686)

1   Citation, commencement and interpretation

(1) These Regulations may be cited as the National Health Service (Existing Liabilities Scheme) Regulations 1996, and shall come into force on 1st April 1996.

(2) In these Regulations, unless the context otherwise requires –

'the Act' means the National Health Service and Community Care Act 1990;

'an eligible body' means a body of a kind described in regulation 3;

'qualifying liability' means a liability of a kind described in regulation 4;

'relevant function' means the function of providing services in England for the purposes of the National Health Service Act 1977 or by virtue of section 7 of the Health and Medicines Act 1988 or under paragraph 14 or 15 of Schedule 2 to the Act;

'the scheme' means the Existing Liabilities Scheme established by regulation 2.

2   Establishment of scheme

There is hereby established a scheme, to be known as the Existing Liabilities Scheme, whereby an eligible body may, in accordance with the following provisions of these Regulations, make provision to meet qualifying liabilities.

3   Eligible bodies

A body is eligible to participate in the Scheme if –

(a) the body is –

(zi) a Strategic Health Authority,

(i) a Health Authority,

(ii) a Special Health Authority,

(iia) a Primary Care Trust,

(iii) a National Health Service trust,

(iiia) an NHS foundation trust, or

(iv) the Health Protection Agency;

(b) the body has –

    (i) during any period falling before 1st April 1995 exercised any relevant function; or

    (ii) had transferred to it the liabilities of any other body which exercised any relevant function during any period falling before that date; and

  (c) the body has applied to the Secretary of State, in such manner as he may require, to participate in the Scheme, and the Secretary of State has admitted the body to the Scheme.

4   Liabilities to which the Scheme applies

The Scheme applies to any liability in tort owed by an eligible body to a third party in respect of or consequent upon personal injury or loss arising out of or in connection with any breach before 1st April 1995 of a duty of care owed by that body, or a body referred to in regulation 3(b)(ii), to any person in connection with the diagnosis of any illness, or the care or treatment of any patient, in consequence of any act or omission to act on the part of a person employed or engaged by such a body in connection with any relevant function of that body.

National Health Service (Liabilities to Third Parties Scheme) Regulations 1999

(SI 1999, No. 873)

1   Citation, commencement and interpretation

(2) In these Regulations, unless the context otherwise requires –

'the Act' means the National Health Service and Community Care Act 1990;

'an eligible body' means a body of a kind described in regulation 3 or a body which before 1 October 2002 was a Health Authority whose area was situated in England;

'member' means an eligible body which is a member of the Scheme;

'membership year' means, in relation to an eligible body, any period of 12 months beginning on 1st April during any part of which that body is a member of the Scheme;

'preceding year' means, in relation to a membership year, the period of 12 months immediately preceding that membership year;

'qualifying liability' means a liability of a kind described in regulation 4;

'relevant function' means the function of providing services in England for the purposes of the National Health Service Act 1977 or by virtue of section 7 of the Health and Medicines Act 1988 or under paragraph 14 or 15 of Schedule 2 to the Act;

'the Scheme' means the Liabilities to Third Parties Scheme established by regulation 2.

2   Establishment of scheme

There is hereby established a scheme, to be known as the Liabilities to Third Parties Scheme, whereby an eligible body may, in accordance with the following provisions of these Regulations, make provision to meet qualifying liabilities.

3   Eligible bodies

A body is eligible to participate in the Scheme if it is –

  (a) a National Health Service trust,

  (aa) an NHS foundation trust,

  (b) a Strategic Health Authority,

  (c) a Special Health Authority, or

  (d) a Primary Care Trust.

4   Liabilities to which the Scheme applies

(1) The Scheme applies to any liability to any third party to which a member is subject in respect of loss, damage or injury which –

  (a) arises out of the carrying out of any relevant function of that member;

(b) is a qualifying liability; and

(c) is not a qualifying liability for the purposes of the National Health Service (Clinical Negligence Scheme) Regulations 1996, the National Health Service (Existing Liabilities Scheme) Regulations 1996 or a qualifying expense for the purposes of the National Health Service (Property Expenses Scheme) Regulations 1999.

(2) In this regulation –

'board member' means, in respect of a member, any member of the board of that member whether or not that person is an employee of that member;

'personal injury' includes bodily injury, death, disease, illness and nervous shock and is to be treated as including wrongful arrest, detention, imprisonment and malicious prosecution;

'relevant person' means, in respect of a member, a person employed or engaged by that member;

'qualifying liability' means, in respect of a member, a liability which falls within one or more of the following categories –

(i) a liability in respect of personal injury sustained by a relevant person arising out of and in the course of his or her employment or engagement by the member;

(ii) a liability in respect of or consequent upon personal injury or loss arising out of or in connection with any breach of a duty of care or breach of any statutory duty or breach of a duty under any of the Occupiers' Liability Act 1957, the Occupiers' Liability Act 1984 or the Defective Premises Act 1972 in each case owed by the member to any person in consequence of any act or omission to act on the part of any relevant person;

(iii) a contractual liability in respect of personal injury to any person or damage to any property of any third party;

(iv) a liability arising out of the act or omission to act on the part of a relevant person which is dishonest, fraudulent, criminal or malicious;

(v) a liability arising out of the making or publishing of any defamatory statement (whether in written or oral form) by the member or a relevant person;

(vi) a contractual liability to make payment to any relevant person in connection with any personal injury sustained by the relevant person directly as a result of assault;

(vii) any legally enforceable liability in respect of or consequent upon personal injury or loss arising out of or in connection with any tortious or other wrongful act committed by any relevant person;

(viii) a liability arising out of any indemnity properly given by any member to any board member;

(ix) any liability in respect of any consequential or ancillary expense which arises in connection with any liability referred to in any of the above categories.

(3) The Secretary of State and a member may agree –

(a) a minimum level of liability which must arise before a payment or other provision in respect of such a liability may be made under the Scheme; and

(b) an amount which is to be the maximum amount of any payment or other provision in respect of such a liability which may be made under the Scheme.

The Unfair Terms in Consumer Contracts Regulations 1999

(SI 1999, No. 2083)

3   Interpretation

(1) In these Regulations –

'the Community' means the European Community;

'consumer' means any natural person who, in contracts covered by these Regulations, is acting for purposes which are outside his trade, business or profession;

'court' in relation to England and Wales and Northern Ireland means a county court or the High Court, and in relation to Scotland, the Sheriff or the Court of Session;

'EEA Agreement' means the Agreement on the European Economic Area signed at Oporto on 2nd May 1992 as adjusted by the protocol signed at Brussels on 17th March 1993;

'Member State' means a State which is a contracting party to the EEA Agreement;

'notified' means notified in writing;

'qualifying body' means a person specified in Schedule 1;

'seller or supplier' means any natural or legal person who, in contracts covered by these Regulations, is acting for purposes relating to his trade, business or profession, whether publicly owned or privately owned;

'unfair terms' means the contractual terms referred to in regulation 5.

4   Terms to which these Regulations apply

(1) These Regulations apply in relation to unfair terms in contracts concluded between a seller or a supplier and a consumer.

(2) These Regulations do not apply to contractual terms which reflect –

(a) mandatory statutory or regulatory provisions (including such provisions under the law of any Member State or in Community legislation having effect in the United Kingdom without further enactment);

(b) the provisions or principles of international conventions to which the Member States or the Community are party.

5   Unfair terms

(1) A contractual term which has not been individually negotiated shall be regarded as unfair if, contrary to the requirement of good faith, it causes a significant imbalance in the parties' rights and obligations arising under the contract, to the detriment of the consumer.

(2) A term shall always be regarded as not having been individually negotiated where it has been drafted in advance and the consumer has therefore not been able to influence the substance of the term.

(3) Notwithstanding that a specific term or certain aspects of it in a contract has been individually negotiated, these Regulations shall apply to the rest of a contract if an overall assessment of it indicates that it is a pre-formulated standard contract.

(4) It shall be for any seller or supplier who claims that a term was individually negotiated to show that it was.

(5) Schedule 2 to these Regulations contains an indicative and non-exhaustive list of the terms which may be regarded as unfair.

6   Assessment of unfair terms

(1) Without prejudice to regulation 12, the unfairness of a contractual term shall be assessed, taking into account the nature of the goods or services for which the contract was concluded and by referring, at the time of conclusion of the contract, to all the circumstances attending the conclusion of the contract and to all the other terms of the contract or of another contract on which it is dependent.

(2) In so far as it is in plain intelligible language, the assessment of fairness of a term shall not relate –

(a) to the definition of the main subject matter of the contract, or

(b) to the adequacy of the price or remuneration, as against the goods or services supplied in exchange.

7   Written contracts

(1) A seller or supplier shall ensure that any written term of a contract is expressed in plain, intelligible language.

(2) If there is doubt about the meaning of a written term, the interpretation which is most favourable to the consumer shall prevail but this rule shall not apply in proceedings brought under regulation 12.

8 Effect of unfair term

(1) An unfair term in a contract concluded with a consumer by a seller or supplier shall not be binding on the consumer.

(2) The contract shall continue to bind the parties if it is capable of continuing in existence without the unfair term.

9 Choice of law clauses

These Regulations shall apply notwithstanding any contract term which applies or purports to apply the law of a non-Member State, if the contract has a close connection with the territory of the Member States.

10 Complaints – consideration by OFT

(1) It shall be the duty of the OFT to consider any complaint made to it that any contract term drawn up for general use is unfair, unless –

(a) the complaint appears to the OFT to be frivolous or vexatious; or

(b) a qualifying body has notified the OFT that it agrees to consider the complaint.

12 Injunctions to prevent continued use of unfair terms

(1) The OFT or, subject to paragraph (2), any qualifying body may apply for an injunction (including an interim injunction) against any person appearing to the OFT or that body to be using, or recommending use of, an unfair term drawn up for general use in contracts concluded with consumers.

(3) The court on an application under this regulation may grant an injunction on such terms as it thinks fit.

(4) An injunction may relate not only to use of a particular contract term drawn up for general use but to any similar term, or a term having like effect, used or recommended for use by any person.

Data Protection (Subject Access Modification) (Health) Order 2000

(SI 2000, No. 413)

2 Interpretation

In this Order –

'the Act' means the Data Protection Act 1998;

'the appropriate health professional' means –

(a) the health professional who is currently or was most recently responsible for the clinical care of the data subject in connection with the matters to which the information which is the subject of the request relates; or

(b) where there is more than one such health professional, the health professional who is the most suitable to advise on the matters to which the information which is the subject of the request relates; or

(c) where –

(i) there is no health professional available falling within paragraph (a) or (b), or

(ii) the data controller is the Secretary of State and data to which this Order applies are processed in connection with the exercise of the functions conferred on him by or under the Child Support Act 1991 and the Child Support Act 1995 or his functions in relation to social security or war pensions, a health professional who has the necessary experience and qualifications to advise on the matters to which the information which is the subject of the request relates;

'care' includes examination, investigation, diagnosis and treatment;

'request' means a request made under section 7;

'section 7' means section 7 of the Act.

3   Personal data to which Order applies

(1) Subject to paragraph (2), this Order applies to personal data consisting of information as to the physical or mental health or condition of the data subject.

(2) This Order does not apply to any data which are exempted from section 7 by an order made under section 38(1) of the Act.

4   Exemption from the subject information provisions

(1) Personal data falling within paragraph (2) and to which this Order applies are exempt from the subject information provisions.

(2) This paragraph applies to personal data processed by a court and consisting of information supplied in a report or other evidence given to the court by a local authority, Health and Social Services Board, Health and Social Services Trust, probation officer or other person in the course of any proceedings to which the Family Proceedings Courts (Children Act 1989) Rules 1991, the Magistrates' Courts (Children and Young Persons) Rules 1992, the Magistrates' Courts (Criminal Justice (Children)) Rules (Northern Ireland) 1999, the Act of Sederunt (Child Care and Maintenance Rules) 1997 or the Children's Hearings (Scotland) Rules 1996 apply where, in accordance with a provision of any of those Rules, the information may be withheld by the court in whole or in part from the data subject.

5   Exemptions from section 7

(1) Personal data to which this Order applies are exempt from section 7 in any case to the extent to which the application of that section would be likely to cause serious harm to the physical or mental health or condition of the data subject or any other person.

(2) Subject to article 7(1), a data controller who is not a health professional shall not withhold information constituting data to which this Order applies on the ground that the exemption in paragraph (1) applies with respect to the information unless the data controller has first consulted the person who appears to the data controller to be the appropriate health professional on the question whether or not the exemption in paragraph (1) applies with respect to the information.

(3) Where any person falling within paragraph (4) is enabled by or under any enactment or rule of law to make a request on behalf of a data subject and has made such a request, personal data to which this Order applies are exempt from section 7 in any case to the extent to which the application of that section would disclose information.

(a) provided by the data subject in the expectation that it would not be disclosed to the person making the request;

(b) obtained as a result of any examination or investigation to which the data subject consented in the expectation that the information would not be so disclosed; or

(c) which the data subject has expressly indicated should not be so disclosed, provided that sub-paragraphs (a) and (b) shall not prevent disclosure where the data subject has expressly indicated that he no longer has the expectation referred to therein.

(4) A person falls within this paragraph if –

(a) except in relation to Scotland, the data subject is a child, and that person has parental responsibility for that data subject;

(b) in relation to Scotland, the data subject is a person under the age of sixteen, and that person has parental responsibilities for that data subject; or

(c) the data subject is incapable of managing his own affairs and that person has been appointed by a court to manage those affairs.

6   Modification of section 7 relating to data controllers who are not health professionals

(1) Subject to paragraph (2) and article 7(3), section 7 of the Act is modified so that a data controller who is not a health professional shall not communicate information constituting data to which this Order applies in response to a request unless the data controller has first consulted the person who appears to the data controller to be the appropriate health professional on the question

whether or not the exemption in article 5(1) applies with respect to the information.

(2) Paragraph (1) shall not apply to the extent that the request relates to information which the data controller is satisfied has previously been seen by the data subject or is already within the knowledge of the data subject.

7   Additional provision relating to data controllers who are not health professionals

(1) Subject to paragraph (2), article 5(2) shall not apply in relation to any request where the data controller has consulted the appropriate health professional prior to receiving the request and obtained in writing from that appropriate health professional an opinion that the exemption in article 5(1) applies with respect to all of the information which is the subject of the request.

(2) Paragraph (1) does not apply where the opinion either –

    (a) was obtained before the period beginning six months before the relevant day (as defined by section 7(10) of the Act) and ending on that relevant day, or

    (b) was obtained within that period and it is reasonable in all the circumstances to re-consult the appropriate health professional.

(3) Article 6(1) shall not apply in relation to any request where the data controller has consulted the appropriate health professional prior to receiving the request and obtained in writing from that appropriate health professional an opinion that the exemption in article 5(1) does not apply with respect to all of the information which is the subject of the request.

8   Further modifications of section 7

In relation to data to which this Order applies –

    (a) section 7(4) of the Act shall have effect as if there were inserted after paragraph (b) of that subsection 'or, (c) the information is contained in a health record and the other individual is a health professional who has compiled or contributed to the health record or has been involved in the care of the data subject in his capacity as a health professional';

    (b) section 7(9) shall have effect as if –

        (i) there was substituted –

            '(9) If a court is satisfied on the application of –

        (a) any person who has made a request under the foregoing provisions of this section, or

        (b) any other person to whom serious harm to his physical or mental health or condition would be likely to be caused by compliance with any such request in contravention of those provisions, that the data controller in question is about to comply with or has failed to comply with the request in contravention of those provisions, the court may order him not to comply or, as the case may be, to comply with the request.'; and

        (ii) the reference therein to a contravention of the foregoing provisions of that section included a reference to a contravention of the provisions contained in this Order.

Public Health

The Vaccine Damage Payments (Specified Disease) Order 2001

(SI 2001, No. 1652)

1   Citation, commencement and interpretation

(2) In this Order, 'the Act' means the Vaccine Damage Payments Act 1979.

2   Addition to the diseases to which the Act applies

Meningococcal Group C is specified as a disease to which the Act applies.

3   Modification of conditions of entitlement

The condition of entitlement in section 2(1)(b) of the Act (age or time at which vaccination was carried out) shall be omitted in relation to vaccination against Meningococcal Group C.

National Health Service, England and Wales

The Health Service (Control of Patient Information) Regulations 2002

(SI 2002, No. 1438)

1   Citation, commencement, interpretation and extent

(2) In these Regulations –

'the Act' means the Health and Social Care Act 2001;

'public authority' has the same meaning as in section 3(1) of the Freedom of Information Act 2000;

'public health laboratory service' means the microbiological service provided by the Public Health Laboratory Service Board under section 5(2)(c) and (4) of the National Health Service Act 1977;

'research ethics committee' means –

    (a) an ethics committee established or recognised in accordance with Part 2 of the Medicines for Human Use (Clinical Trials) Regulations 2004, or

    (b) any other committee established to advise on the ethics of research investigations in human beings, and recognised for that purpose by or on behalf of the Secretary of State.

(3) Any notice given under these Regulations shall be –

    (a) in writing; or

    (b) transmitted by electronic means in a legible form which is capable of being used for subsequent reference.

2   Medical purposes related to the diagnosis or treatment of neoplasia

(1) Subject to paragraphs (2) to (4) and regulation 7, confidential patient information relating to patients referred for the diagnosis or treatment of neoplasia may be processed for medical purposes which comprise or include –

    (a) the surveillance and analysis of health and disease;

    (b) the monitoring and audit of health and health related care provision and outcomes where such provision has been made;

    (c) the planning and administration of the provision made for health and health related care;

    (d) medical research approved by research ethics committees;

    (e) the provision of information about individuals who have suffered from a particular disease or condition where –

        (i) that information supports an analysis of the risk of developing that disease or condition; and

        (ii) it is required for the counseling and support of a person who is concerned about the risk of developing that disease or condition.

(2) For the purposes of this regulation, 'processing' includes (in addition to the use, disclosure or obtaining of information) any operations, or set of operations, which are undertaken in order to establish or maintain databases for the purposes set out in paragraph (1), including –

    (a) the recording and holding of information;

    (b) the retrieval, alignment and combination of information;

(c) the organisation, adaption or alteration of information;

(d) the blocking, erasure and destruction of information.

(3) The processing of confidential patient information for the purposes specified in paragraph (1) may be undertaken by persons who (either individually or as members of a class) are –

(a) approved by the Secretary of State, and

(b) authorized by the person who lawfully holds the information.

(4) Where the Secretary of State considers that it is necessary in the public interest that confidential patient information is processed for a purpose specified in paragraph (1), he may give notice to any person who is approved and authorized under paragraph (3) to require that person to process that information for that purpose and any such notice may require that the information is processed forthwith or within such period as is specified in the notice.

(5) A person who processes confidential patient information under this regulation shall inform the Patient Information Advisory Group of that processing and shall make available to the Secretary of State such information as he may require to assist him in the investigation and audit of that processing and in his annual consideration of the provisions of these Regulations which is required by section 60(4) of the Act.

3   Communicable disease and other risks to public health

(1) Subject to paragraphs (2) and (3) and regulation 7, confidential patient information may be processed with a view to –

(a) diagnosing communicable diseases and other risks to public health;

(b) recognising trends in such diseases and risks;

(c) controlling and preventing the spread of such diseases and risks;

(d) monitoring and managing –

(i) outbreaks of communicable disease;

(ii) incidents of exposure to communicable disease;

(iii) the delivery, efficacy and safety of immunisation programmes;

(iv) adverse reactions to vaccines and medicines;

(v) risks of infection acquired from food or the environment (including water supplies);

(vi) the giving of information to persons about the diagnosis of communicable disease and risks of acquiring such disease.

(2) For the purposes of this regulation, 'processing' includes any operations, or set of operations set out in regulation 2(2) which are undertaken for the purposes set out in paragraph (1).

(3) The processing of confidential patient information for the purposes specified in paragraph (1) may be undertaken by –

(a) the Public Health Laboratory Service;

(b) persons employed or engaged for the purposes of the health service;

(c) other persons employed or engaged by a Government Department or other public authority in communicable disease surveillance.

(4) Where the Secretary of State considers that it is necessary to process patient information for a purpose specified in paragraph (1), he may give notice to any body or person specified in paragraph (2) to require that person or body to process that information for that purpose and any such notice may require that the information is processed forthwith or within such period as is specified in the notice.

(5) Where confidential information is processed under this regulation, the bodies and persons specified in paragraph (2) shall make available to the Secretary of State such information as he may require to assist him in the investigation and audit of that processing and in his annual consideration of the provisions of these Regulations which is required by section 60(4) of the Act.

4   Modifying the obligation of confidence

Anything done by a person that is necessary for the purpose of processing confidential patient information in accordance with these Regulations shall be taken to be lawfully done despite any obligation of confidence owed by that person in respect of it.

5   General

Subject to regulation 7, confidential patient information may be processed for medical purposes in the circumstances set out in the Schedule to these Regulations provided that the processing has been approved –

    (a) in the case of medical research, by both the Secretary of State and a research ethics committee, and

    (b) in any other case, by the Secretary of State.

6   Registration

(1) Where an approval granted by the Secretary of State under regulation 5 permits the transfer of confidential patient information between persons who may determine the purposes for which, and the manner in which, the information may be processed, he shall record in a register the name and address of each of those persons together with the particulars specified in paragraph (2).

(2) The following particulars are specified for inclusion in each entry in the register –

    (a) a description of the confidential patient information to which the approval relates;

    (b) the medical purposes for which the information may be processed;

    (c) the provisions in the Schedule to these Regulations under which the information may be processed; and

    (d) such other particulars as the Secretary of State may consider appropriate to enter in the register.

(3) The Secretary of State shall retain the particulars of each entry in the register for so long as confidential patient information may be processed under an approval and for not less than 12 months after the termination of an approval.

(4) The Secretary of State shall, in such manner and to the extent to which he considers it appropriate, publish entries in the register.

7   Restrictions and exclusions

(1) Where a person is in possession of confidential patient information under these Regulations, he shall not process that information more than is necessary to achieve the purposes for which he is permitted to process that information under these Regulations and, in particular, he shall –

    (a) so far as it is practical to do so, remove from the information any particulars which identify the person to whom it relates which are not required for the purposes for which it is, or is to be, processed;

    (b) not allow any person access to that information other than a person who, by virtue of his contract of employment or otherwise, is involved in processing the information for one or more of those purposes and is aware of the purpose or purposes for which the information may be processed;

    (c) ensure that appropriate technical and organisational measures are taken to prevent unauthorised processing of that information;

    (d) review at intervals not exceeding 12 months the need to process confidential patient information and the extent to which it is practicable to reduce the confidential patient information which is being processed;

    (e) on request by any person or body, make available information on the steps taken to comply with these Regulations.

(2) No person shall process confidential patient information under these Regulations unless he is a health professional or a person who in the circumstances owes a duty of confidentiality which is equivalent to that which would arise if that person were a health professional.

(3) For the purposes of paragraph (2) 'health professional' has the same meaning as in section 69(1) of the Data Protection Act 1998.

8   Enforcement procedure

(1) Any person who does not comply with a requirement imposed on him under regulation 2(4) or (5), 3(4) or (5) or 7 may be subject to a civil penalty of not exceeding £5000.

(2) The Secretary of State may determine whether any person has not complied with such a requirement and he may assess whether it is appropriate to impose the maximum civil penalty, a lesser penalty or no penalty having regard to the seriousness of any non-compliance, the circumstances of any person who has not complied and the need to ensure the compliance in respect of any such future requirements.

(3) Any penalty payable under this regulation shall be recoverable by the Secretary of State as a civil debt.

The Schedule

Regulations 5 and 6(2)(c)

General Provisions

Circumstances in which confidential patient information may be processed for medical purposes under regulation 5 of these Regulations.

1. The processing of confidential patient information for medical purposes with a view to making the patient in question less readily identifiable from that information.

2. The processing of confidential patient information that relates to the present or past geographical locations of patients (including where necessary information from which patients may be identified) which is required for medical research into the locations at which disease or other medical conditions may occur.

3. The processing of confidential patient information to enable the lawful holder of that information to identify and contact patients for the purpose of obtaining consent –

    (a) to participate in medical research;

    (b) to use the information for the purposes of medical research, or

    (c) to allow the use of tissue or other samples for medical purposes.

4. The processing of confidential patient information for medical purposes from more than one source with a view to –

    (a) linking information from more than one of those sources;

    (b) validating the quality or completeness of –

        (i) confidential patient information, or

        (ii) data derived from such information;

    (c) avoiding the impairment of the quality of data derived from confidential patient information by incorrect linkage or the unintentional inclusion of the same information more than once.

5. The audit, monitoring and analysing of the provision made by the health service for patient care and treatment.

6. The granting of access to confidential patient information for one or more of the above purposes.

The National Health Service (General Medical Services Contracts) Regulations 2004

(SI 2004, No. 291)

Part I General

Interpretation

2.—(1) In these Regulations –

'the Act' means the National Health Service Act 1977; [*sic*]

'the 1990 Act' means the National Health Service and Community Care Act 1990;

'the 2003 Order' means the General and Specialist Medical Practice (Education, Training and Qualifications) Order 2003;

'additional services' means one or more of –

(a) cervical screening services,

(b) contraceptive services,

(c) vaccinations and immunisations,

(d) childhood vaccinations and immunisations,

(e) child health surveillance services,

(f) maternity medical services, and

(g) minor surgery;

'adjudicator' means the Secretary of State or a person or persons appointed by the Secretary of State under section 4(5) of the 1990 Act or paragraph 101(5) of Schedule 6;

'approved medical practice' shall be construed in accordance with section 11(4) of the Medical Act 1983;

'assessment panel' means a committee or sub-committee of a Primary Care Trust (other than the Primary Care Trust which is a party to the contract in question) appointed to exercise functions under paragraphs 31 and 35 of Schedule 6;

'cervical screening services' means the services described in paragraph 2(2) of Schedule 2;

'child' means a person who has not attained the age of 16 years;

'child health surveillance services' means the services described in paragraph 6(2) of Schedule 2;

'childhood vaccinations and immunisations' means the services described in paragraph 5(2) of Schedule 2;

'closed', in relation to the contractor's list of patients, means closed to applications for inclusion in the list of patients other than from immediate family members of registered patients;

'contraceptive services' means the services described in paragraph 3(2) of Schedule 2;

'contract' means, except where the context otherwise requires, a general medical services contract under section 28Q of the Act;

'contractor's list of patients' means the list prepared and maintained by the Primary Care Trust under paragraph 14 of Schedule 6;

'core hours' means the period beginning at 8am and ending at 6.30pm on any day from Monday to Friday except Good Friday, Christmas Day or bank holidays;

'enhanced services' are–

(a) services other than essential services, additional services or out of hours services, or

(b) essential services, additional services or out of hours services or an element of such a service that a contractor agrees under the contract to provide in accordance with specifications set out in a plan, which requires of the contractor an enhanced level of service provision compared to that which it needs generally to provide in relation to that service or element of service;

'essential services' means the services required to be provided in accordance with regulation 15;

'FHSAA' means the Family Health Services Appeal Authority constituted under section 49S of the Act;

'general medical practitioner' means –

(a) from the coming into force of article 10 of the 2003 Order, a medical practitioner whose name is included in the General Practitioner Register otherwise than by virtue of paragraph 1(d) of Schedule 6 to that Order;

'General Practitioner Register' means the register kept by the General Medical Council under article 10 of the 2003 Order;

'global sum' has the same meaning as in the GMS Statement of Financial Entitlements;

'health care professional' has the same meaning as in section 28M of the Act and 'health care profession' shall be construed accordingly;

'health service body' has, unless the context otherwise requires, the meaning given to it in section 4(2) of the 1990 Act;

'immediate family member' means –

(a) a spouse,

(b) a person (whether or not of the opposite sex) whose relationship with the registered patient has the characteristics of the relationship between husband and wife,

(c) a parent or step-parent,

(d) a son,

(e) a daughter,

(f) a child of whom the registered patient is –

(i) the guardian, or

(ii) the carer duly authorised by the local authority to whose care the child has been committed under the Children Act 1989, or

(g) a grandparent;

'Local Medical Committee' means a committee recognised under section 45A of the Act;

'maternity medical services' means the services described in paragraph 7(1) of Schedule 2;

'medical card' means a card issued by a Primary Care Trust, Local Health Board, Health Authority, Health Board or Health and Social Services Board to a person for the purpose of enabling him to obtain, or establishing his title to receive, primary medical services;

'medical officer' means a medical practitioner who is –

(a) employed or engaged by the Department for Work and Pensions, or

(b) provided by an organisation in pursuance of a contract entered into with the Secretary of State for Work and Pensions;

'medical performers list' means a list of medical practitioners prepared in accordance with regulations made under section 28X of the Act;

'Medical Register' means the registers kept under section 2 of the Medical Act 1983;

'minor surgery' means the services described in paragraph 8(2) of Schedule 2;

'NCAA' means the National Clinical Assessment Authority established as a Special Health Authority under section 11 of the Act;

'national disqualification' means –

(a) a decision made by the FHSAA under section 49N of the Act;

'NHS contract' has the meaning assigned to it in section 4 of the 1990 Act;

'the NHS dispute resolution procedure' means the procedure for resolution of disputes specified –

(a) in paragraphs 101 and 102 of Schedule 6; or

(b) in a case to which paragraph 36 of Schedule 6 applies, in that paragraph;

'normal hours' means those days and hours on which and the times at which services under the contract are normally made available and may be different for different services;

'open', in relation to a contractor's list of patients, means open to applications from patients in accordance with paragraph 15 of Schedule 6;

'out of hours period' means –

(a) the period beginning at 6.30pm on any day from Monday to Thursday and ending at 8am on the following day,

(b) the period between 6.30pm on Friday and 8am on the following Monday, and

(c) Good Friday, Christmas Day and bank holidays,

and 'part' of an out of hours period means any part of any one or more of the periods described in paragraphs (a) to (c); 'out of hours services' means services required to be provided in all or part of the out of hours period which –

(a) would be essential services if provided in core hours, or

(b) are included in the contract as additional services funded under the global sum;

'parent' includes, in relation to any child, any adult who, in the opinion of the contractor, is for the time being discharging in respect of that child the obligations normally attaching to a parent in respect of his child;

'patient' means –

(a) a registered patient,

(b) a temporary resident,

(c) persons to whom the contractor is required to provide immediately necessary treatment under regulation 15(6) or (8) respectively,

(d) any other person to whom the contractor has agreed to provide services under the contract,

(e) any person for whom the contractor is responsible under regulation 31, and

(f) any person for whom the contractor is responsible under arrangements made with another contractor in accordance with Schedule 7;

'PCT Patients' Forum' means a Patients' Forum established for a Primary Care Trust under section 15 of the National Health Service Reform and Health Care Professions Act 2002;

'practice' means the business operated by the contractor for the purpose of delivering services under the contract;

'practice area' means the area referred to in regulation 18(1)(d);

'practice leaflet' means a leaflet drawn up in accordance with paragraph 76 of Schedule 6;

'practice premises' means an address specified in the contract as one at which services are to be provided under the contract;

'primary care list' means –

(a) a list of persons performing primary medical or dental services prepared in accordance with regulations made under section 28X of the Act,

(b) a list of persons undertaking to provide general medical services, general dental services, general ophthalmic services or, as the case may be, pharmaceutical services prepared in accordance with regulations made under sections 29, 36, 39, 42 or 43 of the Act,

(c) a list of persons approved for the purposes of assisting in the provision of any services mentioned in paragraph (b) prepared in accordance with regulations made under section 43D of the Act,

(d) a services list referred to in section 8ZA of the National Health Service (Primary Care) Act 1997,

(e) a list corresponding to a services list prepared by virtue of regulations made under section 41 of the Health and Social Care Act 2001;

'Primary Care Trust' means, unless the context otherwise requires, the Primary Care Trust which is a party, or prospective party, to the contract;

'primary carer' means, in relation to an adult, the adult or organisation primarily caring for him;

'registered patient' means –

(a) a person who is recorded by the Primary Care Trust as being on the contractor's list of patients, or

(b) a person whom the contractor has accepted for inclusion on its list of patients, whether or not notification of that acceptance has been received by the Primary Care Trust and who has not been notified by the Primary Care Trust as having ceased to be on that list;

'relevant Strategic Health Authority' means the Strategic Health Authority established for an area which includes the area for which the Primary Care Trust is established;

'section 28C provider' means a person who is providing services under a pilot scheme or in accordance with section 28C arrangements;

'temporary resident' means a person accepted by the contractor as a temporary resident under paragraph 16 of Schedule 6 and for whom the contractor's responsibility has not been terminated in accordance with that paragraph;

'walk-in centre' means a centre at which information and treatment for minor conditions is provided to the public under arrangements made by or on behalf of the Secretary of State;

'working day' means any day apart from Saturday, Sunday, Christmas Day, Good Friday or a bank holiday;

'writing', except in paragraph 104(1) of Schedule 6 and unless the context otherwise requires, includes electronic mail and 'written' shall be construed accordingly.

(2) In these Regulations, the use of the term 'it' in relation to the contractor shall be deemed to include a reference to a contractor that is an individual medical practitioner or two or more individuals practising in partnership and related expressions shall be construed accordingly.

Part II Contractors

Conditions: general

3. Subject to the provisions of any order made by the Secretary of State under section 176 of the Health and Social Care (Community Health and Standards) Act 2003 (general medical services: transitional), a Primary Care Trust may only enter into a contract if the conditions set out in regulations 4 and 5 are met.

Conditions relating solely to medical practitioners

4.—(1) In the case of a contract to be entered into with a medical practitioner, that practitioner must be a general medical practitioner.

(2) In the case of a contract to be entered into with two or more individuals practising in partnership –

(a) at least one partner (who must not be a limited partner) must be a general medical practitioner; and

(b) any other partner who is a medical practitioner must –

(i) be a general medical practitioner, or

(ii) be employed by a Primary Care Trust, a Local Health Board, (in England and Wales and Scotland) an NHS Trust, an NHS foundation trust, (in Scotland) a Health Board or (in Northern Ireland) a Health and Social Services Trust.

(3) In the case of a contract to be entered into with a company limited by shares –

(a) at least one share in the company must be legally and beneficially owned by a general medical practitioner; and

(b) any other share or shares in the company that are legally and beneficially owned by a medical practitioner must be so owned by –

(i) a general medical practitioner, or

(ii) a medical practitioner who is employed by a Primary Care Trust, a Local Health Board, (in England and Wales and Scotland) an NHS Trust, an NHS foundation trust, (in Scotland) a Health Board or (in Northern Ireland) a Health and Social Services Trust.

General condition relating to all contracts

5.—(1) It is a condition in the case of a contract to be entered into –

    (a) with a medical practitioner, that the medical practitioner;

    (b) with two or more individuals practising in partnership, that any individual or the partnership; and

    (c) with a company limited by shares, that –

        (i) the company,

        (ii) any person legally and beneficially owning a share in the company, and

        (iii) any director or secretary of the company, must not fall within paragraph (2).

 (2) A person falls within this paragraph if –

    (a) he or it is the subject of a national disqualification;

    (b) subject to paragraph (3), he or it is disqualified or suspended (other than by an interim suspension order or direction pending an investigation) from practising by any licensing body anywhere in the world;

    (c) within the period of five years prior to the signing of the contract or commencement of the contract, whichever is the earlier, he has been dismissed (otherwise than by reason of redundancy) from any employment by a health service body, unless he has subsequently been employed by that health service body or another health service body and paragraph (4) applies to him or that dismissal was the subject of a finding of unfair dismissal by any competent tribunal or court;

    (d) within the period of five years prior to signing the contract or commencement of the contract, whichever is the earlier, he or it has been removed from, or refused admission to, a primary care list by reason of inefficiency, fraud or unsuitability (within the meaning of section 49F(2), (3) and (4) of the Act respectively) unless his name has subsequently been included in such a list;

    (e) he has been convicted in the United Kingdom of murder;

    (f) he has been convicted in the United Kingdom of a criminal offence other than murder, committed on or after 14th December 2001, and has been sentenced to a term of imprisonment of over six months;

    (g) subject to paragraph (5) he has been convicted elsewhere of an offence –

        (i) which would, if committed in England and Wales, constitute murder, or

        (ii) committed on or after 14th December 2001, which would if committed in England and Wales, constitute a criminal offence other than murder, and been sentenced to a term of imprisonment of over six months;

    (h) he has been convicted of an offence referred to in Schedule 1 to the Children and Young Persons Act 1933 (offences against children and young persons with respect to which special provisions of this Act apply) or Schedule 1 to the Criminal Procedure (Scotland) Act 1995 (offences against children under the age of 17 years to which special provisions apply) committed on or after 1st March 2004;

    (i) he or it has –

        (i) been adjudged bankrupt or had sequestration of his estate awarded unless (in either case) he has been discharged or the bankruptcy order has been annulled,

        (ii) been made the subject of a bankruptcy restrictions order or an interim bankruptcy restrictions order under Schedule 4A to the Insolvency Act 1986 unless that order has ceased to have effect or has been annulled, or

        (iii) made a composition or arrangement with, or granted a trust deed for, his or its creditors unless he or it has been discharged in respect of it;

    (j) an administrator, administrative receiver or receiver is appointed in respect of it;

    (k) he has been –

(i) removed from the office of charity trustee or trustee for a charity by an order made by the Charity Commissioners or the High Court on the grounds of any misconduct or mismanagement in the administration of the charity for which he was responsible or to which he was privy, or which he by his conduct contributed to or facilitated ...

(l) he is subject to a disqualification order under the Company Directors Disqualification Act 1986 or to an order made under section 429(2)(b) of the Insolvency Act 1986 (failure to pay under county court administration order).

(3) A person shall not fall within paragraph (2)(b) where the Primary Care Trust is satisfied that the disqualification or suspension from practising is imposed by a licensing body outside the United Kingdom and it does not make the person unsuitable to be –

(a) a contractor;

(b) a partner, in the case of a contract with two or more individuals practising in partnership;

(c) in the case of a contract with a company limited by shares –

(i) a person legally and beneficially holding a share in the company, or

(ii) a director or secretary of the company, as the case may be.

(4) Where a person has been employed as a member of a health care profession any subsequent employment must also be as a member of that profession.

(5) A person shall not fall within paragraph (2)(g) where the Primary Care Trust is satisfied that the conviction does not make the person unsuitable to be –

(a) a contractor;

(b) a partner, in the case of a contract with two or more individuals practising in partnership;

(c) in the case of a contract with a company limited by shares –

(i) a person legally and beneficially holding a share in the company, or

(ii) a director or secretary of the company, as the case may be.

Part IV Health Service Body Status

Health service body status

10.—(1) Where a proposed contractor elects in a written notice served on the Primary Care Trust at any time prior to the contract being entered into to be regarded as a health service body for the purposes of section 4 of the 1990 Act, it shall be so regarded from the date on which the contract is entered into.

Part V Contracts: Required Terms

Parties to the contract

11. A contract must specify –

(a) the names of the parties;

(b) in the case of a partnership –

(i) whether or not it is a limited partnership, and

(ii) the names of the partners and, in the case of a limited partnership, their status as a general or limited partner; and

(c) in the case of each party, the address to which official correspondence and notices should be sent.

Health service contract

12. If the contractor is to be regarded as a health service body pursuant to regulation 10, the contract must state that it is an NHS contract.

Contracts with individuals practising in partnership

13.—(1) Where the contract is with two or more individuals practising in partnership, the contract shall be treated as made with the partnership as it is from time to time constituted, and the contract shall make specific provision to this effect.

Essential services

15.—(1) For the purposes of section 28R(1) of the Act (requirement to provide certain primary medical services), the services which must be provided under a general medical services contract ('essential services') are the services described in paragraphs (3), (5), (6) and (8).

(2) Subject to regulation 20, a contractor must provide the services described in paragraphs (3) and (5) throughout the core hours.

(3) The services described in this paragraph are services required for the management of its registered patients and temporary residents who are, or believe themselves to be –

    (a) ill, with conditions from which recovery is generally expected;

    (b) terminally ill; or

    (c) suffering from chronic disease, delivered in the manner determined by the practice in discussion with the patient.

(4) For the purposes of paragraph (3) –

'disease' means a disease included in the list of three-character categories contained in the tenth revision of the International Statistical Classification of Diseases and Related Health Problems; and

    'management' includes –

    (a) offering consultation and, where appropriate, physical examination for the purpose of identifying the need, if any, for treatment or further investigation; and

    (b) the making available of such treatment or further investigation as is necessary and appropriate, including the referral of the patient for other services under the Act and liaison with other health care professionals involved in the patient's treatment and care.

(5) The services described in this paragraph are the provision of appropriate ongoing treatment and care to all registered patients and temporary residents taking account of their specific needs including –

    (a) the provision of advice in connection with the patient's health, including relevant health promotion advice; and

    (b) the referral of the patient for other services under the Act.

(6) A contractor must provide primary medical services required in core hours for the immediately necessary treatment of any person to whom the contractor has been requested to provide treatment owing to an accident or emergency at any place in its practice area.

(7) In paragraph (6), 'emergency' includes any medical emergency whether or not related to services provided under the contract.

(8) A contractor must provide primary medical services required in core hours for the immediately necessary treatment of any person falling within paragraph (9) who requests such treatment, for the period specified in paragraph (10).

(9) A person falls within paragraph (8) if he is a person –

    (a) whose application for inclusion in the contractor's list of patients has been refused in accordance with paragraph 17 of Schedule 6 and who is not registered with another provider of essential services (or their equivalent) in the area of the Primary Care Trust;

    (b) whose application for acceptance as a temporary resident has been rejected under paragraph 17 of Schedule 6; or

    (c) who is present in the contractor's practice area for less than 24 hours.

(10) The period referred to in paragraph (8) is –

    (a) in the case of paragraph (9)(a), 14 days beginning with the date on which that person's application was refused or until that person has been subsequently registered elsewhere for the provision of essential services (or their equivalent), whichever occurs first;

(b) in the case of paragraph (9)(b), 14 days beginning with the date on which that person's application was rejected or until that person has been subsequently accepted elsewhere as a temporary resident, whichever occurs first; and

(c) in the case of paragraph (9)(c), 24 hours or such shorter period as the person is present in the contractor's practice area.

Services generally

18.—(1) A contract must specify –

(a) the services to be provided;

(b) subject to paragraph (2), the address of each of the premises to be used by the contractor or any sub-contractor for the provision of such services;

(c) to whom such services are to be provided;

(d) the area as respects which persons resident in it will, subject to any other terms of the contract relating to patient registration, be entitled to –

(i) register with the contractor, or

(ii) seek acceptance by the contractor as a temporary resident; and

(e) whether, at the date on which the contract comes into force, the contractor's list of patients is open or closed.

(2) The premises referred to in paragraph (1)(b) do not include –

(a) the homes of patients; or

(b) any other premises where services are provided on an emergency basis.

20.   A contract must contain a term which requires the contractor in core hours –

(a) to provide –

(i) essential services, and

(ii) additional services funded under the global sum, at such times, within core hours, as are appropriate to meet the reasonable needs of its patients; and

(b) to have in place arrangements for its patients to access such services throughout the core hours in case of emergency.

Fees and charges

24.—(1) The contract must contain terms relating to fees and charges which have the same effect as those set out in paragraphs (2) to (4).

(2) The contractor shall not, either itself or through any other person, demand or accept from any patient of its a fee or other remuneration, for its own or another's benefit, for –

(a) the provision of any treatment whether under the contract or otherwise; or

(b) any prescription or repeatable prescription for any drug, medicine or appliance, except in the circumstances set out in Schedule 5.

(3) Where a person applies to a contractor for the provision of essential services and claims to be on that contractor's list of patients, but fails to produce his medical card on request and the contractor has reasonable doubts about that person's claim, the contractor shall give any necessary treatment and shall be entitled to demand and accept a reasonable fee in accordance with paragraph 1(e) of Schedule 5, subject to the provision for repayment contained in paragraph (4).

Part VI Functions of Local Medical Committees

27.—(1) The functions of a Local Medical Committee which are prescribed for the purposes of section 45A(9) (Local Medical Committees) of the Act are –

(a) the consideration of any complaint made to it by any medical practitioner against a medical practitioner specified in paragraph (2) providing services under a contract in the relevant area involving any question of the efficiency of those services;

(b) the reporting of the outcome of the consideration of any such complaint to the Primary Care Trust with whom the contract is held in cases where that consideration gives rise to any concerns relating to the efficiency of services provided under a contract;

(c) the making of arrangements for the medical examination of a medical practitioner specified in paragraph (2), where the contractor or the Primary Care Trust is concerned that the medical practitioner is incapable of adequately providing services under the contract and it so requests with the agreement of the medical practitioner concerned; and

(d) the consideration of the report of any medical examination arranged in accordance with sub-paragraph (c) and the making of a written report as to the capability of the medical practitioner of adequately providing services under the contract to the medical practitioner concerned, the contractor and the Primary Care Trust with whom the contractor holds a contract.

(2) The medical practitioner referred to in paragraph (1)(a) and (c) is a medical practitioner who is –

(a) a contractor;

(b) one of two or more individuals practising in partnership who hold a contract; or

(c) a legal and beneficial shareholder in a company which holds a contract.

Schedule 2, Regulation 16: Additional Services

Additional services generally

1. The contractor shall provide, in relation to each additional service, such facilities and equipment as are necessary to enable it properly to perform that service.

Cervical screening

2.—(1) A contractor whose contract includes the provision of cervical screening services shall –

(a) provide all the services described in sub-paragraph (2); and

(b) make such records as are referred to in sub-paragraph (3).

(2) The services referred to in sub-paragraph (1)(a) are –

(a) the provision of any necessary information and advice to assist women identified by the Primary Care Trust as recommended nationally for a cervical screening test in making an informed decision as to participation in the NHS Cervical Screening Programme;

(b) the performance of cervical screening tests on women who have agreed to participate in that Programme;

(c) arranging for women to be informed of the results of the test; and

(d) ensuring that test results are followed up appropriately.

(3) The records referred to in sub-paragraph (1)(b) are an accurate record of the carrying out of a cervical screening test, the result of the test and any clinical follow up requirements.

Contraceptive services

3.—(1) A contractor whose contract includes the provision of contraceptive services shall make available to all its patients who request such services the services described in sub-paragraph (2).

(2) The services referred to in sub-paragraph (1) are –

(a) the giving of advice about the full range of contraceptive methods;

(b) where appropriate, the medical examination of patients seeking such advice;

(c) the treatment of such patients for contraceptive purposes and the prescribing of contraceptive substances and appliances (excluding the fitting and implanting of intrauterine devices and implants);

(d) the giving of advice about emergency contraception and where appropriate, the supplying or prescribing of emergency hormonal contraception or, where the contractor has a conscientious objection to emergency contraception, prompt referral to another provider of primary medical services who does not have such conscientious objections;

(e) the provision of advice and referral in cases of unplanned or unwanted pregnancy, including advice about the availability of free pregnancy testing in the practice area and, where appropriate, where the contractor has a conscientious objection to the termination of pregnancy, prompt referral to another provider of primary medical services who does not have such conscientious objections;

(f) the giving of initial advice about sexual health promotion and sexually transmitted infections; and

(g) the referral as necessary for specialist sexual health services, including tests for sexually transmitted infections.

Vaccinations and immunisations

4.—(1) A contractor whose contract includes the provision of vaccinations and immunisations shall comply with the requirements in sub-paragraphs (2) and (3).

(2) The contractor shall –

(a) offer to provide to patients all vaccinations and immunisations (excluding childhood vaccinations and immunisations) of a type and in the circumstances for which a fee was provided for under the 2003–04 Statement of Fees and Allowances made under regulation 34 of the National Health Service (General Medical Services) Regulations 1992 other than influenza vaccination;

(b) provide appropriate information and advice to patients about such vaccinations and immunisations;

(c) record in the patient's record kept in accordance with paragraph 73 of Schedule 6 any refusal of the offer referred to in paragraph (a);

(d) where the offer is accepted, administer the vaccinations and immunisations and include in the patient's record kept in accordance with paragraph 73 of Schedule 6 –

(i) the patient's consent to the vaccination or immunisation or the name of the person who gave consent to the vaccination or immunisation and his relationship to the patient,

(ii) the batch numbers, expiry date and title of the vaccine,

(iii) the date of administration,

(iv) in a case where two vaccines are administered in close succession, the route of administration and the injection site of each vaccine,

(v) any contraindications to the vaccination or immunisation, and

(vi) any adverse reactions to the vaccination or immunisation.

(3) The contractor shall ensure that all staff involved in administering vaccines are trained in the recognition and initial treatment of anaphylaxis.

Childhood vaccinations and immunisations

5.—(1) A contractor whose contract includes the provision of childhood vaccinations and immunisations shall comply with the requirements in sub-paragraphs (2) and (3).

(2) The contractor shall –

(a) offer to provide to children all vaccinations and immunisations of a type and in the circumstances for which a fee was provided for under the 2003–04 Statement of Fees and Allowances made under regulation 34 of the National Health Service (General Medical Services) Regulations 1992;

(b) provide appropriate information and advice to patients and, where appropriate, their parents, about such vaccinations and immunisations;

(c) record in the patient's record kept in accordance with paragraph 73 of Schedule 6 any refusal of the offer referred to in paragraph (a);

(d) where the offer is accepted, administer the vaccinations and immunisations and include in the patient's record kept in accordance with paragraph 73 of Schedule 6 –

(i) the name of the person who gave consent to the vaccination or immunisation and his relationship to the patient;

    (ii) the batch numbers, expiry date and title of the vaccine;

    (iii) the date of administration;

    (iv) in a case where two vaccines are administered in close succession, the route of administration and the injection site of each vaccine;

    (v) any contraindications to the vaccination or immunisation; and

    (vi) any adverse reactions to the vaccination or immunisation.

(3) The contractor shall ensure that all staff involved in administering vaccines are trained in the recognition and initial treatment of anaphylaxis.

Child health surveillance

6.—(1) A contractor whose contract includes the provision of child health surveillance services shall, in respect of any child under the age of five for whom it has responsibility under the contract –

    (a) provide all the services described in sub-paragraph (2), other than any examination so described which the parent refuses to allow the child to undergo, until the date upon which the child attains the age of five years; and

    (b) maintain such records as are specified in sub-paragraph (3).

(2) The services referred to in sub-paragraph (1)(a) are –

    (a) the monitoring –

        (i)by the consideration of any information concerning the child received by or on behalf of the contractor, and

        (ii)on any occasion when the child is examined or observed by or on behalf of the contractor (whether pursuant to paragraph (b) or otherwise), of the health, well-being and physical, mental and social development (all of which characteristics are referred to in this paragraph as 'development') of the child while under the age of 5 years with a view to detecting any deviations from normal development;

    (b) the examination of the child at a frequency that has been agreed with the Primary Care Trust in accordance with the nationally agreed evidence based programme set out in the fourth edition of 'Health for all Children'.

(3) The records mentioned in sub-paragraph (1)(b) are an accurate record of –

    (a) the development of the child while under the age of 5 years, compiled as soon as is reasonably practicable following the first examination of that child and, where appropriate, amended following each subsequent examination; and

    (b) the responses (if any) to offers made to the child's parent for the child to undergo any examination referred to in sub-paragraph (2)(b).

Maternity medical services

7.—(1) A contractor whose contract includes the provision of maternity medical services shall –

    (a) provide to female patients who have been diagnosed as pregnant all necessary maternity medical services throughout the antenatal period;

    (b) provide to female patients and their babies all necessary maternity medical services throughout the postnatal period other than neonatal checks;

    (c) provide all necessary maternity medical services to female patients whose pregnancy has terminated as a result of miscarriage or abortion or, where the contractor has a conscientious objection to the termination of pregnancy, prompt referral to another provider of primary medical services who does not have such conscientious objections.

(2) In this paragraph –

'antenatal period' means the period from the start of the pregnancy to the onset of labour;

'maternity medical services' means –

    (a) in relation to female patients (other than babies) all primary medical services relating to pregnancy, excluding intra partum care, and

    (b) in relation to babies, any primary medical services necessary in their first 14 days of life;

'postnatal period' means the period starting from the conclusion of delivery of the baby or the patient's discharge from secondary care services, whichever is the later, and ending on the fourteenth day after the birth.

Minor surgery

8.—(1) A contractor whose contract includes the provision of minor surgery shall comply with the requirements in sub-paragraphs (2) and (3).

    (2) The contractor shall make available to patients where appropriate –

        (a) curettage;

        (b) cautery; and

        (c) cryocautery of warts, verrucae and other skin lesions.

    (3) The contractor shall ensure that its record of any treatment provided under this paragraph includes the consent of the patient to that treatment.

Schedule 5, Regulation 24: Fees and Charges

1. The contractor may demand or accept a fee or other remuneration –

    (a) from any statutory body for services rendered for the purposes of that body's statutory functions;

    (b) from any body, employer or school for a routine medical examination of persons for whose welfare the body, employer or school is responsible, or an examination of such persons for the purpose of advising the body, employer or school of any administrative action they might take;

    (c) for treatment which is not primary medical services or otherwise required to be provided under the contract and which is given –

        (i) pursuant to the provisions of section 65 of the Act (accommodation and services for private patients), or

        (ii) in a registered nursing home which is not providing services under that Act, if, in either case, the person administering the treatment is serving on the staff of a hospital providing services under the Act as a specialist providing treatment of the kind the patient requires and if, within 7 days of giving the treatment, the contractor or the person providing the treatment supplies the Primary Care Trust, on a form provided by it for the purpose, with such information about the treatment as it may require;

    (d) under section 158 of the Road Traffic Act 1988 (payment for emergency treatment of traffic casualties);

    (e) when it treats a patient under regulation 24(3), in which case it shall be entitled to demand and accept a reasonable fee (recoverable in certain circumstances under regulation 24(4)) for any treatment given, if it gives the patient a receipt;

    (f) for attending and examining (but not otherwise treating) a patient –

        (i) at his request at a police station in connection with possible criminal proceedings against him,

        (ii) at the request of a commercial, educational or not-for-profit organisation for the purpose of creating a medical report or certificate,

        (iii) for the purpose of creating a medical report required in connection with an actual or potential claim for compensation by the patient;

    (g) for treatment consisting of an immunisation for which no remuneration is payable by the Primary Care Trust and which is requested in connection with travel abroad;

    (h) for prescribing or providing drugs, medicines or appliances (including a collection of such drugs, medicines or appliances in the form of a travel kit) which a patient requires to have in his possession solely in anticipation of the onset of an ailment or occurrence of an injury while he is outside the United Kingdom but for which he is not requiring treatment when the medicine is prescribed;

(i) for a medical examination –

    (i) to enable a decision to be made whether or not it is inadvisable on medical grounds for a person to wear a seat belt, or

    (ii) for the purpose of creating a report –

        (aa) relating to a road traffic accident or criminal assault, or

        (bb) that offers an opinion as to whether a patient is fit to travel;

(j) for testing the sight of a person to whom none of paragraphs (a), (b) or (c) of section 38 (1) of the Act (arrangements for general ophthalmic services) applies (including by reason of regulations under section 38(6) of that Act);

(k) where it is a contractor which is authorised or required by a Primary Care Trust under regulation 20 of the Pharmaceutical Regulations or paragraphs 47 or 49 of Schedule 6 to provide drugs, medicines or appliances to a patient and provides for that patient, otherwise than by way of pharmaceutical services or dispensing services, any Scheduled drug;

(l) for prescribing or providing drugs or medicines for malaria chemoprophylaxis.

Schedule 6, Regulation 26: Other Contractual Terms

Part 1 Provision of Services

Premises

1. Subject to any plan which is included in the contract pursuant to regulation 18(3), the contractor shall ensure that the premises used for the provision of services under the contract are –

    (a) suitable for the delivery of those services; and

    (b) sufficient to meet the reasonable needs of the contractor's patients.

Attendance at practice premises

2.—(1) The contractor shall take steps to ensure that any patient who –

    (a) has not previously made an appointment; and

    (b) attends at the practice premises during the normal hours for essential services,

is provided with such services by an appropriate health care professional during that surgery period except in the circumstances specified in sub-paragraph (2).

    (2) The circumstances referred to in sub-paragraph (1) are that –

        (a) it is more appropriate for the patient to be referred elsewhere for services under the Act; or

        (b) he is then offered an appointment to attend again within a time which is appropriate and reasonable having regard to all the circumstances and his health would not thereby be jeopardised.

Attendance outside practice premises

3.—(1) In the case of a patient whose medical condition is such that in the reasonable opinion of the contractor –

    (a) attendance on the patient is required; and

    (b) it would be inappropriate for him to attend at the practice premises,

the contractor shall provide services to that patient at whichever in its judgement is the most appropriate of the places set out in sub-paragraph (2).

    (2) The places referred to in sub-paragraph (1) are –

        (a) the place recorded in the patient's medical records as being his last home address;

        (b) such other place as the contractor has informed the patient and the Primary Care Trust is the place where it has agreed to visit and treat the patient; or

        (c) some other place in the contractor's practice area.

(3) Nothing in this paragraph prevents the contractor from –
  (a) arranging for the referral of a patient without first seeing the patient, in a case where the medical condition of that patient makes that course of action appropriate; or
  (b) visiting the patient in circumstances where this paragraph does not place it under an obligation to do so.

Newly registered patients

4.—(1) Where a patient has been –
  (a) accepted on a contractor's list of patients under paragraph 15; or
  (b) assigned to that list by the Primary Care Trust,
the contractor shall, in addition and without prejudice to its other obligations in respect of that patient under the contract, invite the patient to participate in a consultation either at its practice premises or, if the medical condition of the patient so warrants, at one of the places referred to in paragraph 3(2).

(2) An invitation under sub-paragraph (1) shall be issued within six months of the date of the acceptance of the patient on, or their assignment to, the contractor's list.

(3) Where a patient (or, where appropriate, in the case of a patient who is a child, his parent) agrees to participate in a consultation mentioned in sub-paragraph (1) the contractor shall, in the course of that consultation make such inquiries and undertake such examinations as appear to it to be appropriate in all the circumstances.

Patients not seen within three years

5. Where a registered patient who –
  (a) has attained the age of 16 years but has not attained the age of 75 years; and
  (b) has attended neither a consultation with, nor a clinic provided by, the contractor within the period of three years prior to the date of his request,
requests a consultation the contractor shall, in addition and without prejudice to its other obligations in respect of that patient under the contract, provide such a consultation in the course of which it shall make such inquiries and undertake such examinations as appear to it to be appropriate in all the circumstances.

Patients aged 75 years and over

6.—(1) Where a registered patient who –
  (a) has attained the age of 75 years; and
  (b) has not participated in a consultation under this paragraph within the period of twelve months prior to the date of his request,
requests a consultation, the contractor shall, in addition and without prejudice to its other obligations in respect of that patient under the contract, provide such a consultation in the course of which it shall make such inquiries and undertake such examinations as appear to it to be appropriate in all the circumstances.

(2) A consultation under sub-paragraph (1) shall take place in the home of the patient where, in the reasonable opinion of the contractor, it would be inappropriate, as a result of the patient's medical condition, for him to attend at the practice premises.

Clinical reports

7.—(1) Where the contractor provides any clinical services, other than under a private arrangement, to a patient who is not on its list of patients, it shall, as soon as reasonably practicable, provide a clinical report relating to the consultation, and any treatment provided, to the Primary Care Trust.

(2) The Primary Care Trust shall send any report received under sub-paragraph (1) –
  (a) to the person with whom the patient is registered for the provision of essential services or their equivalent; or
  (b) if the person referred to in paragraph (a) is not known to it, to the Primary Care Trust in whose area the patient is resident.

Criteria for out of hours services

10. A contractor whose contract includes the provision of out of hours services shall only be required to provide such services if, in the reasonable opinion of the contractor in the light of the patient's medical condition, it would not be reasonable in all the circumstances for the patient to wait for the services required until the next time at which he could obtain such services during core hours.

Standards for out of hours services

11. From 1st January 2005, a contractor which provides out of hours services must, in the provision of such services, meet the quality standards set out in the document entitled 'Quality Standards in the Delivery of GP Out of Hours Services' published on 20th June 2002.

Duty of co-operation in relation to additional, enhanced and out of hours services

12.—(1) A contractor which does not provide to its registered patients or to persons whom it has accepted as temporary residents –

    (a) a particular additional service;

    (b) a particular enhanced service; or

    (c) out of hours services, either at all or in respect of some periods or some services,

shall comply with the requirements specified in sub-paragraph (2).

    (2) The requirements referred to in sub-paragraph (1) are that the contractor shall –

        (a) co-operate, insofar as is reasonable, with any person responsible for the provision of that service or those services;

        (b) comply in core hours with any reasonable request for information from such a person or from the Primary Care Trust relating to the provision of that service or those services; and

        (c) in the case of out of hours services, take reasonable steps to ensure that any patient who contacts the practice premises during the out of hours period is provided with information about how to obtain services during that period.

    (3) Nothing in this paragraph shall require a contractor whose contract does not include the provision of out of hours services to make itself available during the out of hours period.

13. Where a contractor is to cease to be required to provide to its patients –

    (a) a particular additional service;

    (b) a particular enhanced service; or

    (c) out of hours services, either at all or in respect of some periods or some services,

it shall comply with any reasonable request for information relating to the provision of that service or those services made by the Primary Care Trust or by any person with whom the Trust intends to enter into a contract for the provision of such services.

Part II Patients

List of patients

14. The Primary Care Trust shall prepare and keep up to date a list of the patients –

    (a) who have been accepted by the contractor for inclusion in its list of patients under paragraph 15 and who have not subsequently been removed from that list under paragraphs 19 to 27; and

    (b) who have been assigned to the contractor under paragraph 32 or 33 and whose assignment has not subsequently been rescinded.

Application for inclusion in a list of patients

15.—(1) The contractor may, if its list of patients is open, accept an application for inclusion in its list of patients made by or on behalf of any person whether or not resident in its practice area or included, at the time of that application, in the list of patients of another contractor or provider of primary medical services.

(2) The contractor may, if its list of patients is closed, only accept an application for inclusion in its list of patients from a person who is an immediate family member of a registered patient whether or not resident in its practice area or included, at the time of that application, in the list of patients of another contractor or provider of primary medical services.

(3) Subject to sub-paragraph (4), an application for inclusion in a contractor's list of patients shall be made by delivering to the practice premises a medical card or an application signed (in either case) by the applicant or a person authorised by the applicant to sign on his behalf.

(4) An application may be made –

    (a) on behalf of any child –

        (i) by either parent, or in the absence of both parents, the guardian or other adult who has care of the child,

        (ii) by a person duly authorised by a local authority to whose care the child has been committed under the Children Act 1989, or

        (iii) by a person duly authorised by a voluntary organisation by which the child is being accommodated under the provisions of that Act; or

    (b) on behalf of any adult who is incapable of making such an application, or authorising such an application to be made on their behalf, by a relative or the primary carer of that person.

(5) A contractor which accepts an application for inclusion in its list of patients shall notify the Primary Care Trust in writing as soon as possible.

(6) On receipt of a notice under sub-paragraph (5), the Primary Care Trust shall –

    (a) include that person in the contractor's list of patients from the date on which the notice is received; and

    (b) notify the applicant (or, in the case of a child or incapable adult, the person making the application on their behalf) of the acceptance.

Temporary residents

16.—(1) The contractor may, if its list of patients is open, accept a person as a temporary resident provided it is satisfied that the person is –

    (a) temporarily resident away from his normal place of residence and is not being provided with essential services (or their equivalent) under any other arrangement in the locality where he is temporarily residing; or

    (b) moving from place to place and not for the time being resident in any place.

(2) For the purposes of sub-paragraph (1), a person shall be regarded as temporarily resident in a place if, when he arrives in that place, he intends to stay there for more than 24 hours but not more than three months.

(3) A contractor which wishes to terminate its responsibility for a person accepted as a temporary resident before the end of –

    (a) three months; or

    (b) such shorter period for which it agreed to accept him as a patient,

shall notify him either orally or in writing and its responsibility for that patient shall cease 7 days after the date on which the notification was given.

(4) At the end of three months, or on such earlier date as its responsibility for the temporary resident has come to an end, the contractor shall notify the Primary Care Trust in writing of any person whom it accepted as a temporary resident.

Refusal of applications for inclusion in the list of patients or for acceptance as a temporary resident

17.—(1) The contractor shall only refuse an application made under paragraph 15 or 16 if it has reasonable grounds for doing so which do not relate to the applicant's race, gender, social class, age, religion, sexual orientation, appearance, disability or medical condition.

(2) The reasonable grounds referred to in paragraph (1) shall, in the case of applications made under paragraph 15, include the ground that the applicant does not live in the contractor's practice area.

(3) A contractor which refuses an application made under paragraph 15 or 16 shall, within 14 days of its decision, notify the applicant (or, in the case of a child or incapable adult, the person making the application on their behalf) in writing of the refusal and the reason for it.

(4) The contractor shall keep a written record of refusals of applications made under paragraph 15 and of the reasons for them and shall make this record available to the Primary Care Trust on request.

Patient preference of practitioner

18.—(1) Where the contractor has accepted an application for inclusion in its list of patients, it shall –

    (a) notify the patient (or, in the case of a child or incapable adult, the person who made the application on their behalf) of the patient's right to express a preference to receive services from a particular performer or class of performer either generally or in relation to any particular condition; and

    (b) record in writing any such preference expressed by or on behalf of the patient.

(2) The contractor shall endeavour to comply with any reasonable preference expressed under sub-paragraph (1) but need not do so if the preferred performer –

    (a) has reasonable grounds for refusing to provide services to the patient; or

    (b) does not routinely perform the service in question within the practice.

Removal from the list at the request of the patient

19.—(1) The contractor shall notify the Primary Care Trust in writing of any request for removal from its list of patients received from a registered patient.

(2) Where the Primary Care Trust –

    (a) receives notification from the contractor under sub-paragraph (1); or

    (b) receives a request from the patient to be removed from the contractor's list of patients,

it shall remove that person from the contractor's list of patients. (3) A removal in accordance with sub-paragraph (2) shall take effect –

    (a) on the date on which the Primary Care Trust receives notification of the registration of the person with another provider of essential services (or their equivalent); or

    (b) 14 days after the date on which the notification or request made under sub-paragraph (1) or (2) respectively is received by the Primary Care Trust, whichever is the sooner.

(4) The Primary Care Trust shall, as soon as practicable, notify in writing –

    (a) the patient; and

    (b) the contractor, that the patient's name will be or has been removed from the contractor's list of patients on the date referred to in sub-paragraph (3).

(5) In this paragraph and in paragraphs 20(1)(b) and (10), 21(6) and (7), 23 and 26, a reference to a request received from or advice, information or notification required to be given to a patient shall include a request received from or advice, information or notification required to be given to –

    (a) in the case of a patient who is a child, a parent or other person referred to in paragraph 15(4)(a); or

    (b) in the case of an adult patient who is incapable of making the relevant request or receiving the relevant advice, information or notification, a relative or the primary carer of the patient.

Removal from the list at the request of the contractor

20.—(1) Subject to paragraph 21, a contractor which has reasonable grounds for wishing a patient to be removed from its list of patients which do not relate to the applicant's race, gender, social class, age, religion, sexual orientation, appearance, disability or medical condition shall –

    (a) notify the Primary Care Trust in writing that it wishes to have the patient removed; and

    (b) subject to sub-paragraph (2), notify the patient of its specific reasons for requesting removal.

(2) Where, in the reasonable opinion of the contractor –

(a) the circumstances of the removal are such that it is not appropriate for a more specific reason to be given; and

(b) there has been an irrevocable breakdown in the relationship between the patient and the contractor,

the reason given under sub-paragraph (1) may consist of a statement that there has been such a breakdown.

(3) Except in the circumstances specified in sub-paragraph (4), a contractor may only request a removal under sub-paragraph (1), if, within the period of 12 months prior to the date of its request to the Primary Care Trust, it has warned the patient that he is at risk of removal and explained to him the reasons for this.

(4) The circumstances referred to in sub-paragraph (3) are that –

(a) the reason for removal relates to a change of address;

(b) the contractor has reasonable grounds for believing that the issue of such a warning would –

(i) be harmful to the physical or mental health of the patient, or

(ii) put at risk the safety of one or more of the persons specified in sub-paragraph (5); or

(c) it is, in the opinion of the contractor, not otherwise reasonable or practical for a warning to be given.

(5) The persons referred to in sub-paragraph (4) are –

(a) the contractor, where it is an individual medical practitioner;

(b) in the case of a contract with two or more individuals practising in partnership, a partner in that partnership;

(c) in the case of a contract with a company, a legal and beneficial owner of shares in that company;

(d) a member of the contractor's staff;

(e) a person engaged by the contractor to perform or assist in the performance of services under the contract; or

(f) any other person present –

(i) on the practice premises, or

(ii) in the place where services are being provided to the patient under the contract.

(6) The contractor shall record in writing –

(a) the date of any warning given in accordance with sub-paragraph (3) and the reasons for giving such a warning as explained to the patient; or

(b) the reason why no such warning was given.

(7) The contractor shall keep a written record of removals under this paragraph which shall include –

(a) the reason for removal given to the patient;

(b) the circumstances of the removal; and

(c) in cases where sub-paragraph (2) applies, the grounds for a more specific reason not being appropriate, and shall make this record available to the Primary Care Trust on request.

(8) A removal requested in accordance with sub-paragraph (1) shall, subject to sub-paragraph (9), take effect from –

(a) the date on which the Primary Care Trust receives notification of the registration of the person with another provider of essential services (or their equivalent); or

(b) the eighth day after the Primary Care Trust receives the notice referred to in sub-paragraph (1)(a), whichever is the sooner.

(9) Where, on the date on which the removal would take effect under sub-paragraph (8), the contractor is treating the patient at intervals of less than seven days, the contractor shall notify the Primary Care Trust in writing of the fact and the removal shall take effect –

    (a) on the eighth day after the Trust receives notification from the contractor that the person no longer needs such treatment; or

    (b) on the date on which the Primary Care Trust receives notification of the registration of the person with another provider of essential services (or their equivalent), whichever is the sooner.

(10) The Primary Care Trust shall notify in writing –

    (a) the patient; and

    (b) the contractor,

that the patient's name has been or will be removed from the contractor's list of patients on the date referred to in sub-paragraph (8) or (9).

Removals from the list of patients who are violent

21.—(1) A contractor which wishes a patient to be removed from its list of patients with immediate effect on the grounds that –

    (a) the patient has committed an act of violence against any of the persons specified in sub-paragraph (2) or behaved in such a way that any such person has feared for his safety; and

    (b) it has reported the incident to the police, shall notify the Primary Care Trust in accordance with sub-paragraph (3).

(2) The persons referred to in sub-paragraph (1) are –

    (a) the contractor where it is an individual medical practitioner;

    (b) in the case of a contract with two or more individuals practising in partnership, a partner in that partnership;

    (c) in the case of a contract with a company, a legal and beneficial owner of shares in that company;

    (d) a member of the contractor's staff;

    (e) a person engaged by the contractor to perform or assist in the performance of services under the contract; or

    (f) any other person present –

        (i) on the practice premises, or

        (ii) in the place where services were provided to the patient under the contract.

(3) Notification under sub-paragraph (1) may be given by any means including telephone or fax but if not given in writing shall subsequently be confirmed in writing within seven days (and for this purpose a faxed notification is not a written one).

(4) The Primary Care Trust shall acknowledge in writing receipt of a request from the contractor under sub-paragraph (1).

(5) A removal requested in accordance with sub-paragraph (1) shall take effect at the time that the contractor –

    (a) makes the telephone call to the Primary Care Trust; or

    (b) sends or delivers the notification to the Primary Care Trust.

(6) Where, pursuant to this paragraph, the contractor has notified the Primary Care Trust that it wishes to have a patient removed from its list of patients, it shall inform the patient concerned unless –

    (a) it is not reasonably practicable for it to do so; or

    (b) it has reasonable grounds for believing that to do so would –

        (i) be harmful to the physical or mental health of the patient, or

        (ii) put at risk the safety of one or more of the persons specified in sub-paragraph (2).

(7) Where the Primary Care Trust has removed a patient from the contractor's list of patients in accordance with sub-paragraph (5) it shall give written notice of the removal to that patient.

(8) Where a patient is removed from the contractor's list of patients in accordance with this paragraph, the contractor shall record in the patient's medical records that the patient has been removed under this paragraph and the circumstances leading to his removal.

Termination of responsibility for patients not registered with the contractor

28.—(1) Where a contractor –

   (a) has received an application for the provision of medical services other than essential services –

   (i) from a person who is not included in its list of patients,

   (ii) from a person whom it has not accepted as a temporary resident, or

   (iii) on behalf of a person mentioned in sub-paragraph (i) or (ii), from one of the persons specified in paragraph 15(4); and

   (b) has accepted that person as a patient for the provision of the service in question, its responsibility for that patient shall be terminated in the circumstances referred to in sub-paragraph (2).

(2) The circumstances referred to in sub-paragraph (1) are –

   (a) the patient informs the contractor that he no longer wishes it to be responsible for provision of the service in question;

   (b) in cases where the contractor has reasonable grounds for terminating its responsibility which do not relate to the person's race, gender, social class, age, religion, sexual orientation, appearance, disability or medical condition, the contractor informs the patient that it no longer wishes to be responsible for providing him with the service in question; or

   (c) it comes to the notice of the contractor that the patient –

   (i) no longer resides in the area for which the contractor has agreed to provide the service in question, or

   (ii) is no longer included in the list of patients of another contractor to whose registered patients the contractor has agreed to provide that service.

(3) A contractor which wishes to terminate its responsibility for a patient under sub-paragraph (2)(b) shall notify the patient of the termination and the reason for it.

(4) The contractor shall keep a written record of terminations under this paragraph and of the reasons for them and shall make this record available to the Primary Care Trust on request.

(5) A termination under sub-paragraph (2)(b) shall take effect –

   (a) from the date on which the notice is given where the grounds for termination are those specified in paragraph 21(1); or

   (b) in all other cases, 14 days from the date on which the notice is given.

Part III Prescribing and Dispensing

Excessive prescribing

46.—(1) The contractor shall not prescribe drugs, medicines or appliances whose cost or quantity, in relation to any patient, is, by reason of the character of the drug, medicine or appliance in question in excess of that which was reasonably necessary for the proper treatment of that patient.

(2) In considering whether a contractor has breached its obligations under sub-paragraph (1) the Primary Care Trust shall seek the views of the Local Medical Committee (if any) for its area.

Part IV Persons Who Perform Services

Qualifications of performers

53.—(1) Subject to sub-paragraph (2), no medical practitioner shall perform medical services under the contract unless he is –

   (a) included in a medical performers list for a Primary Care Trust in England;

   (b) not suspended from that list or from the Medical Register; and

   (c) not subject to interim suspension under section 41A of the Medical Act 1983 (interim orders).

(2) Sub-paragraph (1)(a) shall not apply in the case of –

   (a) a medical practitioner employed by an NHS trust, an NHS foundation trust, (in Scotland) a Health Board, or (in Northern Ireland) a Health and Social Services Trust who is providing services other than primary medical services at the practice premises;

   (b) a person who is provisionally registered under section 15 (provisional registration), 15A (provisional registration for EEA nationals) or 21 (provisional registration) of the Medical Act 1983 acting in the course of his employment in a resident medical capacity in an approved medical practice; or

   (c) a GP Registrar during the first two months of his training period.

54. No health care professional other than one to whom paragraph 53 applies shall perform clinical services under the contract unless he is appropriately registered with his relevant professional body and his registration is not currently suspended.

55. Where the registration of a health care professional or, in the case of a medical practitioner, his inclusion in a primary care list is subject to conditions, the contractor shall ensure compliance with those conditions insofar as they are relevant to the contract.

56. No health care professional shall perform any clinical services unless he has such clinical experience and training as are necessary to enable him properly to perform such services.

Conditions for employment and engagement

60.—(1) Before employing or engaging any person to assist it in the provision of services under the contract, the contractor shall take reasonable care to satisfy itself that the person in question is both suitably qualified and competent to discharge the duties for which he is to be employed or engaged.

   (2) The duty imposed by sub-paragraph (1) is in addition to the duties imposed by paragraphs 57 to 59.

   (3) When considering the competence and suitability of any person for the purpose of sub-paragraph (1), the contractor shall have regard, in particular, to –

   (a) that person's academic and vocational qualifications;

   (b) his education and training; and

   (c) his previous employment or work experience.

Training

61. The contractor shall ensure that for any health care professional who is –

   (a) performing clinical services under the contract; or

   (b) employed or engaged to assist in the performance of such services, there are in place arrangements for the purpose of maintaining and updating his skills and knowledge in relation to the services which he is performing or assisting in performing.

62. The contractor shall afford to each employee reasonable opportunities to undertake appropriate training with a view to maintaining that employee's competence.

Level of skill

67. The contractor shall carry out its obligations under the contract with reasonable care and skill.

Part V Records, Information, Notifications and Rights of Entry

Patient records

73.—(1) In this paragraph, 'computerised records' means records created by way of entries on a computer.

   (2) The contractor shall keep adequate records of its attendance on and treatment of its patients and shall do so –

   (a) on forms supplied to it for the purpose by the Primary Care Trust; or

   (b) with the written consent of the Primary Care Trust, by way of computerised records, or in a combination of those two ways.

(3) The contractor shall include in the records referred to in sub-paragraph (2) clinical reports sent in accordance with paragraph 7 of this Schedule or from any other health care professional who has provided clinical services to a person on its list of patients.

(6) The contractor shall send the complete records relating to a patient to the Primary Care Trust –

> (a) where a person on its list dies, before the end of the period of 14 days beginning with the date on which it was informed by the Primary Care Trust of the death, or (in any other case) before the end of the period of one month beginning with the date on which it learned of the death; or
>
> (b) in any other case where the person is no longer registered with the contractor, as soon as possible at the request of the Primary Care Trust.

Confidentiality of personal data

75. The contractor shall nominate a person with responsibility for practices and procedures relating to the confidentiality of personal data held by it.

Practice leaflet

76. The contractor shall –

> (a) compile a document (in this paragraph called a practice leaflet) which shall include the information specified in Schedule 10;
>
> (b) review its practice leaflet at least once in every period of 12 months and make any amendments necessary to maintain its accuracy; and
>
> (c) make available a copy of the leaflet, and any subsequent updates, to its patients and prospective patients.

Requests for information from Patients' Forums

78.—(1) Subject to sub-paragraph (2), where the contractor receives a written request from the Patients' Forum established for the Primary Care Trust to produce any information which appears to the Forum to be necessary for the effective carrying out of its functions it shall comply with that request promptly and in any event no later than the twentieth working day following the date the request was made.

(2) The contractor shall not be required to produce information under sub-paragraph (1) which –

> (a) is confidential and relates to a living individual, unless at least one of the conditions specified in sub-paragraph (3) applies; or
>
> (b) is prohibited from disclosure by or under any enactment or any ruling of a court of competent jurisdiction or is protected by the common law, unless sub-paragraph (4) applies.

(3) The conditions referred to in sub-paragraph (2)(a) are –

> (a) the information can be disclosed in a form from which the identity of the individual cannot be ascertained; or
>
> (b) the individual consents to the information being disclosed.

Reports to a medical officer

80.—(1) The contractor shall, if it is satisfied that the patient consents –

> (a) supply in writing to a medical officer within such reasonable period as that officer, or an officer of the Department for Work and Pensions on his behalf and at his direction, may specify, such clinical information as the medical officer considers relevant about a patient to whom the contractor or a person acting on the contractor's behalf has issued or has refused to issue a medical certificate; and
>
> (b) answer any inquiries by a medical officer, or by an officer of the Department for Work and Pensions on his behalf and at his direction, about a prescription form or medical certificate issued by the contractor or on its behalf or about any statement which the contractor or a person acting on the contractor's behalf has made in a report.

(2) For the purpose of satisfying himself that the patient has consented as required by paragraph (1), the contractor may (unless it has reason to believe the patient does not consent) rely on an assurance in writing from the medical officer, or any officer of the Department for Work and Pensions, that he holds the patient's written consent.

Notifications to the Primary Care Trust

82. In addition to any requirements of notification elsewhere in the regulations, the contractor shall notify the Primary Care Trust in writing, as soon as reasonably practicable, of –

> (a) any serious incident that, in the reasonable opinion of the contractor, affects or is likely to affect the contractor's performance of its obligations under the contract;
>
> (b) any circumstances which give rise to the Primary Care Trust's right to terminate the contract under paragraph 111, 112 or 113(1);
>
> (c) any appointments system which it proposes to operate and the proposed discontinuance of any such system;
>
> (d) any change of which it is aware in the address of a registered patient; and
>
> (e) the death of any patient of which it is aware.

Notification of deaths

87.—(1) The contractor shall report in writing to the Primary Care Trust the death on its practice premises of any patient no later than the end of the first working day after the date on which the death occurred.

> (2) The report shall include –
>
> > (a) the patient's full name;
> >
> > (b) the patient's National Health Service number where known;
> >
> > (c) the date and place of death;
> >
> > (d) a brief description of the circumstances, as known, surrounding the death;
> >
> > (e) the name of any medical practitioner or other person treating the patient whilst on the practice premises; and
> >
> > (f) the name, where known, of any other person who was present at the time of the death.

(3) The contractor shall send a copy of the report referred to in sub-paragraph (1) to any other Primary Care Trust in whose area the deceased was resident at the time of his death.

Part VI Complaints

Complaints procedure

92.—(1) The contractor shall establish and operate a complaints procedure to deal with any complaints in relation to any matter reasonably connected with the provision of services under the contract ...

> (2) The contractor shall take reasonable steps to ensure that patients are aware of –
>
> > (a) the complaints procedure;
> >
> > (b) the role of the Primary Care Trust and other bodies in relation to complaints about services under the contract; and
> >
> > (c) their right to assistance with any complaint from independent advocacy services provided under section 19A of the Act (independent advocacy services).

(3) The contractor shall take reasonable steps to ensure that the complaints procedure is accessible to all patients.

Making of complaints

93. A complaint may be made by or, with his consent, on behalf of a patient, or former patient, who is receiving or has received services under the contract, or –

> (a) where the patient is a child –
>
> > (i) by either parent, or in the absence of both parents, the guardian or other adult who has care of the child,

     (ii) by a person duly authorised by a local authority to whose care the child has been committed under the provisions of the Children Act 1989; or

     (iii) by a person duly authorised by a voluntary organisation by which the child is being accommodated under the provisions of that Act;

    (a) where the patient is incapable of making a complaint, by a relative or other adult who has an interest in his welfare.

94. Where a patient has died a complaint may be made by a relative or other adult person who had an interest in his welfare or, where the patient falls within paragraph 93(a)(ii) or (iii), by the authority or voluntary organisation.

Period for making complaints

95.—(1) Subject to sub-paragraph (2), the period for making a complaint is –

    (a) six months from the date on which the matter which is the subject of the complaint occurred; or

    (b) six months from the date on which the matter which is the subject of the complaint comes to the complainant's notice provided that the complaint is made no later than 12 months after the date on which the matter which is the subject of the complaint occurred.

    (2) Where a complaint is not made during the period specified in sub-paragraph (1), it shall be referred to the person nominated under paragraph 96(2)(a) and if he is of the opinion that –

    (a) having regard to all the circumstances of the case, it would have been unreasonable for the complainant to make the complaint within that period; and

    (b) notwithstanding the time that has elapsed since the date on which the matter which is the subject matter of the complaint occurred, it is still possible to investigate the complaint properly,

the complaint shall be treated as if it had been received during the period specified in sub-paragraph (1).

Further requirements for complaints procedures

96.—(1) A complaints procedure shall also comply with the requirements set out in sub-paragraphs (2) to (6).

    (2) The contractor must nominate –

    (a) a person (who need not be connected with the contractor and who, in the case of an individual, may be specified by his job title) to be responsible for the operation of the complaints procedure and the investigation of complaints; and

    (b) a partner, or other senior person associated with the contractor, to be responsible for the effective management of the complaints procedure and for ensuring that action is taken in the light of the outcome of any investigation.

    (3) All complaints must be –

    (a) either made or recorded in writing;

    (b) acknowledged in writing within the period of three working days beginning with the day on which the complaint was made or, where that is not possible, as soon as reasonably practicable; and

    (c) properly investigated.

    (4) Within the period of 10 working days beginning with the day on which the complaint was received by the person specified under sub-paragraph (2)(a) or, where that is not possible, as soon as reasonably practicable, the complainant must be given a written summary of the investigation and its conclusions.

    (5) Where the investigation of the complaint requires consideration of the patient's medical records, the person specified under sub-paragraph (2)(a) must inform the patient or person acting on his behalf if the investigation will involve disclosure of information contained in those records to a person other than the contractor or an employee of the contractor.

    (6) The contractor must keep a record of all complaints and copies of all correspondence relating to complaints, but such records must be kept separate from patients' medical records.

Provision of information about complaints

98. The contractor shall inform the Primary Care Trust, at such intervals as required, of the number of complaints it has received under the procedure established in accordance with this Part.

Part IX Miscellaneous

Clinical governance

121.—(1) The contractor shall have an effective system of clinical governance.

(2) The contractor shall nominate a person who will have responsibility for ensuring the effective operation of the system of clinical governance.

(3) The person nominated under sub-paragraph (2) shall be a person who performs or manages services under the contract.

(4) In this paragraph 'system of clinical governance' means a framework through which the contractor endeavours continuously to improve the quality of its services and safeguard high standards of care by creating an environment in which clinical excellence can flourish.

Insurance

122.—(1) The contractor shall at all times hold adequate insurance against liability arising from negligent performance of clinical services under the contract.

(2) The contractor shall not sub-contract its obligations to provide clinical services under the contract unless it has satisfied itself that the sub-contractor holds adequate insurance against liability arising from negligent performance of such services.

123. The contractor shall at all times hold adequate public liability insurance in relation to liabilities to third parties arising under or in connection with the contract which are not covered by the insurance referred to in paragraph 122(1).

Compliance with legislation and guidance

125. The contractor shall –

(a) comply with all relevant legislation; and

(b) have regard to all relevant guidance issued by the Primary Care Trust, the relevant Strategic Health Authority or the Secretary of State.

Third party rights

126. The contract shall not create any right enforceable by any person not a party to it.

The National Health Service (Complaints) Regulations 2004

(SI 2004, No. 1768)

Part I Introduction

Interpretation

2.—(1) In these Regulations –

'the 1977 Act' means the National Health Service Act 1977; [sic]

'the 2003 Act' means the Health and Social Care (Community Health and Standards) Act 2003;

'complainant' in Part II means any person who makes or has made a complaint in accordance with regulation 9 to an NHS body and in Part III means any person who has made a complaint in accordance with regulation 14 or 15 to the Healthcare Commission;

'complaints manager' means the person designated in accordance with regulation 5;

'disciplinary proceedings' means any procedure for disciplining employees adopted by an NHS body;

'general medical services contractor' means a person who has entered into a general medical services contract with a Primary Care Trust in accordance with section 28Q of the 1977 Act;

'the Healthcare Commission' means the Commission for Healthcare, Audit and Inspection established under section 41 of the 2003 Act;

'health care professional' means a person who is a member of a profession which is regulated by a health regulatory body;

'health regulatory body' means a body mentioned in section 25(3) of the National Health Service Reform and Health Care Professions Act 2002;

'Health Service Commissioner' means the person appointed Health Service Commissioner for England in accordance with section 1 of, and Schedule 1 to, the Health Service Commissioners Act 1993;

'independent provider' means a person or body, including a voluntary organisation but excluding an NHS foundation trust, which is providing services under arrangements made with an NHS body in accordance with section 16CC(2) or section 23 of the 1977 Act;

'Independent Regulator' means the Independent Regulator of NHS Foundation Trusts established under section 2 of the 2003 Act;

'NHS body' means a Strategic Health Authority, an NHS Trust which operates from premises wholly or mainly in England, a Primary Care Trust and a Special Health Authority to which section 2 of the Health Service Commissioners Act 1993 applies;

'NHS contract' has the meaning given in section 4 of the National Health Service and Community Care Act 1990;

'NHS foundation trust' has the meaning given in section 1 of the 2003 Act;

'patient' in regulation 8 means a person who is receiving or has received services from an NHS body or an independent provider and in regulation 15 means a person who is receiving or has received services from an NHS foundation trust;

'patients' forum' means a patients' forum established in accordance with section 15 of the National Health Service Reform and Health Care Professions Act 2002;

'primary care services' means services provided by a primary care provider;

'primary care provider' has the meaning given in paragraph (2);

'Primary Care Trust' means a body established under section 16A of the 1977 Act;

'relevant patients' forum' in relation to an NHS trust or a Primary Care Trust, means the patients' forum established for the NHS trust or Primary Care Trust;

'relevant Primary Care Trust' means, in relation to a primary care provider, the Primary Care Trust which has made arrangements with that primary care provider for the provision of primary care services;

'relevant Strategic Health Authority' means, in relation to an NHS trust or a Primary Care Trust, the Strategic Health Authority in whose area the NHS trust or Primary Care Trust wholly or mainly exercises its functions;

'staff' means any person who is employed by, or engaged to provide services to, an NHS body;

(2) A primary care provider means –

(a) a general medical services contractor;

(b) a person who has entered into a default contract with a Primary Care Trust;

(c) a person who provides primary medical services in accordance with arrangements made either under section 28C of the 1977 Act or under a transitional agreement.

Part II Handling and Consideration of Complaints By NHS Bodies

Arrangements for the handling and consideration of complaints

3.—(1) Each NHS body must make arrangements in accordance with these Regulations for the handling and consideration of complaints.

(2) The arrangements must be accessible and such as to ensure that complaints are dealt with speedily and efficiently, and that complainants are treated courteously and sympathetically and as far as possible involved in decisions about how their complaints are handled and considered.

(3) The arrangements must be in writing and a copy must be given, free of charge, to any person who makes a request for one.

(4) Where an NHS trust or a Primary Care Trust makes arrangements for the provision of services with an independent provider, it must ensure that the independent provider has in place arrangements for the handling and consideration of complaints about any matter connected with its provision of services as if these Regulations applied to it.

Responsibility for complaints arrangements

4. Each NHS body must designate one of its members, or in the case of an NHS trust a member of its board of directors, to take responsibility for ensuring compliance with the arrangements made under these Regulations and that action is taken in the light of the outcome of any investigation.

Complaints manager

5. (1) Each NHS body must designate a person, in these Regulations referred to as a complaints manager, to manage the procedures for handling and considering complaints and in particular –

(a) to perform the functions of the complaints manager under this Part; and

(b) to perform such other functions in relation to complaints as the NHS body may require.

Complaints to NHS bodies

6. Subject to regulation 7, a complaint to an NHS body may be about any matter reasonably connected with the exercise of its functions including in particular, in the case of an NHS trust or Primary Care Trust, any matter reasonably connected with –

(a) its provision of health care or any other services, including in the case of a Primary Care Trust, its provision of primary medical services under section 16CC of the 1977 Act; and

(b) the function of commissioning health care or other services under an NHS contract or making arrangements for the provision of such care or other services with an independent provider or with an NHS foundation trust.

Matters excluded from consideration under the arrangements

7. The following complaints are excluded from the scope of the arrangements required under this Part –

(a) a complaint made by an NHS body which relates to the exercise of its functions by another NHS body;

(b) a complaint made by a primary care provider which relates either to the exercise of its functions by an NHS body or to the contract or arrangements under which it provides primary care services;

(c) a complaint made by an employee of an NHS body about any matter relating to his contract of employment;

(d) a complaint made by an independent provider or an NHS foundation trust about any matter relating to arrangements made by an NHS body with that independent provider or NHS foundation trust;

(e) a complaint which relates to the provision of primary medical services in accordance with arrangements made by a Primary Care Trust with a Strategic Health Authority under section 28C of the 1977 Act or under a transitional agreement;

(f) a complaint which is being or has been investigated by the Health Service Commissioner;

(g) a complaint arising out of an NHS body's alleged failure to comply with a data subject request under the Data Protection Act 1998 or a request for information under the Freedom of Information Act 2000;

(h) a complaint about which the complainant has stated in writing that he intends to take legal proceedings;

(i) a complaint about which an NHS body is taking or is proposing to take disciplinary proceedings in relation to the substance of the complaint against a person who is the subject of the complaint;

(j) a complaint the subject matter of which has already been investigated under these Regulations

Persons who may make complaints

8.—(1) A complaint may be made by –

(a) a patient; or

(b) any person who is affected by or likely to be affected by the action, omission or decision of the NHS body which is the subject of the complaint.

(2) A complaint may be made by a person (in these Regulations referred to as a representative) acting on behalf of a person mentioned in paragraph (1) in any case where that person –

(a) has died;

(b) is a child;

(c) is unable by reason of physical or mental incapacity to make the complaint himself; or

(d) has requested the representative to act on his behalf.

(3) In the case of a patient or person affected who has died or who is incapable, the representative must be a relative or other person who, in the opinion of the complaints manager, had or has a sufficient interest in his welfare and is a suitable person to act as representative.

(4) If in any case the complaints manager is of the opinion that a representative does or did not have a sufficient interest in the person's welfare or is unsuitable to act as a representative, he must notify that person in writing, stating his reasons.

(5) In the case of a child, the representative must be a parent, guardian or other adult person who has care of the child and where the child is in the care of a local authority or a voluntary organisation, the representative must be a person authorised by the local authority or the voluntary organisation.

(6) In these Regulations any reference to a complainant includes a reference to his representative.

Making a complaint

9.—(1) Where a person wishes to make a complaint under these Regulations, he may make the complaint to the complaints manager or any other member of the staff of the NHS body which is the subject of the complaint.

(2) A complaint may be made orally or in writing (including electronically) and –

(a) where it is made orally, the complaints manager must make a written record of the complaint which includes the name of the complainant, the subject matter of the complaint and the date on which it was made; and

(b) where it is made in writing, the complaints manager must make a written record of the date on which it was received.

Time limit for making a complaint

10.—(1) Subject to paragraph (2) a complaint must be made within –

    (a) six months of the date on which the matter which is the subject of the complaint occurred; or

    (b) six months of the date on which the matter which is the subject of the complaint came to the notice of the complainant.

(2) Where a complaint is made after the expiry of the period mentioned in paragraph (1), the complaints manager may investigate it if he is of the opinion that –

    (a) having regard to all the circumstances, the complainant had good reasons for not making the complaint within that period; and

    (b) notwithstanding the time that has elapsed it is still possible to investigate the complaint effectively and efficiently.

Acknowledgement and record of complaint

11.—(1) The complaints manager must send to the complainant a written acknowledgement of the complaint within 2 working days of the date on which the complaint was made.

(2) Where a complaint was made orally, the acknowledgement must be accompanied by the written record mentioned in regulation 9(2)(a) with an invitation to the complainant to sign and return it.

(3) The complaints manager must send a copy of the complaint and his acknowledgement to any person identified in the complaint as the subject of the complaint.

(4) The acknowledgement sent to the complainant under paragraph (1) must include information about the right to assistance from the independent advocacy services provided under section 19A of the 1977 Act.

Investigation

12.—(1) The complaints manager must investigate the complaint to the extent necessary and in the manner which appears to him most appropriate to resolve it speedily and efficiently.

(2) The complaints manager may, in any case where he thinks it would be appropriate to do so and with the agreement of the complainant, make arrangements for conciliation, mediation or other assistance for the purposes of resolving the complaint, and in any such case the NHS body must ensure that appropriate conciliation or mediation services are available.

(3) The complaints manager must take such steps as are reasonably practicable to keep the complainant informed about the progress of the investigation.

Response

13.—(1) The complaints manager must prepare a written response to the complaint which summarises the nature and substance of the complaint, describes the investigation under regulation 12 and summarises its conclusions.

(2) The response must be signed by the chief executive of the NHS body except in cases where for good reason the chief executive is not himself able to sign it, in which case it may be signed by a person acting on his behalf.

(3) Subject to paragraph (4), the response must be sent to the complainant within 25 working days beginning on the date on which the complaint was made, unless the complainant agrees to a longer period in which case the response may be sent within that longer period.

(4) The response must notify the complainant of his right to refer the complaint to the Healthcare Commission in accordance with regulation 14.

(5) Copies of the response mentioned in paragraph (1) must be sent to any other person to whom the complaint was sent under regulation 11(3).

Part III Handling and Consideration of Complaints By the Healthcare Commission

General complaints remit of the Healthcare Commission

14.—(1) Subject to paragraph (1A), in any case where –

(a) a complainant is not satisfied with the result of an investigation –

(i) by an NHS body under regulation 12, or

(ii) by an independent provider, with whom an NHS trust or Primary Care Trust has made arrangements as mentioned in regulation 6, in accordance with its arrangements for the handling and consideration of complaints;

(b) for any reason an investigation mentioned in paragraph (1)(a) has not been completed within 6 months of the date on which the complaint was made, or

(c) a complaints manager has decided not to investigate a complaint on the grounds that it was not made within the time limit mentioned in regulation 10;

he may request the Healthcare Commission to consider the complaint in accordance with this Part.

(2) In any case where a person has made a complaint to a primary care provider and is not satisfied with the outcome of an investigation of his complaint by the primary care provider, in accordance with its procedures for the handling and investigation of complaints, he, or a person who acted as his representative in accordance with those procedures, may request the Healthcare Commission to consider the complaint in accordance with this Part.

Remit of Healthcare Commission in relation to complaints about NHS foundation trusts

15.—(1) Subject to paragraphs (2) to (7), where a person has made a complaint to an NHS foundation trust and either –

(a) he is not satisfied with the outcome of any investigation of that complaint by the NHS foundation trust in accordance with any procedures it may have; or

(b) the NHS foundation trust has no complaints procedures,

he may request the Healthcare Commission to consider the complaint in accordance with this Part.

(2) The Healthcare Commission's remit in relation to NHS foundation trusts is limited to consideration only of a complaint which –

(a) is made by a patient or any other person who is affected by, or likely to be affected by, the action or omission of the NHS foundation trust which forms the subject matter of the complaint; and

(b) is reasonably connected with the provision of health care or other services to such persons by or for the NHS foundation trust.

(3) The Healthcare Commission may not consider a complaint made under this regulation where the complaint –

(a) is one about which the complainant has stated in writing that he intends to take legal proceedings;

(b) is one about which the NHS foundation trust has stated in writing that it is taking or is proposing to take disciplinary proceedings in relation the substance of the complaint against a person who is the subject of the complaint;

(c) arises out of the NHS foundation trust's alleged failure to comply with a data subject request under the Data Protection Act 1998 or a request for information under the Freedom of Information Act 2000; or

(d) which is being or has been investigated by the Health Service Commissioner.

(4) Where the Healthcare Commission consider that a complaint or any part of a complaint made under this regulation does not fall within paragraph (2), it must refer that complaint or part of a complaint to the Independent Regulator.

(7) The Healthcare Commission shall make a report to the Independent Regulator each month and when the Independent Regulator shall otherwise require, which—

    (a) specifies the number of complaints received about NHS foundation trusts in that month, or other period specified in the request;

    (b) identifies the subject matter of those complaints; and

    (c) summarises how any complaints concluded during that month, or other period specified in the request, were handled, including their outcome.

(8) The Healthcare Commission may, provided that it has the consent, which may be either express or implied, of the complainant send a copy of any complaint that it has received about an NHS foundation trust to the Independent Regulator.

(9) The Independent Regulator may request that the Healthcare Commission send him any complaint about an NHS foundation trust that the Healthcare Commission receives.

(10) For the purposes of paragraph (9) the Independent Regulator may make a standing request that identifies a type of complaint that he wishes to receive.

(11) Where the Healthcare Commission receives a request under paragraph (9) it must, provided that it has the consent, which may be either express or implied, of the complainant, send a copy of the complaint to the Independent Regulator—

    (a) in the case of an individual request, within two days of receiving the request; or

    (b) in the case of a standing request, within two days of receipt of a complaint which falls within the terms of that request.

(12) On receipt of a copy of a complaint under paragraph (8) or (11) the Independent Regulator may give his views on the complaint or its handling to the Healthcare Commission and, where he wishes to give such views, must do so as soon as reasonably practicable.

Decision on handling of complaint

16.—(1) On receipt of the complaint the Healthcare Commission must assess the nature and substance of the complaint and decide how it should be handled having regard to –

    (a) the views of the complainant;

    (b) the views of the body complained about;

    (c) in the case of a complaint about an NHS foundation trust which falls within regulation 15(2), any views given by the Independent Regulator pursuant to regulation 15(12);

    (d) any investigation of the complaint, whether under Part II or otherwise, and any action taken as a result of such investigation; and

    (e) any other relevant circumstances.

(2) As soon as reasonably practicable the Healthcare Commission must notify the complainant as to whether it has decided –

    (a) to take no further action;

    (b) to make recommendations to the body which is the subject of the complaint as to what action might be taken to resolve it;

    (c) to investigate the complaint further in accordance with regulation 17, whether by establishing a panel to consider it or otherwise;

    (d) to consider the subject matter of the complaint as part of or in conjunction with any other investigation or review which it is conducting or proposes to conduct in the exercise of its functions under the 2003 Act;

    (e) to refer the complaint to a health regulatory body;

    (f) in the case of a complaint about an NHS foundation trust which falls within regulation 15(2), to refer the complaint to the Independent Regulator; or

    (g) to refer the complaint to the Health Service Commissioner in accordance with section 10 of the Health Service Commissioners Act 1993.

(3) The notice of decision mentioned in paragraph (2) –

    (a) must be sent to any person who or body which is the subject of the complaint;

    (b) may be sent to any other body which the Healthcare Commission considers has an interest in it;

    (c) must include the Healthcare Commission's reasons for its decision; and

    (d) in the case of a notification under paragraph (2)(a), must inform the complainant of his right to refer his complaint to the Health Service Commissioner.

(4) For the purposes of its decision under this regulation, the Healthcare Commission may –

    (a) distinguish one part of a complaint from another and make different proposals in respect of those different parts; and

    (b) take such advice as appears to it to be required.

Investigation by the Healthcare Commission

17.—(1) Where the Healthcare Commission proposes to investigate a complaint itself, it must, within 10 working days of the date on which it sent the notice mentioned in regulation 16(2), or where that is not possible, as soon as reasonably practicable, send to the complainant and any other person to whom the notice was sent its proposed terms of reference for its investigation.

(2) The complainant and any person or body to whom the terms of reference are sent as mentioned in paragraph (1) may comment in writing on the proposed terms of reference provided that they do so within 10 working days of the date on which they were sent.

(3) The Healthcare Commission may conduct its investigation in any manner which seems to it appropriate, may take such advice as appears to it to be required and, having regard in particular to the views of the complainant and any person who or body which is the subject of the complaint, may appoint a panel to hear and consider the complaint in accordance with regulation 18.

(4) The Healthcare Commission may request any person or body to produce such information and documents as it considers necessary to enable a complaint to be considered properly.

(5) A request under paragraph (4) must be in writing (which may be electronically), must specify what information is requested and state why it is relevant to the consideration of the complaint.

(6) The Healthcare Commission may not make a request under paragraph (4) for information which is confidential and relates to a living individual unless the individual to whom the information relates has consented, such consent may be either express or implied, to its disclosure and use for the purposes of the investigation of the complaint.

Panels

18.—(1) Subject to paragraph (2), the Healthcare Commission must prepare and keep up to date a list of people who, in its opinion, are suitable to be members of an independent lay panel to hear and consider complaints.

(2) The following persons are not eligible for membership of an independent lay panel –

    (a) a member or employee of an NHS body;

    (b) any person who is, or who has at any time been, a health care professional or an employee of a health care professional.

(3) Where the Healthcare Commission proposes to refer a complaint to a panel it must make arrangements for the complaint to be considered by a panel of three people selected from the list mentioned in paragraph (1), one of whom must be appointed to be the chairman.

(4) Subject to paragraphs (5) to (7), a panel may consider a complaint in any manner and adopt any procedure which appears to it to be appropriate to resolve the complaint, having regard to any representations to it which may be made by the complainant or by the person who is the subject of the complaint (in this regulation referred to as the participants).

(5) The panel must ensure that the participants are kept informed generally and in particular about –

    (a) the composition of the panel;

    (b) the date and time of any hearing; and

    (c) the names of any person whom the panel proposes to interview or from whom it proposes to take advice or evidence.

(6) A participant before a panel may be accompanied or represented by a friend or advocate but may not be represented by a legal representative acting as such.

(7) In the event of disagreement among members of the panel, the view of the majority shall prevail.

Report of investigation by the Healthcare Commission

19.—(1) Where the Healthcare Commission investigates a complaint it must, as soon as reasonably practicable, prepare a written report of its investigation which –

(a) summarises the nature and substance of the complaint;

(b) describes the investigation and summarises its conclusions including any findings of fact, the Healthcare Commission's opinion of those findings and its reasons for its opinion;

(c) recommends what action should be taken and by whom to resolve the complaint; and

(d) identifies what other action, if any, should be taken and by whom.

(2) The report may include suggestions which it considers would improve the services of an NHS body, an NHS foundation trust or a primary care provider, or which would otherwise be effective for the purpose of resolving the complaint.

(3) Subject to paragraph (4), the report must be sent to –

(a) the complainant together with a letter explaining to him his right to take his complaint to the Health Service Commissioner;

(b) the body which was the subject of the complaint and, in the case of a complaint arising out of services provided by an independent provider, the body which commissioned those services;

(c) in the case of a complaint involving a primary care provider, to the relevant Primary Care Trust;

(d) any relevant Strategic Health Authority; and

(e) in the case of a complaint involving an NHS foundation trust to the Independent Regulator.

(4) The Healthcare Commission must adapt the report to ensure that confidential information from which the identity of a living individual can be ascertained is not disclosed without the express consent of the individual to whom it relates.

Part IV General

Publicity

20.—(1) Each NHS body and the Healthcare Commission must ensure that there is effective publicity for its complaints arrangements.

(2) Each NHS body must take all reasonable steps to ensure that the persons listed in paragraph (3) are informed of its arrangements, the name of its complaints manager and the address at which he can be contacted.

(3) The persons referred to in paragraph (2) are –

(a) patients and their carers;

(b) visitors to any hospital or other premises for the management of which the NHS body is responsible;

(c) staff of the NHS body;

(d) independent providers with whom arrangements have been made under section 16CC or section 23 of the 1977 Act;

(e) any body with which it has made an NHS contract; and

(f) its relevant patients' forum.

Monitoring

21.—(1) For the purpose of monitoring the arrangements under these Regulations each NHS body must prepare a report for each quarter of the year for consideration by its Board.

(2) The reports mentioned in paragraph (1) must –

(a) specify the numbers of complaints received;

(b) identify the subject matter of those complaints;

(c) summarise how they were handled including the outcome of the investigations; and

(d) identify any complaints where the recommendations of the Healthcare Commission were not acted upon, giving the reasons why not.

Annual reports

22. Each NHS body must prepare an annual report on its handling and consideration of complaints and send a copy of that report –

(a) in the case of a Strategic Health Authority or Special Health Authority, to the Healthcare Commission;

(b) in the case of an NHS trust, to its relevant Strategic Health Authority and the Healthcare Commission; and

(c) in the case of a Primary Care Trust, to its relevant Strategic Health Authority and the Healthcare Commission.

The National Health Service (Performers Lists) Regulations 2004

(SI 2004, No. 585)

Part 1 General Provisions as to Performers Lists

Interpretation and modification

2.—(1) In these Regulations –

'the Amendment Regulations' means the National Health Service (Performers Lists) Amendment Regulations 2005

'contingent removal' shall be construed in accordance with regulation 12;

'employment' means any employment, whether paid or unpaid and whether under a contract for services or a contract of service and 'employed' and 'employer' shall be construed accordingly;

'FHSAA' means the Family Health Services Appeal Authority constituted under section 49S;

'fraud case' means a case where a person satisfies the second condition for removal from the performers list, set out in section 49F(3) or, by virtue of section 49H, is treated as doing so;

'licensing or regulatory body' means a body that licenses or regulates any profession of which the performer is, or has been a member, including a body regulating or licensing the education, training or qualifications of that profession, and includes any body which licenses or regulates any such profession, its education, training or qualifications, outside the United Kingdom;

'list' means a list referred to in section 49N(1)(a) to (c), a performers list, a dental list, a medical list, a services list or a supplementary list;

'medical list' means the list prepared by a Primary Care Trust under regulation 4 of the Medical Regulations;

'medical performers list' means a list of medical practitioners prepared and published pursuant to regulation 3(1)(a);

'Medical Regulations' means the National Health Service (General Medical Services) Regulations 1992;

'a national disqualification' means a decision –

(a) made by the FHSAA to nationally disqualify a performer under section 49N;

(b) to nationally disqualify a performer under provisions in force in Scotland or Northern Ireland corresponding to section 49N; or

(c) by the Tribunal, which is treated as a national disqualification by the FHSAA by virtue of regulation 6(4) of the Abolition of the Tribunal Regulations;

'the NCAA' means the National Clinical Assessment Authority established as a Special Health Authority under section 11;

'notice' means a notice in writing (including electronically) and 'notify' shall be construed accordingly;

'performer' means a health care professional;

'performers list' means a list prepared and published pursuant to regulation 3(1);

'previous list' means a list in which the performer's name was included prior to his inclusion in the performers list;

'Primary Care Act' means the National Health Service (Primary Care) Act 1997;

'professional conduct' includes matters relating both to professional conduct and professional performance;

'relevant body' means the body for the time being mentioned in section 25(3) of the National Health Service Reform and Health Care Professions Act 2002, which regulates the profession of the performer;

'relevant performers list' means—

(a) in the case of a medical practitioner, the medical performers list;

'relevant Part' means—

(a) in the case of a medical practitioner, Part 2

'services list' means a list prepared by a Primary Care Trust under regulation 3 of the Services List Regulations;

'suspended', unless the context otherwise requires, means –

(a) suspended by a Primary Care Trust or equivalent body under section 49I or 49J, regulations made under section 43D or under section 8ZA of the Primary Care Act, including these Regulations; and

all references to sections are to sections of the National Health Service Act 1977, except where specified otherwise. [*sic*]

Performers lists

(1) A Primary Care Trust shall prepare and publish, in accordance with this Part, as modified or supplemented by the relevant Part—

(a) a medical performers list

(2) Performers lists shall be available for public inspection.

Application for inclusion in a performers list

4.—(1) An application by a performer for the inclusion of his name in a performers list shall be made by sending the Primary Care Trust an application in writing, which shall include the information mentioned in paragraph (2), the undertakings, certificate and consents required by paragraphs (3) and (6), any declaration required under paragraph (4) or (5) and any further information, undertakings, consents or declarations required under paragraph (7) or the relevant Part.

(2) The performer shall provide the following information –

(a) his full name;

(b) his sex;

(c) his date of birth;

(d) his private address and telephone number;

(e) chronological details of his professional experience (including the starting and finishing dates of each appointment together with an explanation of any gaps between appointments) with any additional supporting particulars, and an explanation of why he was dismissed from any post;

(f) names and addresses of two referees, who are willing to provide clinical references relating to two recent posts (which may include any current post) as a performer which lasted at least three months without a significant break, and, where this is not possible, a full explanation and the names and addresses of alternative referees;

(g) whether he has any outstanding application, including a deferred application, to be included in a list or an equivalent list, and if so, particulars of that application;

(h) details of any list or equivalent list from which he has been removed or contingently removed, or to which he has been refused admission or in which he has been conditionally included, with an explanation as to why;

(i) if he is the director of any body corporate that is included in any list or equivalent list, or which has an outstanding application (including a deferred application) for inclusion in any list or equivalent list, the name and registered office of that body and details of the Primary Care Trust or equivalent body concerned; and

(j) where he is, or was in the preceding six months, or was at the time of the originating events, a director of a body corporate, details of any list or equivalent list to which that body has been refused admission, in which it has been conditionally included, from which it has been removed or contingently removed or from which it is currently suspended, with an explanation as to why and details of the Primary Care Trust or equivalent body concerned.

(3) The performer shall provide the following undertakings, certificate and consent –

(a) undertaking to provide the declarations and document, if applicable, required by regulation 9;

(b) undertaking to notify the Primary Care Trust within 7 days of any material changes to the information provided in the application until the application is finally determined or, if his name is included in the performers list, at any time when his name is included in that list;

(c) undertaking to notify the Primary Care Trust if he is included, or applies to be included, in any other list held by a Primary Care Trust or equivalent body;

(d) undertaking to co-operate with an assessment by the NCAA, when requested to do so by the Primary Care Trust;

(e) undertaking, except where the relevant Part provides to the contrary, to participate in the appraisal system provided by a Primary Care Trust;

(f) an enhanced criminal record certificate, under section 115 of the Police Act 1997, in relation to himself; and

(g) consent to the disclosure of information in accordance with regulation 9.

(4) The performer shall send with the application a declaration as to whether he –

(a) has any criminal convictions in the United Kingdom;

(b) has been bound over following a criminal conviction in the United Kingdom;

(c) has accepted a police caution in the United Kingdom;

(d) has accepted and agreed to pay either a procurator fiscal fine under section 302 of the Criminal Procedure (Scotland) Act 1995 or a penalty under section 115A of the Social Security Administration Act 1992;

(e) has, in summary proceedings in Scotland in respect of an offence, been the subject of an order discharging him absolutely (without proceeding to conviction);

(f) has been convicted elsewhere of an offence, or what would constitute a criminal offence if committed in England and Wales;

(g) is currently the subject of any proceedings which might lead to such a conviction, which have not yet been notified to the Primary Care Trust;

(h) has been subject to any investigation into his professional conduct by any licensing, regulatory or other body, where the outcome was adverse;

(i) is currently subject to any investigation into his professional conduct by any licensing, regulatory or other body;

(j) is to his knowledge, or has been where the outcome was adverse, the subject of any investigation by the NHS Counter Fraud and Security Management Service in relation to fraud;

(k) is the subject of any investigation by another Primary Care Trust or equivalent body, which might lead to his removal from any of that Trust's or body's lists or equivalent lists;

(l)   is, or has been where the outcome was adverse, the subject of any investigation into his professional conduct in respect of any current or previous employment;

(m)   has been removed from, contingently removed from, refused admission to, or conditionally included in any list or equivalent list kept by a Primary Care Trust or equivalent body, or is currently suspended from such a list and if so, why and the name of that Trust or equivalent body; or

(n)   is, or has ever been, subject to a national disqualification,

and, if so, he shall give details, including approximate dates, of where any investigation or proceedings were or are to be brought, the nature of that investigation or proceedings, and any outcome.

(5) If the performer is, has in the preceding six months been, or was at the time of the originating events a director of a body corporate, he shall, in addition, make a declaration to the Primary Care Trust as to whether the body corporate –

(a) has any criminal convictions in the United Kingdom;

(b) has been convicted elsewhere of an offence, or what would constitute a criminal offence if committed in England and Wales;

(c) is currently the subject of any proceedings which might lead to such a conviction, which have not yet been notified to the Primary Care Trust;

(d) has been subject to any investigation into its provision of professional services by any licensing, regulatory or other body, where the outcome was adverse;

(e) is currently subject to any investigation into its provision of professional services by any licensing, regulatory or other body;

(f) is to his knowledge, or has been where the outcome was adverse, the subject of any investigation by the NHS Counter Fraud and Security Management Service in relation to fraud;

(g) is the subject of any investigation by another Primary Care Trust or equivalent body, which might lead to its removal from any list or equivalent list; or

(h) has been removed from, contingently removed from, refused admission to, or conditionally included in any list or equivalent list or is currently suspended from such a list,

and, if so, he shall give the name and registered office of the body corporate and details, including approximate dates, of where any investigation or proceedings were or are to be brought, the nature of that investigation or those proceedings, and any outcome.

(6) The performer shall consent to a request being made by the Primary Care Trust to any employer or former employer, licensing, regulatory or other body in the United Kingdom or elsewhere, for information relating to a current investigation, or an investigation where the outcome was adverse, into him or a body corporate referred to in paragraphs (2) and (5) and, for the purposes of this paragraph, 'employer' includes any partnership of which the performer is or was a member.

(7) If, in the case of any application, the Primary Care Trust finds that the information, references or documentation supplied by the performer are not sufficient for it to decide his application, it shall seek from him such further information, references or documentation as it may reasonably require in order to make a decision and he shall supply it with the material so sought.

Readmission

5.—(1) Where a performer has been removed from its performers list by a Primary Care Trust on the grounds that he had been convicted of a criminal offence, and that conviction is overturned on appeal, it may agree to include him in its performers list without a full application if it –

(a) is satisfied that there are no other matters that need to be considered; and

(b) has received an undertaking from him to comply with the requirements of these Regulations.

(2) In a case to which paragraph (1) applies, if the conviction is reinstated on a further appeal, the previous determination of the Primary Care Trust to remove that performer from its performers list shall once again have effect.

Decisions and grounds for refusal

6. (1) The grounds on which a Primary Care Trust may refuse to include a performer in its performers list are, in addition to any prescribed in the relevant Part, that –

    (a) having considered the declaration required by regulation 4(4) and (if applicable) regulation 4(5), and any other information or documents in its possession relating to him, it considers that he is unsuitable to be included in its performers list;

    (b) having contacted the referees provided by him under regulation 4(2)(f), it is not satisfied with the references;

    (c) having checked with the NHS Counter Fraud and Security Management Service for any facts that it considers relevant relating to past or current fraud investigations involving or related to him, which that Service shall supply, and, having considered these and any other facts in its possession relating to fraud involving or relating to him, the Trust considers these justify such refusal;

    (d) having checked with the Secretary of State for any facts that he considers relevant relating to past or current investigations or proceedings involving or related to the performer, which he shall supply, and, having considered these and any other facts in its possession involving or relating to the performer, the Trust considers these justify such refusal; or

    (e) there are any grounds for considering that admitting him to its performers list would be prejudicial to the efficiency of the services, which those included in that list perform.

(2) The grounds on which a Primary Care Trust must refuse to include a performer in its performers list are, in addition to any prescribed in the relevant Part, that –

    (a) he has not provided satisfactory evidence that he intends to perform the services, which those included in the relevant performers list perform, in its area;

    (b) it is not satisfied he has the knowledge of English which, in his own interests or those of his patients, is necessary in performing the services, which those included in the relevant performers list perform, in its area;

    (c) he has been convicted in the United Kingdom of murder;

    (d) he has been convicted in the United Kingdom of a criminal offence, committed on or after the day prescribed in the relevant Part, and has been sentenced to a term of imprisonment of over six months;

    (e) he is subject to a national disqualification;

    (f) he has not updated his application in accordance with regulation 7(4); or

    (g) in a case to which regulation 15(4) applies, he does not notify it under regulation 15(5) that he wishes to be included in its performers list subject to the specified conditions.

(3) Before making a decision on the performer's application, the Primary Care Trust shall –

    (a) check, as far as reasonably practicable, the information he provided, in particular that provided under regulation 4(4) and (if applicable) (5) or as required by the relevant Part, and shall ensure that it has sight of relevant documents;

    (b) check with the NHS Counter Fraud and Security Management Service whether he has any record of fraud, which information that Service shall supply;

    (c) check with the Secretary of State as to any information held by him as to any record about past or current investigations or proceedings involving or related to that performer, which information he shall supply; and

    (d) take up the references that he provided under regulation 4(2)(f).

(4) Where the Primary Care Trust is considering a refusal of the performer's application under paragraph (1) or (2), it shall consider all facts which appear to it to be relevant and shall in particular take into consideration, in relation to paragraph (1)(a), (c) or (d) –

(a) the nature of any offence, investigation or incident;

(b) the length of time since any offence, incident, conviction or investigation;

(c) whether there are other offences, incidents or investigations to be considered;

(d) any action or penalty imposed by any licensing, regulatory or other body, the police or the courts as a result of any such offence, incident or investigation;

(e) the relevance of any offence, investigation or incident to his performing the services, which those included in the relevant performers list perform, and any likely risk to his patients or to public finances;

(f) whether any offence was a sexual offence to which Part I of the Sexual Offences Act 1997 applies, or if it had been committed in England or Wales, would have applied;

(g) whether he has been refused admission to, or conditionally included in, or removed, contingently removed or is currently suspended from, any list or any equivalent list, and if so, the facts relating to the matter which led to such action and the reasons given by the Primary Care Trust or equivalent body for such action; and

(h) whether he was at the time, has in the preceding six months been, or was at the time of the originating events a director of a body corporate, which was refused admission to, conditionally included in, removed or contingently removed from, any list or equivalent list or is currently suspended from any such list, and if so, what the facts were in each such case and the reasons given by the Primary Care Trust or equivalent body in each case.

(5) When the Primary Care Trust takes into consideration any of the matters set out in paragraph (4), it shall consider the overall effect of all the matters being considered.

(6) When the Primary Care Trust has decided whether or not to include a performer in its performers list, it shall notify him within 7 days of that decision of –

(a) that decision; and

(b) if it has decided not to include him, the reasons for that (including any facts relied upon) and of any right of appeal under regulation 15 against that decision.

(7) When the Primary Care Trust notifies the performer under paragraph (6)(b), it shall—

(a) notify him that if he wishes to exercise a right of appeal, he must do so within the period of 28 days beginning with the date on which it gave him the notice informing him of its decision; and

(b) tell him how to exercise any such right.

Requirements with which a performer in a performers list must comply

9.—(1) A performer, who is included in a performers list of a Primary Care Trust, shall make a declaration to that Trust in writing, within 7 days of its occurrence, if he –

(a) is convicted of any criminal offence in the United Kingdom;

(b) is bound over following a criminal conviction in the United Kingdom;

(c) accepts a police caution in the United Kingdom;

(d) has accepted and agreed to pay either a procurator fiscal fine under section 302 of the Criminal Procedure (Scotland) Act 1995 or a penalty under section 115A of the Social Security Administration Act 1992;

(e) has, in summary proceedings in Scotland in respect of an offence, been the subject of an order discharging him absolutely (without proceeding to conviction);

(f) is convicted elsewhere of an offence, or what would constitute a criminal offence if committed in England and Wales;

(g) is charged in the United Kingdom with a criminal offence, or is charged elsewhere with an offence which, if committed in England and Wales, would constitute a criminal offence;

(h) is informed by any licensing, regulatory or other body of the outcome of any investigation into his professional conduct, and there is a finding against him;

    (i) becomes the subject of any investigation into his professional conduct by any licensing, regulatory or other body;

    (j) becomes subject to an investigation into his professional conduct in respect of any current or previous employment, or is informed of the outcome of any such investigation, where it is adverse;

    (k) becomes to his knowledge the subject of any investigation by the NHS Counter Fraud and Security Management Service in relation to fraud, or is informed of the outcome of such an investigation, where it is adverse;

    (l) becomes the subject of any investigation by another Primary Care Trust or equivalent body, which might lead to his removal from any list or equivalent list; or

    (m) is removed, contingently removed or suspended from, refused admission to, or conditionally included in, any list or equivalent list,

and, if so, he shall give details, including approximate dates, and where any investigation or proceedings were or are to be brought, the nature of that investigation or those proceedings, and any outcome.

    (2) A performer, who is included in a performers list of a Primary Care Trust, and is, was in the preceding six months, or was at the time of the originating events a director of a body corporate, shall make a declaration to that Trust in writing within 7 days of its occurrence if that body corporate –

    (a) is convicted of any criminal offence in the United Kingdom;

    (b) is convicted elsewhere of an offence, or what would constitute a criminal offence if committed in England and Wales;

    (c) is charged in the United Kingdom with a criminal offence, or is charged elsewhere with an offence which, if committed in England and Wales, would constitute a criminal offence;

    (d) is informed by any licensing, regulatory or other body of the outcome of any investigation into its provision of professional services, and there is a finding against it;

    (e) becomes the subject of any investigation into its provision of professional services by any licensing, regulatory or other body;

    (f) becomes to his knowledge the subject of any investigation in relation to fraud, or is informed of the outcome of such an investigation, if adverse;

    (g) becomes the subject of any investigation by another Primary Care Trust or equivalent body, which might lead to its removal from any list or equivalent list; or

    (h) is removed, contingently removed or suspended from, refused admission to, or conditionally included in any list or equivalent list,

and, if so, he shall give the name and registered address of the body corporate and details, including approximate dates, of where any investigation or those proceedings were or are to be brought, the nature of that investigation or proceedings, and any outcome.

    (3) A performer, who is included in a performers list of a Primary Care Trust, shall consent to a request being made by that Trust to any employer or former employer, licensing, regulatory or other body in the United Kingdom or elsewhere for information relating to a current investigation or an investigation, where the outcome was adverse, by that employer or body into the performer or a body corporate referred to in paragraphs (1) and (2) and, for the purposes of this paragraph, 'employer' includes any partnership of which the performer is or was a member.

    (4) A performer, who is included in a performers list of a Primary Care Trust, shall supply it with an enhanced criminal record certificate under section 115 of the Police Act 1997 in relation to himself, if it at any time, for reasonable cause, it requests him to provide such a certificate.

    (5) Subject to paragraph (6), a performer, who is included in a performers list of a Primary Care Trust, shall comply with any undertaking he gave on admission to that list or to any previous list from which he has been transferred pursuant to Schedule 1 to these Regulations or the Schedule to the Amendment Regulations.

(6) A performer, who is included in a relevant performers list of a Primary Care Trust, shall act in accordance with the undertakings that a performer is required by these Regulations to provide when applying for inclusion in that relevant performers list.

(7) A performer, who is included in a performers list of a Primary Care Trust, shall, except where the relevant Part provides to the contrary –

(a) participate in the appraisal system provided by a Primary Care Trust; and

(b) if the appraisal is not conducted by the Trust in whose list he is included, send that Trust a copy of the statement summarising that appraisal.

Removal from performers list

10.—(1) The Primary Care Trust must remove the performer from its performers list where it becomes aware that he –

(a) has been convicted in the United Kingdom of murder;

(b) has been convicted in the United Kingdom of a criminal offence, committed on or after the day prescribed in the relevant Part, and has been sentenced to a term of imprisonment of over six months;

(c) is subject to a national disqualification;

(d) has died; or

(e) is no longer a member of the relevant health care profession.

(2) Where a Primary Care Trust is notified by the FHSAA that it has considered an appeal by a performer against –

(a) a contingent removal by the Trust and has decided to remove him instead; or

(b) a conditional inclusion, where he has been conditionally included in a performers list until the appeal has been decided, and has decided not to include him,

the Trust shall remove him from its performers list and shall notify him immediately that it has done so.

(3) The Primary Care Trust may remove a performer from its performers list where any of the conditions set out in paragraph (4) is satisfied.

(4) The conditions mentioned in paragraph (3) are that –

(a) his continued inclusion in its performers list would be prejudicial to the efficiency of the services which those included in the relevant performers list perform ('an efficiency case');

(b) he is involved in a fraud case in relation to any health scheme; or

(c) he is unsuitable to be included in that performers list ('an unsuitability case').

(5) For the purposes of this regulation, in addition to the services covered by the definition of 'health scheme' in section 49F(8), the following shall also be health schemes –

(a) health services, including medical and surgical treatment, provided by the armed forces;

(b) services provided by Port Health Authorities constituted under the Public Health (Control of Disease) Act 1984;

(c) medical services provided to a prisoner in the care of the medical officer or other such officer of a prison appointed for the purposes of section 7 of the Prison Act 1952; and

(d) publicly-funded health services provided by or on behalf of any organisation anywhere in the world.

(6) Where the performer cannot demonstrate that he has performed the services, which those included in the relevant performers list perform, within the area of the Primary Care Trust during the preceding twelve months, it may remove him from its performers list.

(7) Subject to any provision in the relevant Part, in calculating the period of twelve months referred to in paragraph (6), the Primary Care Trust shall disregard any period during which –

(a) the performer was suspended under these Regulations; or

(b) he was performing whole time service in the armed forces in a national emergency (as a volunteer or otherwise), compulsory whole-time service in the armed forces (including service resulting from reserve liability), or any equivalent service, if liable for compulsory whole-time service in the armed forces.

(8) Where a Primary Care Trust is considering removing a performer from its performers list under paragraphs (3) to (6) or regulations 8(2), 12(3)(c) or 15(6)(b) or contingently removing a performer under regulation 12(1), it shall give him –

    (a) notice of any allegation against him;

    (b) notice of what action it is considering and on what grounds;

    (c) the opportunity to make written representations to it within 28 days of the date of the notification under sub-paragraph (b); and

    (d) the opportunity to put his case at an oral hearing before it, if he so requests, within the 28 day period mentioned in sub-paragraph (c).

(9) If there are no representations within the period specified in paragraph (8)(c), the Primary Care Trust shall decide whether or not to remove the performer and then, within 7 days of making that decision, notify him of –

    (a) that decision and the reasons for it (including any facts relied upon); and

    (b) any right of appeal under regulation 15.

(10) If there are representations, the Primary Care Trust must take them into account before reaching its decision, and shall then, within 7 days of making that decision, notify him of –

    (a) that decision and the reasons for it (including any facts relied upon); and

    (b) any right of appeal under regulation 15.

(11) If the performer requests an oral hearing, this must take place before the Primary Care Trust reaches its decision, and it shall then, within 7 days of making that decision, notify him of –

    (a) that decision and the reasons for it (including any facts relied upon); and

    (b) any right of appeal under regulation 15.

(12) When the Primary Care Trust notifies the performer of any decision, it shall inform him that, if he wishes to exercise a right of appeal, he must do so within the period of 28 days beginning with the date on which it informed him of its decision and it shall tell him how to exercise any such right.

(13) The Primary Care Trust shall also notify the performer of his right to have the decision reviewed in accordance with regulation 14.

(14) Where the Primary Care Trust decides to remove a performer under paragraph (6), he shall not be removed from its performers list, until –

    (a) a period of 28 days starting with the day on which it reaches its decision; or

    (b) any appeal is disposed of by the FHSAA, whichever is the later.

Criteria for a decision on removal

11.—(1) Where a Primary Care Trust is considering whether to remove a performer from its performers list under regulation 10(3) and (4)(c) ('an unsuitability case'), it shall –

    (a) consider any information relating to him which it has received in accordance with any provision of regulation 9;

    (b) consider any information held by the Secretary of State as to any record about past or current investigations or proceedings involving or related to that performer, which information he shall supply if the Trust so requests; and

    (c) in reaching its decision, take into consideration the matters set out in paragraph (2).

(2) The matters referred to in paragraph (1) are –

    (a) the nature of any offence, investigation or incident;

    (b) the length of time since any such offence, incident, conviction or investigation;

    (c) whether there are other offences, incidents or investigations to be considered;

    (d) any action taken or penalty imposed by any licensing or regulatory body, the police or the courts as a result of any such offence, incident or investigation;

    (e) the relevance of any offence, incident or investigation to his performing relevant primary services and any likely risk to any patients or to public finances;

(f) whether any offence was a sexual offence to which Part I of the Sexual Offences Act 1997 applies, or if it had been committed in England and Wales, would have applied;

(g) whether the performer has been refused admittance to, conditionally included in, removed, contingently removed or is currently suspended from any list or equivalent list, and if so, the facts relating to the matter which led to such action and the reasons given by the Primary Care Trust or equivalent body for such action; and

(h) whether he was at the time, has in the preceding six months been, or was at the time of the originating events a director of a body corporate, which was refused admission to, conditionally included in, removed or contingently removed from any list or equivalent list or is currently suspended from any such list, and if so, what the facts were in each such case and the reasons given by the Primary Care Trust or equivalent body in each case for such action.

(3) Where a Primary Care Trust is considering removal of a performer from its performers list under regulation 10(3) and (4)(b) it shall consider –

(a) any information relating to him which it has received in accordance with any provision of regulation 9;

(b) any information held by the Secretary of State as to any record about past or current investigations or proceedings involving or related to that performer, which information he shall supply, if the Trust so requests; and

(c) the matters set out in paragraph (4).

(4) The matters referred to in paragraph (3)(c) are –

(a) the nature of any incidents of fraud;

(b) the length of time since the last incident of fraud occurred, and since any investigation into it was concluded;

(c) whether there are any other incidents of fraud, or other criminal offences to be considered;

(d) any action taken by any licensing, regulatory or other body, the police or the courts as a result of any such offence, investigation or incident;

(e) the relevance of any investigation into an incident of fraud to his performing relevant primary services and the likely risk to patients or to public finances;

(f) whether the performer has been refused admittance to, conditionally included in, removed, or contingently removed or is currently suspended from, any list or equivalent list, and, if so, the facts relating to the matter which led to such action and the reasons given by the Primary Care Trust or equivalent body for such action; and

(g) whether he was at the time, has in the preceding six months been, or was at the time of the originating events a director of a body corporate, which was refused admission to, conditionally included in, or removed or contingently removed from, any list or equivalent list, or is currently suspended from any such list, and if so, what the facts were in each such case and the reasons given by the Primary Care Trust or equivalent body in each case.

(5) Where a Primary Care Trust is considering removal of a performer from its performers list under regulation 10(3) and (4)(a) ('an efficiency case'), it shall –

(a) consider any information relating to him which it has received in accordance with any provision of regulation 9;

(b) consider any information held by the Secretary of State as to any record about past or current investigations or proceedings involving or related to that performer, which information he shall supply, if the Trust so requests; and

(c) in reaching its decision, take into account the matters referred to in paragraph (6).

(6) The matters referred to in paragraph (5)(c) are –

(a) the nature of any incident which was prejudicial to the efficiency of the services, which the performer performed;

(b) the length of time since the last incident occurred and since any investigation into it was concluded;

(c) any action taken by any licensing, regulatory or other body, the police or the courts as a result of any such incident;

(d) the nature of the incident and whether there is a likely risk to patients;

(e) whether the performer has ever failed to comply with a request to undertake an assessment by the NCAA;

(f) whether he has previously failed to supply information, make a declaration or comply with an undertaking required on inclusion in a list;

(g) whether he has been refused admittance to, conditionally included in, removed or contingently removed or is currently suspended from any list or equivalent list, and if so, the facts relating to the matter which led to such action and the reasons given by the Primary Care Trust or the equivalent body for such action; and

(h) whether he was at the time, has in the preceding six months been, or was at the time of the originating events a director of a body corporate, which was refused admission to, conditionally included in, removed or contingently removed from, any list or equivalent list, or is currently suspended from any such list, and if so, what the facts were in each such case and the reasons given by the Primary Care Trust or equivalent body in each case for such action.

(7) In making any decision under regulation 10, the Primary Care Trust shall take into account the overall effect of any relevant incidents and offences relating to the performer of which it is aware, whichever condition it relies on.

(8) When making a decision on any condition in regulation 10(4), the Primary Care Trust shall state in its decision on which condition it relies.

Contingent removal

12.—(1) In an efficiency case or a fraud case the Primary Care Trust may, instead of deciding to remove a performer from its performers list, decide to remove him contingently.

(2) If it so decides, it must impose such conditions as it may decide on his inclusion in its performers list with a view to –

(a) removing any prejudice to the efficiency of the services in question (in an efficiency case); or

(b) preventing further acts or omissions (in a fraud case).

(3) If the Primary Care Trust determines that the performer has failed to comply with a condition, it may decide to –

(a) vary the conditions imposed;

(b) impose new conditions; or

(c) remove him from its performers list.

Suspension

13.—(1) If a Primary Care Trust is satisfied that it is necessary to do so for the protection of members of the public or is otherwise in the public interest, it may suspend a performer from its performers list, in accordance with the provisions of this regulation –

(a) while it decides whether or not to exercise its powers to remove him under regulation 10 or contingently remove him under regulation 12;

(b) while it waits for a decision affecting him of a court anywhere in the world or of a licensing or regulatory body;

(c) where it has decided to remove him, but before that decision takes effect; or

(d) pending appeal under these Regulations.

(2) Subject to paragraph (8), in a case falling within paragraph (1)(a), the Primary Care Trust must specify a period, not exceeding six months, as the period of suspension.

(3) Subject to paragraph (8), in a case falling within paragraph (1)(b), the Primary Care Trust may specify that the performer remains suspended after the decision referred to in that paragraph has been made for an additional period, not exceeding six months.

(8) The Primary Care Trust may extend the period of suspension under paragraph (2) or impose a further period of suspension under paragraph (3), so long as the aggregate does not exceed six months.

(9) Except as provided in paragraph 9(A), the effect of a suspension is that, while a performer is suspended under these Regulations, he is to be treated as not being included in the Primary Care Trust's performers list, even though his name appears in it.

(9A) For the purpose of an application by a performer who is suspended under these Regulations to be included in another performers list, he shall be treated as still included in the list from which he is suspended, notwithstanding that suspension.

(10) The Primary Care Trust may at any time revoke the suspension and notify the performer of its decision.

(11) Where a Primary Care Trust is considering suspending a performer or varying the period of suspension under this regulation, it shall give him –

    (a) notice of any allegation against him;

    (b) notice of what action it is considering and on what grounds; and

    (c) the opportunity to put his case at an oral hearing before it, on a specified day, provided that at least 24 hours notice of the hearing is given.

(12) If the performer does not wish to have an oral hearing or does not attend the oral hearing, the Primary Care Trust may suspend the performer with immediate effect.

(13) If an oral hearing does take place, the Primary Care Trust shall take into account any representations made before it reaches its decision.

(14) The Primary Care Trust may suspend the performer with immediate effect following the hearing.

(15) The Primary Care Trust shall notify the performer of its decision and the reasons for it (including any facts relied upon) within 7 days of making that decision.

Appeals

15.—(1) A performer may appeal (by way of redetermination) to the FHSAA against a decision of a Primary Care Trust mentioned in paragraph (2) by giving notice to the FHSAA.

(2) The Primary Care Trust decisions in question are decisions –

    (a) to refuse admission to a performers list under regulation 6(1);

    (b) to impose a particular condition under regulation 8, or to vary any condition or to impose a different condition under that regulation;

    (c) on a review, under regulation 14, of a conditional inclusion under regulation 8;

    (d) to remove the performer under regulations 8(2), 10(3) or (6), 12(3)(c) or 15(6)(b);

    (e) to impose a particular condition under regulation 12, or to vary any condition or to impose a different condition under that regulation;

    (f) on a review, under regulation 14, of a contingent removal under regulation 12; and

    (g) which the relevant Part prescribes that the performer may appeal to the FHSAA.

(3) On appeal the FHSAA may make any decision which the Primary Care Trust could have made.

(4) Where the decision of the FHSAA on appeal is that the appellant's inclusion in a performers list is to be subject to conditions, whether or not those conditions are identical with the conditions imposed by the Primary Care Trust, the Trust shall ask him to notify it within 28 days of the decision (or such longer period as the Trust may agree) whether he wishes to be included in its performers list subject to those conditions.

(5) If the performer notifies the Primary Care Trust that he does wish to be included in its performers list subject to the conditions, it shall so include him.

(6) Where the FHSAA on appeal decides to impose a contingent removal –

    (a) the Primary Care Trust and the performer may each apply to the FHSAA for the conditions imposed on the performer to be varied, for different conditions to be imposed, or for the contingent removal to be revoked; and

(b) the Primary Care Trust may remove the performer from its performers list if it determines that he has failed to comply with any such condition.

Notification

16.—(1) Where a Primary Care Trust decides to –

(a) refuse to admit a performer to its performers list on the grounds specified in regulation 6, (24(1 or 31 (1);

(b) impose conditions on his inclusion in that list under regulation 8;

(c) remove him from that list under regulation 10;

(d) remove him from that list contingently under regulation 12; or

(e) suspend him from that list under regulation 13, it shall notify the persons or bodies specified in paragraph (2) and shall additionally notify those specified in paragraph (3), if requested to do so by those persons or bodies in writing (including electronically), of the matters set out in paragraph (4).

(2) Where paragraph (1) applies, a Primary Care Trust shall notify within 7 days of that decision –

(a) the Secretary of State;

(b) any other Primary Care Trust or equivalent body that, to the knowledge of the notifying Trust –

(i) has the performer on any list or equivalent list,

(ii) is considering an application for inclusion in any list or equivalent list by him, or

(iii) in whose area he performs services;

(c) the Scottish Executive;

(d) the National Assembly for Wales;

(e) the Northern Ireland Executive;

(f) the relevant body or any other appropriate regulatory body;

(g) the NCAA; and

(h) where it is a fraud case, the NHS Counter Fraud and Security Management Service.

(3) The persons or bodies to be additionally notified in accordance with paragraph (1) are –

(a) persons or bodies that can establish that they are or were employing him, are using or have used his services or are or were considering employing him or using his services in a professional capacity; and

(b) a partnership which provides primary services and can establish that the performer is or was a member of the partnership or that it is considering inviting the performer to become such a member.

(4) The matters referred to in paragraph (1) are –

(a) his name, address and date of birth;

(b) his professional registration number;

(c) the date and a copy of the Primary Care Trust's decision; and

(d) a contact name of a person in the Trust for further enquiries.

(5) The Primary Care Trust shall send to the performer concerned a copy of any information about him provided to the persons or bodies listed in paragraph (2) or (3), and any correspondence with that person or body relating to that information.

(6) Where the Primary Care Trust has notified any of the persons or bodies specified in paragraph (2) or (3) of the matters set out in paragraph (4), it may, in addition, if requested by that person or body, notify that person or body of any evidence that was considered, including any representations from the performer.

(7) Where a Primary Care Trust is notified by the FHSAA that it has imposed a national disqualification on a performer who was, or had applied to be included, in its performers list, it shall notify the persons or bodies listed in paragraph (2)(b), (g) and (h) and paragraph (3).

(8) Where a decision is changed on review or appeal, or a suspension lapses, the Primary Care Trust shall notify the persons or bodies that were notified of the original decision of the later decision or the fact that that suspension has lapsed.

Restrictions on withdrawal from performers lists

18.—(1) Where a Primary Care Trust is investigating a performer –

   (a) for the purpose of deciding whether or not to exercise its powers to remove him under regulation 10 or contingently remove him under regulation 12; or

   (b) who has been suspended under regulation 13(1)(a),

he may not withdraw from any list kept by any Primary Care Trust in which he is included, except where the Secretary of State has given his consent, until the matter has been finally determined by the Trust.

   (2) Where a Primary Care Trust has decided to remove a performer from its performers list under regulation 10(3) to (6) or to contingently remove him from it under regulation 12, but has not yet given effect to its decision, he may not withdraw from any list kept by any Primary Care Trust in which he is included, except where the Secretary of State has given his consent.

   (3) Where a Primary Care Trust has suspended a performer under regulation 13(1)(b), he may not withdraw from any list kept by any Primary Care Trust in which he is included, except where the Secretary of State has given his consent, until the decision of the relevant court or body is known and the matter has been considered and finally determined by the Trust.

18A.— National disqualification

   (1) In this regulation and in regulation 19 'national disqualification' means the disqualification of the performer from inclusion in—

   (a) a performer's list;

   (b) a list referred to in section 49N(1) prepared by a Primary Care Trust;

   (c) a supplementary list prepared by a Primary Care Trust;

   (d) a list of pharmacists performing local pharmaceutical services prepared by a Primary Care Trust,

or only from inclusion in one or more descriptions of such list prepared by a Primary Care Trust or an equivalent list, the description being that specified by the FHSAA in its decision.

   (2) If a performer appeals to the FHSAA under regulation 15 and the FHSAA decides—

   (a) to remove the appellant from a performers list; or

   (b) to refuse to admit him to a performers list,

the FHSAA may also impose a national disqualification on that performer.

   (3) A Primary Care Trust which has—

   (a) removed a performer from its performers list; or

   (b) refused to include him in its performers list,

may apply to the FHSAA for a national disqualification to be imposed on him.

   (4) Any application under paragraph (3) must be made before the end of the period of three months beginning with –

   (a) the date of the removal or the refusal; or

   (b) 1st April 2006, whichever is the later.

   (5) If the FHSAA imposes a national disqualification on a person –

   (a) no Primary Care Trust may include him in any list from which he has been so disqualified; and

   (b) if he is included in any such list, a Primary Care Trust shall remove him from that list forthwith.

   (6) The FHSAA may, at the request of a person upon whom it has imposed a national disqualification, review that disqualification.

   (7) On a review under paragraph (6), the FHSAA may confirm or revoke that disqualification.

   (8) Subject to regulation 19, a request referred to in paragraph (6) may not be made before the end of the period of –

   (a) two years beginning with the date on which the national disqualification was imposed; or

   (b) one year beginning with the date of the FHSAA's decision on the last such Review.

Part 2 Medical Performers Lists

Interpretation

21.—(1) For the purposes of this Part the prescribed description of performer is medical practitioner and the relevant body is the General Medical Council.

(2) In this Part –

'2002 Order' means the Medical Act 1983 (Amendment) Order 2002;

'2003 Order' means the General and Specialist Medical Practice (Education, Training and Qualifications) Order 2003;

'the Board' means the Postgraduate Medical Education and Training Board;

'both registers' means the register of medical practitioners and, after the coming into force of article 10 of the 2003 Order, that register and the GP Register;

'CCT' means Certificate of Completion of Training awarded under article 8 of the 2003 Order, including any such certificate awarded in pursuance of the competent authority functions of the Board specified in article 20(3)(a) of that Order;

'contractor' means a general medical practitioner, who both provides and performs primary medical services in accordance with section 28C arrangements or under a general medical services contract;

'Fitness to Practise Panel' means a panel constituted pursuant to paragraph 19E of Schedule 1 to the Medical Act;

'the GP Register', after the coming into force of article 10 of the 2003 Order, means the register kept by virtue of that article;

'GP Registrar' means a medical practitioner, who is being trained in general practice …

'GP Trainer' means a general medical practitioner, other than a GP Registrar, who is [approved];

'general medical practitioner' means a GP Registrar or –

    (a) on and after the coming into force of article 10 of the 2003 Order, a medical practitioner whose name is included in the GP Register …

'health case' has the meaning ascribed to it by section 35E(4) of the Medical Act;

'Medical Act' means the Medical Act 1983;

'professional registration number' means the number against the general medical practitioner's name in the registers of medical practitioners;

'relevant scheme' means the scheme in respect of which the general medical practitioner is applying to be included in a medical performers list;

'register of medical practitioners' has the meaning given to it by section 2(2) of the Medical Act;

'scheme' means an arrangement to provide primary medical services –

    (a) in accordance with section 28C; or

    (b) under a general medical services contract;

'vocational training scheme' means –

    (a) a pre-arranged programme of training which is designed for the purpose of enabling a medical practitioner to gain the medical experience prescribed by regulation 6(1) of the Vocational Training Regulations; or

    (b) post-graduate medical education and training necessary for the award of a CCT in general practice under that article.

Medical performers list

22.—(1) Subject to paragraphs (2) to (3), a medical practitioner may not perform any primary medical services, unless he is a general medical practitioner and his name is included in a medical performers list.

(2) A medical practitioner, who is provisionally registered under section 15, 15A or 21 of the Medical Act, may perform primary medical services, when his name is not included in a medical performers list, but only whilst acting in the course of his employment in a resident medical capacity in an approved medical practice (within the meaning of section 11(4) of that Act).

(2A) A medical practitioner who falls within paragraph (2B) may perform primary medical services in the area of a Primary Care Trust, but only in so far as the performance of those services constitutes part of a programme of post-registration supervised clinical practice approved by the Board ('a post-registration programme').

(2B) A medical practitioner falls within this paragraph if he –

(a) is not a GP Registrar;

(b) is undertaking a post-registration programme;

(c) has notified the Primary Care Trust that he will be undertaking part or all of a post-registration programme in its area at least 24 hours before commencing any part of that programme taking place in the Primary Care Trust's area; and

(d) has, with that notification, provided the Primary Care Trust with evidence sufficient for it to satisfy itself that he is undergoing a post-registration programme.

(3) A GP Registrar, who has applied in accordance with these Regulations to a Primary Care Trust to have his name included in its medical performers list, may perform primary medical services, despite not being included in that list, until the first of the following events arises –

(a) the Trust notifies him of its decision on that application; or

(b) the end of a period of 2 months, starting with the date on which his vocational training scheme begins.

Grounds for removal from a medical performers list

26.—(1) Subject to paragraph (2) and in addition to the grounds in regulation 10(1), the Primary Care Trust must remove a medical practitioner from its medical performers list where it becomes aware that he is –

(a) the subject of a direction given by the Professional Conduct Committee under section 36(1)(i) or (ii) of the Medical Act (professional misconduct and criminal offences);

(b) the subject of an order or direction made by that Committee under section 38(1) of that Act (order for immediate suspension);

(c) the subject of a direction by a Fitness to Practise Panel for erasure or immediate suspension under section 35D(2)(a) or (b), (5)(a) or (b), (10)(a) or (b), or (12)(a) or (b) (functions of a Fitness to Practise Panel), or section 38(1) (power to order immediate suspension etc) of that Act;

(d) the subject of a direction by a Fitness to Practise Panel suspending him pursuant to rules made under paragraph 5A(3) of Schedule 4 to that Act (professional performance assessments);

(e) included in the medical performers list of another Primary Care Trust; or

(f) if a GP Registrar, in breach of the undertaking provided in accordance with regulation 23(2) and has failed to withdraw from the list after the Primary Care Trust has given him 28 days notice requesting him to do so.

(2) Paragraph (1)(c) shall not apply where a direction that a medical practitioner's registration be suspended is made in a health case.

Additional decision that may be appealed

27. A general medical practitioner may also appeal, under regulation 15, against a decision of the Primary Care Trust to refuse to include his name in its medical performers list under regulation 24(1).

The Human Fertilisation and Embryology (Research Purposes) Regulations 2001

(SI 2001, No. 188)

Citation, commencement and interpretation

(2) In these Regulations 'the Act' means the Human Fertilisation and Embryology Act 1990.

Further purposes for which research licences may be authorised

2.—(1) The Authority may issue a licence for research under paragraph 3 of Schedule 2 to the Act for any of the purposes specified in the following paragraph.

(2) A licence may be issued for the purposes of –

(a) increasing knowledge about the development of embryos;

(b) increasing knowledge about serious disease, or

(c) enabling any such knowledge to be applied in developing treatments for serious disease.

The Medicines for Human Use (Clinical Trials) Regulations 2004

(SI 2004, No. 1031)

Part I Introductory Provisions

Interpretation

2.—(1) In these Regulations –

'the Act' means the Medicines Act 1968;

'adult' means a person who has attained the age of 16 years;

'adverse event' means any untoward medical occurrence in a subject to whom a medicinal product has been administered, including occurrences which are not necessarily caused by or related to that product;

'adverse reaction' means any untoward and unintended response in a subject to an investigational medicinal product which is related to any dose administered to that subject;

'chief investigator' means –

    (a) in relation to a clinical trial conducted at a single trial site, the investigator for that site, or

    (b) in relation to a clinical trial conducted at more than one trial site, the authorised health professional, whether or not he is an investigator at any particular site, who takes primary responsibility for the conduct of the trial;

'clinical trial' means any investigation in human subjects, other than a non-interventional trial, intended –

    (a) to discover or verify the clinical, pharmacological or other pharmacodynamic effects of one or more medicinal products,

    (b) to identify any adverse reactions to one or more such products, or

    (c) to study absorption, distribution, metabolism and excretion of one or more such products, with the object of ascertaining the safety or efficacy of those products;

'Commission Directive 2003/94/EC' means Commission Directive 2003/94/EC laying down the principles and guidelines of good manufacturing practice for medicinal products for human use and for investigational medicinal products for human use;

'conditions and principles of good clinical practice' means the conditions and principles specified in Schedule 1;

'conducting a clinical trial' includes –

    (a) administering, or giving directions for the administration of, an investigational medicinal product to a subject for the purposes of that trial,

    (b) giving a prescription for an investigational medicinal product for the purposes of that trial,

    (c) carrying out any other medical or nursing procedure in relation to that trial, and

    (d) carrying out any test or analysis –

        (i) to discover or verify the clinical, pharmacological or other pharmacodynamic effects of the investigational medicinal products administered in the course of the trial,

        (ii) to identify any adverse reactions to those products, or

        (iii) to study absorption, distribution, metabolism and excretion of those products,

but does not include any activity undertaken prior to the commencement of the trial which consists of making such preparations for the trial as are necessary or expedient;

'the GCP Directive' means Commission Directive 2005/28/EC laying down principles and detailed guidelines for good clinical practice as regards investigational medicinal products for human use, as well as the requirements for authorisation of the manufacturing or importation of such products;

'the Directive' means Directive 2001/20/EC of the European Parliament and of the Council on the approximation of the laws, regulations and administrative provisions of the Member States relating to the implementation of good clinical practice in the conduct of clinical trials on medicinal products for human use;

'Directive 2001/83/EC' means Directive 2001/83/EC of the European Parliament and of the Council on the Community code relating to medicinal products for human use, as amended;

'the European Medicines Agency' means the European Agency for the Evaluation of Medicinal Products established by Council Regulation (EEC) No. 2309/93 laying down Community procedures for the authorization and supervision of medicinal products for human and veterinary use and establishing a European Agency for the Evaluation of Medicinal Products;

'ethics committee' means –

    (a) a committee established or recognised in accordance with Part 2,

    (b) the Ethics Committee constituted by regulations made by the Scottish Ministers under section 51(6) of the Adults with Incapacity (Scotland) Act 2000, or

    (c) the Gene Therapy Advisory Committee;

'the Gene Therapy Advisory Committee' means the Gene Therapy Advisory Committee appointed by the Secretary of State to –

(a) consider and advise on the acceptability of proposals for gene therapy research on human subjects, on ethical grounds, and

(b) provide advice on developments in gene therapy research and their implications;

'health care' means services for or in connection with the prevention, diagnosis or treatment of illness;

'informed consent' shall be construed in accordance with paragraph 3 of Part 1 of Schedule 1;

'investigational medicinal product' means a pharmaceutical form of an active substance or placebo being tested, or to be tested, or used, or to be used, as a reference in a clinical trial, and includes a medicinal product which has a marketing authorization but is, for the purposes of the trial –

(a) used or assembled (formulated or packaged) in a way different from the form of the product authorised under the authorization,

(b) used for an indication not included in the summary of product characteristics under the authorization for that product, or

(c) used to gain further information about the form of that product as authorised under the authorization;

'investigator' means, in relation to a clinical trial, the authorised health professional responsible for the conduct of that trial at a trial site, and if the trial is conducted by a team of authorised health professionals at a trial site, the investigator is the leader responsible for that team;

'licensing authority' shall be construed in accordance with section 6 of the Act;

'medicinal product' means –

(a) a medicinal product within the meaning given by Article 1 of Directive 2001/83/EC, or

(b) any product which is not a medicinal product within the meaning given by Article 1 of Directive 2001/83/EC, but which is a medicinal product within the meaning given by section 130 of the Act;

'minor' means a person under the age of 16 years;

'non-interventional trial' means a study of one or more medicinal products which have a marketing authorization, where the following conditions are met –

(a) the products are prescribed in the usual manner in accordance with the terms of that authorization,

(b) the assignment of any patient involved in the study to a particular therapeutic strategy is not decided in advance by a protocol but falls within current practice,

(c) the decision to prescribe a particular medicinal product is clearly separated from the decision to include the patient in the study,

(d) no diagnostic or monitoring procedures are applied to the patients included in the study, other than those which are ordinarily applied in the course of the particular therapeutic strategy in question, and

(e) epidemiological methods are to be used for the analysis of the data arising from the study;

'Phase I trial' means a clinical trial to study the pharmacology of an investigational medicinal product when administered to humans, where the sponsor and investigator have no knowledge of any evidence that the product has effects likely to be beneficial to the subjects of the trial;

'the principles and guidelines of good manufacturing practice' means the principles and guidelines of good manufacturing practice set out in Commission Directive 2003/94/EC;

'protocol' means a document that describes the objectives, design, methodology, statistical considerations and organisation of a clinical trial;

'serious adverse event', 'serious adverse reaction' or 'unexpected serious adverse reaction' means any adverse event, adverse reaction or unexpected adverse reaction, respectively, that –

(a) results in death,

(b) is life-threatening,

(c) requires hospitalisation or prolongation of existing hospitalisation,

(d) results in persistent or significant disability or incapacity, or

(e) consists of a congenital anomaly or birth defect;

'sponsor' shall be construed in accordance with regulation 3;

'subject' means, in relation to a clinical trial, an individual, whether a patient or not, who participates in a clinical trial –

    (a) as a recipient of an investigational medicinal product or of some other treatment or product, or

    (b) without receiving any treatment or product, as a control;

'third country' means a country or territory outside the European Economic Area;

'trial site' means a hospital, health centre, surgery or other establishment or facility at or from which a clinical trial, or any part of such a trial, is conducted;

'unexpected adverse reaction' means an adverse reaction the nature and severity of which is not consistent with the information about the medicinal product in question set out –

    (a) in the case of a product with a marketing authorization, in the summary of product characteristics for that product,

    (b) in the case of any other investigational medicinal product, in the investigator's brochure relating to the trial in question.

Sponsor of a clinical trial

3.—(1) In these Regulations, subject to the following paragraphs, 'sponsor' means, in relation to a clinical trial, the person who takes responsibility for the initiation, management and financing (or arranging the financing) of that trial.

    (11) A person who is a sponsor of a clinical trial in accordance with this regulation must –

    (a) be established in an EEA State, or

    (b) have a legal representative who is so established.

Part II Ethics Committees

United Kingdom Ethics Committees Authority

5.—(1) The body responsible for establishing, recognising and monitoring ethics committees in the United Kingdom in accordance with these Regulations is the United Kingdom Ethics Committees Authority, which is a body consisting of –

    (a) the Secretary of State for Health;

    (b) the National Assembly for Wales;

    (c) the Scottish Ministers; and

    (d) the Department for Health, Social Services and Public Safety for Northern Ireland.

Establishment of ethics committees

6.—(1) The Authority may establish ethics committees to act –

    (a) for the entire United Kingdom or for such areas of the United Kingdom; and

    (b) in relation to such descriptions or classes of clinical trials,

as the Authority consider appropriate.

Part III Authorisation for Clinical Trials and Ethics Committee Opinion

Requirement for authorisation and ethics committee opinion

12.—(1) No person shall –

    (a) start a clinical trial or cause a clinical trial to be started; or

    (b) conduct a clinical trial,

unless the conditions specified in paragraph (3) are satisfied.

    (2) No person shall –

    (a) recruit an individual to be a subject in a trial;

    (b) issue an advertisement for the purpose of recruiting individuals to be subjects in a trial,

unless the condition specified in paragraph (3)(a) has been satisfied.

(3) The conditions referred to in paragraphs (1) and (2) are –

   (a) an ethics committee to which an application in relation to the trial may be made in accordance with regulation 14 or an appeal panel appointed under Schedule 4 has given a favourable opinion in relation to the clinical trial; and

   (b) the clinical trial has been authorised by the licensing authority.

Application for ethics committee opinion

14.—(1) An application for an ethics committee opinion in relation to a clinical trial shall be made by the chief investigator for that trial.

(2) A chief investigator for a trial shall make an application for an ethics committee opinion in relation to that trial to one ethics committee only, regardless of the number of trial sites at which the trial is to be conducted.

(5) An application for an ethics committee opinion in relation to a clinical trial involving medicinal products for gene therapy, other than a trial falling within paragraph (4), shall be made to the Gene Therapy Advisory Committee.

Ethics committee opinion

15.—(1) Subject to paragraphs (3) and (4), an ethics committee shall within the specified period following receipt of a valid application, give an opinion in relation to the clinical trial to which the application relates.

(2) Where following receipt of a valid application it appears to the committee that further information is required in order to give an opinion on a trial, the committee may, within the specified period and before giving its opinion, send a notice in writing to the applicant requesting that he furnishes the committee with that information.

(5) In preparing its opinion, the committee shall consider, in particular, the following matters –

   (a) the relevance of the clinical trial and its design;

   (b) whether the evaluation of the anticipated benefits and risks as required under paragraph 10of Part 2 of Schedule 1 is satisfactory and whether the conclusions are justified;

   (c) the protocol;

   (d) the suitability of the investigator and supporting staff;

   (e) the investigator's brochure or, where the investigational medicinal product has a marketing authorization and the product is to be used in accordance with the terms of that authorization, the summary of product characteristics relating to that product;

   (f) the quality of the facilities for the trial;

   (g) the adequacy and completeness of the written information to be given, and the procedure to be followed, for the purpose of obtaining informed consent to the subjects' participation in the trial;

   (h) if the subjects are to include minors or persons incapable of giving informed consent, whether the research is justified having regard to the conditions and principles specified in Part 4 or Part 5 respectively of Schedule 1;

   (i) provision for indemnity or compensation in the event of injury or death attributable to the clinical trial;

   (j) any insurance or indemnity to cover the liability of the investigator or sponsor;

   (k) the amounts, and, where appropriate, the arrangements, for rewarding or compensating investigators and subjects;

   (l) the terms of any agreement between the sponsor and the owner or occupier of the trial site which are relevant to the arrangements referred to in sub-paragraph (k); and

   (m) the arrangements for the recruitment of subjects.

(6) If –

   (a) any subject of the clinical trial is to be a minor; and

   (b) the committee does not have a member with professional expertise in paediatric care,

it shall, before giving its opinion, obtain advice on the clinical, ethical and psychosocial problems in the field of paediatric care which may arise in relation to that trial.

(7) If –

    (a) any subject to the clinical trial is to be an adult incapable by reason of physical and mental incapacity to give informed consent to participation in the trial; and

    (b) the committee does not have a member with professional expertise in the treatment of –

        (i) the disease to which the trial relates, and

        (ii) the patient population suffering that disease,

it shall, before giving its opinion, obtain advice on the clinical, ethical and pyschosocial problems in the field of that disease and patient population which may arise in relation to that trial.

(10) In this regulation –

'the specified period' means –

    (a) in the case of a clinical trial involving a medicinal product for gene therapy or somatic cell therapy or a medicinal product containing a genetically modified organism –

        (i) where a specialist group or committee is consulted, 180 days, or

        (ii) where there is no such consultation, 90 days; or

    (b) in any other case, 60 days.

Review and appeal relating to ethics committee opinion

16.—(1) This regulation applies where a chief investigator for a trial has been notified by the ethics committee to which he made an application in accordance with regulation 14 that the committee's opinion in relation to that trial is not favourable.

(3) Where the opinion was given by an ethics committee other than the Gene Therapy Advisory Committee, the chief investigator may within 90 days of being notified that the committee's opinion is not favourable, give a notice to the United Kingdom Ethics Committees Authority –

    (a) stating his wish to appeal against the opinion; and

    (b) setting out his representations with respect to that opinion.

(4) Where the opinion was given by the Gene Therapy Advisory Committee, the chief investigator may, within 14 days of being notified of that opinion –

    (a) give a notice in writing to the Committee requiring the Committee to review its opinion; or

    (b) give a notice in writing to the United Kingdom Ethics Committee Authority –

        (i) stating his wish to appeal against the opinion; and

        (ii) setting out his representations with respect to that opinion.

(5) Where the Gene Therapy Advisory Committee is required by a notice under paragraph (4) to review its opinion, it must do so within 60 days of receipt of the notice.

(6) On a review pursuant to paragraph (5), the Gene Therapy Advisory Committee may vary or confirm their opinion and shall give notice in writing to the chief investigator of the variation or confirmation.

(7) If the Gene Therapy Advisory Committee confirm their opinion pursuant to paragraph (6), a chief investigator may within the 14 days of being notified of the confirmation give notice in writing to the United Kingdom Ethics Committees Authority –

    (a) stating his wish to appeal against the Committee's opinion; and

    (b) setting out his representations with respect to that opinion.

Request for authorisation to conduct a clinical trial

17.—(1) A request for authorisation to conduct a clinical trial shall be made to the licensing authority by the sponsor of the trial.

Part IV Good Clinical Practice and the Conduct of Clinical Trials

Good clinical practice and protection of clinical trial subjects

28.—(1) No person shall –

    (a) conduct a clinical trial; or

(b) perform the functions of the sponsor of a clinical trial (whether that person is the sponsor or is acting under arrangements made with that sponsor), otherwise than in accordance with the conditions and principles of good clinical practice.

(2) Subject to paragraph (5), the sponsor of a clinical trial shall put and keep in place arrangements for the purpose of ensuring that with regard to that trial the conditions and principles of good clinical practice are satisfied or adhered to.

(3) Subject to paragraphs (4) and (5), the sponsor of a clinical trial shall ensure that –

(a) the investigational medicinal products used in the trial, and

(b) any devices used for the administration of such products, are made available to the subjects of the trial free of charge.

Conduct of trial in accordance with clinical trial authorisation etc.

29. Subject to regulation 30, no person shall conduct a clinical trial otherwise than in accordance with –

(a) the protocol relating to that trial, as may be amended from time to time in accordance with regulations 22 to 25;

(b) the terms of –

(i) the request for authorisation to conduct that trial,

(ii) the application for an ethics committee opinion in relation to that trial, and

(iii) any particulars or documents, other than the protocol, accompanying that request or that application, as may be amended from time to time in accordance with regulations 22 to 25; and

(c) any conditions imposed by the licensing authority under regulation 18(2) or (6), 19(8), 20(5), 24 (5) or Schedule 5.

Notification of serious breaches

29A.—(1) The sponsor of a clinical trial shall notify the licensing authority in writing of any serious breach of—

(a) the conditions and principles of good clinical practice in connection with that trial; or

(b) the protocol relating to that trial, as amended from time to time in accordance with regulations 22 to 25, within 7 days of becoming aware of that breach.

(2) For the purposes of this regulation, a 'serious breach' is a breach which is likely to effect to a significant degree –

(a) the safety or physical or mental integrity of the subjects of the trial; or

(b) the scientific value of the trial.

Urgent safety measures

30.—(1) The sponsor and investigator may take appropriate urgent safety measures in order to protect the subjects of a clinical trial against any immediate hazard to their health or safety.

(2) If measures are taken pursuant to paragraph (1), the sponsor shall immediately, and in any event no later than 3 days from the date the measures are taken, give written notice to the licensing authority and the relevant ethics committee of the measures taken and the circumstances giving rise to those measures.

Suspension or termination of clinical trial

31.—(1) If, in relation to a clinical trial –

(a) the licensing authority have objective grounds for considering that –

(i) any condition, restriction or limitation which applies to the conduct of the trial and is set out in the request for authorisation or the particulars or documents accompanying that request, or

(ii) any condition imposed by the licensing authority under regulation 18(2) or (6), 19 (8), 20(5), 24 (5) or Schedule 5, is no longer satisfied (either generally or at a particular trial site); or

(b) the licensing authority have information raising doubts about the safety or scientific validity of the trial, or the conduct of the trial at a particular trial site,

the licensing authority may, by a notice served in accordance with paragraph (2), require that the trial, or the conduct of the trial at a particular trial site, be suspended or terminated.

Part V Pharmacovigilance

Notification of adverse events

32.—(1) An investigator shall report any serious adverse event which occurs in a subject at a trial site at which he is responsible for the conduct of a clinical trial immediately to the sponsor.

(2) An immediate report under paragraph (1) may be made orally or in writing.

(3) Following the immediate report of a serious adverse event, the investigator shall make a detailed written report on the event.

Notification of suspected unexpected serious adverse reactions

33.—(1) A sponsor shall ensure that all relevant information about a suspected unexpected serious adverse reaction which occurs during the course of a clinical trial in the United Kingdom and is fatal or life-threatening is –

(a) recorded; and

(b) reported as soon as possible to –

(i) the licensing authority,

(ii) the competent authorities of any EEA State, other than the United Kingdom, in which the trial is being conducted, and

(iii) the relevant ethics committee, and in any event not later that 7 days after the sponsor was first aware of the reaction.

(5) A sponsor shall ensure that, in relation to each clinical trial in the United Kingdom for which he is the sponsor, the investigators responsible for the conduct of a trial are informed of any suspected unexpected serious adverse reaction which occurs in relation to an investigational medicinal product used in that trial, whether that reaction occurs during the course of that trial or another trial for which the sponsor is responsible.

Clinical trials conducted in third countries

34. If a clinical trial is being conducted at a trial site in a third country in addition to sites in the United Kingdom, the sponsor of that trial shall ensure that all suspected unexpected serious adverse reactions occurring at that site are entered into the European database established in accordance with Article 11 of the Directive.

Annual list of suspected serious adverse reactions and safety report

35.—(1) As soon as practicable after the end of the reporting year, a sponsor shall, in relation to each investigational medicinal product tested in clinical trials in the United Kingdom for which he is the sponsor furnish the licensing authority and the relevant ethics committees with –

(a) a list of all the suspected serious adverse reactions which have occurred during that year in relation to –

(i) those trials, whether at trial sites in the United Kingdom or elsewhere, or

(ii) any other trials relating to that product which are conducted outside the United Kingdom and for which he is the sponsor, including those reactions relating to any investigational medicinal product used as a placebo or as a reference in those trials; and

(b) a report on the safety of the subjects of those trials.

Part VIII Enforcement and Related Provisions

Offences

49.—(1) Any person who contravenes any of the following provisions –

(a) regulation 3A;
    (aa) regulation 12(1) and (2);
(b) regulation 13(1);
(c) regulation 27;
(d) regulation 28(1) to (3);
(e) regulation 29;
    (ee) regulation 29A;
(f) regulation 30(2);
    (ff) regulation 31A(1) to (3) and (5) to (10);
(g) regulation 32(1), (3), and (5) to (9);
(h) regulation 33(1) to (5);
(i) regulation 34;
(j) regulation 35(1);
(k) regulation 36(1);
(l) regulation 42; and
(m) regulation 43(1) and (6), shall be guilty of an offence.

False or misleading information

50.—(1) Any person who in the course of –
    (a) making an application for an ethics committee opinion;
    (b) making a request for authorisation to conduct a clinical trial; or
    (c) making an application for the grant or variation of a manufacturing authorisation,
provides to the licensing authority or an ethics committee any relevant information which is false or misleading in a material particular shall be guilty of an offence.

    (2) Any person who –
    (a) is conducting a clinical trial authorised in accordance with these Regulations;
    (b) is a sponsor of such a clinical trial;
    (c) while acting under arrangements made with a sponsor of such a clinical trial, performs the functions of that sponsor; or
    (d) holds a manufacturing authorisation,
and who, for the purposes of these Regulations, provides to the licensing authority or an ethics committee any relevant information which is false or misleading in a material particular shall be guilty of an offence.

    (4) In this regulation, 'relevant information' means any information which is relevant to an evaluation of –
    (a) the safety, quality or efficacy of an investigational medicinal product;
    (b) the safety or scientific validity of a clinical trial; or
    (c) whether, with regard to a clinical trial, the conditions and principles of good clinical practice are being satisfied or adhered to.

Defence of due diligence

51.—(1) A person does not commit an offence under these Regulations if he took all reasonable precautions and exercised all due diligence to avoid the commission of that offence.

    (2) Where evidence is adduced which is sufficient to raise an issue with respect to that defence, the court or jury shall assume that the defence is satisfied unless the prosecution proves beyond reasonable doubt that it is not.

Penalties

52. A person guilty of an offence under these Regulations shall be liable –
    (a) on summary conviction to a fine not exceeding the statutory maximum or to imprisonment for a term not exceeding three months or to both;
    (b) on conviction on indictment to a fine or to imprisonment for a term not exceeding two years or to both.

Schedule 1 Regulation 2(1), Conditions and Principles of Good Clinical Practice and the Protection of Clinical Trial Subjects

Part I Application and Interpretation

1.—(1) The conditions and principles specified in Part 2 apply to all clinical trials.

(2) If any subject of a clinical trial is –

(a) an adult able to give informed consent, or

(b) an adult who has given informed consent to taking part in the clinical trial prior to the onset of incapacity, the conditions and principles specified in Part 3 apply in relation to that subject.

(3) If any subject of a clinical trial is a minor, the conditions and principles specified in Part 4 apply in relation to that subject.

(4) If any subject –

(a) is an adult unable by virtue of physical or mental incapacity to give informed consent, and

(b) did not, prior to the onset of incapacity, give or refuse to give informed consent to taking part in the clinical trial, the conditions and principles specified in Part 5 apply in relation to that subject.

(5) If any person –

(a) is an adult unable by virtue of physical or mental incapacity to give informed consent, and

(b) has, prior to the onset of incapacity, refused to give informed consent to taking part in the clinical trial, that person cannot be included as a subject in the clinical trial.

3.—(1) For the purposes of this Schedule, a person gives informed consent to take part, or that a subject is to take part, in a clinical trial only if his decision –

(a) is given freely after that person is informed of the nature, significance, implications and risks of the trial; and

(b) either –

(i) is evidenced in writing, dated and signed, or otherwise marked, by that person so as to indicate his consent, or

(ii) if the person is unable to sign or to mark a document so as to indicate his consent, is given orally in the presence of at least one witness and recorded in writing.

(2) For the purposes of this Schedule, references to informed consent –

(a) shall be construed in accordance with paragraph (1); and

(b) include references to informed consent given or refused by an adult unable by virtue of physical or mental incapacity to give informed consent, prior to the onset of that incapacity.

Part 2 Conditions and Principles which Apply to all Clinical Trials

Principles based on Articles 2 to 5 of the GCP Directive

1. The rights, safety and well-being of the trial subjects shall prevail over the interests of science and society.

2. Each individual involved in conducting a trial shall be qualified by education, training and experience to perform his tasks.

3. Clinical trials shall be scientifically sound and guided by ethical principles in all their aspects.

4. The necessary procedures to secure the quality of every aspect of the trial shall be complied with.

5. The available non-clinical and clinical information on an investigational medicinal product shall be adequate to support the proposed clinical trial.

6. Clinical trials shall be conducted in accordance with the principles of the Declaration of Helsinki.

7. The protocol shall provide for the definition of inclusion and exclusion of subjects participating in a clinical trial, monitoring and publication policy.

8. The investigator and sponsor shall consider all relevant guidance with respect to commencing and conducting a clinical trial.

9. All clinical information shall be recorded, handled and stored in such a way that it can be accurately reported, interpreted and verified, while the confidentiality of records of the trial subjects remains protected.

Conditions based on Article 3 of the Directive

10. Before the trial is initiated, foreseeable risks and inconveniences have been weighed against the anticipated benefit for the individual trial subject and other present and future patients. A trial should be initiated and continued only if the anticipated benefits justify the risks.

11. The medical care given to, and medical decisions made on behalf of, subjects shall always be the responsibility of an appropriately qualified doctor or, when appropriate, of a qualified dentist.

12. A trial shall be initiated only if an ethics committee and the licensing authority comes to the conclusion that the anticipated therapeutic and public health benefits justify the risks and may be continued only if compliance with this requirement is permanently monitored.

13. The rights of each subject to physical and mental integrity, to privacy and to the protection of the data concerning him in accordance with the Data Protection Act 1998 are safeguarded.

14. Provision has been made for insurance or indemnity to cover the liability of the investigator and sponsor which may arise in relation to the clinical trial.

Part III Conditions which Apply in Relation to an Adult able to Consent or Who has Given Consent Prior to the Onset of Incapacity

1. The subject has had an interview with the investigator, or another member of the investigating team, in which he has been given the opportunity to understand the objectives, risks and inconveniences of the trial and the conditions under which it is to be conducted.

2. The subject has been informed of his right to withdraw from the trial at any time.

3. The subject has given his informed consent to taking part in the trial.

4. The subject may, without being subject to any resulting detriment, withdraw from the clinical trial at any time by revoking his informed consent.

5. The subject has been provided with a contact point where he may obtain further information about the trial.

Part IV Conditions and Principles which Apply in Relation to a Minor

Conditions

1. Subject to paragraph 6, a person with parental responsibility for the minor or, if by reason of the emergency nature of the treatment provided as part of the trial no such person can be contacted prior to the proposed inclusion of the subject in the trial, a legal representative for the minor has had an interview with the investigator, or another member of the investigating team, in which he has been given the opportunity to understand the objectives, risks and inconveniences of the trial and the conditions under which it is to be conducted.

2. That person or legal representative has been provided with a contact point where he may obtain further information about the trial.

3. That person or legal representative has been informed of the right to withdraw the minor from the trial at any time.

4. That person or legal representative has given his informed consent to the minor taking part in the trial.

5. That person with parental responsibility or the legal representative may, without the minor being subject to any resulting detriment, withdraw the minor from the trial at any time by revoking his informed consent.

6. The minor has received information according to his capacity of understanding, from staff with experience with minors, regarding the trial, its risks and its benefits.

7. The explicit wish of a minor who is capable of forming an opinion and assessing the information referred to in the previous paragraph to refuse participation in, or to be withdrawn from, the clinical trial at any time is considered by the investigator.

8. No incentives or financial inducements are given –

    (a) to the minor; or

    (b) to a person with parental responsibility for that minor or, as the case may be, the minor's legal representative, except provision for compensation in the event of injury or loss.

9. The clinical trial relates directly to a clinical condition from which the minor suffers or is of such a nature that it can only be carried out on minors.

10. Some direct benefit for the group of patients involved in the clinical trial is to be obtained from that trial.

11. The clinical trial is necessary to validate data obtained –

    (a) in other clinical trials involving persons able to give informed consent, or

    (b) by other research methods.

12. The corresponding scientific guidelines of the European Medicines Agency are followed.

Principles

13. Informed consent given by a person with parental responsibility or a legal representative to a minor taking part in a clinical trial shall represent the minor's presumed will.

14. The clinical trial has been designed to minimise pain, discomfort, fear and any other foreseeable risk in relation to the disease and the minor's stage of development.

15. The risk threshold and the degree of distress have to be specially defined and constantly monitored.

16. The interests of the patient always prevail over those of science and society.

Part V Conditions and Principles which Apply in Relation to an Incapacitated Adult

Conditions

1. The subject's legal representative has had an interview with the investigator, or another member of the investigating team, in which he has been given the opportunity to understand the objectives, risks and inconveniences of the trial and the conditions under which it is to be conducted.

2. The legal representative has been provided with a contact point where he may obtain further information about the trial.

3. The legal representative has been informed of the right to withdraw the subject from the trial at any time.

4. The legal representative has given his informed consent to the subject taking part in the trial.

5. The legal representative may, without the subject being subject to any resulting detriment, withdraw the subject from the trial at any time by revoking his informed consent.

6. The subject has received information according to his capacity of understanding regarding the trial, its risks and its benefits.

7. The explicit wish of a subject who is capable of forming an opinion and assessing the information referred to in the previous paragraph to refuse participation in, or to be withdrawn from, the clinical trial at any time is considered by the investigator.

8. No incentives or financial inducements are given to the subject or their legal representative, except provision for compensation in the event of injury or loss.

9. There are grounds for expecting that administering the medicinal product to be tested in the trial will produce a benefit to the subject outweighing the risks or produce no risk at all.

10. The clinical trial is essential to validate data obtained –

      (a) in other clinical trials involving persons able to give informed consent, or

      (b) by other research methods.

11. The clinical trial relates directly to a life-threatening or debilitating clinical condition from which the subject suffers.

Principles

12. Informed consent given by a legal representative to an incapacitated adult in a clinical trial shall represent that adult's presumed will.

13. The clinical trial has been designed to minimise pain, discomfort, fear and any other foreseeable risk in relation to the disease and the cognitive abilities of the patient.

14. The risk threshold and the degree of distress have to be specially defined and constantly monitored.

15. The interests of the patient always prevail over those of science and society.

Schedule 2 Regulations 7(1)(b), 8(a) and 9 Additional Provisions Relating to Ethics Committees

Interpretation

1. In this Schedule –

    'expert member' means a member of an ethics committee who –

      (a) is a health care professional,

      (b) has professional qualifications or experience relating to the conduct of, or use of statistics in clinical trials, unless those professional qualifications or experience relate only to the ethics of clinical research or medical treatment, or

      (c) is not a health care professional, but has been a registered medical practitioner or a person registered in the dentists register under the Dentists Act 1984;

    'lay member' means a member of an ethics committee, other than an expert member.

Membership

3.—(1) An ethics committee shall consist of –

      (a) expert members; and

      (b) lay members.

(2) An ethics committee shall have no more than 18 members.

(3) Subject to paragraph 7, the members of an ethics committee shall be appointed by the appointing authority.

(4) A person shall not be eligible for appointment as a lay member of an ethics committee if, in the course of his employment or business, he –

      (a) provides medical, dental or nursing care, or

      (b) conducts clinical research.

(5) An appointing authority shall, in relation to an ethics committee, exercise their power under sub-paragraph (3) so as to ensure that –

      (a) at least one third of the total membership shall be lay members; and

      (b) at least half of the lay members must be persons who are not, or who never have been –

         (i) health care professionals,

         (ii) persons involved in the conduct of clinical research, other than as a subject of such research, or

         (iii) a chairman, member or director of –

            (aa) a health service body, or

            (bb) a body, other than a health service body, which provides health care.

The Human Fertilisation and Embryology Authority (Disclosure of Donor Information) Regulations 2004

(SI 2004, No. 1511)

Citation, commencement and interpretation

(2) In these Regulations –

'the Act' means the Human Fertilisation and Embryology Act 1990;

'applicant' means a person who has requested information under section 31(4) of the Act;

'donor' means the person who has provided the sperm, eggs or embryos that have been used for treatment services in consequence of which the applicant was, or may have been, born.

Information that the Authority is required to give

2.—(1) Subject to paragraph (4), the information contained in the register which the Authority is required to give an applicant by virtue of section 31(4)(a) of the Act is any information to which paragraph (2) or (3) applies.

(2) This paragraph applies to information as to –

(a) the sex, height, weight, ethnic group, eye colour, hair colour, skin colour, year of birth, country of birth and marital status of the donor;

(b) whether the donor was adopted;

(c) the ethnic group or groups of the donor's parents;

(d) the screening tests carried out on the donor and information on his personal and family medical history;

(e) where the donor has a child, the sex of that child and where the donor has children, the number of those children and the sex of each of them;

(f) the donor's religion, occupation, interests and skills and why the donor provided sperm, eggs or embryos;

(g) matters contained in any description of himself as a person which the donor has provided;

(h) any additional matter which the donor has provided with the intention that it be made available to an applicant;

but does not include information which may identify the donor by itself or in combination with any other information which is in, or is likely to come into, the possession of the applicant.

(3) This paragraph applies to information from which the donor may be identified which he provides after 31st March 2005 to a person to whom a licence applies, being information as to –

(a) any matter specified in sub-paragraphs (a) to (h) of paragraph (2);

(b) the surname and each forename of the donor and, if different, the surname and each forename of the donor used for the registration of his birth;

(c) the date of birth of the donor and the town or district in which he was born;

(d) the appearance of the donor;

(e) the last known postal address of the donor.

(4) The information which the Authority is required to give to the applicant does not include any information which at the time of his request the applicant indicates that he does not wish to receive.

The Human Tissue Act 2004 (Ethical Approval, Exceptions from Licensing and Supply of Information about Transplants) Regulations 2006

(SI 2006, No. 1260)

Citation, commencement and interpretation

(2) In these Regulations –

'the Act' means the Human Tissue Act 2004;

'donor' and 'recipient' have the meaning given by regulation 4; and

'research ethics authority' means –

    (a) an ethics committee established or recognised in accordance with Part 2 of the Medi-cines

for Human Use (Clinical Trials) Regulations 2004, or

    (b) any other committee established or person appointed –

        (i) to advise on, or on matters which include, the ethics of research investigations on relevant material which has come from a human body, and

        (ii) recognised for that purpose by, or on behalf of, the –

            (aa) Secretary of State,

            (bb) National Assembly of Wales, or

            (cc) Department of Health, Social Services and Public Safety;

'transplantable material' has the meaning given in regulation 9 of the Human Tissue Act 2004 (Persons who Lack Capacity to Consent and Transplants) Regulations 2006.

Ethical approval of research

2. Research is ethically approved for the purposes of section 1(9)(a) and paragraph 10(b) of Schedule 4 to the Act where it is approved by a research ethics authority.

Exceptions from licensing requirement

3.—(1) The storage of relevant material by a person who intends to use it for a scheduled purpose is excepted from section 16(2)(e)(ii) of the Act (storage of relevant material which has come from a human body) in the circumstances set out in paragraphs (2) to (4).

    (2) Storage of relevant material which has come from the body of a living person is excepted where the person storing it is intending to use it for –

    (a) any purpose specified in paragraphs 2 to 5 or 8 to 12 of Part 1 of Schedule 1 to the Act (determining the cause of death, establishing after a person's death the efficacy of any drug or treatment administered to him, obtaining information which may be relevant to another person, public display, clinical audit, education or training relating to human health, performance assessment, public health monitoring, quality assurance); or

    (b) the purpose of qualifying research.

    (3) Storage of relevant material which has come from a human body is excepted where the person storing it is intending to use it for the purpose of transplantation and –

    (a) the material is an organ or part of an organ if it is to be used for the same purpose as the entire organ in the human body; or

    (b) the storage is for a period of less than 48 hours.

    (4) Storage of relevant material which has come from the body of a deceased person is excepted where –

    (a) the person storing it is intending to use it for the purpose of qualifying research; or

    (b) the relevant material –

        (i) has come from premises in respect of which a license under section 16(2) is in force,

        (ii) is stored by a person intending to use it for the sole purpose of analysis for a scheduled purpose other than research, and

        (iii) will be returned to premises in respect of which a license under section 16(2) is in force when the analysis is completed.

    (5) In this regulation –

    (a) 'organ' means a differentiated and vital part of the human body, formed by different tissues, that maintains its structure, vascularisation and capacity to develop physio-logical functions with an important level of autonomy;

    (b) 'qualifying research' means –

> (i) research which is ethically approved for the purposes of section 1(9)(a) of the Act; or
> (ii) a specific research project for which such ethical approval is pending;

(c) an application for ethical approval is pending from when it has been submitted to a research ethics authority until the decision of the authority has been communicated to the applicant.

Information about transplant operations

Information to be supplied by medical practitioner who removes transplantable material

4. A person who has removed transplantable material from a human body ('the donor') which is proposed to be transplanted to another person ('the recipient') shall supply to NHS Blood and Transplant the information specified in Schedule 1 to these Regulations.

Information to be supplied by medical practitioner who receives transplantable material

5. A person who has received transplantable material which is proposed to be transplanted to a recipient shall supply to NHS Blood and Transplant the information specified in Schedule 2 to these Regulations.

Schedule 1 Regulation 4

Removal of Transplantable Material

Information about removal

1. Name and address of the hospital or other place at which the transplantable material was removed from the donor.

2. Full name of registered medical practitioner or person who removed the transplantable material, the appointment he holds and the place at which he holds it.

3. In any case where the transplantable material is considered unsuitable for transplanting after removal, a statement of –

(a) the reason for the unsuitability, and
(b) the manner of disposal of the material.

Information about transplantable material and donor

4. Description of the transplantable material.

5. Whether the donor was living or deceased at the time of its removal.

6. Date and time of its removal.

7. Full name of the donor and, where applicable, his hospital case note number.

Schedule 2 Regulation 5

Receipt of Transplantable Material

Information about receipt

1. Name and address of the hospital or other place at which the transplantable material was received.

2. Full name of registered medical practitioner who proposes to carry out the transplant (or who has carried it out), the appointment he holds and the place at which he holds it.

3. In any case where the transplantable material is not transplanted to another person, a statement of –

(a) the reason why not, and

(b) the manner of disposal of the material.

Information about transplantable material

4. Description of the transplantable material.

5. Name and address of the hospital or other place at which the transplantable material was removed from the donor.

6. If the transplantable material was removed outside the United Kingdom –

    (a) the name of the country in which the material was removed, and

    (b) the reference number allocated to the material by NHS Blood and Transplant when arrangements were made to import it.

Information about transplant and recipient

7. Full name of the recipient.

8. Date and time that the transplant was carried out.

9. In any case where the donor is genetically related to the recipient, a description of the relationship.

10. If the transplant was carried out in –

    (a) a health service hospital (within the meaning of the National Health Service Act 1977 or

    (b) a hospital vested in the Department of Health, Social Services and Public Safety or managed by a Health and Social Services Trust,

a statement indicating (if that is the case) that –

    (a) the recipient was entitled to the provision of the treatment by virtue of regulations made by the Council of the European Communities under Article 42 of the Treaty establishing the European Community, or

    (b) the recipient was a national of another country who was entitled to be provided with the treatment by virtue of an agreement entered into between the European Community and that other country, or

    (c) the treatment of the recipient was provided under an arrangement for providing health care mutually agreed between the Government of the United Kingdom and the Government of a country or territory specified in Schedule 2 to the National Health Service (Charges to Overseas Visitors Regulations 1989 or specified in Schedule 2 to the Provision of Health Services to Persons Not Ordinarily Resident Regulations 2005.

The Human Tissue Act 2004 (Persons who Lack Capacity to Consent and Transplants) Regulations 2006

2006 No. 1659

Part 1

Preliminary

Interpretation

2.   In these Regulations –

'the Act' means the Human Tissue Act 2004;

'the Authority' means the Human Tissue Authority;

'the clinical trials regulations' means –

    (a) the Medicines for Human Use (Clinical Trials) Regulations 2004(**a**) and any other regulations replacing those regulations or amending them, and

(b) any other regulations relating to clinical trials and designated by the Secretary of State as clinical trials regulations for the purposes of section 30(5) of the Mental Capacity Act 2005 (research);

'donor' and 'recipient' have the meaning given by regulation 11;

'intrusive research' means research of a kind that would be unlawful if it was carried out

(a) on or in relation to a person who had capacity to consent to it, but

(b) without his consent;

'organ' means a differentiated and vital part of the human body, formed by different tissues, that maintains its structure, vascularisation and capacity to develop physiological functions with an important level of autonomy;

'transplantable material' has the meaning given by –

(a) regulation 9 for the purposes of section 34 of the Act (information about transplant operations), and

(b) regulation 10 for the purposes of section 33 of the Act (restrictions on transplants involving a live donor).

Part 2

Persons Who Lack Capacity to Consent

Storage and use of relevant material

Deemed consent to storage and use of relevant material: England and Wales

3.—(1) This regulation applies in any case falling within paragraphs (a) and (b) of section 6 of the Act (storage and use involving material from adults who lack capacity to consent).

(2) An adult ('P') who lacks capacity to consent to an activity of a kind mentioned in section 1(1)(d) or (f) of the Act (storage or use of material for purposes specified in Schedule 1) which involves material from P's body, is deemed to have consented to the activity where –

(a) the activity is done for a purpose specified in paragraph 4 or 7 of Part 1 of Schedule 1 to the Act (the purposes of obtaining information relevant to another person and of transplantation) by a person who is acting in what he reasonably believes to be P's best interests;

(b) the activity is done for the purpose of a clinical trial which is authorised and conducted in accordance with the clinical trials regulations;

(c) the activity is done on or after the relevant commencement date for the purpose of intrusive research which is carried out in accordance with the requirements of section 30(1)(a) and (b) of the Mental Capacity Act 2005 (approval by appropriate body and compliance with sections 32 and 33 of that Act);

(d) the activity is done on or after the relevant commencement date for the purpose of intrusive research –

(i) section 34 of the Mental Capacity Act 2005 (loss of capacity during research project) applies in relation to that research, and

(ii) the activity is carried out in accordance with regulations made under section 34(2) of that Act; or

(e) the activity is done before the relevant commencement date for the purpose of research which, before that date, is ethically approved within the meaning of regulation 8.

Analysis of DNA

Purposes for which DNA may be analysed without consent: England and Wales

5.—(1) This regulation applies for the purposes of paragraph 12 of Schedule 4 to the Act (excepted purposes relating to DNA of adults who lack capacity to consent).

(2) In any case falling within sub-paragraph (1)(a)(i) and (b) of that paragraph (DNA manufactured by the body of a person who under the law of England and Wales lacks capacity to consent), the purposes for which DNA manufactured by the body of a person ('P') who lacks capacity to consent to analysis of the DNA may be analysed are –

(a) any purpose which the person carrying out the analysis reasonably believes to be in P's best interests;

(b) the purposes of a clinical trial which is authorised and conducted in accordance with the clinical trials regulations;

(c) the purposes of intrusive research which is carried out on or after the relevant commencement date in accordance with the requirements of section 30(1)(a) and (b) of the Mental Capacity Act 2005 (approval by appropriate body and compliance with sections 32 and 33 of that Act);

(d) the purposes of intrusive research –

(i) which is carried out on or after the relevant commencement date,

(ii) in relation to which section 34 of the Mental Capacity Act 2005 (loss of capacity during research project) applies, and

(iii) which is carried out in accordance with regulations made under section 34(2) of that Act; or

(e) research which is carried out before the relevant commencement date and which, before that date, is ethically approved within the meaning of regulation 8.

Ethical approval

Ethical approval for the purposes of regulations 3 to 6

8.—(1) Research is ethically approved within the meaning of this regulation if approval is given by a research ethics authority in the circumstances specified in paragraph (2).

(2) The circumstances are that –

(a) the research is in connection with disorders, or the functioning, of the human body,

(b) there are reasonable grounds for believing that research of comparable effectiveness cannot be carried out if the research has to be confined to, or relate only to, persons who have capacity to consent to taking part in it, and

(c) there are reasonable grounds for believing that research of comparable effectiveness cannot be carried out in circumstances such that the person carrying out the research is not in possession, and not likely to come into possession, of information from which the person from whose body the defined material has come can be identified.

(3) 'Defined material' –

(a) in relation to ethical approval for the purposes of regulations 3(2)(e) and 4(2)(c), means the relevant material involved in an activity of a kind mentioned in section 1(1) (d) or (f) of the Act, and

(b) in relation to ethical approval for the purposes of regulations 5(2)(e) and 6(2)(c), means the bodily material in relation to which an analysis of DNA is to be carried out.

(4) 'Research ethics authority' has the meaning given by regulation 2 of the Human Tissue Act 2004 (Ethical Approval, Exceptions from Licensing and Supply of Information about Transplants) Regulations 2006.

Part 3

Transplants

Meaning of transplantable material for the purposes of section 34 of the Act

9. For the purposes of section 34 of the Act (information about transplant operations) 'transplantable material' means –

(a) the whole or part of any of the following organs if it is to be used for the same purpose as the entire organ in the human body –
(i) kidney,
(ii) heart,
(iii) lung or a lung lobe,
(iv) pancreas,
(v) liver,
(vi) bowel,
(vii) larynx;
(b) face, or
(c) limb.

Meaning of transplantable material for the purposes of section 33 of the Act

10.—(1) Subject to paragraphs (2) and (3), for the purposes of section 33 of the Act (restriction on transplants involving a live donor), 'transplantable material' means –
(a) an organ, or part of an organ if it is to be used for the same purpose as the entire organ in the human body,
(b) bone marrow, and
(c) peripheral blood stem cells, where that material is removed from the body of a living person with the intention that it be transplanted into another person.

(2) The material referred to in paragraph (1)(a) is not transplantable material for the purposes of section 33 of the Act in a case where the primary purpose of removal of the material is the medical treatment of the person from whose body the material is removed.

(3) The material referred to in paragraph (1)(b) and (c) is transplantable material for the purposes of section 33 of the Act only in a case where the person from whose body the material is removed is –
(a) an adult who lacks the capacity, or
(b) a child who is not competent, to consent to removal of the transplantable material.

Cases in which restriction on transplants involving a live donor is disapplied

11.—(1) Section 33(1) and (2) of the Act (offences relating to transplants involving a live donor) shall not apply in any case involving transplantable material from the body of a living person ('the donor') if the requirements of paragraphs (2) to (6) are met.

(2) A registered medical practitioner who has clinical responsibility for the donor must have caused the matter to be referred to the Authority.

(3) The Authority must be satisfied that –
(a) no reward has been or is to be given in contravention of section 32 of the Act (prohibition of commercial dealings in human material for transplantation), and
(b) when the transplantable material is removed –
(i) consent for its removal for the purpose of transplantation has been given, or
(ii) its removal for that purpose is otherwise lawful.

(4) The Authority must take the report referred to in paragraph (6) into account in making its decision under paragraph (3).

(5) The Authority shall give notice of its decision under paragraph (3) to –
(a) the donor of the transplantable material or any person acting on his behalf,
(b) the person to whom it is proposed to transplant the transplantable material ('the recipient') or any person acting on his behalf, and
(c) the registered medical practitioner who caused the matter to be referred to the Authority under paragraph (2).

(6) Subject to paragraph (7), one or more qualified persons must have conducted separate interviews with each of the following –
(a) the donor,

    (b) if different from the donor, the person giving consent, and

    (c) the recipient, and reported to the Authority on the matters specified in paragraphs (8) and (9).

(7) Paragraph (6) does not apply in any case where the removal of the transplantable material for the purpose of transplantation is authorised by an order made in any legal proceedings before a court.

(8) The matters that must be covered in the report of each interview under paragraph (6) are –

    (a) any evidence of duress or coercion affecting the decision to give consent,

    (b) any evidence of an offer of a reward, and

    (c) any difficulties of communication with the person interviewed and an explanation of how those difficulties were overcome.

(9) The following matters must be covered in the report of the interview with the donor and, where relevant, the other person giving consent –

    (a) the information given to the person interviewed as to the nature of the medical procedure for, and the risk involved in, the removal of the transplantable material,

    (b) the full name of the person who gave that information and his qualification to give it, and

    (c) the capacity of the person interviewed to understand –

        (i) the nature of the medical procedure and the risk involved, and

        (ii) that the consent may be withdrawn at any time before the removal of the transplantable material.

(10) A person shall be taken to be qualified to conduct an interview under paragraph (6) if –

    (a) he appears to the Authority to be suitably qualified to conduct the interview,

    (b) he does not have any connection with any of the persons to be interviewed, or with a person who stands in a qualifying relationship to any of those persons, which the Authority considers to be of a kind that might raise doubts about his ability to act impartially, and

    (c) in the case of an interview with the donor or other person giving consent, he is not the person who gave the information referred to in paragraph (9)(a).

Decisions of the Authority: procedure for certain cases

12.—(1) In any case to which paragraph (2), (3) or (4) applies, the Authority's decision as to the matters specified in regulation 11(3) shall be made by a panel of no fewer than 3 members of the Authority.

(2) A case falls within this paragraph if –

    (a) the donor of the transplantable material is a child, and

    (b) the material is an organ or part of an organ if it is to be used for the same purpose as an entire organ in the human body.

(3) A case falls within this paragraph if –

    (a) the donor of the transplantable material is an adult who lacks capacity to consent to removal of the material, and

    (b) the material is an organ or part of an organ if it is to be used for the same purpose as an entire organ in the human body.

(4) A case falls within this paragraph if –

    (a) the donor of the transplantable material is an adult who has capacity to consent to removal of the material, and

    (b) the case involves –

        (i) paired donations,

        (ii) pooled donations, or

        (iii) a non-directed altruistic donation.

(5) In this regulation –

'non-directed altruistic donation' means the removal (in circumstances not amounting to a paired or pooled donation) of transplantable material from a donor for transplant to a person who is not genetically related to the donor or known to him;

'paired donations' means an arrangement under which –
- (a) transplantable material is removed from a donor ('D') for transplant to a person who is not genetically related or known to D, and
- (b) transplantable material is removed from another person for transplant to a person who is genetically related or known to D; and

'pooled donations' means a series of paired donations of transplantable material, each of which is linked to another in the same series (for example, transplantable material from D is transplanted to the wife of another person ('E'), transplantable material from E is transplanted to the partner of a third person ('F') and transplantable material from F is transplanted to D's son).

Right to reconsideration of Authority's decision

13.—(1) The Authority may reconsider any decision made by it under regulation 11(3) if it is satisfied that –
- (a) any information given for the purpose of the decision was in any material respect false or misleading, or
- (b) there has been any material change of circumstances since the decision was made.

(2) A specified person may in any case require the Authority to reconsider any decision made by it under regulation 11(3).

(3) 'Specified persons', in relation to such a decision, are –
- (a) the donor of the transplantable material or any person acting on his behalf,
- (b) the recipient of the material or any person acting on his behalf, and
- (c) the registered medical practitioner who caused the matter to be referred to the Authority under regulation 11(2).

(4) The right under paragraph (2) is exercisable by giving to the Authority, in such manner as it may direct, notice of exercise of the right.

(5) A notice under paragraph (4) shall contain or be accompanied by such other information as the Authority may reasonably require.

(6) On receipt of the information required by paragraph (5), the Authority shall provide to the person requiring the reconsideration –
- (a) a copy of each report made under regulation 11(6) of the interviews that were conducted in the case, and
- (b) a statement of the Authority's reasons for its decision.

(7) Paragraphs (1) to (6) do not apply to a decision made by the Authority on reconsideration in pursuance of a notice under this regulation.

Procedure on reconsideration

14.—(1) Reconsideration shall be by way of fresh decision made at a meeting of the Authority.

(2) The meeting shall take place as soon as reasonably practicable after the provision of the reports and statement required by regulation 13(6), having regard to the need to allow time for the information contained in that material to be taken into account.

(3) Where a member of the Authority has taken part in the making of a decision subject to reconsideration (whether under regulation 12 or otherwise), he is disqualified from participating in the Authority's reconsideration of it.

(4) On reconsideration under regulation 13(2) –
- (a) the person ('A') by whom the reconsideration is required under regulation 13(2) shall be entitled to require that he or his representative be given an opportunity to appear before and be heard at the meeting of the Authority at which the decision is reconsidered, and
- (b) the members of the Authority in attendance at the meeting at which the decision is reconsidered shall consider any such written representations and comments.

(5) The Authority shall give a notice of its decision to A.

(6) If on reconsideration the Authority upholds the previous decision, the notice under paragraph (5) shall include a statement of the reasons for the Authority's decision.

(7) 'Reconsideration' means reconsideration in pursuance of a notice under regulation 13.

The Mental Capacity Act 2005 (Independent Mental Capacity Advocates) (General) Regulations 2006

(SI 2006, No. 1832)

2.— Interpretation

(1) In these Regulations—

'the Act' means the Mental Capacity Act 2005; and

'IMCA' means an independent mental capacity advocate.

(2) In these Regulations, references to instructions given to a person to act as an IMCA are to instructions given under sections 37 to 39 of the Act or under regulations made by virtue of section 41 of the Act.

4.— Meaning of serious medical treatment

(1) This regulation defines serious medical treatment for the purposes of section 37 of the Act.

(2) Serious medical treatment is treatment which involves providing, withdrawing or withholding treatment in circumstances where –

  (a) in a case where a single treatment is being proposed, there is a fine balance between its benefits to the patient and the burdens and risks it is likely to entail for him,

  (b) in a case where there is a choice of treatments, a decision as to which one to use is finely balanced, or

  (c) what is proposed would be likely to involve serious consequences for the patient.

5.— Appointment of independent mental capacity advocates

(1) No person may be appointed to act as an IMCA for the purposes of sections 37 to 39 of the Act, or regulations made by virtue of section 41 of the Act, unless –

  (a) he is for the time being approved by a local authority on the grounds that he satisfies the appointment requirements, or

  (b) he belongs to a class of persons which is for the time being approved by a local authority on the grounds that all persons in that class satisfy the appointment requirements.

(2) The appointment requirements, in relation to a person appointed to act as an IMCA, are that –

  (a) he has appropriate experience or training or an appropriate combination of experience and training;

  (b) he is a person of integrity and good character; and

  (c) he is able to act independently of any person who instructs him.

(3) Before a determination is made in relation to any person for the purposes of paragraph (2) (b), there must be obtained in respect of that person –

  (a) an enhanced criminal record certificate issued pursuant to section 113B of the Police Act 1997; or

  (b) if the purpose for which the certificate is required is not one prescribed under sub-section (2) of that section, a criminal record certificate issued pursuant to section 113A of that Act.

6.— Functions of an independent mental capacity advocate

(1) This regulation applies where an IMCA has been instructed by an authorised person to represent a person ('P').

(2) 'Authorised person' means a person who is required or enabled to instruct an IMCA under sections 37 to 39 of the Act or under regulations made by virtue of section 41of the Act.

(3) The IMCA must determine in all the circumstances how best to represent and support P.

(4) In particular, the IMCA must –

(a) verify that the instructions were issued by an authorised person;

(b) to the extent that it is practicable and appropriate to do so –

(i) interview P, and

(ii) examine the records relevant to P to which the IMCA has access under section 35 (6) of the Act;

(c) to the extent that it is practicable and appropriate to do so, consult –

(i) persons engaged in providing care or treatment for P in a professional capacity or for remuneration, and

(ii) other persons who may be in a position to comment on P's wishes, feelings, beliefs or values; and

(d) take all practicable steps to obtain such other information about P, or the act or decision that is proposed in relation to P, as the IMCA considers necessary.

(5) The IMCA must evaluate all the information he has obtained for the purpose of –

(a) ascertaining the extent of the support provided to P to enable him to participate in making any decision about the matter in relation to which the IMCA has been instructed;

(b) ascertaining what P's wishes and feelings would be likely to be, and the beliefs and values that would be likely to influence P, if he had capacity in relation to the proposed act or decision;

(c) ascertaining what alternative courses of action are available in relation to P;

(d) where medical treatment is proposed for P, ascertaining whether he would be likely to benefit from a further medical opinion.

(6) The IMCA must prepare a report for the authorised person who instructed him.

(7) The IMCA may include in the report such submissions as he considers appropriate in relation to P and the act or decision which is proposed in relation to him.

7.— Challenges to decisions affecting persons who lack capacity

(1) This regulation applies where –

(a) an IMCA has been instructed to represent a person ('P') in relation to any matter, and

(b) a decision affecting P (including a decision as to his capacity) is made in that matter.

(2) The IMCA has the same rights to challenge the decision as he would have if he were a person (other than an IMCA) engaged in caring for P or interested in his welfare.

The Mental Capacity Act 2005 (Appropriate Body) (England) Regulations 2006

(SI 2006, No. 2810)

Citation, commencement and application

(2) These Regulations apply in relation to the carrying out of research in England.

Appropriate Bodies

2. In relation to a research project referred to in sections 30, 31 and 32 of the Mental Capacity Act 2005, the appropriate body is a committee –

(a) established to advise on, or on matters which include, the ethics of intrusive research in relation to people who lack capacity to consent to it; and

(b) recognised for that purpose by the Secretary of State.

The Mental Capacity Act 2005 (Loss of Capacity during Research Project) (England) Regulations 2007

(SI 2007, No 679)

1.— Citation, commencement, territorial application and interpretation

(2) These Regulations apply in relation to the carrying out of research in England.

(3) In these Regulations –

'the Act' means the Mental Capacity Act 2005;

'appropriate body' has the meaning given by section 30(4) of the Act and the Mental Capacity Act 2005 (Appropriate Body) (England) Regulations 2006.

2.   Application

These Regulations apply where –

  (a) a person ('P') –
     (i) has consented before 31 March 2008 to take part in a research project ('the project') begun before 1st October 2007, but
     (ii) before the conclusion of the project, loses capacity to consent to continue to take part in it, and
     (iii) research for the purposes of the project in relation to P would, apart from these Regulations, be unlawful by virtue of section 30 of the Act.

3.   Research which may be carried out despite a participant's loss of capacity

Despite P's loss of capacity, research for the purposes of the project may be carried out using information or material relating to him if –

  (a) that information or material was obtained before P's loss of capacity,
  (b) that information or material is either –
     (i) data within the meaning given in section 1(1) of the Data Protection Act 1998, or
     (ii) material which consists of or includes human cells or human DNA,
  (c) the project satisfies the requirements set out in Schedule 1, and
  (d) the person conducting the project ('R') takes in relation to P such steps as are set out in Schedule 2.

Schedule 1

Requirements which the project must satisfy

Regulation 3(c)

1. A protocol approved by an appropriate body and having effect in relation to the project makes provision for research to be carried out in relation to a person who has consented to take part in the project but loses capacity to consent to continue to take part in it.

2. The appropriate body is satisfied that there are reasonable arrangements in place for ensuring that the requirements of Schedule 2 will be met.

Schedule 2

Steps which the person conducting the project must take

Regulation 3(d)

1. R must take reasonable steps to identify a person who –

(a) otherwise than in a professional capacity or for remuneration, is engaged in caring for P or is interested in P's welfare, and (b)

is prepared to be consulted by R under this Schedule.

2. If R is unable to identify such a person he must, in accordance with guidance issued by the Secretary of State, nominate a person who –

(a) is prepared to be consulted by R under this Schedule, but

(b) has no connection with the project.

3. R must provide the person identified under paragraph 1, or nominated under paragraph 2, with information about the project and ask him –

(a) for advice as to whether research of the kind proposed should be carried out in relation to P, and

(b) what, in his opinion, P's wishes and feelings about such research being carried out would be likely to be if P had capacity in relation to the matter.

4. If, at any time, the person consulted advises R that in his opinion P's wishes and feelings would be likely to lead him to wish to withdraw from the project if he had capacity in relation to the matter, R must ensure that P is withdrawn from it.

5. The fact that a person is the donee of a lasting power of attorney given by P, or is P's deputy, does not prevent him from being the person consulted under paragraphs 1 to 4.

6. R must ensure that nothing is done in relation to P in the course of the research which would be contrary to –

(a) an advance decision of his which has effect, or

(b) any other form of statement made by him and not subsequently withdrawn, of which R is aware.

7. The interests of P must be assumed to outweigh those of science and society.

8. If P indicates (in any way) that he wishes the research in relation to him to be discontinued, it must be discontinued without delay.

9. The research in relation to P must be discontinued without delay if at any time R has reasonable grounds for believing that the requirement set out in paragraph 1 of Schedule 1 is no longer met or that there are no longer reasonable arrangements in place for ensuring that the requirements of this Schedule are met in relation to P.

10. R must conduct the research in accordance with the provision made in the protocol referred to in paragraph 1 of Schedule 1 for research to be carried out in relation to a person who has consented to take part in the project but loses capacity to consent to continue to take part in it.

Part III

Department of Health Circulars and Guidelines

Health Service Guidelines Arrangements for Clinical Negligence Claims in the NHS

[The following guidance was issued with Health Service Guideline (96)48]

Executive summary

Introduction

This is a summary of the main points contained within *NHS Indemnity Arrangements for clinical negligence claims in the NHS*, issued under cover of HSG 96/48. The booklet includes a Q&A section covering the applicability of NHS indemnity to common situations and an annex on sponsored trials. It covers NHS indemnity for clinical negligence but not for any other liability such as product liability, employers liability or liability ftpor NHS trust board members.

Clinical negligence

Clinical negligence is defined as 'a breach of duty of care by members of the health care professions employed by NHS bodies or by others consequent on decisions or judgements made by members of those professions acting in their professional capacity in the course of their employment, and which are admitted as negligent by the employer or are determined as such through the legal process'.

The term health care professional includes hospital doctors, dentists, nurses, midwives, health visitors, pharmacy practitioners, registered ophthalmic or dispensing opticians (working in a hospital setting), members of professions allied to medicine and dentistry, ambulance personnel, laboratory staff and relevant technicians.

Main principles

NHS bodies are vicariously liable for the negligent acts and Omissions of their employees and should have arrangements for meeting this liability.

NHS Indemnity applies where

    (a) the negligent health care professional was:

        (i) working under a contract of employment and the negligence occurred in the course of that employment;

        (ii) not working under a contract of employment but was contracted to an NHS body to provide services to persons to whom that NHS body owed a duty of care;

(iii) neither of the above but otherwise owed a duty of care to the persons injured;

(b) persons, not employed under a contract of employment and who may or may not be a health care professional, who owe a duty of care to the persons injured. These include locums; medical academic staff with honorary contracts; students; those conducting clinical trials; charitable volunteers; persons undergoing further professional education, training and examinations; students and staff working on income generation projects.

Where these principles apply, NHS bodies should accept full financial liability where negligent harm has occurred, and not seek to recover their costs from the health care professional involved.

Who is not covered

NHS Indemnity does not apply to family health service practitioners working under contracts for services, eg GPs (including fundholders), general dental practitioners, family dentists, pharmacists or optometrists; other self employed health care professionals eg independent midwives; employees of FHS practices; employees of private hospitals; local education authorities; voluntary agencies. Exceptions to the normal cover arrangements are set out in the main document.

Circumstances covered

NHS Indemnity covers negligent harm caused to patients or healthy volunteers in the following circumstances: whenever they are receiving an established treatment, whether or not in accordance with an agreed guideline or protocol; whenever they are receiving a novel or unusual treatment which, in the judgement of the health care professional, is appropriate for that particular patient; whenever they are subjects as patients or healthy volunteers of clinical research aimed at benefitting patients now or in the future.

Expenses met

Where negligence is alleged, NHS bodies are responsible for meeting: the legal and administrative costs of defending the claim or, if appropriate, of reaching a settlement; the plaintiffs costs, as agreed by the two parties or as awarded by the court; the damages awarded either as a one-off payment or as a structured settlement.

Clinical negligence – definition

1. Clinical negligence is defined as:

'A breach of duty of care by members of the health care professions employed by NHS bodies or by others consequent on decisions or judgments made by members of those professions acting in their professional capacity in the course of employment, and which are admitted as negligent by the employer or are determined as such through the legal process.'*[1]

2. In this definition 'breach of duty of care' has its legal meaning. NHS bodies will need to take legal advice in individual cases, but the general position will be that the following must all apply before liability for negligence exists:

2.1 There must have been a duty of care owed to the person treated by the relevant professional(s);

2.2 The standard of care appropriate to such duty must not have been attained and therefore the duty breached, whether by action or inaction, advice given or failure to advise;

2.3 Such a breach must be demonstrated to have caused the injury and therefore the resulting loss complained about by the patient;

---

[1]* The NHS (Clinical Negligence Scheme) Regulations 1996, which established the Clinical Negligence Scheme for Trusts, defines clinical negligence in terms of ' . . . a liability in tort owed by a member to a third party in respect of or consequent upon personal injury or loss arising out of or in connection with any breach of a duty of care owed by that body to any person in connection with the diagnosis of any illness, or the care or treatment of any patient, in consequence of any act or omission to act on the part of a person employed or engaged by a member in connection with any relevant function of the member.'

2.4 Any loss sustained as a result of the injury and complained about by the person treated must be of a kind that the courts recognise and for which they allow compensation; and

2.5 The injury and resulting loss complained about by the person treated must have been reasonably foreseeable as a possible consequence of the breach.

3. This booklet is concerned with NHS Indemnity for clinical negligence and does not cover indemnity for any other liability such as product liability, employers liability or liability for NHS trust board members.

Other terms

4. Throughout this guidance:

4.1 The terms 'an NHS body' and 'NHS bodies' include Health Authorities, Special Health Authorities and NHS Trusts but excludes all GP practices whether fundholding or not, general dental practices, pharmacies and opticians' practices.

4.2 The term 'health care professional' includes:

> Doctors, dentists, nurses, midwives, health visitors, hospital pharmacy practitioners, registered ophthalmic or registered dispensing opticians working in a hospital setting, members of professions supplementary to medicine and dentistry, ambulance personnel, laboratory staff and relevant technicians.

Principles

5. NHS bodies are legally liable for the negligent acts and omissions of their employees (the principle of vicarious liability), and should have arrangements for meeting this liability. NHS Indemnity applies where:

5.1 the negligent health care professional was working under a contract of employment (as opposed to a contract for services) and the negligence occurred in the course of that employment; or

5.2 the negligent health care professional, although not working under a contract of employment, was contracted to an NHS body to provide services to persons to whom that NHS body owed a duty of care.

6. Where the principles outlined in paragraph 5 apply, NHS bodies should accept full financial liability where negligent harm has occurred. They should not seek to recover their costs either in part or in full from the health care professional concerned or from any indemnities they may have. NHS bodies may carry this risk entirely or spread it through membership of the Clinical Negligence Scheme for Trusts (CNST – see EL(95)40).

Who is covered

7. NHS Indemnity covers the actions of staff in the course of their NHS employment. It also covers people in certain other categories whenever the NHS body owes a duty of care to the person harmed, including, for example, locums, medical academic staff with honorary contracts, students, those conducting clinical trials, charitable volunteers and people undergoing further professional education, training and examinations. This includes staff working on income generation projects. GPs or dentists who are directly employed by Health Authorities, e.g. as Public Health doctors (including port medical officers and medical inspectors of immigrants at UK air/sea ports), are covered.

8. Examples of the applicability of NHS Indemnity to common situations are set out in question and answer format in Annex A.

Who is not covered

9. NHS Indemnity does not apply to general medical and dental practitioners working under contracts for services. General practitioners, including GP fundholders, are responsible for making their own indemnity arrangements, as are other self-employed health care professionals such as independent midwives. Neither does NHS Indemnity apply to employees of general practices,

whether fundholding or not, or to employees of private hospitals (even when treating NHS patients) local education authorities or voluntary agencies.

10. Examples of circumstances in which independent practitioners or staff who normally work for private employers are covered by NHS Indemnity are given in Annex A. The NHS Executive advises independent practitioners to check their own indemnity position.

11. Examples of circumstances in which NHS employees are not covered by NHS Indemnity are also given in Annex A.

Circumstances covered

12. NHS bodies owe a duty of care to healthy volunteers or patients treated or undergoing tests which they administer. NHS Indemnity covers negligent harm caused to these people in the following circumstances:

12.1 whenever they are receiving an established treatment, whether of not in accordance with an agreed guideline or protocol;

12.2 whenever they are receiving a novel or unusual treatment which in the clinical judgment of the health care professional is appropriate for the particular patient;

12.3 whenever they are subjects of clinical research aimed at benefitting patients now or in the future, whether as patients or as healthy volunteers. (Special arrangements, including the availability of no-fault indemnity apply where research is sponsored by pharmaceutical companies. See Annex B.)

Expenses met

13. Where negligence is alleged NHS bodies are responsible for meeting:

13.1 the legal and administrative costs of defending the claim and, if appropriate, of reaching a settlement, including the cost of any mediation;

13.2 where appropriate, plaintiff's costs, either as agreed between the parties or as awarded by a court of law;

13.3 the damages agreed or awarded, whether as a one-off payment or a structured settlement.

Claims management principles

14. NHS bodies should take the essential decisions on the handling of claims of clinical negligence against their staff, using professional defence organisations or others as their agents and advisers as appropriate.*²

Financial support arrangements

15. Details of the Clinical Negligence Scheme for Trusts (CNST) were announced in EL(95)40 on 29 March 1995.

16. All financial arrangements in respect of clinical negligence costs for NHS bodies have been reviewed and guidance on transitional arrangements (for funding clinical accidents which happened before 1 April 1995), was issued on 27 November 1995 under cover of FDL(95)56. FDL(96) 36 provided further guidance on a number of detailed questions.

Annex A
Questions and Answers on NHS Indemnity

Below are replies to some of the questions most commonly asked about NHS Indemnity

1   Who is covered by NHS Indemnity?

NHS bodies are liable at law for the negligent acts and omissions of their staff in the course of their NHS employment. Under NHS Indemnity, NHS bodies take direct responsibility for costs and

---

²* Editors' note: The handling of claims for clinical negligence has subsequently been taken over by the NHS Litigation Authority, although 'NHS bodies' remain legally responsible for meeting claims.

damages arising from clinical negligence where they (as employers) are vicariously liable for the acts and omissions of their health care professional staff.

2   Would health care professionals opting to work under contracts for services rather than as employees of the NHS be covered?

Where an NHS body is responsible for *providing* care to patients NHS Indemnity will apply whether the health care professional involved is an employee or not. For example a doctor working under a contract for services with an NHS Trust would be covered because the Trust has responsibility for the care of its patients. A consultant undertaking contracted NHS work in a private hospital would also be covered.

3   Does this include clinical academics and research workers?

NHS bodies are vicariously liable for the work done by university medical staff and other research workers (e.g. employees of the MRC) under their honorary contracts, but not for pre-clinical or other work in the university.

4   Are GP practices covered?

GP's whether fundholders or not [and who are not employed by Health Authorities as public health doctors], are independent practitioners and therefore they and their employed staff are not covered by NHS Indemnity.

5   Is a hospital doctor doing a GP locum covered?

This would not be the responsibility of the NHS body since it would be outside the contract of employment. The hospital doctor and the general practitioners concerned should ensure that there is appropriate professional liability cover.

6   Is a GP seeing a patient in hospital covered?

A GP providing medical care to patients in hospital under a contractual arrangement, e.g. where the GP was employed as a clinical assistant, will be covered by NHS Indemnity, as will a GP who provides services in NHS hospitals under staff fund contracts (known as 'bed funds'). Where there is no such contractual arrangement, and the NHS body provides facilities for patient(s) who continue to be the clinical responsibility of the GP, the GP would be responsible and professional liability cover would be appropriate. However, junior medical staff, nurses or members of the professions supplementary to medicine involved in the care of a GP's patients in NHS hospitals under their contract of employment would be covered.

7   Are GP trainees working in general practice covered?

In general practice the responsibility for training and for paying the salary of a GP trainee rests with the trainer. While the trainee is receiving a salary in general practice it is advisable that both the trainee and the trainer, and indeed other members of the practice, should have appropriate professional liability cover as NHS indemnity will not apply.

8   Are NHS employees working under contracts with GP fundholders covered?

If their employing NHS body has agreed a contract to provide services to a GP fundholding practice's patients, NHS employees will be working under the terms of their contracts of employment and NHS Indemnity will cover them. If NHS employees themselves contract with GP fundholders (or any other independent body) to do work outside their NHS contract of employment they should ensure that they have separate indemnity cover.

9   Is academic general practice covered?

The Department his no plans to extend NHS Indemnity to academic departments of general practice. In respect of general medical services, Health Authorities' payments of fees and allowances include an element for expenses, of which medical defence subscriptions are a part.

10   Is private work in NHS hospitals covered by NHS Indemnity?

NHS bodies will not be responsible for a health care professional's private practice, even in an NHS hospital. However, where junior medical staff, nurses or members of professions supplementary to medicine are involved in the care of private patients in NHS hospitals, they would normally be doing so is part of their NHS contract, and would therefore be covered. It remains advisable that health professionals who might be involved in work outside the scope of his or her NHS employment should have professional liability cover.

11   Is Category 2 work covered?

Category 2 work (e.g. reports for insurance companies) is by definition not undertaken for the employing NHS body and is therefore not covered by NHS Indemnity. Unless the work is carried out on behalf of the employing NHS body, professional liability cover would be needed.

12   Are disciplinary proceedings of statutory bodies covered?

NHS bodies are not financially responsible for the defence of staff involved in disciplinary proceedings conducted by statutory bodies such as the GMC (doctors), UKCC (nurses and midwives), GDC (dentists) CPSM (professions supplementary to medicine) and RPSGB (pharmacists). It is the responsibility of the practitioner concerned to take out professional liability cover against such an eventuality.

13   Are clinical trials covered?

In the case of negligent harm, health care professionals undertaking clinical trials or studies on volunteers, whether healthy or patients, in the course of their NHS employment are covered by NHS Indemnity. Similarly, for a trial not involving medicines, the NHS body would take financial responsibility unless the trial were covered by such other indemnity as may have been agreed between the NHS body and those responsible for the trial. In any case, NHS bodies should ensure that they are informed of clinical trials in which their staff are taking part in their NHS employment and that these trials have the required Research Ethics Committee approval. For non-negligent harm, see question 16 below.

14   Is harm resulting from a fault in the drug/equipment covered?

Where harm is caused due to a fault in the manufacture of a drug or piece of equipment then, under the terms of the Consumer Protection Act 1987, it is no defence for the producer to show that he exercised reasonable care. Under normal circumstances, therefore, NHS indemnity would not apply unless there was a question whether the health care professional either knew or should reasonably have known that the drug/equipment was faulty but continued to use it. Strict liability could apply if the drug/equipment had been manufactured by an NHS body itself, for example a prototype as part of a research programme.

15   Are Local Research Ethics Committees (LRECs) covered?

Under the Department's guidelines an LREC is appointed by the Health Authority to provide independent advice to NHS bodies within its area on the ethics of research proposals. The Health Authority should take financial responsibility for members' acts and omissions in the course of performance of their duties as LREC members.

16   Is there liability for non-negligent harm?

Apart from liability for defective products, legal liability does not arise where a person is harmed but no one has acted negligently. An example of this would be unexpected side-effects of drugs during clinical trials. In exceptional circumstances (and within the delegated limit of £50,000) NHS bodies may consider whether an ex-gratia payment could be offered. NHS bodies may not offer advance indemnities or take out commercial insurance for non-negligent harm.

17   What arrangements can non-NHS bodies make for non-negligent harm?

Arrangements will depend on the status of the non-NHS body. Arrangements for clinical trials sponsored by the pharmaceutical industry are set out in Annex B. Other independent sector sponsors of clinical research involving NHS patients (e.g. universities and medical research charities) may also make arrangements to indemnity research subjects for non-negligent harm. Public sector research funding bodies such as the Medical Research Council (MRC) may not offer advance indemnities nor take out commercial insurance for non-negligent harm. The MRC offers the assurance that it will give sympathetic consideration to claims in respect of non-negligent harm arising from an MRC funded trial. NHS bodies should not make ex-gratia payments for non-negligent harm where research is sponsored by a non-NHS body.

18   Would health care professionals be covered if they were working other than in accordance with the duties of their post?

Health care professionals would be covered by NHS Indemnity for actions in the course of NHS employment, and this should be interpreted liberally. For work not covered in this way health care professionals may have a civil, or even, in extreme circumstances, criminal liability for their actions.

19   Are health care professionals attending accident victims ('Good Samaritan' acts) covered?

'Good Samaritan' acts are not part of the health care professional's work for the employing body. Medical defence organisations are willing to provide low-cost cover against the (unusual) event of anyone performing such an act being sued for negligence. Ambulance services can, with the agreement of staff, include an additional term in the individual employee contracts to the effect that the member of staff is expected to provide assistance in any emergency outside of duty hours where it is appropriate to do so.

20   Are NHS staff in public health medicine or in community health services doing work for local authorities covered? Are occupational physicians covered?

Staff working in public health medicine, clinical medical officers or therapists carrying out local authority functions under their NHS contract would be acting in the course of their NHS employment. They will therefore be covered by NHS Indemnity. The same principle applies to occupational physicians employed by NHS bodies.

21   Are NHS staff working for other agencies, e.g. the Prison Service, covered?

In general, NHS bodies are not financially responsible for the acts of NHS staff when they are working on an individual contractual basis for other agencies. (Conversely, they are responsible where, for example, a Ministry of Defence doctor works in an NHS hospital.) Either the non-NHS body commissioning the work would be responsible, or the health care professional should have separate indemnity cover. However, NHS Indemnity should cover work for which the NHS body pays the health care professional a fee, such as domiciliary visits, and family planning services.

22   Are former NHS staff covered?

NHS Indemnity will cover staff who have subsequently left the Service (e.g. on retirement) provided the liability arose in respect of acts or omissions in the course of their NHS employment, regardless of when the claim was notified. NHS bodies may seek the co-operation of former staff in providing statements in the defence of a case.

23   Are NHS staff offering services to voluntary bodies such as the Red Cross or hospices covered?

The NHS body would be responsible for the actions of its staff only if it were contractually responsible for the clinical staffing of the voluntary body. If not, the staff concerned may wish to ensure that they have separate indemnity cover.

24   Do NHS bodies provide cover for locums?

NHS bodies take financial responsibility for the acts and omissions of a locum health care professional, whether 'internal' or provided by an external agency, doing the work of a colleague who would be covered.

25   What are the arrangements for staff employed by one trust working in another?

This depends on the contractual arrangements. If the work is being done as part of a formal agreement between the trusts, then the staff involved will be acting within their normal NHS duties and, unless the agreement states otherwise, the employing trust will be liable. The NHS Executive does not recommend the use of ad hoc arrangements, e.g. a doctor in one trust asking a doctor in another to provide an informal second opinion, unless there is an agreement between the trusts as to which of them will accept liability for the 'visiting' doctor in such circumstances.

26   Are private sector rotations for hospital staff covered?

The medical staff of independent hospitals are responsible for their own professional liability cover, subject to the requirements of the hospital managers. If NHS staff in the training grades work in independent hospitals as part of their NHS training, they would be covered by NHS Indemnity, provided that such work was covered by an NHS contract of employment.

27   Are voluntary workers covered?

Where volunteers work in NHS bodies, they are covered by NHS Indemnity. NHS managers should be aware of all voluntary activity going on in their organisations and should wherever possible confirm volunteers' indemnity position in writing.

28   Are students covered?

NHS Indemnity applies where students are working under the supervision of NHS employees. This should be made clear in the agreement between the NHS body and the students' educational body. This will apply to students of all the health care professions and to school students on, for example, work experience placements. Students working in NHS premises, under supervision of medical academic staff employed by universities holding honorary contracts, are also covered. Students who spend time in a primary care setting will only be covered if this is part of an NHS contract. Potential students making preliminary visits and school placements should be adequately supervised and should not become involved in any clinical work. Therefore, no clinical negligence should arise on their part.

In the unlikely event of a school making a negligent choice of work placement for a pupil to work in the NHS, then the school, and not NHS indemnity, should pick up the legal responsibility for the actions of that pupil. The contractual arrangement between the NHS and the school should make this clear.

29   Are health care professional undergoing on-the-job training covered?

Where an NHS body's staff are providing on-the-job training (e.g. refresher or skills updating courses) for health care professionals, the trainees are covered by NHS Indemnity whether they are normally employed by the NHS or not.

30   Are independent midwives covered?

Independent midwives are self-employed practitioners. In common with all other health care professionals working outside the NHS, they are responsible for making their own indemnity arrangements.

31   Are overseas doctors who have come to the UK temporarily, perhaps to demonstrate a new technique, covered?

The NHS body which has invited the overseas doctor will owe a duty of care to the patients on whom the technique is demonstrated and so NHS Indemnity will apply. NHS bodies, therefore, need to make sure that they are kept informed of any such demonstration visits which are proposed and of the nature of the technique to be demonstrated. Where visiting clinicians are not formally registered as students, or are not employees, an honorary contract should be arranged.

32   Are staff who are qualified in another member state of the European Union covered?

Staff qualified in another member state of the European Union, and who are undertaking an adaptation period in accordance with EEC directive 89/48EEC and the European Communities

(Recognition of Professional Qualifications) Regulations 1991 which implements EEC Directive 89/48/EEC) and EEC Directive 92/51/EEC, must be treated in a manner consistent with their qualified status in another member state, and should be covered.

Health Service Circular HSC 2000/028 Resuscitation Policy

For action by: NHS Trusts – Chief Executives
For information to: NHS Trusts – Medical Directors; NHS Trusts – Directors of Nursing; Primary Care Groups – Chairs; Health Authorities (England) – Chief Executives
It is also available on the Department of Health web site at http://www.doh.gov.uk/coinh.htm

Summary

NHS Trust chief executives are asked to ensure that appropriate resuscitation policies which respect patients' rights are in place, understood by all relevant staff, and accessible to those who need them, and that such policies are subject to appropriate audit and monitoring arrangements.

Action

Recent reports raise serious concerns about standards of resuscitation decision-making in the NHS. **Chief executives** should ensure that:

- patients' rights are central to decision-making on resuscitation;
- the Trust has an agreed resuscitation policy in place which respects patients' rights;
- the policy is published and readily available to those who may wish to consult it, including patients, families and carers;
- appropriate arrangements are in place for ensuring that all staff who may be involved in resuscitation decisions understand and implement the policy;
- appropriate supervision arrangements are in place to review resuscitation decisions;
- induction and staff development programmes cover the resuscitation policy;
- clinical practice in this area is regularly audited;
- clinical audit outcomes are reported in the Trust's annual clinical governance report;
- a non-executive Director of the Trust is given designated responsibility on behalf of the Trust Board to ensure that a resuscitation policy is agreed, implemented, and regularly reviewed within the clinical governance framework.

Backgound and other information

1. Resuscitation decisions are amongst the most sensitive decisions that clinicians, patients and parents may have to make. Patients (and where appropriate their relatives and carers) have as much right to be involved in those decisions as they do other decisions about their care and treatment. As with all decision-making, doctors have a duty to act in accordance with an appropriate and responsible body of professional opinion.

2. In 1991 the Chief Medical Officer of the time wrote to all consultants in England (PL/CMO(91) 22) to emphasise their responsibility for ensuring that resuscitation policy was in place and understood by all staff who may be involved, particularly junior medical staff. Chief executives should ensure that consultants are aware of, and fulfil, this responsibility. Recent reports raise serious concerns concerning the current implementation of resuscitation policy.

3. The revised joint statement from the British Medical Association, Resuscitation Council (UK) and the Royal College of Nursing *Decisions Relating to Cardiopulmonary Resuscitation* (1999) is commended as an appropriate basis for a resuscitation policy. The guidance is available at http://www.resus.org.uk/pages/DNR3.htm.

4. Audit of the implementation of resuscitation policy should involve all relevant clinicians, and identify any areas where improvement is required – for example ensuring that decisions made on admission are properly reviewed by the clinical team and that patients, and where appropriate relatives, have been properly involved in the process. Clinical audit data should be made available to the Trust medical director and the clinical governance lead, and to the Commission for Health Improvement.

5. The Secretary of State has asked the Commission for Health Improvement (CHI) to pay particular attention to resuscitation decision-making processes as part of its rolling programme of reviews of clinical governance arrangements put in place by NHS organisations.

**Department
of Health**

[NHS organisation name]
consent form 1

Patient agreement to investigation
or treatment

Patient details (or pre-printed label)

Patient's surname/family name.................................

Patient's first names ....

Date of birth ....

Responsible health professional.................................

Job title ....

NHS number (or other identifier)..................................

    Male   Female

Special requirements ....
(eg other language/other communication method)

To be retained in patient's notes

Patient identifier/label

Name of proposed procedure or course of treatment (include brief
explanation if medical term not clear) ....
....
....

Statement of health professional (to be filled in by health professional with
appropriate knowledge of proposed procedure, as specified in consent policy)

I have explained the procedure to the patient. In particular, I have explained:

The intended benefits ....
....
....
Serious or frequently occurring risks ....
....
....
Any extra procedures which may become necessary during the procedure

blood transfusion...

other procedure (please specify) ....
....

I have also discussed what the procedure is likely to involve, the benefits and risks of any available alternative treatments (including no treatment) and any particular concerns of this patient.

The following leaflet/tape has been provided ....

This procedure will involve:

general and/or regional anaesthesia   local anaesthesia   sedation

Signed:..   Date .. ..
Name (PRINT) ....   Job title ....

Contact details (if patient wishes to discuss options later) ....

Statement of interpreter (where appropriate)

I have interpreted the information above to the patient to the best of my ability and in a way in which I believe s/he can understand.

Signed ....   Date ....
Name (PRINT) ....

Top copy accepted by patient: yes/no (please ring)

2

Statement of patient

Please read this form carefully. If your treatment has been planned in advance, you should already have your own copy of page 2 which describes the benefits and risks of the proposed treatment. If not, you will be offered a copy now. If you have any further questions, do ask – we are here to help you. You have the right to change your mind at any time, including after you have signed this form.

I agree to the procedure or course of treatment described on this form.

I understand that you cannot give me a guarantee that a particular person will perform the procedure. The person will, however, have appropriate experience.

I understand that I will have the opportunity to discuss the details of anaesthesia with an anaesthetist before the procedure, unless the urgency of my situation prevents this. (This only applies to patients having general or regional anaesthesia.)

I understand that any procedure in addition to those described on this form will only be carried out if it is necessary to save my life or to prevent serious harm to my health.

I have been told about additional procedures which may become necessary during my treatment. I have listed below any procedures **which I do not wish to be carried out** without further discussion. ....
....
....
....

Patient's signature ....   Date.............................
Name (PRINT) ....

A witness should sign below if the patient is unable to sign but has indicated his or her consent. Young people/children may also like a parent to sign here (see notes).

Signature ....   Date ....
Name (PRINT) ....

Confirmation of consent (to be completed by a health professional when the patient is admitted for the procedure, if the patient has signed the form in advance)

On behalf of the team treating the patient, I have confirmed with the patient that s/he has no further questions and wishes the procedure to go ahead.

Signed:..   Date ....
Name (PRINT) ....   Job title ....

Important notes: (tick if applicable)

See also advance directive/living will (eg Jehovah's Witness form)

Patient has withdrawn consent (ask patient to sign /date here) ....

3

Guidance to health professionals (to be read in conjunction with consent policy)

What a consent form is for

This form documents the patient's agreement to go ahead with the investigation or treatment you have proposed. It is not a legal waiver – if patients, for example, do not receive enough information on which to base their decision, then the consent may not be valid, even though the form has been signed. Patients are also entitled to change their mind after signing the form, if they retain capacity to do so. The form should act as an *aide-memoire* to health professionals and patients, by providing a check-list of the kind of information patients should be offered, and by enabling the patient to have a written record of the main points discussed. In no way, however, should the written information provided for the patient be regarded as a substitute for face-to-face discussions with the patient.

The law on consent

See the Department of Health's *Reference guide to consent for examination or treatment* for a comprehensive summary of the law on consent (also available at www.doh.gov.uk/consent).

Who can give consent

Everyone aged 16 or more is presumed to be competent to give consent for themselves, unless the opposite is demonstrated. If a child under the age of 16 has "sufficient understanding and intelligence to enable him or her to understand fully what is proposed", then he or she will be competent to give consent for himself or herself. Young people aged 16 and 17, and legally 'competent' younger children, may therefore sign this form for themselves, but may like a parent to countersign as well. If the child is not able to give consent for himself or herself, some-one with parental responsibility may do so on their behalf and a separate form is available for this purpose. Even where a child is able to give consent for himself or herself, you should always involve those with parental responsibility in the child's care, unless the child specifically asks you not to do so. If a patient is mentally competent to give consent but is physically unable to sign a form, you should complete this form as usual, and ask an independent witness to confirm that the patient has given consent orally or non-verbally.

When NOT to use this form

If the patient is 18 or over and is not legally competent to give consent, you should use form 4 (form for adults who are unable to consent to investigation or treatment) instead of this form. A patient will not be legally competent to give consent if:
• they are unable to comprehend and retain information material to the decision and/or
• they are unable to weigh and use this information in coming to a decision.
You should always take all reasonable steps (for example involving more specialist colleagues) to support a patient in making their own decision, before concluding that they are unable to do so. Relatives **cannot** be asked to sign this form on behalf of an adult who is not legally competent to consent for himself or herself.

Information

Information about what the treatment will involve, its benefits and risks (including side-effects and complications) and the alternatives to the particular procedure proposed, is crucial for patients when making up their minds. The courts have stated that patients should be told about 'significant risks which would affect the judgement of a reasonable patient'. 'Significant' has not been legally defined, but the GMC requires doctors to tell patients about 'serious or frequently occurring' risks. In addition if patients make clear they have particular concerns about certain kinds of risk, you should make sure they are informed about these risks, even if they are very small or rare. You should always answer questions honestly. Sometimes, patients may make it clear that they do not want to have any information about the options, but want you to decide on their behalf. In such circumstances, you should do your best to ensure that the patient receives at least very basic information about what is proposed. Where information is refused, you should document this on page 2 of the form or in the patient's notes.

4

[NHS organisation name]
consent form 2

Parental agreement to investigation or treatment for a child or young person

> **Patient details (or pre-printed label)**
>
> Patient's surname/family name.................................
>
> Patient's first names ....
>
> Date of birth ....
>
> Age ....
>
> Responsible health professional.............................
>
> Job title ....
>
> NHS number (or other identifier)..............................
>
> Male   Female
>
> Special requirements ....
> (eg other language/other communication method)

To be retained in patient's notes

Patient identifier/label

Name of proposed procedure or course of treatment (include brief
explanation if medical term not clear) ....
....
....

Statement of health professional (to be filled in by health professional with
appropriate knowledge of proposed procedure, as specified in consent policy)

I have explained the procedure to the child and his or her parent(s). In particular, I have
explained:

The intended benefits ....
....
Serious or frequently occurring risks ....
....
....

Any extra procedures which may become necessary during the procedure

   blood transfusion..

   other procedure (please specify) ....

....

I have also discussed what the procedure is likely to involve, the benefits and risks of any
available alternative treatments (including no treatment) and any particular concerns of this
patient and his or her parents.

   The following leaflet/tape has been provided ....

This procedure will involve:

   general and/or regional anaesthesia   local anaesthesia   sedation

Signed:...   Date .. ..
Name (PRINT) ....   Job title ....

Contact details (if child/parent wish to discuss options later) ....

Statement of interpreter (where appropriate)

I have interpreted the information above to the child and his or her parents to the best of
my ability and in a way in which I believe they can understand.

Signed ....   Date ....
Name (PRINT) ....

Top copy accepted by patient: yes/no (please ring)

Statement of parent   **Patient identifier/label**

Please read this form carefully. If the procedure has been planned in advance, you should already have your own copy of page 2 which describes the benefits and risks of the proposed treatment. If not, you will be offered a copy now. If you have any further questions, do ask – we are here to help you and your child. You have the right to change your mind at any time, including after you have signed this form.

I agree to the procedure or course of treatment described on this form and **I confirm** that I have 'parental responsibility' for this child.

I understand that you cannot give me a guarantee that a particular person will perform the procedure. The person will, however, have appropriate experience.

I understand that my child and I will have the opportunity to discuss the details of anaesthesia with an anaesthetist before the procedure, unless the urgency of the situation prevents this. (This only applies to children having general or regional anaesthesia.)

I understand hat any procedure in addition to those described on this form will only be carried out if it is necessary to save the life of my child or to prevent serious harm to his or her health.

I have been told about additional procedures which may become necessary during my child's treatment. I have listed below any **procedures which I do not wish to be carried out** without further discussion. ....
....
....
....

Signature ....   Date................................
Name (PRINT) ....Relationship to child...............................

Child's agreement to treatment (if child wishes to sign)

I agree to have the treatment I have been told about.

Name ....   Signature ....
Date ....

Confirmation of consent (to be completed by a health professional when the child is admitted for the procedure, if the parent/child have signed the form in advance)

On behalf of the team treating the patient, I have confirmed with the child and his or her parent(s) that they have no further questions and wish the procedure to go ahead.

Signed:...   Date .. ..
Name (PRINT) ....   Job title ....

Important notes: (tick if applicable)

See also advance directive/living will (eg Jehovah's Witness form)

Parent has withdrawn consent (ask parent to sign /date here) ....…..............

3

Guidance to health professionals (to be read in conjunction with consent policy)

This form

This form should be used to document consent to a child's treatment, where that consent is being given by a person with parental responsibility for the child. The term 'parent' has been used in this form as a shorthand for 'person with parental responsibility'. Where children are legally competent to consent for themselves (see below), they may sign the standard 'adult' consent form (form 1). There is space on that form for a parent to countersign if a competent child wishes them to do so.

Who can give consent

Everyone aged 16 or more is presumed to be competent to give consent for themselves, unless the opposite is demonstrated. The courts have stated that if a child under the age of 16 has "sufficient understanding and intelligence to enable him or her to understand fully what is proposed", then he or she will be competent to give consent for himself or herself. If children are not able to give consent for themselves, some-one with parental responsibility may do so on their behalf.

Although children acquire rights to give consent for themselves as they grow older, people with 'parental responsibility' for a child retain the right to give consent on the child's behalf until the child reaches the age of 18. Therefore, for a number of years, both the child and a person with parental responsibility have the right to give consent to the child's treatment. In law, health professionals only need the consent of one appropriate person before providing treatment. This means that in theory it is lawful to provide treatment to a child under 18 which a person with parental responsibility has authorised, even if the child refuses. As a matter of good practice, however, you should always seek a competent child's consent before providing treatment unless any delay involved in doing so would put the child's life or health at risk. Younger children should also be as involved as possible in decisions about their healthcare. Further advice is given in the Department's guidance *Seeking consent: working with children*. Any differences of opinion between the child and their parents, or between parents, should be clearly documented in the patient's notes.

Parental responsibility

The person(s) with parental responsibility will usually, but not invariably, be the child's birth parents. People with parental responsibility for a child include: the child's mother; the child's father if married to the mother at the child's conception, birth or later; a legally appointed guardian; the local authority if the child is on a care order; or a person named in a residence order in respect of the child. Fathers who have never been married to the child's mother will only have parental responsibility if they have acquired it through a court order or parental responsibility agreement (although this may change in the future).

Information

Information about what the treatment will involve, its benefits and risks (including side-effects and complications) and the alternatives to the particular procedure proposed, is crucial for children and their parents when making up their minds about treatment. The courts have stated that patients should be told about 'significant risks which would affect the judgement of a reasonable patient'. 'Significant' has not been legally defined, but the GMC requires doctors to tell patients about 'serious or frequently occurring' risks. In addition if patients make clear they have particular concerns about certain kinds of risk, you should make sure they are informed about these risks, even if they are very small or rare. You should always answer questions honestly.

Guidance on the law on consent

See the Department of Health publications *Reference guide to consent for examination or treatment* and *Seeking consent: working with children* for a comprehensive summary of the law on consent (also available at www.doh.gov.uk/consent).

4

[NHS organisation name] consent form 3

Patient identifier/label

Patient/parental agreement to investigation or treatment
(procedures where consciousness not impaired)

Name of procedure (include brief explanation if medical term not clear)
....
....

Statement of health professional (to be filled in by health professional with appropriate knowledge of proposed procedure, as specified in consent policy)

I have explained the procedure to the patient/parent. In particular, I have explained:
The intended benefits ....
....
....
Serious or frequently occurring risks:...
....
....

I have also discussed what the procedure is likely to involve, the benefits and risks of any available alternative treatments (including no treatment) and any particular concerns of those involved.

   The following leaflet/tape has been provided ....

Signed: .... Date ....
Name (PRINT) .... Job title ....

Statement of interpreter (where appropriate)
I have interpreted the information above to the patient/parent to the best of my ability and in a way in which I believe s/he/they can understand.

Signed ....Date....................Name (PRINT)...................................

Statement of patient/person with parental responsibility for patient
I agree to the procedure described above.

I understand that you cannot give me a guarantee that a particular person will perform the procedure. The person will, however, have appropriate experience.

I understand that the procedure will/will not involve local anaesthesia.

Signature .... Date ....
Name (PRINT) .... Relationship to patient ....

Confirmation of consent (to be completed by a health professional when the patient is admitted for the procedure, if the patient/parent has signed the form in advance)

I have confirmed that the patient/parent has no further questions and wishes the procedure to go ahead.

Signed: .... Date ....
Name (PRINT) .... Job title ....

Top copy accepted by patient: yes/no (please ring)

Guidance to health professionals (to be read in conjunction with consent policy)

This form
This form documents the patient's agreement (or that of a person with parental responsibility for the patient) to go ahead with the investigation or treatment you have proposed. **It is only designed for procedures where the patient is expected to remain alert throughout and where an anaesthetist is not involved in their care: for example for drug therapy where written consent is deemed appropriate.** In other circumstances you should use either form 1 (for adults/competent children) or form 2 (parental consent for children/young people) as appropriate.

Consent forms are not legal waivers – if patients, for example, do not receive enough information on which to base their decision, then the consent may not be valid, even though the form has been signed. Patients also have every right to change their mind after signing the form.

Who can give consent
Everyone aged 16 or more is presumed to be competent to give consent for themselves, unless the opposite is demonstrated. If a child under the age of 16 has "sufficient understanding and intelligence to enable him or her to understand fully what is proposed", then he or she will be competent to give consent for himself or herself. Young people aged 16 and 17, and legally 'competent' younger children, may therefore sign this form for themselves, if they wish. If the child is not able to give consent for himself or herself, some-one with parental responsibility may do so on their behalf. Even where a child is able to give consent for himself or herself, you should always involve those with parental responsibility in the child's care, unless the child specifically asks you not to do so. If a patient is mentally competent to give consent but is physically unable to sign a form, you should complete this form as usual, and ask an independent witness to confirm that the patient has given consent orally or non-verbally.

When NOT to use this form (see also 'This form' above)
If the patient is 18 or over and is not legally competent to give consent, you should use form 4 (form for adults who are unable to consent to investigation or treatment) instead of this form. A patient will not be legally competent to give consent if:
* they are unable to comprehend and retain information material to the decision and/or
* they are unable to weigh and use this information in coming to a decision.
You should always take all reasonable steps (for example involving more specialist colleagues) to support a patient in making their own decision, before concluding that they are unable to do so. Relatives **cannot** be asked to sign this form on behalf of an adult who is not legally competent to consent for himself or herself.

Information
Information about what the treatment will involve, its benefits and risks (including side-effects and complications) and the alternatives to the particular procedure proposed, is crucial for patients when making up their minds about treatment. The courts have stated that patients should be told about 'significant risks which would affect the judgement of a reasonable patient'. 'Significant' has not been legally defined, but the GMC requires doctors to tell patients about 'serious or frequently occurring' risks. In addition if patients make clear they have particular concerns about certain kinds of risk, you should make sure they are informed about these risks, even if they are very small or rare. You should always answer questions honestly. Sometimes, patients may make it clear that they do not want to have any information about the options, but want you to decide on their behalf. In such circumstances, you should do your best to ensure that the patient receives at least very basic information about what is proposed. Where information is refused, you should document this overleaf or in the patient's notes.

The law on consent
See the Department of Health's *Reference guide to consent for examination or treatment* for a comprehensive summary of the law on consent (also available at www.doh.gov.uk/consent).

[NHS organisation name]
consent form 4

Form for adults who are unable to
consent to investigation or treatment

Patient details (or pre-printed label)

Patient's surname/family name.................................

Patient's first names ....

Date of birth ....

Responsible health professional................................

Job title ....

NHS number (or other identifier)................................

Male   Female

Special requirements ....
(eg other language/other communication method)

To be retained in patient's notes

Patient identifier/label

All sections to be completed by health professional proposing the procedure

A Details of procedure or course of treatment proposed

(NB see guidance to health professionals overleaf for details of situations where court approval must first be sought)

B Assessment of patient's capacity

I confirm that the patient lacks capacity to give or withhold consent to this procedure or course of treatment because:

the patient is unable to comprehend and retain information material to the decision; and/or

the patient is unable to use and weigh this information in the decision-making process; or

the patient is unconscious

Further details (excluding where patient unconscious): for example how above judgements reached; which colleagues consulted; what attempts made to assist the patient make his or her own decision and why these were not successful.

C Assessment of patient's best interests

To the best of my knowledge, the patient has not refused this procedure in a valid advance directive. Where possible and appropriate, I have consulted with colleagues and those close to the patient, and I believe the procedure to be in the patient's best interests because:

(Where incapacity is likely to be temporary, for example if patient unconscious, or where patient has fluctuating capacity)

The treatment cannot wait until the patient recovers capacity because:

2

D Involvement of the patient's family and others close to the patient

The final responsibility for determining whether a procedure is in an incapacitated patient's best interests lies with the health professional performing the procedure. However, it is good practice to consult with those close to the patient (eg spouse/partner, family and friends, carer, supporter or advocate) unless you have good reason to believe that the patient would not have wished particular individuals to be consulted, or unless the urgency of their situation prevents this. "Best interests" go far wider than "best medical interests", and include factors such as the patient's wishes and beliefs when competent, their current wishes, their general well-being and their spiritual and religious welfare.

(to be signed by a person or persons close to the patient, if they wish)

I/We have been involved in a discussion with the relevant health professionals over the treatment of................................(patient's name). I/We understand that he/she is unable to give his/her own consent, based on the criteria set out in this form. I/We also understand that treatment can lawfully be provided if it is in his/her best interests to receive it.

Any other comments (including any concerns about decision)

Name ....Relationship to patient......................................
Address (if not the same as patient..
....
....

Signature ....   Date...............................

If a person close to the patient was not available in person, has this matter been discussed in any other way (eg over the telephone?)

Yes   No

Details:

Signature of health professional proposing treatment

The above procedure is, in my clinical judgement, in the best interests of the patient, who lacks capacity to consent for himself or herself. Where possible and appropriate I have discussed the patient's condition with those close to him or her, and taken their knowledge of the patient's views and beliefs into account in determining his or her best interests.

I have/have not sought a second opinion.

Signature:..   Date .. ..
Name (PRINT) ....   Job title ....

Where second opinion sought, s/he should sign below to confirm agreement:

Signature:..   Date .. ..
Name (PRINT) ....   Job title ....

3

Guidance to health professionals (to be read in conjunction with consent policy)

This form should only be used where it would be usual to seek written consent but an adult patient (18 or over) lacks capacity to give or withhold consent to treatment. If an adult **has** capacity to accept or refuse treatment, you should use the standard consent form and respect any refusal. Where treatment is very urgent (for example if the patient is critically ill), it may not be feasible to fill in a form at the time, but you should document your clinical decisions appropriately afterwards. If treatment is being provided under the authority of Part IV of the *Mental Health Act 1983*, different legal provisions apply and you are required to fill in more specialised forms (although in some circumstances you may find it helpful to use this form as well). If the adult now lacks capacity, but has clearly refused particular treatment in advance of their loss of capacity (for example in an advance directive or 'living will'), then you must abide by that refusal if it was validly made and is applicable to the circumstances. For further information on the law on consent, see the Department of Health's *Reference guide to consent for examination or treatment* (www.doh.gov.uk/consent).

When treatment can be given to a patient who is unable to consent
For treatment to be given to a patient who is unable to consent, the following **must** apply:
* the patient must lack the capacity ('competence') to give or withhold consent to this procedure AND
* the procedure must be in the patient's best interests.

Capacity
A patient will lack capacity to consent to a particular intervention if he or she is:
* unable to comprehend and retain information material to the decision, especially as to the consequences of having, or not having, the intervention in question; and/or
* unable to use and weigh this information in the decision-making process.
Before making a judgement that a patient lacks capacity you must take all steps reasonable in the circumstances to assist the patient in taking their own decisions (this will clearly not apply if the patient is unconscious). This may involve explaining what is involved in very simple language, using pictures and communication and decision-aids as appropriate. People close to the patient (spouse/partner, family, friends and carers) may often be able to help, as may specialist colleagues such as speech and language therapists or learning disability teams, and independent advocates or supporters.

Capacity is 'decision-specific': a patient may lack capacity to take a particular complex decision, but be quite able to take other more straight-forward decisions or parts of decisions.

Best interests
A patient's best interests are not limited to their best medical interests. Other factors which form part of the best interests decision include:
* the wishes and beliefs of the patient when competent
* their current wishes
* their general well-being
* their spiritual and religious welfare

Two incapacitated patients, whose *physical* condition is identical, may therefore have different best interests.

Unless the patient has clearly indicated that particular individuals should not be involved in their care, or unless the urgency of their situation prevents it, you should attempt to involve people close to the patient (spouse/partner, family and friends, carer, supporter or advocate) in the decision-making process. Those close to the patient cannot require you to provide particular treatment which you do not believe to be clinically appropriate. However they will know the patient much better than you do, and therefore are likely to be able to provide valuable information about the patient's wishes and values.

Second opinions and court involvement
Where treatment is complex and/or people close to the patient express doubts about the proposed treatment, a second opinion should be sought, unless the urgency of the patient's condition prevents this. Donation of regenerative tissue such as bone marrow, sterilisation for contraceptive purposes and withdrawal of artificial nutrition or hydration from a patient in PVS must never be undertaken without prior

4

High Court approval. High Court approval can also be sought where there are doubts about the patient's capacity or best interests.

Part IV

General Medical Council

Serious Communicable Diseases

(September 1997)

Use of term 'serious communicable disease'

In this guidance the term serious communicable disease applies to any disease which may he transmitted from human to human and which may result in death or serious illness. It particularly concerns, but is not limited to, infections such as human immunodeficiency virus (HIV), tuberculosis and hepatitis B and C.

Providing a good standard of practice and care

1. All patients are entitled to good standards of practice and care from their doctors, regardless of the nature of their disease or condition.

2. You must not deny or delay investigation or treatment because you believe that the patient's actions or lifestyle may have contributed to their condition. Where patients pose a serious risk to your health or safety you may take reasonable, personal measures to protect yourself before investigating a patient's condition or providing treatment. In the context of serious communicable diseases these will usually be infection control measures. You must follow the guidance in paragraph 4 on consent to testing.

3. You must keep yourself informed about serious communicable diseases, and particularly their means of transmission and control. You should always take appropriate measures to protect yourself and others from infection. YOu must make sure that any staff for whom you are responsible are also appropriately informed and co-operate with measures designed to prevent transmission of infection to other patients.

Consent to testing for a serious communicable disease

4. You must obtain consent from patients before testing for a serious communicable disease, except in the rare circumstances described in paragraphs 6, 7, 9, 11 and 17 below. The information you provide when seeking consent should be appropriate to the circumstances and to the nature of the condition or conditions being tested for. Some conditions, such as HIV, have serious social and financial, as well as medical, implications. In such cases you must make sure that the patient is given appropriate information about the implications of the test, and appropriate time to consider and discuss them.

Children

5. When testing patients under 16 for a serious communicable disease, you must follow the guidance in paragraph 4 if you judge that they have sufficient maturity to understand the implications of testing.

6. Where a child cannot give or withhold consent, you should seek consent from a person with parental responsibility for the child. If you believe that that person's judgment is distorted, for example, because he or she may be the cause of the child's infection, you must decide whether the

medical interests of the child override the wishes of those with parental responsibility. Whenever possible you should discuss the issues with an experienced colleague before making a decision. If you test a child without obtaining consent, you must be prepared to justify that decision.

Unconscious patients

7. You may test unconscious patients for serious communicable diseases, without their prior consent, where testing would be in their immediate clinical interests – for example, to help in making a diagnosis. You should not test unconscious patients for other purposes.

Testing in laboratories

12. It is the responsibility of the doctor treating the patient to obtain consent to testing for diagnostic purposes. If you work in a laboratory you may test blood or other specimens for serious communicable diseases only for the purposes for which the samples have been obtained, or for closely related purposes which are in the direct interests of the patient. See paragraph 14 for guidance on testing undertaken for research purposes.

Unlinked anonymised screening

13. In unlinked anonymised surveillance programmes for serious communicable diseases, you should make sure that patients are provided with information which covers:

- Their right to refuse inclusion of the sample in the programme.
- The fact that their blood sample cannot be identified and there is no way of tracing it back to them.
- The benefits of seeking a test if they think they have been exposed to infection.

Research

14. You may undertake research only where the protocol has been approved by the appropriate, properly constituted research ethics committee. It remains your responsibility to ensure that research does not infringe patients' rights.

Deceased patients

15. When a patient who is brain stem dead is being considered as an organ donor, you should explain to relatives that assessing the suitability of organs for transplantation will involve testing for certain infections, including HIV.

Post-mortem testing

16. Where a post-mortem has been authorised or ordered you may test the deceased patient for communicable diseases where relevant to the investigation into the causes of death.

17. You should not routinely test for serious communicable diseases before performing post-mortems; but you should take precautions to protect yourself and other health care workers. If you have reason to believe the deceased person had a serious communicable disease, you should assume the body to be infectious.

Confidentiality

Informing other health care professionals

18. If you diagnose a patient as having a serious communicable disease, you should explain to the patient:

    a. The nature of the disease and its medical, social and occupational implications, as appropriate.

    b. Ways of protecting others from infection.

    c. The importance to effective care of giving the professionals who will be providing care information which they need to know about the patient's disease or condition. In particular you must make sure that patient understands that general practitioners cannot provide adequate clinical management and care without knowledge of their patients' conditions.

19. If patients still refuse to allow other health care workers to be informed, you must respect the patients' wishes except where you judge that failure to disclose the information would put a health care worker or other patient at serious risk of death or serious harm. Such situations may arise, for example, when dealing with violent patients with severe mental illness or disability. If you are in doubt about whether disclosure is appropriate, you should seek advice from an experienced colleague. You should inform patients before disclosing information. Such occasions are likely to arise rarely and you must be prepared to justify a decision to disclose information against a patient's wishes.

Disclosures to others

20. You must disclose information about serious communicable diseases in accordance with the law. For example, the appropriate authority must be informed where a notifiable disease is diagnosed. Where a communicable disease contributed to the cause of death, this must be recorded on the death certificate. You should also pass information about serious communicable diseases to the relevant authorities for the purpose of communicable disease control and surveillance.

21. As the GMC booklet *Confidentiality* makes clear, a patient's death does not of itself release a doctor from the obligation to maintain confidentiality. But in some circumstances disclosures can be justified because they protect other people from serious harm or because they are required by law.

Giving information to close contacts

22. You may disclose information about a patient, whether living or dead, in order to protect a person from risk of death or serious harm. For example, you may disclose information to a known sexual contact of a patient with HIV where you have reason to think that the patient has not informed that person, and cannot be persuaded to do so. In such circumstances you should tell the patient before you make the disclosure, and you must be prepared to justify a decision to disclose information.

23. You must not disclose information to others, for example relatives, who have not been, and are not, at risk of infection.

Doctors' responsibilities to protect patients from infection

24. You must protect patients from unnecessary exposure to infection by following safe working practices and implementing appropriate infection control measures. This includes following the Control of Substances Hazardous to Health Regulations 1994 and other health and safety at work legislation. These regulations may require you to inform your employer, or the person responsible for health and safety in your organisation, if there are any deficiencies in protection measures in your work place. Failure to do so may amount to a criminal offence.

25. You must follow the UK Health Departments' advice on immunisation against hepatitis B, If you are in direct contact with patients you should protect yourself and your patients by being immunised against other common serious communicable diseases, where vaccines are available.

26. You must always take action to protect patients when you have good reason to suspect that your own health, or that of a colleague, is a risk to them.

27. You must consider how any infection you have may put patients at risk. You must take particular care if you work with patients for whom exposure to infection may be serious, for example pregnant women or immuno-suppressed patients.

28. You must comply promptly with appropriate requests to be tested for serious communicable diseases when there is an investigation into an outbreak of disease amongst patients.

Responsibilities of doctors who have been exposed to a serious communicable disease

29. If you have any reason to believe that you have been exposed to a serious communicable disease you must seek and follow professional advice without delay on whether you should undergo testing and, if so, which tests are appropriate. Further guidance on your responsibilities if your health may put patients at risk is included in our booklet *Good Medical Practice*.

30. If you acquire a serious communicable disease you must promptly seek and follow advice from a suitably qualified colleague – such as a consultant in occupational health, infectious diseases or public health on:

- Whether, and in what ways, you should modify your professional practice.
- Whether you should inform your current employer, your previous employers or any prospective employer, about your condition.

31. You must not rely on your own assessment of the risks you pose to patients.

32. If you have a serious communicable disease and continue in professional practice you must have appropriate medical supervision.

33. If you apply for a new post, you must complete health questionnaires honestly and fully.

Treating colleagues with serious communicable diseases

34. If you are treating a doctor or other health care worker with a serious communicable disease you must provide the confidentiality and support to which every patient is entitled.

35. If you know, or have good reason to believe, that a medical colleague or health care worker who has or may have a serious communicable disease, is practising, or has practised, in a way which places patients at risk, you must inform an appropriate person in the health care worker's employing authority, for example an occupational health physician, or where appropriate, the relevant regulatory body. Such cases are likely to arise very rarely. Wherever possible you should inform the health care worker concerned before passing information to an employer or regulatory body.

Guidance for Doctors Who Are Asked to Circumcise Male Children

(September 1997)

Introduction

Background

1. Issues raised by male circumcision have been drawn to our attention in two ways. First, by complaints that doctors had not provided an acceptable standards of practice when performing this procedure. We have also received inquiries about the ethics of the procedure, asking for our views on whether, and in what circumstances, the procedure would be acceptable for either religious or therapeutic reasons.

2. Circumcision raises difficult questions about the rights and freedoms of individuals. Many people maintain that individuals have a right to practise their religion unhindered. Others feel that it is unequivocally wrong to undertake a surgical procedure, with its attendant risks, on an infant who is unable to consent. These are not solely medical matters and we do not think they can be resolved by the medical profession alone. They are matters for society as a whole to decide. Nonetheless, we have a responsibility to protect patients and to guide doctors and we have therefore undertaken to provide guidance which sets out the principles of good medical practice for those doctors who are asked to perform circumcisions for religious or for medical reasons.

3. The following paragraphs set out the diversity of views on the issues, reflecting the response to our consultation amongst religious groups, civil rights and children's rights groups and the medical profession.

Rights and freedoms

4. Male circumcision considered by many in the Jewish and Islamic faiths to be essential to the practice of their religion; they would regard any restriction or ban on male circumcision as an infringement of a fundamental human right. Many also believe that if doctors were prevented from

carrying out the procedure, parents would turn in greater numbers to individuals who lack the skills and experience to perform it safely and competently.

5. Others, including those who campaign against the practice of male circumcision, strongly believe that, because circumcision for non-therapeutic reasons carries risks, it is wrong to perform the procedure on children who are not old enough to give informed consent.

The legal position

6. In 1995 The Law Commission issued a consultation paper on consent in the criminal law. This paper argues that male circumcision is lawful in the UK, but this point has been challenged.

7. Article 24.3 of the UN Convention on the Rights of the Child (ratified by the UK Government in 1991) states that ratifying states should 'take all effective and appropriate measures with a view to abolishing traditional practices prejudicial to the health of children'. However, this must be balanced against Article 9.2 of the European Convention on Human Rights, which protects the rights of individuals to practise their religion.

8. The legal position is untested in the context of circumcision and therefore remains unclear.

Views about harm and benefit

9. There is also a wide variation of views on the role of the medical profession. Many believe that doctors have a duty to provide the public with objective information about circumcision; and that they should be obliged to provide counselling to parents before, and after, circumcising their child. Others believe that doctors should not put undue emphasis on the risks of the procedure, because there is insufficient evidence to justify worrying parents about them.

10. Similarly, while there is a body of opinion that because circumcision has very few medical benefits, and the potential dangers to the child far outweigh these, circumcision is inappropriate under any circumstances. Other people believe that circumcision causes no harm, and may be beneficial; some would recommend performing the procedure routinely.

Conclusion

11. Our consultation demonstrated widely conflicting views in society, which neither doctors, nor the GMC can resolve.

12. We believe that the welfare of infants who are circumcised must be paramount, whatever the reason for undertaking the procedure. Any medical procedure must be undertaken in hygienic conditions, with appropriate pain relief and aftercare.

13. In drafting our guidance for doctors we have considered, as objectively as possible, all the views and information put to us. Our aim is to provide advice which will help doctors to provide a good standard of care for their patients.

14. Our published guidance does not specifically address the rights of children. However, many of the principles set out in our booklet *Good Medical Practice* are of broad application and should be followed by doctors when they are asked to perform circumcisions. The guidance which follows is based on the principles in this booklet.

Standards of practice for doctors asked to circumcise male children

15. If you decide to circumcise a male child you must:

- Have the necessary skills and experience both to perform the operation and use appropriate measures, including anaesthesia, to minimise pain and discomfort.
- Keep up to date with developments in the practice of male circumcision including when the procedure is, and is not, necessary for medical reasons.
- Explain objectively to those with parental responsibility for the child any benefits or risks of the procedure, taking into account the age of the child.

- Explain to those with parental responsibility that they may invite their religious advisor to be present at the circumcision to give advice on how the procedure should be performed to meet the requirements of their faith.
- Listen to those with parental responsibility and give careful consideration to their views. You are not obliged to act on a request to circumcise a child, but you should explain if you are opposed to circumcision other than for therapeutic reasons. You should also tell those with parental responsibility that they have a right to see another doctor.
- Obtain the permission of both parents whenever possible, but in all cases obtain valid consent, in writing, from a person with parental responsibility before performing the procedure.
- Provide appropriate aftercare.

Seeking Patients' Consent: the Ethical Considerations

(February 1999: under review)

This booklet sets out the principles of good practice which all registered doctors are expected to follow when seeking patients' informed consent to investigations, treatment, screening or research. It enlarges on the general principles set out in paragraph 12 of our booklet *Good Medical Practice*.

Introduction

1. Successful relationships between doctors and patients depend on trust. To establish that trust you must respect patients' autonomy – their right to decide whether or not to undergo any medical intervention even where a refusal may result in harm to themselves or in their own death. Patients must be given sufficient information, in a way that they can understand, to enable them to exercise their right to make informed decisions about their care.

2. This right is protected in law, and you are expected to be aware of the legal principles set by relevant case law in this area. Existing case law gives a guide to what can be considered minimum requirements of good practice in seeking informed consent from patients.

3. Effective communication is the key to enabling patients to make informed decisions. You must take appropriate steps to find out what patients want to know and ought to know about their condition and its treatment. Open, helpful dialogue of this kind with patients leads to clarity of objectives and understanding, and strengthens the quality of the doctor/patient relationship. It provides an agreed framework within which the doctor can respond effectively to the individual needs of the patient. Additionally, patients who have been able to make properly informed decisions are more likely to cooperate fully with the agreed management of their conditions.

Consent to investigation and treatment

Providing sufficient information

4. Patients have a right to information about their condition and the treatment options available to them. The amount of information you give each patient will vary, according to factors such as the nature of the condition, the complexity of the treatment, the risks associated with the treatment or procedure, and the patient's own wishes. For example, patients may need more information to make an informed decision about a procedure which carries a high risk of failure or adverse side effects; or about an investigation for a condition which, if present, could have serious implications for the patient's employment, social or personal life.

5. The information which patients want or ought to know, before deciding whether to consent to treatment or an investigation, may include:

- details of the diagnosis, and prognosis, and the likely prognosis if the condition is left untreated;

- uncertainties about the diagnosis including options for further investigation prior to treatment;
- options for treatment or management of the condition, including the option not to treat;
- the purpose of a proposed investigation or treatment; details of the procedures or therapies involved, including subsidiary treatment such as methods of pain relief; how the patient should prepare for the procedure; and details of what the patient might experience during or after the procedure including common and serious side effects;
- for each option, explanations of the likely benefits and the probabilities of success; and discussion of any serious or frequently occurring risks, and of any lifestyle changes which may be caused by, or necessitated by, the treatment;
- advice about whether a proposed treatment is experimental;
- how and when the patient's condition and any side effects will be monitored or re-assessed;
- the name of the doctor who will have overall responsibility for the treatment and, where appropriate, names of the senior members of his or her team;
- whether doctors in training will be involved, and the extent to which students may be involved in an investigation or treatment;
- a reminder that patients can change their minds about a decision at any time;
- a reminder that patients have a right to seek a second opinion;
- where applicable, details of costs or charges which the patient may have to meet.

6. When providing information you must do your best to find out about patients' individual needs and priorities. For example, patients' beliefs, culture, occupation or other factors may have a bearing on the information they need in order to reach a decision. You should not make assumptions about patients' views, but discuss these matters with them, and ask them whether they have any concerns about the treatment or the risks it may involve. You should provide patients with appropriate information, which should include an explanation of any risks to which they may attach particular significance. Ask patients whether they have understood the information and whether they would like more before making a decision.

7. You must not exceed the scope of the authority given by a patient, except in an emergency. Therefore, if you are the doctor providing treatment or undertaking an investigation, you must give the patient a clear explanation of the scope of consent being sought. This will apply particularly where:

- treatment will be provided in stages with the possibility of later adjustments;
- different doctors (or other health care workers) provide particular elements of an investigation or treatment (for example anaesthesia in surgery);
- a number of different investigations or treatments are involved;
- uncertainty about the diagnosis, or about the appropriate range of options for treatment, may be resolved only in the light of findings once investigation or treatment is underway, and when the patient may be unable to participate in decision making.

In such cases, you should explain how decisions would be made about whether or when to move from one stage or one form of treatment to another. There should be a clear agreement about whether the patient consents to all or only parts of the proposed plan of investigation or treatment, and whether further consent will have to be sought at a later stage.

8. You should raise with patients the possibility of additional problems coming to light during a procedure when the patient is unconscious or otherwise unable to make a decision. You should seek consent to treat any problems which you think may arise and ascertain whether there are any procedures to which the patient would object, or prefer to give further thought to before you proceed. You must abide by patients' decisions on these issues. If in exceptional circumstances you decide, while the patient is unconscious, to treat a condition which falls outside the scope of the patient's consent, your decision may be challenged in the courts, or be the subject of a complaint to your employing authority or the GMC. You should therefore seek the views of an experienced

colleague, wherever possible, before providing the treatment. And you must be prepared to explain and justify your decision. You must tell the patient what you have done and why, as soon as the patient is sufficiently recovered to understand.

Responding to questions

9. You must respond honestly to any questions the patient raises and, as far as possible, answer as fully as the patient wishes. In some cases, a patient may ask about other treatments that are unproven or ineffective. Some patients may want to know whether any of the risks or benefits of treatment are affected by the choice of institution or doctor providing the care. You must answer such questions as fully, accurately and objectively as possible.

Withholding information

10. You should not withhold information necessary for decision making unless you judge that disclosure of some relevant information would cause the patient serious harm. In this context serious harm does not mean the patient would become upset, or decide to refuse treatment.

11. No-one may make decisions on behalf of a competent adult. If patients ask you to withhold information and make decisions on their behalf, or nominate a relative or third party to make decisions for them, you should explain the importance of them knowing the options open to them, and what the treatment they may receive will involve. If they insist they do not want to know in detail about their condition and its treatment, you should still provide basic information about the treatment. If a relative asks you to withhold information, you must seek the views of the patient. Again, you should not withhold relevant information unless you judge that this would cause the patient serious harm.

12. In any case where you withhold relevant information from the patient you must record this, and the reason for doing so, in the patient's medical records and you must be prepared to explain and justify your decision.

Presenting information to patients

13. Obtaining informed consent cannot be an isolated event. It involves a continuing dialogue between you and your patients which keeps them abreast of changes in their condition and the treatment or investigation you propose. Whenever possible, you should discuss treatment options at a time when the patient is best able to understand and retain the information. To be sure that your patient understands, you should give clear explanations and give the patient time to ask questions. In particular, you should:

- use up to date written material, visual and other aids to explain complex aspects of the investigation, diagnosis or treatment where appropriate and/or practicable;
- make arrangements, wherever possible, to meet particular language and communication needs, for example through translations, independent interpreters, signers, or the patient's representative;
- where appropriate, discuss with patients the possibility of bringing a relative or friend, or making a tape recording of the consultation;
- explain the probabilities of success, or the risk of failure of, or harm associated with options for treatment, using accurate data;
- ensure that information which patients may find distressing is given to them in a considerate way. Provide patients with information about counselling services and patient support groups, where appropriate;
- allow patients sufficient time to reflect, before and after making a decision, especially where the information is complex or the severity of the risks is great. Where patients have difficulty understanding information, or there is a lot of information to absorb, it may be appropriate to provide it in manageable amounts, with appropriate written or other back-up material, over a period of time, or to repeat it;
- involve nursing or other members of the health care team in discussions with the patient, where appropriate. They may have valuable knowledge of the patient's background or particular concerns, for example in identifying what risks the patient should be told about;

- ensure that, where treatment is not to start until some time after consent has been obtained, the patient is given a clear route for reviewing their decision with the person providing the treatment.

Who obtains consent

14. If you are the doctor providing treatment or undertaking an investigation, it is your responsibility to discuss it with the patient and obtain consent, as you will have a comprehensive understanding of the procedure or treatment, how it is carried out, and the risks attached to it. Where this is not practicable, you may delegate these tasks provided you ensure that the person to whom you delegate:

- is suitably trained and qualified;
- has sufficient knowledge of the proposed investigation or treatment, and understands the risks involved;
- acts in accordance with the guidance in this booklet.

You will remain responsible for ensuring that, before you start any treatment, the patient has been given sufficient time and information to make an informed decision, and has given consent to the procedure or investigation.

Ensuring voluntary decision making

15. It is for the patient, not the doctor, to determine what is in the patient's own best interests. Nonetheless, you may wish to recommend a treatment or a course of action to patients, but you must not put pressure on patients to accept your advice. In discussions with patients, you should:

- give a balanced view of the options;   .
- explain the need for informed consent.

You must declare any potential conflicts of interest, for example where you or your organisation benefit financially from use of a particular drug or treatment, or treatment at a particular institution.

16. Pressure may be put on patients by employers, insurance companies or others to undergo particular tests or accept treatment. You should do your best to ensure that patients have considered the options and reached their own decision. You should take appropriate action if you believe patients are being offered inappropriate or unlawful financial or other rewards.

17. Patients who are detained by the police or immigration services, or are in prison, and those detained under the provisions of any mental health legislation may be particularly vulnerable. Where such patients have a right to decline treatment you should do your best to ensure that they know this, and are able to exercise this right.

Emergencies

18. In an emergency, where consent cannot be obtained, you may provide medical treatment to anyone who needs it, provided the treatment is limited to what is immediately necessary to save life or avoid significant deterioration in the patient's health. However, you must still respect the terms of any valid advance refusal which you know about, or is drawn to your attention. You should tell the patient what has been done, and why, as soon as the patient is sufficiently recovered to understand.

Establishing capacity to make decisions

19. You must work on the presumption at every adult has the capacity to decide whether to consent to, or refuse, proposed medical intervention, unless it is shown that they cannot understand information presented in a clear way. If a patient's choice appears irrational, or does not accord with your view of what is in the patient's best interests, that is not evidence in itself that the patient lacks competence. In such circumstances it may be appropriate to review with the patient whether all reasonable steps have been taken to identify and meet their information needs (see paragraphs

5–17). Where you need to assess a patient's capacity to make a decision, you should consult the guidance issued by professional bodies.

Fluctuating capacity

20. Where patients have difficulty retaining information, or are only intermittently competent to make a decision, you should provide any assistance they might need to reach an informed decision. You should record any decision made while the patients were competent, including the key elem ents of the consultation. You should review any decision made whilst they were competent, at appropriate intervals before treatment starts, to establish that their views are consistently held and can be relied on.

Mentally incapacitated patients

21. No-one can give or withhold consent to treatment on behalf of a mentally incapacitated patient. You must first assess the patient's capacity to make an informed decision about the treatment. If patients lack capacity to decide, provided they comply, you may carry out an investigation or treatment, which may include treatment for any mental disorder, that you judge to be in their best interests. However, if they do not comply, you may compulsorily treat them for any mental disorder only within the safeguards laid down by the Mental Health Act (1983) and any physical disorder arising from that mental disorder, in line with the guidance in the Code of Practice of the Mental Health Commission. You should seek the courts' approval for any non-therapeutic or controversial treatments which are not directed at their mental disorder.

Advance statements

22. If you are treating a patient who has lost capacity to consent to or refuse treatment, for example through onset or progress of a mental disorder or other disability, you should try to find out whether the patient has previously indicated preferences in an advance statement ('advance directives' or 'living wills'). You must respect any refusal of treatment given when the patient was competent, provided the decision in the advance statement is clearly applicable to the present circumstances, and there is no reason to believe that the patient has changed his/her mind. Where an advance statement of this kind is not available, the patient's known wishes should be taken into account – see paragraph 25 on the 'best interests' principle.

Children

23. You must assess a child's capacity to decide whether to consent to or refuse proposed inves- tigation or treatment before you provide it. In general, a competent child will be able to understand the nature, purpose and possible consequences of the proposed investigation or treatment, as well as the consequences of non-treatment. Your assessment must take account of the relevant laws or legal precedents in this area. You should bear in mind that:

- at age 16 a young person can be treated as an adult and can be presumed to have capacity to decide;
- under age 16 children may have capacity to decide, depending on their ability to understand what is involved;
- where a competent child refuses treatment, a person with parental responsibility or the court may authorise investigation or treatment which is in the child's best interests. The position is different in Scotland, where those with parental responsibility cannot authorise procedures a competent child has refused. Legal advice may be helpful on how to deal with such cases.

24. Where a child under 16 years old is not competent to give or withhold their informed consent, a person with parental responsibility may authorise investigations or treatment which are in the child's best interests. This person may also refuse any intervention, where they consider that refusal to be in the child's best interests, but you are not bound by such a refusal and may seek a ruling from the court. In an emergency where you consider that it is in the child's best interests to proceed, you may treat the child, provided it is limited to that treatment which is reasonably required in that emergency.

'Best interests' principle

25. In deciding what options may be reasonably considered as being in the best interests of a patient who lacks capacity to decide, you should take into account:

- options for treatment or investigation which are clinically indicated;
- any evidence of the patient's previously expressed preferences, including an advance statement;
- your own and the health care team's knowledge of the patient's background, such as cultural, religious, or employment considerations;
- views about the patient's preferences given by a third party who may have other knowledge of the patient, for example the patient's partner, family, carer, tutordative (Scotland), or a person with parental responsibility;
- which option least restricts the patient's future choices, where more than one option (including non-treatment) seems reasonable in the patient's best interest.

Applying to the court

26. Where a patient's capacity to consent is in doubt, or where differences of opinion about his or her best interests cannot be resolved satisfactorily, you should consult more experienced colleagues and, where appropriate, seek legal advice on whether it is necessary to apply to the court for a ruling. You should seek the court's approval where a patient lacks capacity to consent to a medical intervention which is non-therapeutic or controversial, for example contraceptive sterilisation, organ donation, withdrawal of life support from a patient in a persistent vegetative state. Where you decide to apply to a court you should, as soon as possible, inform the patient and his or her representative of your decision and of his or her right to be represented at the hearing.

Forms of consent

27. To determine whether patients have given informed consent to any proposed investigation or treatment, you must consider how well they have understood the details and implications of what is proposed, and not simply the form in which their consent has been expressed or recorded.

Express consent

28. Patients can indicate their informed consent either orally or in writing. In some cases, the nature of the risks to which the patient might be exposed make it important that a written record is available of the patient's consent and other wishes in relation to the proposed investigation and treatment. This helps to ensure later understanding between you, the patient, and anyone else involved in carrying out the procedure or providing care. Except in an emergency, where the patient has capacity to give consent you should obtain written consent in cases where:

- the treatment or procedure is complex, or involves significant risks and/or side effects;
- providing clinical care is not the primary purpose of the investigation or examination;
- there may be significant consequences for the patient's employment, social or personal life;
- the treatment is part of a research programme.

29. You must use the patient's case notes and/or a consent form to detail the key elements of the discussion with the patient, including the nature of information provided, specific requests by the patient, details of the scope of the consent given.

Statutory requirements

30. Some statutes require written consent to be obtained for particular treatments (for example some fertility treatments). You must follow the law in these areas.

Implied consent

31. You should be careful about relying on a patient's apparent compliance with a procedure as a form of consent. For example, the fact that a patient lies down on an examination couch does not in itself indicate that the patient has understood what you propose to do and why.

Reviewing consent

32. A signed consent form is not sufficient evidence that a patient has given, or still gives, informed consent to the proposed treatment in all its aspects. You, or a member of the team, must review the patient's decision close to the time of treatment, and especially where:

- significant time has elapsed between obtaining consent and the start of treatment;
- there have been material changes in the patient's condition, or in any aspects of the proposed treatment plan, which might invalidate the patient's existing consent;
- new, potentially relevant information has become available, for example about the risks of the treatment, or about other treatment options.

Consent to screening

33. Screening (which may involve testing) healthy or asymptomatic people to detect genetic predispositions or early signs of debilitating or life threatening conditions can be an important tool in providing effective care. But the uncertainties involved in screening may be great, for example the risk of false positive or false negative results. Some findings may potentially have serious medical, social or financial consequences not only for the individuals, but for their relatives. In some cases the fact of having been screened may itself have serious implications.

34. You must ensure that anyone considering whether to consent to screening can make a properly informed decision. As far as possible, you should ensure that screening would not be contrary to the individual's interest. You must pay particular attention to ensuring that the information the person wants or ought to have is identified and provided. You should be careful to explain clearly:

- the purpose of the screening;
- the likelihood of positive/negative findings and possibility of false positive/negative results;
- the uncertainties and risks attached to the screening process;
- any significant medical, social or financial implications of screening for the particular condition or predisposition;
- follow up plans, including availability of counselling and support services.

If you are considering the possibility of screening children, or adults who are not able to decide for themselves, you should refer to the guidance at paragraphs 19–25. In appropriate cases, you should take account of the guidance issued by bodies such as the Advisory Committee on Genetic Testing.

Consent to research

35. Research involving clinical trials of drugs or treatments, and research into the causes of, or possible treatment for, a particular condition, is important in increasing doctors' ability to provide effective care for present and future patients. The benefits of the research may, however, be uncertain and may not be experienced by the person participating in the research. In addition, the risk involved for research participants may be difficult to identify or to assess in advance. If you carry out or participate in research involving patients or volunteers, it is particularly important that you ensure:

- as far as you are able, that the research is not contrary to the individual's interests;
- that participants understand that it is research and that the results are not predictable.

36. You must take particular care to be sure that anyone you ask to consider taking part in research is given the fullest possible information, presented in terms and a form that they can understand. This must include any information about possible benefits and risks; evidence that a research ethics committee has given approval; and advice that they can withdraw at any time. You should ensure that participants have the opportunity to read and consider the research information leaflet. You must allow them sufficient time to reflect on the implications of participating in the study. You must not put pressure on anyone to take part in research. You must obtain the person's consent in writing. Before starting any research you must always obtain approval from a properly constituted research ethics committee.

37. You should seek further advice where your research will involve adults who are not able to make decisions for themselves, or children. You should be aware that in these cases the legal position is complex or unclear, and there is currently no general consensus on how to balance the possible risks and benefits to such vulnerable individuals against the public interest in conducting research. (A number of public consultation exercises are under way.) You should consult the guidance issued by bodies such as the Medical Research Council and the medical royal colleges to keep up to date. You should also seek advice from the relevant research ethics committee where appropriate.

Withholding and Withdrawing Life-Prolonging Treatments: Good Practice in Decision-Making

(August 2002)

The GMC advise that this guidance should be read in the light of the judgment in *R. (on the application of Burke) v General Medical Council* [2004] EWHC 1879, [2005] 2 WLR 431. The GMC is appealing against that decision.
http://www.gmc-uk.org/standards/whwd.htm
This guidance develops the advice in *Good Medical Practice* and *Seeking Patients' Consent: The Ethical Considerations*. It sets out the standards of practice expected of doctors when they consider whether to withhold or withdraw life-prolonging treatments.

Introduction
1. Doctors have a responsibility to make the care of their patients their first concern. This is essential when considering any of the growing range of life-prolonging treatments which make it possible to extend the lives of patients who, through organ failure or other life-threatening conditions, might otherwise die.
2. The benefits of modern techniques such as cardiopulmonary resuscitation, renal dialysis, artificial ventilation, and *artificial nutrition and hydration*, are considerable. However, life has a natural end and the existence of such techniques presents doctors, patients and their families with dilemmas.
3. Dilemmas arise where, for example, advanced techniques of life support may be able, in some cases where patients are in a permanent vegetative state or similar condition, to sustain life artificially for many years with little or no hope of recovery. In other cases, they may simply prolong the dying process and cause unnecessary distress to the patient. In these instances the question arises as to whether it is in the best interests of the patient to start or continue the treatment. Reaching a satisfactory answer may mean addressing a number of difficult ethical and legal issues.
4. The main questions that arise are:

- Whether the ethical principle requiring doctors to show respect for human life would mean that doctors should offer all means at their disposal to prolong a patient's life? Or would it allow for the possibility of withholding or withdrawing a life-prolonging treatment?
- Are there circumstances in which withholding or withdrawing life-prolonging treatment would be unlawful?
- What are the responsibilities in the decision-making process of the patient, doctor, healthcare team, family members and other people who are close to the patient? And what weight should be given to their views?

5. These issues have caused considerable debate amongst the profession, public and in the courts, highlighting a number of concerns within the wider community. These include concerns about:

- the possibility of over- or under-treatment towards the end of life;
- concerns that some doctors may make decisions about life-prolonging treatments without access to up to date clinical advice; and

- concerns that doctors may make judgements about the appropriateness of treatment (or non-treatment) on a quality of life basis regarding patients, particularly the very young or very old, which patients or society as a whole may not support.

It is also clear that the profession and patients want more guidance on what is considered ethically and legally permissible in this area; and that patients and their families want greater involvement in making these decisions, with better arrangements to support them when facing these distressing situations.

6. The guidance which follows first sets out a number of guiding principles (Part 1: paragraphs 9–30), and then provides a framework for putting the principles into practice (Part 2: paragraphs 32–95) when doctors are faced with making a decision whether to withhold or withdraw a life-prolonging treatment. It includes advice about the need to ensure that there is proper care for dying patients, and that their families and others close to them are involved in that care where appropriate.

7. The guidance is based on long established ethical principles which include doctors' obligations to show respect for human life; protect the health of their patients; and to make their patients' best interests their first concern (as outlined in paragraph 9). It takes account of those areas of broad consensus so far established within the Council, the medical profession and the public about what can be regarded as good practice in applying the principles to decisions about life-prolonging treatment.

8. Good practice also encompasses doctors' obligation to work within the law. The guidance takes account of law affecting practice in this area, in particular the law prohibiting killing (including euthanasia) and assisted suicide. A brief summary of the current legal background against which decisions should be made about withholding or withdrawing treatment is provided at Appendix A. However, it is not intended as a substitute for up to date legal advice in individual cases. So wherever there is uncertainty about how a particular decision might be viewed in law, legal advice must be sought, for example from a medical defence body or employer's solicitor.

Part 1   Guiding Principles

Respect for human life and best interests

9. Doctors have an ethical obligation to show respect for human life; protect the health of their patients; and to make their patients' best interests their first concern. This means offering those treatments where the possible benefits outweigh any burdens or risks associated with the treatment, and avoiding those treatments where there is no net benefit to the patient.

10. Benefits and burdens for the patient are not always limited to purely medical considerations, and doctors should be careful, particularly when dealing with patients who cannot make decisions for themselves, to take account of all the other factors relevant to the circumstances of the particular patient. It may be very difficult to arrive at a view about the preferences of patients who cannot decide for themselves, and doctors must not simply substitute their own values or those of the people consulted.

11. Prolonging life will usually be in the best interests of a patient, provided that the treatment is not considered to be excessively burdensome or disproportionate in relation to the expected benefits. Not continuing or not starting a potentially life-prolonging treatment is in the best interests of a patient when it would provide no net benefit to the patient. In cases of acute critical illness where the outcome of treatment is unclear, as for some patients who require intensive care, survival from the acute crisis would be regarded as being in the patient's best interests.

End of natural life

12. Life has a natural end, and doctors and others caring for a patient need to recognise that the point may come in the progression of a patient's condition where death is drawing near. In these circumstances doctors should not strive to prolong the dying process with no regard to the patient's

wishes, where known, or an up to date assessment of the benefits and burdens of treatment or non-treatment.

Adult patients who can decide for themselves

13. Adult competent patients have the right to decide how much weight to attach to the benefits, burdens, risks, and the overall acceptability of any treatment. They have the right to refuse treatment even where refusal may result in harm to themselves or in their own death, and doctors are legally bound to respect their decision. Adult patients who have the capacity to make their own decision can express their wishes about future treatment in an advance statement.

Adult patients who cannot decide for themselves

14. Any valid advance refusal of treatment – one made when the patient was competent and on the basis of adequate information about the implications of his/her choice – is legally binding and must be respected where it is clearly applicable to the patient's present circumstances and where there is no reason to believe that the patient had changed his/her mind.

15. Where adult patients lack capacity to decide for themselves, an assessment of the benefits, burdens and risks, and the acceptability of proposed treatment must be made on their behalf by the doctor, taking account of their wishes, where they are known. Where a patient's wishes are not known it is the doctor's responsibility to decide what is in the patient's best interests. However, this cannot be done effectively without information about the patient which those close to the patient will be best placed to know. Doctors practising in Scotland need additionally to take account of the Scottish legal framework for making decisions on behalf of adults with incapacity.

Choosing between options: difference of view about best interests

16. Applying these principles may result in different decisions in each case, since patients' assessments of the likely benefits and burdens or risks, and what weight or priority to give to these, will differ according to patients' different values, beliefs and priorities. Doctors must take account of patients' preferences when providing treatment. However, where a patient wishes to have a treatment that – in the doctor's considered view – is not clinically indicated, there is no ethical or legal obligation on the doctor to provide it. Where requested, patients' right to a second opinion should be respected.

17. Where a patient lacks capacity to decide, the doctor, health care team or those close to the patient involved in making the decision, may reach different conclusions about the patient's preferences and what course of action might be in the patient's best interests. In these cases it is important to take time to try to reach a consensus about treatment and it may be appropriate to seek a second opinion, or other independent or informal review.

18. In the rare circumstances where any significant disagreement about best interests cannot be resolved, legal advice should be sought on whether it is necessary to apply to the court for a ruling. Doctors practising in Scotland would need to take account of the statutory procedures for resolving disagreements.

Concerns about starting then stopping treatment

19. Although it may be emotionally more difficult for the health care team, and those close to the patient, to withdraw a treatment from a patient rather than to decide not to provide a treatment in the first place, this should not be used as a reason for failing to initiate a treatment which may be of some benefit to the patient. Where it has been decided that a treatment is not in the best interests of the patient, there is no ethical or legal obligation to provide it and therefore no need to make a distinction between not starting the treatment and withdrawing it.

20. Where patients lack capacity to make decisions about treatment, and there is a reasonable degree of uncertainty about the appropriateness of providing a particular treatment, treatment which may be of some benefit to the patient should be started until a clearer assessment can be made. It must be explained clearly to all those involved in caring for the patient that the treatment

will be reviewed, and may be withdrawn at a later stage, if it is proving to be ineffective or too burdensome for the patient.

21. This is particularly important where time is needed for consultation and a more detailed assessment, in emergencies, and also where there is doubt about the severity of a condition, the likelihood of recovery, or the ability of a particular treatment to benefit the patient. In these cases patients, their families and carers should be reassured that symptom assessment and relief and nursing care would always be provided, whatever decision is made about particular treatments.

Artificial nutrition and hydration

22. Decisions involving artificial nutrition or hydration may be particularly difficult and/or contentious. In part this is because the benefits and burdens of either nutrition or hydration may not be well known and involve difficult assessments of the patient. For example, patients in the later stages of a progressive or severely disabling condition, where their body systems begin to shut down, may increasingly lose interest in food or drink. For some patients not taking nutrition or hydration may be part of the natural dying process. Problems in making assessments can arise because some patients may under-report their symptoms, while perceptions may differ between doctors, members of the health care team and those close to a patient, about the presence or severity of symptoms such as pain.

23. In the face of such uncertainties, there may be concern about the possibility that a patient who is unconscious or semi-conscious, and whose wishes cannot be determined, might experience distressing symptoms and complications or otherwise be suffering, because their needs for nutrition or hydration are not being met. Alternatively there may be concern that attempts to meet the patient's needs may cause avoidable suffering. For some people there may be emotional difficulties in deciding not to provide what they see as basic nurture for the patient.

24. In view of these considerations, it is essential that doctors ensure that those involved in making the decision are provided with clear and up-to-date information about what is known of the benefits, burdens and risks of providing nutrition and hydration through artificial means, and information about the basis on which the particular patient's needs have been assessed. It is also essential that doctors making decisions about artificial nutrition and hydration take careful account of the principles of good practice set out in this guidance (see also advice at paragraphs 78–83).

Non-discrimination

25. Doctors have a duty to give priority to patients on the basis of clinical need, while seeking to make the best use of resources using up to date evidence about the clinical efficacy of treatments. Doctors must not allow their views about, for example, a patient's age, disability, race, colour, culture, beliefs, sexuality, gender, lifestyle, social or economic status to prejudice the choices of treatment offered or the general standard of care provided.

Care for the dying

26. Patients who are dying should be afforded the same respect and standard of care as all other patients. Patients and their families and others close to them should be treated with understanding and compassion. Where the likely progression of a patient's condition is known, and their death is seen as an inevitable outcome, it is important to ensure that the patient's palliative care or terminal care needs are identified and met appropriately. This should include consideration of their wishes regarding such matters as the appropriate place for receiving care (which may affect the treatment options available), and their needs for religious, spiritual or other personal support. Every attempt should be made to ensure that they are afforded privacy, dignity, and good quality care in comfortable surroundings. This includes assessment of, and adequate relief from, pain and other distressing symptoms, and appropriate support and nursing care.

27. Discussion about the dying process allows patients the opportunity they may want to decide what arrangements should be made to manage the final stages of their illness, and to attend to personal and other concerns that they consider important towards the end of their life.

Conscientious objections

28. Where a decision to withhold or withdraw life-prolonging treatment has been made by a competent adult patient, or made by the senior clinician responsible for the care of a patient who lacks capacity to decide (following discussions with those close to the patient and the health care team) doctors who have a conscientious objection to the decision may withdraw from the care of that patient. In doing so they must ensure, without delay, that arrangements have been made for another suitably qualified colleague to take over their role, so that the patient's care does not suffer.

29. Junior doctors in this position must make their conscientious objection known to the doctor responsible for the patient's care who should then ensure that arrangements are made for another colleague to take over from the junior doctor.

Accountability

30. Doctors are responsible to their patients and society at large, while being individually accountable to the GMC and in the courts for their decisions about withholding and withdrawing life-prolonging treatments.

Part 2 Good Practice Framework

31. The guidance which follows provides a framework for putting the principles into practice in reaching, implementing and reviewing decisions on withholding or withdrawing life-prolonging treatments. It identifies other sources of advice where these are known.

Clinical responsibility for decisions

32. If you are the consultant or general practitioner in charge of a patient's care, it is your responsibility to make the decision about whether to withhold or withdraw a life-prolonging treatment, taking account of the views of the patient or those close to the patient as set out in paragraphs 41–48 and 53–57. Exceptionally, in an emergency where the senior clinician cannot be contacted in time, if you are an appropriately experienced junior hospital doctor or deputising general practitioner you may take responsibility for making the decision, but it must be discussed with the senior clinician as soon as possible.

Diagnosis and prognosis

33. Before a decision is made to withhold or withdraw treatment, as the treating doctor you must carry out a thorough assessment of the patient's condition and the likely prognosis, taking account of current guidance on good clinical practice and the views and assessments of the clinical team.

34. Where there is significant disagreement within the clinical team, you must do your best to resolve it and to ensure clarity and consistency in the information provided to the patient or those close to the patient.

35. You should always give consideration to seeking a second opinion. You must seek a second opinion in cases where you are not sufficiently experienced or knowledgeable, or where there is significant disagreement within the team about clinical aspects of a patient's care. In life threatening emergencies, where seeking a second opinion is not possible, follow the guidance at paragraphs 39–40.

Options for treatment

36. You must identify appropriate treatment options based on up to date clinical evidence about efficacy, side effects and other risks, referring to any relevant clinical guidelines on the treatment and management of the patient's condition, or of patients with similar underlying risk factors.

37. You must reach a considered judgement on the likely clinical and personal benefits, burdens and risks, for the particular patient, of each of the treatment (or non-treatment) options identified.

38. Always consult a clinician with relevant experience (who may be from another discipline such as nursing) in cases where:

- You and the health care team have limited experience of a condition.
- You are in doubt about the range of options, or the benefits, burdens and risks of a particular option for the individual patient.
- You are considering withholding or withdrawing artificial nutrition or hydration from a patient who is not imminently dying, although in a very serious condition, and whose views cannot be determined (see paragraph 81 below).
- You and other members of the health care team have a serious difference of opinion about the appropriate options for a patient's care.

Emergencies: with limited information about the patient

39. A life-threatening emergency might arise where you and the healthcare team have no previous knowledge of, or inadequate information about, the patient's medical history or wishes regarding treatment, and where any delay might prejudice the outcome. In these circumstances you may consider that it is not possible to obtain all relevant information or hold any consultations – as outlined in this guidance – before making a decision.

40. In deciding whether to withhold or withdraw a particular treatment you must respect the terms of any valid and applicable advance refusal that is in the patient's notes or is drawn to your attention. Otherwise you must make a considered judgement about the patient's best interests. Where there is a reasonable degree of uncertainty about the appropriateness of any treatment, you should follow the advice at paragraph 20 above. You should give a clear explanation of the reasons for your decisions to the patient where they recover sufficiently to understand or – if the patient does not recover – to those close to the patient.

Choosing between options: patients who can decide for themselves

Seeking the patient's views

41. Where a patient has the capacity to decide, you must raise with the patient the need to discuss your conclusions about diagnosis, prognosis and which options you consider may be in the patient's best interests. It is for the patient to judge what weight or priority to give to any benefits, burdens or risks; and to decide whether any of the options would be acceptable.

42. You should bear in mind that you are bound to respect an adult patient's competently made refusal of treatment even where complying with the decision will lead to the patient's death. If a specific treatment is requested which, in your considered view is clinically inappropriate, you are not legally or ethically bound to provide it. However, you should give the patient a clear explanation of the reasons for your view, and respect their request to have a second opinion.

43. Where the possibility of withholding or withdrawing a life-prolonging treatment is an option, you should offer the patient the opportunity to discuss how their care would be managed if such a decision were made. This should include:

- arrangements for providing nursing care and other appropriate treatments;
- the patient's preferences about who should be involved in decision making or in providing additional support if they become incapacitated;
- what might be their palliative or terminal care needs should death become inevitable and how these would be met.

Discussions of this sort, handled sensitively, may help to build trust and provide an opportunity for you to get information about the patient's values and priorities that might be helpful in later decision making.

Sensitive handling of discussions

44. Discussions about the possibility of withholding or withdrawing a potentially life-prolonging treatment may be difficult and distressing. But this does not mean that discussion should be avoided, rather that it should be handled sensitively, and with appropriate support being provided to the patient. You should ensure the patient knows that they can invite a relative or other person they trust, including a religious or spiritual adviser, to be present during the discussion.

45. Discussions of this kind may need to be conducted over several meetings. You should hold discussions at a time when the patient is best able to understand and retain information. You should allow the patient sufficient time to reflect and ask questions before deciding, and discuss the patient's right to change their mind about the decision.

46. Where patients clearly indicate that they do not wish to know about or discuss particular aspects of their condition or treatment, you should not force this information on them. However, you should explain the impact this might have on decision making; explore whether they have unmet needs for support; and do your best to clarify their wishes about how treatment decisions should be made in these circumstances.

47. Where a patient has an existing condition and the likely progression of the disorder is known, for example in some forms of cancer or Alzheimer's disease, you should consider formulating an advance care plan with the patient and the health care team, to allow as much time as possible for the issues to be explored sensitively and effectively. A record of the plan should be available to the patient and others involved in their care, so that everyone is clear about what has been agreed.

48. The advice about sensitive handling is particularly important in relation to decisions about cardiopulmonary resuscitation, and may be relevant to some decisions about artificial nutrition and hydration (see also paragraphs 78–94).

Choosing between options: patients who cannot decide for themselves

Assessing capacity to decide

49. In cases where the dying process itself affects capacity, the correct course of action for the patient may have been decided previously, following the guidance above and the principles in Part 1. Where no such advance care plan has been agreed, or the plan has not been reviewed recently or is not relevant to the patient's current condition, you should follow the advice below.

50. Where patients have difficulty retaining information, communicating their views or are only intermittently competent, you should provide any assistance a patient might need to enable them to reach and communicate a decision. Failure to communicate may not be due to incapacity. The fact that the patient's choice appears irrational or does not accord with your own or others' views of what is in the patient's best interests, is not evidence in itself that a patient lacks capacity.

51. Where there are doubts about a patient's capacity to make a decision, you should carry out a thorough assessment consulting relevant professional guidelines, and taking into account any legal tests of capacity. Where appropriate, you should seek a second opinion – for example, as described in paragraph 38 above. Where these steps have been taken and a patient's capacity to decide remains in doubt, you must seek legal advice, which may include asking a court to determine capacity.

52. Generally you should start any necessary treatment, which is considered to be of some benefit to the patient, whilst the patient's capacity is being determined. This decision must be reviewed in the light of the outcome of the assessment. However, if you are practising in Scotland, only treatment which is necessary for the preservation of the patient's life or to prevent serious deterioration in the patient's health should be started whilst capacity is being determined.

Meeting the responsibility for assessing the patient's best interests

53. Where a patient lacks capacity to decide, you should take reasonable steps to ascertain whether they have previously expressed their wishes in an advance statement, as described at paragraphs 14–15. You must respect any valid and clinically relevant advance refusal of treatment where you have no reason to believe that the patient has changed his/her mind. In making this assessment, it is necessary to consider whether the patient had foreseen the particular circumstances which have subsequently materialised, or would have been aware of and weighed up any advances in treatment options since their decision was made.

54. Where a patient's wishes are not known and you are not aware of an advance refusal, you – as the senior clinician responsible for the patient's care – have responsibility to make a decision about what course of action would be in the patient's best interests. However, you should consult the

healthcare team and those close to the patient for any information that may be relevant to the decision, including their views about what the patient's wishes might have been. You should pay due regard to any previous wishes of the patient about not disclosing information to particular individuals.

55. If the patient is new to you at the time decisions are needed, you must satisfy yourself as to whether such consultations have previously been carried out and find out what has been agreed. If you are practising in Scotland you should take steps to find out whether someone has been appointed to make health care decisions on behalf of the patient and seek their views.

Aiming for a consensus

56. Your discussions about treatment and how best to manage the patient's palliative or other care needs should take account of the considerations set out in paragraphs 41–48. You should take time to try to reach a consensus about treatment. In doing so, you should be careful to explain the participants' roles in reaching a decision and where ultimate responsibility for the decision rests. You should give careful consideration to how much weight it would be reasonable to attach to each person's views.

57. You should do your best to ensure that participants in the decision making have access to any additional support that might be needed, and are aware of any local arrangements for independent review should it become necessary. It may be helpful in trying to reach agreement, for those involved to be provided with some information about the ethical and legal considerations which may be relevant to the decision making, including making available copies of this and other relevant guidance.

Resolving disagreements about best interests

58. It is usually possible to reach a consensus about treatment, given adequate time for discussions between the parties. Individuals may be helped by the opportunity to consult others, medical or non-medical, whose views they respect. In complex cases where it is difficult to reach agreement, or cases where particular individuals participating in the decision-making advance strong arguments as to why an option may be considered controversial, you may also find it helpful to seek multi-disciplinary clinical or ethical review, independent of the healthcare team.

59. Where informal review fails to resolve any significant disagreement, you must seek legal advice. This may be available from your Trust or other employing organisation, or your defence body. If you are practising in Scotland and a dispute arises which cannot be resolved informally, you should take legal advice on the statutory procedures for dispute resolution. Patients, or those close to the patient where appropriate, should be informed as early as possible of any decision to seek independent review or a legal opinion, so that they have the opportunity to participate or can be represented.

Communicating decisions

60. Whatever decision is made, you must do your best to ensure that all those consulted, and especially those responsible for delivering care, are consistently informed of the decision and are clear about the goals and the agreed care plan. You should check that hand-over arrangements between professional and other carers include suitable arrangements for passing on the information.

61. It is particularly important that where a patient's death is seen as an inevitable outcome of a decision to withhold or withdraw treatment, that everyone involved is clear about the arrangements for providing appropriate palliative or terminal care, and their roles. You should discuss what the role of the family or other carers will be; what religious, spiritual or other personal support the patient might need; and what support the patient and those close to the patient will receive from yourself or the healthcare team.

62. You should bear in mind that, in circumstances where individuals may be under stress, any important information provided verbally might need to be reinforced in writing.

Recording decisions

63. You must ensure that decisions are properly documented, including the relevant clinical findings; details of discussions with the patient, health care team, or others involved in decision making; details of treatment given with any agreed review dates; and outcomes of treatment or other significant factors which may affect future care. You should record the information at the time of, or soon after, the events described. The record should be legible, clear, accurate and unambiguous, for example avoiding abbreviations or other terminology that may cause confusion to those providing care. You should ensure that the records are appropriately accessible to the patient, team members and others involved in providing care to the patient.

Reviewing decisions

64. You must review your decisions at appropriate intervals during the agreed treatment or the period of palliative or terminal care, to determine whether the goals of treatment or the care plan remain appropriate in the patient's present condition. In doing so, you should talk to the patient where possible, and consult those involved in the patient's care.

65. You should consider seeking a second opinion where, for example, the patient's condition is not progressing as expected. Clinical scenarios may change rapidly and it may become necessary to restart treatment that has been withheld, or vice versa. You also should bear in mind that patients might change their minds about decisions.

Audit and education

66. As in other areas of practice, you must participate in clinical audit of your decisions to help improve knowledge of the outcomes of treatment and non-treatment decisions. Where possible you should help to disseminate best practice, for example, by contributing to the education of students and colleagues about good practice in this area.

Areas for special consideration

Children

67. All the advice in this booklet – the guiding principles, the good practice framework, the advice on artificial nutrition and hydration and on cardiopulmonary resuscitation – also applies to decision making in cases involving children. This includes premature babies and children with disabilities where the decisions may be particularly difficult for everyone involved.

68. In all cases you, and others involved in making decisions on behalf of a child, have a duty to consider what is in the child's best interests on the basis of an assessment of the benefits, burdens and risks for the child. Children's roles in determining what their interests are, and their preferences in relation to treatment, increase with maturity and experience. You should always encourage and help them to understand what is proposed and to participate in decision making as much as they are able and willing to do so.

69. You must assess a child's capacity to decide whether to consent to or refuse a proposed investigation or treatment. In general, children can be considered as having capacity to make a particular decision where they are able to understand the nature, purpose and possible consequences of the proposed investigation or treatment, as well as the consequences of non-treatment.

70. You must also take account of the relevant laws or legal precedents in this area, which vary significantly between Scotland, England and Wales, and Northern Ireland. In particular you should bear in mind that:

- At age 16 a young person can be treated as an adult and can be presumed to have capacity to decide.
- Under age 16 children may have capacity to decide, depending on their ability to understand what is involved.

- Where a child lacks capacity to decide, a person with parental responsibility for the child may authorise or refuse treatment where they consider that to be in the child's best interests.

71. The wishes of a child who has the capacity to decide whether to consent to or refuse a proposed treatment should normally be respected. However, the legal position in England and Wales means that, in some circumstances where a child has made a competent refusal of a treatment, a person with parental responsibility, or the courts, may nevertheless authorise the treatment where it is in the child's best interests. You may need to seek legal advice on how to deal with such cases.

72. Where a child lacks capacity to make his or her own decision, you should note that authorisation given by one person with parental responsibility cannot be vetoed by a refusal from another person who also holds parental responsibility. In such circumstances you should do your best, in the child's interest, to try to achieve a consensus between those with parental responsibility.

73. It is important that you work sensitively, and in partnership with the child (where that is possible), those who have parental responsibility for the child, members of the healthcare team and other carers, and aim to achieve consensus with them about the best course of action. You should take steps to ensure that those who have a share in the responsibility for making decisions are clear about their roles. As the treating clinician you will take the lead in judging the clinical factors, and the parents will lead in judging more generally what might be in the child's best interests.

74. When considering how best to provide the information and support needed by a child's parents or other carers, and in trying to resolve any significant disagreements amongst those involved in the decision making, you should follow the guidance at paragraphs 44–48 and 53–59 above. Remember that effective communication, careful deliberation, compassion and sensitivity are particularly important in cases involving children.

75. Where there is disagreement between those with parental responsibility and the healthcare team and this cannot be resolved satisfactorily through informal review, you should seek legal advice about obtaining a ruling from the courts.

76. Where none of those holding parental responsibility are willing to authorise treatment, you should consider yourself bound by their refusal unless you obtain a ruling from the court. In an emergency where you consider that it is in the child's best interests to provide treatment, you may treat the child provided it is limited to that treatment which is reasonably required either to save the child's life, or to prevent deterioration in the child's health.

77. This advice takes account of the legal position at the time of writing this guidance, but you should take steps to ensure access to up to date legal advice and seek specific advice in any cases of doubt.

Artificial nutrition and hydration

78. Where a patient has a problem in taking fluids or food orally, you must carry out an appropriate assessment of their condition and their particular requirements for nutrition or hydration. There are a number of means which you should consider for meeting the patient's assessed needs, including nasogastric tube, percutaneous endoscopic gastrostomy (gastric 'PEG'), subcutaneous hydration, or intravenous cannula, all commonly termed 'artificial' nutrition or hydration. However, the benefits and burdens are different for artificial nutrition and artificial hydration and you should assess these separately. In doing so you should take and follow up to date professional advice on the particular clinical considerations affecting respectively artificial nutrition and artificial hydration.

79. In all cases you should assess the patient for the presence of distressing symptoms, for example signs of pain, breathing difficulties, confusion, and dry mouth. Symptoms should be alleviated appropriately following up-to-date professional guidance.

80. In deciding which of the options for providing artificial nutrition or hydration are appropriate in meeting a patient's assessed need, you must ensure that the patient (where able to decide), the health care team, and those close to the patient (where the patient's wishes cannot be determined), are fully involved in the decision making. You should take appropriate steps to help those participating in the decision making to understand your assessment of the patient's requirements for

nutrition or hydration, and any uncertainties underlying the options you consider appropriate for meeting those needs.

81. Where patients have capacity to decide for themselves, they may consent to, or refuse, any proposed intervention of this kind. In cases where patients lack capacity to decide for themselves and their wishes cannot be determined, you should take account of the following considerations: Where there is a reasonable degree of uncertainty about the likely benefits or burdens for the patient of providing either artificial nutrition or hydration, it may be appropriate to provide these for a trial period with a pre-arranged review to allow a clearer assessment to be made.

Where death is imminent, in judging the benefits, burdens or risks, it usually would not be appropriate to start either artificial hydration or nutrition, although artificial hydration provided by the less invasive measures may be appropriate where it is considered that this would be likely to provide symptom relief.

Where death is imminent and artificial hydration and/or nutrition are already in use, it may be appropriate to withdraw them if it is considered that the burdens outweigh the possible benefits to the patient.

Where death is not imminent, it usually will be appropriate to provide artificial nutrition or hydration. However, circumstances may arise where you judge that a patient's condition is so severe, and the prognosis so poor that providing artificial nutrition or hydration may cause suffering, or be too burdensome in relation to the possible benefits. In these circumstances, as well as consulting the health care team and those close to the patient, you must seek a second or expert opinion from a senior clinician (who might be from another discipline such as nursing) who has experience of the patient's condition and who is not already directly involved in the patient's care. This will ensure that, in a decision of such sensitivity, the patient's interests have been thoroughly considered, and will provide necessary reassurance to those close to the patient and to the wider public. It can be extremely difficult to estimate how long a patient will live, especially for patients with multiple underlying conditions. Expert help in this should be sought where you, or the health care team, are uncertain about a particular patient.

82. Where significant conflicts arise about whether artificial nutrition or hydration should be provided, either between you and other members of the health care team or between the team and those close to the patient, and the disagreement cannot be resolved after informal or independent review, you should seek legal advice on whether it is necessary to apply to the court for a ruling.

83. Where you are considering withdrawing artificial nutrition and hydration from a patient in a permanent vegetative state (PVS), or condition closely resembling PVS, the courts in England, Wales and Northern Ireland currently require that you approach them for a ruling. The courts in Scotland have not specified such a requirement, but you should seek legal advice on whether a court declaration may be necessary in an individual case. (For leading cases see the legal summary at Appendix A).

Cardiopulmonary resuscitation

84. Cardiopulmonary resuscitation (CPR), if attempted promptly in appropriate situations, may be effective in restarting the heart and lungs of some patients. However CPR is known to have a low success rate, especially for patients with serious conditions who are in poor general health. CPR carries some risk of complications and harmful side effects, and if used inappropriately it may do more harm than good by prolonging the dying process and the pain or suffering of a seriously ill patient, in a manner which could be seen as degrading and undignified. For example, if a patient is at the end-stage of an incurable illness and death is imminent, attempts to resuscitate them are likely to be futile and not in the patient's best interests.

85. Advice on when it is appropriate to attempt to resuscitate a patient, and circumstances when it is appropriate to make an advance decision not to attempt resuscitation (DNAR order), is available from professional bodies.

86. Where a patient is already seriously ill with a foreseeable risk of cardiopulmonary arrest, or a patient is in poor general health and nearing the end of their life, decisions about whether to attempt CPR in particular circumstances ideally should be made in advance as part of the care plan

for that patient. A patient's own views, about whether the level of burden or risk outweighs the likely benefits from successful CPR, would be central in deciding whether CPR should be attempted. It is important in these cases to offer competent patients or, if a patient lacks capacity to decide, those close to the patient, an early opportunity to discuss their future care and the circumstances in which CPR should or should not be attempted.

87. Discussions about circumstances in which CPR should not be attempted can be difficult and distressing for all concerned. However, failing to give patients or, where appropriate, those close to the patient, the opportunity to be involved in reaching a decision can cause more distress at a later stage, when the patient or a relative discovers a DNAR order was made, than if the issue were tackled sensitively at the outset.

88. Some patients may not wish to be given the details or to make decisions about CPR themselves. The wishes of these patients should be followed. Many patients – including some for whom CPR is likely to be futile – will want to be involved in the decision, and you must provide these patients with appropriate information about CPR, including up to date details about its effectiveness and appropriate use, to ensure a sufficient understanding of what is involved. There may be other patients for whom cardiopulmonary arrest is not a foreseeable risk who nevertheless raise the issue. You should respond honestly to their questions.

89. You should always take the patient's wishes into account. You must respect a competent patient's decision to refuse CPR. You should usually comply with patients' requests to provide CPR, although there is no obligation to provide treatment that you consider futile. The patient's decision must be recorded appropriately and communicated clearly to the health care team.

90. Where patients lack capacity to make a decision about CPR, you should consult the health care team, the patient's proxy decision maker – in Scotland, where appointed – or others close to the patient, taking account of any request made by the patient when competent not to discuss their care with particular individuals. Where, after appropriate consultation, it is your considered judgement that attempting CPR would not be in the patient's best interests, the reasons for that decision should be explained clearly to those consulted.

91. In holding discussions about CPR, you should make clear to the patient, the health care team and others consulted about the patient's care, that the provision of all other appropriate treatment and care would be unaffected by a decision not to attempt CPR.

92. Whilst the final decision about the clinical merits of attempting resuscitation rests with the consultant or general practitioner in charge of the patient's care, good consistent communication between the doctor, nurses, patient and carers is the key to ensuring that the patient's rights are respected, and misunderstanding and dissent are minimised.

93. Once a decision is made, you or a senior medical member of the team should record fully any advance decision not to attempt to resuscitate a patient, including the basis on which the decision was reached and the names of those with whom it was discussed. You should ensure that the decision is communicated to all those involved in providing care to the patient. A DNAR order should be reviewed regularly to ensure it remains appropriate in the patient's present condition.

94. In putting this guidance into practice, you should take account of relevant guidance from professional bodies, and relevant protocols within the healthcare setting in which you work.

Accountability

95. If you decide not to follow any part of the guidance in this document, you must be prepared to explain and justify your actions and decisions, to patients and their families, your colleagues and, where necessary, the courts and the GMC.

Appendix B Glossary

This defines some key terms used within this document. These definitions have no wider or legal significance.

Advance statements

Also referred to as 'advance directives' or 'living wills', these are statements made by adults at a time they have capacity to decide for themselves about the treatments they wish to accept or refuse, in circumstances in the future where they are no longer able to make decisions or communicate their preferences. An advance statement cannot authorise a doctor to do anything that is illegal. Where a specific treatment is requested, doctors are not bound to provide it, if in their professional view it is clinically inappropriate. An advance refusal of treatment made when an adult patient was competent, on the basis of adequate information about the implications of his/her choice, is legally binding and must be respected where it is clearly applicable to the patient's present circumstances and where there is no reason to believe that the patient had changed his/her mind.

Artificial nutrition and hydration

This term is commonly used in medicine to refer to techniques such as the use of nasogastric tubes, percutaneous endoscopic gastrostomy ('gastric PEG'), subcutaneous hydration, or intravenous cannula, to provide a patient with nutrition and hydration where a patient has a problem taking fluids or food orally. A distinction is generally made between such 'artificial' means and 'oral' nutrition and hydration where food or drink is given by mouth, the latter being regarded as part of nursing care.

Nursing care

Sometimes also referred to as 'basic care' there is no legal or commonly accepted definition of what is covered by this term. In the medical profession it is most often used to refer to procedures or medications which are solely or primarily aimed at providing comfort to a patient or alleviating that person's pain, symptoms or distress. It includes the offer of oral nutrition and hydration.

Proxy decision maker

A patient who has lost capacity to make decisions may have previously indicated whom they wish to represent their views or take decisions on their behalf. In Scotland under provisions in the Adults with Incapacity (Scotland) Act 2000 a welfare attorney, welfare guardian or a person authorised under an intervention order, may be granted authority to make medical decisions on behalf of an adult patient with incapacity. These persons can be referred to as proxy decision-makers. ('Proxy decision maker' is not an accepted legal term in England and Wales.) There is a Code of Practice under the Act for making decisions on behalf of adults with incapacity. Advice on the powers of welfare attorneys, welfare guardians or a person authorised under an intervention order, and on the Code of Practice can be obtained from medical defence bodies, the Scottish Executive, Health Department and the BMA.

'Those close to the patient'

This phrase is intended to include any of the following – a professional or other carer, a partner, a close family member, an informal advocate. It will also include, in Scotland, any proxy decision maker appointed under the Adults with Incapacity (Scotland) Act 2000, and a 'nearest relative' or 'person claiming an interest' – such as a public guardian, mental welfare commissioner, local authority – as referred to in this Act or under the provisions of Scottish mental health legislation. In England and Wales under mental health legislation, a 'nearest relative' or 'guardian' may have been appointed.

Starting then stopping treatment

Some people find it difficult to contemplate withdrawing a life-prolonging treatment once started, either because of the emotional distress that can accompany such a decision, or because they have concerns about what might be seen as their 'responsibility' for the patient's death. This sense of responsibility may particularly arise for those who understand withdrawing treatment as a positive 'act' which is morally more blameworthy than not starting treatment. (An example often given is the position held by some within the Jewish faith who make this distinction.) However, within the current broad consensus about ethical practice in medicine and taking account of the legal position, there is no ethical or legal obligation to continue to provide a treatment where it has been decided that the treatment is not in the best interests of the patient.

Research: The Role and Responsibilities of Doctors

(February 2002)

[Footnotes and links omitted]

Good Practice in Research

This guidance sets out the standards expected of all doctors working in research in the NHS, universities and the private sector or other circumstances. It develops the general principles and standards on research set out in our other guidance documents and should be used in conjunction with them. You must always follow the principles in this guidance and take note of other governance and good practice guidelines issued by the Departments of Health and other authoritative bodies. You must observe and keep up to date with the laws and statutory codes of practice which affect your work.

Introduction

1. Research involving people directly or indirectly is vital in improving care for present and future patients and the health of the population as a whole.
2. Doctors involved in research have an ethical duty to show respect for human life and respect peoples' autonomy. Partnership between participants and the health care team is essential to good research practice and such partnerships are based on trust. You must respect patients' and volunteers' rights to make decisions about their involvement in research. It is essential to listen to and share information with them, respect their privacy and dignity, and treat them politely and considerately at all times.

Scope of the guidance

3. Research in this document refers to any experimental study into the causes, treatment or prevention of ill health and disease in humans, involving people or their tissues or organs or data. It includes toxicity studies, clinical trials, genetic studies, epidemiological research including analyses of medical records, and other collections and analyses of data about health and illness, whether anonymised or not. It covers clinical research which may be therapeutic, that is of potential benefit to patients who participate, and non-therapeutic, where no immediate benefit to those patients or volunteers who participate is expected.
4. This guidance does not apply to clinical audit which involves no experimental study. Nor does it cover innovative therapeutic interventions designed to benefit individual patients. These activities are covered by the standards and principles set out in our other guidance.

Principles governing research practice

5. Because the benefits of the research are not always certain and may not be experienced by the participants, you must be satisfied that the research is not contrary to their interests. In particular:

- you must be satisfied that, in therapeutic research, the foreseeable risks will not outweigh the potential benefits to the patients. The development of treatments and furthering of knowledge should never take precedence over the patients' best interests;
- in non-therapeutic research, you must keep the foreseeable risks to participants as low as possible. In addition the potential benefits from the development of treatments and furthering of knowledge must far outweigh any such risks;
- before starting any research you must ensure that ethical approval has been obtained from a properly constituted and relevant research ethics committee – such committees abide by the guidance for local and multi-centre research ethics committees, whether they are within the NHS, the university sector, the pharmaceutical industry, or elsewhere;
- you must conduct research in an ethical manner and one that accords with best practice;
- you must ensure that patients or volunteers understand that they are being asked to participate in research and that the results are not predictable;

- you must obtain and record the participants' consent; save in exceptional circumstances where specific approval not to obtain consent must have been given by the research ethics committee;
- respect participants' right to confidentiality;
- with participants' consent, keep GPs, and other clinicians responsible for participants' care, informed of the participants' involvement in the research and provide the GPs with any information necessary for their continuing care;
- you must complete research projects involving patients or volunteers, or do your best to ensure that they are completed by others, except where results indicate a risk that participants may be harmed or no benefit can be expected;
- you must record and report results accurately;
- you must be prepared to explain and justify your actions and decisions.

6. If you undertake records based research which does not involve patients or volunteers directly you are still bound by the principles on which this guidance is based. You must be satisfied that you have appropriate authority to access any identifiable data; advice on access to, and use of, data is in paragraphs 30 to 42 below.

7. The principles set out in our guidance Good Medical Practice, Seeking patients' consent: the ethical considerations and Confidentiality: Protecting and Providing information must be followed when undertaking research.

Putting the principles into practice

Protecting the autonomy and interests of participants

8. You must conduct all research with honesty and integrity and, in designing, organising and executing research, you must always put the protection of participants' interests first. You must:

- not put pressure on patients or volunteers to participate in the research;
- ensure that no real or implied coercion is used on participants who are in a dependent relationship to you, for example, medical students, a junior colleague, nurse in your practice or employee in your company;
- keep to all aspects of the research protocol and make significant changes to, or deviations from, the protocol only with the agreement of the research ethics committee and the research funder.

9. If you have good reason to believe that participants are being put at risk by participating in the research or by the behaviour of anyone conducting the research, you should report your concerns to a senior colleague. If you remain concerned, you should inform the research ethics committee, and the research sponsor together with the employer or contracting body if appropriate.

10. You must report evidence of financial or scientific fraud or other contravention of this guidance to an appropriate person or authority, including where appropriate the GMC or other statutory regulatory body.

Research Design

11. All research must be based on a properly developed protocol that has been approved by a research ethics committee. It must be prepared according to the good practice guidelines given in this guidance and that of other relevant bodies, for example, the Departments of Health, Royal College of Physicians of London and the Medical Research Council, and where appropriate, the International Conference on Harmonisation.

12. You must ensure that:

- the aims, design and methodology of the project are justifiable, verifiable and scientifically valid;
- over-use of patient groups or individuals is avoided.

Conflicts of interest

13. You must always act in the participants' best interests when carrying out research. You must ensure that your judgement about the research is not influenced, or seen by others to be influenced, by financial, personal, political or other external interests at any stage of the process. You should always declare any conflicts that may arise to an appropriate person, authority or organisation, as well as to the participants.

Funding and payments

14. You must be open and honest in all financial and commercial matters relating to your research and its funding. In particular you must:

- declare to research ethics committees, prior to the research being approved, all financial interests and sums of money which you know, or estimate, will be paid for the research undertaken; accept only those payments and benefits approved by the research ethics committee;
- give participants information on how the research is funded, including any benefits which will accrue to researchers and/or their departments;
- respond honestly and fully to participants' questions, including inquiries about direct payments made to you and any financial interests you have in the research project or its sponsoring organisations;
- ensure that everyone in the research team, including nurses and non-medical staff, is informed about the way in which the research is being financed and managed;
- not offer payments at a level which could induce research participants to take risks that they would otherwise not take, or to volunteer more frequently than is advisable or against their better interests or judgement;
- not allow your conduct in the research to be influenced by payment or gifts.

Consent

15. Seeking consent is fundamental to research involving people.

Valid consent

16. Participants' consent is legally valid and professionally acceptable only where participants are competent to give consent, have been properly informed, and have agreed without coercion.

Consent for research

17. Obtaining consent is a process involving open and helpful dialogue, and is essential in clarifying objectives and understanding between doctors and research participants.

18. Effective communication is the key to enabling participants to make informed decisions. When providing information you must do your best to find out about participants' individual needs and priorities. For example, participants' current understanding of their condition and treatment, beliefs, culture, occupation or other factors may have a bearing on the information they require. You must not make assumptions about participants' views, but discuss matters with them, and ask whether they have any concerns about the treatment or the risks involved in the research programme.

19. You must ensure that any individuals whom you invite to take part in research are given the information which they want or ought to know, and that is presented in terms and a form that they can understand. You must bear in mind that it may be difficult for participants to identify and assess the risks involved. Giving the information will usually include an initial discussion supported by a leaflet or sound recording, where possible taking into account any particular communication or language needs of the participants. You must give participants an opportunity to ask questions and to express any concerns they may have.

20. The information provided should include:

- what the research aims to achieve, an outline of the research method, and confirmation that a research ethics committee has approved the project;

- the legal rights and safeguards provided for participants;
- the reasons that the patient or volunteer has been asked to participate;
- if the project involves randomisation, the nature of the process and reasons for it, and the fact that in double-blind research trials neither the patient nor the treatment team will know whether the patient is receiving the treatment being tested or is in the control group;
- information about possible benefits and risks;
- an explanation of which parts of the treatment are experimental or not fully tested;
- advice that they can withdraw at any time and, where relevant, an assurance that this will not adversely affect their relationship with those providing care;
- an explanation of how personal information will be stored, transmitted and published;
- what information will be available to the participant about the outcome of the research, and how that information will be presented;
- arrangements for responding to adverse events;
- details of compensation available should participants suffer harm as a result of their participation in the research.

21. You must allow people sufficient time to reflect on the implications of participating in the study, and provide any further information they request, including a copy of the protocol approved by the research ethics committee. You must not put pressure on anyone to take part in the research. You should make a record of the discussion and the outcome.

22. When seeking consent it is also important to consider the needs of particular groups of people and situations that require special consideration, advice is given in paragraphs 43 to 58.

Seeking consent to obtain organs, tissues or body fluids from living patients or volunteers

23. Samples of body fluids, tissues and organs can form a valuable archive for research purposes. You must obtain appropriate consent or authorisation before taking or retaining organs, tissues or body fluids, from patients or volunteers, for research purposes. This applies whether the material is obtained solely for research purposes or retained following a clinical or surgical treatment.

24. When seeking participants' consent, you must be satisfied that participants understand the amount and nature of tissues, organs or body fluids which will be taken. Where material is being obtained for a specific project, you must explain how the sample will be used; where a sample is to be stored and used in further research projects, this must be made clear. You must be prepared to respond honestly and sensitively to any questions which the participants may ask.

25. You must be open and honest about any financial transactions associated with the use of tissues, organs or body fluids (see paragraph 14). Financial remuneration for supplying such material to other organisations or individuals should be limited to administrative costs involved, and you should not be involved, directly or indirectly, in buying or selling human organs, tissues or body fluids.

26. Obtaining human organs, tissue and body fluids for use in research raises complex issues, and you must ensure that you take account of the relevant guidance. Professional guidance on post-mortem examinations, and the removal and retention of human material has been issued by a number of bodies; advice from the UK Health Departments is in preparation (see Appendix).

Post-mortems

27. The legislation relating to post-mortems and retention of organs is currently being reviewed in the UK. You must keep up to date with and observe the law which governs this area of practice.

28. Different legal requirements arise in post-mortems undertaken at the direction of the coroner or procurator fiscal, from those undertaken at the instigation of the hospital. Nonetheless in all cases it is essential that the deceased's relatives are involved in the decision if it is planned to remove and retain any tissue, body fluids or organs for the purposes of research:

- where a child has died, the parental consent to the removal, storage and use of such material for research must be obtained;

- where an adult has died, reasonable efforts should be made to ascertain what the person would have wanted, for example by discussing the issues with their relatives or representatives, and reading any 'living will' or other statements made by that person.

29. It is essential that clear information is provided to the family or representatives of a deceased patient about the extent of the tissue and fluid or organs to be taken, and as far as possible, the nature of the research for which it will or may be used. You must be prepared to respond honestly and sensitively to any questions that they may ask and you should be considerate when giving information to and obtaining consent from them.

Confidentiality

30. Patients and people who volunteer to participate in research are entitled to expect that doctors will respect their privacy and autonomy. Where data is needed for research, epidemiology or public health surveillance you should:
    1. Seek consent to the disclosure of any information wherever that is practicable;
    2. Anonymise data where unidentifiable data will serve the purpose;
    3. Keep disclosures to the minimum necessary;
    4. Keep up to date with, and abide by, the requirements of statute and common law, including the Data Protection Act 1998 and orders made under the Health and Social Care Act 2001.

Use of existing records in research

Obtaining consent

31. Records made for one purpose, for example the provision of care, should not usually be disclosed for another purpose without the patient's consent. If you are asked to disclose, or seek access to, records containing personal information for research, you must be satisfied that express consent has been sought from the participant, wherever that is practicable.

32. Where it is not practicable for the person who holds the records either to obtain express consent to disclosure, or to anonymise records, data may be disclosed for research, provided participants have been given information about access to their records, and about their right to object. Any objection must be respected. Usually such disclosures will be made to allow a person outside the research team to anonymise the records, or to identify participants who may be invited to participate in a study. Such disclosures must be kept to the minimum necessary for the purpose. In all such cases you must be satisfied that participants have been told, or have had access to written material informing them:

- that their records may be disclosed to persons outside the team which provided their care.
- of the purpose and extent of the disclosure, for example, to produce anonymised data for use in research, epidemiology or surveillance.
- that the person given access to records will be subject to a duty of confidentiality.
- that they have a right to object to such a process, and that their objection will be respected, except where the disclosure is essential to protect the patient, or someone else, from risk of death or serious harm.

33. Where you control personal information or records about patients or volunteers, you must not allow anyone access, unless the person has been properly trained and authorised by the health authority, NHS trust or comparable body and is subject to a duty of confidentiality in their employment or because of their registration with a statutory regulatory body.

Where consent cannot be obtained

34. Where it is not practicable to contact participants to seek their consent to the anonymisation of data or use of identifiable data in research, this fact should be drawn to the attention of a research ethics committee so that it can consider whether the likely benefits of the research outweigh the loss of confidentiality to the patient. Disclosures may otherwise be improper, even if the recipients of the

information are registered medical practitioners. The decision of a research ethics committee would be taken into account by a court if a claim for breach of confidentiality were made, but the court's judgment would be based on its own assessment of whether the public interest was served.

Projects which are not approved by research ethics committees

35. Some epidemiology, health surveillance and monitoring is, for good reason, undertaken without research ethics committee approval. Data can be used in these cases where there is a statutory requirement to do so, for example where the data relates to a known or suspected 'notifiable' disease, or where there is a relevant order under the Health and Social Care Act 2001.

36. Where there is no statutory duty to disclose information, disclosures must be made in accordance with the principles set out in paragraph 30 above. Where it is not practicable to seek consent, nor to anonymise data, information may be disclosed or accessed where the disclosure is justified in the public interest.

Disclosures in the public interest

37. Personal information may be disclosed in the public interest, without the individual's consent, where the benefits to an individual or to society of the disclosure outweigh the public and the individual's interest in keeping the information confidential. In all cases where you consider disclosing information without consent from the individual, you must weigh the possible harm (both to the individual, and the overall trust between doctors and participants) against the benefits which are likely to arise from the release of information.

38. Before considering whether disclosure of personal information would be justified, you must be satisfied that:

      a. the participants are not competent to give consent; or,

      b. it is not practicable to seek consent, for example because:

- the records are of such age and/or number that reasonable efforts to trace patients are unlikely to be successful;
- the patient has been or may be violent;
- action must be taken quickly (for example in the detection or control of outbreaks of some communicable diseases) and there is insufficient time to contact participants; or
      c. participants have been asked, but have withheld consent.

39. In considering whether the public interest in the research outweighs the privacy interests of the individual and society, you will need to consider the nature of the information to be disclosed, how long identifiable data will be preserved, how many people may have access to the data, as well as the potential benefits of the research project. A participant's wishes about the use of data can be overridden only in exceptional circumstances and you must be prepared to explain and justify such a decision.

40. Other circumstances in which disclosures may be made without consent are discussed below.

Records made during research

41. Records made during research should be kept securely and disclosed to people outside the research team only in accordance with the guidance in our booklet Confidentiality: Protecting and Providing Information.

Recording and reporting research results

42. When you are involved in a research project you must:

- maintain complete and accurate records and retain them for purposes of audit;
- record and report research results accurately and in a way that is transparent and open to audit;
- report adverse findings as soon as possible to the research participants who are affected, to those responsible for their medical care, to the research sponsor and primary funder and to

bodies responsible for protecting the public, such as the Medicines Control Agency or other licensing bodies;

- make every effort to inform participants of the outcome of the research; or make the information publicly available if it is not practicable to inform individual participants;
- ensure that claims of authorship are justified;
- publish results whenever possible, including adverse findings, preferably through peer reviewed journals. You must always try to ensure that your research results appear in such journals before they are reported in other media, and if you are presenting your research findings to the non-medical press you should make every effort to ensure that your research findings are reported in a balanced way;
- explain to the relevant research ethics committee if, exceptionally, you believe there are valid reasons not to publish the results of a study.

People and situations requiring special consideration

Vulnerable adults

43. Competent but vulnerable adults may find it difficult to withhold consent if they are put under implicit or explicit pressures from institutions or health care professionals. But the treatments being researched might be of significant benefit to such people, and to exclude vulnerable groups could be a form of discrimination. Frail elderly people, people living in institutions and adults with learning difficulties or mental illness who remain competent should all be considered vulnerable. Pregnant women may also be subjected to hidden pressures to become involved in research, and their inclusion in a project may need special consideration.

44. Careful consideration should therefore be given to involving vulnerable adults in research, and particular attention should be given to the consent process, ensuring that they have sufficient information provided in a suitable format, and enough time to consider the issues. You should give consideration to their vulnerability and difficulties they may have in understanding or retaining information. You may need to encourage them to seek the help of a relative/close friend, support worker/advocate. You should proceed with the research only if you believe that the participant's consent is voluntary and based on an understanding of the information they have been given.

Assessing capacity

45. No one can give or withhold consent on behalf of an adult with mental incapacity. Before involving participants who, by reason of mental disorder or inability to communicate, lack mental capacity, you must first assess their capacity to make an informed decision about participating in research.

Fluctuating capacity

46. Where participants have difficulty retaining information, or are only intermittently competent to make a decision, you should provide any assistance they might need to reach an informed decision. You should record any decision made while they were competent, including the key elements of the consultation. You should review any decision made whilst they were competent at appropriate intervals before the research starts, and at intervals during the study, to establish that their views are consistently held and can be relied on.

Adults who lack capacity

47. In England, Wales and Northern Ireland there is no legislation setting out the circumstances in which research involving adults with mental incapacity may be undertaken.

48. Research into conditions that are not linked to incapacity should never be undertaken with adults with incapacity if it could equally well be done with other adults. It should be limited to areas of research related to the participants' incapacity or to physical illnesses that are linked to their incapacity. If you involve this group of people in research you must demonstrate that:

- it could be of direct benefit to their health; or
- it is of special benefit to the health of people in the same age group with the same state of health; or
- that it will significantly improve the scientific understanding of the adult's incapacity leading to a direct benefit to them or to others with the same incapacity; and
- the research is ethical and will not cause the participants emotional, physical or psychological harm; and
- the person does not express objections physically or verbally.

49. You must also ensure that participants' right to withdraw from the research is respected at all times. Any sign of distress, pain or indication of refusal irrespective of whether or not it is given in a verbal form should be considered as implied refusal.

Advance Statements

50. If you are involving adults who have lost capacity to consent to, or refuse to participate in research, for example through onset or progress of a mental disorder, you should try to find out whether they have previously indicated preferences in an advance statement ('advance directives' or 'living wills'). Adults can express their wishes about forms of treatment and about participation in research in an advance statement and their views should be taken into account. Any refusal to participate in a research trial or project, given when an adult patient was competent, which remains valid and clearly applicable, is legally binding and must be respected.

Research into treatment in emergencies

51. In an emergency where consent cannot be obtained, treatment can be given only if it is limited to what is immediately necessary to save life or avoid significant deterioration in the patient's health. This may include treatment that is part of a therapeutic research project, where the risks of the new treatment are not believed to exceed the known risks of standard treatment. If, during treatment, the patient regains capacity, the patient should be told about the research as soon as possible and their consent to continue should be sought.

52. If it is possible, you should discuss the situation with relatives and/or partners of the patient unless you have what you judge to be good reason to believe that the patient would wish otherwise.

53. You must always respect the terms of any valid advance refusal that you know about, or is drawn to your attention.

54. If there is time, you may want to seek the opinion or advice of another member of the research team to discuss the course of action you are intending to take.

Children and young people

55. Research involving children and young people is important in promoting their health and to validate in them the beneficial results of research conducted with adults. However, to the degree that they are unable to recognise their best interests, express their own needs, protect themselves from harm, or make informed choices about the potential risks and benefits of research, children and young people are vulnerable members of society.

56. When involving children and young people in research you must protect their ethical, physical, mental and emotional rights and ensure that they are not exploited. It is important to assess carefully the potential benefits and harm to them, at all stages of any research.

57. You must always ensure that you have obtained consent before undertaking any research on children and young people. If they are not competent, independently, to consent to treatment then they should not participate in research without the consent of someone with parental responsibility. GMC guidance Seeking patients' consent: the ethical considerations gives advice on consent.

58. A full exposition of the issues concerning research that involve children is contained in 'Guidelines for the ethical conduct of medical research involving children'.

Teaching, training and management

Teaching and supervision

59. All students should be introduced to the basic principles of good research practice as undergraduates. This should include the ethical importance of informed consent and the practical importance of related communication skills. It should also provide the basis for continuing, appropriate training at all stages of their education and professional development.

60. If you have special responsibilities for supervision of research or teaching you must develop and demonstrate the skills, attitudes and practices of a competent teacher because you will be a significant role model. You must make sure that students and junior colleagues who undertake research are properly supervised. Junior staff and research students who are being trained or supervised should always be given clear information about the roles and responsibilities of supervisors, teachers and mentors.

Keeping up to date

61. As a researcher you should keep your knowledge and skills up to date throughout your working life. You should take part regularly in educational activities that develop your competence and performance in research methods.

Managerial responsibilities for research

62. If you have management responsibility in an organisation undertaking research, or are leading a research team or a research project, the management tasks you undertake will have to meet the standards set by the GMC.

63. If you have responsibility to act on concerns brought to your attention about the quality and integrity of the research including allegations of fraud or misconduct, you must ensure that systems are in place to deal with such concerns. Where such a concern is brought to your attention, you must take action promptly:

- taking account of participants' safety;
- establishing the facts as far as you are able, separating genuine concerns from those made mischievously or maliciously;
- protecting the person who has made the allegations and the person about whom the allegation is made, from harmful criticisms or actions.

64. If you are leading a team, you must:

- ensure the research plans are clearly explained to the appropriate ethics committee(s), the health care organisations in which the research will take place, and other bodies with supervisory or regulatory responsibilities;
- ensure that all members of the team are competent and in a position to carry out their research responsibilities with integrity;
- take responsibility for ensuring that the team carries out the research in a manner which is safe, effective and efficient;
- do your best to make sure that the whole team understands the need to provide a polite, responsive and accessible service that respects the research participants' dignity and treats their information as confidential;
- ensure that research participants and colleagues understand your role and responsibilities in the team.

This booklet is not exhaustive. It cannot cover all the questions that may arise. You must therefore always be prepared to explain and justify your actions and decisions.

Confidentiality: Protecting and Providing Information

(April 2004)

Being registered with the GMC gives you rights and privileges. In return, you have a duty to meet the standard of competence, care and conduct set by the GMC.

Doctors hold information about patients which is private and sensitive. This information must not be given to others unless the patient consents or you can justify the disclosure.

When you are satisfied that information should be released, you should act promptly to disclose all relevant information. This is often essential to the best interests of the patient, or to safeguard the well-being of others.

Patients' right to confidentiality

Principles

1. Patients have a right to expect that information about them will be held in confidence by their doctors. Confidentiality is central to trust between doctors and patients. Without assurances about confidentiality, patients may be reluctant to give doctors the information they need in order to provide good care. If you are asked to provide information about patients you must:

- inform patients about the disclosure, or check that they have already received information about it;
- anonymise data where unidentifiable data will serve the purpose;
- be satisfied that patients know about disclosures necessary to provide their care, or for local clinical audit of that care, that they can object to these disclosures but have not done so;
- seek patients' express consent to disclosure of information, where identifiable data is needed for any purpose other than the provision of care or for clinical audit – save in the exceptional circumstances described in this booklet;
- keep disclosures to the minimum necessary; and
- keep up to date with and observe the requirements of statute and common law, including data protection legislation.

2. You must always be prepared to justify your decisions in accordance with this guidance.

3. This booklet develops the advice in Good Medical Practice (2001). It sets out the standards of practice expected of doctors when they hold or share information about patients. Additional advice on how the guidance in this booklet should be put into practice, and on the law relating to the use and disclosure of information about patients, is available in our Frequently Asked Questions.

Protecting information

4. When you are responsible for personal information about patients you must make sure that it is effectively protected against improper disclosure at all times.

5. Many improper disclosures are unintentional. You should not discuss patients where you can be overheard or leave patients' records, either on paper or on screen, where they can be seen by other patients, unauthorised health care staff or the public. You should take all reasonable steps to ensure that your consultations with patients are private.

Sharing information with patients

6. Patients have a right to information about the health care services available to them, presented in a way that is easy to follow and use.

7. Patients also have a right to information about any condition or disease from which they are suffering. This should be presented in a manner easy to follow and use, and include information

about diagnosis, prognosis, treatment options, outcomes of treatment, common and/or serious side-effects of treatment, likely time-scale of treatments and costs where relevant. You must always give patients basic information about treatment you propose to provide, but you should respect the wishes of any patient who asks you not to give them detailed information. This places a considerable onus upon health professionals. Yet, without such information, patients cannot make proper choices as partners in the health care process. Our booklet Seeking Patients' Consent: The Ethical Considerations (1998) gives further advice on providing information to patients.

8. You should tell patients how information about them may be used to protect public health, to undertake research and audit, to teach or train clinical staff and students and to plan and organise health care services. See paragraphs 13–15 for further information.

Disclosing information about patients

9. You must respect patients' confidentiality. Seeking patients' consent to disclosure of information is part of good communication between doctors and patients. When asked to provide information you must follow the guidance in paragraph 1 of this booklet.

Circumstances where patients may give implied consent to disclosure

Sharing information in the health care team or with others providing care

10. Most people understand and accept that information must be shared within the health care team in order to provide their care. You should make sure that patients are aware that personal information about them will be shared within the health care team, unless they object, and of the reasons for this. It is particularly important to check that patients understand what will be disclosed if you need to share identifiable information with anyone employed by another organisation or agency who is contributing to their care. You must respect the wishes of any patient who objects to particular information being shared with others providing care, except where this would put others at risk of death or serious harm.

11. You must make sure that anyone to whom you disclose personal information understands that it is given to them in confidence, which they must respect. All staff members receiving personal information in order to provide or support care are bound by a legal duty of confidence, whether or not they have contractual or professional obligations to protect confidentiality.

12. Circumstances may arise where a patient cannot be informed about the sharing of information, for example because of a medical emergency. In these cases you must pass relevant information promptly to those providing the patient's care.

Disclosing information for clinical audit

13. Clinical audit is essential to the provision of good care. All doctors in clinical practice have a duty to participate in clinical audit. Where an audit is to be undertaken by the team which provided care, or those working to support them, such as clinical audit staff, you may disclose identifiable information, provided you are satisfied that patients:

- have been informed that their data may be disclosed for clinical audit, and their right to object to the disclosure; and
- have not objected.

14. If a patient does object you should explain why information is needed and how this may benefit their care. If it is not possible to provide safe care without disclosing information for audit, you should explain this to the patient and the options open to them.

15. Where clinical audit is to be undertaken by another organisation, information should be anonymised wherever that is practicable. In any case where it is not practicable to anonymise data, or anonymised data will not fulfil the requirements of the audit, express consent must be obtained before identifiable data is disclosed.

Disclosures where express consent must be sought

16. Express consent is usually needed before the disclosure of identifiable information for purposes such as research, epidemiology, financial audit or administration. When seeking express consent to disclosure you must make sure that patients are given enough information on which to base their decision, the reasons for the disclosure and the likely consequences of the disclosure. You should also explain how much information will be disclosed and to whom it will be given. If the patient withholds consent, or consent cannot be obtained, disclosures may be made only where they are required by law or can be justified in the public interest. Where the purpose is covered by a regulation made under s60 of the Health and Social Care Act 2001, disclosures may also be made without patients' consent. You should make a record of the patient's decision, and whether and why you have disclosed information.

17. Where doctors have contractual obligations to third parties, such as companies or organisations, they must obtain patients' consent before undertaking any examination or writing a report for that organisation. Before seeking consent they must explain the purpose of the examination or report and the scope of the disclosure. Doctors should offer to show patients the report, or give them copies, whether or not this is required by law.

Disclosure in connection with judicial or other statutory proceedings

Disclosures required by law

18. You must disclose information to satisfy a specific statutory requirement, such as notification of a known or suspected communicable disease. You should inform patients about such disclosures, wherever that is practicable, but their consent is not required.

Disclosures to courts or in connection with litigation

19. You must also disclose information if ordered to do so by a judge or presiding officer of a court. You should object to the judge or the presiding officer if attempts are made to compel you to disclose what appear to you to be irrelevant matters, for example matters relating to relatives or partners of the patient, who are not parties to the proceedings.

20. You must not disclose personal information to a third party such as a solicitor, police officer or officer of a court without the patient's express consent, except in the circumstances described in the paragraphs which follow.

Disclosures to statutory regulatory bodies

21. Patient records or other patient information may be needed by a statutory regulatory body for investigation into a health professional's fitness to practise. If you are referring concerns about a health professional to a regulatory body, you must seek the patient's consent before disclosing identifiable information, wherever that is practicable. Where patients withhold consent or it is not practicable to seek their consent, you should contact the GMC, or other appropriate regulatory body, which will advise you on whether the disclosure of identifiable information would be justified in the public interest or for the protection of other patients. Wherever practicable you should discuss this with the patient. There may be exceptional cases where, even though the patient objects, disclosure is justified.

The public interest

Disclosures in the public interest

22. Personal information may be disclosed in the public interest, without the patient's consent, and in exceptional cases where patients have withheld consent, where the benefits to an individual or to society of the disclosure outweigh the public and the patient's interest in keeping the information confidential. In all cases where you consider disclosing information without consent from the patient, you must weigh the possible harm (both to the patient, and the overall trust between doctors and patients) against the benefits which are likely to arise from the release of information.

23. Before considering whether a disclosure of personal information 'in the public interest' would be justified, you must be satisfied that identifiable data are necessary for the purpose, or that it is not

practicable to anonymise the data. In such cases you should still try to seek patients' consent, unless it is not practicable to do so, for example because:

- the patients are not competent to give consent (see paragraphs 28 and 29); or
- the records are of such age and/or number that reasonable efforts to trace patients are unlikely to be successful; or
- the patient has been, or may be violent; or obtaining consent would undermine the purpose of the disclosure (eg disclosures in relation to crime); or
- action must be taken quickly (for example in the detection or control of outbreaks of some communicable diseases) and there is insufficient time to contact patients.

24. In cases where there is a serious risk to the patient or others, disclosures may be justified even where patients have been asked to agree to a disclosure, but have withheld consent (for further advice see paragraph 27).

25. You should inform patients that a disclosure will be made, wherever it is practicable to do so. You must document in the patient's record any steps you have taken to seek or obtain consent and your reasons for disclosing information without consent.

26. Ultimately, the 'public interest' can be determined only by the courts; but the GMC may also require you to justify your actions if a complaint is made about the disclosure of identifiable information without a patient's consent. The potential benefits and harms of disclosures made without consent are also considered by the Patient Information Advisory Group in considering applications for Regulations under the Health and Social Care Act 2001. Disclosures of data covered by a Regulation are not in breach of the common law duty of confidentiality.

Disclosures to protect the patient or others

27. Disclosure of personal information without consent may be justified in the public interest where failure to do so may expose the patient or others to risk of death or serious harm. Where the patient or others are exposed to a risk so serious that it outweighs the patient's privacy interest, you should seek consent to disclosure where practicable. If it is not practicable to seek consent, you should disclose information promptly to an appropriate person or authority. You should generally inform the patient before disclosing the information. If you seek consent and the patient withholds it you should consider the reasons for this, if any are provided by the patient. If you remain of the view that disclosure is necessary to protect a third party from death or serious harm, you should disclose information promptly to an appropriate person or authority. Such situations arise, for example, where a disclosure may assist in the prevention, detection or prosecution of a serious crime, especially crimes against the person, such as abuse of children.

Children and other patients who may lack competence to give consent

Disclosures in relation to the treatment sought by children or others who lack capacity to give consent

28. Problems may arise if you consider that a patient lacks capacity to give consent to treatment or disclosure. If such patients ask you not to disclose information about their condition or treatment to a third party, you should try to persuade them to allow an appropriate person to be involved in the consultation. If they refuse and you are convinced that it is essential, in their medical interests, you may disclose relevant information tó an appropriate person or authority. In such cases you should tell the patient before disclosing any information, and where appropriate, seek and carefully consider the views of an advocate or carer. You should document in the patient's record your discussions with the patient and the reasons for decidingto disclose information.

Disclosures where a patient may be a victim of neglect or abuse

29. If you believe a patient to be a victim of neglect or physical, sexual or emotional abuse and that the patient cannot give or withhold consent to disclosure, you must give information promptly to an appropriate responsible person or statutory agency, where you believe that the disclosure is in the

patient's best interests. If, for any reason, you believe that disclosure of information is not in the best interests of an abused or neglected patient, you should discuss the issues with an experienced colleague. If you decide not to disclose information, you must be prepared to justify your decision.

Disclosure after a patient's death

30. You still have an obligation to keep personal information confidential after a patient dies. The extent to which confidential information may be disclosed after a patient's death will depend on the circumstances. If the patient had asked for information to remain confidential, his or her views should be respected. Where you are unaware of any directions from the patient, you should consider requests for information taking into account:

- whether the disclosure of information may cause distress to, or be of benefit to, the patient's partner or family;
- whether disclosure of information about the patient will in effect disclose information about the patient's family or other people;
- whether the information is already public knowledge or can be anonymised;
- the purpose of the disclosure.

If you decide to disclose confidential information you must be prepared to explain and justify your decision.

Glossary

This defines the terms used within this document. These definitions have no wider or legal significance.

Anonymised data Data from which the patient cannot be identified by the recipient of the information. The name, address, and full post code must be removed together with any other information which, in conjunction with other data held by or disclosed to the recipient, could identify the patient. Unique numbers may be included only if recipients of the data do not have access to the 'key' to trace the identity of the patient.

Clinical audit Evaluation of clinical performance against standards or through comparative analysis, to inform the management of services. Studies that aim to derive, scientifically confirm and publish generalisable knowledge constitute research and are not encompassed within the definition of clinical audit in this document.

Consent Agreement to an action based on knowledge of what the action involves and its likely consequences.

Express consent Consent which is expressed orally or in writing (except where patients cannot write or speak, when other forms of communication may be sufficient).

Identifiable data Data from which a patient can be identified. Name, address and full postcode will identify patients; combinations of data may also do so, even where name and address are not included.

Implied consent Agreement to disclosure where patients have been informed about the information to be disclosed, the purpose of the disclosure, and that they have a right to object to the disclosure, but have not done so.

Health care team The health care team comprises the people providing clinical services for each patient and the administrative staff who directly support those services.

Patients Used throughout the guidance to mean competent patients. Parents of, or those with parental responsibility for, children who lack maturity to make decisions for themselves, are generally entitled to make decisions about disclosures on behalf of their children.

Personal information Information about people which doctors learn in a professional capacity and from which individuals can be identified.

Public interest: The interests of the community as a whole, or a group within the community or individuals.

Good Medical Practice (GMC, 2006)

(Footnotes and endnotes omitted)

Patients must be able to trust doctors with their lives and health. To justify that trust you must show respect for human life and you must:

- Make the care of your patient your first concern

- Protect and promote the health of patients and the public
- Provide a good standard of practice and care
    - Keep your professional knowledge and skills up to date
    - Recognise and work within the limits of your competence
    - Work with colleagues in the ways that best serve patients' interests
- Treat patients as individuals and respect their dignity
    - Treat patients politely and considerately
    - Respect patients' right to confidentiality
- Work in partnership with patients
    - Listen to patients and respond to their concerns and preferences
    - Give patients the information they want or need in a way they can understand
    - Respect patients' right to reach decisions with you about their treatment and care
    - Support patients in caring for themselves to improve and maintain their health
- Be honest and open and act with integrity
    - Act without delay if you have good reason to believe that you or a
    - colleague may be putting patients at risk
    - Never discriminate unfairly against patients or colleagues
    - Never abuse your patients' trust in you or the public's trust in the profession.

You are personally accountable for your professional practice and must always be prepared to justify your decisions and actions.

About Good Medical Practice

Good Medical Practice sets out the principles and values on which good practice is founded; these principles together describe medical professionalism in action. The guidance is addressed to doctors, but it is also intended to let the public know what they can expect from doctors.

We have provided links to other guidance and information which illustrate how the principles in Good Medical Practice apply in practice, and how they may be interpreted in other contexts; for example, in undergraduate education, in revalidation, or in our consideration of a doctor's conduct, performance or health through our fitness to practise procedures. There are links to:

- supplementary guidance and other information from the GMC
- cases heard by GMC fitness to practise panels, which provide examples of where a failure to follow the guidance in Good Medical Practice has put a doctor's registration at risk (available on-line only)
- external (non-GMC) sources of advice and information.
- You can access all these documents on our website, or order printed versions of the GMC documents by contacting publications@gmc-uk.org (phone: 0161 923 6315).

How Good Medical Practice applies to you

The guidance that follows describes what is expected of all doctors registered with the GMC. It is your responsibility to be familiar with Good Medical Practice and to follow the guidance it contains. It is guidance, not a statutory code, so you must use your judgement to apply the principles to the various situations you will face as a doctor, whether or not you routinely see patients. You must be prepared to explain and justify your decisions and actions.

In Good Medical Practice the terms 'you must' and 'you should' are used in the following ways:

- 'You must' is used for an overriding duty or principle.
- 'You should' is used when we are providing an explanation of how you will meet the overriding duty.
- 'You should' is also used where the duty or principle will not apply in all situations or circumstances, or where there are factors outside your control that affect whether or how you can comply with the guidance.

Serious or persistent failure to follow this guidance will put your registration at risk.

Good Doctors

1 Patients need good doctors. Good doctors make the care of their patients their first concern: they are competent, keep their knowledge and skills up to date, establish and maintain good relationships with patients and colleagues*, are honest and trustworthy, and act with integrity.

Good clinical care

Providing good clinical care
2 Good clinical care must include:
- (a) adequately assessing the patient's conditions, taking account of the history (including the symptoms, and psychological and social factors), the patient's views, and where necessary examining the patient
- (b) providing or arranging advice, investigations or treatment where necessary
- (c) referring a patient to another practitioner, when this is in the patient's best interests.

3 In providing care you must:
- (a) recognise and work within the limits of your competence
- (b) prescribe drugs or treatment, including repeat prescriptions, only when you have adequate knowledge of the patient's health, and are satisfied that the drugs or treatment serve the patient's needs
- (c) provide effective treatments based on the best available evidence
- (d) take steps to alleviate pain and distress whether or not a cure may be possible
- (e) respect the patient's right to seek a second opinion
- (f) keep clear, accurate and legible records, reporting the relevant clinical findings, the decisions made, the information given to patients, and any drugs prescribed or other investigation or treatment
- (g) make records at the same time as the events you are recording or as soon as possible afterwards
- (h) be readily accessible when you are on duty
- (i) consult and take advice from colleagues, when appropriate
- (j) make good use of the resources available to you.

Supporting self-care
4 You should encourage patients and the public to take an interest in their health and to take action to improve and maintain it. This may include advising patients on the effects of their life choices on their health and well-being and the possible outcomes of their treatments.

Avoid treating those close to you
5 Wherever possible, you should avoid providing medical care to anyone with whom you have a close personal relationship.

---

* Those a doctor works with, whether or not they are also doctors.

Raising concerns about patient safety

6 If you have good reason to think that patient safety is or may be seriously compromised by inadequate premises, equipment, or other resources, policies or systems, you should put the matter right if that is possible. In all other cases you should draw the matter to the attention of your employing or contracting body. If they do not take adequate action, you should take independent advice on how to take the matter further. You must record your concerns and the steps you have taken to try to resolve them.

Decisions about access to medical care

7 The investigations or treatment you provide or arrange must be based on the assessment you and the patient make of their needs and priorities, and on your clinical judgement about the likely effectiveness of the treatment options. You must not refuse or delay treatment because you believe that a patient's actions have contributed to their condition. You must treat your patients with respect whatever their life choices and beliefs. You must not unfairly discriminate against them by allowing your personal views* to affect adversely your professional relationship with them or the treatment you provide or arrange. You should challenge colleagues if their behaviour does not comply with this guidance.

8 If carrying out a particular procedure or giving advice about it conflicts with your religious or moral beliefs, and this conflict might affect the treatment or advice you provide, you must explain this to the patient and tell them they have the right to see another doctor. You must be satisfied that the patient has sufficient information to enable them to exercise that right. If it is not practical for a patient to arrange to see another doctor, you must ensure that arrangements are made for another suitably qualified colleague to take over your role.

9 You must give priority to the investigation and treatment of patients on the basis of clinical need, when such decisions are within your power. If inadequate resources, policies or systems prevent you from doing this, and patient safety is or may be seriously compromised, you must follow the guidance in paragraph 6.

10 All patients are entitled to care and treatment to meet their clinical needs. You must not refuse to treat a patient because their medical condition may put you at risk. If a patient poses a risk to your health or safety, you should take all available steps to minimise the risk before providing treatment or making suitable alternative arrangements for treatment.

Treatment in emergencies

11 In an emergency, wherever it arises, you must offer assistance, taking account of your own safety, your competence, and the availability of other options for care.

Maintaining good medical practice

Keeping up to date

12 You must keep your knowledge and skills up to date throughout your working life.You should be familiar with relevant guidelines and developments that affect your work. You should regularly take part in educational activities that maintain and further develop your competence and performance.

13 You must keep up to date with, and adhere to, the laws and codes of practice relevant to your work.

Maintaining and improving your performance

14 You must work with colleagues and patients to maintain and improve the quality of your work and promote patient safety.

In particular, you must:

      (a) maintain a folder of information and evidence, drawn from your medical practice

      (b) reflect regularly on your standards of medical practice in accordance with GMC guidance on licensing and revalidation

      (c) take part in regular and systematic audit

---

* This includes your views about a patient's age, colour, culture, disability, ethnic or national origin, gender, lifestyle, marital or parental status, race, religion or beliefs, sex, sexual orientation, or social or economic status.

(d) take part in systems of quality assurance and quality improvement

(e) respond constructively to the outcome of audit, appraisals and performance reviews, undertaking further training where necessary

(f) help to resolve uncertainties about the effects of treatments

(g) contribute to confidential inquiries and adverse event recognition and reporting, to help reduce risk to patients

(h) report suspected adverse drug reactions in accordance with the relevant reporting scheme

(i) co-operate with legitimate requests for information from organisations monitoring public health – when doing so you must follow the guidance in Confidentiality: Protecting and providing information.

Teaching and training, appraising and assessing

15 Teaching, training, appraising and assessing doctors and students are important for the care of patients now and in the future. You should be willing to contribute to these activities.

16 If you are involved in teaching you must develop the skills, attitudes and practices of a competent teacher.

17 You must make sure that all staff for whom you are responsible, including locums and students, are properly supervised.

18 You must be honest and objective when appraising or assessing the performance of colleagues, including locums and students. Patients will be put at risk if you describe as competent someone who has not reached or maintained a satisfactory standard of practice.

19 You must provide only honest, justifiable and accurate comments when giving references for, or writing reports about, colleagues. When providing references you must do so promptly and include all information that is relevant to your colleague's competence, performance or conduct.

Relationships with patients

The doctor–patient partnership

20 Relationships based on openness, trust and good communication will enable you to work in partnership with your patients to address their individual needs.

21 To fulfil your role in the doctor–patient partnership you must:

(a) be polite, considerate and honest

(b) treat patients with dignity

(c) treat each patient as an individual

(d) respect patients' privacy and right to confidentiality

(e) support patients in caring for themselves to improve and maintain their health

(f) encourage patients who have knowledge about their condition to use this when they are making decisions about their care.

Good communication

22 To communicate effectively you must:

(a) listen to patients, ask for and respect their views about their health, and respond to their concerns and preferences

(b) share with patients, in a way they can understand, the information they want or need to know about their condition, its likely progression, and the treatment options available to them, including associated risks and uncertainties

(c) respond to patients' questions and keep them informed about the progress of their care

(d) make sure that patients are informed about how information is shared within teams and among those who will be providing their care.

23 You must make sure, wherever practical, that arrangements are made to meet patients' language and communication needs.

Children and young people

24 The guidance that follows in paragraphs 25–27 is relevant whether or not you routinely see children and young people as patients. You should be aware of the needs and welfare of children and young people when you see patients who are parents or carers, as well as any patients who may represent a danger to children or young people.

25 You must safeguard and protect the health and well-being of children and young people.

26 You should offer assistance to children and young people if you have reason to think that their rights have been abused or denied.

27 When communicating with a child or young person you must:

       (a) treat them with respect and listen to their views

       (b) answer their questions to the best of your ability

       (c) provide information in a way they can understand.

28 The guidance in paragraphs 25–27 is about children and young people, but the principles also apply to other vulnerable groups.

Relatives, carers and partners

29 You must be considerate to relatives, carers, partners and others close to the patient, and be sensitive and responsive in providing information and support, including after a patient has died. In doing this you must follow the guidance in Confidentiality: Protecting and providing information.

Being open and honest with patients if things go wrong

30 If a patient under your care has suffered harm or distress, you must act immediately to put matters right, if that is possible. You should offer an apology and explain fully and promptly to the patient what has happened, and the likely short-term and long-term effects.

31 Patients who complain about the care or treatment they have received have a right to expect a prompt, open, constructive and honest response including an explanation and, if appropriate, an apology. You must not allow a patient's complaint to affect adversely the care or treatment you provide or arrange.

Maintaining trust in the profession

32 You must not use your professional position to establish or pursue a sexual or improper emotional relationship with a patient or someone close to them.

33 You must not express to your patients your personal beliefs, including political, religious or moral beliefs, in ways that exploit their vulnerability or that are likely to cause them distress.

34 You must take out adequate insurance or professional indemnity cover for any part of your practice not covered by an employer's indemnity scheme, in your patients' interests as well as your own.

35 You must be familiar with your GMC reference number. You must make sure you are identifiable to your patients and colleagues, for example by using your registered name when signing statutory documents, including prescriptions. You must make your registered name and GMC reference number available to anyone who asks for them.

Consent

36 You must be satisfied that you have consent or other valid authority before you undertake any examination or investigation, provide treatment or involve patients in teaching or research. Usually this will involve providing information to patients in a way they can understand, before asking for their consent. You must follow the guidance in Seeking patients' consent: The ethical considerations, which includes advice on children and patients who are not able to give consent.

Confidentiality

37 Patients have a right to expect that information about them will be held in confidence by their doctors. You must treat information about patients as confidential, including after a patient has died. If you are considering disclosing confidential information without a patient's consent, you must follow the guidance in Confidentiality: Protecting and providing information.

Ending your professional relationship with a patient

38 In rare circumstances, the trust between you and a patient may break down, and you may find it necessary to end the professional relationship. For example, this may occur if a patient has been violent to you or a colleague, has stolen from the premises, or has persistently acted inconsiderately or unreasonably. You should not end a relationship with a patient solely because of a complaint the patient has made about you or your team, or because of the resource implications* of the patient's care or treatment.

39 Before you end a professional relationship with a patient, you must be satisfied that your decision is fair and does not contravene the guidance in paragraph 7. You must be prepared to justify your decision. You should inform the patient of your decision and your reasons for ending the professional relationship, wherever practical in writing.

40 You must take steps to ensure that arrangements are made promptly for the continuing care of the patient, and you must pass on the patient's records without delay.

Working with colleagues

Working in teams

41 Most doctors work in teams with colleagues from other professions. Working in teams does not change your personal accountability for your professional conduct and the care you provide. When working in a team, you should act as a positive role model and try to motivate and inspire your colleagues. You must:

- (a) respect the skills and contributions of your colleagues
- (b) communicate effectively with colleagues within and outside the team
- (c) make sure that your patients and colleagues understand your role and responsibilities in the team, and who is responsible for each aspect of patient care
- (d) participate in regular reviews and audit of the standards and performance of the team, taking steps to remedy any deficiencies
- (e) support colleagues who have problems with performance, conduct or health.

42 If you are responsible for leading a team, you must follow the guidance in Management for doctors.

Conduct and performance of colleagues

43 You must protect patients from risk of harm posed by another colleague's conduct, performance or health. The safety of patients must come first at all times. If you have concerns that a colleague may not be fit to practise, you must take appropriate steps without delay, so that the concerns are investigated and patients protected where necessary. This means you must give an honest explanation of your concerns to an appropriate person from your employing or contracting body, and follow their procedures.

44 If there are no appropriate local systems, or local systems do not resolve the problem, and you are still concerned about the safety of patients, you should inform the relevant regulatory body. If you are not sure what to do, discuss your concerns with an impartial colleague or contact your defence body, a professional organisation, or the GMC for advice.

45 If you have management responsibilities you should make sure that systems are in place through which colleagues can raise concerns about risks to patients, and you must follow the guidance in Management for doctors.

Respect for colleagues

46 You must treat your colleagues fairly and with respect. You must not bully or harass them, or unfairly discriminate against them by allowing your personal views** to affect adversely your

---

* If you charge fees, you may refuse further treatment for patients unable or unwilling to pay for services you have already provided. You must follow the guidance in paragraph 39.

** This includes your views about a colleague's age, colour, culture, disability, ethnic or national origin, gender, lifestyle, marital or parental status, race, religion or beliefs, sex, sexual orientation, or social or economic status.

professional relationship with them. You should challenge colleagues if their behaviour does not comply with this guidance.

47 You must not make malicious and unfounded criticisms of colleagues that may undermine patients' trust in the care or treatment they receive, or in the judgement of those treating them.

Arranging cover

48 You must be satisfied that, when you are off duty, suitable arrangements have been made for your patients' medical care. These arrangements should include effective hand-over procedures, involving clear communication with healthcare colleagues. If you are concerned that the arrangements are not suitable, you should take steps to safeguard patient care and you must follow the guidance in paragraph 6.

46. See GMC guidance on valuing diversity

Taking up and ending appointments

49 Patient care may be compromised if there is not sufficient medical cover. Therefore, you must take up any post, including a locum post, you have formally accepted, and you must work your contractual notice period, unless the employer has reasonable time to make other arrangements.

Sharing information with colleagues

50 Sharing information with other healthcare professionals is important for safe and effective patient care.

51 When you refer a patient, you should provide all relevant information about the patient, including their medical history and current condition.

52 If you provide treatment or advice for a patient, but are not the patient's general practitioner, you should tell the general practitioner the results of the investigations, the treatment provided and any other information necessary for the continuing care of the patient, unless the patient objects.

53 If a patient has not been referred to you by a general practitioner, you should ask for the patient's consent to inform their general practitioner before starting treatment, except in emergencies or when it is impractical to do so. If you do not inform the patient's general practitioner, you will be responsible for providing or arranging all necessary after-care.

Delegation and referral

54 Delegation involves asking a colleague to provide treatment or care on your behalf. Although you will not be accountable for the decisions and actions of those to whom you delegate, you will still be responsible for the overall management of the patient, and accountable for your decision to delegate. When you delegate care or treatment you must be satisfied that the person to whom you delegate has the qualifications, experience, knowledge and skills to provide the care or treatment involved. You must always pass on enough information about the patient and the treatment they need.

55 Referral involves transferring some or all of the responsibility for the patient's care, usually temporarily and for a particular purpose, such as additional investigation, care or treatment that is outside your competence. You must be satisfied that any healthcare professional to whom you refer a patient is accountable to a statutory regulatory body or employed within a managed environment. If they are not, the transfer of care will be regarded as delegation, not referral. This means you remain responsible for the overall management of the patient, and accountable for your decision to delegate.

Probity

Being honest and trustworthy

56 Probity means being honest and trustworthy, and acting with integrity: this is at the heart of medical professionalism.

57 You must make sure that your conduct at all times justifies your patients' trust in you and the public's trust in the profession.

58 You must inform the GMC without delay if, anywhere in the world, you have accepted a caution, been charged with or found guilty of a criminal offence, or if another professional body has made a finding against your registration as a result of fitness to practise procedures.

59 If you are suspended by an organisation from a medical post, or have restrictions placed on your practice you must, without delay, inform any other organisations for which you undertake medical work and any patients you see independently.

Providing and publishing information about your services
60 If you publish information about your medical services, you must make sure the information is factual and verifiable.
61 You must not make unjustifiable claims about the quality or outcomes of your services in any information you provide to patients. It must not offer guarantees of cures, nor exploit patients' vulnerability or lack of medical knowledge.
62 You must not put pressure on people to use a service, for example by arousing ill-founded fears for their future health.

Writing reports and CVs, giving evidence and signing documents
63 You must be honest and trustworthy when writing reports, and when completing or signing forms, reports and other documents.
64 You must always be honest about your experience, qualifications and position, particularly when applying for posts.
65 You must do your best to make sure that any documents you write or sign are not false or misleading. This means that you must take reasonable steps to verify the information in the documents, and that you must not deliberately leave out relevant information.
66 If you have agreed to prepare a report, complete or sign a document or provide evidence, you must do so without unreasonable delay.
67 If you are asked to give evidence or act as a witness in litigation or formal inquiries, you must be honest in all your spoken and written statements. You must make clear the limits of your knowledge or competence.
68 You must co-operate fully with any formal inquiry into the treatment of a patient and with any complaints procedure that applies to your work. You must disclose to anyone entitled to ask for it any information relevant to an investigation into your own or a colleague's conduct, performance or health. In doing so, you must follow the guidance in Confidentiality: Protecting and providing information.
69 You must assist the coroner or procurator fiscal in an inquest or inquiry into a patient's death by responding to their enquiries and by offering all relevant information. You are entitled to remain silent only when your evidence may lead to criminal proceedings being taken against you.

Research
70 Research involving people directly or indirectly is vital in improving care and reducing uncertainty for patients now and in the future, and improving the health of the population as a whole.
71 If you are involved in designing, organising or carrying out research, you must:
    (a) put the protection of the participants' interests first
    (b) act with honesty and integrity
    (c) follow the appropriate national research governance guidelines and the guidance in Research: The role and responsibilities of doctors.

Financial and commercial dealings
72 You must be honest and open in any financial arrangements with patients. In particular:
    (a) you must inform patients about your fees and charges, wherever possible before asking for their consent to treatment
    (b) you must not exploit patients' vulnerability or lack of medical knowledge when making charges for treatment or services
    (c) you must not encourage patients to give, lend or bequeath money or gifts that will directly or indirectly benefit you

(d) you must not put pressure on patients or their families to make donations to other people or organisations

(e) you must not put pressure on patients to accept private treatment

(f) if you charge fees, you must tell patients if any part of the fee goes to another healthcare professional.

73 You must be honest in financial and commercial dealings with employers, insurers and other organisations or individuals. In particular:

(a) before taking part in discussions about buying or selling goods or services, you must declare any relevant financial or commercial interest that you or your family might have in the transaction

(b) if you manage finances, you must make sure the funds are used for the purpose for which they were intended and are kept in a separate account from your personal finances.

Conflicts of interest

74 You must act in your patients' best interests when making referrals and when providing or arranging treatment or care. You must not ask for or accept any inducement, gift or hospitality which may affect or be seen to affect the way you prescribe for, treat or refer patients. You must not offer such inducements to colleagues.

75 If you have financial or commercial interests in organisations providing healthcare or in pharmaceutical or other biomedical companies, these interests must not affect the way you prescribe for, treat or refer patients.

76 If you have a financial or commercial interest in an organisation to which you plan to refer a patient for treatment or investigation, you must tell the patient about your interest. When treating NHS patients you must also tell the healthcare purchaser.

Health

77 You should be registered with a general practitioner outside your family to ensure that you have access to independent and objective medical care. You should not treat yourself.

78 You should protect your patients, your colleagues and yourself by being immunised against common serious communicable diseases where vaccines are available.

79 If you know that you have, or think that you might have, a serious condition that you could pass on to patients, or if your judgement or performance could be affected by a condition or its treatment, you must consult a suitably qualified colleague. You must ask for and follow their advice about investigations, treatment and changes to your practice that they consider necessary. You must not rely on your own assessment of the risk you pose to patients.

Further reading

You can access these documents when viewing Good Medical Practice on our website (http://www.gmc-uk.org).

Supplementary ethical guidance from the GMC

This guidance expands upon the principles in Good Medical Practice to show how the principles apply in practice:

- Confidentiality: Protecting and providing information (April 2004)
- Conflicts of interest (November 2006)
- Maintaining boundaries (November 2006)
- Management for doctors (February 2006)
- Good practice in prescribing medicines (May 2006)
- Raising concerns about patient safety (November 2006)
- Reporting criminal and regulatory proceedings within and outside the UK (November 2006)
- Research: The role and responsibilities of doctors (February 2002)
- Seeking patients' consent: The ethical considerations (November 1998)
- Withholding and withdrawing life prolonging treatments: Good practice in decision making (August 2002)

Maintaining Boundaries (GMC: November 2006)

1. In our core guidance for doctors, *Good Medical Practice* we advise that:

- You must not use your professional position to establish or pursue a sexual or improper emotional relationship with a patient or someone close to them.
- You must treat patients with dignity.
- You must protect patients from risk of harm posed by another colleague's conduct . . . The safety of patients must come first at all times. If you have concerns that a colleague may not be fit to practise, you must take appropriate steps without delay, so that the concerns are investigated and patients protected where necessary.

This supplementary guidance is intended to provide more detail about how to comply with these principles.

2. Trust is a critical component in the doctor–patient partnership: patients must be able to trust doctors with their lives and health. In most successful doctor–patient relationships a professional boundary exists between doctor and patient. If this boundary is breached, this can undermine the patient's trust in their doctor, as well as the public's trust in the medical profession.

3. The doctor–patient relationship may involve an imbalance of power between the doctor and the patient. This could arise, for example, from the doctor having access to expertise and healthcare resources which the patient needs, or the possible vulnerability – emotional or physical – of a patient seeking healthcare. This may be particularly acute in some specialties such as psychiatry but can arise in any relationship between doctor and patient.

Sexual and Improper Emotional Relationships with Current and Former Patients

4. In order to maintain professional boundaries, and the trust of patients and the public, you must not establish or pursue a sexual or improper emotional relationship with a patient. You must not use your professional relationship with a patient to establish or pursue a relationship with someone close to them. For example, you must not use home visits to pursue a relationship with a member of a patient's family.

5. You must not pursue a sexual relationship with a former patient, where at the time of the professional relationship the patient was vulnerable, for example because of mental health problems, or because of their lack of maturity.

6. Pursuing a sexual relationship with a former patient may be inappropriate, regardless of the length of time elapsed since the therapeutic relationship ended. This is because it may be difficult to be certain that the professional relationship is not being abused.

7. If circumstances arise in which social contact with a former patient leads to the possibility of a sexual relationship beginning, you must use your professional judgement and give careful consideration to the nature and circumstances of the relationship, taking account of the following:

- when the professional relationship ended and how long it lasted
- the nature of the previous professional relationship
- whether the patient was particularly vulnerable at the time of the professional relationship, and whether they are still vulnerable
- whether you will be caring for other members of the patient's family.

8. If you are not sure whether you are – or could be seen to be – abusing your professional position, it may help to discuss your situation with an impartial colleague, a defence body, medical association or (confidentially) with a member of the GMC Standards and Ethics team.

Intimate Examinations

9. It is particularly important to maintain a professional boundary when examining patients: intimate examinations can be embarrassing or distressing for patients. Whenever you examine a patient you should be sensitive to what they may perceive as intimate. This is likely to include

examinations of breasts, genitalia and rectum, but could also include any examination where it is necessary to touch or even be close to the patient.

Chaperones

10. Wherever possible, you should offer the patient the security of having an impartial observer (a 'chaperone') present during an intimate examination. This applies whether or not you are the same gender as the patient.

11. A chaperone does not have to be medically qualified but will ideally:

- be sensitive, and respectful of the patient's dignity and confidentiality
- be prepared to reassure the patient if they show signs of distress or discomfort
- be familiar with the procedures involved in a routine intimate examination
- be prepared to raise concerns about a doctor if misconduct occurs.

In some circumstances, a member of practice staff, or a relative or friend of the patient may be an acceptable chaperone.

12. If either you or the patient does not wish the examination to proceed without a chaperone present , or if either of you is uncomfortable with the choice of chaperone, you may offer to delay the examination to a later date when a chaperone (or an alternative chaperone) will be available, if this is compatible with the patients best interests.

13. You should record any discussion about chaperones and its outcome. If a chaperone is present, you should record that fact and make a note of their identity. If the patient does not want a chaperone, you should record that the offer was made and declined.

Intimate examinations

14. Before conducting an intimate examination you should:

- explain to the patient why an examination is necessary and give the patient an opportunity to ask questions;
- explain what the examination will involve, in a way the patient can understand, so that the patient has a clear idea of what to expect, including any potential pain or discomfort;
- obtain the patient's permission before the examination and record that permission has been obtained;
- give the patient privacy to undress and dress and keep the patient covered as much as possible to maintain their dignity. Do not assist the patient in removing clothing unless you have clarified with them that your assistance is required.

15. During the examination you should:

- explain what you are going to do before you do it and, if this differs from what you have already outlined to the patient, explain why and seek the patient's permission;
- be prepared to discontinue the examination if the patient asks you to;
- keep discussion relevant and do not make unnecessary personal comments.

16. You must follow the guidance in *Seeking patients' consent: The ethical considerations*.

17. By highlighting some of the issues associated with intimate examinations, this guidance does not intend to deter you from carrying them out when necessary. Following this guidance and making detailed and accurate records at the time of examination, or shortly afterwards, will help you to justify your decisions and actions.

Intimate examinations of anaesthetised patients

18. You must obtain consent prior to anaesthetisation, usually in writing, for the intimate examination of anaesthetised patients.

19. If you are supervising a student you should ensure that valid consent has been obtained before they carry out any intimate examination under anaesthesia.

Sexualised Behaviour and Your Duty to Report

20. In order to maintain professional boundaries and the trust of patients and the public you must never make a sexual advance towards a patient nor display 'sexualised behaviour'. Sexualised behaviour has been defined as 'acts, words or behaviour designed or intended to arouse or gratify sexual impulses and desires'.

21. If you have grounds to believe that a colleague has, or may have demonstrated sexualised behaviour when with a patient, you must take appropriate steps without delay so that your concerns are investigated and patients protected where necessary. Where there is a suspicion that a sexual assault or other criminal activity has taken place, it should be reported to the police.

22. Guidance on steps you should take is included in *Good Medical Practice*, in *Management for doctors* and in the supplementary guidance, *Raising concerns about patient safety*.

23. If you are not sure what to do, discuss your concerns with an impartial colleague or contact your defence body, a professional organisation or the GMC for advice.

24. You should respect patient confidentiality wherever possible when reporting your concerns. Nevertheless, the safety of patients must come first at all times and therefore takes precedence over maintaining confidentiality. If you are satisfied that it is necessary to identify the patient, wherever practical you should seek the patient's consent to disclosure of any information and, if this is refused, inform the patient of your intention to disclose the information.

25. In all cases where a patient reports a breach of sexual boundaries, appropriate support and assistance must be offered to the patient. All such reports must be properly investigated, whatever the apparent credibility of the patient.

26. If a patient displays sexualised behaviour, wherever possible treat them politely and considerately and try to re-establish a professional boundary. If you should find it necessary to end the professional relationship you must follow the guidance in paragraphs 38–40 of Good Medical Practice.

A Guide for Doctors Referred to the GMC (2005)

(Excerpts)

Introduction

This booklet explains how the General Medical Council (GMC) deals with concerns about doctors that have been referred to us by patients, employers, the police and other bodies. This is only a guide to our procedures. It is not a substitute for obtaining independent advice from your defence organisation or solicitor. We have also produced a series of fact sheets that provide more detailed information on specific aspects of our procedures.

What is the GMC and what does it do?

The General Medical Council (GMC) regulates doctors in the United Kingdom. Its governing body – the Council – is made up of both doctors and members of the public.

The GMC:

- sets the standards of good medical practice which it expects of doctors throughout their working lives;
- assures the quality of undergraduate medical education in the UK and co-ordinates all stages of medical education;
- the GMC administers systems for the registration of doctors to control their entry to medical practice in the UK;
- deals firmly and fairly with doctors whose fitness to practise is questioned.

The reformed fitness to practise procedures implemented on 1 November 2004 allow us to look at all aspects of a doctor's fitness to practise. There are no longer separate streams for different types of cases. The nature of the investigation will vary according to the types of concerns that have been raised.

When can the GMC take action?

We can take action if the doctor's fitness to practise is impaired. This may be for a number of reasons:

- misconduct;
- deficient performance;
- a criminal conviction or caution in the British Isles (or elsewhere for an offence which would be a criminal offence if committed in England or Wales);
- physical or mental ill-health;
- a determination (decision) by a regulatory body either in the British Isles or overseas.

We can also issue a warning to a doctor where the doctor's fitness to practise is not impaired but there has been a significant departure from the principles set out in the GMC's guidance for doctors, *Good Medical Practice*. This will be disclosed to a doctor's employer and to any other enquirer during a five-year period. A warning will not be appropriate where the concerns relate exclusively to a doctor's physical or mental health.

Some of the concerns raised with us may not need any formal GMC action. Our procedures will consider the nature of the concerns and the evidence to assess what action, if any, may be required.

What action will the GMC take?

The GMC's procedures are divided into two separate stages: 'Investigation' and 'Adjudication'. In the investigation stage, we investigate cases to assess whether we need to refer them for adjudication. The adjudication stage consists of a hearing of the cases which we have referred to a Fitness to Practise panel.

Investigation

We will first consider any concerns to assess whether we need to investigate further, and if so, what form the investigation should take. In some cases, it will be clear from the start, that it is not appropriate for the GMC to investigate (for example, because it is not about a doctor or because the case clearly falls outside our criteria for taking action in relation to a doctor).

The GMC will not normally investigate complaints about matters that took place more than five years ago, unless it considers that it is in the public interest for the case to proceed. If we proceed with an investigation, we will inform you of the complaint and request details of your employer(s). You will also be given an opportunity to comment on the issues. The GMC's guidance to doctors, *Good Medical Practice,* makes it clear that doctors must co-operate fully with any formal inquiry into the treatment of a patient and with any complaints procedures that apply to their work. We will ask your employer(s) (normally the chief executive or medical director of the relevant Trust) if they have any other concerns about your practice. This ensures that we have a fuller picture about your fitness to practise and also allows us to feed into local clinical governance. At this stage we recognise that, in many cases, the concerns have not been investigated. Very often, the early dialogue with the doctor's employer means that we can conclude our investigation without taking any further action. Our investigation will depend very much on the nature of the concerns raised with us. Our investigation staff will decide on the most effective forms of investigation for the case. An investigation may include:

- obtaining further documentary evidence from employers, the complainant or other parties;
- obtaining witness statements;
- obtaining expert reports on clinical matters;
- an assessment of the doctor's performance;
- an assessment of the doctor's health.

If we consider that a doctor could be an immediate risk to patients, or it is in his/her own interest or the public interest, we can take immediate action to stop a doctor working by suspending their registration or by restricting their practice while we continue our investigations.

How long will the investigation take?

The length of the investigation depends on the complexity and seriousness of the concerns. We will complete the investigation as quickly and efficiently as we can and will keep you informed of progress.

What will happen at the end of the investigation?

At the end of the investigation by the GMC, the case will be considered by two senior GMC staff known as case examiners (one medical and one non-medical). They can:

- conclude the case with no further action;
- issue a warning;
- refer the case to a Fitness to Practise or an Interim Orders panel; or
- agree undertakings on health and performance issues following a health or performance assessment.

No case can be concluded or referred to a Fitness to Practise panel without the agreement of both a medical and non-medical case examiner. If they fail to agree, the matter will be considered by the Investigation Committee, a statutory committee of the GMC.

If the case examiners or the Investigation Committee decide that the doctor's fitness to practise is not impaired, they may issue a warning. A warning will be appropriate where the concerns indicate a significant departure from the standards set out in the GMC's guidance for doctors, *Good Medical Practice*, or if there is a significant cause for concern following assessment. The Investigation Committee will also consider cases where case examiners consider that a warning is appropriate, but where the doctor has disputed the facts, or requested a hearing of the Investigation Committee. The hearing will take place in public. We will inform both the doctor and the complainant of the case examiners' decision and their reasons.

Referring a doctor to a Fitness to Practise panel

Fitness to Practise panels form the final stage of our procedures. A panel consists of specially trained people who will hear all the evidence and will decide at the end of the hearing whether they need to take action regarding the doctor's registration. If we refer a case to a Fitness to Practise panel, we will write to the doctor setting out the specific allegations and explaining the process leading up to the panel hearing. Again, it will be important to seek advice from your defence organisation. Fitness to Practise panels will normally be held in public, except where a panel is considering evidence about a doctor's health. We also have special arrangements for vulnerable witnesses.

What happens at the end of a Fitness to Practise panel hearing?

At the end of the hearing the Fitness to Practise panel may decide that the doctor's fitness to practise is not impaired and will either take no action or issue a warning. Where they make a finding that the doctor's fitness to practise is impaired they may do one of the following:

- put conditions on the doctor's registration (this might mean the doctor is only allowed to do medical work under supervision or might restrict him/her to certain areas of practice);
- suspend the doctor's name from the medical register so that s/he cannot practise during the period of suspension;
- erase (remove) the doctor's name from the medical register so that s/he will not be able to work as a doctor in Great Britain for at least five years; the GMC's expectation is that erasure should normally be for life.

In deciding on the appropriate outcome, the panel my take into account any written undertakings made by the doctor.

If the panel decides to impose conditions on the doctor's registration, they may also impose an order for immediate conditions. If the panel directs that the doctor's registration should be suspended or that his/her name should be erased from the register, they may also impose an order for immediate suspension.

Warnings

A warning will be appropriate where concerns indicate a significant departure from the principles set out in the GMC's guidance for doctors, *Good Medical Practice*, or if there is a significant cause for concern following assessment but a restriction on the doctor's registration is not necessary. For more information on warnings please see the fact sheet which can be downloaded from our website.

Undertakings

Undertakings are an enforceable agreement between the GMC and the doctor about the doctor's future practice. They allow the GMC to deal effectively with cases where the issues relate to a doctor's health or performance without having to refer to a Fitness to Practise panel. Such undertakings might include restrictions on the practitioner's practice or behaviour, or commitments to have medical supervision or retraining. For more information on undertakings please see the fact sheet which can be downloaded from our website.

Interim Orders Panel

At any stage in the proceedings we may refer the doctor to the Interim Orders Panel (IOP). An IOP can suspend or restrict a doctor from practising while the investigation continues. For more information on the Interim Orders Panel please see the fact sheet which can be downloaded from our website.

Convictions and decisions by other regulatory bodies

Our rules allow us to deal quickly with doctors who have received a criminal conviction or caution or who have been subject to a decision by a regulatory body either in the British Isles or overseas. We treat convictions, cautions and determinations by other regulatory bodies as proof of that offence. In many cases, particularly where the doctor has received a custodial sentence, the case will be referred directly to a Fitness to Practise panel for a hearing. Certain categories of conviction cases (such as parking offences) will be closed at a very early stage with no further investigation or action.

Appeal

A doctor has 28 days in which to appeal to the High Court or Court of Sessions against any decision by a Fitness to Practise panel. The panel's decision will not take effect until either the appeal period expires or the appeal is determined. However, the panel can impose an immediate order for suspension or conditions if it believes it needs to protect the public or if it is in the best interests of the doctor.

Council for Healthcare Regulatory Excellence

The Council for Healthcare Regulatory Excellence (CHRE) has the power to refer a decision by a Fitness to Practise panel to the High Court (or its equivalent elsewhere in the UK) for the protection of the public, if it considers that the decision is unduly lenient. The CHRE has 28 days to decide whether to refer a decision following the doctor's 28-day appeal period.

Advice

If you are subject to investigation or action by the GMC you should contact your medical defence organisation straight away. The defence organizations know our procedures well and are a good source of advice. They can offer you legal support if you need it.

If you are not a member of a defence organisation, you could contact the British Medical Association or another professional organisation of which you are a member. They may not be able to provide legal representation but they are a good source of expert advice and support.

Alternatively, you can get your own legal advice, at your own expense. Legal aid is not available to doctors being investigated under our procedures. You cannot claim costs from the other parties involved.

Part V

Human Fertilisation and Embryology Code of Practice (2004)

(6th Edition, 2003)

[Footnotes omitted]

Part 3 Welfare of the Child and the Assessment of Those Seeking Treatment

General Obligations

Human Fertilisation and Embryology Act 1990

Section 13

(1) The following shall be conditions of every licence under paragraph 1 of Schedule 2 to this Act . . .

(5) A woman shall not be provided with treatment services unless account has been taken of the welfare of any child who may be born as a result of the treatment (including the need of that child for a father) and of any other child who may be affected by the birth.

3.1 When considering the treatment of any woman, treatment centres must take into account the welfare of the child that may be born as a result of treatment. Treatment centres are expected to also consider the welfare of any children the woman may already have responsibility for and the effect that treatment could have on these children. Treatment centre staff are expected to be aware of the need to show both care and sensitivity in this decision making process. Consideration is expected to be taken regarding the wishes and needs of those seeking treatment and the needs of any children involved.

3.2 Treatment centres are expected to take reasonable steps to ensure:

    (i)   The safety of those seeking treatment and

    (ii) The protection of any resulting or affected child or children.

3.3 Treatment centres are expected to ensure that they have clear written criteria for assessing the welfare of any child or children which may be born or which may be affected by the birth of such child or children. Those criteria are expected to include the importance of a stable and supportive environment for any and all children who are part of an existing or prospective family group.

3.4 Best practice is expected to include an assessment of the welfare of the child upon first contact for licensed treatment with the prospective patients. If there is a delay before treatment takes place, treatment centres are expected to establish that no changes of circumstances have occurred since the original assessment of the welfare of the child before proceeding with treatment.

3.5 Treatment centres are expected to repeat the welfare of the child assessment where there has been:

> (i) A gap of two years or more in contact between the clinic and the patient(s) or
> (ii) A change of partner or
> (iii) A child born to the patient(s) since the previous assessment or
> (iv) A significant change in the prospective patient's medical or social circumstances.

3.6 Treatment centres are expected to take all reasonable steps to verify the identity of those seeking treatment. This might be achieved through information from both partners' GP. However, if consent to this disclosure of information from both partners' GP is not given, or the patient(s) are from abroad, the patient is expected to be required to provide additional confirmation of identity e.g. birth certificate, passport.

3.7 Women over 35 and men over 45 are expected – like all patients – to be offered clinical advice and counselling at the outset. Advice and counselling is expected to focus on the implications of age for success in treatment. Gametes of patients in these age groups are expected to be used only for their own or their partner's treatment.

3.8 Gametes for use in treatment may only be taken from patients under the age of 18 in the following exceptional circumstances:

> (i) If it is the intention to use such gametes for the patient's own treatment or for the use of the patient's partner and
> (ii) If the centre is able to satisfy itself that the patient is capable of giving and actually gives effective consent to the use or storage of those gametes.

3.9 Sperm to be used for the purposes of research may be taken from a male under the age of 18 only if the centre is able to satisfy itself that the donor is capable of giving, and actually gives, effective consent to such use.

3.10 It is expected that eggs shall not to be taken from a female under the age of 18 for the purposes of storage or licensed research without informing the HFEA.

Welfare Of The Child

3.11 Treatment centres are expected to:

> (i) Take reasonable steps to determine who will have parental responsibility for the child or children which may be born as a result of treatment and
> (ii) Take reasonable steps to determine the person or persons responsible for raising such child or children and
> (iii) Take particular care where the child is to be raised in another country and where the law may be different from that in this jurisdiction. In such cases patients are expected to have counselling on the implications for the potential child and all others who could be affected (particularly when using donated gametes) especially if the treatment requested is considered illegal in the country of origin.

3.12 Those seeking treatment are entitled to a fair assessment. Treatment centres are expected to conduct the assessment with skill and care, and have regard to the wishes and sensitivities of all those involved. This assessment is expected to take into account the following factors relating to patients:

> (i) The commitment to raise children
> (ii) The ability to provide a stable and supportive environment for a child/children
> (iii) Immediate and family medical histories
> (iv) The age, health and ability to provide for the needs of a child/children
> (v) The risk of harm to children including:
> > (a) inherited disorders or transmissible disease
> > (b) multiple births
> > (c) problems arising during pregnancy
> > (d) neglect or abuse
> > (e) the effect of a new baby or babies upon any existing child of the family.

3.13 Where donated gametes are used, treatment centres are expected to take into account the following additional factors:
- (i) A child's potential need to know about their origins and whether or not the prospective parents are prepared for the questions which may arise while the child is growing up
- (ii) Family attitudes towards such a child
- (iii) Implications which may arise if the donor is known within the child's family or social circle
- (iv) The possibility of disputed fatherhood.

Other Issues To Be Taken Into Account

3.14 **Where the child will have no legal father** the treatment centre is expected to assess the prospective mother's ability to meet the child's/children's needs and the ability of other persons within the family or social circle willing to share responsibility for those needs.

3.15 **Where the couple are not married** couples are expected to be advised that their legal position as parents, whether or not donated gametes are used, may require legal advice in order for full parental responsibility to be achieved.

Surrogate Pregnancy

3.16 **Where the child will not be raised by the carrying mother** all involved parties are expected to be made aware that the child's legal parent will be the carrying mother (and in certain circumstances could be her husband or partner) unless relevant court proceedings are carried out. Treatment centres are expected to – where possible – assess the possibility of a dispute in such circumstances and the effect upon the child, and the effect of any proposed arrangement upon a child or children of the family of the carrying mother or commissioning parents.

3.17 Treatment centres are expected to consider the use of assisted conception techniques to produce a surrogate pregnancy only where the commissioning mother is unable for physical or other medical reasons to carry a child or where her health may be impaired by doing so.

Selection Of Donated Gametes

3.18 Where treatment is provided for a man and woman together, treatment centres are expected to strive as far as possible to match the physical characteristics and ethnic background of the donor to those of the infertile partner, or in the case of embryo donation, to both partners, unless there are good reasons for departing from this procedure.

3.19 When discussing the selection of potential donors, treatment centres are expected to be sensitive to the wishes of those seeking treatment for information, whilst avoiding the possibility that this information could be used to select a donor possessing certain characteristics for reasons that are incompatible with or not relevant to the welfare of the child. For example, those seeking treatment are expected not to be treated with gametes provided by a donor of different physical characteristics unless there are compelling reasons for doing so. Those seeking treatment with donated gametes (or embryos) are expected to be advised that no guarantees can be given where an attempt is made to match physical characteristics.

Enquiries To Be Made

3.20 In their assessment of prospective patients, treatment centres are expected to:
- (i) Take medical and social histories from each prospective parent and see each couple together and separately
- (ii) Obtain the patients' consent to make enquiries of each of their GPs. Refusal by the patients, or either of them, to give such consent is a factor to be taken into consideration in the decision to provide treatment. In such circumstances, the treatment centre is expected to ask the patient's reason for the refusal and record the answer in the patient's medical records. In the absence of such consent, treatment centres are expected to seek to establish the identity of the patient(s) by appropriate evidence, e.g. passport, photocard driving licence and birth certificate

(iii) Once the relevant consents have been received from the prospective patients, ask the GP of both partners if he/she knows of any reason why the patient(s) might not be suitable for treatment and if he/she knows of anything which might adversely affect the welfare of any resulting child

(iv) Where unsatisfactory responses or no responses to enquiries are received, obtain the further consent from the prospective patient(s) to approach any individuals, agencies or authorities for such further information as the centre deems to be required for a satisfactory assessment. (A response may be deemed to be unsatisfactory, for example, where prospective parents have had children removed from their care or committed a relevant criminal offence.) Refusal by the prospective parents or either of them to give such consent is a factor to be taken into consideration in the decision whether or not to provide treatment.

Multidisciplinary Assessment

3.21 In deciding whether to provide treatment, treatment centres are expected to take into account views from the staff who have had involvement with the prospective patients. Those seeking treatment are expected to be given the opportunity to respond to adverse comments and objections before a final decision is made.

3.22 Where adverse information has been provided in confidence to a member of staff at the treatment centre, consent is expected to be sought from the information provider to discuss it with other members of staff. Where such consent is refused but the member of staff considers the matter as crucial to the decision to be taken, treatment centres are expected to use their discretion based upon good professional practice before breaking that confidence.

3.23 Treatment centres are expected to base their decision to refuse to provide treatment upon all available information. Treatment may be refused if the treatment centre concludes:

(i)   That it would not be in the interests of any resulting child or
(ii) That it would not be in the interests of any other child or
(iii) That it is unable to obtain sufficient information or advice upon which to base a proper assessment or
(iv) That, having regard to all the circumstances, it is inappropriate to offer such treatment.

3.24 Where treatment is refused treatment centres are expected to:

(i)   Explain the reasons for such refusal to the woman and – where appropriate – her partner, together with any circumstances which may cause the treatment centre to reconsider its decision and
(ii) Explain any remaining options and
(iii) Explain opportunities for obtaining appropriate counselling.

Written Record In Respect Of The Welfare Of The Child

3.25 Treatment centres are expected to record in writing information that has been considered in respect of the welfare of the child. This record is expected to reflect the views of those who were consulted in reaching the decision and the views of those seeking treatment.

Additional Information For Those Seeking Long Term Storage Of Gametes And Embryos

3.26 Centres are expected to seek to obtain the clients' consent to approach the GPs of each partner. Failure to give such consent is expected to be taken into account in the decision whether or not to store or accept gametes or embryos for treatment or research.

3.27 Where such consent is given, centres are expected to ask the GP(s) if they have information relevant to the storage of such gametes or embryos which they are prepared to disclose to the HFEA.

Additional Information For Those Seeking An Egg Sharing Arrangement

3.28 In addition to considering the general advice given above (paragraphs 3.1 – 3.10), treatment centres are expected to have clear written procedures for welfare of the child assessments in respect of:

(i)   The egg provider

(ii) The egg recipient(s)

(iii) The partners of the egg provider and the egg recipient.

3.29 Treatment centres are expected to ensure that:

(i)   Care is taken in the selection of egg providers in egg sharing arrangements and

(ii) Egg providers are fully assessed and medically suitable and

(iii) The treatment offered is the most suitable available to satisfy the needs of the egg provider and recipient(s).

3.30 Treatment centres are expected to offer counselling to egg providers and recipients and to the partners of women donating and receiving eggs and any other individuals directly affected. There is expected to be the opportunity for the donor to receive counselling from a different counsellor from the one providing counselling to the recipient.

3.31 Treatment centres are expected to provide any additional impartial support (e.g. a member of the nursing staff not involved in the treatment of either donor or recipient) to all parties during the egg sharing cycle.

Part 4 Assessing and Screening Potential Donors

General Standards

4.1 Where individuals are considering donation, from the outset treatment centres are expected to:

(i)   Ensure that those individuals considering donation understand which tests must be carried out and why they are necessary and

(ii) Inform these individuals that the tests may reveal previously unsuspected conditions, including low sperm counts, genetic anomalies and HIV infection and

(iii) Enquire of these individuals whether they have previously provided gametes at a different treatment centre, and if so, establish that the limit of 10 live birth events per donor will not be exceeded (see also paragraph 8.30) and

(iv) Inform them that they can withdraw from the process of donation at any time until embryos or gametes have been used in treatment and

(v)   Ensure that no pressure or undue influence is applied to donate sperm, eggs or embryos by clinic staff, friends or relatives and

(vi) Give full, up-to-date advice on the position of the HFEA Register regarding circumstances under which donors' information, both identifying and non-identifying, might be disclosed and

(vii) Ensure that any donor and their partner are given the opportunity to be seen by an independent counsellor to explore the implications of donation for all concerned.

Human Fertilisation and Embryology Act 1990

Section 12

The following shall be conditions of every licence granted under this Act – (e) that no money or other benefit shall be given or received in respect of any supply of gametes or embryos unless authorised by directions.

4.2 Payments or benefits may be provided in exchange for gametes or embryos only in accordance with Directions made by the HFEA (see 4.26 below). These include those payments or benefits which, to the knowledge of the treatment centre, have been made to an agency or other intermediary.

4.3 Reasonable expenses incurred by an egg donor who becomes ill as a direct result of donating, may also be reimbursed by the treatment centre.

Family And Other Relevant History

4.4 Before gametes are provided, medical and family histories are expected to be taken and are expected to include details of previous donations. Donors are also expected to be encouraged to provide as much other non-identifying biographical information as possible, so that it may be available to prospective parents and resulting children. If a donor cannot give a full and accurate family history, treatment centres are expected to record this fact.

4.5 Treatment centres are expected to, wherever possible, ask prospective donors' GPs if they know of any reason why the prospective donor should not donate for the treatment of others. Failure to obtain relevant information is expected to be taken into account when deciding whether or not to accept gametes or embryos for treatment.

4.6 Before approaching the relevant GP, treatment centres are expected to obtain the donor's consent. Failure to give such consent or obtain relevant information is expected to be taken into account in deciding whether or not to accept gametes or embryos for treatment.

4.7 Where consent to approach the GP is refused, treatment centres are expected to consider asking for proof of identification in the form of a birth certificate, passport or similar documentation. Failure to provide satisfactory evidence of identification is expected to be taken into account in deciding whether or not to accept gametes or embryos for treatment.

Suitability As Donors

4.8 Before accepting gametes for the treatment of others, treatment centres are expected to consider the suitability of the intending donor. All potential donors must be given suitable opportunities to receive counselling. Where this involves embryos the counselling is expected to be offered to both partners of the donating couple. The views of all treatment centre personnel involved with the prospective donor are expected to be taken into account. In particular, treatment centres are expected to consider:

    (i)   Personal or family history of heritable disorders and

    (ii) Personal history of transmissible infection and

    (iii) The level of potential fertility indicated by semen analysis (where appropriate) and

    (iv) If the prospective donor has children, the implications for the prospective donor in respect of the donation for themselves and their existing families and any offspring born of their donation both in the short and longer term and

    (v) If the prospective donor does not have children, the implications for themselves and any future family.

Potential Donors Undergoing Treatment

4.9 It is expected that the possibility of donating gametes should be raised before and not during a potential donor's treatment cycle. It is expected to be raised by the counsellor rather than by anyone directly involved in that person's treatment. There must be no pressure or undue influence on a patient to donate supernumerary gametes or embryos. It is expected that counselling should be offered in all cases.

Scientific Tests

4.10 It is expected that all reasonable steps should be taken to prevent the transmission of serious genetic disorders. This will usually be served by taking a thorough history from the prospective donor.

4.11 It is expected that genetic testing should be limited to the determination of carrier status for inherited recessive disorders in which abnormal test results carry no significant direct health implications for the prospective donor.

4.12 Centres are expected to ensure that where prospective donors are genetically tested, they have the same level of support and counselling as recipients. They are expected to be informed of the test results and offered post test counselling as applicable.

4.13 **Cystic Fibrosis**. Normally, treatment centres are expected to screen prospective donors especially if they emanate from a population group which contains a high frequency of cystic fibrosis carriers. Where a treatment centre uses unscreened donors it is expected to inform the patient concerned and offer screening and counselling. Where a treatment centre uses screened donors, it is expected to caution the patient about the limits of the test and the likelihood that a screened donor could be a cystic fibrosis carrier. In exceptional circumstances (e.g. difficulty in replacing a donor) treatment centres may use a cystic fibrosis positive donor. In such circumstances, the patient is expected to be made aware of the risks associated with this practice and offered relevant screening and counselling.

4.14 **Tay-Sachs, Thalassaemia and Sickle Cell anaemia.** It is expected that screening should be carried out in appropriate population groups.

4.15 **HIV testing.** The minimum procedure to be adopted is expected to be that set out in the HFEA and Department of Health's HIV Screening For People Providing Gametes And/Or Embryos For Donation guide (see Appendix C).

4.16 **Cytomegalovirus (CMV) antibodies.** Treatment centres are expected to screen all those considering such donation for cytomegalovirus antibodies. Wherever possible, treatment centres are expected to use CMV seronegative donors, and are expected to ensure that gametes from those who are CMV seropositive are used only for CMV seropositive recipients. Only those seropositive prospective donors who are unlikely to have an active infection (IgG positive and IgM negative) are expected to be used. Gametes from a seronegative potential donor who seroconverts during the course of donation must not be used for treatment services.

4.17 Testing of potential donors for other infections is expected to (for sperm) follow the British Andrology Society guidelines and (for eggs and embryos) the British Fertility Society guidelines (see Appendix F).

4.18 It is essential that all recipients of gamete donations receive information explaining the limitations of testing procedures and the risks associated with treatment. If any concerns are raised appropriate counselling is expected to be made available.

4.19 Centres are expected to re-screen people considering donation where appropriate, and adopt any other test which may come to be regarded as a matter of good practice by the standards of professional colleagues in relevant specialities or may be indicated in a particular case while this *Code* is in force.

4.20 Where an embryo is donated for clinical treatment, each donating party is expected to undergo full screening as recommended for potential gamete donors (see paragraphs 4.10–4.19 above).

4.21 Gamete providers in surrogacy arrangements are expected to be screened in accordance with the usual requirements for potential donors. The screening is expected to comply with the advice given in paragraphs 4.10–4.20 above and that are set out in Appendix C of this *Code of Practice*.

Age Of People Considering Donation

4.22 Unless there are exceptional reasons for doing so, it is expected that sperm should not be taken for the treatment of others from donors over the age of 45. Such exceptional reasons are expected to be explained in the treatment records.

4.23 Unless there are exceptional reasons for doing so, it is expected that eggs should not be taken for the treatment of others from donors over the age of 35. Such exceptional reasons are expected to be explained in the treatment records.

4.24 It is expected that gametes for the treatment of others shall not be taken from anyone under the age of 18.

4.25 Where gametes are used to produce embryos specifically for donation, or embryos are donated following licensed fertility treatment, treatment centres are expected to follow the age limits that exist for gamete donors – 35 for egg donors and 45 for sperm donors – unless there are exceptional reasons for not doing so. If there are exceptional reasons, these are expected to be explained in the treatment records.

Payment And Expenses For People Providing Gametes For Donation

4.26 Gamete donors must be paid no more than £15 for each donation plus reasonable expenses in accordance with HFEA Directions (see guidance in Appendix G).

People Unsuitable As Donors

4.27 Where a treatment centre decides that a potential donor is unsuitable for donation, it is expected to record the reasons and also explain these to the individual concerned. The reasoning behind the treatment centre's decision should be presented to the relevant individual sensitively and any questions answered in a straightforward and comprehensive manner.

4.28 It is expected that counselling should be offered to all potential donors who are deemed to be unsuitable for any reason. Where a treatment centre refuses to accept a potential gamete donor because of physical or psychological problems that require separate treatment or specialist counselling, the treatment centre is expected to provide reasonable assistance to the individual in obtaining relevant treatment or counselling.

4.29 Where information affecting the suitability of a potential donor becomes known after the selection process is complete, the treatment centre is expected to review the potential donor's suitability and take appropriate action.

4.30 Where a treatment centre learns that a gamete donor has a previously unsuspected genetic disease or is the carrier of a deleterious recessively inherited condition (e.g. through the birth of a baby with cystic fibrosis), the treatment centre is expected to:

> (i) Notify the supplying centre and the HFEA immediately. (The supplying centre is expected to notify other centres of the carrier status of the gamete donor) and
>
> (ii) Consider notifying the gamete donor of their condition, and where the gamete donor has been informed of their condition, offer counselling and testing and
>
> (iii) Inform patients who have received treatment using those donor gametes where the treatment has resulted in a live birth, and offer these patients counselling and
>
> (iv) Where a woman is pregnant as a result of treatment with those donor gametes, carefully consider when and how the woman should be given this information.

4.31 Centres are expected to advise gamete donors that where, subsequent to a donation being made, the donor discovers they are affected by a previously unsuspected genetic disease or finds they are a carrier of a deleterious recessively inherited condition (e.g. through the birth of a baby with cystic fibrosis), they are expected to inform the centre which accepted the donation as soon as possible. The centre is expected to then proceed as in paragraph 4.28 above.

People Involved In An Egg Sharing Arrangement

4.32 It is expected that egg providers shall be treated in the same way as other potential gamete donors (see paragraphs 4.10–4.18 above and Appendix C).

4.33 It is expected that egg providers and recipients shall be made aware, prior to consent, of the screening that will be undertaken before treatment is commenced.

Part VI

Scotland

Age of Legal Capacity (Scotland) Act 1991

1991 c. 50

Age of legal capacity.
1.—(1) As from the commencement of this Act –

    (a) a person under the age of 16 years shall, subject to section 2 below, have no legal capacity to enter into any transaction;

    (b) a person of or over the age of 16 years shall have legal capacity to enter into any transaction.

Exceptions to general rule.
2.—(1) A person under the age of 16 years shall have legal capacity to enter into a transaction—

    (a) of a kind commonly entered into by persons of his age and circumstances, and

    (b) on terms which are not unreasonable.

    (4) A person under the age of 16 years shall have legal capacity to consent on his own behalf to any surgical, medical or dental procedure or treatment where, in the opinion of a qualified medical practitioner attending him, he is capable of understanding the nature and possible consequences of the procedure or treatment.

Adults with Incapacity (Scotland) Act 2000

2000 asp 4

Part 1

General

1 General principles and fundamental definitions

(1) The principles set out in subsections (2) to (4) shall be given effect to in relation to any intervention in the affairs of an adult under or in pursuance of this Act, including any order made in or for the purpose of any proceedings under this Act for or in connection with an adult.

(2) There shall be no intervention in the affairs of an adult unless the person responsible for authorising or effecting the intervention is satisfied that the intervention will benefit the adult and that such benefit cannot reasonably be achieved without the intervention.

(3) Where it is determined that an intervention as mentioned in subsection (1) is to be made, such intervention shall be the least restrictive option in relation to the freedom of the adult, consistent with the purpose of the intervention.

(4) In determining if an intervention is to be made and, if so, what intervention is to be made, account shall be taken of –

(a) the present and past wishes and feelings of the adult so far as they can be ascertained by any means of communication, whether human or by mechanical aid (whether of an interpretative nature or otherwise) appropriate to the adult;

(b) the views of the nearest relative and the primary carer of the adult, in so far as it is reasonable and practicable to do so;

(c) the views of –

(i) any guardian, continuing attorney or welfare attorney of the adult who has powers relating to the proposed intervention; and

(ii) any person whom the sheriff has directed to be consulted, in so far as it is reasonable and practicable to do so; and

(d) the views of any other person appearing to the person responsible for authorising or effecting the intervention to have an interest in the welfare of the adult or in the proposed intervention, where these views have been made known to the person responsible, in so far as it is reasonable and practicable to do so.

(5) Any guardian, continuing attorney, welfare attorney or manager of an establishment exercising functions under this Act or under any order of the sheriff in relation to an adult shall, in so far as it is reasonable and practicable to do so, encourage the adult to exercise whatever skills he has concerning his property, financial affairs or personal welfare, as the case may be, and to develop new such skills.

(6) For the purposes of this Act, and unless the context otherwise requires –

'adult' means a person who has attained the age of 16 years;

'incapable' means incapable of –

(a) acting; or

(b) making decisions; or

(c) communicating decisions; or

(d) understanding decisions; or

(e) retaining the memory of decisions, as mentioned in any provision of this Act, by reason of mental disorder or of inability to communicate because of physical disability; but a person shall not fall within this definition by reason only of a lack or deficiency in a faculty of communication if that lack or deficiency can be made good by human or mechanical aid (whether of an interpretative nature or otherwise); and

'incapacity' shall be construed accordingly.

(7) In subsection (4)(c)(i) any reference to –

(a) a guardian shall include a reference to a guardian (however called) appointed under the law of any country to, or entitled under the law of any country to act for, an adult during his incapacity, if the guardianship is recognised by the law of Scotland;

(b) a continuing attorney shall include a reference to a person granted, under a contract, grant or appointment governed by the law of any country, powers (however expressed), relating to the granter's property or financial affairs and having continuing effect notwithstanding the granter's incapacity;

(c) a welfare attorney shall include a reference to a person granted, under a contract, grant or appointment governed by the law of any country, powers (however expressed) relating to the granter's personal welfare and having effect during the granter's incapacity.

Appeal against decision as to incapacity

14   Appeal against decision as to incapacity

A decision taken for the purposes of this Act, other than by the sheriff, as to the incapacity of an adult may be appealed by –

(a) the adult; or

(b) any person claiming an interest in the adult's property, financial affairs or personal welfare relating to the purpose for which the decision was taken, to the sheriff or, where the decision was taken by the sheriff, to the sheriff principal and thence, with the leave of the sheriff principal, to the Court of Session.

Human Tissue (Scotland) Act 2006

2006 asp 4

Part 1 Transplantation Etc.

General functions of the Scottish Ministers

1   Duties of the Scottish Ministers as respects transplantation, donation of body parts etc.

It is the duty of the Scottish Ministers to –

(a) promote, support and develop programmes of transplantation;

(b) promote information and awareness about the donation for transplantation of parts of a human body;

(c) promote the taking of any necessary measures relating to the quality and safety, storage and use of any such part donated for that purpose.

Use of part of body of deceased person for transplantation, research etc.

3   Use of part of body of deceased person for transplantation, research etc.

(1) Part of the body of a deceased person may be removed from the body and used, for the purposes of –

(a) transplantation;

(b) research;

(c) education or training;

(d) audit, only if the requirements of subsection (2) are satisfied as respects the part.

(2) The requirements are that –

(a) the removal and use for the purpose in question are authorised in accordance with section 6, 7, 8, 9 or, as the case may be, 10; and

(b) the removal is carried out in accordance with section 11.

4 Disapplication of sections 3, 6 to 11 and 16 in certain circumstances

Sections 3, 6 to 11 and 16 do not apply –

(a) to anything done for the purposes of the functions or under the authority of the procurator fiscal ...

5 Consent by procurator fiscal to removal of part of body

(1) Where a person knows, or has reason to believe, that an examination of the body of a deceased person is, or may be, required for the purposes of the functions of the procurator fiscal, the person may not, except with the consent of the procurator fiscal, remove from the body any part of it, or authorise such removal, for a purpose referred to in section 3(1).

6 Authorisation: adult

(1) An adult may authorise the removal and use of a part of the adult's body after the adult's death for one or more of the purposes referred to in section 3(1).

(2) Authorisation by virtue of subsection (1) –

(a) must be –

(i) in writing; or

(ii) expressed verbally;

(b) subject to subsections (3) and (4), may be withdrawn in writing.

(3) If the adult is blind or unable to write, withdrawal of authorisation by virtue of subsection (2)(b) may be signed by another adult (a 'signatory') on the adult's behalf and if it is so signed it must be witnessed by one witness.

(4) Withdrawal of authorisation which is signed by a signatory on behalf of an adult by virtue of subsection (3) must contain a statement signed by both the signatory and the witness in the presence of the adult and of each other that the adult, in the presence of them both, expressed the intention to withdraw the authorisation and requested the signatory to sign the withdrawal on behalf of the adult.

(5) Nothing in subsection (3) prevents an adult who is blind from withdrawing, in accordance with subsection (2)(b), any authorisation by virtue of subsection (1).

(6) In subsection (2)(a)(i), 'writing' includes, in relation to the requirement there for authorisation to be in writing, representation of a character in visible form.

7 Authorisation by adult's nearest relative

(1) If there is in force immediately before an adult's death no authorisation by the adult by virtue of section 6(1) of removal and use of any part of the adult's body for transplantation, the nearest relative of the deceased adult may, subject to subsection (4), authorise the removal and use of any part for one or more of the purposes referred to in section 3(1).

(2) If –

(a) there is in force immediately before an adult's death authorisation by the adult by virtue of section 6(1) of removal and use of a part of the adult's body for transplantation;

(b) the authorisation does not expressly include removal and use of the part for a particular purpose referred to in paragraphs (b) to (d) of section 3(1), the nearest relative of the deceased adult may, subject to subsection (4), authorise the removal and use of the part for the particular purpose in question which is not included in the authorisation.

(3) If –

(a) there is in force immediately before an adult's death authorisation by the adult by virtue of section 6(1) of removal and use of a particular part of the adult's body for transplantation;

(b) the authorisation does not expressly include removal and use of another particular part, the nearest relative of the deceased adult may, subject to subsection (4), authorise the removal and use of the other particular part which is not so included for one or more of the purposes referred to in paragraphs (b) to (d) of section 3(1).

(4) The nearest relative may not give authorisation under –

(a) subsection (1) if the relative has actual knowledge that the adult was unwilling for any part of the adult's body, or the part in question, to be used for transplantation;

(b) subsection (2) if the relative has actual knowledge that the adult was unwilling for the part to be used for the purpose in question;

(c) subsection (3) if the relative has actual knowledge that the adult was unwilling for any other part of the adult's body or, as the case may be, the other particular part in question, to be used for transplantation.

(5) For the purposes of –

(a) subsection (4)(a), the mere fact that there is no authorisation by the adult in force is not to be regarded as unwillingness by the adult referred to in that subsection;

(b) subsection (4)(b), the mere fact that the authorisation does not include a particular purpose referred to in paragraphs (b) to (d) of section 3(1) is not to be regarded as unwillingness by the adult referred to in that subsection;

(c) subsection (4)(c), the mere fact that there is no authorisation by the adult in force as respects the removal and use of other parts, or the other particular part in question, for transplant- ation is not to be regarded as unwillingness by the adult referred to in that subsection.

(6) Authorisation by virtue of subsection (1), (2) or (3) –

(a) must be –

(i)   in writing and signed; or

(ii) expressed verbally, by the nearest relative;

(b) subject to subsection (7), may be withdrawn in writing so signed.

(7) To the extent that authorisation by virtue of subsection (1) is for the purposes of trans- plantation, it may not be withdrawn.

8   Authorisation: child 12 years of age or over

(1) A child who is 12 years of age or over may authorise the removal and use of a part of the child's body after the child's death for one or more of the purposes referred to in section 3(1).

(2) Subject to subsections (3) to (5), authorisation by virtue of subsection (1) –

(a) must be in writing;

(b) may be withdrawn in writing.

(3) If the child is blind or unable to write, authorisation by virtue of subsection (1) and withdrawal of such authorisation may be signed by an adult (a 'signatory') on the child's behalf and if it is so signed it must be witnessed by one witness.

(4) Authorisation by virtue of subsection (1), or withdrawal of such authorisation, which is signed by a signatory on behalf of a child by virtue of subsection (3) must contain a statement signed by both the signatory and the witness in the presence of the child and of each other that the child, in the presence of them both, expressed the intention to give the authorisation or, as the case may be, withdraw the authorisation and requested the signatory to sign the authorisation or, as the case may be, the withdrawal on behalf of the child.

(5) Authorisation by virtue of subsection (1) which is signed by a signatory on behalf of a child by virtue of subsection (3) must contain or be accompanied by –

(a) certification in writing signed by the signatory that, in the opinion of the signatory;

(b) certification in writing signed by the witness that, in the opinion of the witness, the child understands the effect of the authorisation and is not acting under undue influ- ence in giving it.

(6) Nothing in subsection (3) prevents a child who is blind from giving authorisation by virtue of subsection (1) in accordance with subsection (2)(a) or withdrawing, in accordance with sub- section (2)(b), any authorisation by the child by virtue of subsection (1) (including authorisation signed by a signatory in accordance with subsection (3)).

(7) In subsection (2)(a), 'writing' includes, in relation to the requirement there for author- isation to be in writing, but only where the authorisation in writing is not signed by a signatory on behalf of the child, representation of a character in visible form.

9   Authorisation as respects child who dies 12 years of age or over by person with parental rights and responsibilities

(1) If there is in force immediately before the death of a child who died 12 years of age or over no authorisation by the child by virtue of section 8(1) of removal and use of any part of the child's body for transplantation, a person who, immediately before the death, had parental rights and parental responsibilities in relation to the child (but who is not a local authority) may, subject to subsection (4), authorise removal and use of any part for one or more of the purposes referred to in section 3(1).

(2) If –

    (a) there is in force immediately before the death of a child who died 12 years of age or over authorisation by the child by virtue of section 8(1) of removal and use of a part of the child's body for transplantation;

    (b) the authorisation does not expressly include removal and use of the part for a particular purpose referred to in paragraphs (b) to (d) of section 3(1), a person who, immediately before the death, had parental rights and parental responsibilities in relation to the child (but who is not a local authority) may, subject to subsection (4), authorise the removal and use of the part for the particular purpose in question which is not included in the authorisation.

(3) If –

    (a) there is in force immediately before the child's death authorisation by the child by virtue of section 8(1) of removal and use of a particular part of the child's body for transplantation;

    (b) the authorisation does not expressly include removal and use of another particular part, a person who, immediately before the death, had parental rights and parental responsibilities in relation to the child (but who is not a local authority) may, subject to subsection (4), authorise the removal and use of the other particular part which is not so included for one or more of the purposes referred to in paragraphs (b) to (d) of section 3(1).

(4) A person may not give authorisation under –

    (a) subsection (1) if the person has actual knowledge that the child was unwilling for any part of the child's body, or the part in question, to be used for transplantation;

    (b) subsection (2) if the person has actual knowledge that the child was unwilling for the part to be used for the purpose in question;

    (c) subsection (3) if the person has actual knowledge that the child was unwilling for any other part of the child's body or, as the case may be, the other particular part in question, to be used for transplantation.

(5) For the purposes of –

    (a) subsection (4)(a), the mere fact that there is no authorisation by the child in force is not to be regarded as unwillingness by the child referred to in that subsection;

    (b) subsection (4)(b), the mere fact that the authorisation by the child does not include a particular purpose referred to in paragraphs (b) to (d) of section 3(1) is not to be regarded as unwillingness by the child referred to in that subsection;

    (c) subsection (4)(c), the mere fact that there is no authorisation by the child in force as respects the removal and use of other parts, or the other particular part in question, for transplantation is not to be regarded as unwillingness by the child as referred to in that subsection.

(6) Authorisation by virtue of subsection (1), (2) or (3) –

    (a) must be –

        (i)   in writing and signed; or

        (ii) expressed verbally, by the person who gives the authorisation in accordance with that subsection;

    (b) subject to subsection (7), may be withdrawn in writing signed by the person.

(7) To the extent that authorisation by virtue of subsection (1) is for the purposes of transplantation, it may not be withdrawn.

10   Authorisation as respects child who dies under 12 years of age

(1) A person who immediately before the death of a child who died under 12 years of age had parental rights and parental responsibilities in relation to the child (but who is not a local authority) may authorise removal and use of a part of the body of the child for one or more of the purposes referred to in section 3(1).

(2) Authorisation by virtue of subsection (1) –

    (a) must be –

        (i)   in writing and signed; or

        (ii) expressed verbally, by the person who gives the authorisation in accordance with that subsection;

    (b) subject to subsection (3), may be withdrawn in writing signed by the person.

(3) To the extent that authorisation by virtue of subsection (1) is for the purposes of transplantation, it may not be withdrawn.

11   Removal of part of body of deceased person: further requirements

(1) The removal of a part of the body of a deceased person for any of the purposes referred to in section 3(1) may be carried out only by –

    (a) a registered medical practitioner; or

    (b) a person authorised to do so in accordance with regulations made by the Scottish Ministers.

16   Offences: removal or use of part of body of deceased person for transplantation, research etc.

(1) A person commits an offence if the person removes, after the day on which section 3 comes into force, a part of the body of a deceased person for any of the purposes referred to in section 3(1) or uses after that day any part so removed for any such purpose and –

    (a) the removal or, as the case may be, the use for the purpose in question is not authorised in accordance with section 6, 7, 8, 9 or, as the case may be, 10; or

    (b) any of the requirements in section 11(1) or (4)(a) is not satisfied as respects the part.

(2) Where a person is charged with an offence under subsection (1) it is a defence for the person to show that, at the time of carrying out the activity, the person reasonably believed that the removal and use were authorised as referred to in paragraph (a) of that subsection or, as the case may be, the requirements in question referred to in paragraph (b) of that subsection were satisfied as respects the part.

(3) A person guilty of an offence under subsection (1) is liable –

    (a) on summary conviction, to –

        (i)   imprisonment for a term not exceeding 12 months;

        (ii) a fine not exceeding the statutory maximum; or

        (iii) both;

    (b) on conviction on indictment, to –

        (i)   imprisonment for a term not exceeding 3 years;

        (ii) a fine; or

        (iii) both.

Restrictions on transplants involving live donor

17   Restrictions on transplants involving live donor

(1) Subject to subsections (3) to (5) and (8), a person commits an offence –

    (a) if –

        (i)   the person removes an organ, part of an organ, or any tissue from the body of a living child intending that it be used for transplantation; and

  (ii) when the person removes the organ, part or tissue, the person knows, or might reasonably be expected to know, that the other person from whose body the person removes it is a living child;

 (b) if –

  (i) the person removes an organ or part of an organ from the body of a living adult intending that it be used for transplantation; and

  (ii) when the person removes the organ or part, the person knows, or might reasonably be expected to know, that the adult from whose body the person removes it is alive; or

 (c) if –

  (i) the person removes any tissue from the body of a living adult with incapacity intending that it be used for transplantation; and

  (ii) when the person removes the tissue the person knows, or might reasonably be expected to know, that the adult from whose body the person removes it is alive and an adult with incapacity.

(2) Subject to subsections (3) to (5) and (8), a person commits an offence –

 (a) if –

  (i) the person uses for transplantation an organ, part of an organ or any tissue which has come from the body of a living child; and

  (ii) when the person does so, the person knows, or might reasonably be expected to know, that it has come from the body of a living child;

 (b) if –

  (i) the person uses for transplantation an organ or part of an organ which has come from the body of a living adult; and

  (ii) when the person does so, the person knows, or might reasonably be expected to know, that it has come from the body of a living adult; or

 (c) if –

  (i) the person uses for transplantation any tissue which has come from the body of a living adult with incapacity; and

  (ii) when the person does so, the person knows, or might reasonably be expected to know, that it has come from the body of a living adult with incapacity.

(3) The Scottish Ministers may by regulations provide that subsection (1)(b) or (2)(b) does not apply in a case where –

 (a) the Ministers are satisfied that –

  (i) no reward has been or is to be given in contravention of section 20; and

  (ii) such other conditions as may be specified in the regulations are satisfied; and

 (b) such other requirements as may be specified in the regulations are complied with.

(4) The Scottish Ministers may by regulations provide that subsection (1)(a) or (c) or (2)(a) or (c) does not apply in a case where –

 (a) a person –

  (i) removes regenerative tissue; or

  (ii) uses such tissue;

 (b) the Ministers are satisfied that –

  (i) no reward has been or is to be given in contravention of section 20;

  (ii) such other conditions, as may be specified in the regulations are satisfied; and

 (c) such other requirements as may be specified in the regulations are complied with.

(5) The Scottish Ministers may by regulations provide that subsection (1)(a) or (b) or (2)(a) or (b) does not apply in a case where –

 (a) a person –

  (i) removes an organ or part of an organ as described in subsection (6); or

  (ii) uses such an organ or part so removed;

 (b) the Ministers are satisfied that –

      (i)   no reward has been or is to be given in contravention of section 20;

      (ii) such other conditions, as may be specified in the regulations are satisfied; and

   (c) such other requirements as may be specified in the regulations are complied with.

(6) The organ or part of an organ is one that –

   (a) during a domino organ transplant operation, is necessarily removed from –

      (i)   a child; or

      (ii) an adult with incapacity; and

   (b) is in turn intended to be used for transplantation in respect of another living person.

(9) A person guilty of an offence under this section is liable on summary conviction to –

   (a) imprisonment for a term not exceeding 12 months;

   (b) a fine not exceeding level 5 on the standard scale; or

   (c) both.

(10) In this section –

'adult with incapacity' is –

   (a) for the purposes of subsections (1)(c) and (2)(c), an adult to whom section 18 applies;

   (b) for the purposes of subsection (6)(a)(ii), an adult in respect of whom section 47 of the Adults with Incapacity (Scotland) Act 2000 applies in relation to the domino organ transplant operation in question;

'domino organ transplant operation' means a transplant operation performed on a living person by a registered medical practitioner –

   (a) which is designed to safeguard or promote the physical health of the person by transplanting organs or parts of organs into the person; and

   (b) by so doing, necessitates the removal of an organ or part of an organ from the person which in turn is intended to be used for transplantation in respect of another living person;

'regenerative tissue' means tissue which is able to be replaced in the body of a living person by natural processes if the tissue is injured or removed;

'reward' means any description of financial or other material advantage, but does not include any payment in money or money's worth for defraying or reimbursing –

   (a) the cost of removing, transporting, preparing, preserving or storing the organ (or part) or tissue;

   (b) any liability incurred in respect of expenses incurred by a third party in, or in connection with, any of the activities referred to in paragraph (a);

   (c) any expenses or loss of earnings incurred by the person from whose body the organ (or part) or tissue comes so far as reasonably and directly attributable to the person's supplying it from the person's body.

18 Meaning of adult with incapacity for purposes of section 17(1)(c) and (2)(c)

(1) This section applies to an adult –

   (a) who, in the opinion of the Scottish Ministers, is an adult who is incapable in relation to a decision about the removal from the adult of regenerative tissue for transplantation; and

   (b) in respect of whom a certificate has been issued by the Ministers in accordance with subsection (2) that they are of this opinion.

(3) In this section, 'incapable' has the same meaning as it has in section 1(6) of the Adults with Incapacity (Scotland) Act 2000.

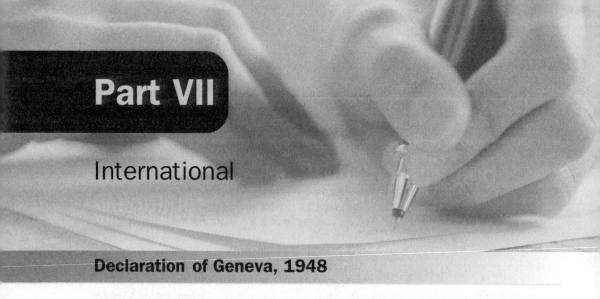

Part VII

International

Declaration of Geneva, 1948

At the time of being admitted as a member of the medical profession I solemnly pledge myself to consecrate my life to the service of humanity: I will give to my teachers the respect and gratitude which is their due; I will practice my profession with conscience and dignity; The health and life of my patient will be my first consideration; I will respect the secrets which are confided in me; I will maintain by all means in my power, the honor and the noble traditions of the medical profession; My colleagues will be my brothers: I will not permit considerations of religion, nationality, race, party politics or social standing to intervene between my duty and my patient; I will maintain the utmost respect for human life, from the time of its conception, even under threat, I will not use my medical knowledge contrary to the laws of humanity; I make these promises solemnly, freely and upon my honor ...

(The Second General Assembly of the World Medical Association 1948)

Convention for the Protection of Human Rights and Dignity of the Human Being With Regard to the Application of Biology and Medicine: Convention on Human Rights and Biomedicine 1997

European Treaty Series – No. 164

Chapter I General Provisions

Article 1   Purpose and object

Parties to this Convention shall protect the dignity and identity of all human beings and guarantee everyone, without discrimination, respect for their integrity and other rights and fundamental freedoms with regard to the application of biology and medicine.

Each Party shall take in its internal law the necessary measures to give effect to the provisions of this Convention.

Article 2   Primacy of the human being

The interests and welfare of the human being shall prevail over the sole interest of society or science.

Article 3   Equitable access to health care

Parties, taking into account health needs and available resources, shall take appropriate measures with a view to providing, within their jurisdiction, equitable access to health care of appropriate quality.

Article 4 Professional standards

Any intervention in the health field, including research, must be carried out in accordance wi___ relevant professional obligations and standards.

Chapter II Consent

Article 5 General rule

An intervention in the health field may only be carried out after the person concerned has given free and informed consent to it.

This person shall beforehand be given appropriate information as to the purpose and nature of the intervention as well as on its consequences and risks.

The person concerned may freely withdraw consent at any time.

Article 6 Protection of persons not able to consent

1. Subject to Articles 17 and 20 below, an intervention may only be carried out on a person who does not have the capacity to consent, for his or her direct benefit.

2. Where, according to law, a minor does not have the capacity to consent to an intervention, the intervention may only be carried out with the authorisation of his or her representative or an authority or a person or body provided for by law.

The opinion of the minor shall be taken into consideration as an increasingly determining factor in proportion to his or her age and degree of maturity.

3. Where, according to law, an adult does not have the capacity to consent to an intervention because of a mental disability, a disease or for similar reasons, the intervention may only be carried out with the authorisation of his or her representative or an authority or a person or body provided for by law.

The individual concerned shall as far as possible take part in the authorisation procedure.

4. The representative, the authority, the person or the body mentioned in paragraphs 2 and 3 above shall be given, under the same conditions, the information referred to in Article 5.

5. The authorisation referred to in paragraphs 2 and 3 above may be withdrawn at any time in the best interests of the person concerned.

Article 7 Protection of persons who have a mental disorder

Subject to protective conditions prescribed by law, including supervisory, control and appeal procedures, a person who has a mental disorder of a serious nature may be subjected, without his or her consent, to an intervention aimed at treating his or her mental disorder only where, without such treatment, serious harm is likely to result to his or her health.

Article 8 Emergency situation

When because of an emergency situation the appropriate consent cannot be obtained, any medically necessary intervention may be carried out immediately for the benefit of the health of the individual concerned.

Article 9 Previously expressed wishes

The previously expressed wishes relating to a medical intervention by a patient who is not, at the time of the intervention, in a state to express his or her wishes shall be taken into account.

Chapter III Private Life and Right to Information

Article 10 Private life and right to information

1. Everyone has the right to respect for private life in relation to information about his or her health.

2. Everyone is entitled to know any information collected about his or her health. However, the wishes of individuals not to be so informed shall be observed.

3. In exceptional cases, restrictions may be placed by law on the exercise of the rights contained in paragraph 2 in the interests of the patient.

Chapter IV Human Genome

Article 11   Non-discrimination

Any form of discrimination against a person on grounds of his or her genetic heritage is prohibited.

Article 12   Predictive genetic tests

Tests which are predictive of genetic diseases or which serve either to identify the subject as a carrier of a gene responsible for a disease or to detect a genetic predisposition or susceptibility to a disease may be performed only for health purposes or for scientific research linked to health purposes, and subject to appropriate genetic counselling.

Article 13   Interventions on the human genome

An intervention seeking to modify the human genome may only be undertaken for preventive, diagnostic or therapeutic purposes and only if its aim is not to introduce any modification in the genome of any descendants.

Article 14   Non-selection of sex

The use of techniques of medically assisted procreation shall not be allowed for the purpose of choosing a future child's sex, except where serious hereditary sex-related disease is to be avoided.

Chapter V Scientific Research

Article 15   General rule

Scientific research in the field of biology and medicine shall be carried out freely, subject to the provisions of this Convention and the other legal provisions ensuring the protection of the human being.

Article 16   Protection of persons undergoing research

Research on a person may only be undertaken if all the following conditions are met:

    i   there is no alternative of comparable effectiveness to research on humans;

    ii the risks which may be incurred by that person are not disproportionate to the potential benefits of the research;

    iii the research project has been approved by the competent body after independent examination of its scientific merit, including assessment of the importance of the aim of the research, and multidisciplinary review of its ethical acceptability,

    iv the persons undergoing research have been informed of their rights and the safeguards prescribed by law for their protection;

    v the necessary consent as provided for under Article 5 has been given expressly, specifically and is documented. Such consent may be freely withdrawn at any time.

Article 17   Protection of persons not able to consent to research

1. Research on a person without the capacity to consent as stipulated in Article 5 may be undertaken only if all the following conditions are met:

    i   the conditions laid down in Article 16, sub-paragraphs i to iv, are fulfilled;

    ii the results of the research have the potential to produce real and direct benefit to his or her health;

    iii research of comparable effectiveness cannot be carried out on individuals capable of giving consent;

    iv the necessary authorisation provided for under Article 6 has been given specifically and in writing; and

    v the person concerned does not object.

2. Exceptionally and under the protective conditions prescribed by law, where the research has not the potential to produce results of direct benefit to the health of the person concerned, such research may be authorised subject to the conditions laid down in paragraph 1, sub-paragraphs i, iii, iv and v above, and to the following additional conditions:

    i   the research has the aim of contributing, through significant improvement in the scientific understanding of the individual's condition, disease or disorder, to the ultimate attainment of results capable of conferring benefit to the person concerned or to other persons in the same age category or afflicted with the same disease or disorder or having the same condition;

ii   the research entails only minimal risk and minimal burden for the individual concerned.

Article 18 Research on embryos *in vitro*

1. Where the law allows research on embryos *in vitro*, it shall ensure adequate protection of the embryo.

2. The creation of human embryos for research purposes is prohibited.

Chapter VI Organ and Tissue Removal from Living Donors for Transplantation Purposes

Article 19   General rule

1. Removal of organs or tissue from a living person for transplantation purposes may be carried out solely for the therapeutic benefit of the recipient and where there is no suitable organ or tissue available from a deceased person and no other alternative therapeutic method of comparable effectiveness.

2. The necessary consent as provided for under Article 5 must have been given expressly and specifically either in written form or before an official body.

Article 20   Protection of persons not able to consent to organ removal

1. No organ or tissue removal may be carried out on a person who does not have the capacity to consent under Article 5.

2. Exceptionally and under the protective conditions prescribed by law, the removal of regenerative tissue from a person who does not have the capacity to consent may be authorised provided the following conditions are met:

i   there is no compatible donor available who has the capacity to consent;

ii   the recipient is a brother or sister of the donor;

iii the donation must have the potential to be life-saving for the recipient;

iv   the authorisation provided for under paragraphs 2 and 3 of Article 6 has been given specifically and in writing, in accordance with the law and with the approval of the competent body;

v   the potential donor concerned does not object.

Chapter VII Prohibition of Financial Gain and Disposal of A Part of the Human Body

Article 21   Prohibition of financial gain

The human body and its parts shall not, as such, give rise to financial gain.

Article 22   Disposal of a removed part of the human body

When in the course of an intervention any part of a human body is removed, it may be stored and used for a purpose other than that for which it was removed, only if this is done in conformity with appropriate information and consent procedures.

Chapter VIII Infringements of the Provisions of the Convention

Article 23 Infringement of the rights or principles

The Parties shall provide appropriate judicial protection to prevent or to put a stop to an unlawful infringement of the rights and principles set forth in this Convention at short notice.

Article 24 Compensation for undue damage

The person who has suffered undue damage resulting from an intervention is entitled to fair compensation according to the conditions and procedures prescribed by law.

Article 25   Sanctions

Parties shall provide for appropriate sanctions to be applied in the event of infringement of the provisions contained in this Convention.

Chapter IX Relation Between this Convention and Other Provisions

Article 26   Restrictions on the exercise of the rights

1. No restrictions shall be placed on the exercise of the rights and protective provisions contained in this Convention other than such as are prescribed by law and are necessary in a democratic society in the interest of public safety, for the prevention of crime, for the protection of public health or for the protection of the rights and freedoms of others.

2. The restrictions contemplated in the preceding paragraph may not be placed on Articles 11, 13, 14, 16, 17, 19, 20 and 21.

Article 27   Wider protection

None of the provisions of this Convention shall be interpreted as limiting or otherwise affecting the possibility for a Party to grant a wider measure of protection with regard to the application of biology and medicine than is stipulated in this Convention.

Chapter X Public Debate

Article 28   Public debate

Parties to this Convention shall see to it that the fundamental questions raised by the developments of biology and medicine are the subject of appropriate public discussion in the light, in particular, of relevant medical, social, economic, ethical and legal implications, and that their possible application is made the subject of appropriate consultation.

Chapter XI Interpretation and Follow-Up of the Convention

Article 29   Interpretation of the Convention

The European Court of Human Rights may give, without direct reference to any specific proceedings pending in a court, advisory opinions on legal questions concerning the interpretation of the present Convention at the request of:

- — the Government of a Party, after having informed the other Parties;
- — the Committee set up by Article 32, with membership restricted to the Representatives of the Parties to this Convention, by a decision adopted by a two-thirds majority of votes cast.

Article 30   Reports on the application of the Convention

On receipt of a request from the Secretary General of the Council of Europe any Party shall furnish an explanation of the manner in which its internal law ensures the effective implementation of any of the provisions of the Convention.

Additional Protocol to the Convention for the Protection of Human Rights and Dignity of the Human Being With Regard to the Application of Biology and Medicine, On the Prohibition of Cloning Human Beings

(Paris, 12.I.1998)

European Treaty Series – No. 168

Article 1

1. Any intervention seeking to create a human being genetically identical to another human being, whether living or dead, is prohibited.

2. For the purpose of this article, the term human being 'genetically identical' to another human being means a human being sharing with another the same nuclear gene set.

Article 2
No derogation from the provisions of this Protocol shall be made under Article 26, paragraph 1, of the Convention.

Additional Protocol to the Convention On Human Rights and Biomedicine Concerning Transplantation of Organs and Tissues of Human Origin

(Strasbourg, 24.I.2002)

European Treaty Series – No. 186

Chapter I Object and Scope

Article 1 Object
Parties to this Protocol shall protect the dignity and identity of everyone and guarantee, without discrimination, respect for his or her integrity and other rights and fundamental freedoms with regard to transplantation of organs and tissues of human origin.

Article 2 Scope and definitions
1. This Protocol applies to the transplantation of organs and tissues of human origin carried out for therapeutic purposes.
2. The provisions of this Protocol applicable to tissues shall apply also to cells, including haematopoietic stem cells.
3. The Protocol does not apply:
     a. to reproductive organs and tissue;
     b. to embryonic or foetal organs and tissues;
     c. to blood and blood derivatives.
4. For the purposes of this Protocol:
     — the term 'transplantation' covers the complete process of removal of an organ or tissue from one person and implantation of that organ or tissue into another person, including all procedures for preparation, preservation and storage;
     — subject to the provisions of Article 20, the term 'removal' refers to removal for the purposes of implantation.

Chapter II General Provisions

Article 3 Transplantation system
Parties shall guarantee that a system exists to provide equitable access to transplantation services for patients.

Subject to the provisions of Chapter III, organs and, where appropriate, tissues shall be allocated only among patients on an official waiting list, in conformity with transparent, objective and duly justified rules according to medical criteria. The persons or bodies responsible for the allocation decision shall be designated within this framework.

In case of international organ exchange arrangements, the procedures must also ensure justified, effective distribution across the participating countries in a manner that takes into account the solidarity principle within each country.

The transplantation system shall ensure the collection and recording of the information required to ensure traceability of organs and tissues.

Article 4   Professional standards

Any intervention in the field of organ or tissue transplantation must be carried out in accordance with relevant professional obligations and standards.

Article 5   Information for the recipient

The recipient and, where appropriate, the person or body providing authorisation for the implantation shall beforehand be given appropriate information as to the purpose and nature of the implantation, its consequences and risks, as well as on the alternatives to the intervention.

Article 6   Health and safety

All professionals involved in organ or tissue transplantation shall take all reasonable measures to minimise the risks of transmission of any disease to the recipient and to avoid any action which might affect the suitability of an organ or tissue for implantation.

Article 7   Medical follow-up

Appropriate medical follow-up shall be offered to living donors and recipients after transplantation.

Article 8   Information for health professionals and the public

Parties shall provide information for health professionals and for the public in general on the need for organs and tissues. They shall also provide information on the conditions relating to removal and implantation of organs and tissues, including matters relating to consent or authorisation, in particular with regard to removal from deceased persons.

Chapter III Organ and Tissue Removal from Living Persons

Article 9   General rule

Removal of organs or tissue from a living person may be carried out solely for the therapeutic benefit of the recipient and where there is no suitable organ or tissue available from a deceased person and no other alternative therapeutic method of comparable effectiveness.

Article 10   Potential organ donors

Organ removal from a living donor may be carried out for the benefit of a recipient with whom the donor has a close personal relationship as defined by law, or, in the absence of such relationship, only under the conditions defined by law and with the approval of an appropriate independent body.

Article 11   Evaluation of risks for the donor

Before organ or tissue removal, appropriate medical investigations and interventions shall be carried out to evaluate and reduce physical and psychological risks to the health of the donor. The removal may not be carried out if there is a serious risk to the life or health of the donor.

Article 12   Information for the donor

The donor and, where appropriate, the person or body providing authorisation according to Article 14, paragraph 2, of this Protocol, shall beforehand be given appropriate information as to the purpose and nature of the removal as well as on its consequences and risks.

They shall also be informed of the rights and the safeguards prescribed by law for the protection of the donor. In particular, they shall be informed of the right to have access to independent advice about such risks by a health professional having appropriate experience and who is not involved in the organ or tissue removal or subsequent transplantation procedures.

Article 13   Consent of the living donor

Subject to Articles 14 and 15 of this Protocol, an organ or tissue may be removed from a living donor only after the person concerned has given free, informed and specific consent to it either in written form or before an official body.

The person concerned may freely withdraw consent at any time.

Article 14   Protection of persons not able to consent to organ or tissue removal

1. No organ or tissue removal may be carried out on a person who does not have the capacity to consent under Article 13 of this Protocol.

2. Exceptionally, and under the protective conditions prescribed by law, the removal of regenerative tissue from a person who does not have the capacity to consent may be authorised provided the following conditions are met:

> i   there is no compatible donor available who has the capacity to consent;
> ii   the recipient is a brother or sister of the donor;
> iii the donation has the potential to be life-saving for the recipient;
> iv   the authorisation of his or her representative or an authority or a person or body provided for by law has been given specifically and in writing and with the approval of the competent body;
> v   the potential donor concerned does not object.

Article 15   Cell removal from a living donor

The law may provide that the provisions of Article 14, paragraph 2, indents ii and iii, shall not apply to cells insofar as it is established that their removal only implies minimal risk and minimal burden for the donor.

Chapter IV Organ and Tissue Removal From Deceased Persons

Article 16   Certification of death

Organs or tissues shall not be removed from the body of a deceased person unless that person has been certified dead in accordance with the law.

The doctors certifying the death of a person shall not be the same doctors who participate directly in removal of organs or tissues from the deceased person, or subsequent transplantation procedures, or having responsibilities for the care of potential organ or tissue recipients.

Article 17   Consent and authorisation

Organs or tissues shall not be removed from the body of a deceased person unless consent or authorisation required by law has been obtained.

The removal shall not be carried out if the deceased person had objected to it.

Article 18   Respect for the human body

During removal the human body must be treated with respect and all reasonable measures shall be taken to restore the appearance of the corpse.

Article 19   Promotion of donation

Parties shall take all appropriate measures to promote the donation of organs and tissues.

Chapter V Implantation of an Organ or Tissue Removed for a Purpose Other than Donation for Implantation

Article 20   Implantation of an organ or tissue removed for a purpose other than donation for implantation

1. When an organ or tissue is removed from a person for a purpose other than donation for implantation, it may only be implanted if the consequences and possible risks have been explained to that person and his or her informed consent, or appropriate authorisation in the case of a person not able to consent, has been obtained.

2. All the provisions of this Protocol apply to the situations referred to in paragraph 1, except for those in Chapter III and IV.

Chapter VI Prohibition of Financial Gain

Article 21   Prohibition of financial gain

1. The human body and its parts shall not, as such, give rise to financial gain or comparable advantage.

The aforementioned provision shall not prevent payments which do not constitute a financial gain or a comparable advantage, in particular:

— compensation of living donors for loss of earnings and any other justifiable expenses caused by the removal or by the related medical examinations;

— payment of a justifiable fee for legitimate medical or related technical services rendered in connection with transplantation;

— compensation in case of undue damage resulting from the removal of organs or tissues from living persons.

2. Advertising the need for, or availability of, organs or tissues, with a view to offering or seeking financial gain or comparable advantage, shall be prohibited.

Article 22   Prohibition of organ and tissue trafficking

Organ and tissue trafficking shall be prohibited.

Chapter VII Confidentiality

Article 23   Confidentiality

1. All personal data relating to the person from whom organs or tissues have been removed and those relating to the recipient shall be considered to be confidential. Such data may only be collected, processed and communicated according to the rules relating to professional confidentiality and personal data protection.

2. The provisions of paragraph 1 shall be interpreted without prejudice to the provisions making possible, subject to appropriate safeguards, the collection, processing and communication of the necessary information about the person from whom organs or tissues have been removed or the recipient(s) of organs and tissues in so far as this is required for medical purposes, including traceability, as provided for in Article 3 of this Protocol.

Chapter VIII Infringements of the Provisions of the Protocol

Article 24   Infringements of rights or principles

Parties shall provide appropriate judicial protection to prevent or to put a stop to an unlawful infringement of the rights and principles set forth in this Protocol at short notice.

Article 25   Compensation for undue damage

The person who has suffered undue damage resulting from transplantation procedures is entitled to fair compensation according to the conditions and procedures prescribed by law.

Article 26   Sanctions

Parties shall provide for appropriate sanctions to be applied in the event of infringement of the provisions contained in this Protocol.

Chapter IX Co-operation between Parties

Article 27   Co-operation between Parties

Parties shall take appropriate measures to ensure that there is efficient co-operation between them on organ and tissue transplantation, *inter alia* through information exchange.

In particular, they shall undertake appropriate measures to facilitate the rapid and safe transportation of organs and tissues to and from their territory.

Additional Protocol to the Convention on Human Rights and Biomedicine Concerning Biomedical Research

European Treaty Series – No. 195
Opened for signature 25 January 2005

Article 1   Object and purpose
Parties to this Protocol shall protect the dignity and identity of all human beings and guarantee everyone, without discrimination, respect for their integrity and other rights and fundamental freedoms with regard to any research involving interventions on human beings in the field of biomedicine.

Article 2   Scope
1. This Protocol covers the full range of research activities in the health field involving interventions on human beings.
2. This Protocol does not apply to research on embryos in vitro. It does apply to research on foetuses and embryos in vivo.
3. For the purposes of this Protocol, the term 'intervention' includes:
   i. a physical intervention, and
   ii. any other intervention in so far as it involves a risk to the psychological health of the person concerned.

Article 3   Primacy of the human being
The interests and welfare of the human being participating in research shall prevail over the sole interest of society or science.

Article 4   General rule
Research shall be carried out freely, subject to the provisions of this Protocol and the other legal provisions ensuring the protection of the human being.

Article 5   Absence of alternatives
Research on human beings may only be undertaken if there is no alternative of comparable effectiveness.

Article 6   Risks and benefits
1. Research shall not involve risks and burdens to the human being disproportionate to its potential benefits.
2. In addition, where the research does not have the potential to produce results of direct benefit to the health of the research participant, such research may only be undertaken if the research entails no more than acceptable risk and acceptable burden for the research participant. This shall be without prejudice to the provision contained in Article 15 paragraph 2, sub-paragraph ii for the protection of persons not able to consent to research.

Article 7   Approval
Research may only be undertaken if the research project has been approved by the competent body after independent examination of its scientific merit, including assessment of the importance of the aim of research, and multidisciplinary review of its ethical acceptability.

Article 8   Scientific quality
Any research must be scientifically justified, meet generally accepted criteria of scientific quality and be carried out in accordance with relevant professional obligations and standards under the supervision of an appropriately qualified researcher.

Article 9   Independent examination by an ethics committee
1. Every research project shall be submitted for independent examination of its ethical acceptability to an ethics committee. Such projects shall be submitted to independent examination in each State in which any research activity is to take place.

2. The purpose of the multidisciplinary examination of the ethical acceptability of the research project shall be to protect the dignity, rights, safety and well-being of research participants. The assessment of the ethical acceptability shall draw on an appropriate range of expertise and experience adequately reflecting professional and lay views.

3. The ethics committee shall produce an opinion containing reasons for its conclusion.

Article 10   Independence of the ethics committee

1. Parties to this Protocol shall take measures to assure the independence of the ethics committee. That body shall not be subject to undue external influences.

2. Members of the ethics committee shall declare all circumstances that might lead to a conflict of interest. Should such conflicts arise, those involved shall not participate in that review.

Article 11   Information for the ethics committee

1. All information which is necessary for the ethical assessment of the research project shall be given in written form to the ethics committee.

2. In particular, information on items contained in the appendix to this Protocol shall be provided, in so far as it is relevant for the research project.

Article 12   Undue influence

The ethics committee must be satisfied that no undue influence, including that of a financial nature, will be exerted on persons to participate in research. In this respect, particular attention must be given to vulnerable or dependent persons.

Article 13   Information for research participants

1. The persons being asked to participate in a research project shall be given adequate information in a comprehensible form. This information shall be documented.

2. The information shall cover the purpose, the overall plan and the possible risks and benefits of the research project, and include the opinion of the ethics committee. Before being asked to consent to participate in a research project, the persons concerned shall be specifically informed, according to the nature and purpose of the research:

    i.   of the nature, extent and duration of the procedures involved, in particular, details of any burden imposed by the research project;

    ii. of available preventive, diagnostic and therapeutic procedures;

    iii. of the arrangements for responding to adverse events or the concerns of research participants;

    iv. of arrangements to ensure respect for private life and ensure the confidentiality of personal data;

    v. of arrangements for access to information relevant to the participant arising from the research and to its overall results;

    vi. of the arrangements for fair compensation in the case of damage;

    vii. of any foreseen potential further uses, including commercial uses, of the research results, data or biological materials;

    vii. of the source of funding of the research project.

3. In addition, the persons being asked to participate in a research project shall be informed of the rights and safeguards prescribed by law for their protection, and specifically of their right to refuse consent or to withdraw consent at any time without being subject to any form of discrimination, in particular regarding the right to medical care.

Article 14   Consent

1. No research on a person may be carried out, subject to the provisions of both Chapter V and Article 19, without the informed, free, express, specific and documented consent of the person. Such consent may be freely withdrawn by the person at any phase of the research.

2. Refusal to give consent or the withdrawal of consent to participation in research shall not lead to any form of discrimination against the person concerned, in particular regarding the right to medical care.

3. Where the capacity of the person to give informed consent is in doubt, Arrangements shall be in place to verify whether or not the person has such capacity.

Article 15   Protection of persons not able to consent to research

1. Research on a person without the capacity to consent to research may be undertaken only if all the following specific conditions are met:
    i. the results of the research have the potential to produce real and direct benefit to his or her health;
    ii. research of comparable effectiveness cannot be carried out on individuals capable of giving consent;
    iii. the person undergoing research has been informed of his or her rights and the safeguards prescribed by law for his or her protection, unless this person is not in a state to receive the information;
    iv. the necessary authorisation has been given specifically and in writing by the legal representative or an authority, person or body provided for by law, and after having received the information required by Article 16, taking into account the person's previously expressed wishes or objections. An adult not able to consent shall as far as possible take part in the authorisation procedure. The opinion of a minor shall be taken into consideration as an increasingly determining factor in proportion to age and degree of maturity;
    v. the person concerned does not object.

2. Exceptionally and under the protective conditions prescribed by law, where the research has not the potential to produce results of direct benefit to the health of the person concerned, such research may be authorised subject to the conditions laid down in paragraph 1, sub-paragraphs ii, iii, iv, and v above, and to the following additional conditions:
    i. the research has the aim of contributing, through significant improvement in the scientific understanding of the individual's condition, disease or disorder, to the ultimate attainment of results capable of conferring benefit to the person concerned or to other persons in the same age category or afflicted with the same disease or disorder or having the same condition;
    ii. the research entails only minimal risk and minimal burden for the individual concerned; and any consideration of additional potential benefits of the research shall not be used to justify an increased level of risk or burden.

3. Objection to participation, refusal to give authorisation or the withdrawal of authorisation to participate in research shall not lead to any form of discrimination against the person concerned, in particular regarding the right to medical care.

Article 16   Information prior to authorisation

1. Those being asked to authorise participation of a person in a research project shall be given adequate information in a comprehensible form. This information shall be documented.

2. The information shall cover the purpose, the overall plan and the possible risks and benefits of the research project, and include the opinion of the ethics committee. They shall further be informed of the rights and safeguards prescribed by law for the protection of those not able to consent to research and specifically of the right to refuse or to withdraw authorisation at any time, without the person concerned being subject to any form of discrimination, in particular regarding the right to medical care. They shall be specifically informed according to the nature and purpose of the research of the items of information listed in Article 13.

3. The information shall also be provided to the individual concerned, unless this person is not in a state to receive the information.

Article 17   Research with minimal risk and minimal burden

1. For the purposes of this Protocol it is deemed that the research bears a minimal risk if, having regard to the nature and scale of the intervention, it is to be expected that it will result, at the most, in a very slight and temporary negative impact on the health of the person concerned.

2. It is deemed that it bears a minimal burden if it is to be expected that the discomfort will be, at the most, temporary and very slight for the person concerned. In assessing the burden for an individual, a person enjoying the special confidence of the person concerned shall assess the burden where appropriate.

Article 18 Research during pregnancy or breastfeeding

1. Research on a pregnant woman which does not have the potential to produce results of direct benefit to her health, or to that of her embryo, foetus or child after birth, may only be undertaken if the following additional conditions are met:

    i.   the research has the aim of contributing to the ultimate attainment of results capable of conferring benefit to other women in relation to reproduction or to other embryos, foetuses or children;

    ii. research of comparable effectiveness cannot be carried out on women who are not pregnant;

    iii. the research entails only minimal risk and minimal burden.

2. Where research is undertaken on a breastfeeding woman, particular care shall be taken to avoid any adverse impact on the health of the child.

Article 19   Research on persons in emergency clinical situations

1. The law shall determine whether, and under which protective additional conditions, research in emergency situations may take place when:

    i.   a person is not in a state to give consent, and

    ii. because of the urgency of the situation, it is impossible to obtain in a sufficiently timely manner, authorisation from his or her representative or an authority or a person or body which would in the absence of an emergency situation be called upon to give authorisation.

2. The law shall include the following specific conditions:

    i.   research of comparable effectiveness cannot be carried out on persons in nonemergency situations;

    ii. the research project may only be undertaken if it has been approved specifically for emergency situations by the competent body;

    iii. any relevant previously expressed objections of the person known to the researcher shall be respected;

    iv. where the research has not the potential to produce results of direct benefit to the health of the person concerned, it has the aim of contributing, through significant improvement in the scientific understanding of the individual's condition, disease or disorder, to the ultimate attainment of results capable of conferring benefit to the person concerned or to other persons in the same category or afflicted with the same disease or disorder or having the same condition, and entails only minimal risk and minimal burden.

3. Persons participating in the emergency research project or, if applicable, their representatives shall be provided with all the relevant information concerning their participation in the research project as soon as possible. Consent or authorisation for continued participation shall be requested as soon as reasonably possible.

Article 20   Research on persons deprived of liberty

Where the law allows research on persons deprived of liberty, such persons may participate in a research project in which the results do not have the potential to produce direct benefit to their health only if the following additional conditions are met:

    i.   research of comparable effectiveness cannot be carried out without the participation of persons deprived of liberty;

    ii. the research has the aim of contributing to the ultimate attainment of results capable of conferring benefit to persons deprived of liberty;

    iii. the research entails only minimal risk and minimal burden.

Article 21   Minimisation of risk and burden

1. All reasonable measures shall be taken to ensure safety and to minimise risk and burden for the research participants.

2. Research may only be carried out under the supervision of a clinical professional who possesses the necessary qualifications and experience.

Article 22   Assessment of health status

1. The researcher shall take all necessary steps to assess the state of health of human beings prior to their inclusion in research, to ensure that those at increased risk in relation to participation in a specific project be excluded.

2. Where research is undertaken on persons in the reproductive stage of their lives, particular consideration shall be given to the possible adverse impact on a current or future pregnancy and the health of an embryo, foetus or child.

Article 23   Non-interference with necessary clinical interventions

1. Research shall not delay nor deprive participants of medically necessary preventive, diagnostic or therapeutic procedures.

2. In research associated with prevention, diagnosis or treatment, participants assigned to control groups shall be assured of proven methods of prevention, diagnosis or treatment.

3. The use of placebo is permissible where there are no methods of proven effectiveness, or where withdrawal or withholding of such methods does not present an unacceptable risk or burden.

Article 23   Non-interference with necessary clinical interventions

1. Research shall not prevent or delay nor deprive participants of medically necessary preventive, diagnostic or therapeutic procedures.

2. In research associated with prevention, diagnosis or treatment, participants assigned to control groups shall be assured of proven methods of prevention diagnosis or treatment.

3. The use of placebo is permissible where there are no methods of proven effectiveness, or where withdrawal or withholding of such methods does not present an unacceptable risk or burden.

Article 24   New developments

1. Parties to this Protocol shall take measures to ensure that the research project is re-examined if this is justified in the light of scientific developments or events arising in the course of the research.

2. The purpose of the re-examination is to establish whether:
   i.   the research needs to be discontinued or if changes to the research project are necessary for the research to continue;
   ii. research participants, or if applicable their representatives, need to be informed of the developments or events;
   iii. additional consent or authorisation for participation is required.

3. Any new information relevant to their participation shall be conveyed to the research partici- pants, or, if applicable, to their representatives, in a timely manner.

4. The competent body shall be informed of the reasons for any premature termination of a research project.

Article 25   Confidentiality

1. Any information of a personal nature collected during biomedical research shall be considered as confidential and treated according to the rules relating to the protection of private life.

2. The law shall protect against inappropriate disclosure of any other information related to a research project that has been submitted to an ethics committee in compliance with this Protocol.

Article 26   Right to information

1. Research participants shall be entitled to know any information collected on their health in conformity with the provisions of Article 10 of the Convention.

2. Other personal information collected for a research project will be accessible to them in con- formity with the law on the protection of individuals with regard to processing of personal data.

Article 27   Duty of care

If research gives rise to information of relevance to the current or future health or quality of life of research participants, this information must be offered to them. That shall be done within a framework of health care or counselling. In communication of such information, due care must be taken in order to protect confidentiality and to respect any wish of a participant not to receive such information.

Article 28   Availability of results

1. On completion of the research, a report or summary shall be submitted to the ethics committee or the competent body.

2. The conclusions of the research shall be made available to participants in reasonable time, on request.

3. The researcher shall take appropriate measures to make public the results of research in reasonable time.

Article 29   Research in States not parties to this Protocol

Sponsors or researchers within the jurisdiction of a Party to this Protocol that plan to undertake or direct a research project in a State not party to this Protocol shall ensure that, without prejudice to the provisions applicable in that State, the research project complies with the principles on which the provisions of this Protocol are based. Where necessary, the Party shall take appropriate measures to that end.

Appendix to the Additional Protocol on Biomedical Research

Information to be given to the ethics committee

Information on the following items shall be provided to the ethics committee, in so far as it is relevant for the research project:

Description of the project

   i.   the name of the principal researcher, qualifications and experience of researchers and, where appropriate, the clinically responsible person, and funding arrangements;

   ii. the aim and justification for the research based on the latest state of scientific knowledge;

   iii. methods and procedures envisaged, including statistical and other analytical techniques;

   iv. a comprehensive summary of the research project in lay language;

   v.   a statement of previous and concurrent submissions of the research project for assessment or approval and the outcome of those submissions; Participants, consent and information

   vi. justification for involving human beings in the research project;

   vii. the criteria for inclusion or exclusion of the categories of persons for participation in the research project and how those persons are to be selected and recruited;

   viii. reasons for the use or the absence of control groups;

   ix. a description of the nature and degree of foreseeable risks that may be incurred through participating in research;

   x.   the nature, extent and duration of the interventions to be carried out on the research participants, and details of any burden imposed by the research project;

   xi. arrangements to monitor, evaluate and react to contingencies that may have consequences for the present or future health of research participants;

   xii. the timing and details of information for those persons who would participate in the research project and the means proposed for provision of this information;

   xiii. documentation intended to be used to seek consent or, in the case of persons not able to consent, authorisation for participation in the research project;

   xiv. arrangements to ensure respect for the private life of those persons who would participate in research and ensure the confidentiality of personal data;

xv.   arrangements foreseen for information which may be generated and be relevant to the present or future health of those persons who would participate in research and their family members;

Other information

xvi.   details of all payments and rewards to be made in the context of the research project;

xvii.   details of all circumstances that might lead to conflicts of interest that may affect the independent judgement of the researchers;

xviii. details of any foreseen potential further uses, including commercial uses, of the research results, data or biological materials;

xix.   details of all other ethical issues, as perceived by the researcher;

xx.   details of any insurance or indemnity to cover damage arising in the context of the research project.

The ethics committee may request additional information necessary for evaluation of the research project.

World Medical Association Declaration of Helsinki

Ethical principles for medical research involving human subjects

A Introduction

1. The World Medical Association has developed the Declaration of Helsinki as a statement of ethical principles to provide guidance to physicians and other participants in medical research involving human subjects. Medical research involving human subjects includes research on identifiable human material or identifiable data.

2. It is the duty of the physician to promote and safeguard the health of the people. The physician's knowledge and conscience are dedicated to the fulfillment of this duty.

3. The Declaration of Geneva of the World Medical Association binds the physician with the words, 'The health of my patient will be my first consideration,' and the International Code of Medical Ethics declares that, 'A physician shall act only in the patient's interest when providing medical care which might have the effect of weakening the physical and mental condition of the patient.'

4. Medical progress is based on research which ultimately must rest in part on experimentation involving human subjects.

5. In medical research on human subjects, considerations related to the well-being of the human subject should take precedence over the interests of science and society.

6. The primary purpose of medical research involving human subjects is to improve prophylactic, diagnostic and therapeutic procedures and the understanding of the aetiology and pathogenesis of disease. Even the best proven prophylactic, diagnostic, and therapeutic methods must continuously be challenged through research for their effectiveness, efficiency, accessibility and quality.

7. In current medical practice and in medical research, most prophylactic, diagnostic and therapeutic procedures involve risks and burdens.

8. Medical research is subject to ethical standards that promote respect for all human beings and protect their health and rights. Some research populations are vulnerable and need special protection. The particular needs of the economically and medically disadvantaged must be recognized. Special attention is also required for those who cannot give or refuse consent for themselves, for

who may be subject to giving consent under duress, for those who will not benefit personally
he research and for those for whom the research is combined with care.

earch Investigators should be aware of the ethical, legal and regulatory requirements for
research on human subjects in their own countries as well as applicable international requirements.
No national ethical, legal or regulatory requirement should be allowed to reduce or eliminate any of
the protections for human subjects set forth in this Declaration.

B Basic Principles for all Medical Research

10. It is the duty of the physician in medical research to protect the life, health, privacy, and dignity
of the human subject.

11. Medical research involving human subjects must conform to generally accepted scientific
principles, be based on a thorough knowledge of the scientific literature, other relevant sources of
information, and on adequate laboratory and, where appropriate, animal experimentation.

12. Appropriate caution must be exercised in the conduct of research which may affect the
environment, and the welfare of animals used for research must be respected.

13. The design and performance of each experimental procedure involving human subjects should
be clearly formulated in an experimental protocol. This protocol should be submitted for consideration, comment, guidance, and where appropriate, approval to a specially appointed ethical
review committee, which must be independent of the investigator, the sponsor or any other kind of
undue influence. This independent committee should be in conformity with the laws and regulations of the country in which the research experiment is performed. The committee has the right to
monitor ongoing trials. The researcher has the obligation to provide monitoring information to the
committee, especially any serious adverse events. The researcher should also submit to the committee, for review, information regarding funding, sponsors, institutional affiliations, other
potential conflicts of interest and incentives for subjects.

14. The research protocol should always contain a statement of the ethical considerations involved
and should indicate that there is compliance with the principles enunciated in this Declaration.

15. Medical research involving human subjects should be conducted only by scientifically qualified
persons and under the supervision of a clinically competent medical person. The responsibility for
the human subject must always rest with a medically qualified person and never rest on the subject
of the research, even though the subject has given consent.

16. Every medical research project involving human subjects should be preceded by careful
assessment of predictable risks and burdens in comparison with foreseeable benefits to the subject
or to others. This does not preclude the participation of healthy volunteers in medical research. The
design of all studies should be publicly available.

17. Physicians should abstain from engaging in research projects involving human subjects unless
they are confident that the risks involved have been adequately assessed and can be satisfactorily
managed. Physicians should cease any investigation if the risks are found to outweigh the potential
benefits or if there is conclusive proof of positive and beneficial results.

18. Medical research involving human subjects should only be conducted if the importance of the
objective outweighs the inherent risks and burdens to the subject. This is especially important when
the human subjects are healthy volunteers.

19. Medical research is only justified if there is a reasonable likelihood that the populations in
which the research is carried out stand to benefit from the results of the research.

20. The subjects must be volunteers and informed participants in the research project.

21. The right of research subjects to safeguard their integrity must always be respected. Every
precaution should be taken to respect the privacy of the subject, the confidentiality of the patient's
information and to minimize the impact of the study on the subject's physical and mental integrity
and on the personality of the subject.

22. In any research on human beings, each potential subject must be adequately informed of the
aims, methods, sources of funding, any possible conflicts of interest, institutional affiliations of the

researcher, the anticipated benefits and potential risks of the study and the discomfort it may entail. The subject should be informed of the right to abstain from participation in the study or to withdraw consent to participate at any time without reprisal. After ensuring that the subject has understood the information, the physician should then obtain the subject's freely-given informed consent, preferably in writing. If the consent cannot be obtained in writing, the non-written consent must be formally documented and witnessed.

23. When obtaining informed consent for the research project the physician should be particularly cautious if the subject is in a dependent relationship with the physician or may consent under duress. In that case the informed consent should be obtained by a well-informed physician who is not engaged in the investigation and who is completely independent of this relationship.

24. For a research subject who is legally incompetent, physically or mentally incapable of giving consent or is a legally incompetent minor, the investigator must obtain informed consent from the legally authorized representative in accordance with applicable law. These groups should not be included in research unless the research is necessary to promote the health of the population represented and this research cannot instead be performed on legally competent persons.

25. When a subject deemed legally incompetent, such as a minor child, is able to give assent to decisions about participation in research, the investigator must obtain that assent in addition to the consent of the legally authorized representative.

26. Research on individuals from whom it is not possible to obtain consent, including proxy or advance consent, should be done only if the physical/mental condition that prevents obtaining informed consent is a necessary characteristic of the research population. The specific reasons for involving research subjects with a condition that renders them unable to give informed consent should be stated in the experimental protocol for consideration and approval of the review committee. The protocol should state that consent to remain in the research should be obtained as soon as possible from the individual or a legally authorized surrogate.

27. Both authors and publishers have ethical obligations. In publication of the results of research, the investigators are obliged to preserve the accuracy of the results. Negative as well as positive results should be published or otherwise publicly available. Sources of funding, institutional affiliations and any possible conflicts of interest should be declared in the publication. Reports of experimentation not in accordance with the principles laid down in this Declaration should not be accepted for publication.

C Additional Principles for Medical Research Combined with Medical Care

28. The physician may combine medical research with medical care, only to the extent that the research is justified by its potential prophylactic, diagnostic or therapeutic value. When medical research is combined with medical care, additional standards apply to protect the patients who are research subjects.

29. The benefits, risks, burdens and effectiveness of a new method should be tested against those of the best current prophylactic, diagnostic, and therapeutic methods. This does not exclude the use of placebo, or no treatment, in studies where no proven prophylactic, diagnostic or therapeutic method exists.*[1]

30. At the conclusion of the study, every patient entered into the study should be assured of access to the best proven prophylactic, diagnostic and therapeutic methods identified by the study.

---

[1]* The WMA hereby reaffirms its position that extreme care must be taken in making use of a placebo-controlled trial and that in general this methodology should only be used in the absence of existing proven therapy. However, a placebo-controlled trial may be ethically acceptable, even if proven therapy is available, under the following circumstances:

— Where for compelling and scientifically sound methodological reasons its use is necessary to determine the efficacy or safety of a prophylactic, diagnostic or therapeutic method; or

— Where a prophylactic, diagnostic or therapeutic method is being investigated for a minor condition and the patients who receive placebo will not be subject to any additional risk of serious or irreversible harm.

All other provisions of the Declaration of Helsinki must be adhered to, especially the need for appropriate ethical and scientific review.

31. The physician should fully inform the patient which aspects of the care are related to the research. The refusal of a patient to participate in a study must never interfere with the patient-physician relationship.

32. In the treatment of a patient, where proven prophylactic, diagnostic and therapeutic methods do not exist or have been ineffective, the physician, with informed consent from the patient, must be free to use unproven or new prophylactic, diagnostic and therapeutic measures, if in the physician's judgement it offers hope of saving life, re-establishing health or alleviating suffering. Where possible, these measures should be made the object of research, designed to evaluate their safety and efficacy. In all cases, new information should be recorded and, where appropriate, published. The other relevant guidelines of this Declaration should be followed.

The Declaration of Helsinki is an official policy document of the World Medical Association, the global representative body for physicians. It was first adopted in 1964 (Helsinki, Finland) and revised in 1975 (Tokyo, Japan), 1983 (Venice, Italy), 1989 (Hong Kong), 1996 (Somerset-West, South Africa) and 2000 (Edinburgh, Scotland). Note of clarification on Paragraph 29 added by the WMA General Assembly, Washington 2002.

Directive 2004/23/EC of the European Parliament and of the Council of 31 March 2004 on setting standards of quality and safety for the donation, procurement, testing, processing, preservation, storage and distribution of human tissues and cells

General Provisions

Article 1

Objective

This Directive lays down standards of quality and safety for human tissues and cells intended for human applications, in order to ensure a high level of protection of human health.

Article 2

Scope

1. This Directive shall apply to the donation, procurement, testing, processing, preservation, storage and distribution of human tissues and cells intended for human applications and of manufactured products derived from human tissues and cells intended for human applications. Where such manufactured products are covered by other directives, this Directive shall apply only to donation, procurement and testing.

2. This Directive shall not apply to:
> (a) tissues and cells used as an autologous graft within the same surgical procedure;
> (b) blood and blood components as defined by Directive 2002/98/EC;
> (c) organs or parts of organs if it is their function to be used for the same purpose as the entire organ in the human body.

Article 3

Definitions

For the purposes of this Directive:
> (a) 'cells' means individual human cells or a collection of human cells when not bound by any form of connective tissue;

(b) 'tissue' means all constituent parts of the human body formed by cells;

(c) 'donor' means every human source, whether living or deceased, of human cells or tissues;

(d) 'donation' means donating human tissues or cells intended for human applications;

(e) 'organ' means a differentiated and vital part of the human body, formed by different tissues, that maintains its structure, vascularisation and capacity to develop physiological functions with an important level of autonomy;

(f) 'procurement' means a process by which tissue or cells are made available;

(g) 'processing' means all operations involved in the preparation, manipulation, preservation and packaging of tissues or cells intended for human applications;

(h) 'preservation' means the use of chemical agents, alterations in environmental conditions or other means during processing to prevent or retard biological or physical deterioration of cells or tissues;

(i) 'quarantine' means the status of retrieved tissue or cells, or tissue isolated physically or by other effective means, whilst awaiting a decision on their acceptance or rejection;

(j) 'storage' means maintaining the product under appropriate controlled conditions until distribution;

(k) 'distribution' means transportation and delivery of tissues or cells intended for human applications;

(l) 'human application' means the use of tissues or cells on or in a human recipient and extracorporal applications;

(m) 'serious adverse event' means any untoward occurrence associated with the procurement, testing, processing, storage and distribution of tissues and cells that might lead to the transmission of a communicable disease, to death or life-threatening, disabling or incapacitating conditions for patients or which might result in, or prolong, hospitalization or morbidity;

(n) 'serious adverse reaction' means an unintended response, including a communicable disease, in the donor or in the recipient associated with the procurement or human application of tissues and cells that is fatal, life-threatening, disabling, incapacitating or which results in, or prolongs, hospitalisation or morbidity;

(o) 'tissue establishment' means a tissue bank or a unit of a hospital or another body where activities of processing, preservation, storage or distribution of human tissues and cells are undertaken. It may also be responsible for procurement or testing of tissues and cells;

(p) 'allogeneic use' means cells or tissues removed from one person and applied to another;

(q) 'autologous use' means cells or tissues removed from and applied in the same person.

Obligations on Member States' Authorities

Article 5

Supervision of human tissue and cell procurement

1. Member States shall ensure that tissue and cell procurement and testing are carried out by persons with appropriate training and experience and that they take place in conditions accredited, designated, authorised or licensed for that purpose by the competent authority or authorities.

2. The competent authority or authorities shall take all necessary measures to ensure that tissue and cell procurement complies with the requirements referred to in Article 28(b), (e) and (f). The tests required for donors shall be carried out by a qualified laboratory accredited, designated, authorised or licensed by the competent authority or authorities.

Chapter III
Donor Selection and Evaluation

Article 12

Principles governing tissue and cell donation

1. Member States shall endeavour to ensure voluntary and unpaid donations of tissues and cells. Donors may receive compensation, which is strictly limited to making good the expenses and inconveniences related to the donation. In that case, Member States define the conditions under which compensation may be granted.

Member States shall report to the Commission on these measures before 7 April 2006 and thereafter every three years. On the basis of these reports the Commission shall inform the European Parliament and the Council of any necessary further measures it intends to take at Community level.

2. Member States shall take all necessary measures to ensure that any promotion and publicity activities in support of the donation of human tissues and cells comply with guidelines or legislative provisions laid down by the Member States. Such guidelines or legislative provisions shall include appropriate restrictions or prohibitions on advertising the need for, or availability of, human tissues and cells with a view to offering or seeking financial gain or comparable advantage. Member States shall endeavour to ensure that the procurement of tissues and cells as such is carried out on a non-profit basis.

Article 13

Consent

1. The procurement of human tissues or cells shall be authorised only after all mandatory consent or authorization requirements in force in the Member State concerned have been met.

2. Member States shall, in keeping with their national legislation, take all necessary measures to ensure that donors, their relatives or any persons granting authorisation on behalf of the donors are provided with all appropriate information as referred to in the Annex.

Article 14

Data protection and confidentiality

1. Member States shall take all necessary measures to ensure that all data, including genetic information, collated within the scope of this Directive and to which third parties have access, have been rendered anonymous so that neither donors nor recipients remain identifiable.

2. For that purpose, they shall ensure that:

    (a) data security measures are in place, as well as safeguards against any unauthorised data additions, deletions or modifications to donor files or deferral records, and transfer of information;

    (b) procedures are in place to resolve data discrepancies; and (c) no unauthorised disclosure of information occurs, whilst guaranteeing the traceability of donations.

3. Member States shall take all necessary measures to ensure that the identity of the recipient (s) is not disclosed to the donor or his family and vice versa, without prejudice to legislation in force in Member States on the conditions for disclosure, notably in the case of gametes donation.

Annex
Information to be Provided on the Donation of Cells and/or Tissues

A. Living donors

1. The person in charge of the donation process shall ensure that the donor has been properly informed of at least those aspects relating to the donation and procurement process outlined in paragraph 3. Information must be given prior to the procurement.

2. The information must be given by a trained person able to transmit it in an appropriate and clear manner, using terms that are easily understood by the donor.

3. The information must cover: the purpose and nature of the procurement, its consequences and risks; analytical tests, if they are performed; recording and protection of donor data, medical confidentiality; therapeutic purpose and potential benefits and information on the applicable safeguards intended to protect the donor.

4. The donor must be informed that he/she has the right to receive the confirmed results of the analytical tests, clearly explained.

5. Information must be given on the necessity for requiring the applicable mandatory consent, certification and authorisation in order that the tissue and/or cell procurement can be carried out.

B. Deceased donors

1. All information must be given and all necessary consents and authorisations must be obtained in accordance with the legislation in force in Member States.

2. The confirmed results of the donor's evaluation must be communicated and clearly explained to the relevant persons in accordance with the legislation in Member States.

Index